Treasures for Scholars Worldwide

中国商业文化遗产文库

英国剑桥大学图书馆藏
怡和洋行中文商业档案辑考

Examination of the Chinese Commercial Documents
in Jardine Matheson Archive,
Collection of the Cambridge University Library, UK

冷 东　潘剑芬　沈晓鸣　主编

下

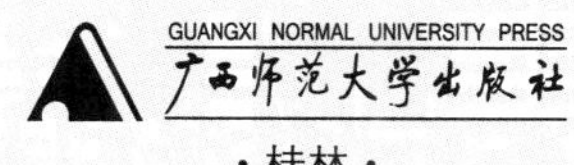

·桂林·

五〇、约道光八年李结坤[1]贩运鸦片书信及鸦片清单

1. 约道光八年李结坤贩运鸦片书信（H1/50/01）

中国鸦片商人李结坤向英国鸦片商人孖地臣[2]汇报联袂巴斯鸦片商人前往印度孟买购买并走私鸦片入境的情况。李结坤依附于外国鸦片资本，建立了自己的商行“坤记”从事鸦片走私贸易。

这份鸦片档案文书格式上很有特点。盖有两枚印章，长方形印章印文“坤记图章”、随形印印章印文“吉呈”。在数额、品种等关键内容处皆盖以印章，说明当时鸦片走私贸易等级精细繁多，具有规模化、程序化的特点。该文献揭露的鸦片走私细节，打破了以往中国商人只是在中国境内接应销售鸦片的看法，使人对19世纪鸦片走私的模式有了新的认识。

Letter re opium business. The letter records that the opium at the port of Wangmi has been checked, where the quality was found to be poor, and 115 chases have been purchased. A further 609 chases were carefully selected and bought from a farmer inland under the order of Jamsetjee of head office. The boxes have been marked with Chinese words chosen from the first lines of the book ‘Thousand Words’. The letter is in Chinese, but includes a few English annotations. The date of the document is unclear: according to the Western and Chinese dates of purchase given in the text, it originates from either 1828 (during the 8th year of the reign of Daoguang, 1821–1850) or 1866 (during the 5th year of the reign of Tongzhi, 1862–1874). 1 item.circa 1828

---

① 李结坤：中国鸦片商人。

② 孖地臣：即詹姆士·马地臣（James Matheson），1796—1878年，英国鸦片商人，怡和洋行（Jardine, Matheson & Co.）的创立者之一。

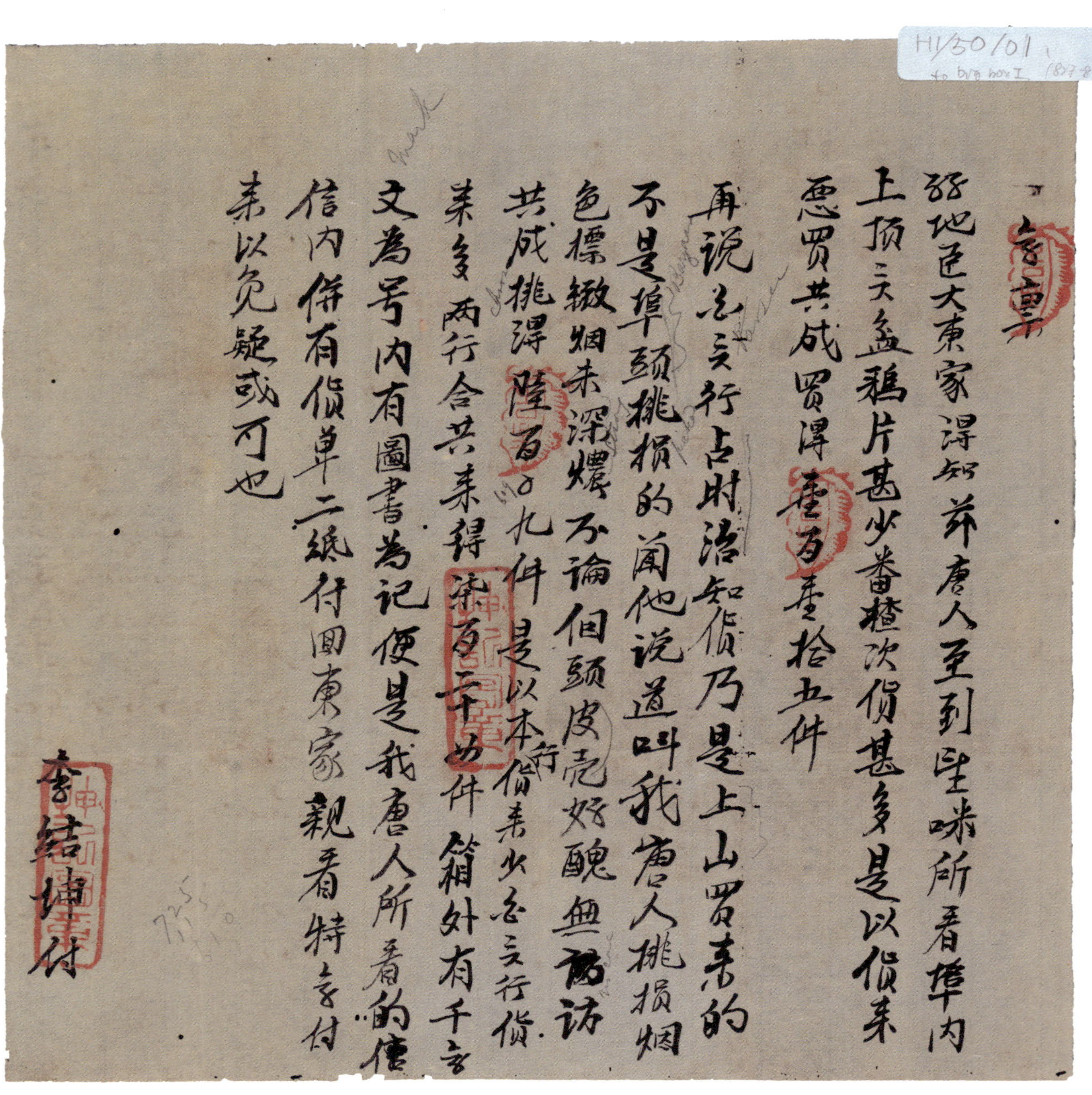

啓者
勿地臣大東家得知 弟唐人至到呈咪所看埠内
上頂三五盒鴉片甚少番棧次貨甚多是以貨未
愿買共成買得壹百叁拾五件
再說各文行占时洽知貨乃是上山買来的
不是埠頭挑損的聞他說道叫我唐人挑損烟
色標緻烟未深爛不論個頭皮亮好醜無論訪
共成挑得陸百〇九件是以本行貨未少各文行貨
未多兩行合共未得柒百二十四件 箱外有千字
文為號内有圖書為記便是我唐人所看的貨
信内併有貨單二紙付回東家親看特字付
未以免疑惑可也

李結由付

2. 约道光八年白头行[①]占时治[②]贩运鸦片的清单（H1/50/02）

巴斯鸦片商人白头行占时治（Jamsetjee）的鸦片货单，记录了十一月初五日至次年正月初三日期间所购买的609箱、14个字号的鸦片，详细注明了这批走私鸦片的购买时间、数量、等级等细节。

Opium invoice. An invoice (in Chinese), provided by Jamsetjee of head office, for 609 chases of opium, including 14 marks of opium, purchased between 22 November and 17 February[③]. The document contains some English annotations. It dates from either 1828 or 1866 (see H1/50/1). 1 item. circa 1828

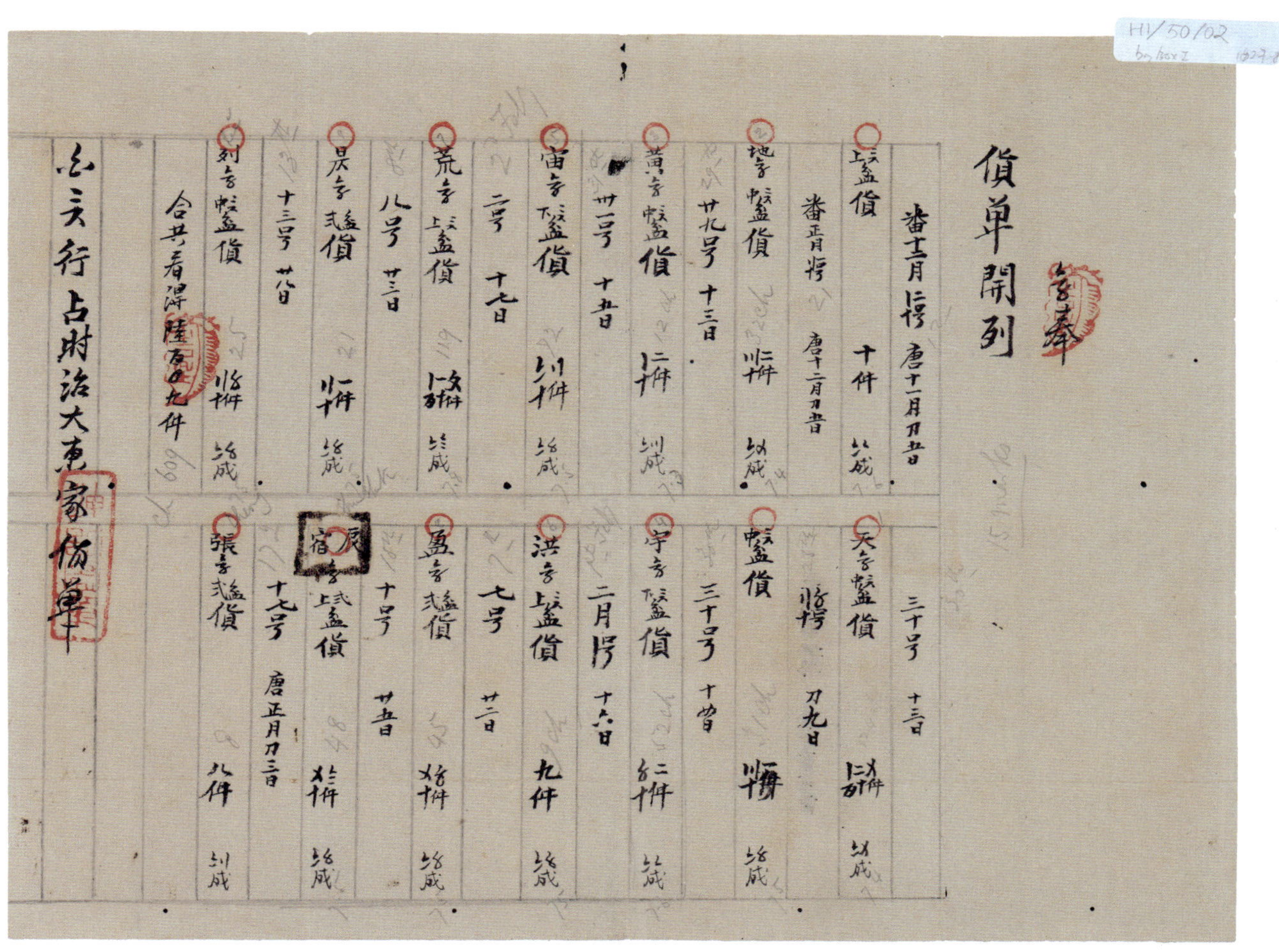
H1/50/02

貨單開列

白頭行占時治大班家貨單

① 白头行：巴斯鸦片商人在广州开设的商行。

② 占时治：Jamsetjee，巴斯鸦片商人。

③ 勘误：英文提要注明这批鸦片购买时间为11月22日至2月17日，根据原文献内容可知购买的起止时间为十一月初五日至次年正月初三日，且原文献中对应的公历时间为12月12日至次年的2月17日，起止时间的阴阳历时间并不完全对应，疑其公历时间存在错误，似应为12月22日至次年的2月17日。此处英文提要中的时间既不同于原文献中所记公历时间，亦不同于所推时间，疑误。

3. 约道光八年李结坤[①]贩运鸦片的清单（H1/50/03）

中国鸦片商人李结坤的鸦片货单，汇报包括十二月十二日至十九日期间所购买的115件、2个字号的鸦片，详细注明了这批走私鸦片的购买时间、数量、等级等细节。

Opium invoice. An invoice, provided by the Hong, for 115 chases of opium, including 2 marks, purchased between 28 January and 4 February. The document contains some English annotations. It dates from either 1828 or 1866 (see H1/50/1). 1 item. circa 1828

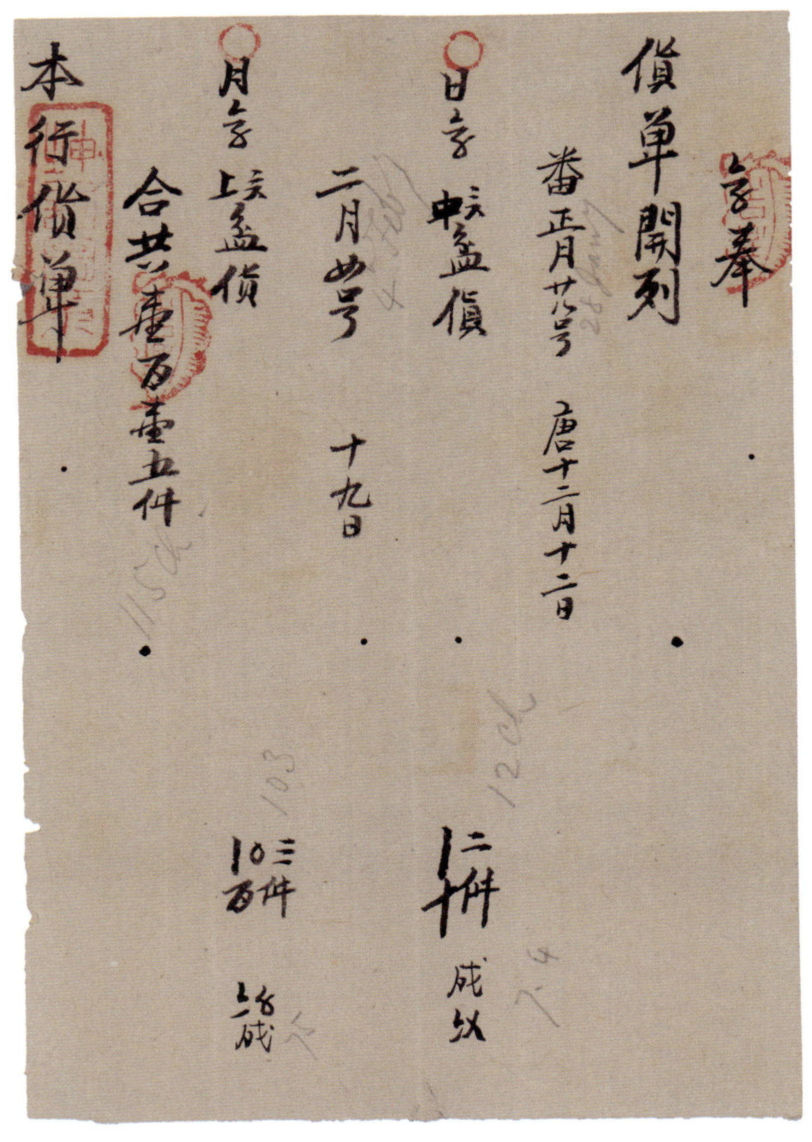
H1/50/03
貨單開列
番正月廿八號
唐十二月十二日
二月四號
十九日
合共壹百壹拾五件
本行貨單

① 李结坤：中国鸦片商人。

五一、道光十七年李船主①相关书信

1. 道光十七年李船主、老先生锦兄通报清军稽查鸦片的书信（H1/51/01）

道光十七年五月初七日（1837年6月9日），福建“李船主”和“老先生锦兄”向怡和洋行鸦片商人通报清朝官府禁烟的法令和行动计划，要求鸦片商人立即将大船驶入公海以逃避官府的缉捕。落款印章，印文“尘茂利记”。

Letter from Ch’en-mao li-chi. A letter (in Chinese) from Ch’en-mao li-chi (Chenmao liji) in Tsin-kiang (sometimes appearing as Ch’in-chow, the present day Ch’uanchou/Quanzhou) to Captain Lee (Li) and Chin (Ji) (first name), 9 June 1837, requesting that they move their ship to the high sea immediately following the government’s raid on opium business in the region. There is also a cover for the letter, which includes two brief English notes. 2 items; Fair condition, but missing some sections. 1837

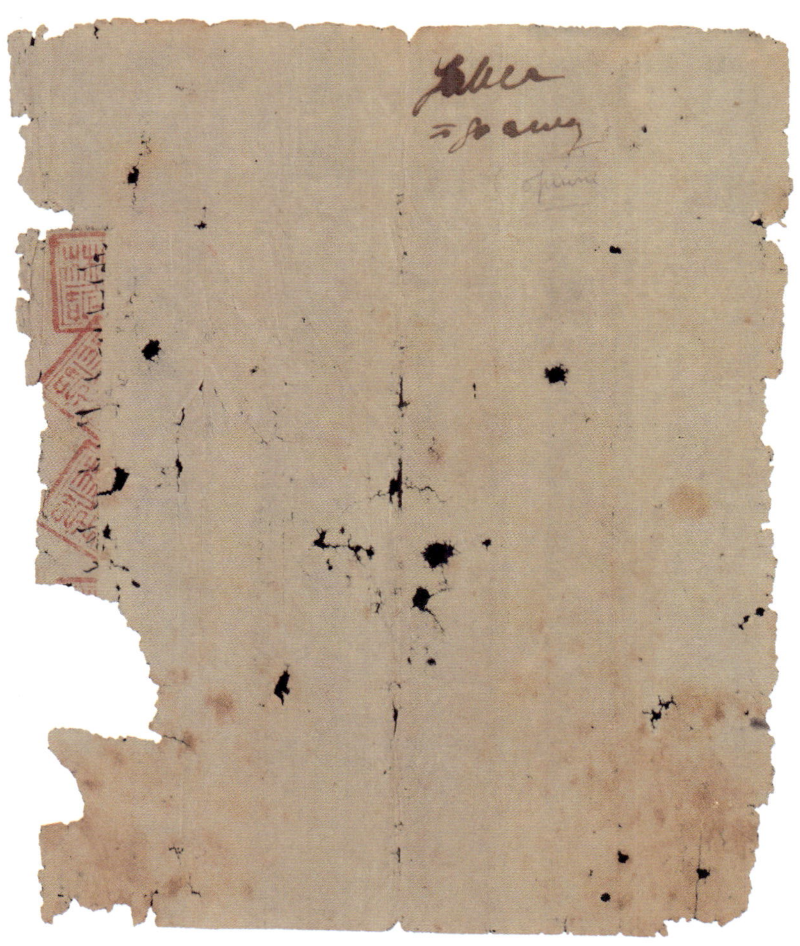

① 李船主：中国福建沿海贩卖鸦片的商人。

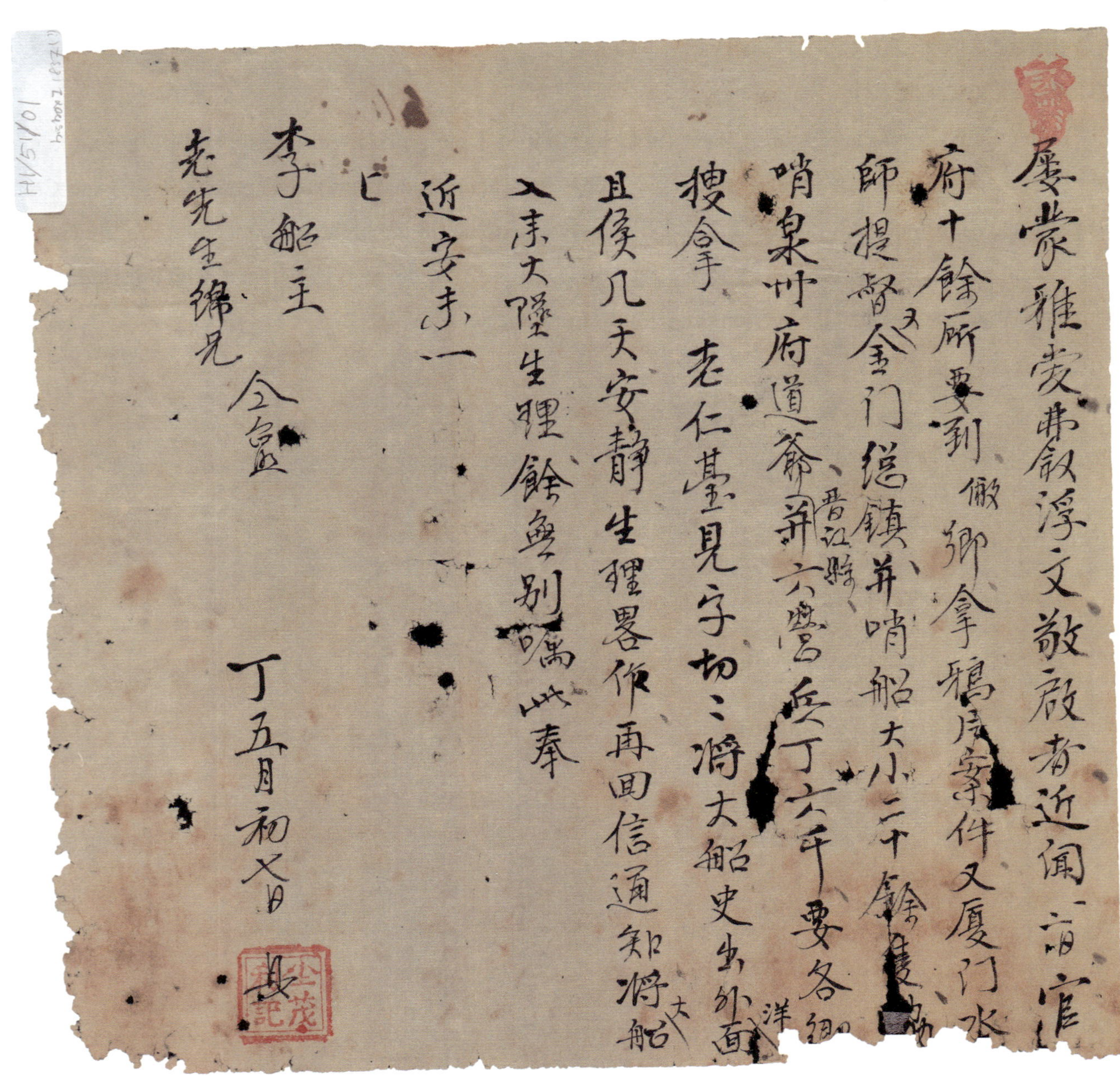

屡蒙雅爱弗叙浮文敬启者近闻一[illegible]官
府十餘所要到 敝 鄉拿賊爲案件又厦门水
師提督又金门總鎮并哨船大小二十餘隻[illegible]
哨泉州府道爺晋江縣并六營兵丁六千要各[illegible]
搜拿 老仁臺見字切〻將大船史出外面洋
且候几天安靜生理畧作再回信通知將大船
入來大墜生理餘無別囑此奉
近安未一
ㄈ
李船主
老先生錦兄 仝覽
丁五月初六日 [illegible]

2. 道光十七年亚丛、平伯、亚朕致李船主[①]的书信（H1/51/02）

道光十七年五月初八日（1837年6月10日），亚丛、平伯、亚朕联合致信李船主，告知其官府在福建晋江查禁鸦片，"捉人烧屋"，并派了七八艘警船到金门。信中还提及政府船只和贩卖鸦片的夹板船之间的争斗，因此要求李船主见字即把他的夹板船移到广东躲避几个月。

Letter from P'ing-po, Ya-ts'ung and Ya-chen. A letter (in Chinese) from P'ing-po (Pingbo), Ya-ts'ung (Yacong) and Ya-chen (Yazhen) to Captain Lee (Li), 10 June 1837, regarding the government's raid on opium in Tsin-kiang county, during which several persons were arrested and police boats were sent to Chinmen. The letter also reports a fight between government boats and clippers. The authors ask Lee to move his ships to Kwangtung for a couple of months. The document includes a brief English note. 1 item; Moderate conditions, in three pieces and missing some sections. 1837

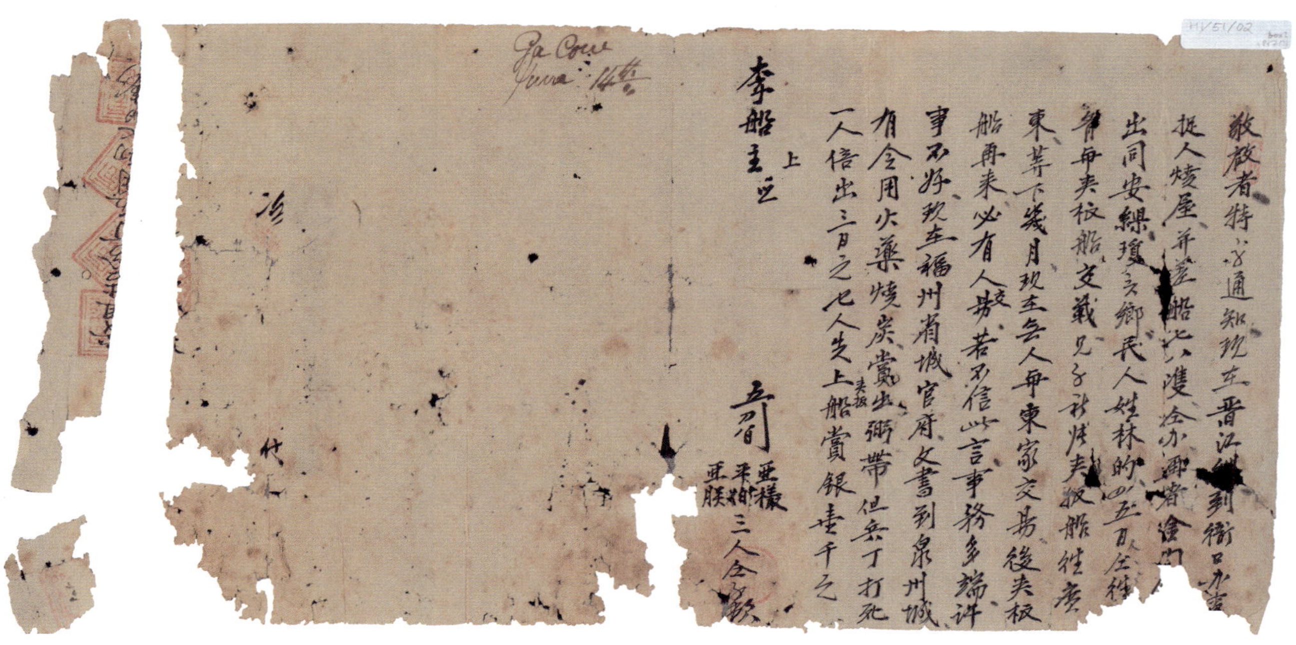

H1/51/02

敬啟者，特此通知，現在晉江[illegible]到衙口[illegible]
捉人燒屋，并差船七八隻往金門[illegible]
出同安縣[illegible]鄉民人姓林的四五月[illegible]
[illegible]與夾板船交戰，兄弟[illegible]夾板船往廣
東暫下幾月，現在無人與東家交易，後夾板
船再來，必有人與交，若不信此言，事務多端，許
事不好，現在福州省城官府文書到泉州城
有令用火藥燒炭，賞出衙帶，但兵丁打死
一人，信出三月之七人先上夾板船，賞銀壹千之

李船主　上

亞欉　平伯　亞朕　三人全啟

---

① 李船主：中国福建沿海贩卖鸦片的商人。

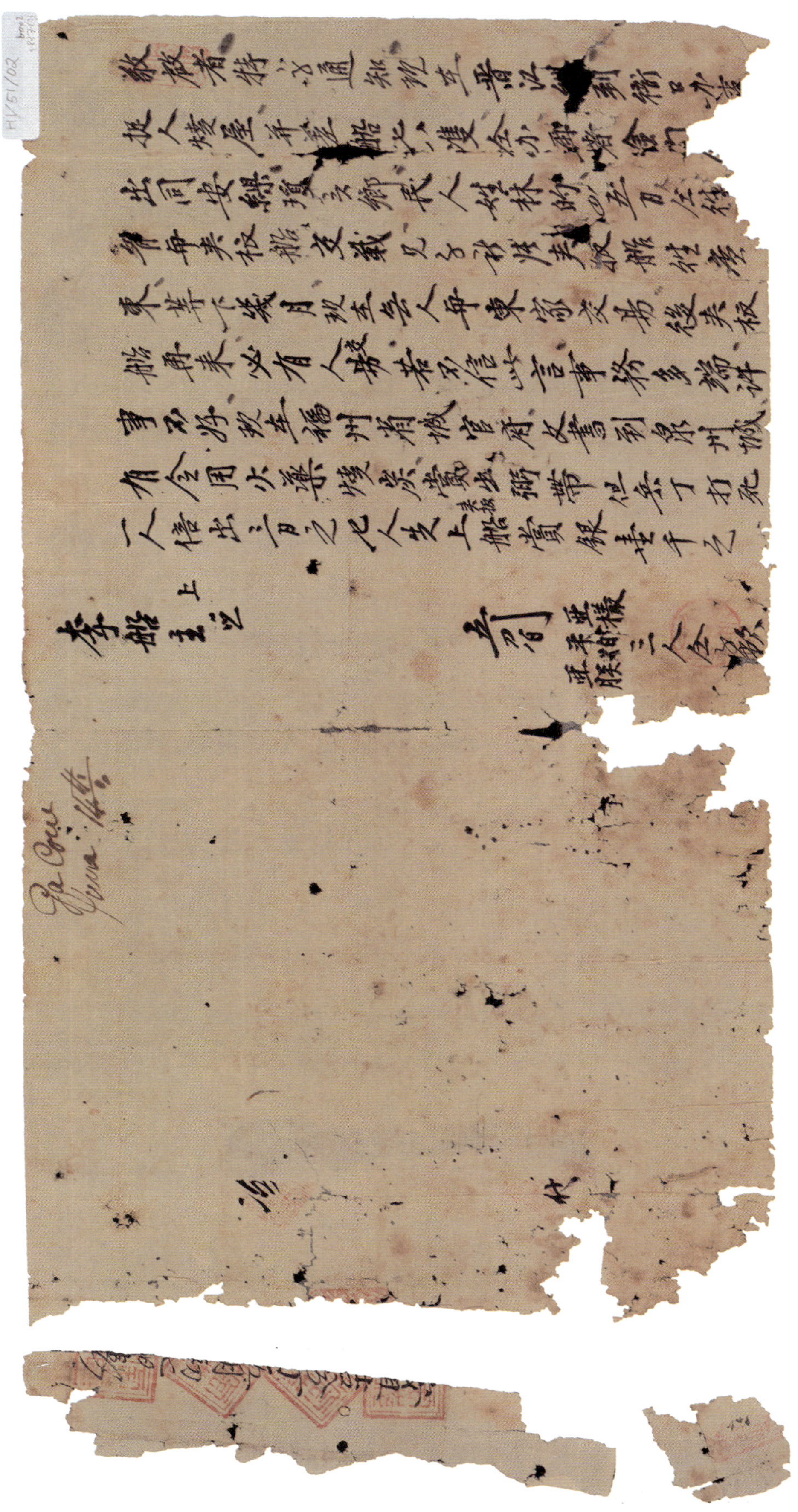

（局部图）

五二、道光二十九年广州丝绸行会《锦联堂[①]公启》[②]（H1/52）

道光二十九年二月初六日（1849年2月28日），广东广州丝绸行会锦联堂印制的关于禁止与外商贸易的通知。据通知内容可知，中英第一次鸦片战争以来，丝绸行业的贸易已经衰落，获利甚微。因传闻说英国人要入城，他们对此消息表示震惊："向来外夷数百年来未闻进城，各国皆守分乐业，华夷并安，今英夷忽有此举，以至人情惶恐，客心疑惑。在粤之商，早决归计，远方之客，闻风不来，则货物何处销售，更恐意外骚扰，又于何处寄顿。是以爰集同人，定议章程，暂停与夷人交易。"

Notice of Chin lien tang. A printed notice by Chin lien tang (Jin lian tang), a cloth and silk guild in Kwangtung (Guangdong province), 20 March 1849[③], concerning the foreign merchants. The notice begins by stating that since the trouble with Britain in 1841 the guild's business has declined. The authors record that there have been rumours recently that the English have been entering the city, and they express their shock at this news, because for hundred years none of the foreign businessmen have ever been allowed to open businesses in Kwangtung. They call for a meeting to be held to establish regulations for governing trade with the foreigners.

---

① 锦联堂：广州丝绸行业行会。

② 《锦联堂公启》:"一口通商"时期，广绣迅速发展，形成以广州为中心的刺绣行业，技艺以男工为主。乾隆年间，广绣形成了行业，广州有绣坊、绣庄50多家，分布在状元坊、新胜街、沙面一带，从业人员3000多人。乾隆五十八年（1793），广州成立了刺绣行会——锦绣行，会址设在杨巷瑞兴里，会名"绮兰堂"，只有男工（花佬）才能入行。行会由各大绣庄轮流担任执事，行内设"值理""行老"等职管理事务。行会的宗旨是支持与保护本土绣业发展，遏制外来绣品的渗入，对遍布城内的绣庄进行管理，协调同行业内部各绣坊之间的矛盾。《锦联堂公启》即是广州丝绸行业为保护本土绣业而禁止与外商贸易的文献之一。

③ 勘误：英文提要日期为1849年3月20日(20 March 1849)，按原中文文献"道光贰拾九年贰月初陆日"，应为1849年2月28日。

嘗聞近悅遠來，經營方得順遂；河清海晏，貨殖自置
流。如我民願一行買賣，自外夷行來，各有一向相安無異。
道光廿一年，英夷滋擾，我各家生理日見短少。試問數年
來，我行中能獲纔頭者，有幾人乎？容凝閩粵夷有
入城之議，不勝駭異。向來外夷數百年來，未聞進城，
各國皆守分樂業，華夷並安。今英夷忽有此舉，以
至人情惶恐，客心疑慮。本粵之商，決歸計遠方之
客，聞風不來，則貨物何處銷售？更恐意外騷擾，又於
何處著頭？是以眾集同人定議，嗣後停與夷人交
易。所有入口之貨，不准私買，即夷館開設零星貨
物，亦不准往投。務祈合志同心，足見義憤。況紬羅
紗綢皆可為衣，吳綢蜀錦亦可謀利，豈必呢羽等
物乎？如夷人果議入城，我行中再行照常交易。
時各安生理，共獲無窮之利矣。謹議條款開
於後：

一議本行各店不得買受夷人貨物
一議本行各店不得與洋行、行莊店及買辦買受貨物
一議本行各店不得到夷館投受貨物
一議本行各店不得與外行並客商買受夷人之頭
　貨物
一議本行各店不得假手別行客店轉受夷人貨物
一議本行各店不得與莊店私相投受
　以上六款，倘本行各宜凜遵。如有犯者，察出違例者
　眾議罰銀四百兩。如知情報信者，公所謝花紅銀貳
　百兩。如該店夥伴知情不報，本行永不雇用。
一議本行經紀並外行經紀不得將夷人貨物轉售各客
　商，本店出亦不交易。
一議洋行並莊店如有靠貨與外行及客商，本行
　永不交易。
一議城廂內外並外行各客如有到夷館投貨者，本行
　永停交易。
一議每月初一日各店同貴出一紙到公所清心

道光貳拾九年貳月初陸日錦聯堂公議

五三、咸丰四年收支账目[①]（H1/53）

咸丰四年三月初八日至六月十七日（1854年4月5日—7月11日）的收支账目，涉及40家商行，包括怡和洋行。文献中有铅笔注释。

Account of receipts and payments. An account of receipts and payments for 5 April to 11 July 1854, mentioning forty names, including Jardine. The document includes pencil annotations. 1 item. 1854

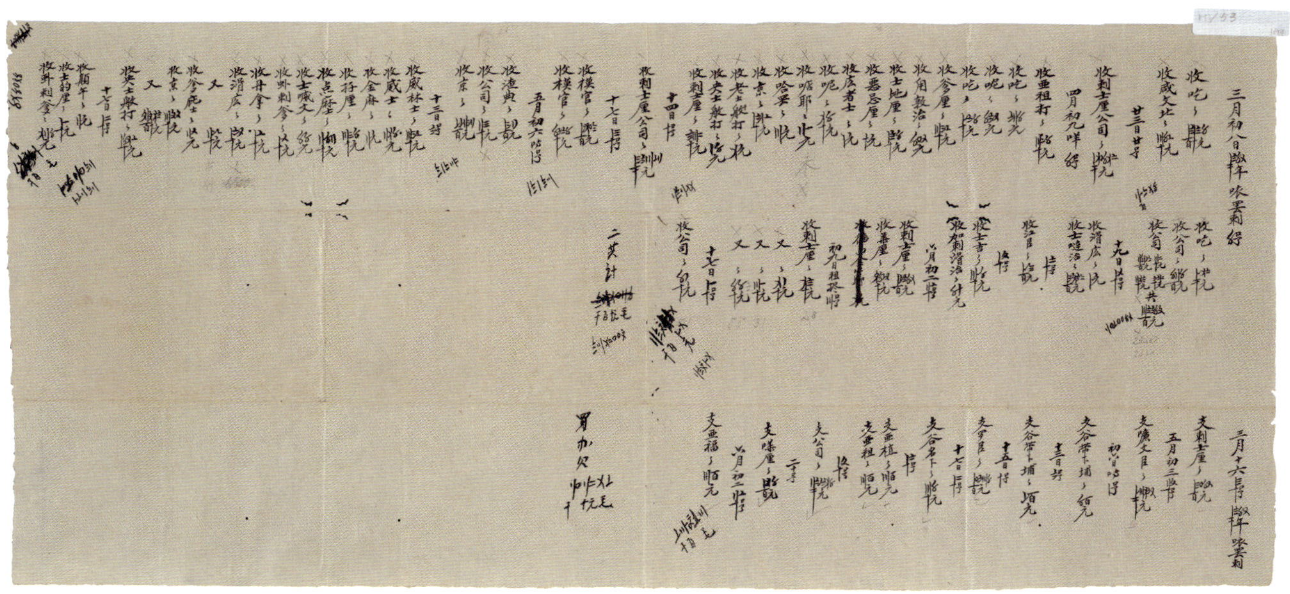

2 | 1

① 该文献以苏州码记录账目。

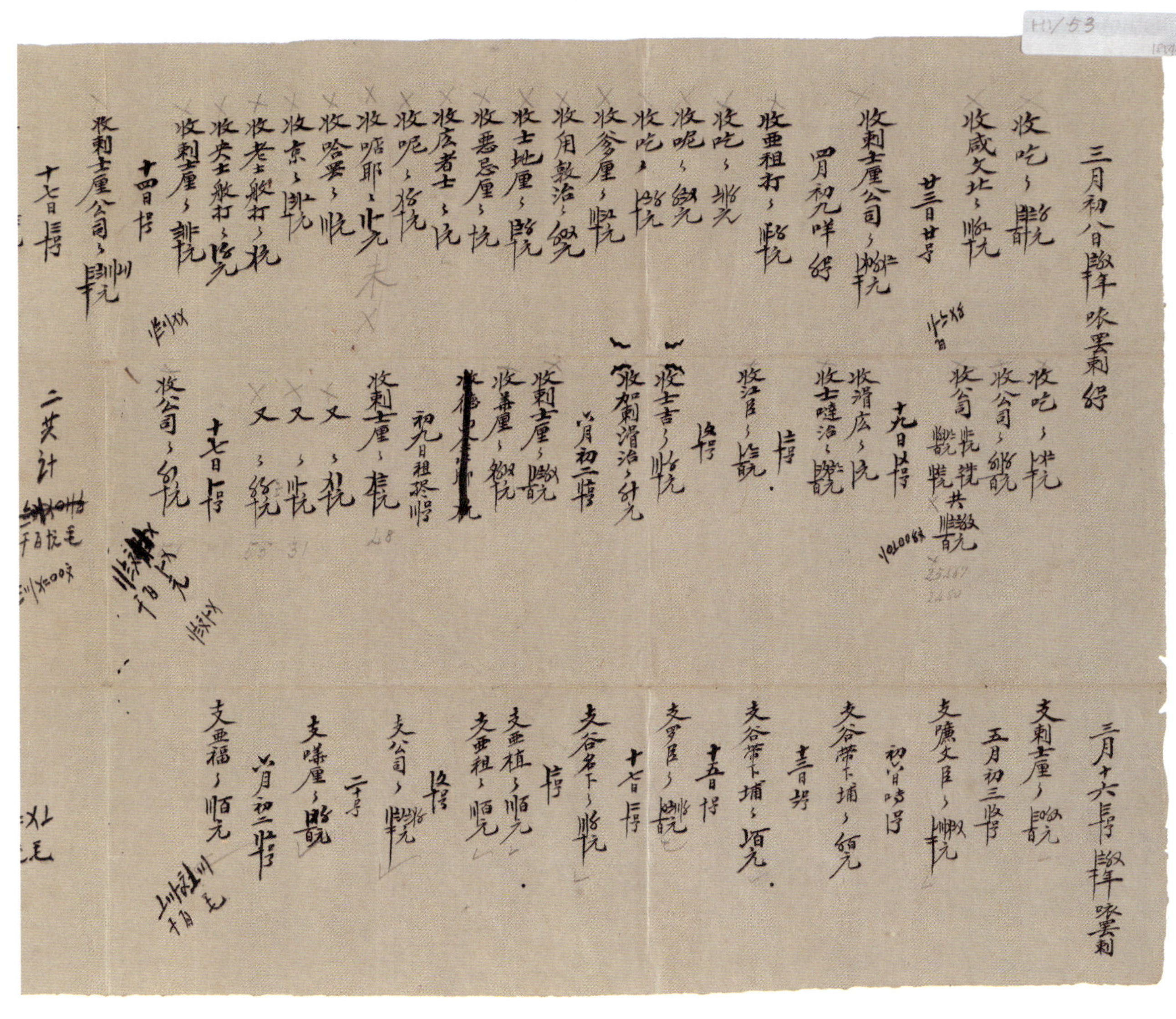

（局部图1）

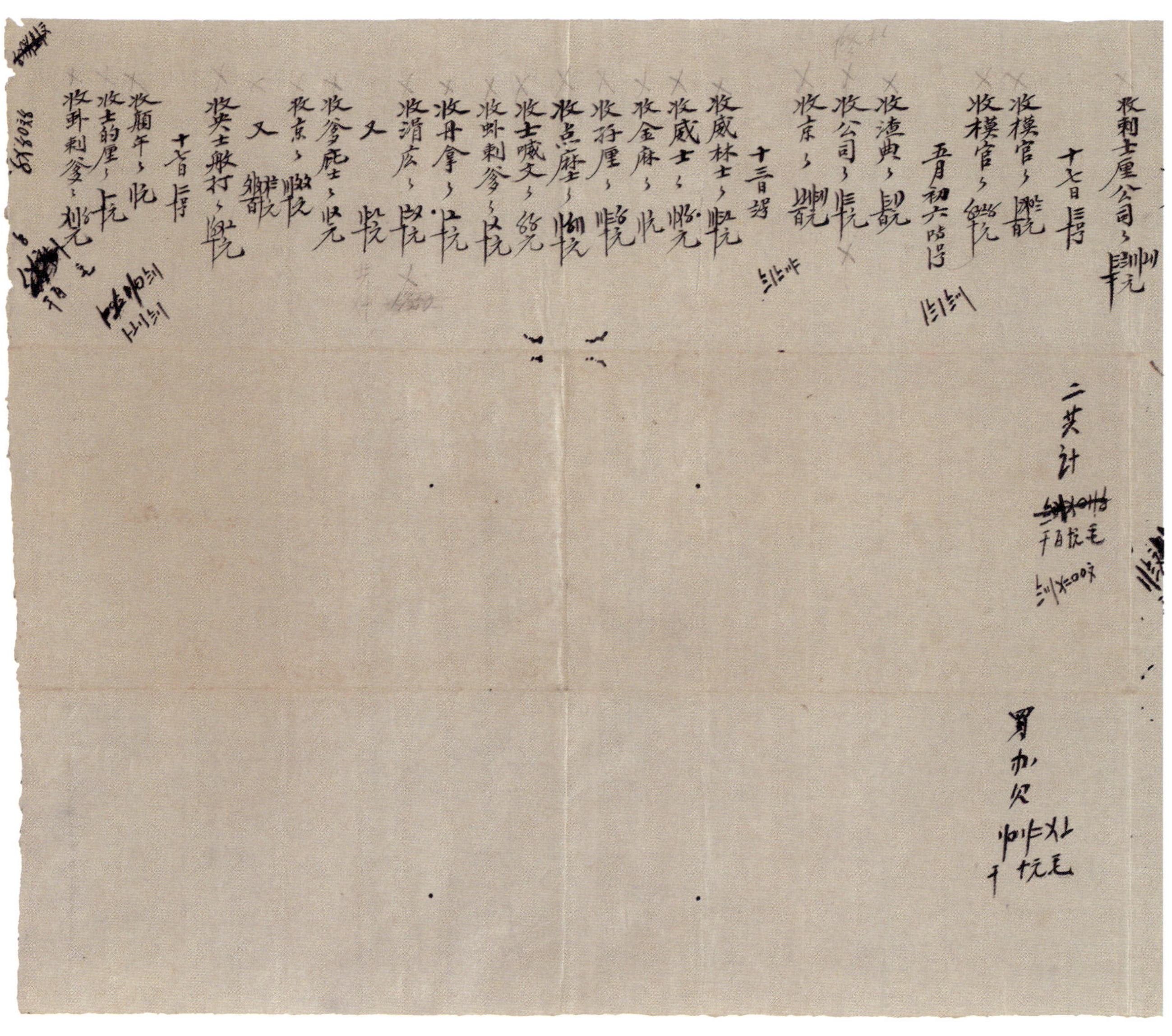

（局部图2）

五四、咸丰七年怡泰茶庄黄沛章[①]与查碘公司[②]签订的借约（H1/54）

咸丰七年四月初一日（1857年4月24日），怡泰茶庄黄沛章向查碘公司借款30,000元的借约，双方约定“同办湖北工夫茶，太平通商，将所办各茶载回广东或上海过交就将银数扣除外多除少补。其银按月一分算，俟交茶日止息”。黄沛章签名上方盖有印章，印文“黄沛章印”。见证人为亚祝。

Contract from Huang P’ei-chang. A contract from Huang P’ei-chang (Huang Peizhang) to Jardine, Matheson & Co. for $30,000, 24 April 1857, for the purchase tea in Hupei (Hubei province) and its transportation to Kwangtung and Shanghai jointly with I-t’ai ch’a-chuang (Yitai chazhuang). One copy of the contract was to be kept by Wu Tsung-fan (Wu Zongfan), witnessed by Ya-chu (Ya Zhu). 1 item. 1857

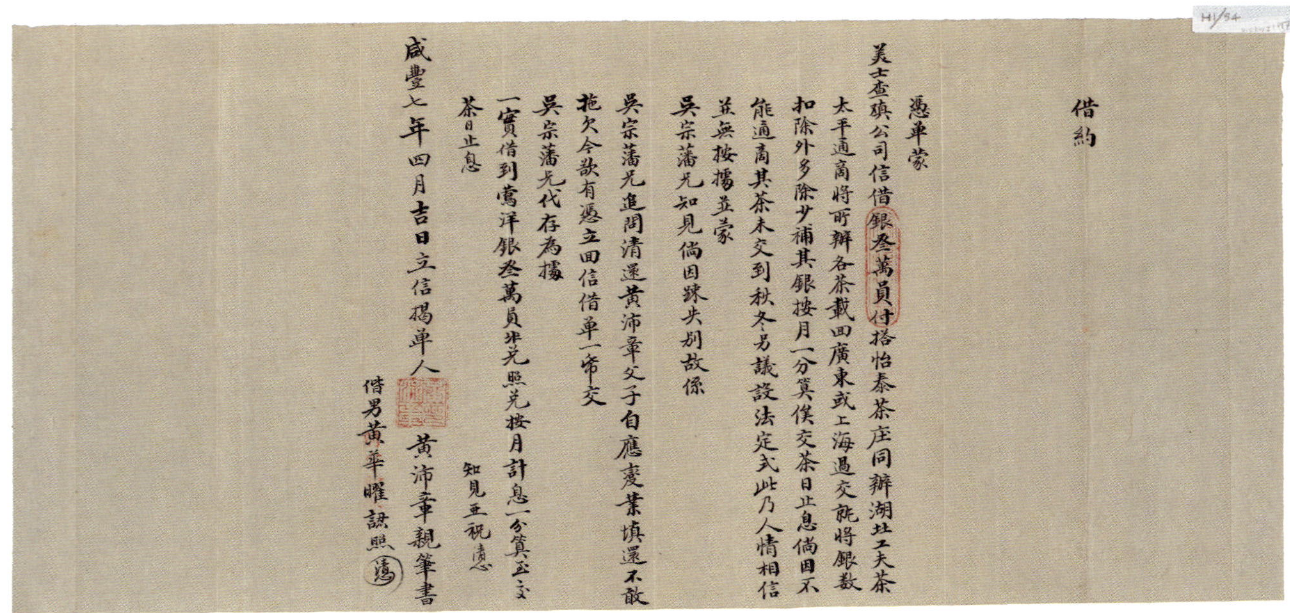

借約

憑單蒙
美士查甸公司信借銀叁萬員付搭怡泰茶庄同辦湖北工夫茶
太平通商將所辦各茶載回廣東或上海過交就將銀數
扣除外多除少補其銀按月一分算俟交茶日止息倘因不
能通商其茶未交到秋冬另議設法定式此乃人情相信
並無按揭並蒙
吳宗藩兄知見倘因疎失別故係
吳宗藩兄進問清還黃沛章父子自應變業填還不敢
拖欠今欲有憑立回信借單一帋交
吳宗藩兄代存為據
一實借到鷹洋銀叁萬員此批照批按月計息一分算至交
茶日止息
知見亞祝遠
咸豐七年四月吉日立信揭單人 黃沛章親筆書
借男黃華曜謹照（憑）

① 黄沛章：中国怡泰茶庄商人。

② 查碘公司：即怡和洋行（Jardine, Matheson & Co.），英国商人威廉·查顿（William Jardine）等创办。

借約

憑單蒙
美士查旗公司信借銀叁萬員付搭怡泰茶庄同辦湖北工夫茶
太平通商將所辦各茶載回廣東或上海過交就將銀數
扣除外多除少補其銀按月一分算俟交茶日止息倘因不
能通商其茶未交到秋冬另議設法定式此乃人情相信
並無按據並蒙
吳宗藩兄知見倘因踈失刓故係
吳宗藩兄追問清還黃沛章父子自應變業填還不敢
拖欠今欲有憑立回信借單一帋交
吳宗藩兄代存為據
一實借到鷹洋銀叁萬員北兑照兑按月計息一分算至交
茶日止息
知見亞祝清心
咸豐七年四月吉日立信揭單人 黃沛章親筆書
借男黃華曜謹照

（局部图）

五五、咸丰八年裕生行[1]与渣甸[2]关于存货品质的契约（H1/55）

咸丰八年（1858）春季，裕生行与英国商人渣甸关于绣巾、扯花素巾等存货品质的契约。由于这批货物（共120件）办备时间长，双方约定，如货物颜色转坏，可将变色之货退货给卖方，若是因买方运输过程遗失或导致布匹湿水，则与卖方无关。白文印“护封”，朱文印“AYUN”。

Storage receipt from Ayun. A storage receipt from Ayun of Yusheng [Hong] to Jardine for silk scarves, spring 1858. 1 item. 1858

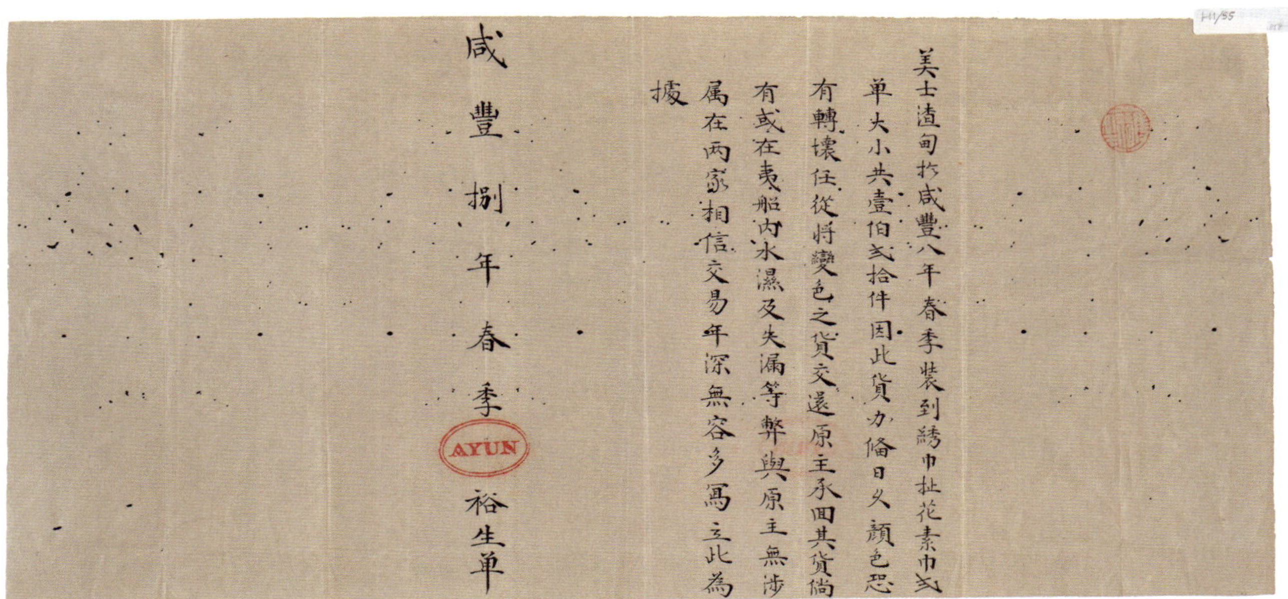
美士渣甸於咸豐八年春季裝到綉巾扯花素巾弍
單大小共壹伯弍拾件因此貨办備日久顏色恐
有轉壞任從將變色之貨交還原主承回其貨倘
有或在夷船內水濕及失漏等弊與原主無涉
属在兩家相信交易年深無容多寫立此為
據
咸豐捌年春季
AYUN
裕生单

① 裕生行：中国商行。

② 渣甸：即英国商人威廉·查顿（William Jardine），又译为渣颠、渣顿、赞典，为怡和洋行（Jardine, Matheson & Co.）创始人之一。

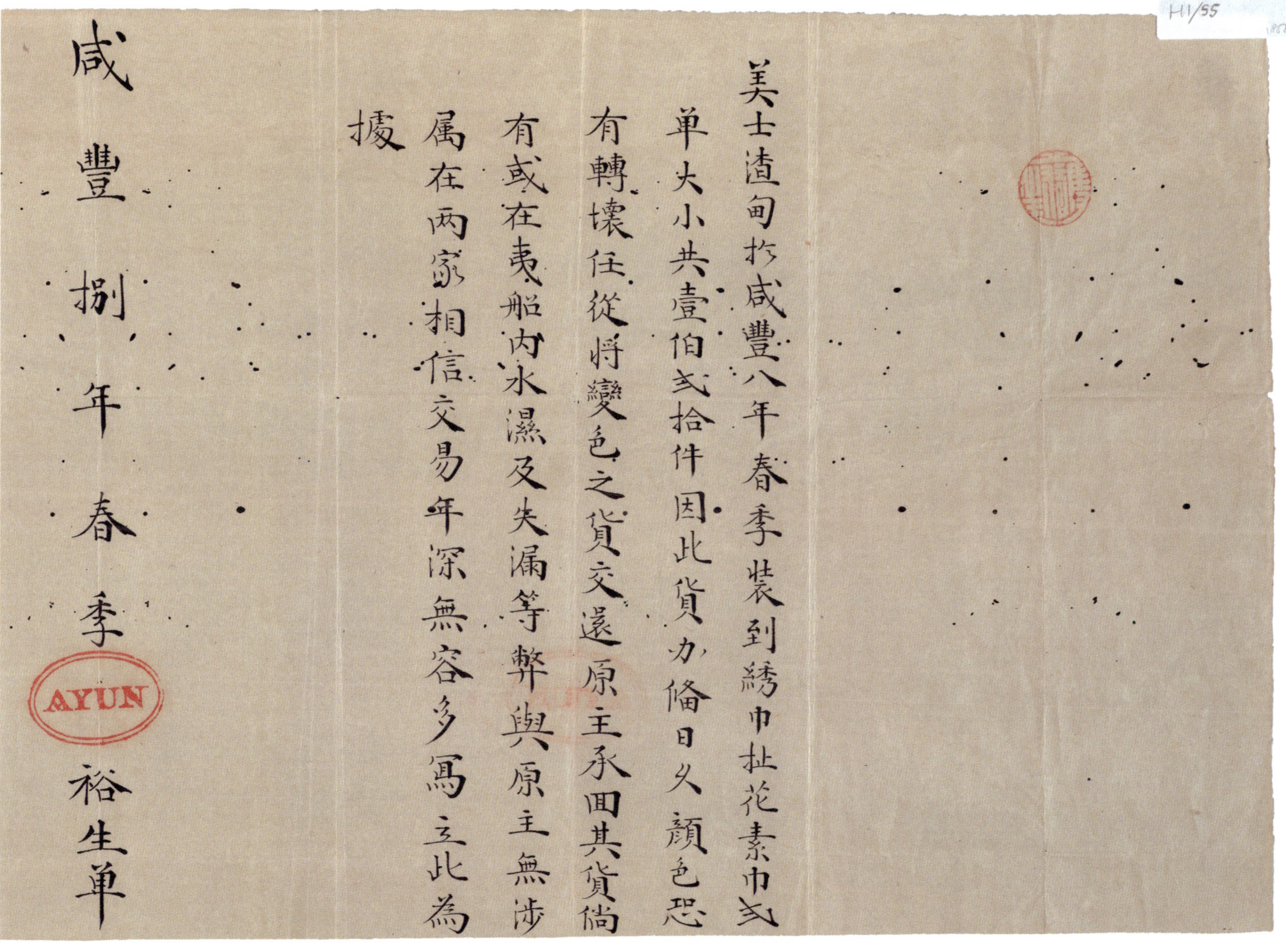

美士渣甸於咸豐八年春季裝到綉巾扯花素巾弍
单大小共壹伯弍拾件因此貨力倫日久顔色恐
有轉壞任從將變色之貨交還原主承回其貨倘
有或在夷船内水濕及失漏等弊與原主無涉
屬在兩家相信交易年深無容多寫立此為
據

咸豐捌年春季裕生单

（局部图）

五六、咸丰九年亚宁[①]致渣甸[②]的信函（H1/56）

咸丰九年六月十八日（1859年7月17日），买办亚宁写给英国商人渣甸的信函。据信中内容可知，渣甸十余年前提拔亚宁“委办厦门看银事职业”，现船主辉士加宾拟提携他兼办茶务，因其与英籍验茶师爹鼻士（Tie pi shih）关系不好，亚宁礼貌地拒绝兼任此职。右上方开头处随形印印文“如意”；末尾随形印印文“谨封”。

Letter from Ya-ning. A letter from Ya-ning, Jardine's Chinese shroffer in Amoy, to Jardine, 17 July 1859, politely but firmly declining the new post for the tea business because of his poor relations with the tea taster, Tie pi shih（Die bi shi）. 1 item. 1859

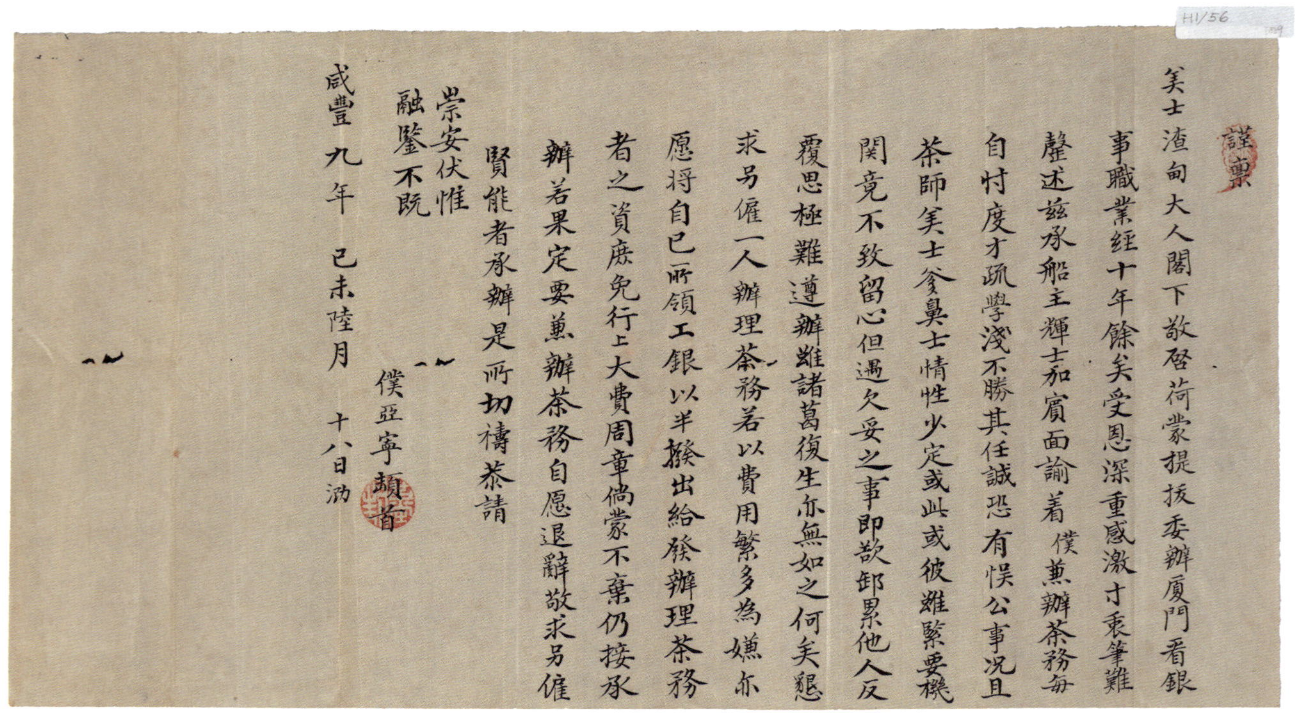

美士渣甸大人閣下敬啓荷蒙提拔委辦廈門看銀
事職業經十年餘矣受恩深重感激寸衷筆難
罄述茲承船主輝士加賓面諭着僕兼辦茶務每
自忖度才疏學淺不勝其任誠恐有悞公事況且
茶師美士爹鼻士情性少定或此或彼難緊要機
関竟不致留心但遇欠妥之事即欲卸累他人反
覆思極難遵辦雖諸葛復生亦無如之何矣懇
求另僱一人辦理茶務若以費用繁多為嫌亦
愿將自己所領工銀以半撥出給發辦理茶務
者之資庶免行上大費周章倘蒙不棄仍接承
辦若果定要兼辦茶務自愿退辭敬求另僱
賢能者承辦是所切禱恭請
崇安伏惟
融鑒不既　　僕亞寧頓首
咸豐九年　己未陸月　十八日泐

---

① 亚宁：中国买办。

② 渣甸：即英国商人威廉·查顿（William Jardine），又译为渣颠、渣顿、赞典，为怡和洋行（Jardine, Matheson & Co.）创始人之一。

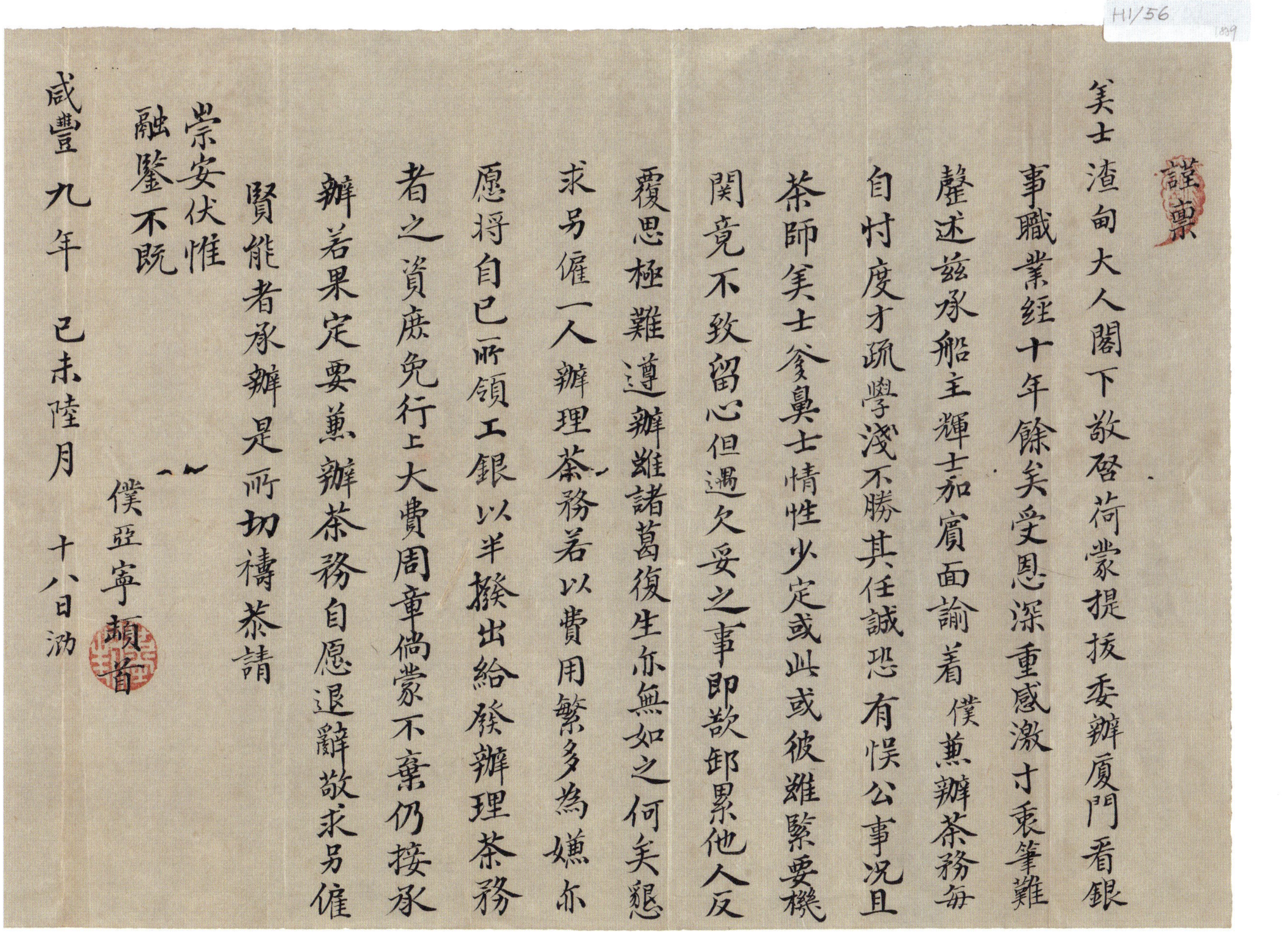

実士浩甸大人閣下敬啓者荷蒙提拔委辦廈門看銀
事職業經十年餘矣受恩深重感激寸衷筆難
殫述茲承船主濮士加賔面諭着僕兼辦茶務第
自忖度才疏學淺不勝其任誠恐有悞公事況且
茶師実士拿畢士情性少定或此或彼雖緊要機
關竟不致留心但遇久要之事即敬邸累他人反
覆思極難遵辦雖諸葛復生亦無如之何矣懇
求另僱一人辦理茶務若以費用繁多為嫌亦
願將自己所領工銀以半撥出給彼辦理茶務
若之資庶免行上大費周章倘蒙不棄仍接承
辦看銀若果定要兼辦茶務自願退辭敬求另僱
賢能者承辦是所切禱恭請
崇安伏惟
賜鑒不既
僕亞高拜
咸豐九年　己未陸月　十八日泐

（局部图）

五七、怡和洋行与福建茶商相关信函

1. 约咸丰五年茶叶买办阿禧[①]致茶师叻件[②]的信函（H1/57/1）

约咸丰五年四月初五日（1855年5月20日），怡和洋行在福建的茶叶买办阿禧致信品茶师叻件（Le Chien）。信中谈及受到竞争对手大成和隆顺商号等影响，导致在福建沙县收购茶叶困难，且沙县只有青庄乌龙而没有工夫茶；并且谈及建宁府城和延平的太平天国起义所造成的政治不确定性及其对茶叶运输的影响。

Letter from Ahee. A letter from Ahee to Jardine regarding tea products and the market in Sha county (Sha xian), Fukien; rival companies such as Tach'eng (Dacheng) and Lungshun (Longshun); and the political uncertainty caused by the Taiping rebellion around Chien-ning fu (Jianning fu) and Yen-p'ing (Yanping) and the impact on shipping. Ahee sends his regards to Mr. Le Chien (Le jian), Jardine's tea-taster, and states that he has not let Wu Pin-yuan (Awei) and Ch'en Kui-kuan (Chen Guiguan) read his letter[③]. The document dates from the 1850s. 1 item. circa 1855

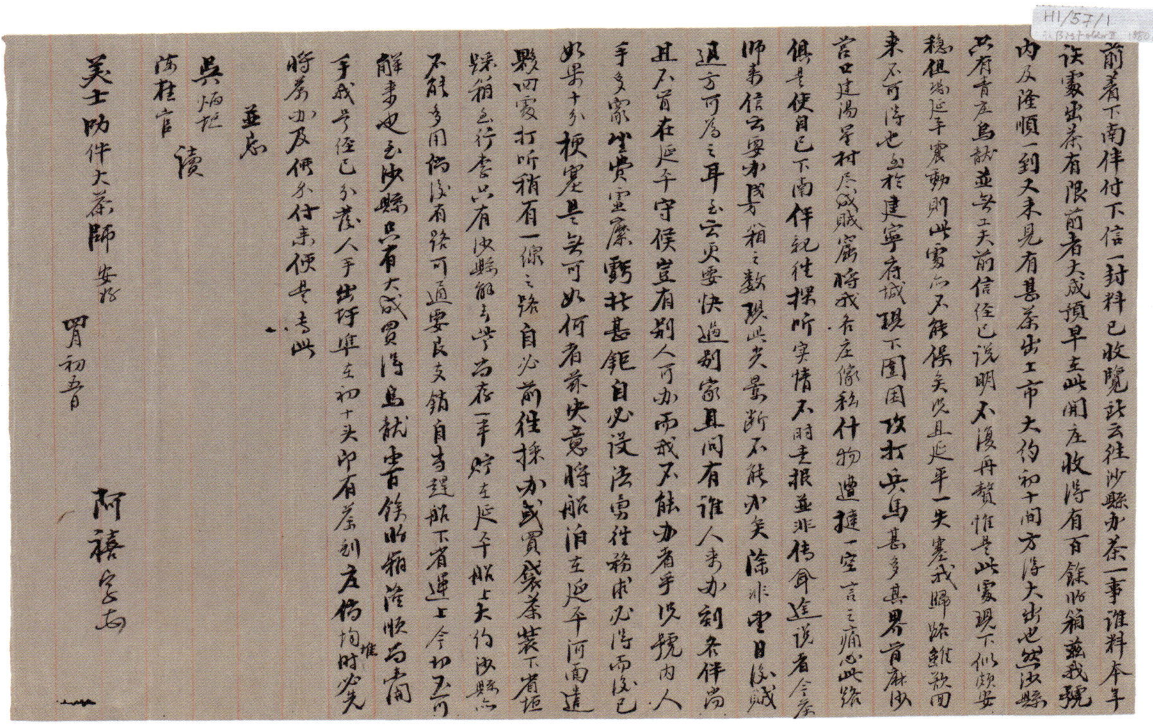

① 阿禧：怡和洋行（Jardine, Matheson & Co.）在福建的茶叶买办，应是H1/57/7信中提及的买办韩纯禧。

② 叻件：怡和洋行（Jardine, Matheson & Co.）的品茶师。

③ 勘误：英文提要中将信末“并恳吴炳垣、陈桂官读”解读为“他没有让吴炳垣和陈桂官读他的信”，似有误。估计是将信中“恳”字错读为“忘”。应解读为“并恳请吴炳垣、陈桂官阅读信件”。

（局部图）

2. 约咸丰五年茶叶买办阿禧[①]向渣甸[②]通报福州茶叶生意的书信（H1/57/2）

约咸丰五年九月二十五日（1855年11月4日），茶叶买办阿禧写信给渣甸，告知他福州茶叶生意的情况。“因界首、建阳等处土匪滋扰，人心惊惶，是以山上之茶无人采摘，故此圩场所出亦无甚好茶可买。其做茶之工人，俱系江西及河口等处者居多，因江西省反乱，其做茶之工人少来，是以工价太高，摘下之茶卖出不合算。其现年出茶之少，乃为此故也。大约计算，比往年少得四份之一”。可知太平天国起义导致茶叶产量较往年减少了四分之一。信中还列举了在此收购茶叶的英国和美国公司。阿禧签名处盖有朱文印章，印文“福臻栈”。

Letter from Ahee. A letter from Ahee to Jardine reporting on the tea business in Foochow. He reports a decrease of a fourth in tea products due to the shortage of manual labourers from Kianghsi (Jiangxi) as a result of the Taiping rebellion, and lists the English and American firms in business: English - Dent & Co. (Diandi), Lien chih chia (Lian zhi jia), Chi li wen (Ji li wen), Chie shih (Jie shi) of Fuho (Fuhe), Chien ni ti (Jian ni di), Lien wen ch'en (Lian wen chen), Tan na (Dan na), Ping ling chien lo chen (Bing ling jian luo chen) and Ching (Jing); American - La shih li (La shi li), Yang ho (Yang he) and Le li fen (Le li fen). The document dates from the 1850s. 1 item; Fair condition, but damage by insects. circa 1855

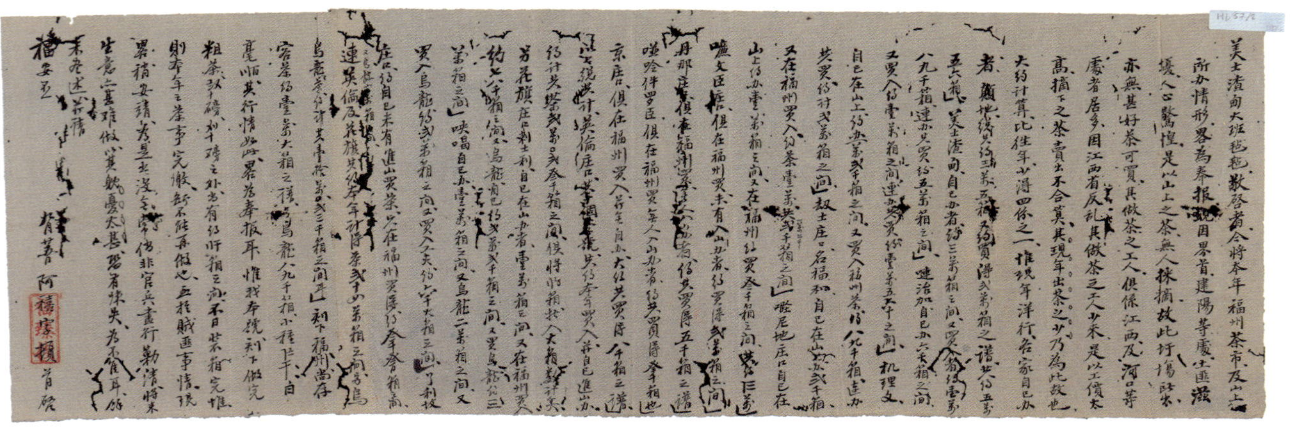

2|1

① 阿禧：怡和洋行（Jardine, Matheson & Co.）在福建的茶叶买办，应是H1//57/7信中提及的买办韩纯禧。

② 渣甸：即英国商人威廉·查顿（William Jardine），又译为渣颠、渣顿、赞典，为怡和洋行（Jardine, Matheson & Co.）创始人之一。

美士渣甸大班毡毡敬启者，今将本年福州茶市及山上所办情形略为奉报。现因界首、建阳等处土匪滋扰，人心惊惶，是以山上之茶无人采摘，故此圩塲□出，亦无甚好茶可买。其做茶之工人俱系江西及河口等处者居多，因江西省反乱，其做茶之工人少来，是以工价太高，摘下之茶卖出不合算。其现年出茶之少，乃为此故也。大约计算比往年少得四份之一。惟现年洋行各家自己办者，颠地约共办三万五箱，又约买得贰万箱之谱，共约五万五六箱。美士渣甸自己办者约三万箱之间，又买入看约壹万八九千箱，连办共买约五万箱之间。琏治加自己办六千箱之间，又买入约壹万箱之间，连办共买约壹万五六千之间。机理文自己在山上约办贰千箱之间，又买入福州茶约八九千箱，连办共买约计贰万箱之间。叔士庄口名福和，自己在山上办贰千箱，又在福州买入约茶壹万（一万二千）共贰千箱之间。咾尼地庄口自己在山上约办壹万箱之间，又在福州约买叁千箱之间，共约柒万之谱。嚧文臣庄口，俱在福州买，未有入山办者，约买得贰万箱之间。丹那庄口，俱在福州买，未入山办者，约共买得五千箱之谱。哋唅件罗臣，俱在福州买，无人入山办者，约共买得叁千箱也。京庄口，俱在福州买入，今年自办，大约共买得八千箱之谱。

（局部图1）

（局部图2）

3. 约咸丰五年茶叶买办阿禧[1]向渣甸[2]通报福州形势的书信（H1/57/3）

约咸丰五年（1855）新月初九日，茶叶买办阿禧给渣甸写信报告福州形势。土匪（指太平天国起义军）因官兵攻杀，已从建阳各处撤退，远窜邵武等郡的偏僻深山，与官兵处于僵持状态。因此，他建议不要在邵武开茶庄采办茶叶，最好把钱存到建宁、建阳两处（此二地俱有城池），然后到各处圩场采购茶叶。他认为新茶一出必将被各商号抢购，因此建议公司为采购新茶预备好银两，并将茶叶箱提前运达福州。

Letter from Ahee. A letter from Ahee to Jardine reporting that the Taiping rebels have withdrawn from Chienyang (Jianyang), but the position in the city is at a stalemate. He advises that it is not suitable to open a branch at Shaowu because it is very close to the border, and that money would be better deposited at Chienyang and Chienning. He also states that money should be prepared for the new tea coming in. The document dates from the 1850s. 1 item. circa 1855

① 阿禧：怡和洋行（Jardine, Matheson & Co.）在福建的茶叶买办，应是 H1/57/7 信中提及的买办韩纯禧。

② 渣甸：即英国商人威廉·查顿（William Jardine），又译为渣颠、渣顿、赞典，为怡和洋行（Jardine, Matheson & Co.）创始人之一。

敬啓者.昨前寄上一信.探得土匪從事.因此報達.
茲因官兵攻殺.於建陽各處.業已退走.遠竄邵
武等郡.藏在山僻之處.暫時從此時後.往來非止.不敢遠
出劫掠.官兵不敢深入攻打.殊非盡善除根.日後
恐再發作.亦未可料也.况且邵武隔界者.不過數十
里之遥.倘若在此開莊.辦茶.實不穩當.爲今之
計.必須將銀兩.存在建寧.建陽.兩處.此二地.俱有城池.
况且内地堅固.非同山僻.險阻可比.然後到各處打[illegible]採
買.將茶運回麻沙.[illegible].其銀兩每人隨身挑帶.不
數百.如此行之.則縱有賊匪.亦不能[illegible]其劫掠矣.
惟是福州茶市.現日甚高.各客亦未[illegible].[illegible]得利息.補
恐辦茶一事.大家[illegible]料想.[illegible]亦不能相應也.至銀兩一節.即
亦要早爲預備.倘有滯手.恐不能多辦.其銀要中儎.[illegible]設法
[illegible].[illegible]茶價之高.仍自有行情.[illegible]千秋等
[illegible].[illegible]不敢入[illegible].其[illegible]一個.[illegible]仍用[illegible]之要
早日運來.以[illegible].[illegible]稍待等語.[illegible]一去.即便[illegible]
行之.乃得快便.此事

[illegible]士德甸大班 [illegible]

[illegible]月初九日 阿[illegible]字 Ahee

（局部图）

4. 约咸丰五年茶叶买办阿熙[①]向渣甸[②]通报在福州采购新茶的书信（H1/57/4）

约咸丰五年（1855），茶叶买办阿熙致信渣甸，信中内容谈及福州茶叶市场的情况。其中包括太平、隆顺、连利、同顺、颠地等六七家洋行在福州采购茶叶。由于颠地的买办格鸦于二十四号圩期先行开手抢买，每百斤出价银二十三四两之多，其余各家被迫随此行情购买新茶，导致茶叶价格居高不下。渣甸曾吩咐阿熙以每百斤十七八两的价格购买三十余个字号的头春好茶，由于价格偏高，阿熙只购买了十四五个字号的茶叶，待茶叶价格跌落之后再继续购买，此情形已告知新茶师勒件（Le Chien）。

Letter from Ahee. A letter from Ahee to Jardine recording how he arrived in Foochow according to plan on 13 March and set off on 30 March to carry out purchases upcountry. He records that there are only six or seven foreign tea men in Foochow, including Chi li wen (Ji li wen) of T'aip'ing (Taiping), Yangho (Yang he) of Lungshun (Longshun), Lien chi (Lian zhi) of Lien Li (Lian li), La shih li (La shi li) of T'ungshun, and Ke-chi (Ge ji) of Dent (Diandi). Among these, Dent & Co. was the first to buy new tea when the season started, and this forced up the prices. As a result of the price rise, Ahee only bought 14 or 15 brands of tea. As Fei sha (Fisher ?) was on sick leave, he has reported these details personally to Mr. Le chien (Le jian), the successor to Fei sha. The document is undated, but probably originates from the 1850s. 1 item. circa 1855

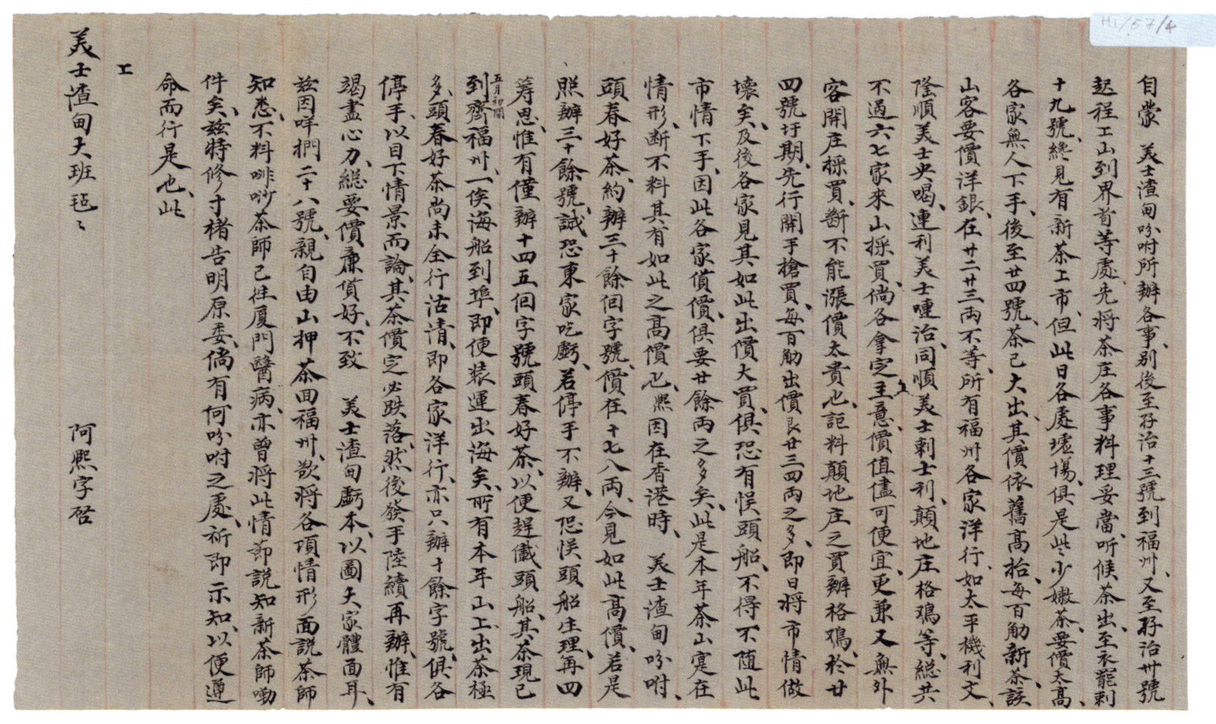
H1/57/4

自蒙 美士渣甸吩咐所辦各事，別後至孖治十三號到福州，又至孖治廿號
起程上山，到界首等處，先將茶庄各事料理妥當，聽候茶出。至永龍剩
十九號，總見有新茶上市，但此日各處墟場，俱是些少嫩茶，要價太高，
各家無人下手。後至廿四號，茶已大出，其價依舊高抬，每百觔新茶該
山客要價洋銀在廿二廿三兩不等。所有福州各家洋行，如太平機利文、
隆順美士央喝、連利美士嗹治、同順美士剌士利、顛地庄格鴉等，總共
不過六七家來山採買，倘各拿定主意，價值儘可便宜，更兼又無外
客開庄採買，斷不能漲價太貴也。詎料顛地庄之買辦格鴉，於廿
四號圩期先行開手搶買，每百觔出價銀廿三四兩之多，即日將市情做
壞矣。及後各家見其如此出價大買，俱恐有悞頭船，不得不隨此
市情下手，因此各家貨價俱要廿餘兩之多矣。此是本年茶山寔在
情形，斷不料其有如此之高價也。照因在香港時，美士渣甸吩咐
頭春好茶，約辦三十餘個字號，價在十七八兩，今見如此高價，若是
照辦三十餘號，誠恐東家吃虧，若停手不辦，又恐悞頭船生理。再四
籌思，惟有僅辦十四五個字號頭春好茶，以便趕儎頭船。其茶現已
五月初開
到齊福州，一俟海船到埠，即便裝運出海矣。所有本年山上出茶極
多，頭春好茶尚未全行沽清，即各家洋行亦只辦十餘字號，俱各
停手，以目下情景而論，其茶價定必跌落，然後發手陸續再辦，惟有
竭盡心力，總要價廉貨好，不致 美士渣甸虧本，以圖大家體面耳。
茲因咩[illegible]二十八號，親自由山押茶回福州，欲將各項情形面說茶師
知悉，不料啡吵茶師已往廈門醫病，亦曾將此情節說知新茶師嘞
件矣。茲特修寸楮，告明原委，倘有何吩咐之處，祈即示知，以便遵
命而行是也。此
上
美士渣甸大班臣 阿熙字啓

---

① 阿熙：怡和洋行（Jardine, Matheson & Co.）在福建的茶叶买办，应是 H1/57/7 信中提及的买办韩纯禧。

② 渣甸：即英国商人威廉·查顿（William Jardine），又译为渣颠、渣顿、赞典，为怡和洋行（Jardine, Matheson & Co.）创始人之一。

自蒙 美士渣甸吩咐所辦各事，到後至馬治十三號到福州，又至馬治卅號
起程上山到界首等處，先將茶莊各事料理妥當，吩咐備茶，出至亞罷剝
十九號。然見有新茶上市，但此日各處墟場，俱是些少嫩茶，要價太高，
各家無人下手。後至廿四號，茶已大出，其價依舊高抬，每百觔新茶，議
山客要價洋銀，在廿二廿三兩不等。所有福州各家洋行，如太平、機利文、
隆順、美士米𠷈、建利、美士建治、同順、美士剌士利、願此莊、格鴉等，總共
不過六七家來山採買。尚各拿定主意，價值儘可便宜，更兼大熟，外
客開莊採買，斷不能漲價太貴。詎料願此莊之買辦格鴉，於廿
四號行期，先行開手搶買，每百觔出價銀廿三四兩之多，即日將市情做
壞矣。及後各家見其如此出價太貴，俱恐有誤頭船，不得不隨此
市情下手。因此各家貨價，俱要廿餘兩之多矣。此是本年茶山實在
情形，斷不料其有如此之高價也。照因在香港時， 美士渣甸吩咐，若是
頭春好茶，約辦三十餘個字號，價在十七八兩，今見如此高價，若是
照辦三十餘號，誠恐東家吃虧，若停手不辦，又恐誤頭船。生理再四
籌思，惟有僅辦十四五個字號頭春好茶，以便趕載頭船。其茶現已
到齊（五月初間）福州，一俟港船到埠，即便裝運出洋矣。所有本年上山茶極
多，頭春好茶出自本行者，即各家洋行亦只辦十餘字號，俱各
停手，以目下情景而論，其茶價定必跌落，然後發手陸續再辦。惟有
竭盡心力，總要價廉貨好，不致 美士渣甸虧本，以圖主家體面耳。
茲因呼捫二十八號，親自由山押茶回福州，欲將各項情形面説茶師
知悉，不料舊時茶師已往廈門醫病，未曾將此情節説知新茶師[illegible]
件矣。茲特修寸楮，告明原委，倘有何吩咐之處，祈即示知，以便遵
命而行是也。此

上

美士渣甸大班廷〻

阿照字啓

（局部图）

5. 四月三十日茶商吴炳垣[①]致栋臣及叻件茶师的书信（年份不详[②]）（H1/57/5）

四月三十日，福建茶商吴炳垣致栋臣及叻件茶师的书信，谈及战乱不能前往战区采购茶叶，转往峡阳和洋口等地采购茶叶的情况。

Letter from Wu Ping-yuan. A two-page letter from Wu Ping-yuan to Mr. Le chien (Le jian) c/o Tung-ch'en (Dongchen) reporting his tea purchases at Hsia-yang and Yang-k'ou and the arrangements for its transport by water. There is no year, but the letter may date from the 1850s. 2 items. circa 1855

---

① 吴炳垣：怡和洋行（Jardine, Matheson & Co.）在福建的茶叶代理商。

② 原中文文献文末署"四月三十日"，英文提要中推测年份为1855年，但咸丰五年（1855）无四月三十日，故此件年份存疑。

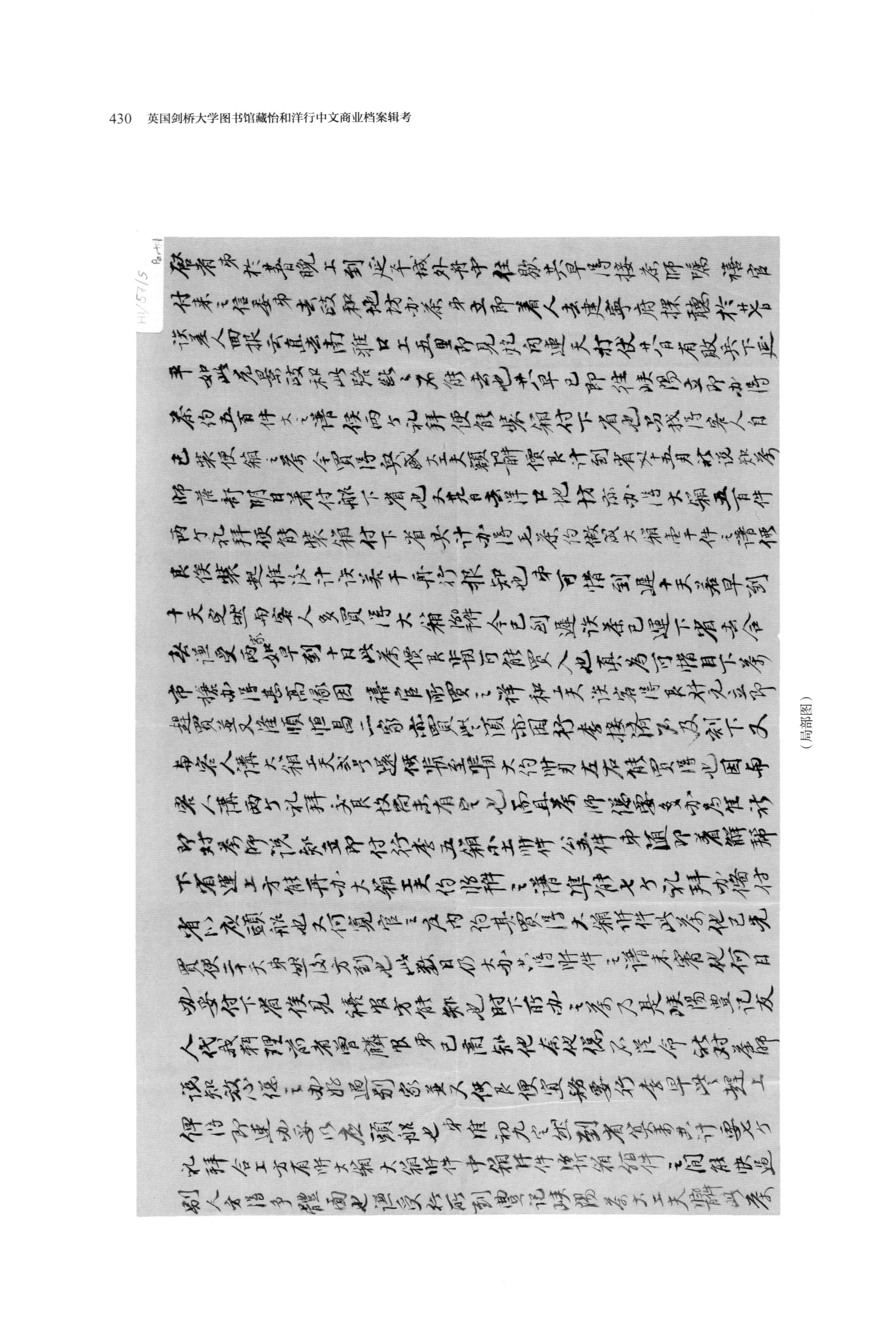

（局部图）

已与客人講過不能做别人行着謹受何先生將茶發去義和社
閩茶師故生行李一半小生一半即付我帮船運上俾得照市情候弟
返省方能定奪也目下汝縣烏龍茶價甚高又探得建寧府
之東乃東豐塘政和各處地坊有头春茶其时尚未有賊到所
以建寧府之客人有十餘帮到北處收買數千件此客弟已知
識一半刻下進退不能弟已探聽何路可走過數天再為报
上然星村苦口蘇汝界首一帶今年头春茶數之不能办也
刻下峡陽洋口兩處头春茶此數天完了惟是二春必好茶
细嫩因雨水調匀之故也本號所买入之奥盛工夫明日再专
馬信付下小办先第料此數天奥盛大箱必到省弟是月在洋
口明早又回峡陽但各琳之工夫办与不办亦要緊惟各茶務要
號名琳庄理办社对茶師說知盛啟良二三箱着　欽先索取此峡
陽洋口兩處斷無有各茶办也尚此

即請

穗记大兄大人刻安

祈即照讀与

四月二十日

弟吳炳垣字上

美士叻件　茶師名証

（局部图）

6. 约咸丰五年福建茶商吴炳垣[①]致栋臣及叻件[②]茶师的书信（H1/57/6）

约咸丰五年五月初一日（1855年6月14日），福建茶商吴炳垣致信栋臣及叻件，告知他们兴盛工夫茶“已着船装运下省”，并且谈及峡阳和洋口的茶叶行情，若无战事，建宁府的政和、松溪必能有头春茶，但“建阳营口、蔴沙、界首、星村一带，倘刻下能平静亦无头春茶也，所因此数处头春茶无人采择，将来二春仍复少出”。

Letter from Wu Ping-yuan. A letter from Wu Ping-yuan to Mr. Le chien (Le jian) c/o Tung-ch'en (Dongchen) enclosing a receipt for Hsingsheng kungfu tea (not included) and reporting sources of tea in the eastern region of the area of Cheng-ho and Chien-ning fu. There is no year, but the letter may date from the 1850s. 1 item. circa 1855

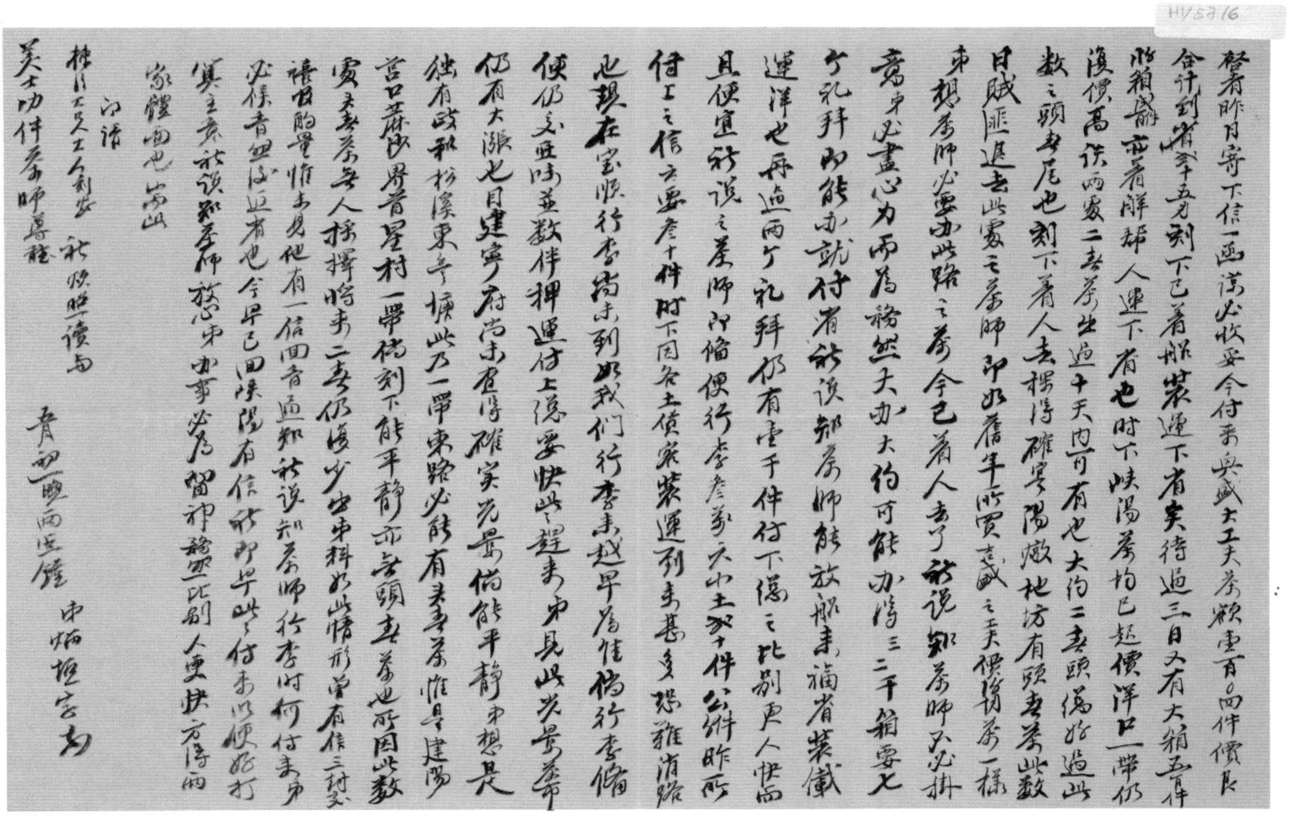

① 吴炳垣：怡和洋行（Jardine, Matheson & Co.）在福建的茶叶代理商。

② 叻件：怡和洋行（Jardine, Matheson & Co.）的品茶师。

（局部图）

7. 咸丰十年福建茶帮公告（H1/57/7）

咸丰十年（1860）六月，福建茶帮关于义和洋行拒绝支付已购茶叶款项的公告。义和行的茶司叻见[①]（Le-chien）、买办韩纯禧[②]、茶商吴炳垣[③]、林阿钦[④]共购买箱茶7000余件，价值共11万余元，不料收到茶叶之后，茶司叻见把阿钦藏在他们的“马毋地”船上，改扮为茶司从北河火船逃脱，试图将茶银骗吞伙分。在听取了案情后，府宪和英国领事“断令该行按数清偿，并饬义和亲书票据存领事执收，限期领银”。随后，该案件被转到上级机关审批。但领事宣布“此案被上司翻驳”，行会因此宣布，在义和洋行偿还所欠茶款之前，茶帮成员不得与该行做任何生意。

Public notice of Fukien Tea Guild. A public notice of July 1860 regarding the case of the refusal of the foreign firm I-ho (Yihe) to make payment for a supply of tea. The notice records that during January and February I-ho’s tea taster Le-chien (Le jian), comprador Han Ch’un-sha (Han Chunshan), and their Chinese tea men Wu Ping-yuan (Wu Bingyuan, namely Awei) and Lin Ah-ch’in (Lin Aqin, namely Acum) purchased about seven thousand cases of tea, valued at around $11,000[⑤]. They dressed Acum as a foreign taster, hide him in their ship the ‘Ma wu ti’, and tried to avoid payment. Having heard the case, the prefecture magistrate and British consul ordered I-ho to sign a document for the payment of the tea money. The case was then forwarded to a higher authority for examination and approval. Recently the consul has announced that the case was turned down. The guild therefore announces that none of its members will be allowed to do any business with I-ho until the debt is settled. 1 item. 1860

---

① 叻见：怡和洋行（Jardine, Matheson & Co.）的品茶师。前文亦称为“叻件”。

② 韩纯禧：怡和洋行（Jardine, Matheson & Co.）在福建的茶叶买办。

③ 吴炳垣：怡和洋行（Jardine, Matheson & Co.）在福建的茶商。

④ 林阿钦：怡和洋行（Jardine, Matheson & Co.）在福建的茶叶买办。

⑤ 勘误：原中文文献中作“拾壹万余元”，英文提要中此数字有误。

閩省自咸豐三年開口招商運茶與各洋行交易，一向由買辦茶樓經手議盤受茶兑銀歷久
無異緣本年正二月間義和洋行茶司叻哯與買辦韓純禧茶樓吴炳垣即阿瑋等串同素所重用林
阿欽指為該洋行新用茶樓向各商議盤先後共買箱茶七千餘件計價銀共拾壹萬餘元不至
料騙茶入手叻等即将欽藏匿本行馬毋地船昷復改扮茶司衣裝帶從北河火船逃脫希
圖将茶銀騙呑夥分經各商具稟本府憲領事官蒙傳義和茶司秉公訊實斷令該行按數清償并
飭義和親書票據存　領事执妝限期領銀只候申詳上司乃静候至今忽據　領事傳稱
此案被上司翻駁竟欲卸肩安知非煒等捏聳上司妝點挾制抑或　領事暗中袒護朝令
夕更似此人面獸心名為洋商實同强盗若再與交易勢必效尤日甚貽害無窮茲集公帮
會議如義和所欠茶銀一不清理嗣後各商務宜一体相関共伸公憤永不得與義和洋行
交易本帮亦不得代為出身包辦自議之後凡我同帮如有私相授受一經察覔各號被欠
茶銀公着認賠并將私易之銀貨繳　官分充各會館公用決不狥情預此佈白

咸豐一拾年六月　日茶帮公具

五八、咸丰十年茶叶买办鲍廉[1]“欠单”

1. 咸丰十年鲍廉“欠单”(H1/58/1)

咸丰十年二月二十一日(1860年3月13日)，怡和洋行买办鲍廉因业务亏损，写给英国商人渣颠[2](Jardine)和急顿赞臣[3](Chi-tun-tsan-ch’en)5600余元的欠单，注明一年内还清2800元，其余的在两年内清还。在“欠单”及鲍廉签名处分别盖有朱文正方形印章，印文“鲍廉图章”，欠款数额“伍仟陆百余员”处盖有方形印章菱形印迹，印文“鲍廉图章”。附有英文注释。

Promissory note to Jardine and Chi-tun-tsan-ch’en. A promissory note (in Chinese) from Alum (Pao Lien, Pao Lian) to Jardine and Chi-tun-tsan-ch’en (Ji dun zan chen) for $5670.67, 3 March 1860[4], incurred as a result of business losses, due for repayment in two years. The document is witnessed by Wu Ya-chu (Wu Yazhu) and Huang K’ai-ch’ing (Huang Kaiqing). It includes a short English note about its terms. 1 item. 1860

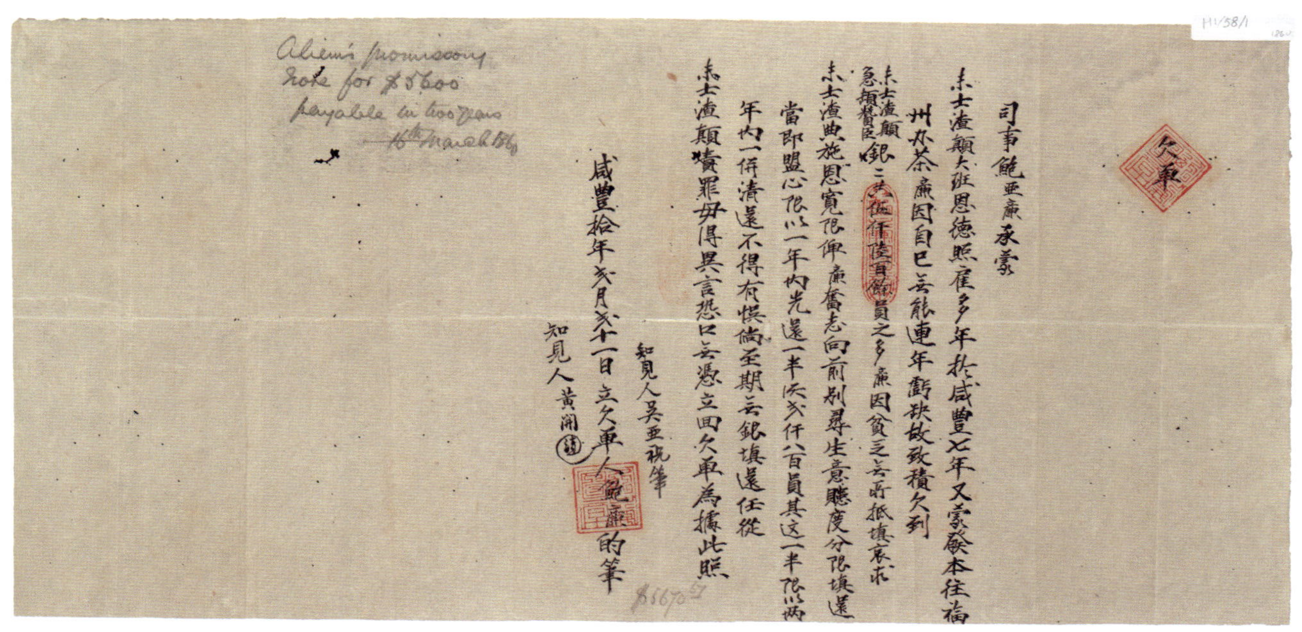
H1/58/1

欠單

司事鮑亞廉承蒙
未士渣顛大班恩德照雇多年於咸豐七年又蒙發本往福
州办茶廉因自己無能連年虧缺致積欠到
未士渣顛
急頓贊臣銀伍仟陸百餘員之多廉因貧乏無可抵填哀求
未士渣典施恩寬限俾廉奮志向前别尋生意聽度分限填還
當即盟心限以一年内先還一半弍仟八百員其这一半限以两
年内一併清還不得有悞倘至期無銀填還任從
未士渣顛饋罪毋得異言恐口無憑立回欠單為據此照
咸豐拾年弍月弍十一日立欠單人鮑廉的筆
知見人吴亞稅筆
知見人黄開

Aliem's promissory note for $5600 payable in two years 16th March 1860

$5670.67

① 鲍廉：中国茶叶买办。

② 渣颠：即英国商人威廉·查顿(William Jardine)，又译为渣顿、赞典，为怡和洋行(Jardine, Matheson & Co.)创始人之一。

③ 急顿赞臣：英国怡和洋行(Jardine, Matheson & Co.)大班。

④ 勘误：英文提要日期为1860年3月3日(3 March 1860)，按原中文文献“咸丰拾年弍月弍十一日”，应为1860年3月13日。

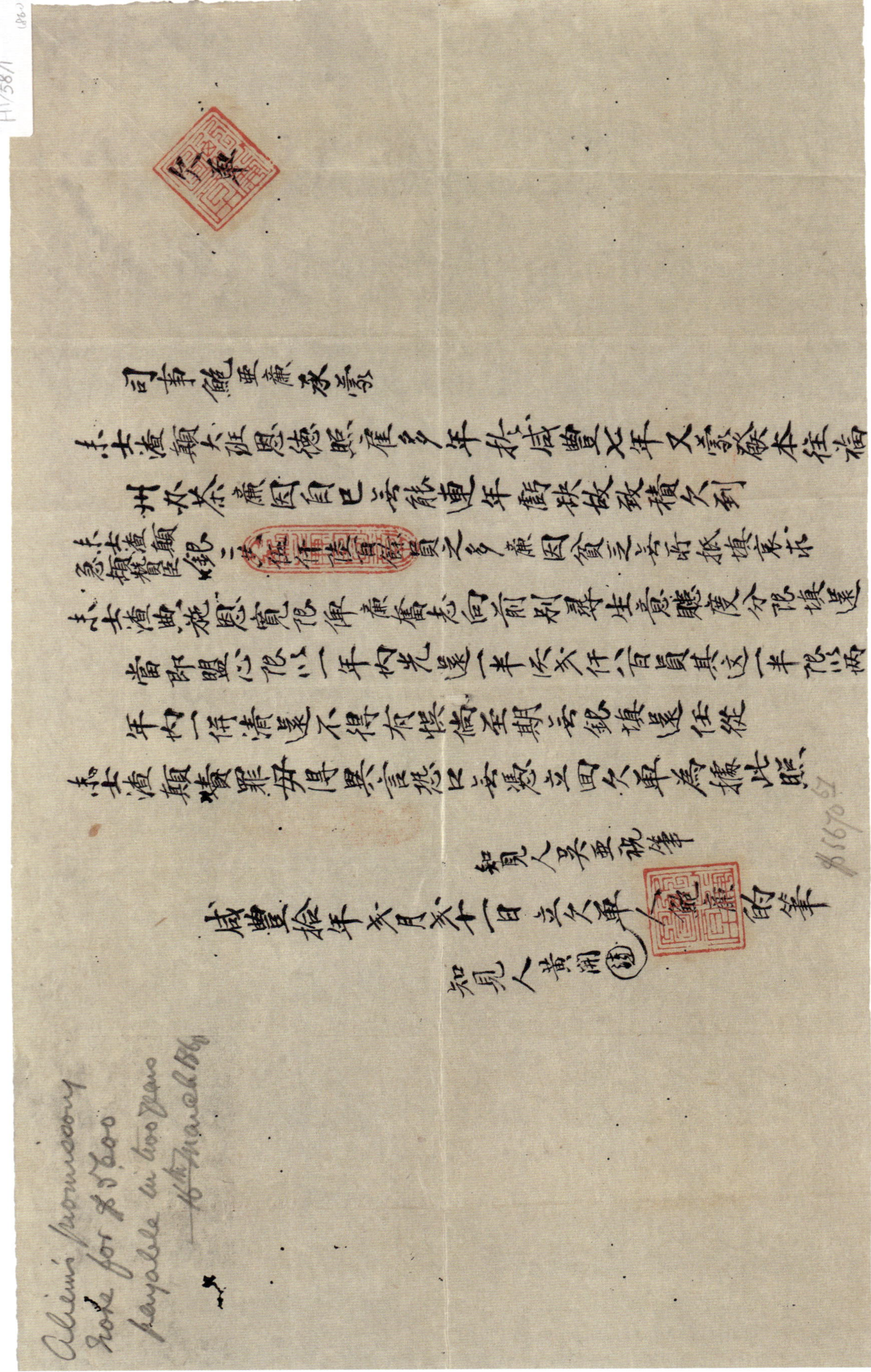

（局部图）

2. 咸丰十年鲍廉“欠单”信封（H1/58/2）

咸丰十年二月二十四日（1860年3月16日），装有鲍廉“欠单”的信封，上印有“顺昌”字样，有两种笔迹的英文注释：以铅笔书写“内附鲍廉的‘欠单’”；以钢笔书写“$5670.67，1860年3月16日放在铁箱内”。

Envelope for promissory note. A Chinese envelope used to hold H1/58/1 and including an English note on the front: ‘Alum①’s Promissory note enclosed $5670.67 Kept in the Iron Chest 16th March 1860.’ 1 item. 1860

① Alum：亚廉，即鲍廉，中国茶叶买办。

五九、咸丰十年亚光[①]给渣颠公司[②]的收据（H1/59）

咸丰十年九月十七日（1860年10月30日），亚光收到渣颠公司70元的收据。

Receipt from Ah-kuang. A receipt from Ah-kuang or Yaguang to Jardine, Matheson & Co. for $70, 30 October 1860. 1 item. 1860

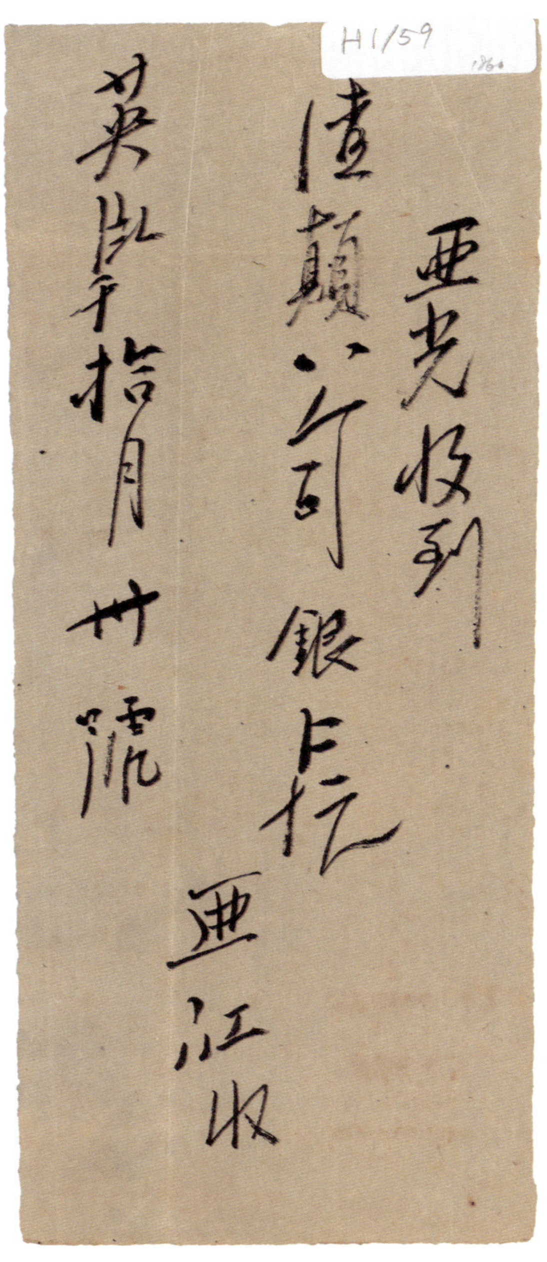
H1/59

亞光收到
渣顛公司銀七拾

---

① 亚光：中国买办。

② 渣颠公司：即英国商人威廉·查顿（William Jardine）等创办的怡和洋行（Jardine, Matheson & Co.）。

六〇、咸丰十一年万济堂[①]收单（H1/60）

咸丰十一年正月初六日（1861年2月15日），万济堂收到查丁[②]大船运来翠毛3箱的收单，因原“起货纸”丢失，万济堂立此收单交给查丁。

Receipt from Wan-chi tang. A receipt from Wan-chi tang (Wan ji tang) for cargo shipped by Jardine, Matheson & Co.'s steamship, 15 February 1861, the original shipping bill being lost. 1 item; Fair condition, but some damage by insects. 1861

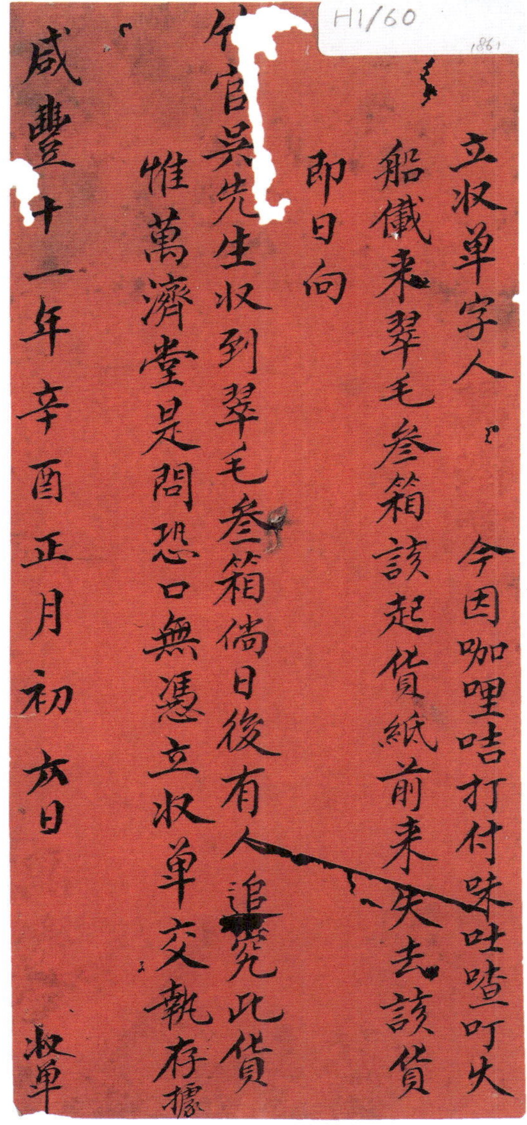
H1/60
1861

立收单字人 今因咖喱咭打付咪吐嗹吖大
船儎来翠毛叁箱該起貨紙前来失去該貨
即日向
[illegible]官吴先生收到翠毛叁箱倘日後有人追究此貨
惟萬濟堂是問恐口無憑立收单交執存據
咸豐十一年辛酉正月初六日 收单

---

① 万济堂：中国商号。

② 查丁：英国怡和洋行（Jardine, Matheson & Co.）。

六一、咸丰十一年《选录船头夜冷纸》（H1/61）

咸丰十一年十月十八日（1861年11月20日），香港中文商业报纸《选录船头夜冷纸》，刊登有各类广告。据报中“本馆启”所载，该报由孖剌新闻纸馆发行，每周印刊3次，全年订阅为每年3大元。

Newspaper advertisements. The newspaper ‘Chih-leng ye-t’ou-ch’uan lo-hsuan’ (‘Zhi leng ye tou chuan lu xuan’)① for 20 December 1861②, containing advertisements. 1 item. 1861

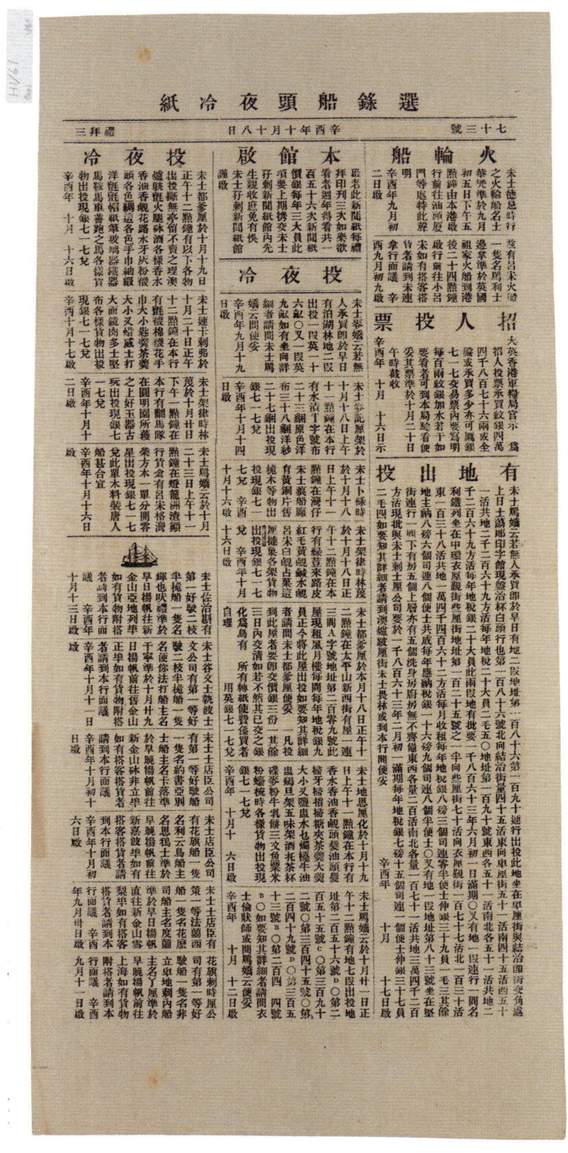

選錄船頭夜冷紙

七十三號　辛酉年十月十八日　禮拜三

火輪船

未士德忌時行之火輪船名士華咒準於九月初五日下午五點鐘由本港啟行前往油頭厦門等處特此布明

辛酉年九月初二日啟

本館啟

啟者此新聞紙每禮拜印刊三次如樂欲看者週年得看共一百五十六次新聞紙價銀每年三大員此項要上期携交未士孖刺新聞紙館內先生親收庶免有悞

末士孖剌新聞紙館謹啟

投夜冷

招人投票

有地出投

---

① 勘误：《选录船头夜冷纸》是香港《孖剌报》的中文商业版报纸。英文提要按西方阅读习惯，把报刊名从左往右误读作“Zhi leng ye tou chuan lu xuan”（《纸冷夜头船录选》）。

② 勘误：英文提要日期为1861年12月20日（20 Decemer 1861），按原中文文献“辛酉年十月十八日”，应为1861年11月20日。

選錄船頭夜冷紙

七十三號　辛酉年十月十八日　禮拜三

火輪船

末士德忌時行之火輪船名士華梵準於九月初五日下午五點鐘由本港啟行前往汕頭厦門等處特此聲明

辛酉年九月初二日啟

茲有呂宋火船一隻名騖利士邊拿準於英國祖家火船到港後二十四點鐘啟行前往小呂宋如有搭客搭貨者請到末連拿行面議　辛酉九月初九啟

招人投票

大英香港軍糧局官示　爲招人投票承買紋銀四萬四千八百七十六兩或全盤或承買多少亦可鷹銀七一七交易票內要寫明每百兩紋銀加水若干如要看者可到本局驗看便妥其票準於十月二十日午時截收

辛酉年　十月　十六日示

有地出投

末士鷹嬌云若無人承買即於早日有地二段地址第一百八十六第一百九十連行出投此地坐在皐厘街與結治卽街交角處上日士滿郎印字館現盤治杯白頭行也第一百八十六號北向結治街量四十五活東向皐厘街五十一活南四十五活西五十一活共地二千二百六十九方活每年地稅二十大員二毛五〇地址第一百九十號東西各五十一活南北各五十一活共地二千二百六十九方活每年地稅銀二十大員此兩段地有批要一千八百六十三年六月初一日滿期〇又有地一段連行一間名利鐵列坐在中環衣厘覲街些厘街地址第一百二十五號之一半向些厘街七十活向衣厘覲街一百七十七活北一百三十活東一百三十八活共地一萬四千四百六十二方活每月收租每年地稅銀八磅三個司連零半便士仲銀三十九員一毛三其餘地主納八磅六個司連八個便士共成每年應納稅銀一十六磅九個司連八個半便士〇又有地一段地址第八十三號坐在堅街連行一間下有房五個上層亦有五個洗身房廚房無不齊備東西各量二百活南北各量一百七十一活共地三萬四千二百方活現批與末士剌士厘公司要於一千八百六十三年二月初一滿期每年地稅銀七磅十五個司連一個便士仲銀三十七員二毛四如要知其詳細者請到澳爐跛厘街末士畏林或到本行問便妥

辛酉年　十月　十七日啟

本館啟

啟者此新聞紙每禮拜印刊三次如樂欲看者週年得看共一百五十六次新聞紙價銀每年三大員此項要上期携交末士孖剌新聞紙館內先生親收庶免有悞

末士孖剌新聞紙館謹啟

投夜冷

末士麥嬌云若無人承買卽於早日有泊湖林地二段出投一段英一十六畝〇又一段英九畝如有坐向詳細者請問末士鷹嬌云問便妥

辛酉年九月十九日啟

末士麥託厘架於十月十八日上午十一點鐘在本行有水漬T字號布二十三綑原色洋布三十八綑洋紗二十七綑出投現銀七一七兌

辛酉年十月十四日啟

末士卜絲時於十月十八日上午十一點鐘在灣仔末士濱船廠有黃銅片舊梳木等物出投現銀七一七兌　辛酉十月十六啟

末士架律時林蔑於十月十八日正午十二點鐘在本行有綠荳來路皮紅毛黃梘鹹水梘呂宋白梘占巢這厘攞梟各架貨物出投現銀七一七兌　辛酉年十月十六日啟

末士都爹厘於本月十八日正午十二點鐘在太平山新西街有屋一連三間A字號地址第二百零九號此屋現租風月樓每間每年地稅銀九員正今將此屋出投如要知其詳細者請問末士都爹厘便妥　一凡投到此屋者要卽交價銀三份一其餘三日內交清如若不然其已交之銀化爲烏有　所有轉紙使費係買者自理　用英銀七一七兌

末士地思厘化於十月十九日上午十一點鐘在本行有香水香油香梘頭髮油頭髮梳牙梳指梳糖夾茶㔶大㔶大小叉鹽盅木乜燭檯牛油盅鷄旦架五味架酒托茶杯碟麥粉牛乳餅三文魚粟米粉蠔梳時各樣貨物出投現銀七一七兌

辛酉年　十月十六日啟

末士鷹嬌云於十月廿一日正午十二點鐘有地七段出投地址第二百五十六號D〇第二百五十五號C〇第三百九十二號〇第三百四十五號〇第二百四十九號D〇第三百五十三號B〇第二百四四號B〇如要知其詳細者請問衣士倫狀師或問鷹嬌云便妥

辛酉年　十月　十二日啟

投夜冷

末士都爹厘於十月十九日正午十二點鐘有以下各物出投斷無亭留不賣之理澳爐駝氈火腿砵酒各樣香水香油香梘花路水牙灰粉襪頭各色綢這各色手巾紬緞洋氈氈帽紙筆玻璃器鐵器馬鞍馬車善跑之馬各樣貨物出投現銀七一七兌

辛酉年　十月　十六日啟

末士運卡剌弗於十月二十日正午十二點鐘在本行有氈襪棉襪花手巾大小匙㔶茶㔶大小叉蠟威士打大面鏡肉多士堅布各樣貨物出投現銀七一七兌

辛酉十月十七啟

末士架律時林蔑於十月廿日下午一點鐘在本行有翻馬隊在圓明園所獲之上好玉器古玩出投現銀七一七兌

辛酉年十月十二日啟

末士鷹嬌云於十月二十三日上午十一點鐘在燈籠洲渣顛行貨倉有呂宋格灣柴方木一單分開零星出投現銀七一七兌此單木料裝唐人船甚合宜

辛酉年十月十六日啟

末士佐治樹有第一好駛二枝半桅船一隻名輝也吠禮準於早日揚帆往新金山亞地列埠如有貨物附搭者請到本行面議　辛酉年十月十三日啟

末士谷文士執波士文公司有第一等好駛二枝半桅船一隻名便你法打船主名于寧準於十月廿九日揚帆前往舊金山正埠如有貨物附搭者請到本行面議

辛酉年十月十一日啟

末士士店臣公司有第一等好駛船一隻名約書亞別士船主名卡落準於早晚揚帆前往新金山砵非立埠如有搭客搭貨者請到本行面議

辛酉年十月初十日啟

末士店臣公司有花旗船一隻名利云鳥船主名思鴉士準於早晚揚帆前往新嘉波埠如有搭客搭貨者請到本行面議

辛酉年十月初六日啟

末士士店臣有第一等法蘭西船一隻名花壓司船主名度蘭準於早日揚帆直往新金山雪梨埠如有搭客搭貨者請到本行面議　辛酉年九月卅日啟

花旗剌時厘公司有第一等好駛船一隻名非立卑地剌內船主名了厘準於早晚揚帆前往上海如有貨物附搭者請到本行面議　辛酉九月十一日啟

（局部图）

六二、香港祺记宝行单据

1. 同治元年卢大昌[①]写给祺记宝行订单的收据（H1/62/01）

同治元年六月二十八日（1862年7月24日），卢大昌写给祺记宝行陈先生的收据（六月十二日祺记订风扇一把、配柜桶锁匙两条），盖有两枚随形印印章，一枚印文“吉星”；另一枚印文“护封”，盖在款项汇总处。有简单英文注释。

Receipt from Lu Ta-ch’ang. A receipt (in Chinese) from Lu Ta-ch’ang (Lu Dachang) to Mr. Ch’en (Chen) of Ch’i-chi Hong for a fan and locks, 24 July 1862, including a brief English note about the receipt. 1 item. 1862

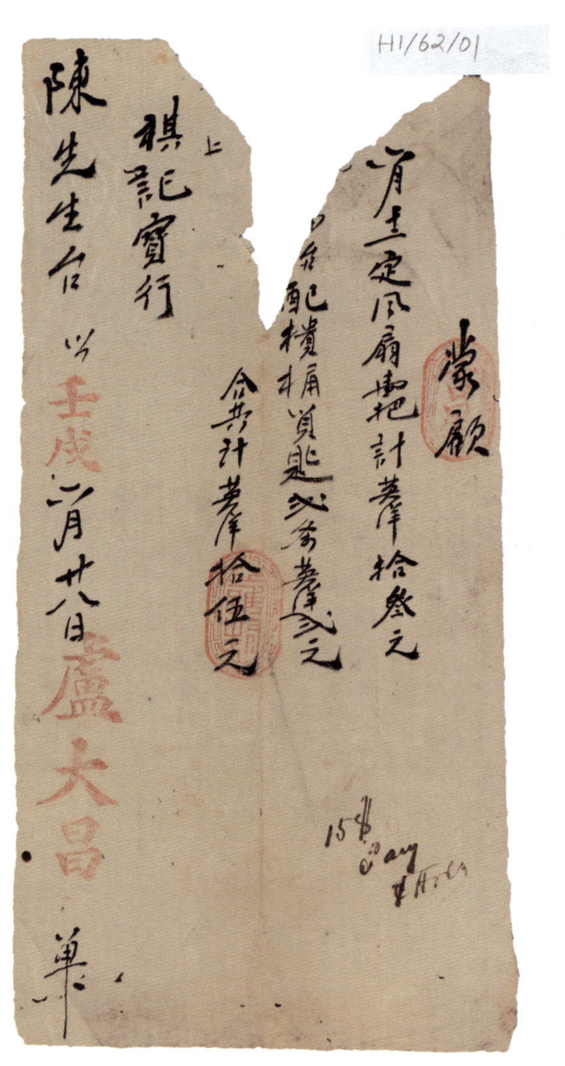
H1/62/01

蒙顧

六月十二定風扇壹把 計英洋拾叁元

六月十二日配櫃桶鎖匙兩條 英洋貳元

合共計英洋拾伍元

祺記寶行 上

陳先生台 收

壬戌六月廿八日盧大昌單

① 卢大昌：工匠。

2. 同治元年香港陆万顺盛冰窖[①]给祺记宝行的发票（H1/62/02）

同治元年七月初五日（1862年7月31日），陆万顺盛冰窖付给祺记宝行的发票（七月初二祺记订购船用白冰），盖有朱文印章，印文“陆万顺盛冰窖发票”。

Receipt from Lu-wan shun-sheng ping-chiao. A receipt from Lu-wan shun-sheng ping-chiao (Lu wan shun sheng bing jiao) to Ch’i-chi Hong for ice used in a ship, 31 July 1862. 1 item. 1862

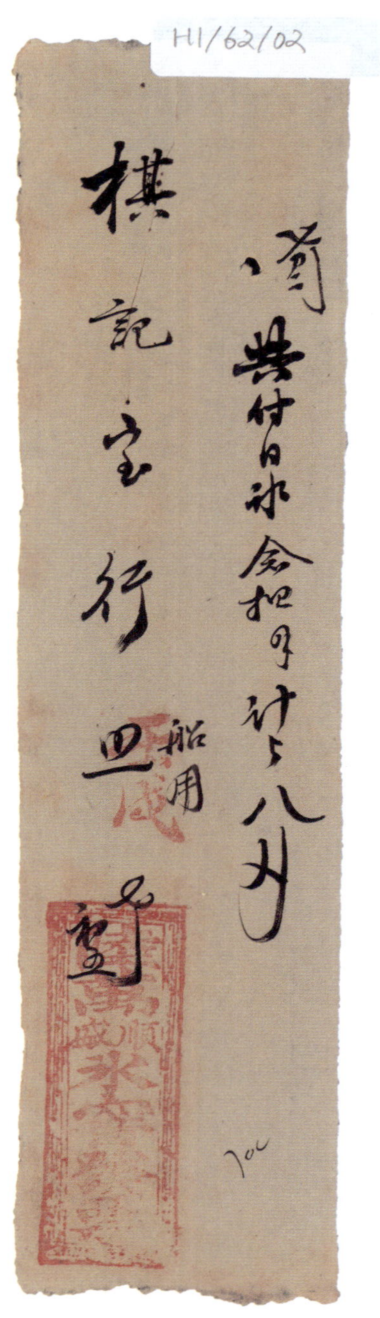

① 陆万顺盛冰窖：制冰商铺。

3. 同治元年香港陆万顺盛冰窖[①]给祺记宝行的发票（H1/62/03）

同治元年七月初五日（1862年7月31日），陆万顺盛冰窖付给祺记宝行的发票，记录了六月初五至七月初五祺记宝行船上用冰的数量及价钱，盖有两枚朱文印章，印文分别为“陆万顺盛冰窖发票”“上洋北门外二桃渡”。

Receipt from Lu-wan shun-sheng ping-chiao. A receipt from Lu-wan shun-sheng ping-chiao (Lu wan shun sheng bing jiao) to Ch’i-chi Hong for ice ordered during June and July, 31 July 1862. 1 item. 1862

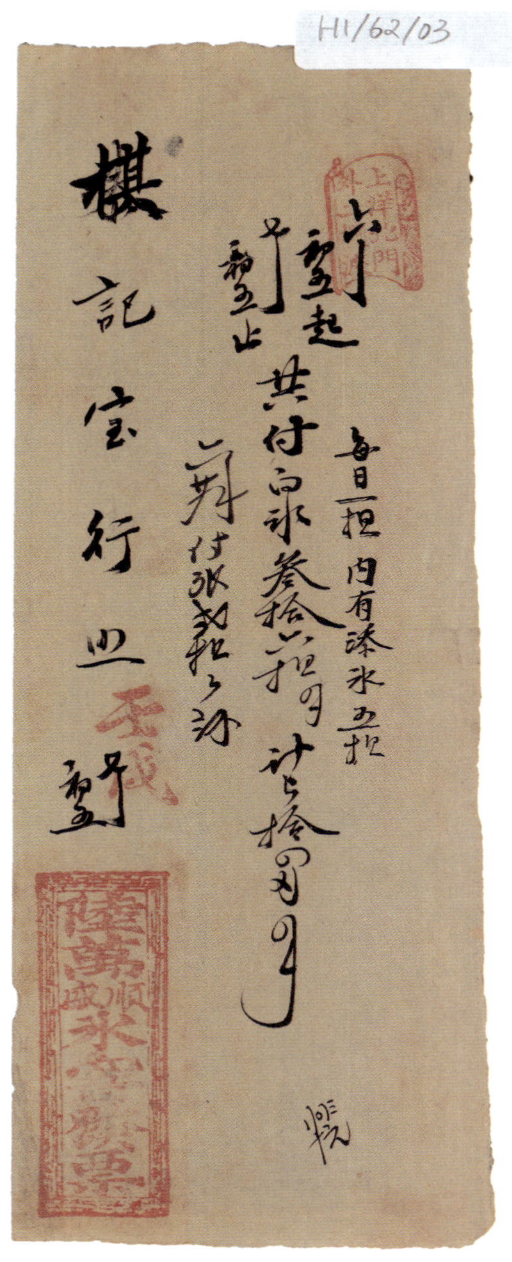

H1/62/03

祺記宝行

---

① 陆万顺盛冰窖：制冰商铺。

4. 同治二年香港成号瑞记付给祺记宝号的丝绸订单收据（H1/62/04）

同治二年（1863）二月，成号瑞记付给祺记宝号的丝绸订单收据，盖有朱文印章，印文“Chun haou Sae Kee 成号瑞记”。上有英文注释，注明这批货“给阿姆斯特朗先生，香港，$28.00”。

Receipt from Chunhaou. A receipt (in Chinese) from Chunhaou (Cheng hao rui ji) Sae Kee (Grocery) to Ch’i-chi Hong for silk, March 1863, including an English note recording that the order was ‘for Mr. Armstrong, Hong Kong’. 1 item. 1863

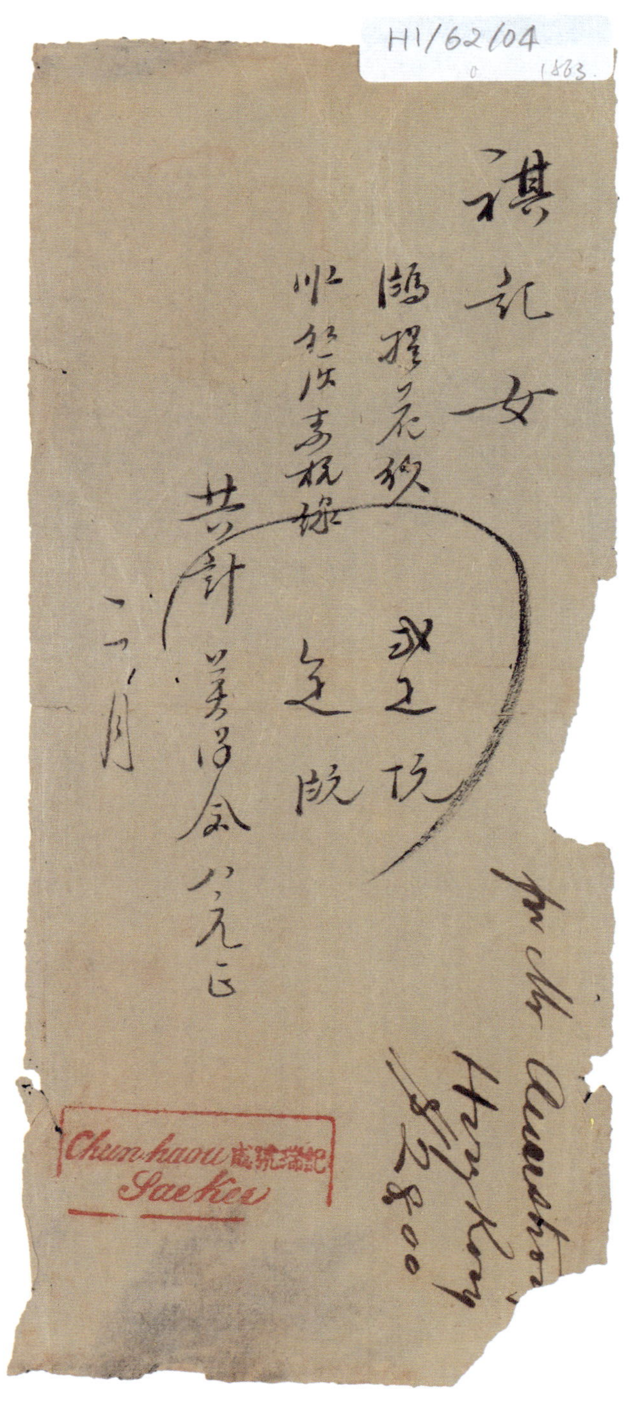

5. 同治二年香港成号瑞记付给旗记宝号的订单收据（H1/62/05）

同治二年三月初三日（1863年4月20日），成号瑞记付给旗记宝行的订单收据（旗记订购麻子油18罐，马口铁罐18只），盖有朱文印章，印文“Chun haou 成号瑞记 Sae Kee”。附有英文注释。

Receipt from Chunhaou. A receipt (in Chinese) from Chunhaou (Cheng hao jui ji) Sae Kee (Grocery) to Ch’i-chi Hong for castor oil and tins, 20 April 1863, including English annotations. 1 item. 1863

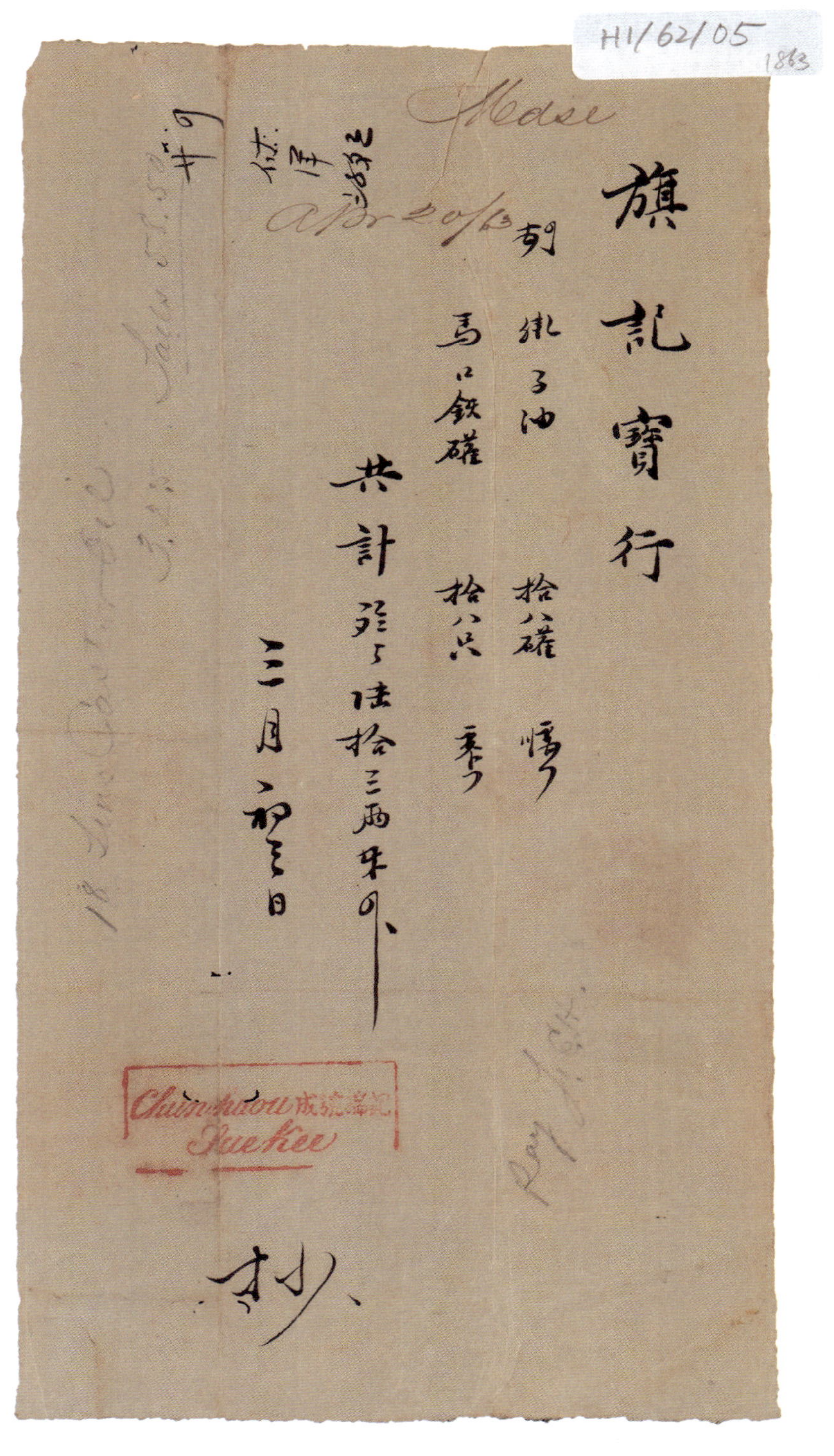

6. 同治二年香港万丰洋货店付给祺记洋行的发票（H1/62/06）

同治二年三月初七日（1863年4月24日），万丰洋货店付给祺记洋行的发票，盖有三枚印章，下方印章印文“万丰洋货发票”，上方两枚印章内容分别为“客意”和“癸亥”。背面有英文注释。

Receipt from Wan-feng yang-huo tian. A receipt (in Chinese) from Wan-feng yang-huo tian (Wan feng yang huo dian) to Mr. Hai-er of Ch'i-chi Hong for mattings, 24 April 1863, including an English note about the receipt. 1 item. 1863

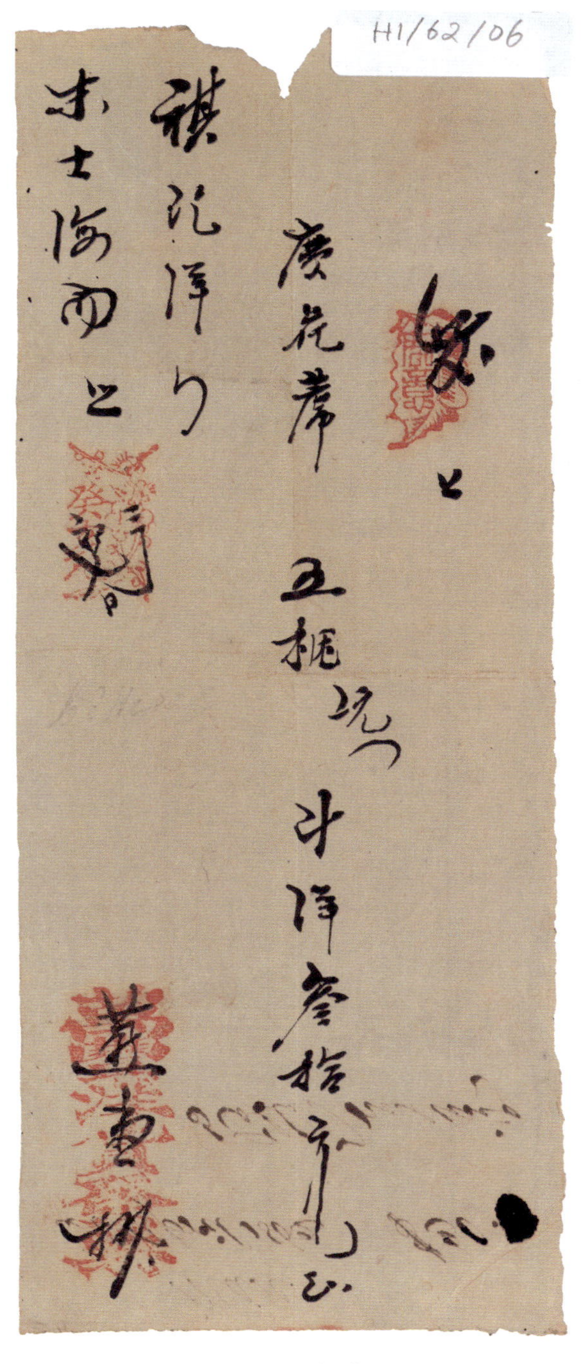

（正）

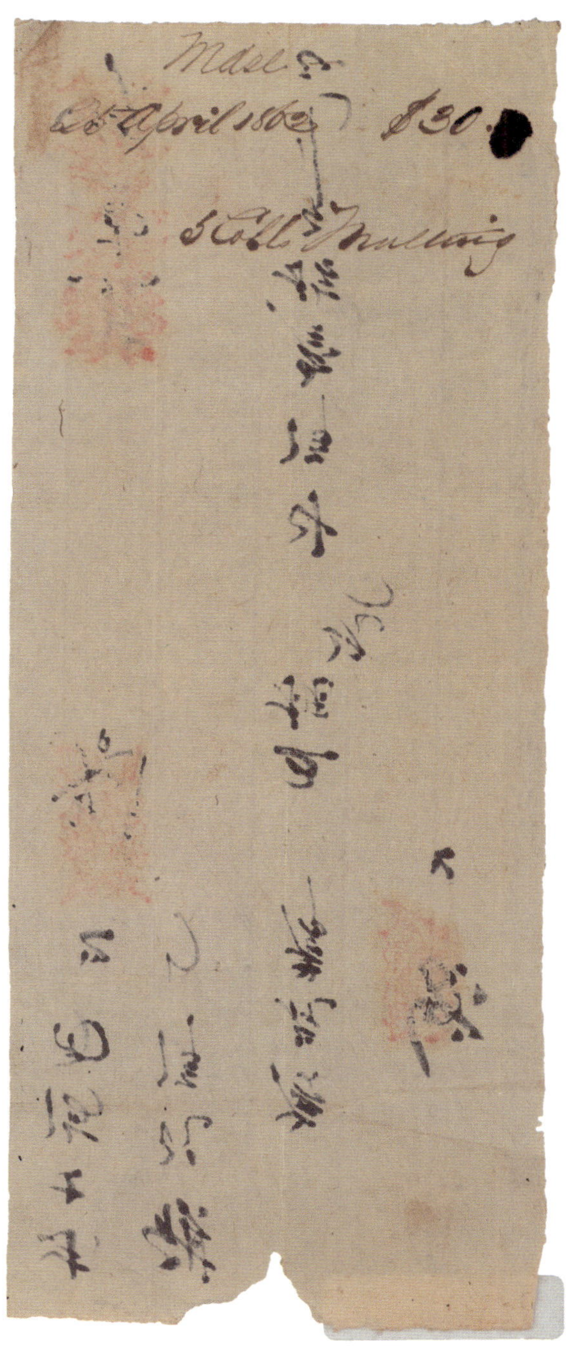

（反）

7. 香港“祺记书柬”（日期不详）（H1/62/07）

香港祺记宝行优惠券，注明“凭票取钱壹佰文”，盖有朱文印“祺记书柬”。

Coupon of Ch’i-chi Hong. An undated coupon issued by Ch’i-chi Hong valued at 100 wen. 1 item.

H1/62/07 n.d.

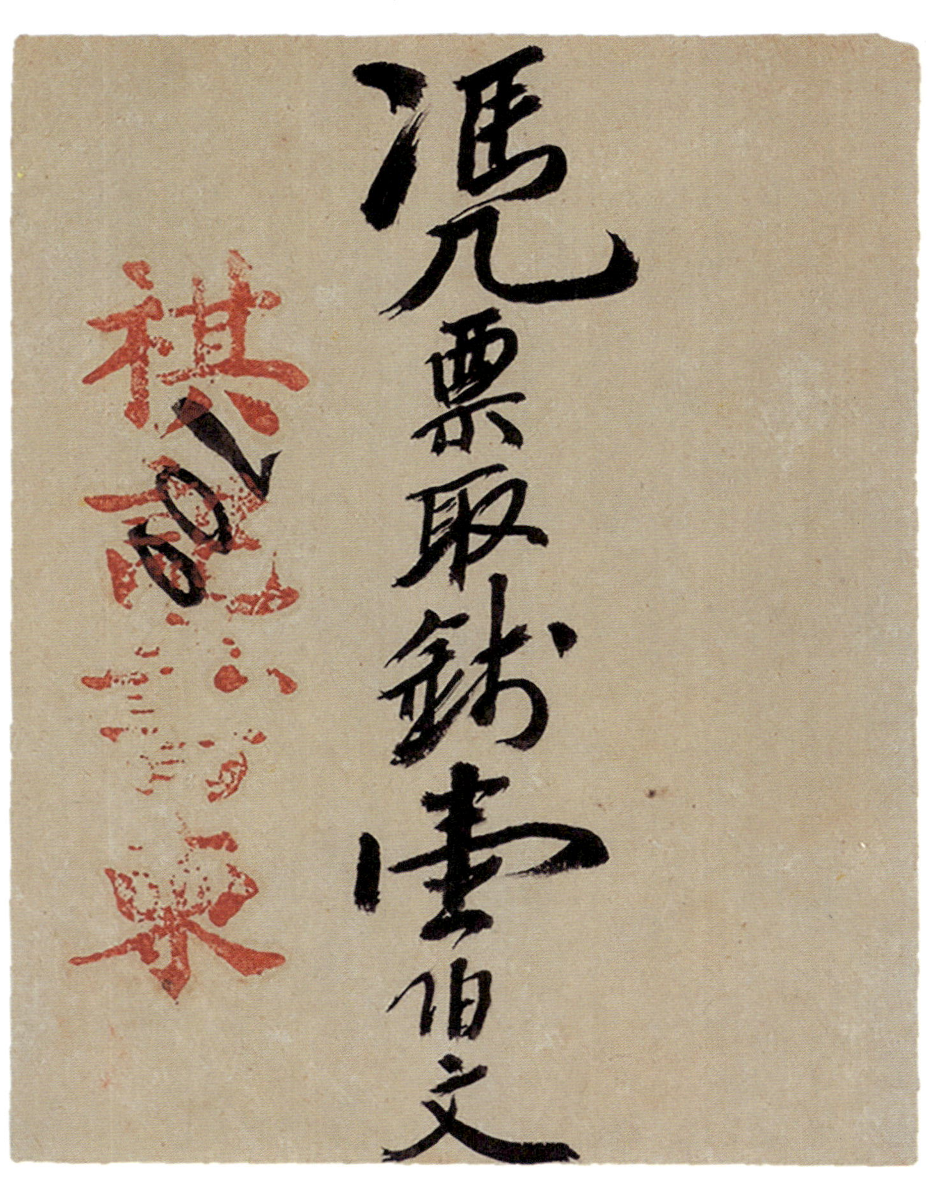
憑票取錢壹佰文

祺記書柬

六三、同治元年香港协记洋货店单据（H1/63）

同治元年七月初五日（1862年7月31日），协记洋货店付给泰兴宝行的发票（泰兴宝行购牛油200斤），盖有朱文印章，印文“协记洋货发票”，抬头盖有一枚随形印。用铅笔写有英文注释。

Receipt from Hsie-chi yang-huo tien. A receipt (in Chinese) from Hsie-chi yang-huo tien (Xie ji yang huo dian) to T’ai-hsing hong (Taixing) for butter, 31 July 1862, including a brief English note about the receipt. 1 item.

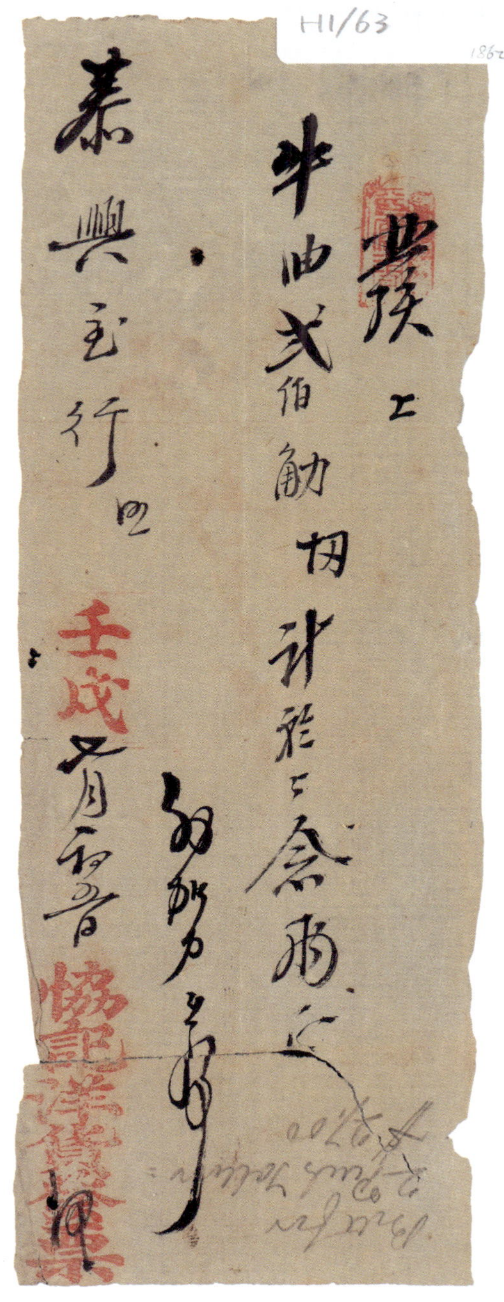

六四、日本单据

1. 同治元年订购柴火的收据（H1/64/1）

同治元年（1862），日文书写的订购188担柴火的收据，盖有印章，印文不清。有简单英文注释。

Receipt for firewood. A receipt (in Japanese) for 188 piculs of firewood from the ‘Banshee’, including English notes about the receipt. 1 item. 1862

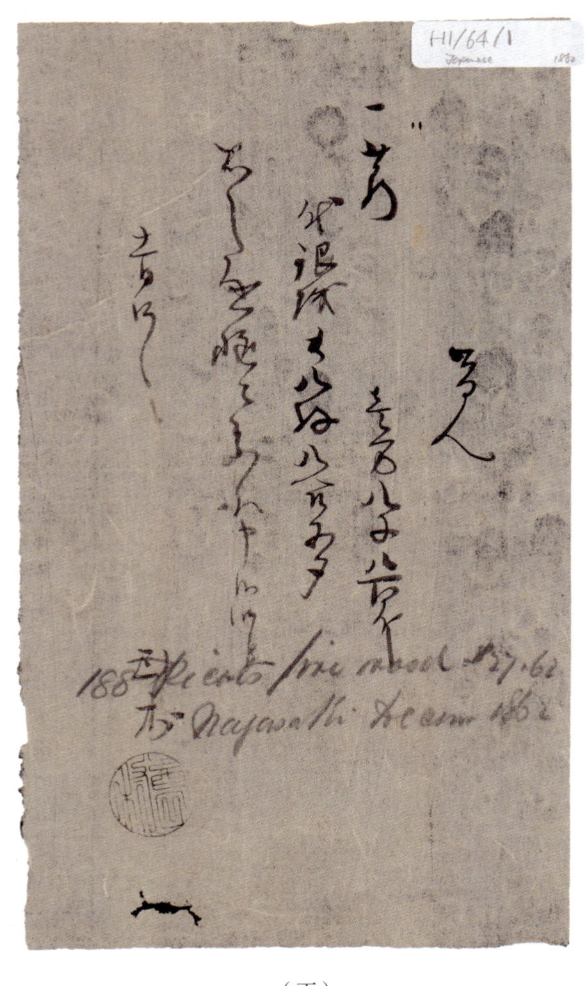

（正）

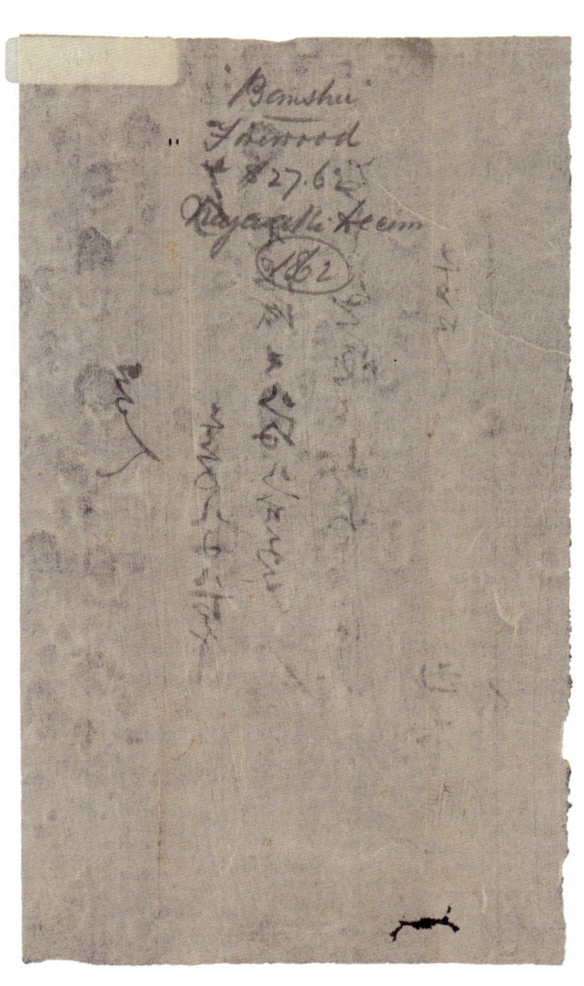

（反）

2. 同治元年日本订购火油的收据（H1/64/2）

同治元年（1862），日文书写的订购火油的收据，盖有印章，印文不清，有简单英文注释。

Receipt for oil. A receipt (in Japanese) for oil from the 'Banshee', including English notes about the receipt. 1 item. 1862

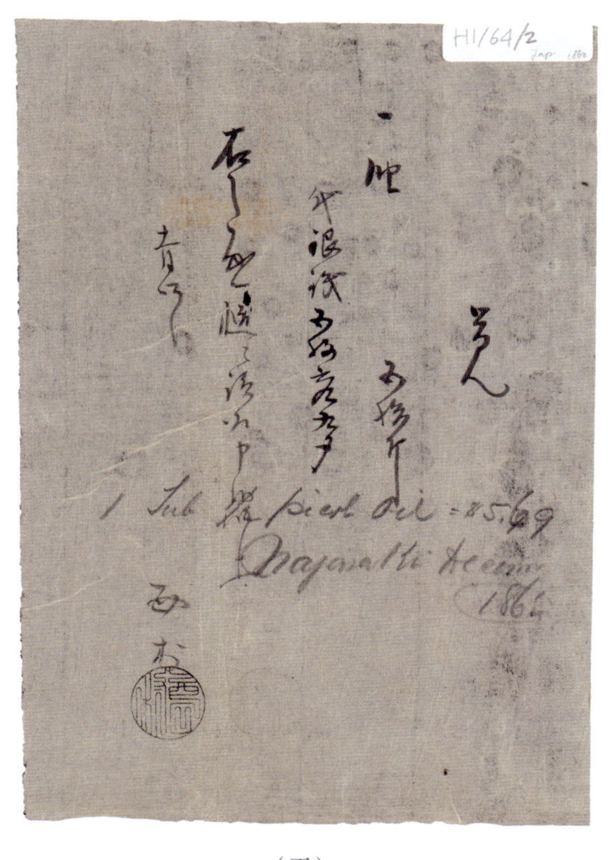

（正）

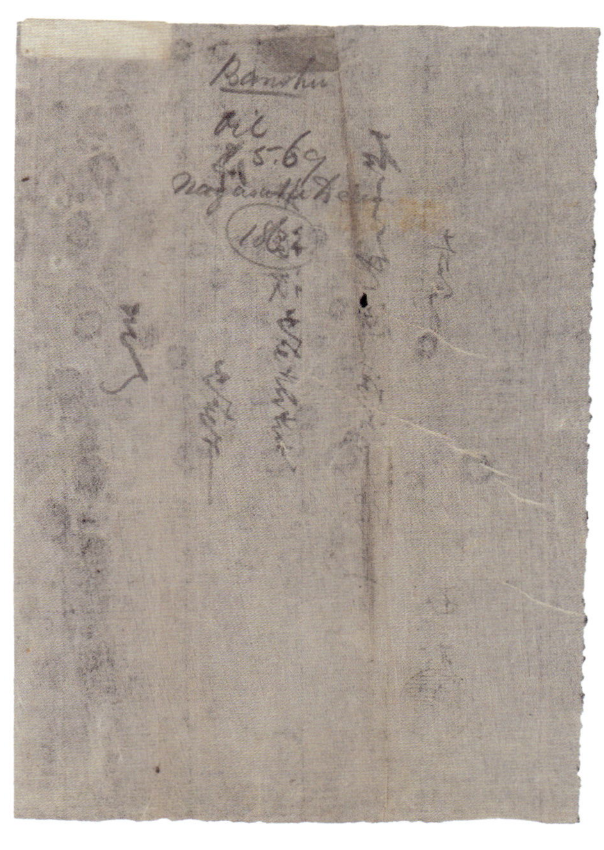

（反）

3. 八月日本订购火油的收据（年份不详）（H1/64/3）

八月，日文书写的订购火油收据，盖有印章，印文不清。由简单英文注释，可知订购1650担油。

Receipt for coals. A receipt (in Japanese) for 1650 piculs of oil, including English notes about the receipt. The date is not known. 1 item.

4. 同治四年货物收据（H1/64/4）

同治四年八月二十一日（1865年10月10日），英国商人向日本商人订购货物的记录。信封背面为日文，正面为英文，写给总工程师 John McArthur[①]，注明收到该轮货物。

Notes re goods for S. S. ‘Glengyle’. An envelope with Japanese on the back and English notes on the front, the latter recording the receipt of goods on board S. S. ‘Glengyle’, 10 October 1865, and addressed to John McArthur, Chief Engineer. 1 item. 1865

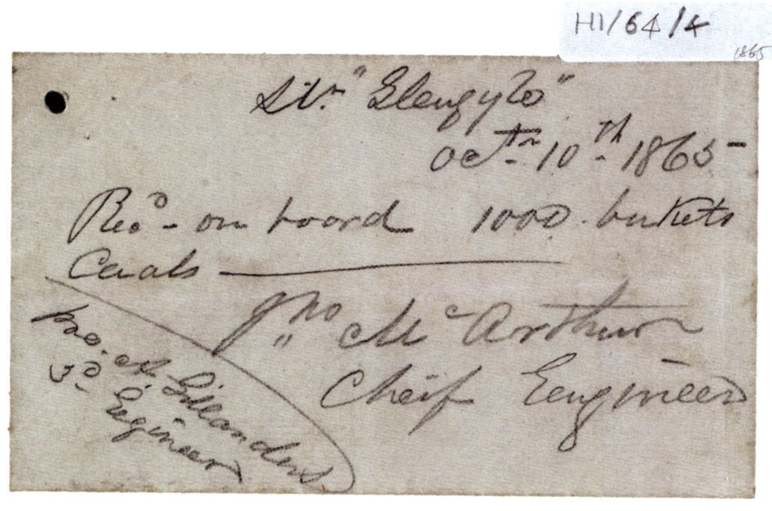

H1/64/4

Str. "Glengyle"
Oct. 10th 1865

Recd. on board 1000 baskets
Coals

Jno McArthur
Chief Engineer

（正）

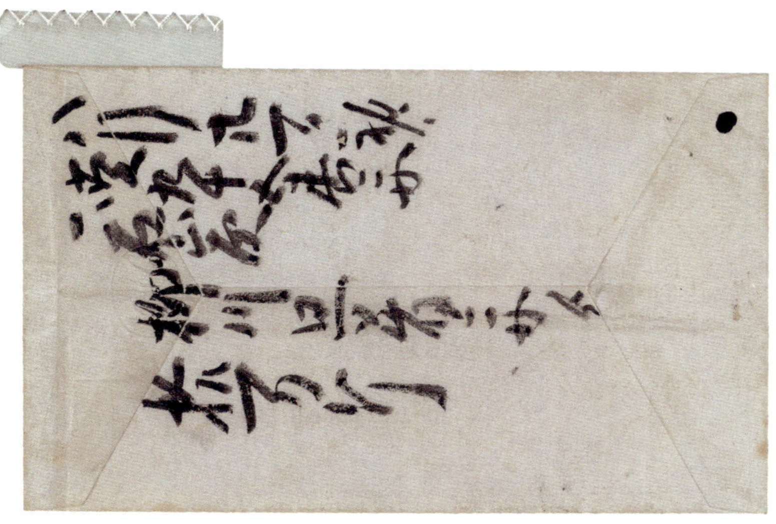

（反）

① John McArthur：约翰·麦克阿瑟，英国总工程师。

六五、同治二年谦信[①]付给渣甸公司[②]的收单（H1/65）

同治二年五月十一日（1863年6月26日），谦信商行收到渣甸公司付寄香港的货物收单，盖有谦信印章，印文“谦信饷漂”。

Receipt from Ch-ien-hsin. A receipt (in Chinese) from Ch'ien-hsin (Qianxin), Hong Kong, to Jardine, Matheson & Co., 26 June 1863, including English notes about the receipt. 1 item. 1863

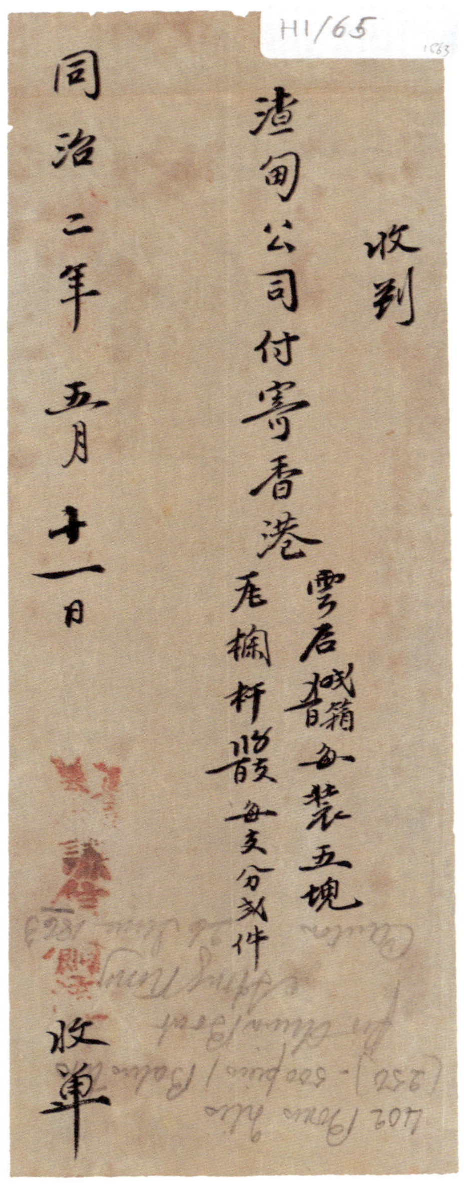
H1/65
收到
渣甸公司付寄香港
同治二年五月十一日
收單

① 谦信：中国商行。

② 渣甸公司：即怡和洋行（Jardine, Matheson & Co），英国商行。

六六、同治四年买办收据（H1/66）

同治四年四月十二日（1865年5月6日），外国商人威利斯（J. Willis）用中文和英文注明付给买办0.25元的收据。

Note of payment to compradore. A note of payment (given in both Chinese and English) from J. Willis (?) to the compradore for a quarter dollar, 12 April 1865[①]. 1 item. 1865

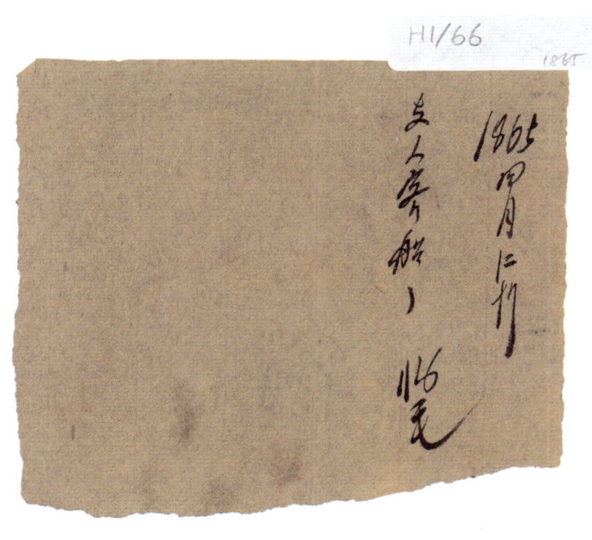

（正）

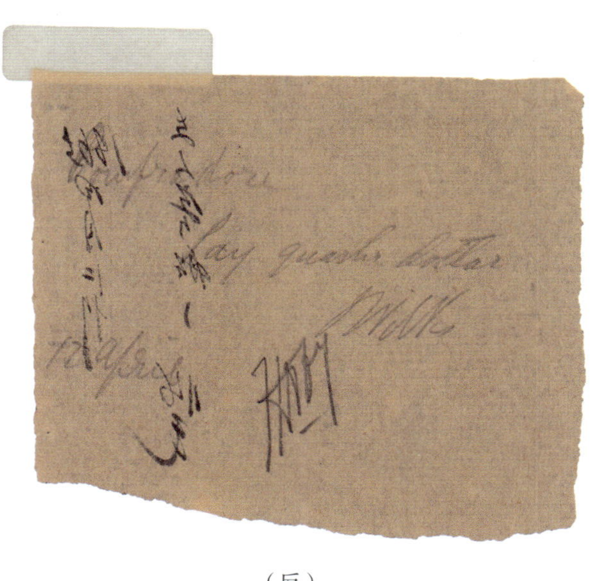

（反）

① 英文提要此时间疑为照录中文档案时间，未转换为公元日期。

六七、同治五年同昌[①]收据（H1/67）

同治五年十二月三十日（1867年2月4日），同昌商行收到英国商人万益500元收据。

Receipt from Huang Nan-shan. A receipt from Huang Nan-shan (Huang Nanshan) of T'ung-ch'ang (Tongchang) Hong to Magniac for $500, 3 February 1867[②]. 1 item. 1867

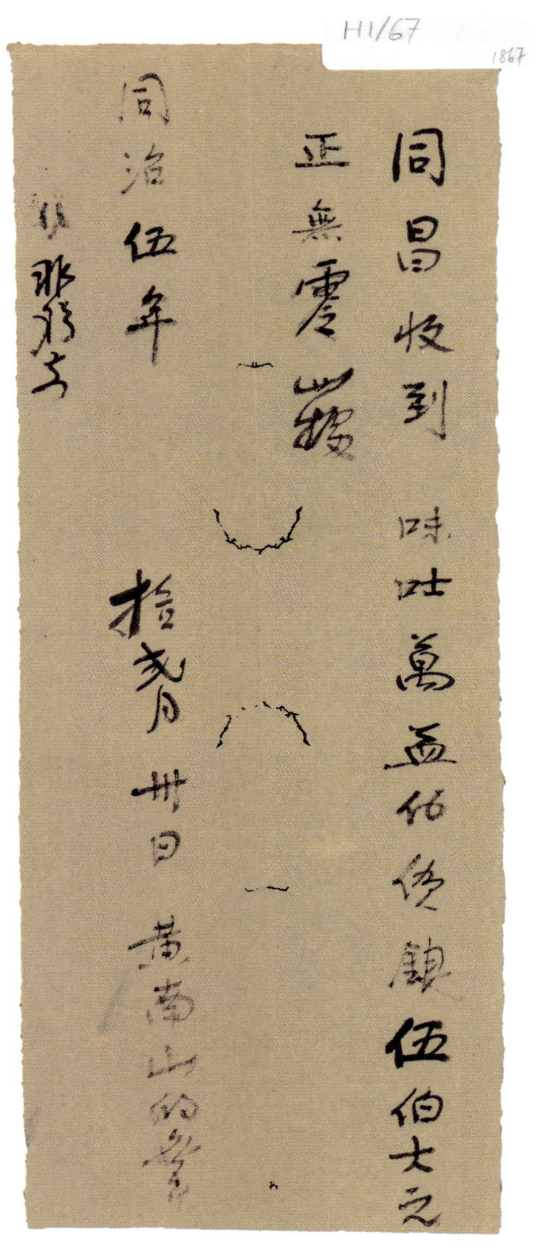
H1/67
1867

同昌收到咭吐萬益[illegible][illegible]銀伍伯大元
正無零一毫
同治伍年拾弍月卅日黃南山的筆
[illegible]

① 同昌：中国商行。

② 勘误：英文提要日期为1867年2月3日（3 February 1867），按原中文文献“同治伍年拾弍月卅日”，应为1867年2月4日。

六八、同治七年振泰①聪记收据（H1/68）

同治七年三月初二日（1868年3月25日），振泰聪记付给怡记宝号的青糖收据，由新兴行云臣代怡记宝号交付30,685.49元。盖有四枚印章，右上方印章内容为“顺吉”；两枚随形印印文均为“振泰图记”；长方形印章中间印文“振泰聪记”，上方印文“汕头”，两旁分别是“发货图书”“支揭不准”。

Receipt from Chintai. A receipt (in Chinese) from Chintai (Zhentai), Swatow, to I-chi (Yi ji) for sugar, 25 March 1868, with $30,685.49 having been delivered by Mr. Yun-ch’en (Yun chen) of Hsin-hsing (Xinxing) Hong on I-chi’s behalf. The receipt includes an English note about its contents. 1 item.

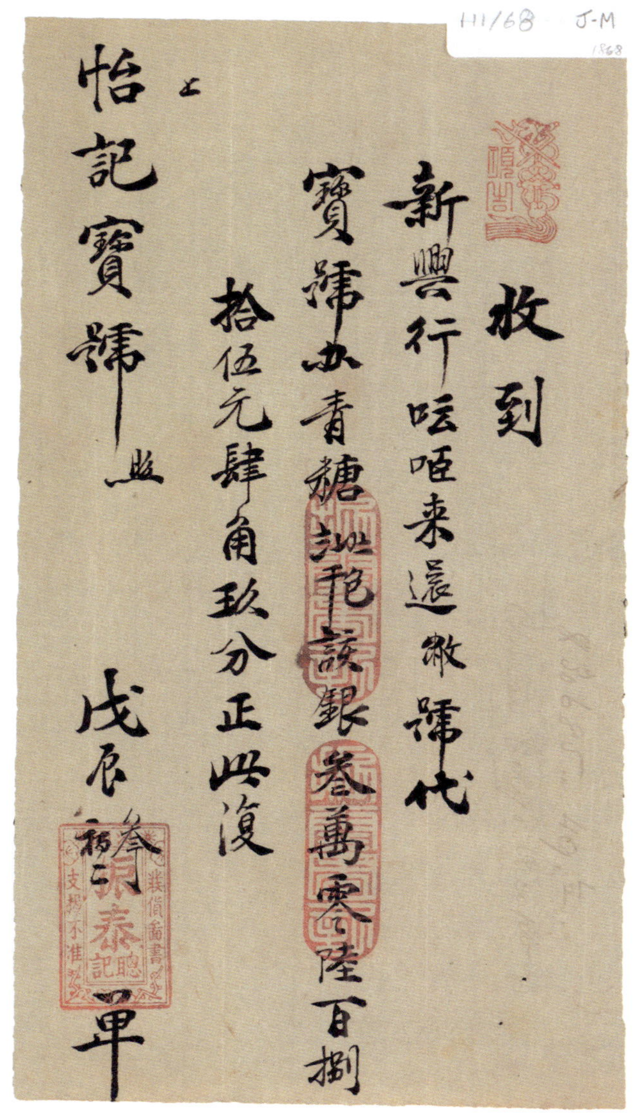
H1/68　J-M
1868

收到
新興行呍咺來還敝號代
寶號出青糖扣艳該銀叁萬零陸百捌
拾伍元肆角玖分正此復
怡記寶號
戊辰 [illegible] 單

① 振泰：中国商行。

六九、同治八年黎辉记[①]翻修美国旧战船的契约（H1/69）

同治八年九月十八日（1869年10月22日），黎辉记翻修美国战船契约，约定在订立合同之日起四个星期内完工，皇家验船人勿孖度验或其他验船人验收合格后，安南国王即把船价银91,000元交给赞职。盖有黎辉记印章，印文“黎辉信记”。

Contract for the re-equipping ‘Yao-na-tie-la-pi’. A contract (in Chinese) for the re-equipment of the old American warship ‘Yao-na-tie-la-pi’ (‘Yao nan die la bi’) under order of Annam’s emperor, 22 October 1869, including five articles. An English note at the bottom records that the contract was signed by Pha Vien, royal commissioner of Annam (Vietnam), and John Jack in the presence of William H. Brereton, Hong Kong. 1 item. 1869

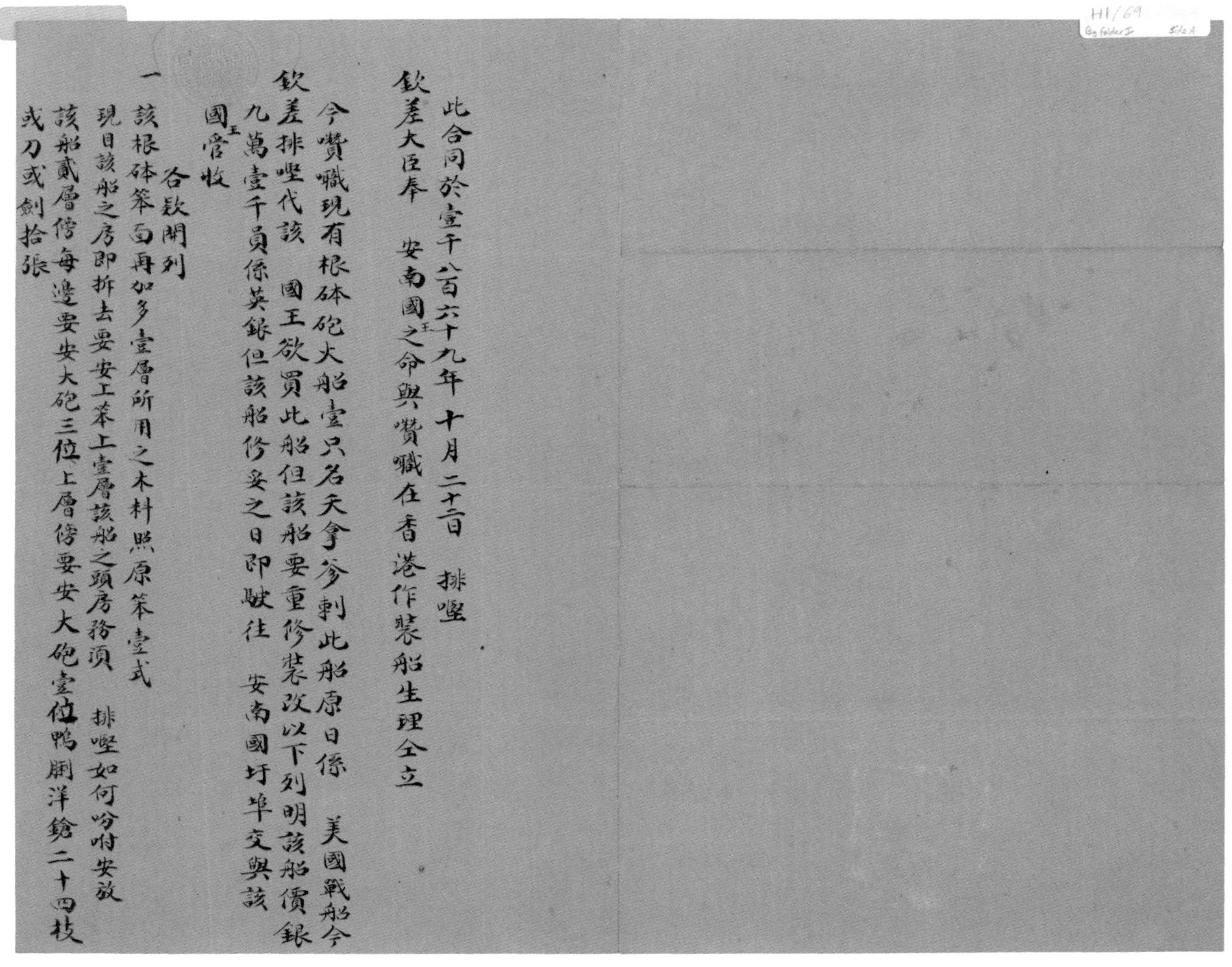
H1/69

此合同於壹千八百六十九年十月二十二日　排㘴
欽差大臣奉　安南國王之命與賛職在香港作裝船生理仝立
今賛職現有根砵砲大船壹只名天拿爹剌此船原日係　美國戰船今
欽差排㘴代該　國王欲買此船但該船要重修裝改以下列明該船價銀
九萬壹千員係英銀但該船修妥之日即駛往　安南國圩埠交與該
國王官收
各欵開列
一　該根砵笨面再加多壹層所用之木料照原笨壹式
現日該船之房即拆去要安工笨上壹層該船之頭房務須　排㘴如何吩咐安放
該船貳層傍每邊要安大砲三位上層傍要安大砲壹位鴨脷洋鎗二十四枝
或刀或劍拾張

① 黎辉记：中国商行。

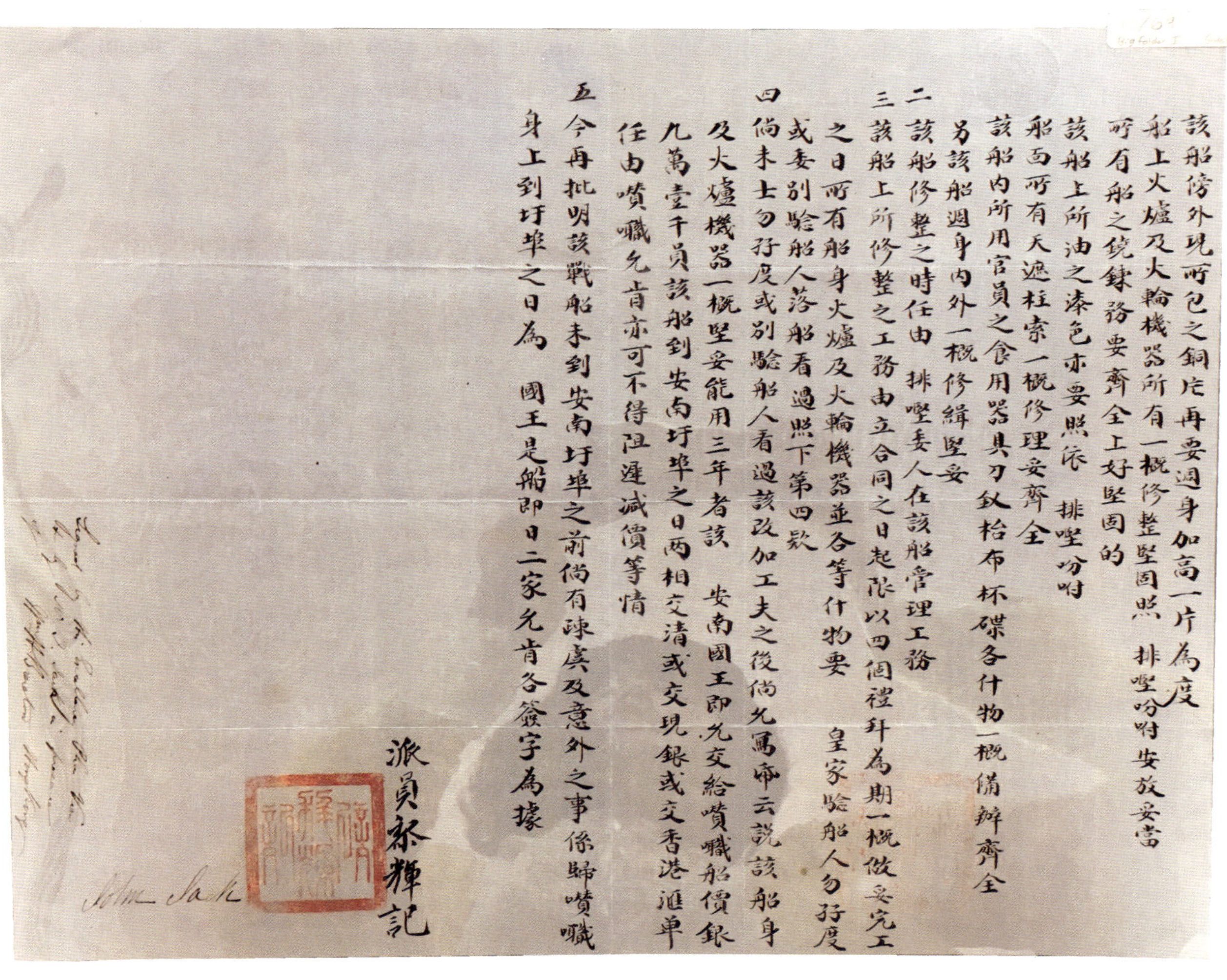

該船傍外現所包之銅片再要週身加高一片為度
船上火爐及火輪機器所有一概修整堅固照　排嘡吩咐安放妥當
所有船之鋭鍊務要齊全上好堅固的
該船上所油之漆色亦要照依　排嘡吩咐
船面所有天遮柱索一概修理妥齊全
該船内所用官員之食用器具刀釵枱布杯碟各什物一概備辦齊全
另該船週身内外一概修緝堅妥
二該船修整之時任由　排嘡委人在該船管理工務
三該船上所修整之工務由立合同之日起限以四個禮拜為期一概做妥完工
之日所有船身火爐及火輪機器並各等什物要　皇家驗船人勿孖度
或委別驗船人落船看過照下第四欵
四倘未士勿孖度或別驗船人看過該改加工夫之後倘允屬席云說該船身
及火爐機器一概堅妥能用三年者該　安南國王即允交給嘖嘰船價銀
九萬壹千員該船到安南圩埠之日兩相交清或交現銀或交香港滙單
任由嘖嘰允肯亦可不得阻遲減價等情
五今再批明該戰船未到安南圩埠之前倘有疎虞及意外之事係歸嘖嘰
身上到圩埠之日為　國王是船即日二家允肯各簽字為據
派員黎輝記

七〇、同治十二年怡和洋行唐景星与香港轮船主遮吸臣签订的航运保险单（H1/70）

同治十二年二月二十三日（1873年3月21日），怡和洋行总买办唐景星（唐廷枢）与香港轮船主遮吸臣签订的上海至黄浦货物运输保险单，货值2300两，保险费十七两二钱五分，包括有“船在洋面遇风打破照保若干如数赔偿”等16个条款，盖有怡和洋行保险印章，印文“怡和保险图记”。

Insurance agreement with Tong King-sing. A printed insurance agreement between Tong King-sing (T’ang Ching-hsing), i.e. T’ang T’ing-shu (Tang Tingshu), and Ewo Insurance for the shipment of cargo from Shanghai to Whampoa, 21 March 1873, including sixteen articles. 1 item. 1873

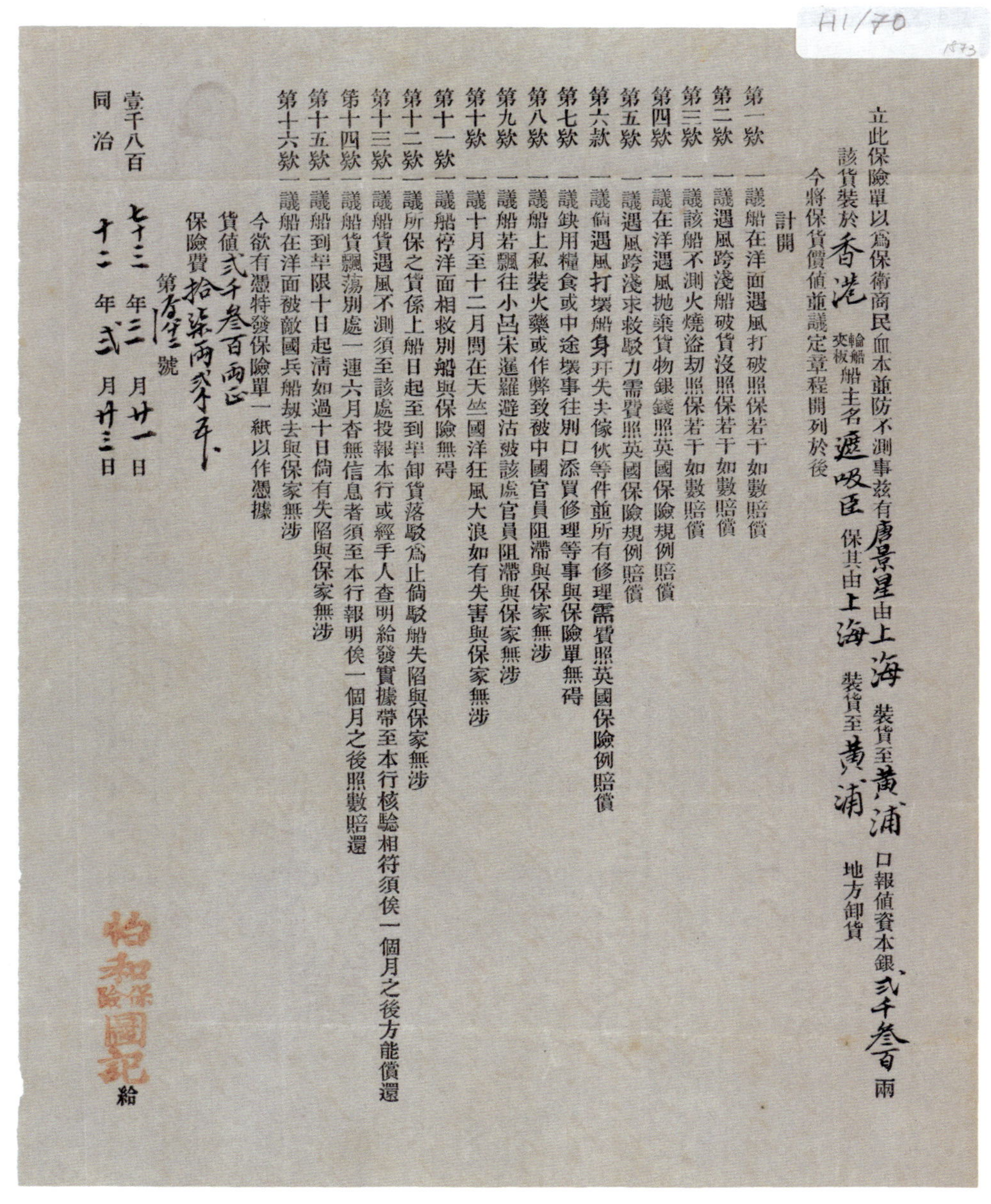

H1/70
1873

立此保險單以爲保衛商民血本並防不測事茲有唐景星由上海裝貨至黃浦口報値資本銀弍千叁百兩
該貨裝於香港輪船夾板船主名遮吸臣保其由上海裝貨至黃浦地方卸貨
今將保貨價値並議定章程開列於後

計開

第一欵一議船在洋面遇風打破照保若干如數賠償
第二欵一議遇風跨淺船破貨沒照保若干如數賠償
第三欵一議該船不測火燒盜刼照保若干如數賠償
第四欵一議在洋遇風抛棄貨物銀錢照英國保險規例賠償
第五欵一議遇風跨淺求救駁力需費照英國保險規例賠償
第六款一議倘遇風打壞船身幷失夫傢伙等件並所有修理需費照英國保險例賠償
第七欵一議缺用糧食或中途壞事往別口添買修理等事與保險單無碍
第八欵一議船上私裝火藥或作弊致被中國官員阻滯與保家無涉
第九欵一議船若飄往小呂宋暹羅避沽被該處官員阻滯與保家無涉
第十欵一議十月至十二月間在天竺國洋狂風大浪如有失害與保家無涉
第十一欵一議船停洋面相救別船與保險無碍
第十二欵一議所保之貨係上船日起至到埠卸貨落駁爲止倘駁船失陷與保家無涉
第十三欵一議船貨遇風不測須至該處投報本行或經手人查明給發實據帶至本行核驗相符須俟一個月之後方能償還
第十四欵一議船貨飄蕩別處一連六月杳無信息者須至本行報明俟一個月之後照數賠還
第十五欵一議船到埠限十日起清如過十日倘有失陷與保家無涉
第十六欵一議船在洋面被敵國兵船刼去與保家無涉

今欲有憑特發保險單一紙以作憑據
貨値弍千叁百兩正
保險費拾柒兩弍錢五分
第[illegible]號

壹千八百七十三年三月廿一日
同治十二年弍月廿三日

怡和保險圖記 給

七一、同治十三年山东烟台同升泰的欠单（H1/71）

同治十三年六月初八日（1874年7月21日），山东烟台同升泰欠英国商行运输费用一千〇九十二两九钱，由同升泰李寿田签立此欠单，盖有同升泰印章，印文“山东烟台同升泰单”，款项文字处盖有随形印印章“同升泰图记”。

Receipt from T’ung-sheng-t’ai. A receipt from Li Shou-tien (Li Shoutian) of T’ung-sheng-t’ai (Tong sheng tai), Yent’ai (Yantai), Shangtung (Shangdong), concerning 1090.02 Tls[①] for loading cargo at Yent’ai, Shangtung, 21 July 1874. 1 item.

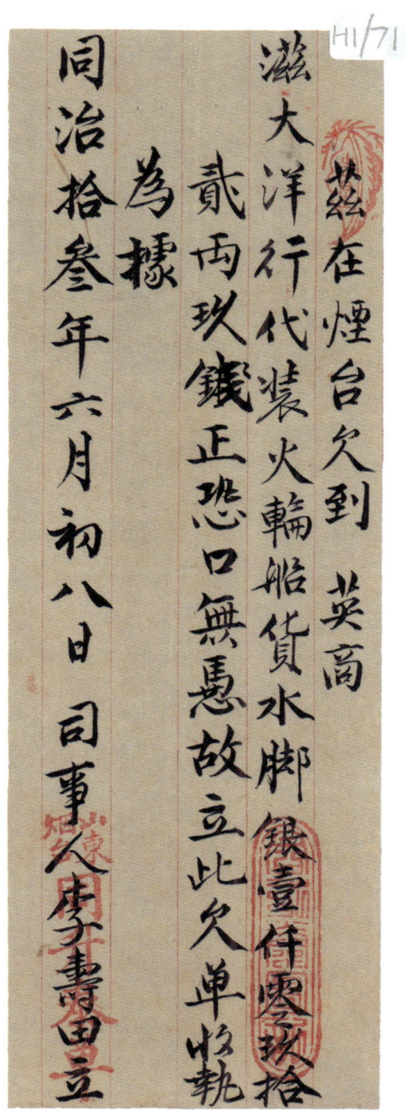

H1/71

兹在烟台欠到 英商
滋大洋行代装火輪船貨水脚銀壹仟零玖拾
貳両玖錢正恐口無憑故立此欠单收執
為據
同治拾叁年六月初八日 司事人李壽田立

① 勘误：英文提要中，把同升泰欠款数“壹仟零玖拾贰两玖钱”误写为“1090.02两”。

七二、光绪元年李节[1]写给布理顿的股份收单（H1/72）

光绪元年十二月初一日（1875年12月28日），李节收到布理顿（Pu-li-tun）抵押给他的香港火烛燕梳公司[2]股份10份，“按欠本息银五仟叁伯元正，限至光绪弍年闰五月初七日如数清还”，倘有拖欠，这些股份将归李节所有，另注明“每月付揭五千元”。

Receipt from Li Chie. A receipt from Li Chie (Li Jie) to Mr. Pu-li-tun (Bu li dun) (Britian?) for 10 shares in Hong Kong Huo-chu Yen-shu Kong-ssu, 28 December 1875, with repayment due in two years. 1 item. 1875

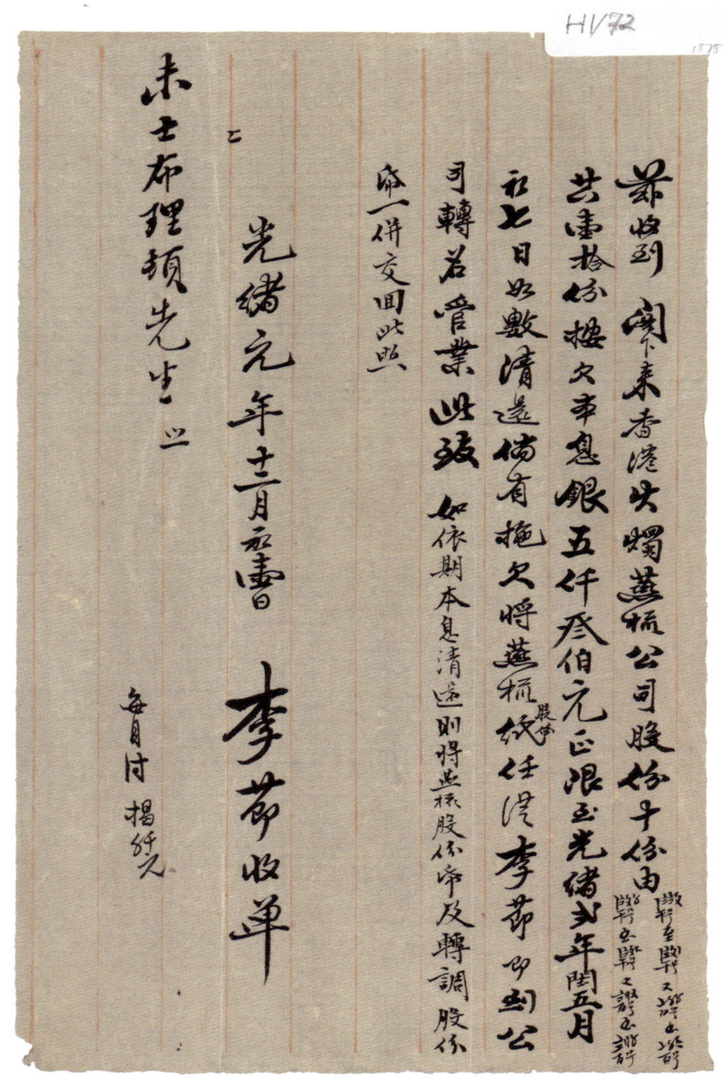

兹收到 閣下來香港火燭燕梳公司股份十份由
共壹拾份按欠本息銀五仟叁伯元正限至光緒弍年閏五月
初七日如數清還倘有拖欠將燕梳股份紙任從李節即出公
司轉名管業此據 如依期本息清還則將燕梳股份帶及轉調股份
除一併交回此照
光緒元年十二月初一日 李節收单
未士布理頓先生 照
每月付 揭仟元

① 李节：中国商人。

② 火烛燕梳公司：保险公司，“燕梳”是保险的英文“Insure”的音译。

七三、光绪四年张子勋①查验渣甸行②“云尔士③”的船运清单（H1/73）

光绪四年二月十三日（1878年3月16日），香港志南④公司张子勋查验英国渣甸行大船“云尔士”装运的第三批货物清单，其将此清单转交给其公司炯堂仁兄大人。盖有朱文印章，印文“香港南记号”“南记图章”，有多枚圆形印章，印文不清。

Invoice from Chang Tsu-hsun. An invoice for the third group of cargo shipped by Jardine, Matheson & Co.'s vessel 'Yun-er-shih', 16 March 1878. The received goods were marked and checked by Chang Tsu-hsun (Zhang Zixun) of Hong Kong Nan-chi hao, and the invoice was forwarded to Chiung-tang (Jiongtang) of the same firm. 1 item. 1878

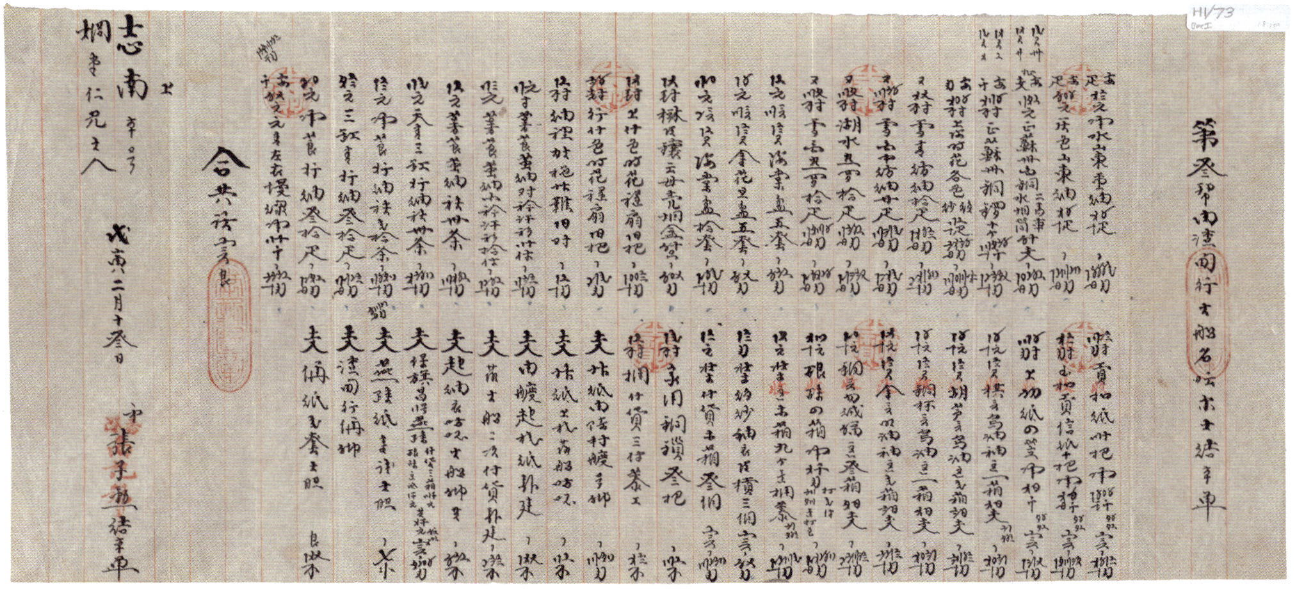

2 | 1

① 张子勋：志南公司商人。
② 渣甸行：即怡和洋行（Jardine, Matheson & Co.），英国商行。
③ 云尔士：怡和洋行（Jardine, Matheson & Co.）的大船。
④ 志南：商号，英文提要中误写为“南志号”（“Nan-chi hao”）。

（局部图1）

（局部图2）

七四、光绪四年权记[①]渔网发货单（H1/74）

光绪四年正月二十一日（1878年2月22日），权记发货单，凭单可取一张36英尺（10.9728米）的渔网，价格3元，盖有权记印章，印文“权记图记”。

Receipt from Ch’uan-chi. A receipt from Ch’uan-chi (Quan ji) for fishnet collected by Chih-hsie-fo, who is owed $3, 22 February 1878. 1 item; Fair condition, but some damage by insects. 1878

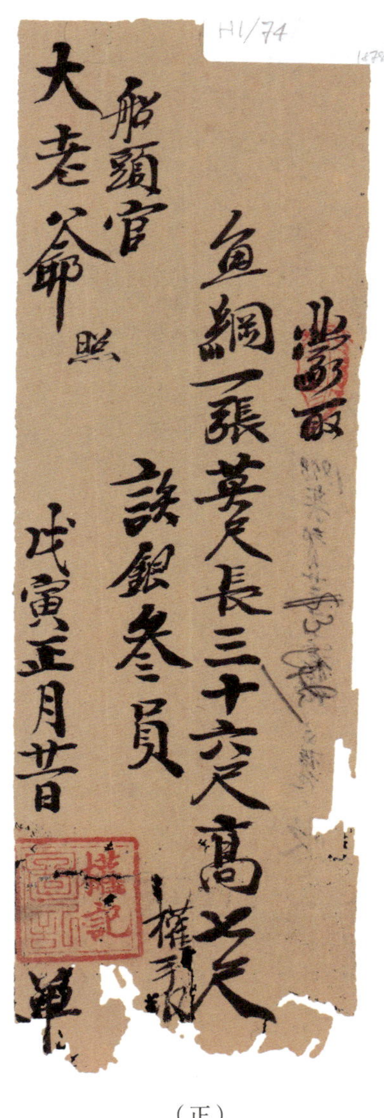

憑取
魚網一張英尺長三十六尺高七尺
該銀叁員
權記
大老爺
船頭官
照
戊寅正月廿一
單

（正）

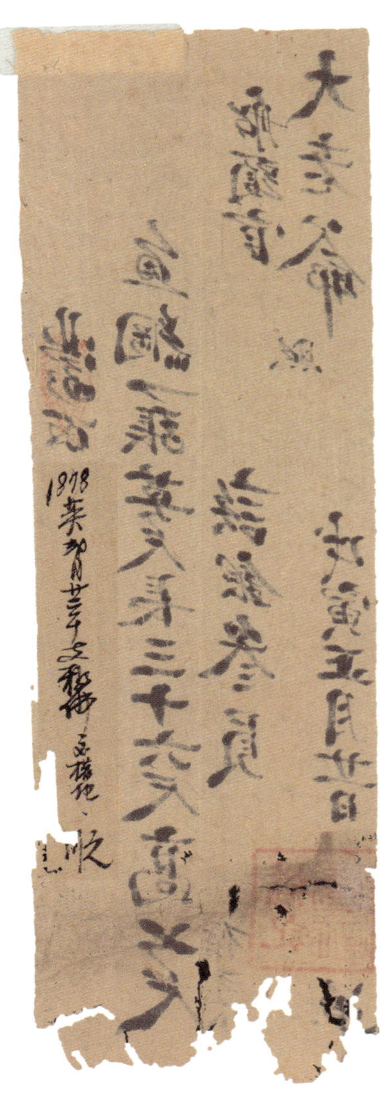

（反）

① 权记：中国商户。

七五、光绪五年香港怡记鱿鱼收据（H1/75）

光绪五年十二月初八日（1880年1月19日），香港怡记收到英国渣甸宝行忘连那揸火船运来鱿鱼一批的收据，盖有怡记印章，印文“香港怡记书柬”，附有英文注释。

Receipt from Hong Kong I-chih. A receipt (in Chinese) from Hong Kong I-chih (Yi ji) to Jardine, Matheson & Co. for squid, 19 January 1880, including English annotations. 1 item. 1880

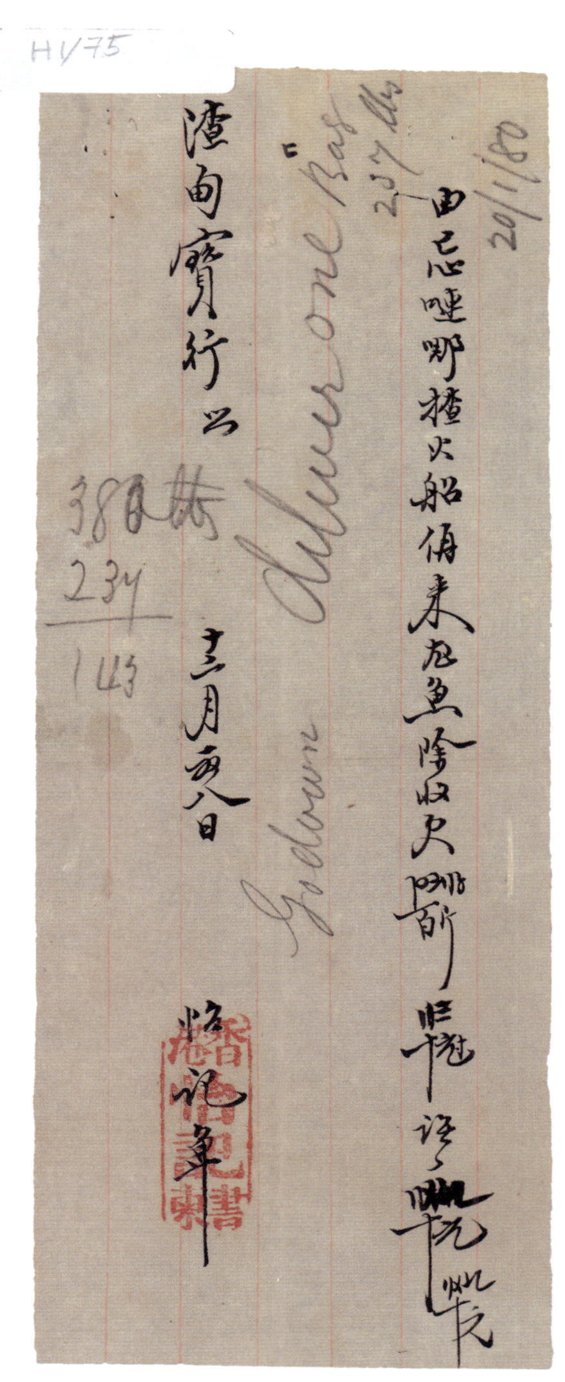
H1/75
20/1/80
257 lbs
one Bag
由忘嗹哪楂火船付來魷魚
渣甸寶行 上
deliver
234
143
Godown
十二月初八日
怡記

七六、光绪六年至七年信宜公司收据

1. 光绪六年新广安维记给信宜公司的收据（H1/76/1）

光绪六年正月初一日（1880年2月10日），新广安维记收到信宜公司雇“柯伦治个罗父”船运来的生油，写此收据交信宜公司，盖有新广安维记印章，印文“新山大埠新广安维记”。

Receipt from Hsin-kuang-an wei-chi. A receipt from Hsin-kuang-an wei-chi (Xin guang an wei ji) to Hsin-I Co. for oil from the ‘K’e-lun-chi-ke-lo-fu’ (‘Ke lun zhi ge luo fu’), 10 February 1880. 1 item; Fair condition, but damage by insects. 1880

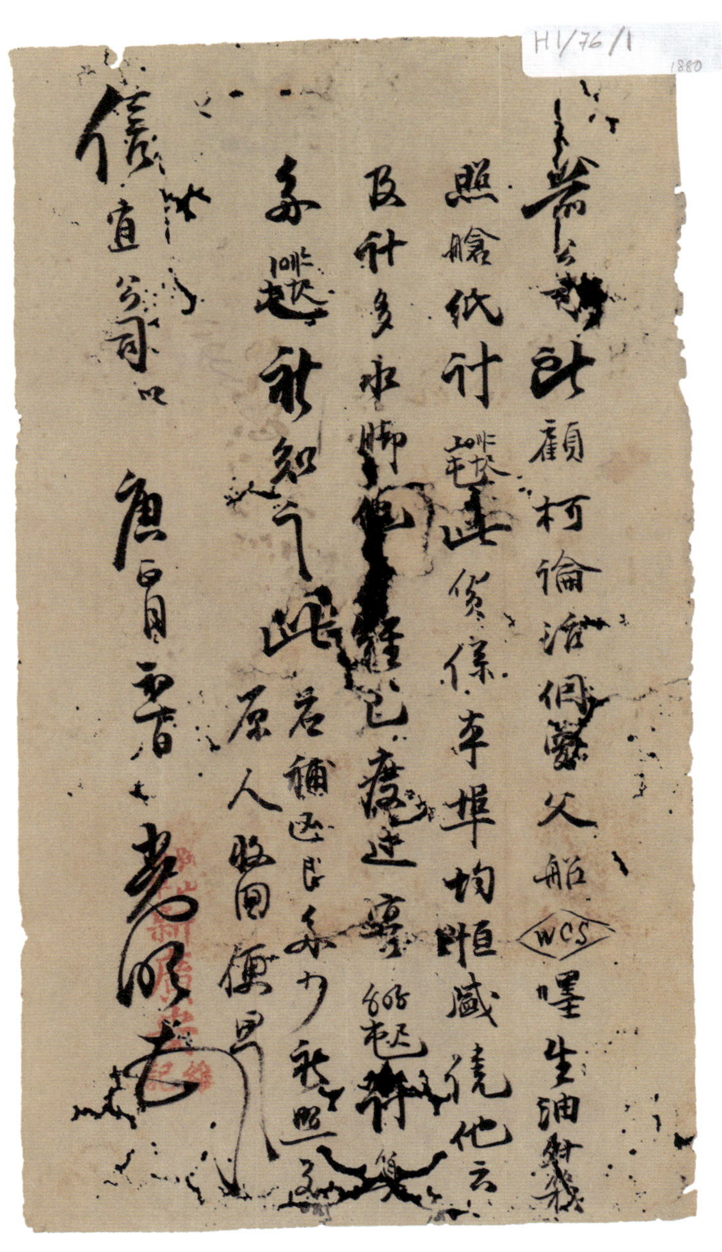

2. 光绪六年永昌生致信宜公司的信函（H1/76/2）

光绪六年十一月二十二日（1880年12月23日），永昌生致信宜公司有关大米贸易的信函，盖有永昌生印章，印文“新山大埠永昌生付”。

Letter from Yung-ch’ang-sheng. A letter from Yung-ch’ang-sheng (Yong chang sheng) yong in Hsin-shan ta-pu to Hsin-I Co., 2 March 1880[①], regarding the rice business. 1 item. 1880

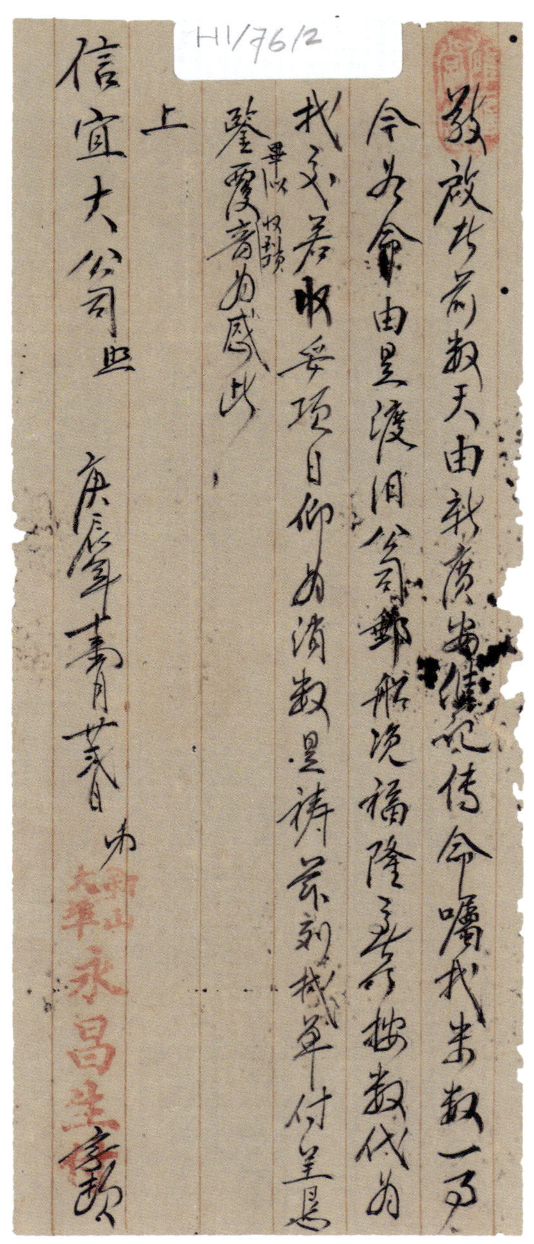

H1/76/2

上

信宜大公司照

庚辰年十壹月廿弍日

新山大埠永昌生付

---

① 勘误：英文提要日期为1880年3月2日（2 March 1880），按原中文文献“庚辰年十壹月廿弍日”，应为1880年12月23日。

3. 光绪六年香港和栈号给信宜公司的收据[①]（H1/76/3）

光绪六年十二月十六日（1881年1月15日），香港和栈号收到“了仑治个罗乎”船的货款，写此收据给信宜公司。收据盖有和栈号印章，印文“香港上环和栈号”。附有英文注释。贴有一枚印花税票。

Receipt from Wo-chan. A receipt (in Chinese) from Wo-chan (Ho-chan, He zhan), Hong Kong, to Hsin-I Co. for the payment of cargo unloaded from the ‘Le-lun-chi-ke-lo-hu’ (‘Le lun zhi ge luo hu’), 15 January 1881, including a brief note in English. 1 item; Fair condition, but some damage by insects. 1881

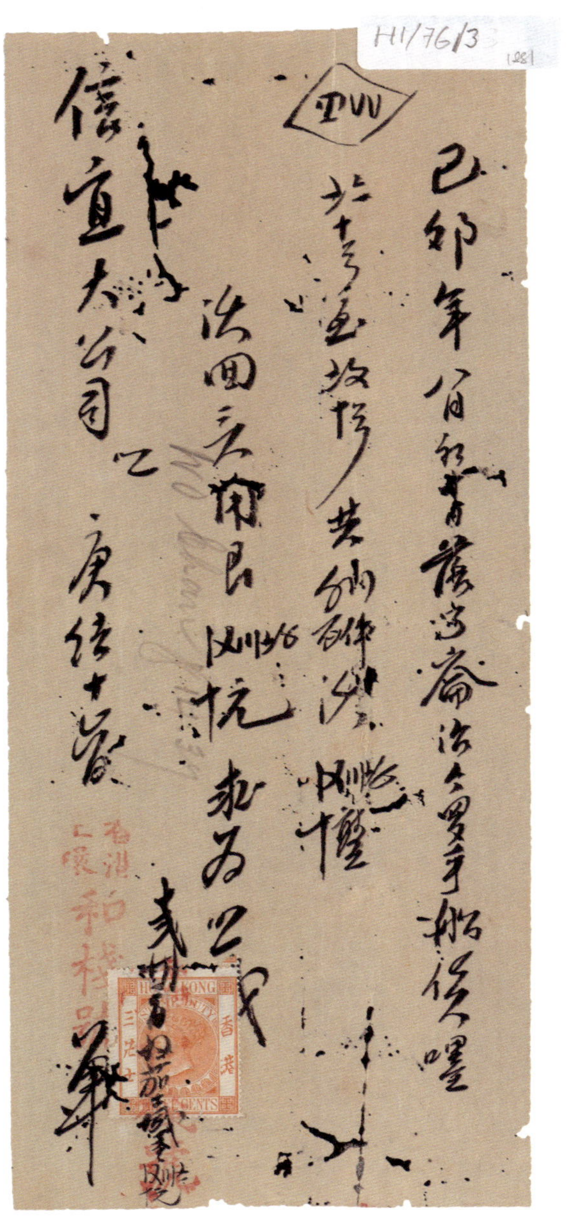

---

① 收据上贴有一枚印花税票（不是邮票，上面注明是“Stamp Duty”），通常纳税人自贴自销。

4. 光绪六年香港公源给信宜公司的收据[①]（H1/76/4）

光绪六年十二月十五日（1881年1月14日），公源收到信宜公司茶叶货款收据，盖有公源印章，印文“公源”“公源图记”“上环公源单”。附有英文注释。贴有一枚印花税票。

Receipt from Kung yuen. A receipt (in Chinese) from Kung yuen (Gong yuan) in Hong Kong Shang-huan to Hsin-I Co. for tea and payment, 15 January 1881[②], including a brief note in English. 1 item. 1881

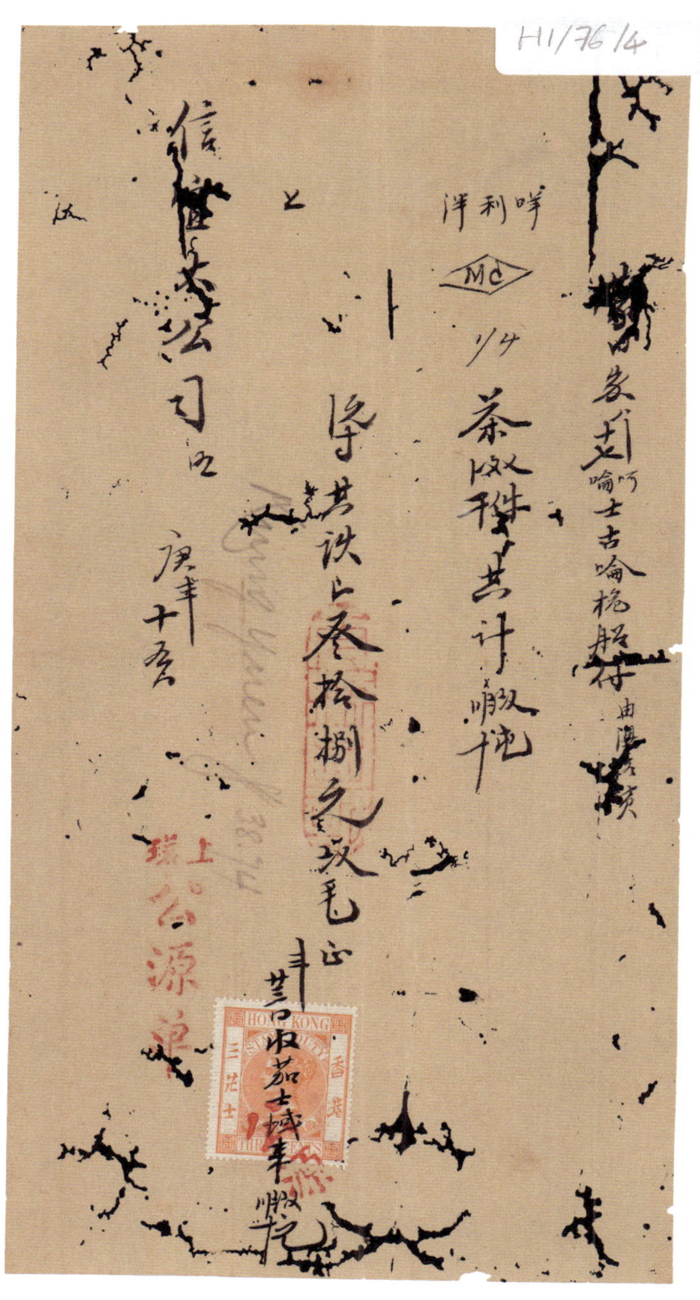

① 收据上贴有一枚印花税票（不是邮票，上面注明是“Stamp Duty”），通常纳税人自贴自销。

② 勘误：英文提要为1881年1月15日（15 January 1881），按原中文文献落款“庚十二月十五日”，应为1881年1月14日。

5. 光绪六年义生栈给信宜公司的收据[①]（H1/76/5）

光绪六年十二月十六日（1881年1月15日），香港义生栈收到信宜公司茶叶、玉米、杂货的收据，盖有两枚印章，印文分别为“香港上环义生栈书柬”及“上环义生栈给部图章”。附有英文注释。贴有一枚印花税票。

Receipt from E Sheng Chan. A receipt (in Chinese) from E Sheng Chan (I-sheng chan, Yi sheng zhan) in Hong Kong Shang-huan to Hsin-I Co. for tea, oil, peas, rice, etc., from the ‘Le-lun-chi-ke-lo-hu’ (‘Le lun zhi ge luo hu’), 15 January 1881, including a brief note in English. 1 item; Fair condition, but with damage by insects, including a missing section in the centre. 1881

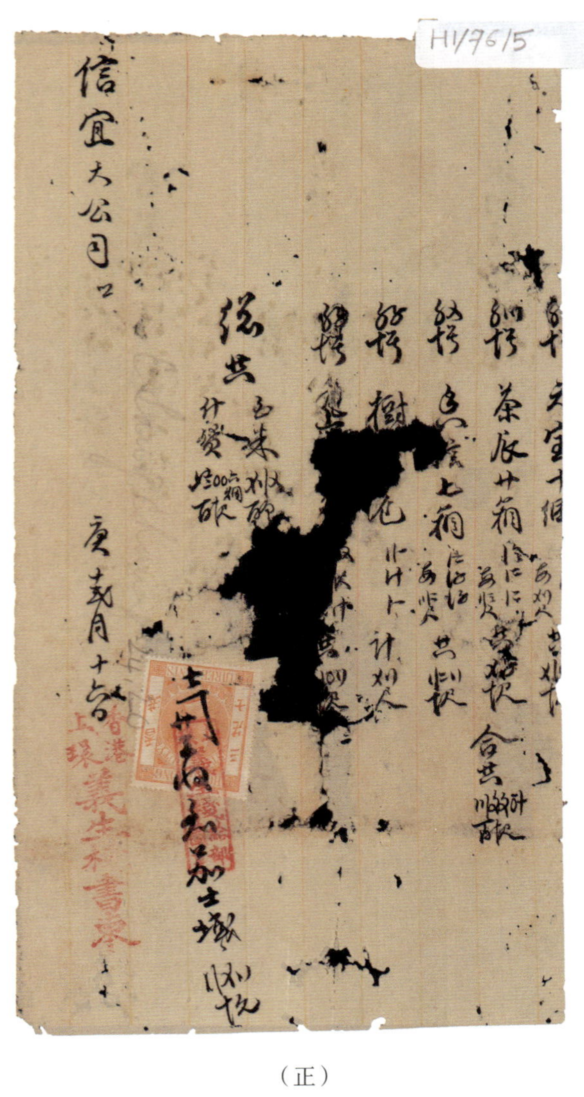

（正）

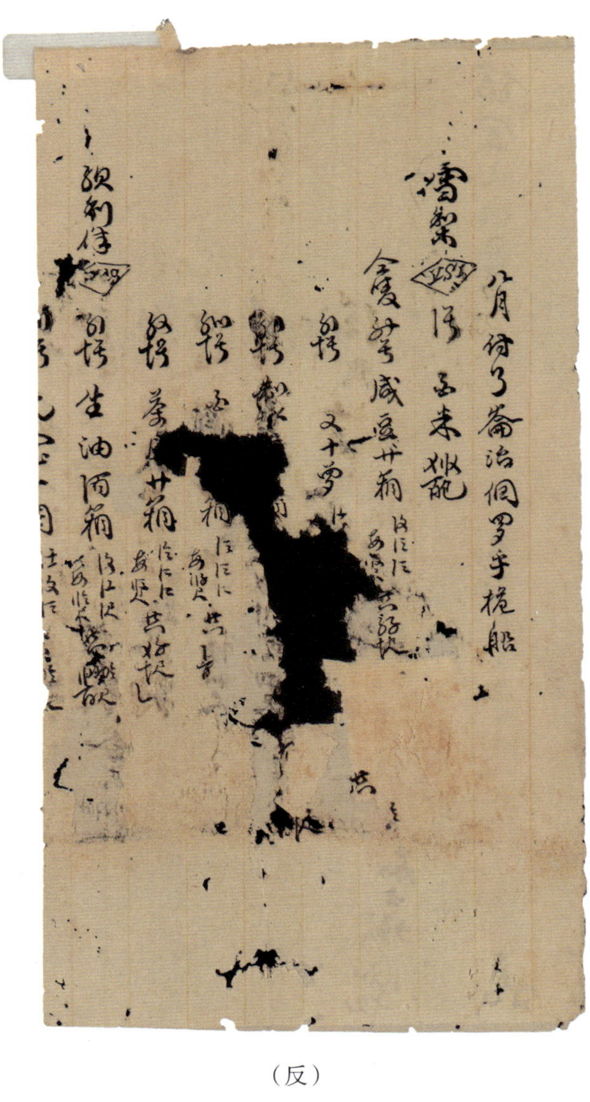

（反）

① 收据上贴有一枚印花税票（不是邮票，上面注明是“Stamp Duty”），通常纳税人自贴自销。

6. 光绪六年香港永祥盛给信宜公司的收据[①]（H1/76/6）

光绪六年十二月十六日（1881年1月15日），永祥盛收到信宜公司生油等货款的收据，盖有永祥盛印章，印文“香港上环永祥盛附”。附有英文注释。贴有一枚印花税票。

Receipt from Wing Chiang Sing. A receipt (in Chinese) from Wing Chiang Sing (Yung-hsiang-sheng, Yong xiang sheng) in Hong Kong Shang-huan to Hsin-I Co. for the purchase of three brands of goods, QHL, SK and WCS (Oil), 15 January 1881, including a brief note in English. 1 item; Fair condition, but some damage by insects. 1881

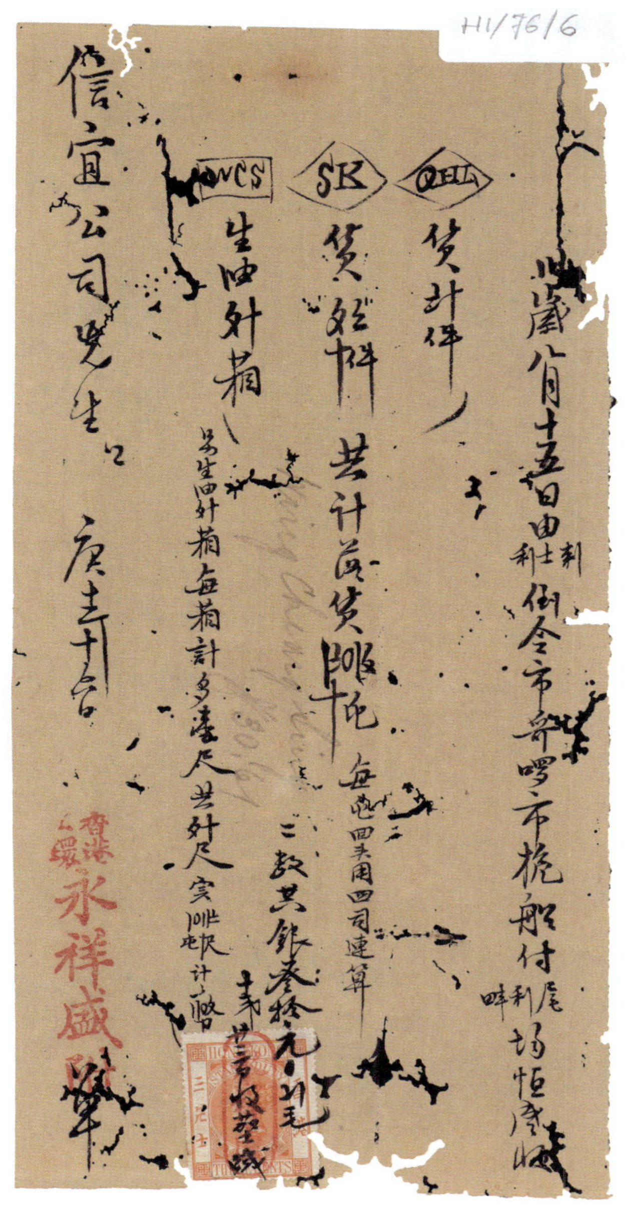

① 收据上贴有一枚印花税票（不是邮票，上面注明是“Stamp Duty”），通常纳税人自贴自销。

7. 光绪六年香港维盛给信宜公司的收据[①]（H1/76/7）

光绪六年十二月（1880年12月31日—1881年1月29日），维盛收到信宜公司茶叶、大米等货款的收据，盖有维盛印章，印文“香港中环维盛”。附有英文注释。贴有一枚印花税票，上面书写有日期“十弍月廿三日”。

Receipt from Wai Sing. A receipt (in Chinese) from Wai Sing (Wei-sheng, Wei sheng) in Hong Kong Chung-huan to Hsin-I Co. for the purchase of tea and rice, 15 January 1881, including a brief note in English. 1 item; Fair condition, but damage by insects. 1881

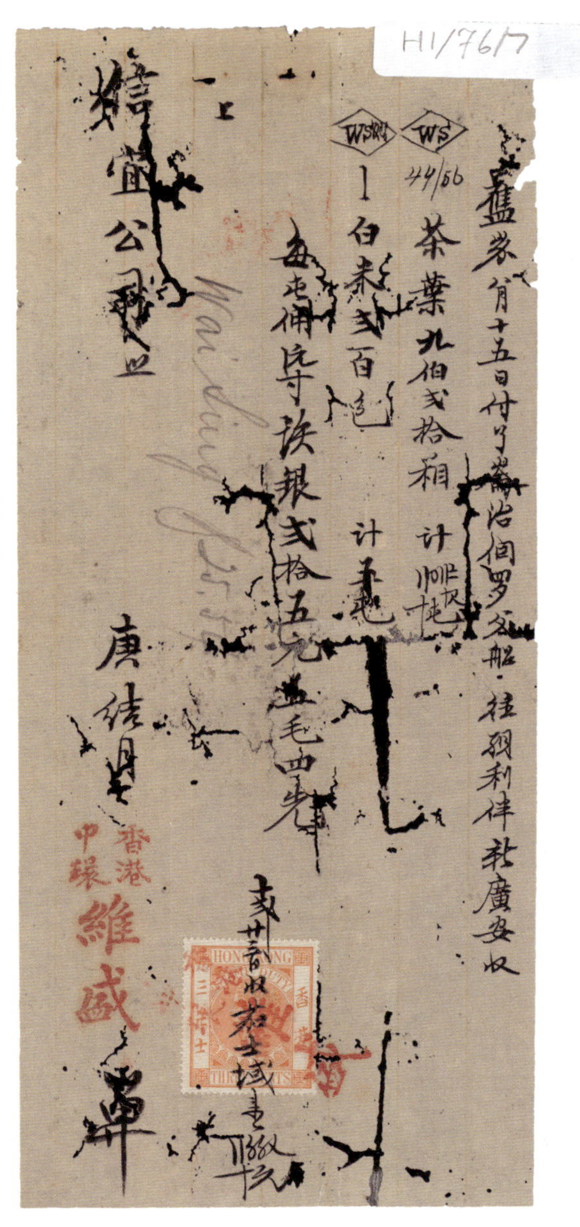
H1/76/7
Wai Sing

① 收据上贴有一枚印花税票（不是邮票，上面注明是“Stamp Duty”），通常纳税人自贴自销。

8. 光绪七年新锦安恒记给信宜公司的收据（H1/76/8）

光绪七年正月初五日（1881年2月3日），新锦安恒记收到信宜公司大米等货款的收据，落款“新锦安恒记”，盖有朱文印章，印文“□□锦安”。

Letter from Hsin-chin-an heng-chi. A letter from Hsin-chin-an heng-chi (Xin jin an heng ji) to Hsin-I Co. regarding money received for rice, 3 February 1881. 1 item. 1881

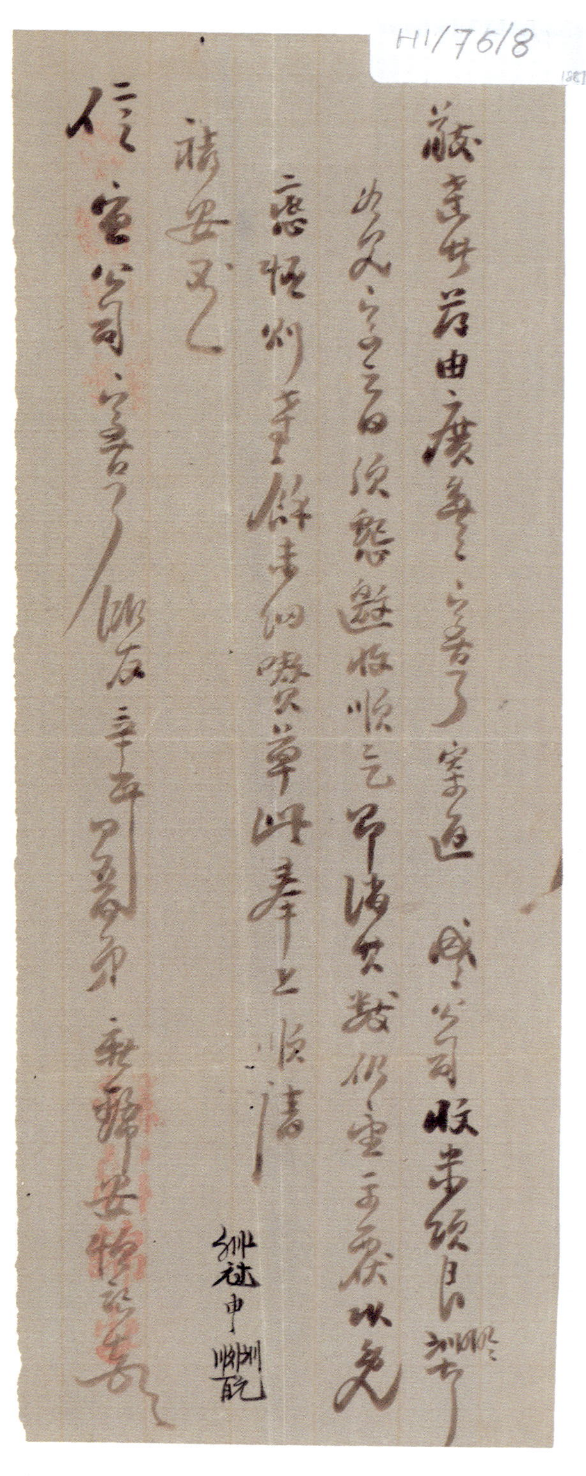

9. 光绪七年澳门马阁信宜栈[①]致孖治臣行机士域大班的账单（H1/76/9）

光绪七年二月初九日（1881年3月8日），澳门马阁信宜栈一月份的开支账单（杂用伙食等合共75元），注明交给孖治臣行机士域（Chi-shi-yu）大班，盖有信宜公司印章，印文“香港信宜公司书柬”。附有英文注释。

Account of Macao godown. An account (in Chinese) of the expenditure of the Hsin-I godown in Macao in the first month of 1881, dated 8 March 1881, sent to Mr. Chi-shi-yu (Ji shi yu), Taipan of Hsin-I Co., Hong Kong, including English notes about the account. 1 item. 1881

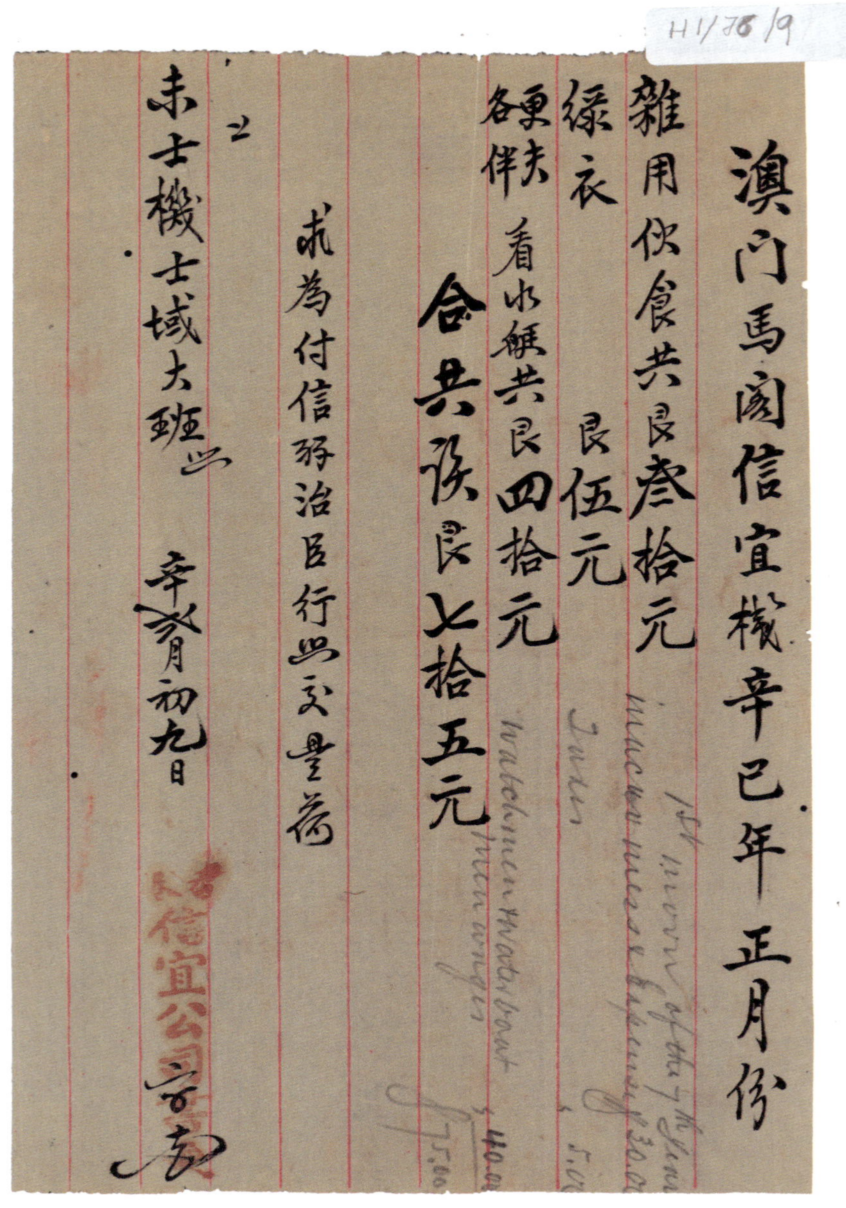

H1/76/9

澳门馬閣信宜棧辛巳年正月份

雜用伙食共艮叁拾元

縫衣　艮伍元

更夫各伴看水艇共艮四拾元

合共該艮七拾五元

求為付信孖治臣行照交是荷

之

未士機士域大班照

辛巳二月初九日

信宜公司

---

① 澳门马阁信宜栈：信宜公司的澳门分公司。

10. 光绪七年信宜公司陶海谦[①]寄给麦忌尤架的开支账单[②]（H1/76/10）

光绪七年八月二十五日（1881年10月17日），信宜公司陶海谦把本年度闰七月及八月份的铺租、伙食杂费、生活费及工银开支账目寄给麦忌尤架（Mei-chi-yu-chia）。账单盖有信宜公司印章，印文“香港信宜公司书柬”。附有英文注释。贴有一枚印花税票。

Account of Hsin-I Co.. An account (in Chinese) of the expenditure of Hsin-I Co., Hong Kong, on maintenance and salaries in the seventh and eighth months of 1881[③], dated 17 October 1881, sent by T'ao Hai-ch'ien (Tao Haiqian) of Hsin-I Co., Hong Kong, to Mr. Mei-chi-yu-chia (Mai ji you jia), including English notes about the account. 1 item; Fair condition, but damage by insects. 1881

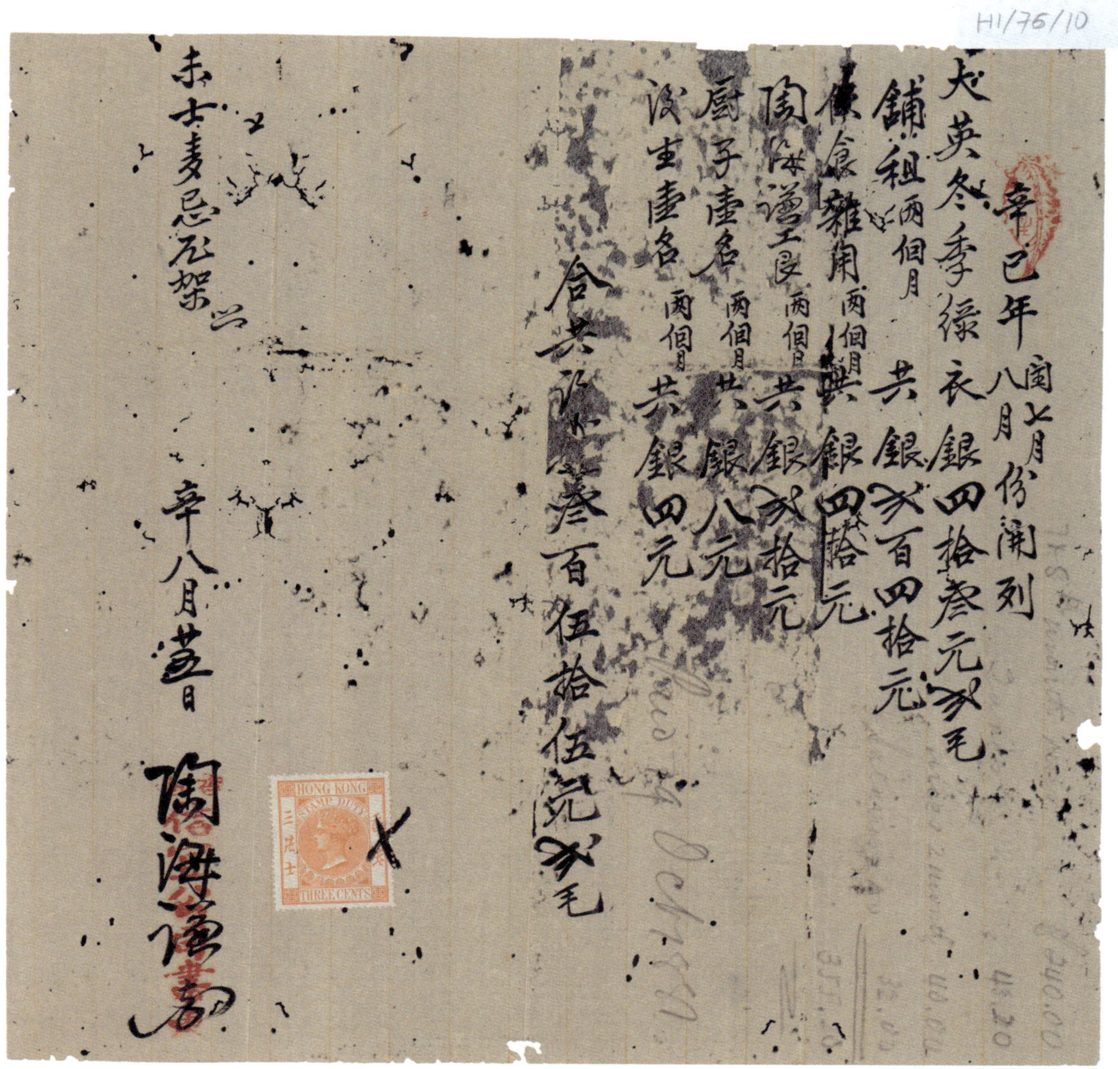
H1/76/10

辛巳年閏七月八月份開列
大英冬季綠衣銀四拾叁元貳毛
鋪租兩個月 共銀貳百四拾元
伙食雜用兩個月 共銀四拾元
陶海謙工食兩個月 共銀貳拾元
廚子壹名兩個月 共銀八元
跟主壹名兩個月 共銀四元
合共銀叁百伍拾伍元貳毛
未士麦忌尤架台
辛八月廿五日
陶海謙

---

① 陶海谦：信宜公司员工。

② 账单上贴有一枚印花税票（不是邮票，上面注明是“Stamp Duty”），通常纳税人自贴自销。

③ 勘误：英文提要谓此账单是1881年7月和8月的账单，按原中文文献，实际为1881年“闰七月、八月”的账单。

11. 光绪七年福昌荣号给香港信宜公司的收据（H1/76/11）

光绪七年九月二十一日（1881年11月12日），福昌荣号给香港信宜公司的收据（家私杂物出价银550元）。

Receipt from Fu-ch’ang-jung hao. A receipt from Fu-ch’ang-jung (Fu Chang rong) hao for domestic goods sold by Hsin-i Co., Hong Kong, 21 November 1881[①]. 1 item; Fair condition, but damage by insects. 1881

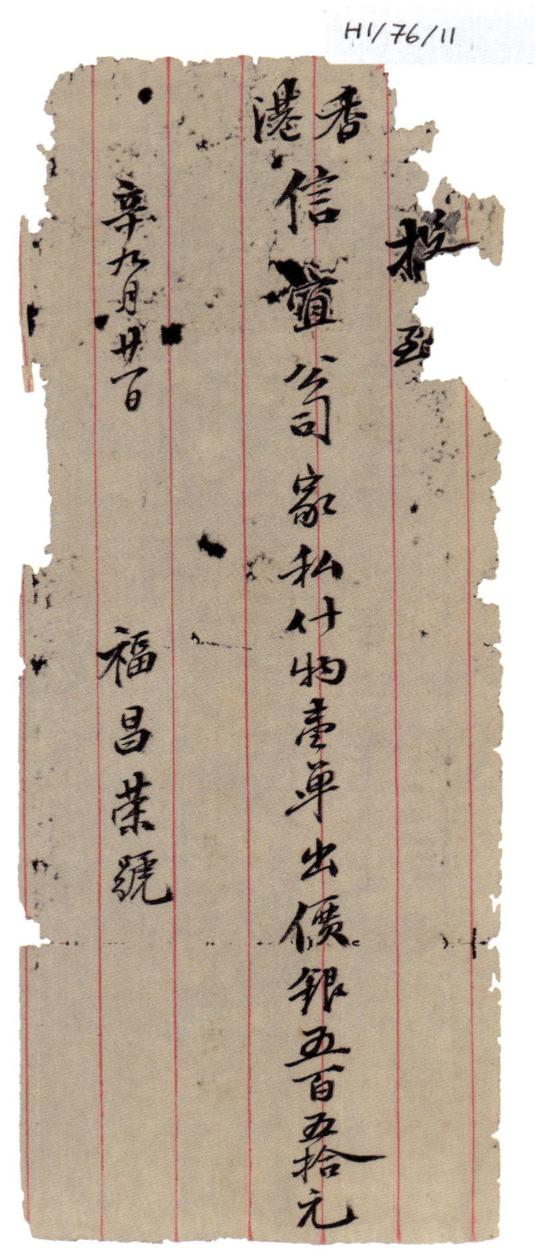

H1/76/11

香港信宜公司家私什物壹單出價銀五百五拾元

辛九月廿一日

福昌榮號

① 勘误：英文提要日期为1881年11月21日（21 November 1881），按原中文文献“辛九月廿一日”，应为1881年11月12日。

七七、光绪八年宝裕行邱焕彩给义和[①]公司的收据（H1/77）

光绪八年正月二十日（1882年3月9日），宝裕行邱焕彩给义和公司的收据，记录光绪七年八月十四日（1881年10月6日）收到“上海燕梳[②]一千元”，以及光绪八年正月二十日（1882年3月9日）收到怡和194.82元。

Receipt from Pao-yu hong. A receipt from Ch’iu Huan-ts’ai (Qiu Huancai) of Pao-yu hong (Bao yu) of 9 March 1882 for $1000 received from Shanghai Yen-shu (Yan shu) Co., 6 October 1881, and £194.82 received from Ewo, 9 March 1882. 1 item. 1882

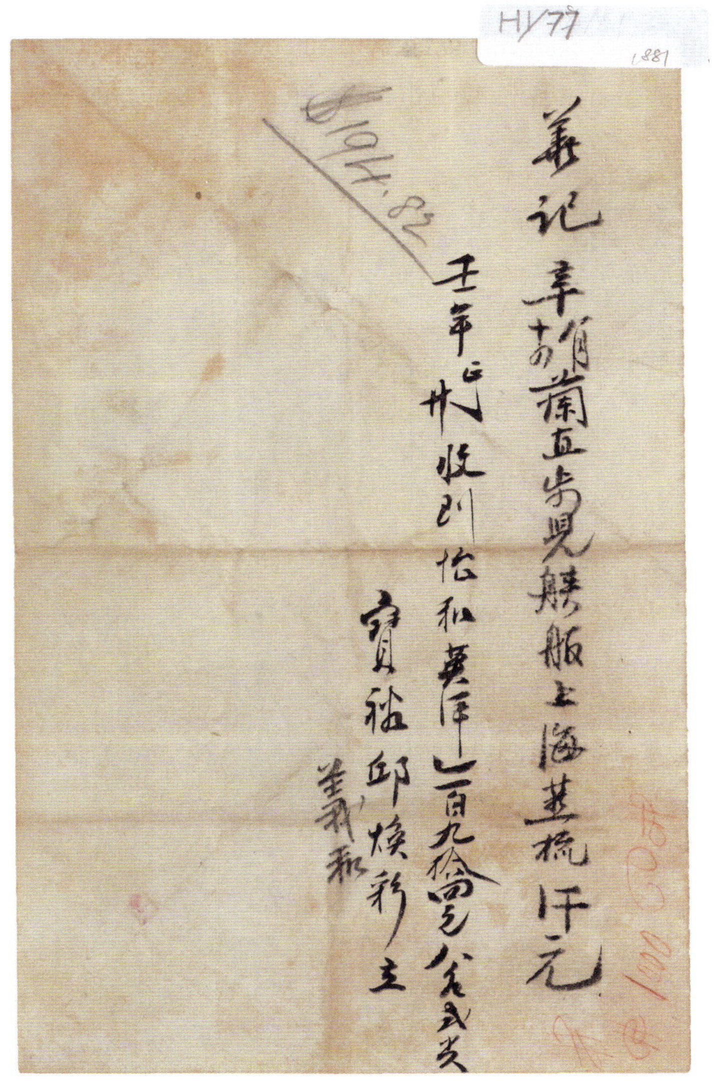
H1/77
1881
$194.82
義記 辛巳八月十四[illegible]上海燕梳仟元
壬午正月廿收到怡和英洋一百九拾四元八[illegible]
寶裕邱煥彩 主
[illegible]

① 义和：即怡和洋行（Jardine, Matheson & Co.），英国商行。
② 燕梳：保险，“燕梳”是保险的英文“Insure”的音译。

七八、光绪十一年潮邦公[①]致怡和宝行[②]的信和电报

1. 光绪十一年潮邦公向怡和宝行索赔的信（H1/78/1）

光绪十一年（1885），潮邦公向怡和宝行索赔的信，报告去年七月二十九日由“罗士练”号轮船装载鲁麟洋行的糖在运输途中打湿了。经在汕头议赔，其他公司已支付了保险赔款，但怡和宝行负责的保本之款1700元尚未赔偿，因此要求怡和宝行尽快赔偿。

Letter from Ch’ao-pang kung. A letter from Ch’ao-pang kung (Chao bang gong) to Ewo reporting that German Lu lin hong’s sugar, which was loaded on Jardine, Matheson & Co.’s steamer ‘Lo-shih-lien’ (‘Luo shi lian’) on 18 September 1884, got wet during the journey. Following negotiations at Swatow, the other companies have paid the insurance claimed, but Ewo has not done so. The author requests that Ewo settle the case soon, otherwise the merchants in Hankow will not use the company’s steamer. 1 item. 1885

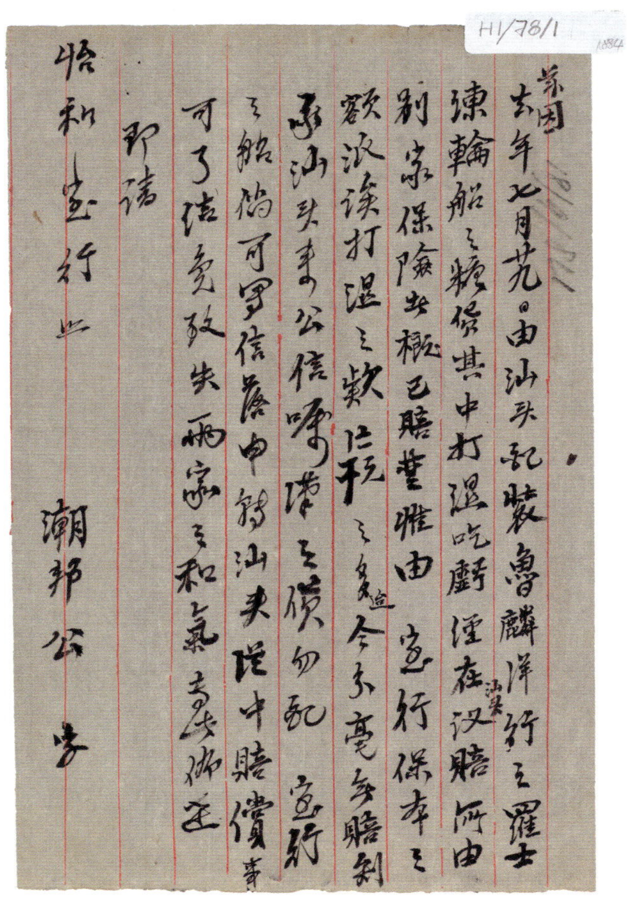

H1/78/1
1884

敬启 去年七月廿九日由汕头配装鲁麟洋行之罗士
练轮船之糖货其中打湿吃亏经在汕头议赔所由
别家保险者概已赔楚惟由 宝行保本之
款派该打湿之款一千七百元之久迄今分毫无赔刻
承汕头来公信嘱帮之货勿配 宝行
之船倘可买信应由汉汕来从中赔偿当
可了结免致失两家之和气 专此布达
即请
怡和宝行照 潮邦公 字

① 潮邦公：中国汕头商人。

② 怡和宝行：即怡和洋行（Jardine, Matheson & Co.），英国商行。

2. 光绪十一年致潮义公[①]的电报（H1/78/2）

光绪十一年十月十八日（1885年11月24日），致汕头商人潮义公的中文电报，配有电报内容的英文翻译，报告汉口老栈怡和[②]已支付了保险赔款，并指示他通知诸商号可使用怡和公司的轮船装运货物。

Telegram to Ch'ao-pang kung. A telegram (in Chinese) to Ch'ao-pang kung (Chao bang gong), Swatow merchant, 24 November 1885, reporting that Hankow Low Chung Ewo have settled and paid the insurance claims, and instructing him to notify the merchants to ship their cargo using Jardine, Matheson & Co.'s steamers. There is an accompanying English translation. 2 items. 1885

H1/78/2

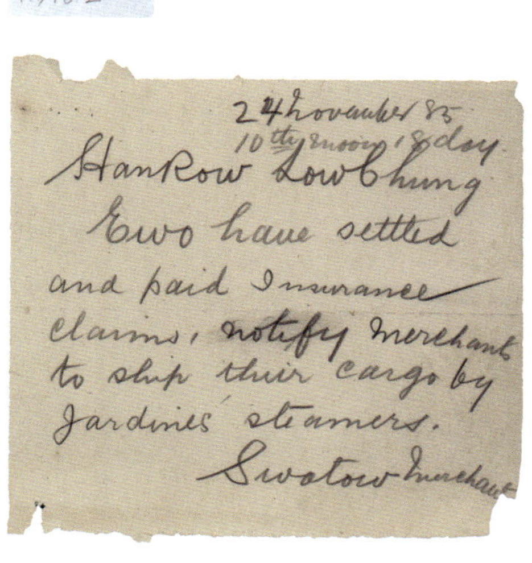
24 November 85
10th moon 18 day
Hankow Low Chung
Ewo have settled
and paid Insurance
claims, notify merchants
to ship their cargo by
Jardines' steamers.
Swatow merchant

（正）

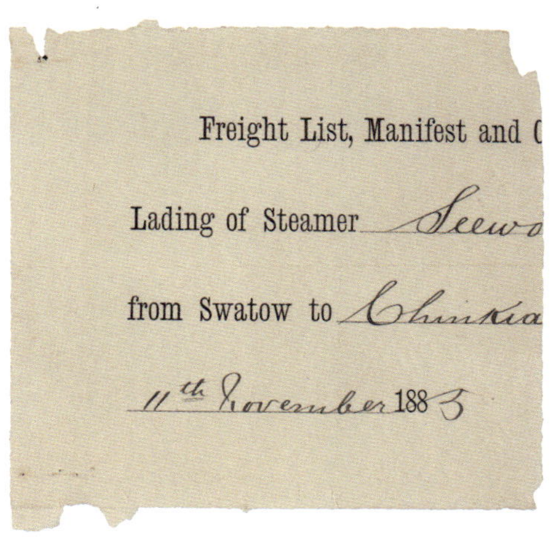
Freight List, Manifest and
Lading of Steamer
from Swatow to
11th November 1885

（反）

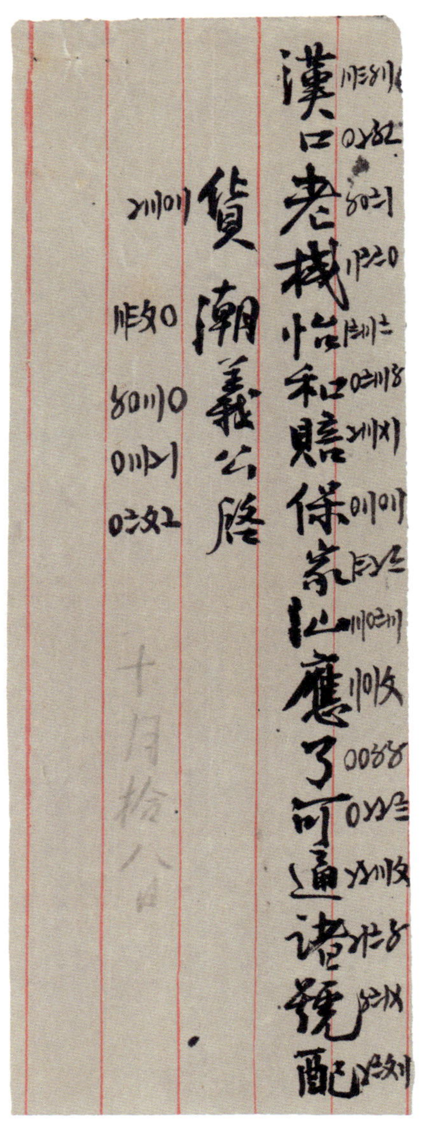
漢口老棧怡和賠保家弘應了可通諸號配
貨潮義公啓
十月拾八日

① 潮义公：中国汕头商人。
② 怡和：即怡和洋行（Jardine, Matheson & Co.），英国商行。

七九、光绪十年谢孟桂[①]告禀怡和大东翁米司格斯惠（H1/79）

光绪十年（1885）十二月，谢孟桂告禀怡和洋行，投诉怡和洋行名下福和轮船买办严昭明的不法行为。

Report from Hsie Meng-kui. A report from Hsie Meng-kui (Xie Menggui) to Mr. Ke-ssu-hui (Ge si hui), Ewo taipan, 2 January 1885[②], regarding the bad behaviour of Yen Chao-ming (Yan Zhaoming), comprador manager of the ship 'Foowo'. 1 item. 1885

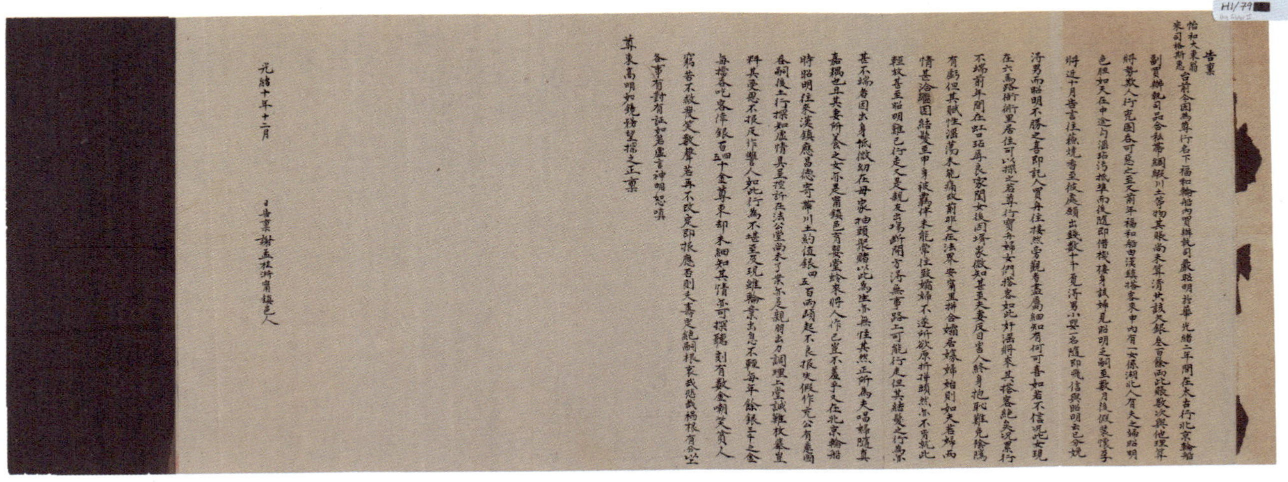

2 | 1

① 谢孟桂：中国浙宁镇邑人。

② 勘误：英文提要日期为1885年1月2日（2 January 1885），换算为农历为"光绪十年十一月十七日"，与原中文文献中的"光绪十年十二月"不符。

（局部图1）

吞騙後土行探知虛情具呈控訴在法公堂尚未了案亦是親明出力調理上堂誠難枚舉皇

料其受恩不報反作讎害人如此行為不堪至及現銀輸書出自心不輕每年餘銀三千之金

上海擺吞吃咬除銀百四五十金萬事東却未細知其情亦可探聽刻有數金嘲笑賓人

痛哉若不救援受救聲若再不設定即求應否則夫妻定絕嗣根哀哉悲哉禍根有分比

各事有對有証如若虛言神明昭鑒

萬東高明如鏡諸望垂之上稟

光緒十年十二月　　日告稟謝孟桂浙甯鎮邑人

（局部图2）

八〇、十月十三日昌顺[1]致外商孝仁的信函（年份不详）（H1/80）

十月十三日，昌顺致函外国商人孝仁（Hsiao-jen）。信件分成两部分，外封盖有护封印及昌顺行的中文印章，印文“昌顺”，注明昌顺托人将此重要信件带到灯龙洲交给韦其兄，再由其转交孝仁。据信函内容可知，前月昌顺从孖地臣[2]处购买了羽纱、棉纱等货物，要求孝仁将货物送至昌顺。盖有昌顺印章，印文“CHEONGSOON”。

Letter from Cheongsoon. A letter in two parts from Cheongsoon (Ch’ang-shun, Changshun) to Mr. Hsiao-jen (Xiaoren) instructing that the cotton yarn and camlet bought from Matheson should be taken to Cheongsoon hong (Ch’ang- shun, Changshun) if a ship can be found for this purpose. The year is not given. 2 items; Fair condition, but damage by insects, including missing sections.

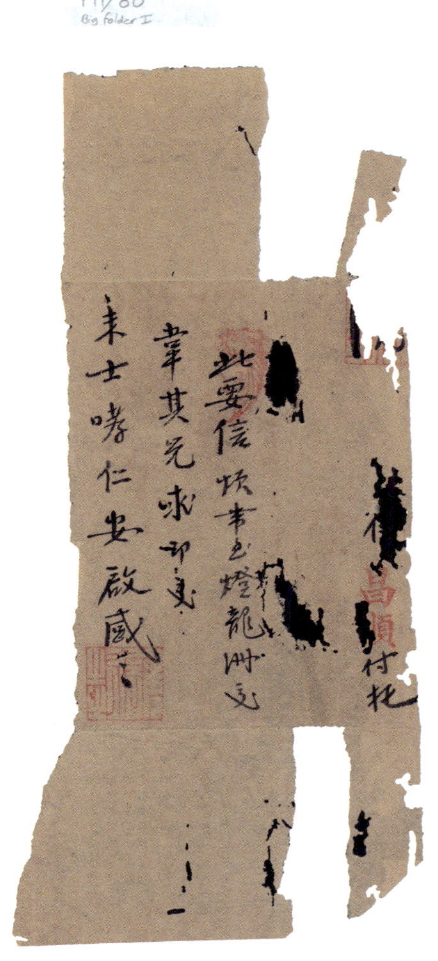
H1/80
Big folder I
此要信煩帶至燈龍洲交
韋其兄求即交
來士嗐仁安啟緘
信 昌順付托

① 昌顺：中国商行。
② 孖地臣：英国商人 Matheson，怡和洋行（Jardine, Matheson & Co.）创始人之一。

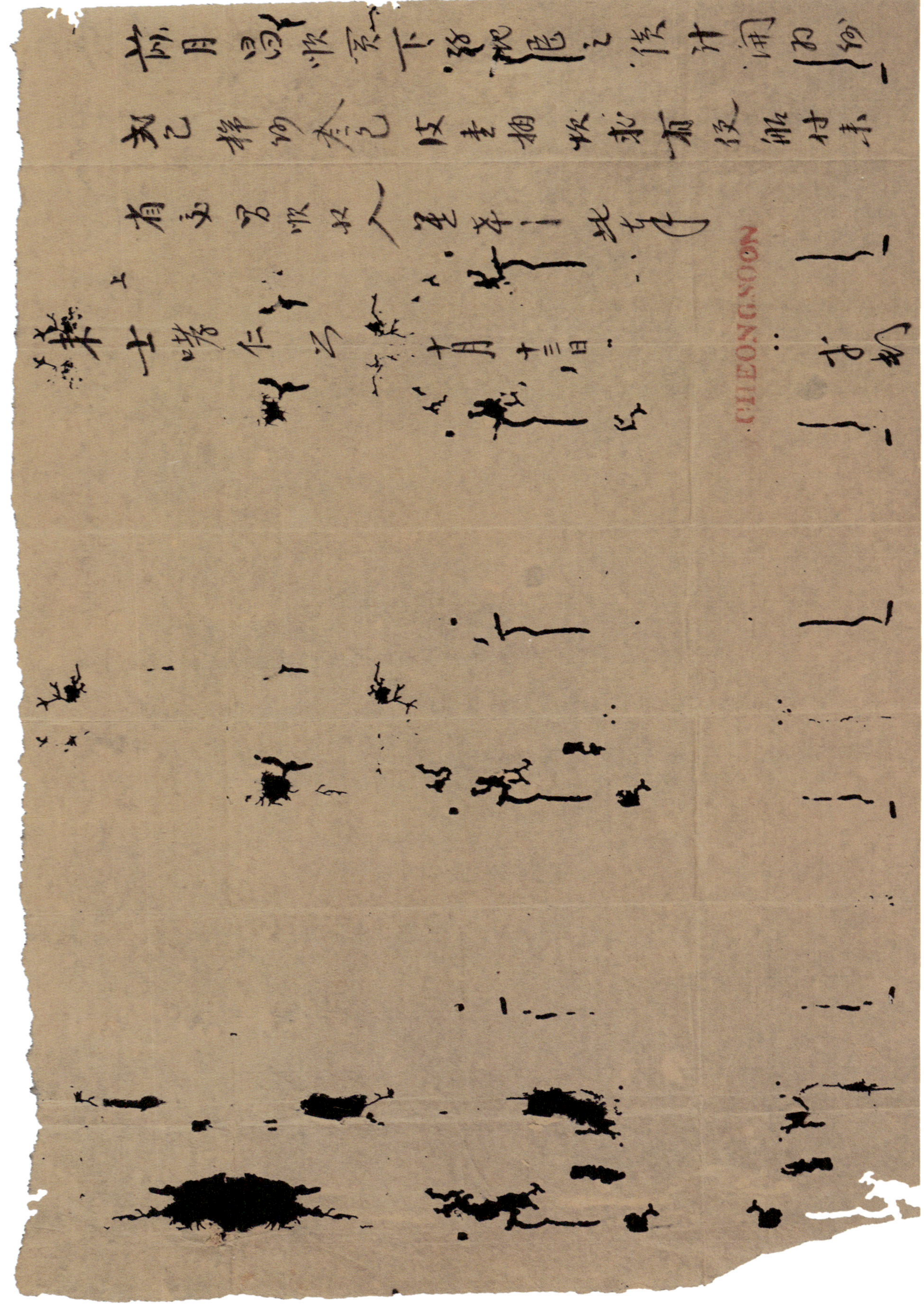

八一、三月十三日香港曹能铁匠铺订单（年份不详）（H1/81）

三月十三日，未士好大宝号[①]向曹能铁匠铺订制钩子等各种器物的订单，附有简短的英文说明。盖有曹能铁匠铺印章，印文不清。

Bill from Hui-neng[②]. A bill (in Chinese) from Hui-neng (Huineng) to Mr. A. Howell for hooks of various kinds from Hui-neng's blacksmith shop, including a brief English note about the bill. The year is not given. 1 item.

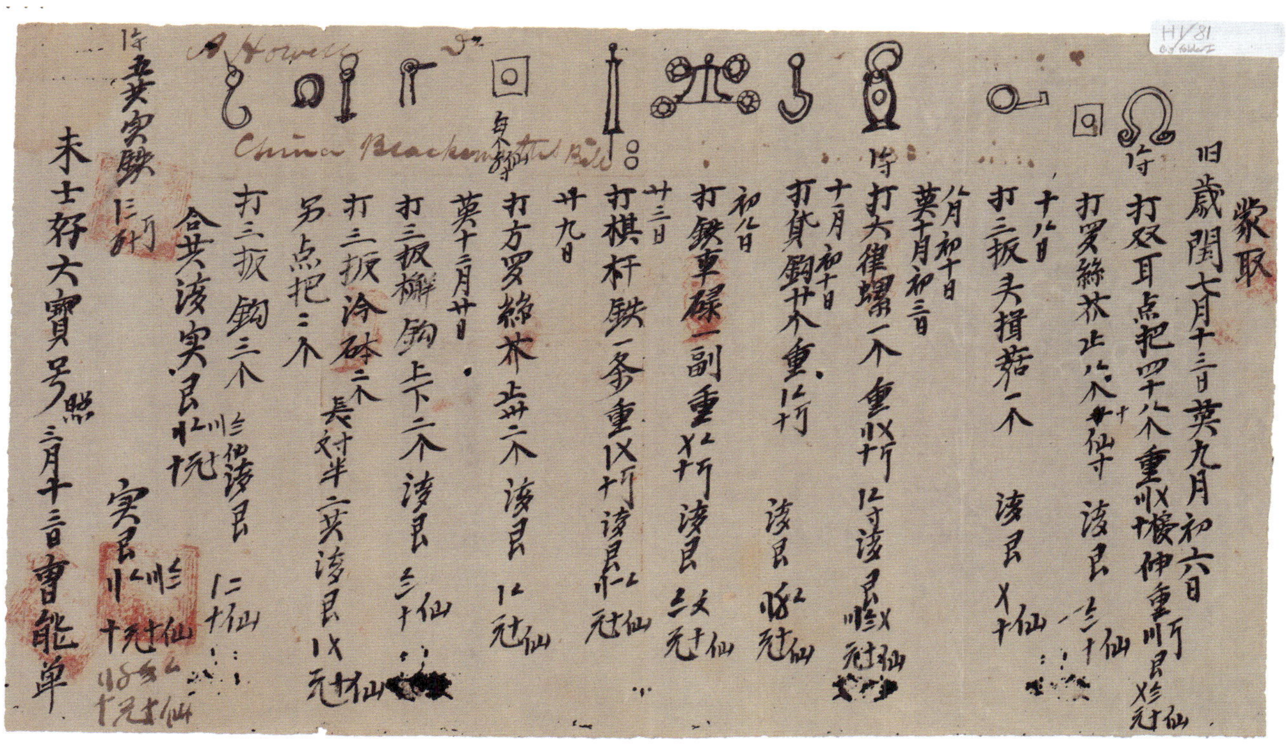

① 未士好大宝号：外国商号。
② 勘误：英文提要误将“曹”认作“会”。

八二、义和行①装修合同（日期不详）（H1/82）

这是一份19世纪义和行的装修合约，里边规定了详细的装修要求，可以大致反映义和行的装修风格。规定义和行门口用青白石砌的墙脚，高度比照公司行②一样；地面用红石铺就，而两个天台用东安阶砖石铺好；四围窗扇用红木，大门用油木，楼板用油木，地下苍门用油木；门口石阶高四级、内打灰砂，住房铺阶砖；楼下窗户用铁窗，楼上窗用玻璃架，窗扇样式均按照公司行样式；栏杆用瓦的，栏杆面铺东安石。此二样价银未入单内，其余各样照式图外并合约为据。特别值得注意的是合约最后的说明“上增楼一十二桁，中一十五桁，下一十二桁”。广州古建筑专家汤国华教授认为，清代广州民居一桁宽度为24厘米，说明义和行底层宽度增加288厘米，中层宽度增加360厘米，上层宽增加288厘米，而且是新建的三楼，说明义和行在不断扩建中，可谓清代中期广州的豪宅了。

Order to I-ho yi. An undated order to I-ho (Yihe) yi for house alterations. 1 item.

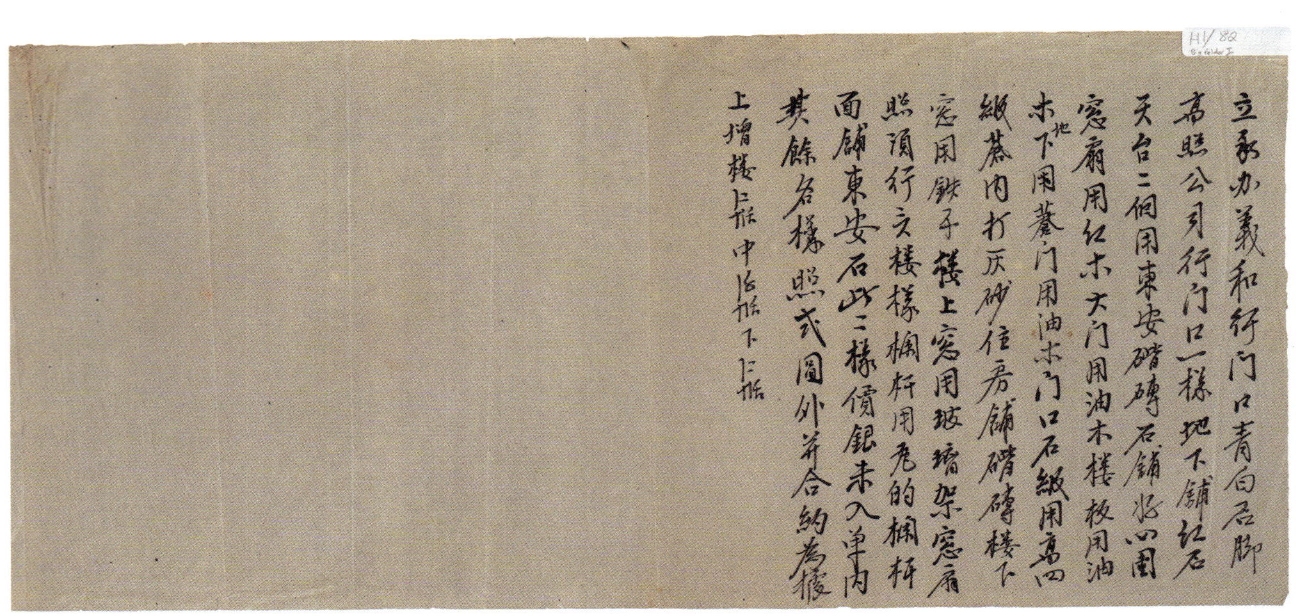
H1/82

立承办義和行门口青白石脚
高照公司行门口一樣 地下鋪紅石
天台二個用東安階磚石鋪好 四圍
窗扇用紅木 大门用油木 樓板用油
木 地下用蒼门用油木 门口石級用高四
級 蓋内打灰砂 住房鋪階磚 樓下
窗用鐵子 樓上窗用玻璃架 窗扇
照頂行之樣樣 欄杆用瓦的 欄杆
面鋪東安石 此二樣價銀未入单内
其餘各樣照式圖外并合約為據
上增樓一十二桁 中一十五桁 下一十二桁

① 义和行：应即义和夷馆，即小溪馆，1832年刊载于《广州纪事报》(*Canton Register*)上的马礼逊绘十三行商馆区地图中，将其标记为“Creek factory, or I'ho(E'wo hong)”。

② 公司行：应即英国馆（English factory），或译新英国馆，又称宝和行（Pauho hong），位于猪巷（Hog lane）与荷兰馆（Dutch factory，或称集义行）之间。

八三、义和行[①]装修合同附录（日期不详）（H1/83）

装修义和行的材料清单，详细列举了装修材料价格及人工费用，是展现当时物价及房产装修情况的宝贵资料。掘地打庄工银150元，庄杉料价银300元，共450元；石料共价银700元，做石工银600元，共1300元；砖40方，每26.5寸价银1060元，坭（泥）水砌砖工银350元，共1410元；纸碎、禾草石羔（膏）价350元，坭（泥）场墙灰工银400元，共750元；木料价银2000元，做木工银1000元，共3000元；铁窗子拱头550元，钉锁铰玻璃120元，共670元；厂栈房租料350元，管工使用500元，共850元[②]；阶砖瓦价银190元，油漆工料银220元，共410元；共计实银8840元[③]。

Bill for construction materials. Undated. 1 item.

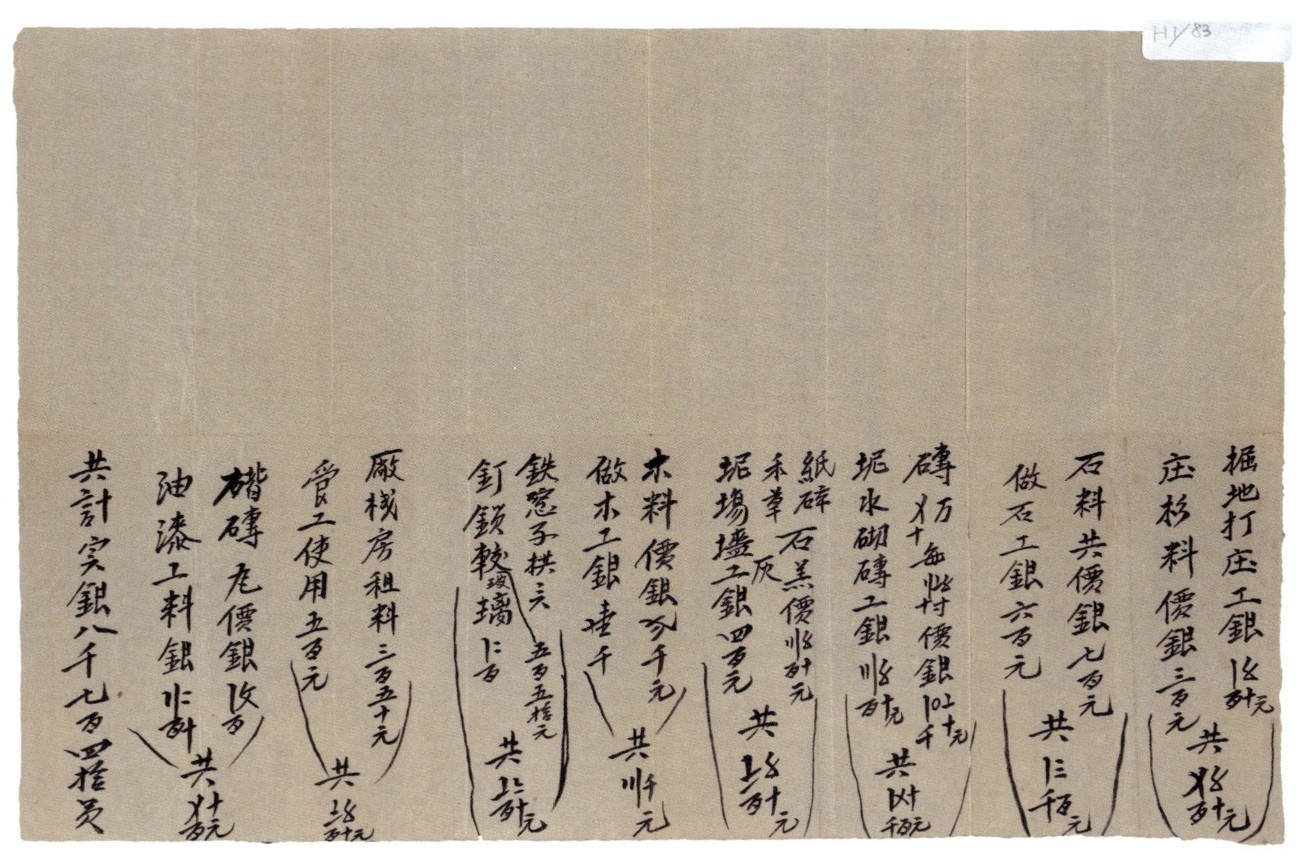

H1/83

掘地打庄工銀一百五十元
庄杉料價銀三百元 共四百五十元
石料共價銀七百元
做石工銀六百元 共一千三百元
磚四十方每廿六寸半價銀一千零六十元
坭水砌磚工銀三百五十元 共一千四百一十元
紙碎禾草石羔價三百五十元
坭場墻灰工銀四百元 共七百五十元
木料價銀二千元
做木工銀壹千 共三千元
鉄窗子拱头五百五十元
釘鎖鉸玻璃一百二十元 共六百七十元
廠棧房租料三百五十元
管工使用五百元 共七百五十元
階磚瓦價銀一百九十元
油漆工料銀二百二十元 共四百一十元
共計實銀八千七百四拾元

---

① 义和行：应即义和夷馆，即小溪馆，1832年刊载于《广州纪事报》(*Canton Register*)上的马礼逊绘十三行商馆区地图中，将其标记为“Creek factory, or I’ho(E’wo hong)”。

② 原文献此处两项费用合计750元，以致其最终与其他项的总计结果为8740元，实际此处两项合计费用为850元。

③ 原文献此处的总计结果为8740元，系厂栈房租料及管工使用合计费用少算100元所致，实际总计费用为8840元。

八四、外国船员名单（日期不详）（H1/84）

中文书写的外国船员名单，附有简单英文注释。名单包括8名米利坚国人[①]（有医生、舵工等）、4名葡萄牙人（水手）和28名徹第缸人[②]（水手）。

Roll of seamen. An undated roll of seamen (in Chinese), including the names of 8 Americans, 4 Portuguese and 28 Chittagong men, with short English notes about the contents of the roll. 1 item.

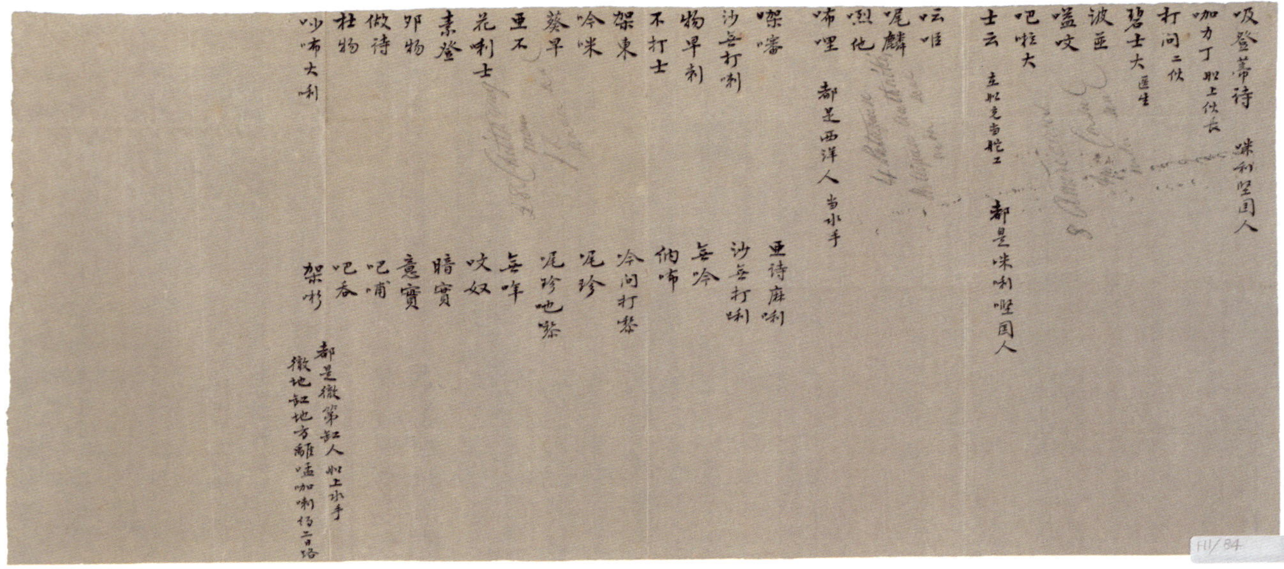

吸登蒂诗　咪利坚国人
加力丁　船上伙长
打问　二伙
碧士　大医生
波亚
嗌文
吧啦大
士云　主船兑当舵工
都是咪唎㗂国人
呍唯
尼麟
烈他
咘哩
都是西洋人　当水手
嚓嚅
沙吾打唎
物早利
不打士
架東
吟咪
葵早
亚不
花唎士
素登
耶物
做诗
杜物
吵咘大唎
亚诗麻唎
沙吾打唎
吾吟
仰咘
吟问打蔡
尼珍
尼珍吔蔡
吾咋
吠奴
暗實
意實
吧哺
吧吞
架彬
都是微第缸人　船上水手
微地缸地方離嗌咖喇伯二日路

H1/84

① 米利坚国人：美国人。
② 徹第缸人：孟加拉人。

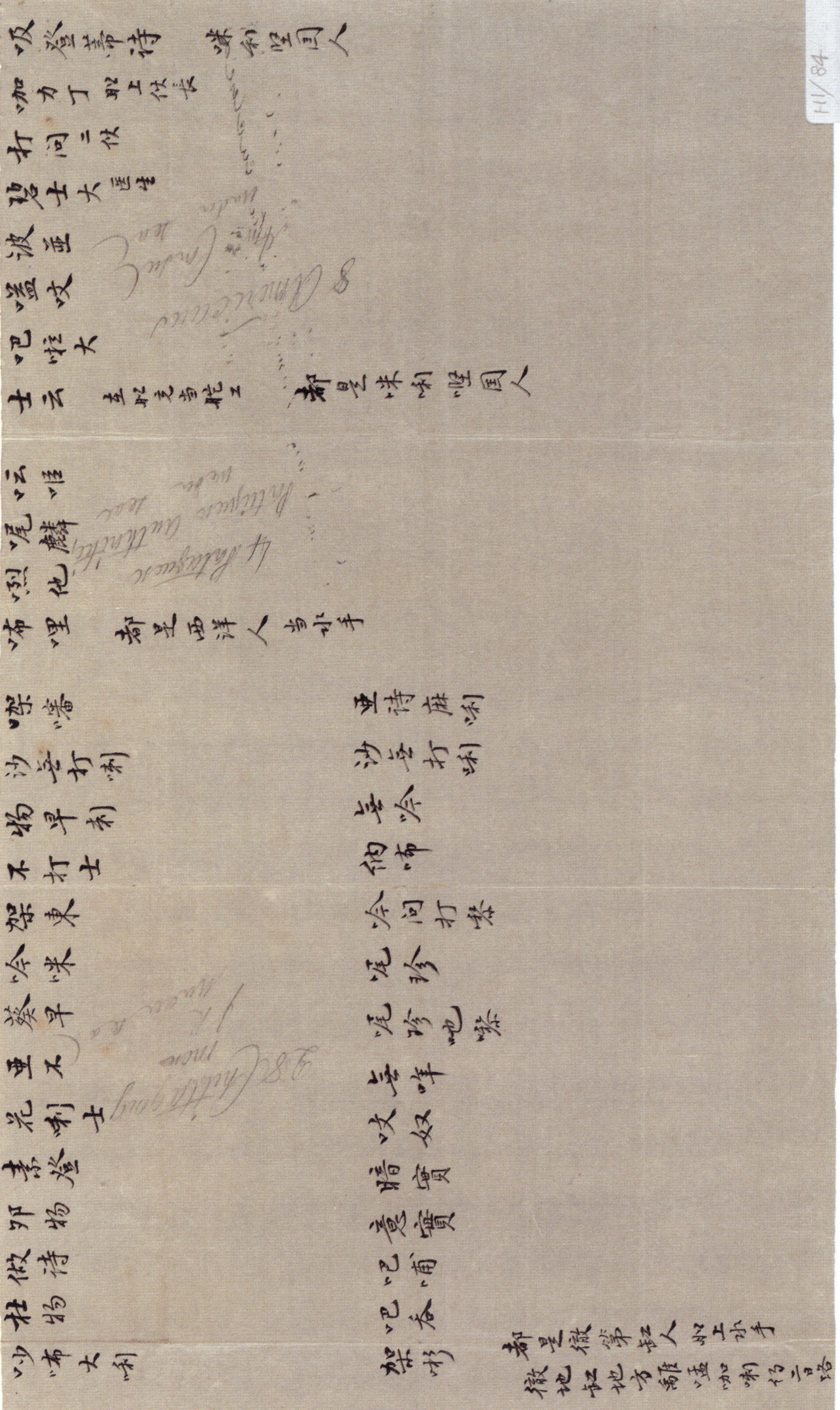

（局部图）

八五、佛山华丰号文房店广告（日期不详）（H1/85）

佛山华丰号文房店的广告，印有“文房第一，价重三都”的宣传，介绍各色纸张及颜料等，注明该铺“在佛山舍人庙[①]右街西向开张”。

Chinese stationery shop poster. Undated. 1 item.

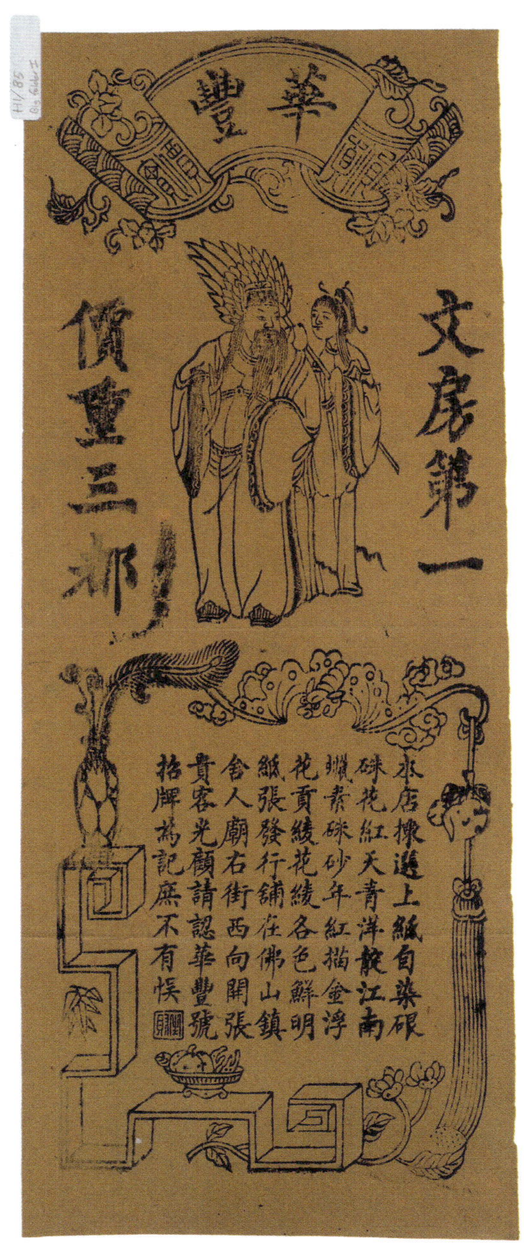

① 舍人庙：原建于佛山燎原路舍人大街，供奉梁舍人，今已不存。

八六、买办又隆[①]致英国商人渣顿[②]大班的信函

1. 正月初九日买办又隆为渣顿大班寻找栈房的信函（年份不详）（H1/86/1）

正月初九日，买办又隆致信英国商人渣顿大班，报告已在广州找寻到两三间栈房，其中一间颇为合适，是原慎昌在河南洲头嘴的栈房，只是租价略高。

Letters from Yowloong (Yu-lung, Youlong), Jardine, Matheson & Co.'s compradore, to Mr. Jardine. Letter re the search for a godown. The year is not given. 1 item.

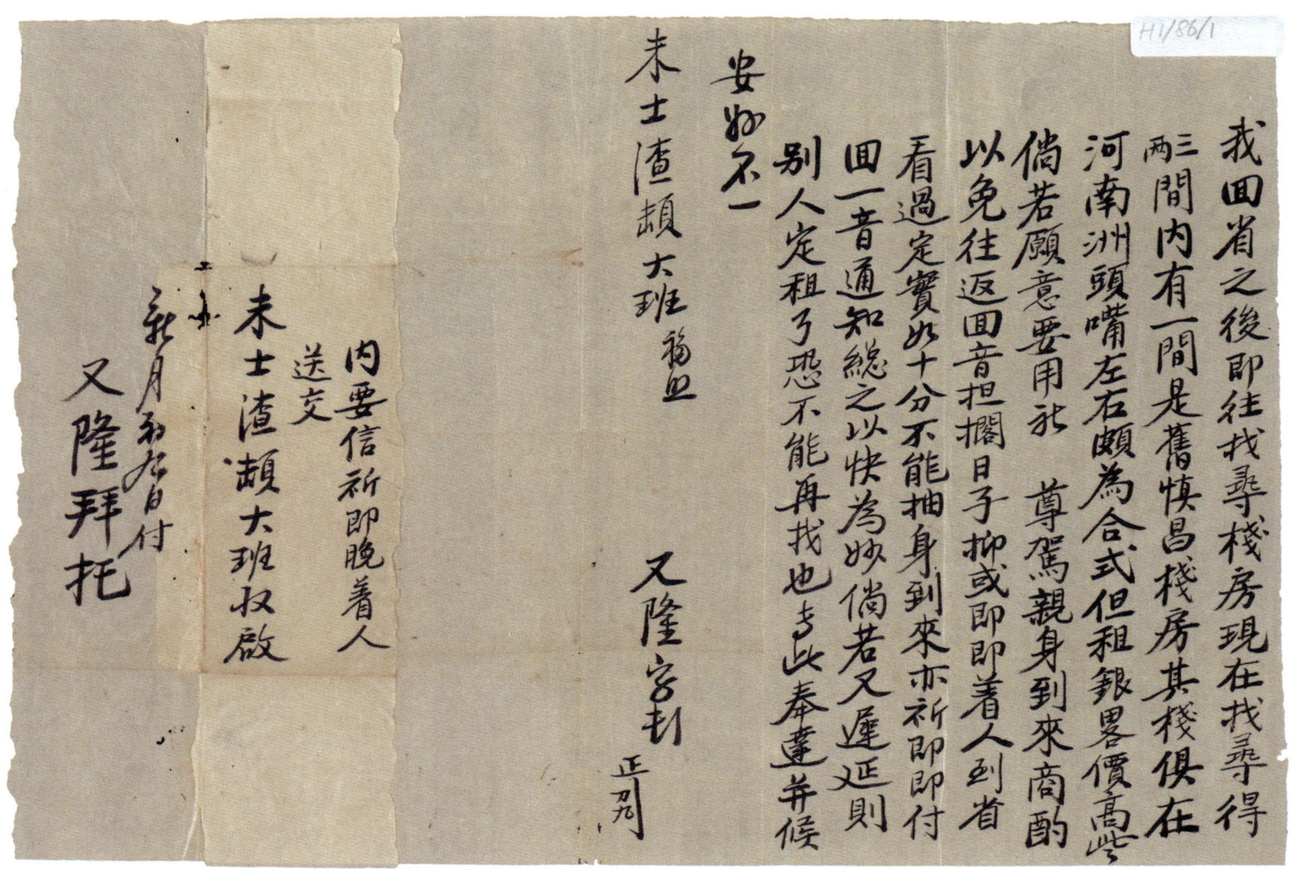

H1/86/1

我回省之後即往找尋棧房現在找尋得兩三間內有一間是舊慎昌棧房其棧係在河南洲頭嘴左右頗為合式但租銀畧價高些倘若願意要用祈 尊駕親身到來商酌以免往返回音担擱日子抑或即即着人到省看過定實如十分不能抽身到來亦祈即即付回一音通知總之以快為妙倘若又遲延則別人定租了恐不能再找也专此奉達并候

安好不一

末士渣顛大班

又隆字剳

正月初九

內要信祈即晚着人送交

末士渣顛大班收啟

新月初九日付

又隆拜托

① 又隆：中国人，怡和洋行（Jardine, Matheson & Co.）的买办。

② 渣顿：即英国商人威廉·查顿（William Jardine），又译为渣颠、渣甸、赞典，为怡和洋行（Jardine, Matheson & Co.）创始人之一。

2. 五月十二日买办又隆[①]致英国商人渣颠[②]的信函（年份不详）(H1/86/2)

该信由买办又隆于五月十二日写给英国商人渣颠，信的开头已散佚，只剩下后半部分及以铅笔撰写的英文注释。他在信中报告了未交银的会单三张，其中一张是亚荣的，还有色瓜和亚好之会单，此二人皆已回乡，建议派人去广州催促其交银。附有铅笔撰写的英文注释。

Letter re unpaid bills. An incomplete letter (in Chinese) in two parts enclosing bills of Awung (Ya-jung, Yarong), Sicqua (Sse-kua, Segua) and Ahoo (Ya-hao, Yahao) (not included). Yowloong reports that Sicqua (Sse-kua, Segua) and Ahoo (Ya-hao, Yahao) have gone into the countryside, and advises that someone should be sent to Canton to look for them and get them to pay their debts. The year is not given. The document includes an incomplete English translation in pencil. 2 items; Fair condition, but damage by insects and missing some sections.

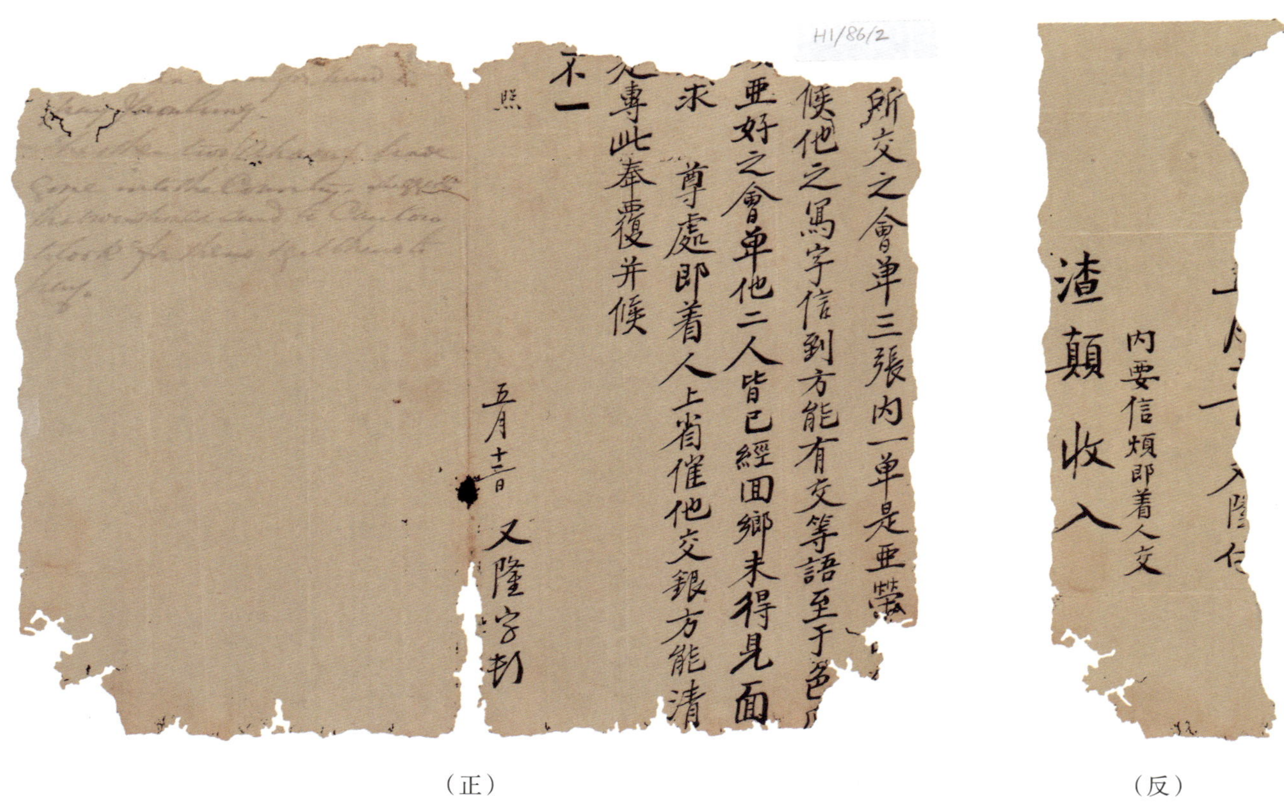
H1/86/2

所交之會单三張内一单是亞榮

候他之寫字信到方能有交等語至于色[瓜]

亞好之會单他二人皆已經回鄉未得見面

求 尊處即着人上省催他交銀方能清

又專此奉覆并候

不一

照

五月十二日 又隆字扎

渣顛收入

内要信煩即着人交

（正）　　（反）

① 又隆：中国人，怡和洋行（Jardine, Matheson & Co.）的买办。

② 渣颠：即英国商人威廉·查顿（William Jardine），又译为渣顿、渣甸、赞典，为怡和洋行（Jardine, Matheson & Co.）创始人之一。

3. 买办又隆[①] 致英国商人渣颠[②] 的信函（日期不详）（H1/86/3）

买办又隆致英国商人渣颠的信，他在信中报告，亚荣要求延长他的交款日期，色瓜和亚好没有找到，要求渣颠派人到广州去催其交银。另附有铅笔撰写的英文注释。

Letter re unpaid bills. An undated letter (in Chinese) regarding three unpaid bills originally enclosed with H1/86/2. Yowloong reports that Awung (Ya-jung, Yarong) has asked for an extension of his repayment date, and that Sicqua (Sse-kua, Segua) and Ahoo (Ya-hao, Yahao) could not be found. He requests that a trustworthy man be sent to Canton to receive back the orders and settle the account. There is also a second sheet containing a partial English translation. 2 items; Fair condition, but damage by insects and missing some sections.

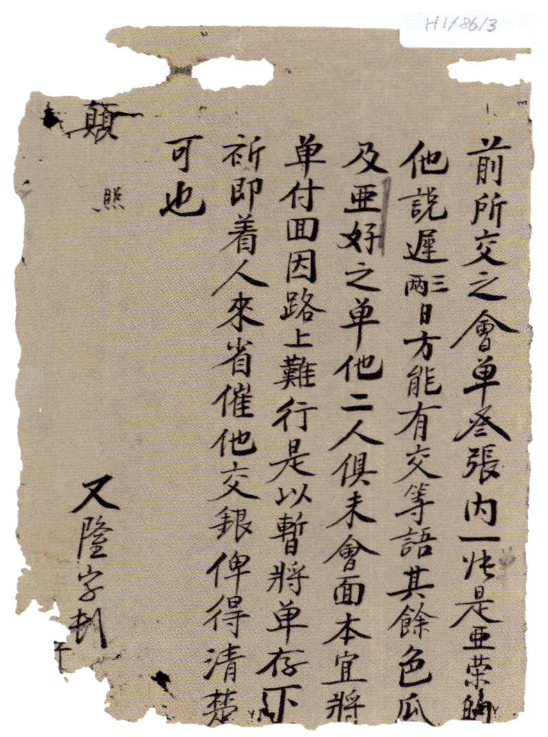
H1/86/3

前所交之會单叁張內一件是亞榮的
他說遲兩三日方能有交等語其餘色瓜
及亞好之单他二人俱未會面本宜將
单付回因路上難行是以暫將单存下
祈即着人來省催他交銀俾得清楚
可也
顛　照
又隆字扎

H1/86/3

Sicqua & Ahoo not
to be found. Asks
to send up a trusty
-worthy man to
Canton, to receive
back the orders &
settle the account.

---

① 又隆：中国人，怡和洋行（Jardine, Matheson & Co.）的买办。

② 渣颠：即英国商人威廉·查顿（William Jardine），又译为渣顿、渣甸、赞典，为怡和洋行（Jardine, Matheson & Co.）创始人之一。

4. 买办又隆[①]致英国商人查顿[②]的信函（日期不详）（H1/86/4）

又隆通报英国商人查顿租赁商馆信函。

Letter re unpaid bills. Two fragments of an undated letter (in Chinese) referring to Yowloong's two previous letters concerning three unpaid bills (H1/86/2–3) and reporting that only Awung has made payment. The document includes part of an English translation in pencil. 2 items; Moderate condition, with damage by insects and missing much of the document.

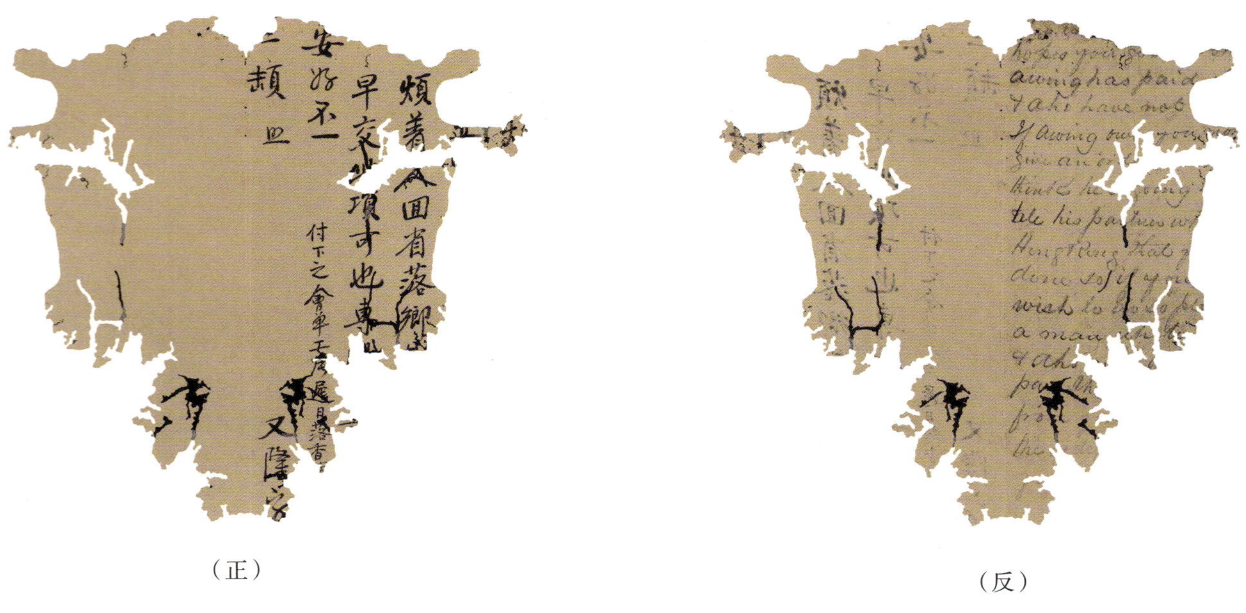

（正）　　（反）

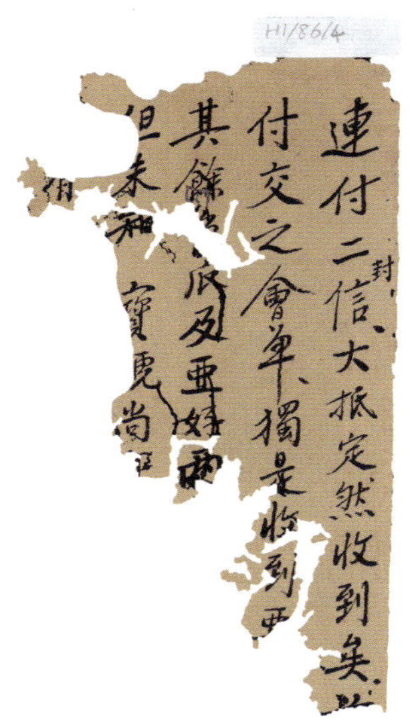

連付二信、封大抵定然收到矣
付交之會單、獨是
其餘
但未知

① 又隆：中国人，怡和洋行（Jardine, Matheson & Co.）的买办。

② 查顿：即英国商人威廉·查顿（William Jardine），又译为渣颠、渣顿、渣甸、赞典，为怡和洋行（Jardine, Matheson & Co.）创始人之一。

八七、新昌[①]单据（日期不详）

1. 轩利[②]致新昌先生要求发货的单据（H1/87/1）

轩利（Hsuan-li）致新昌先生的单据，要求其见字即交烟头（鸦片）一箱。

Receipt from Hsuan-li. An undated receipt from Hsuan-li (Xuanli) (Henry?) to Mr. Hsin-ch’ang for one case of opium. 1 item.

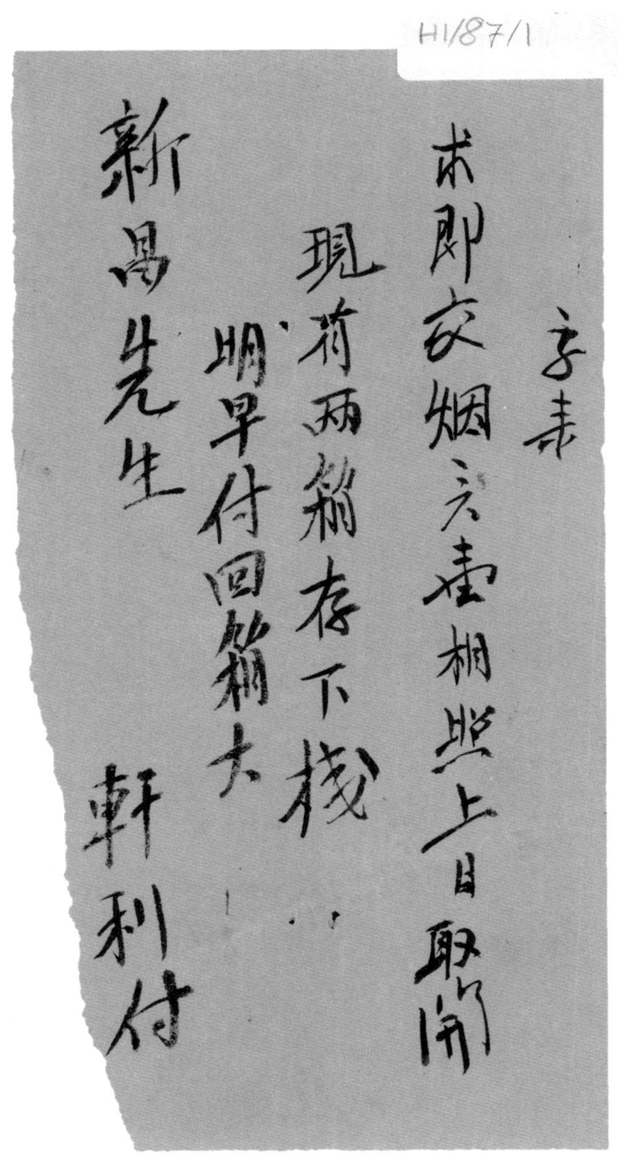

H1/87/1

字来
求即交烟头壹相照上日取開
現荷兩箱存下棧
明早付回箱大
新昌先生
軒利付

---

① 新昌：中国商人，参与贩卖鸦片。

② 轩利：外国鸦片贩子。

2. 痕子致新昌[①]先生要求发货的单据（H1/87/2）

痕子（Hen-tsu）致新昌先生的单据，要求其见字即“请船取面粉四百四十五桶”。

Bill from Hen-tsu. A undated bill (in Chinese) from Hen-tsu (Henzi) to Mr. Hsin-ch’ang for the collection of goods, including English notes about the bill. 1 item.

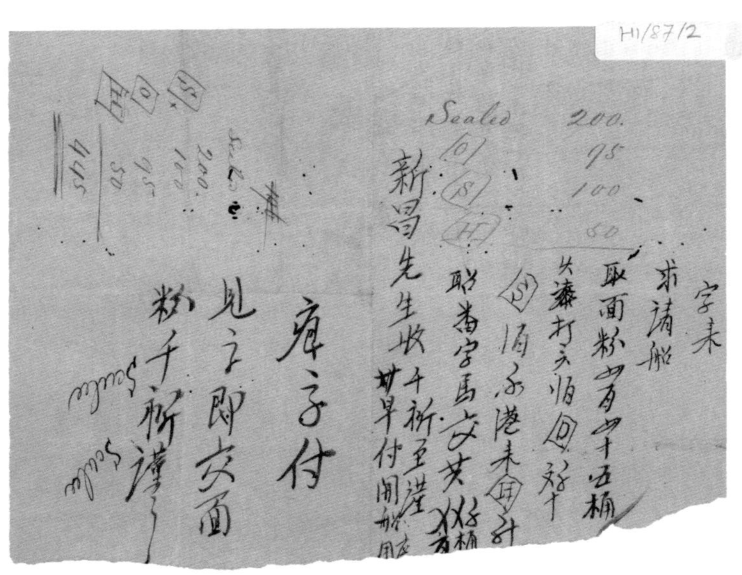

（正）

（反）

① 新昌：中国商人，参与贩卖鸦片。

八八、九月二十一日石艇致烟地吉宝行的收据（年份不详）（H1/88）

九月二十一日石艇致烟地吉宝行的收据，由冯连代收水脚银40元。有简单英文注释。

Receipt to Yen-ti-chi Hong. A receipt (in Chinese) from Shih-t'ing (Shiting) to Yen-ti-chi (Yan di ji) Hong for $40, including an English note about the receipt. The year is not given. 1 item.

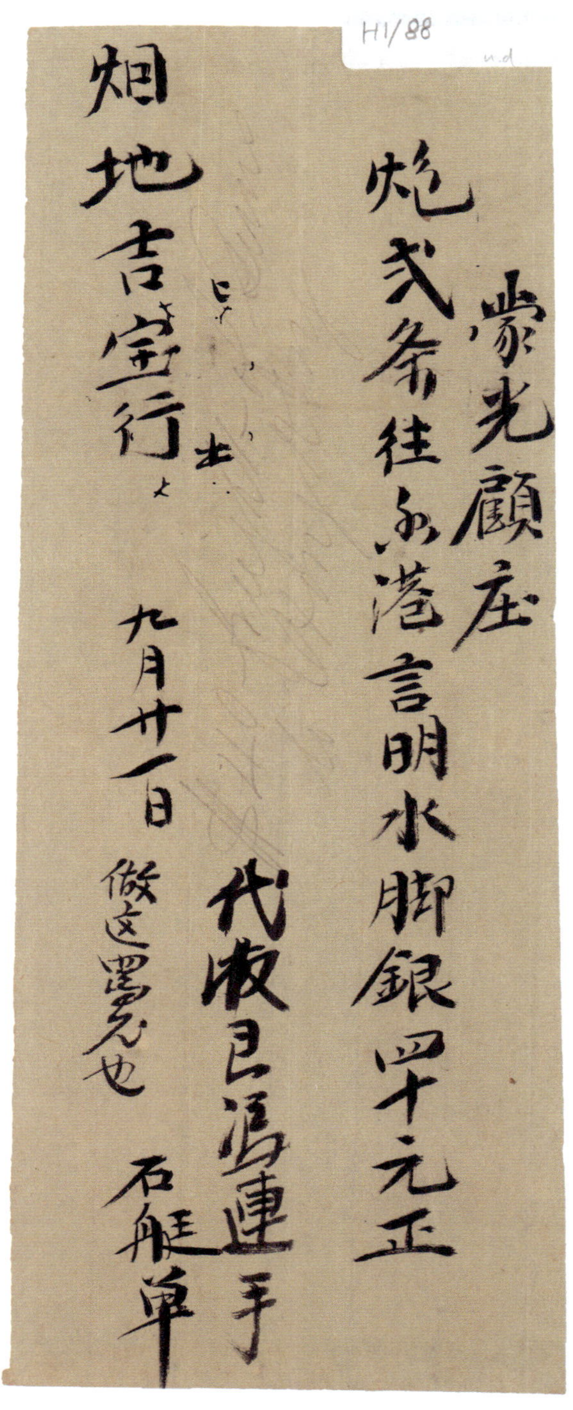

H1/88

蒙光顾庄

炮弍条往来港言明水脚银四十元正

代收己冯连手

石艇单

九月廿一日

烟地吉宝行

八九、金星门[1]唧唎船鸦片拍卖广告（日期不详）（H1/89）

英国鸦片商人发布的明目张胆的中文鸦片广告，在金星门海域进行大规模的鸦片拍卖活动："于五月拾伍日拾点钟金星门唧唎船有头□□盆金花烟四拾余箱出投，如有贵客欲□□，请至唧唎船便知。每投货银壹百，定银拾元，限期七日出货，过期不出，定银不追，勿谓不先言□，风雨不改。"

Opium sale advertisement. An advertisement for the sale of more than 40 cases of opium on the 5th month and 15th day on the ship 'Lang-li' at Gold Star Gate, deposit 100.10 Tls[2]. The year is not given. 1 item; Fair condition, but damage by insects and missing some sections.

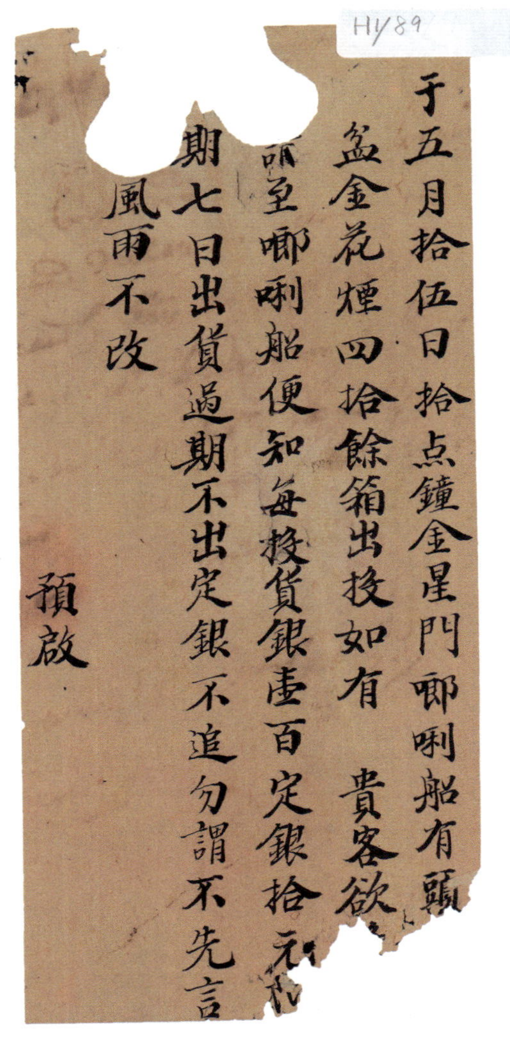
H1/89

于五月拾伍日拾点鐘金星門唧唎船有頭
盆金花煙四拾餘箱出投如有　貴客欲
請至唧唎船便知每投貨銀壹百定銀拾元
期七日出貨過期不出定銀不追勿謂不先言
風雨不改
預啟

① 金星门：伶仃洋海域，清代中期著名鸦片走私地点。

② 原中文文献中谓"每投货银壹百，定银拾元"，此处英文提要有误。

九〇、鸦片提货单据（日期不详）（H1/90）

鸦片提货单据，主要内容为：“三月十一日存下细烟头五箱。细箱四月初二日取三箱。细箱又卅日取式箱。去清的。”

Opium receipt. A receipt for the deposit of 5 cases of opium on the 3rd month and 11th day. The year is not given. 1 item.

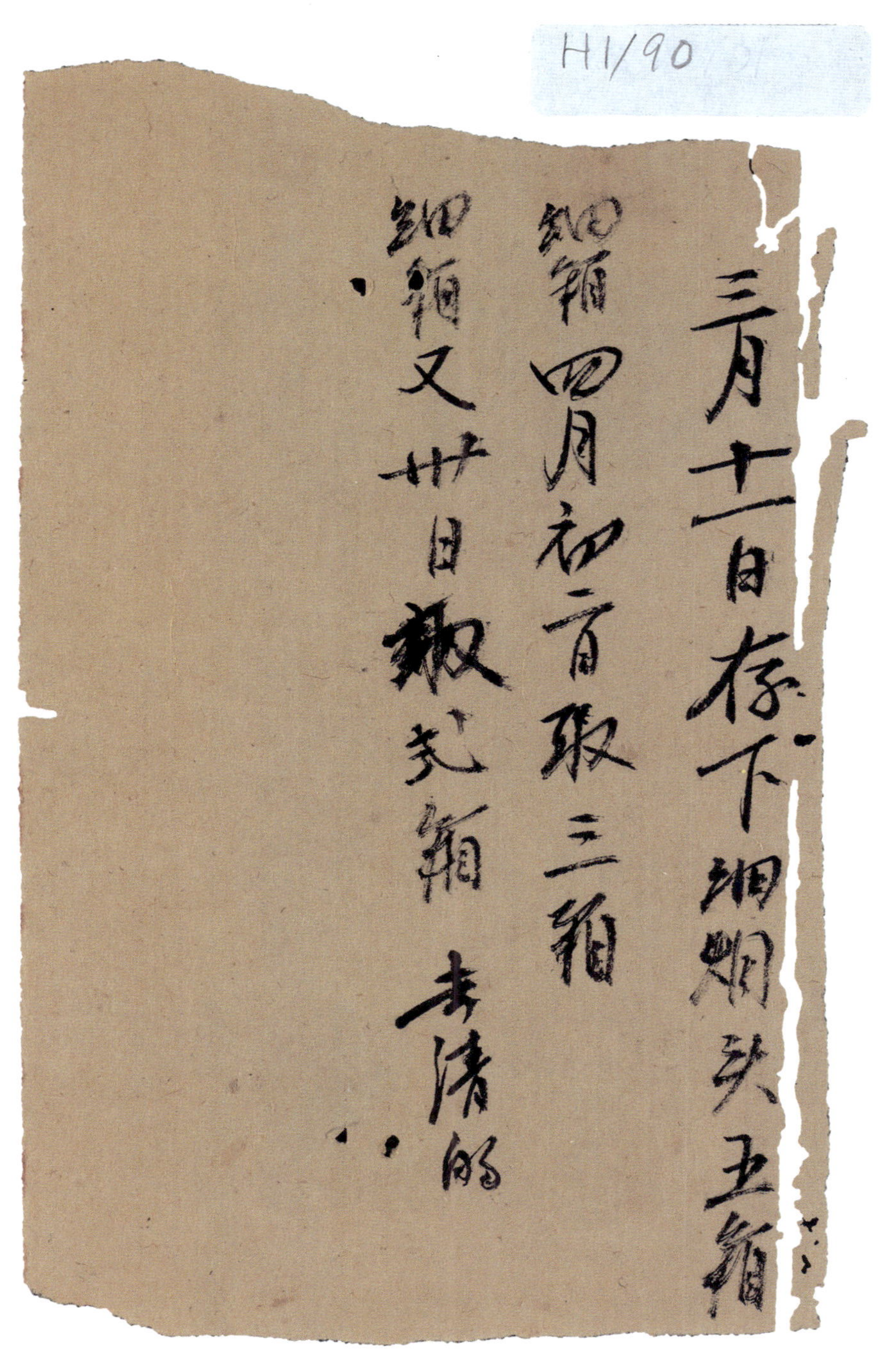

H1/90

三月十一日存下细烟头五箱
细箱四月初二日取三箱
细箱又卅日取式箱
去清的

九一、安记[①]单据（年份不详）

1. 三月十三日安记致痕谷的牛油订单（H1/91/1）

三月十三日，安记致痕谷（Hen-ku）的牛油订单，主要内容为："字来祈取牛油二桶，烦交明日信艇带来是幸。"盖有安记印章，印文"省城德兴街安记"。

Butter order to Mr. Hen-ku. An order from An-chi to Mr. Hen-ku (Hengu) for butter. The year is not given. 1 item.

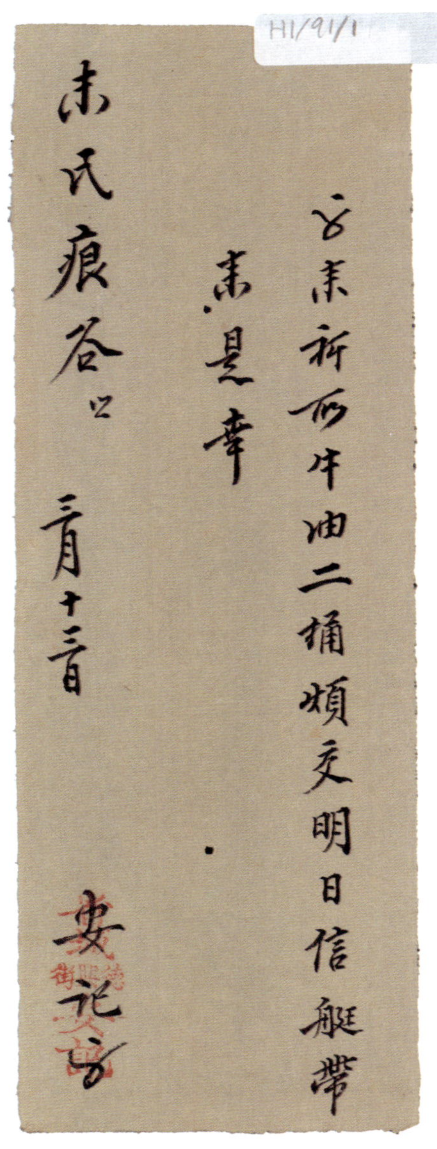
H1/91/1

字來祈取牛油二桶煩交明日信艇帶
來是幸
來氏痕谷
三月十三
安記字

① 安记：中国商号，位于广州德兴街。

2. 四月十六日安记[①]致痕谷的牛油订单（H1/91/2）

四月十六日，安记致痕谷的牛油订单：“见字祈付细桶牛油二桶。”

Butter order to Mr. Hen-ku. An order from An-chi to Mr. Hen-ku (Hengu) for butter. The year is not given. 1 item.

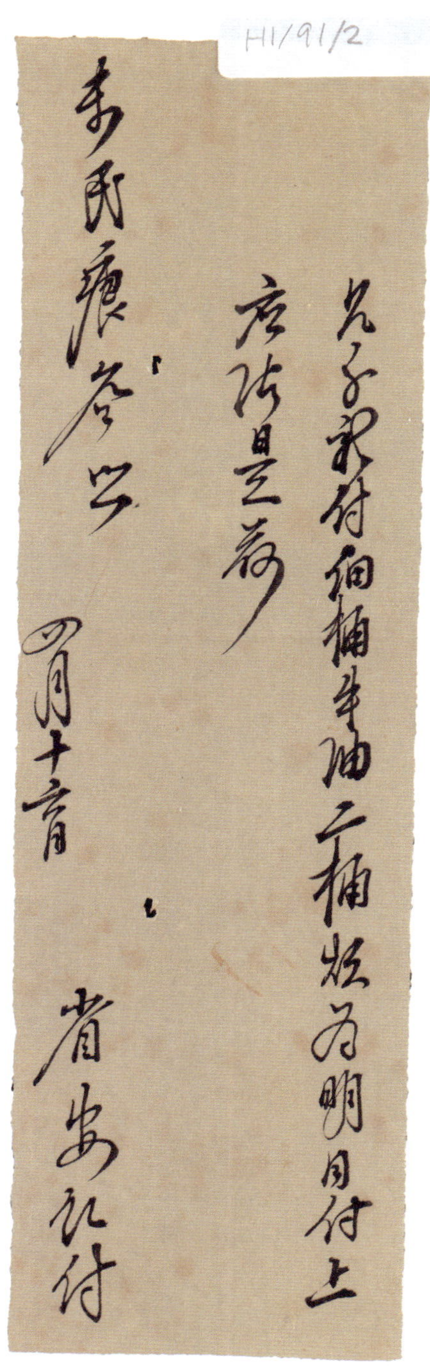

H1/91/2

見字祈付細桶牛油二桶收為明日付上

痕谷

四月十六日

安記付

---

① 安记：中国商号，位于广州德兴街。

3. 六月二十五日安记[①] 致痕谷的饼干订单（H1/91/3）

六月二十五日，安记致痕谷的饼干订单，主要内容为："字来求取水并干四箱，祈交明日来人带上是幸。"盖有安记印章，印文"安记"。

Biscuit order to Mr. Hen-ku. An order from An-chi to Mr. Hen-ku (Hengu) for biscuits. The year is not given. 1 item.

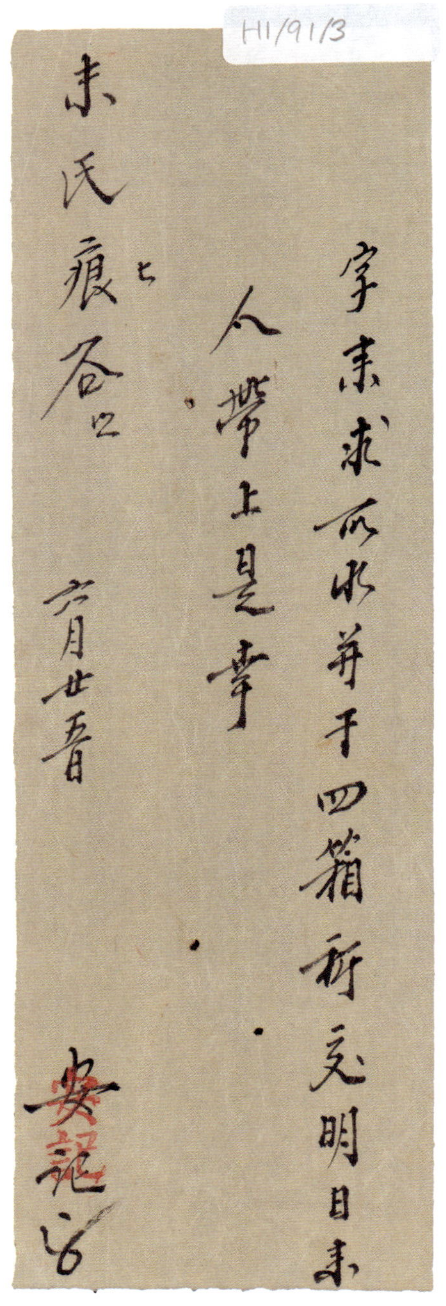
H1/91/3

字来求取水并干四箱祈交明日来
人带上是幸
氏痕谷
六月廿五
安记

① 安记：中国商号，位于广州德兴街。

4. 七月十五日安记[1]致痕谷的牛油订单（H1/91/4）

七月十五日，安记致痕谷的牛油订单，“字来求取牛油四桶”。

Biscuit[2] order to Mr. Hen-ku. An order from An-chi to Mr. Hen-ku (Hengu) for biscuits. The year is not given. 1 item.

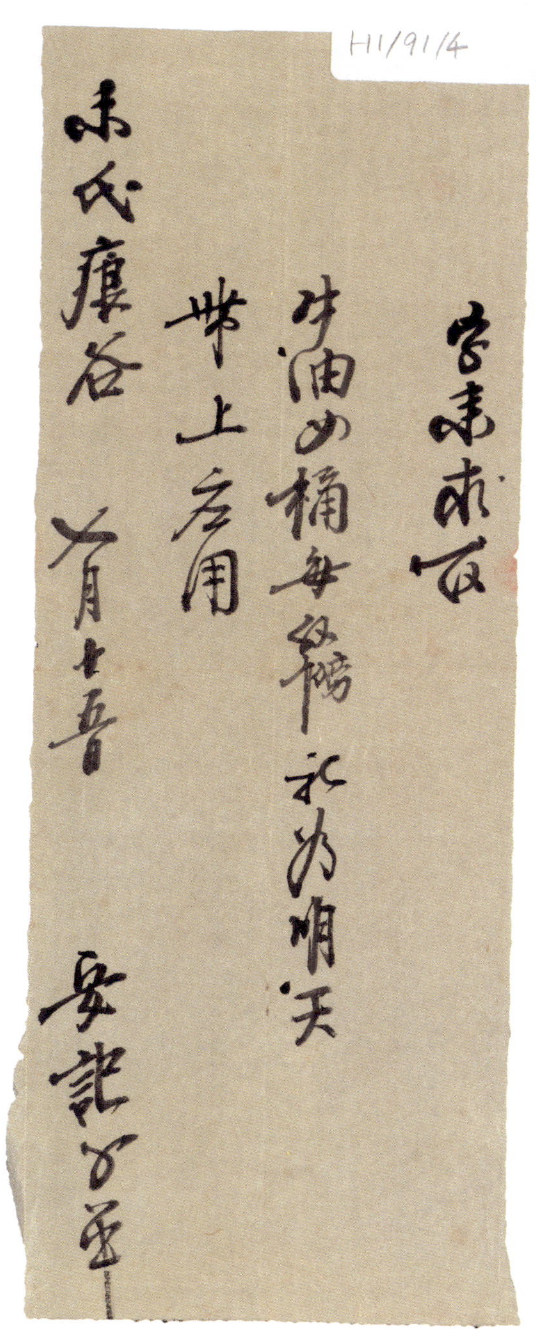

H1/91/4

字来求取

牛油四桶每[illegible]祈为明天

带上应用

[illegible]氏痕谷

七月十五日

安记[illegible]

---

① 安记：中国商号，位于广州德兴街。

② 勘误：此为牛油订单，英文提要有误（此处及第二句末尾处）。

5. 六月初九日安记[①]致痕谷的牛油订单（H1/91/5）

六月初九日，安记致痕谷的牛油订单，主要内容为：“字来求取好牛油弍桶，即明日付上应用。”

Biscuit[②] order to Mr. Hen-ku. An order from An-chi to Mr. Hen-ku (Hengu) for biscuits. The year is not given. 1 item.

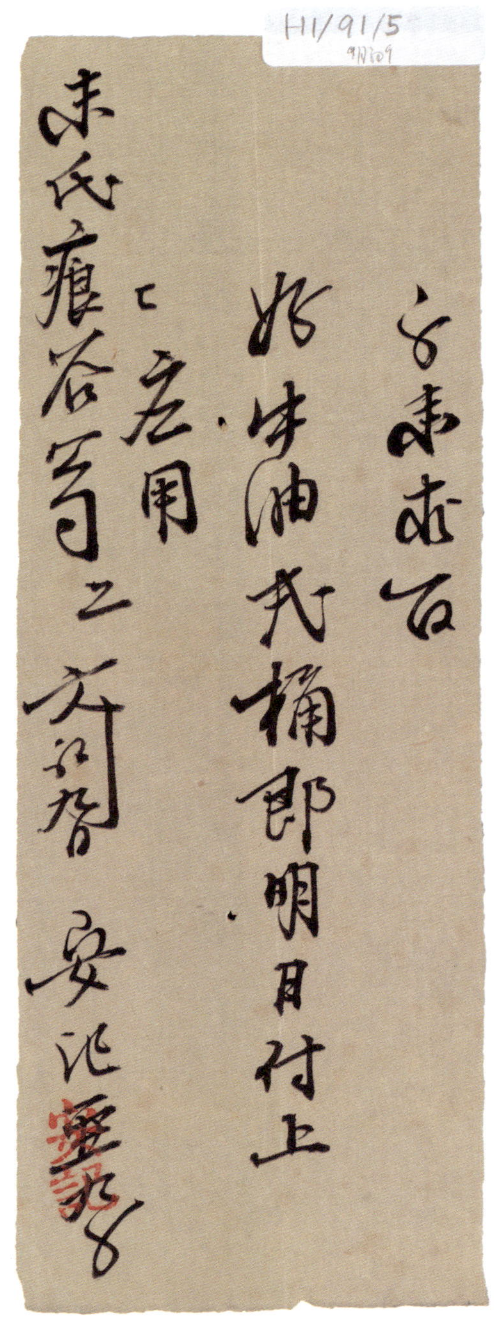

H1/91/5

字来求取
好牛油弍桶即明日付上
应用
来氏痕谷写台 之
六月初九
安记

---

① 安记：中国商号，位于广州德兴街。

② 勘误：此为牛油订单，英文提要有误（此处及第二句末尾处）。

6. 十二月初七日安记[①]致急顿记列的杂货账单（H1/91/6）

十二月初七日，安记致急顿记列（Chi-tun-chi-lie）的杂货账单。盖有安记印章，印文“德兴街安记单”。另有一处方形印章，印文不清。

Grocery bill to Mr. Chi-tun-chi-lie. A bill from An-chi to Mr. Chi-tun-chi-lie (Ji dun ji lie) for groceries, 1 January 1848 (?). 1 item. 1848

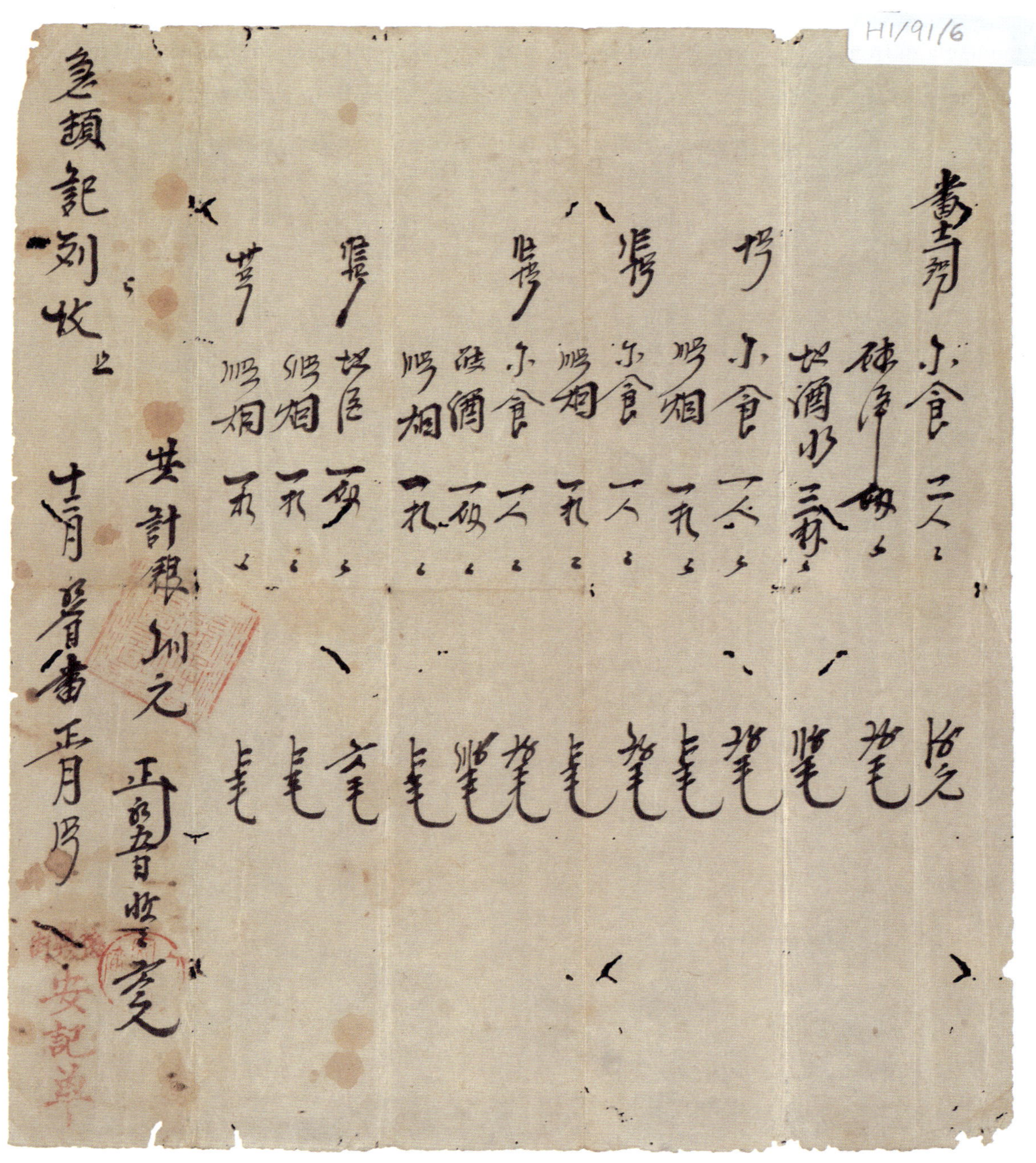

① 安记：中国商号，位于广州德兴街。

九二、十一月初五日兴盛利①、广发裕②致澳顺宝船③的索赔单据（年份不详）（H1/92）

十一月初五日，广发裕、兴盛利因委托澳顺宝船运输的豆饼损坏，而提交此索赔单据。单据盖有广发裕和兴盛利的印章，印文“广发裕”“顺风得利”“兴盛利”，兴盛利的印章较精美，两旁还刻有印文“支取不准”“发货图书”。另附有该单内容的英文翻译。

Freight claim from Hsing shing lee and Kwong faat yeu. A freight claim (in Chinese) from Hsing shing lee (Xing sheng li) and Kwong faat yeu (Guang fa yu) to S. S. ‘Ocean’ for a damaged cargo of bean cakes. There is also a separate English translation. The year is not given. 2 items.

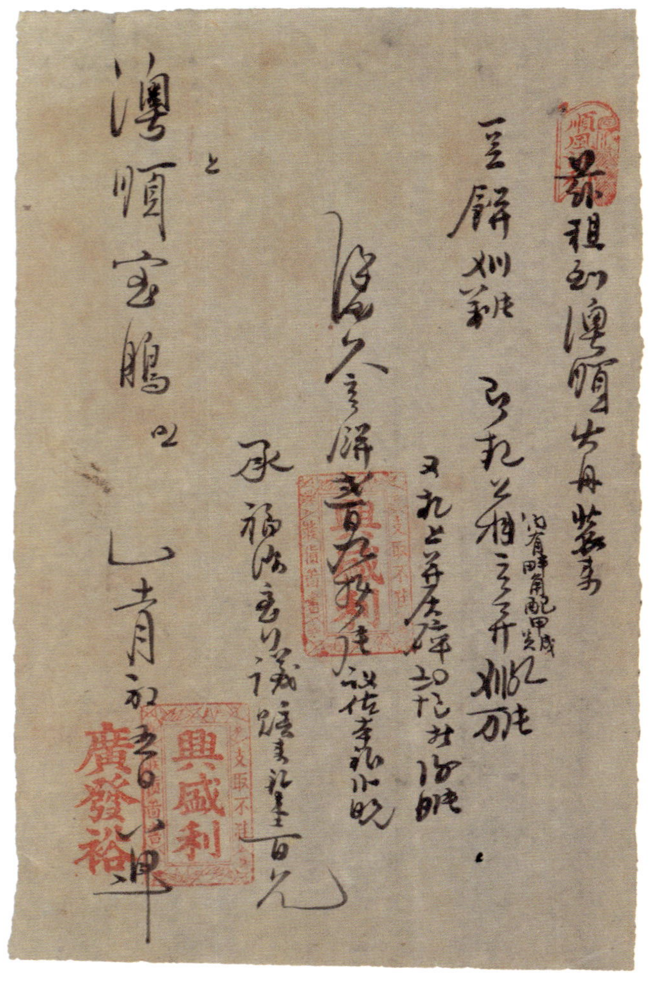
廣發裕
興盛利

H1/92

We had shipped on board the S.S. "Ocean"
43000 pieces Bean Cakes.

Delivered in Godown 42560 pieces
And 70 Bag Broken cakes said 150 pieces

The Balance is 290 pieces being short delivery
adjust price $210

Mr. Look Yuen promised to pay the claim only
One Hundred Dollars

Hing Shing Lee
and
Kwong faat Yeu

---

① 兴盛利：中国商号。

② 广发裕：中国商号。

③ 澳顺宝船：外国轮船 S. S.‘Ocean’，“澳顺”是其英文名“Ocean”的译音。

九三、厦门亚配舍[①]丝绸营销单据（日期不详）（H1/93）

厦门亚配舍丝绸营销单据，背面附有英文注释，可知外商 Reed 向亚配舍购买湖丝三札。

Bill from J. Reed. An undated bill (in Chinese) from J. Reed to Ya-p'ei-she (Ya pei she) in Amoy for three chops of silk, including a new balance, with an English note on the back. 1 item; Fair condition, but damage by insects.

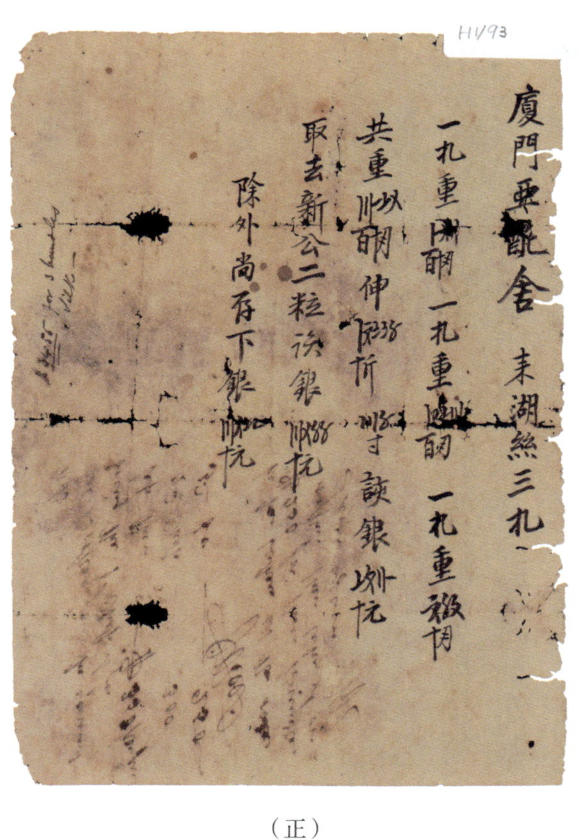

H1/93

廈門亞配舍　來湖絲三札

一札重[illegible]　一札重[illegible]　一札重[illegible]

共重[illegible]　伸[illegible]折[illegible]　該銀[illegible]

取去新公二粒　該銀[illegible]

除外尚存下銀[illegible]

（正）

（反）

① 亚配舍：中国商人。

九四、萃和祥[①]毛重单（日期不详）（H1/94）

萃和祥毛重单，即船运清单。

Shipping list of Ts'ui-ho-hsiang. An undated shipping list (rough weight) of Ts'ui-ho-hsiang (Cui he xiang). 1 item.

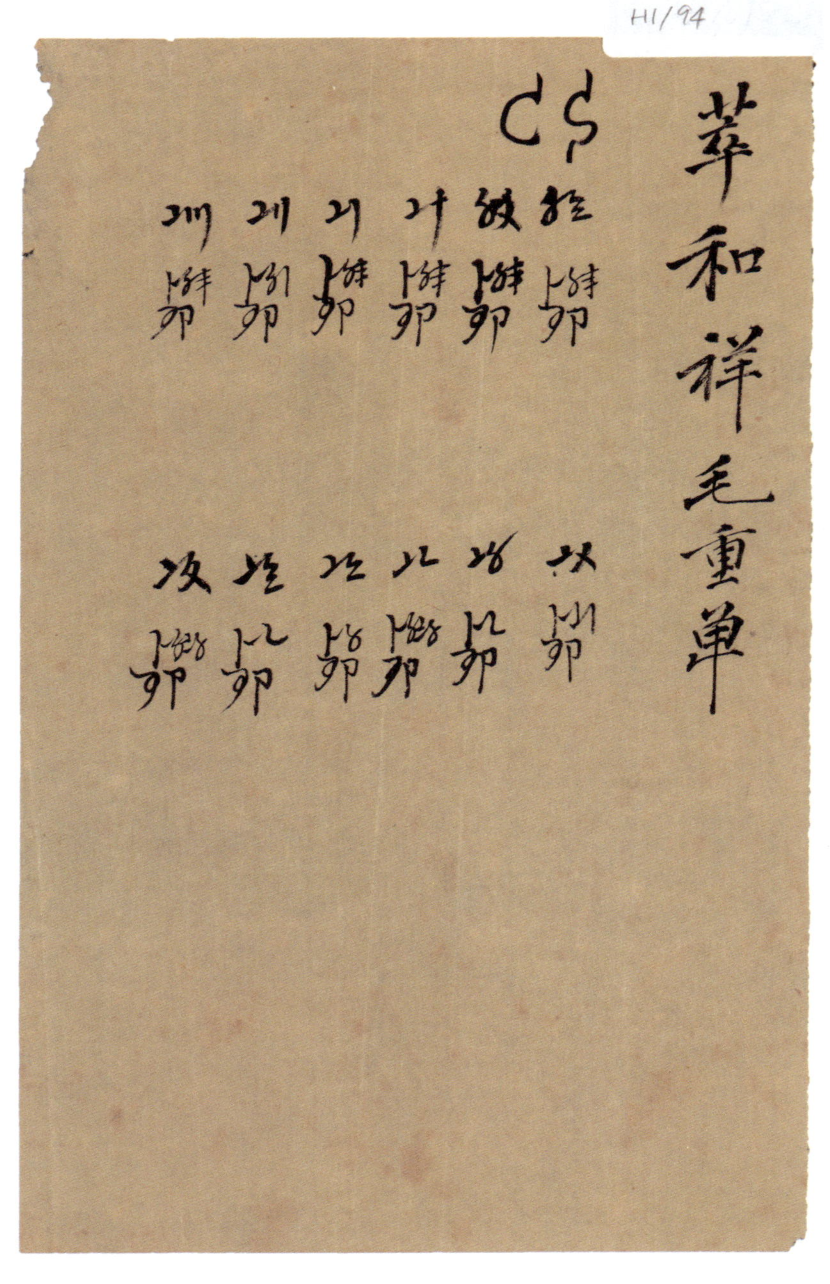

H1/94

萃和祥毛重单

CS

① 萃和祥：中国商号。

九五、亚中[①]致渣甸[②]的信函（年份不详）

1. 六月十九日亚中致渣甸的信函（H1/95/1）

六月十九日，亚中致渣甸的信函，报告他为渣甸营销棉花的情况。

Letter re purchased cotton. Three fragments of a letter regarding cotton purchased on the 11th day of 6th month(31 July). The document dates from 8 August in either 1838 or 1857. 3 items; Moderate condition, with damage by insects and missing much of the document. circa 1838

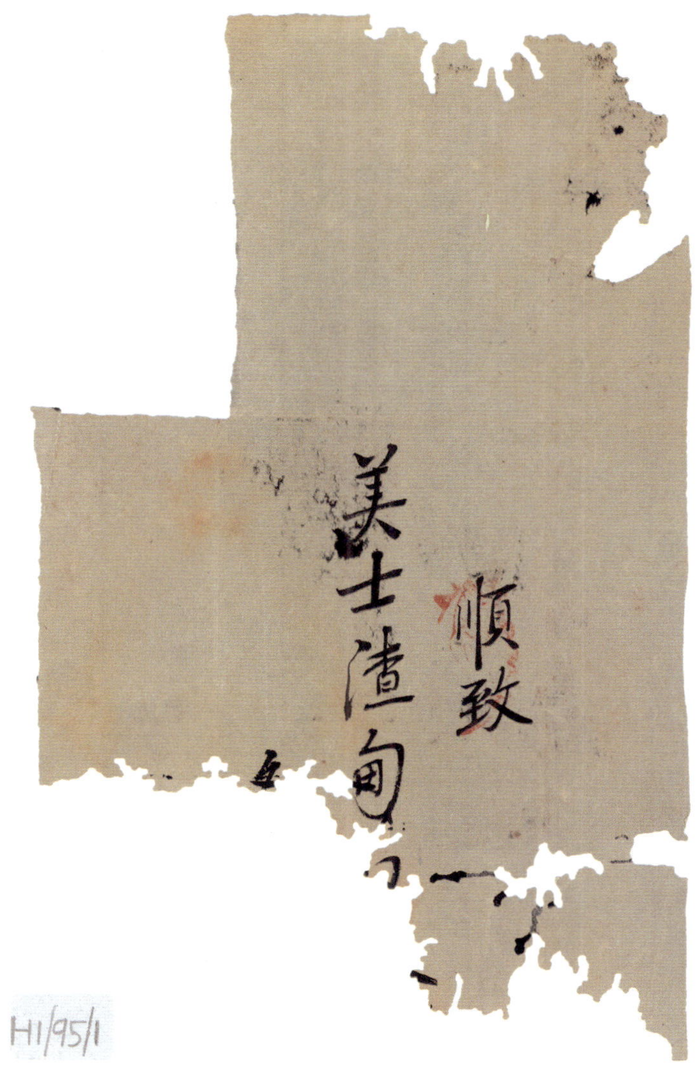
顺致
美士渣甸

H1/95/1

① 亚中：中国商人，落款英文名写作“Achoon”。

② 渣甸：即英国商人威廉·查顿（William Jardine），又译为渣颠、渣顿、赞典，为怡和洋行（Jardine, Matheson & Co.）创始人之一。

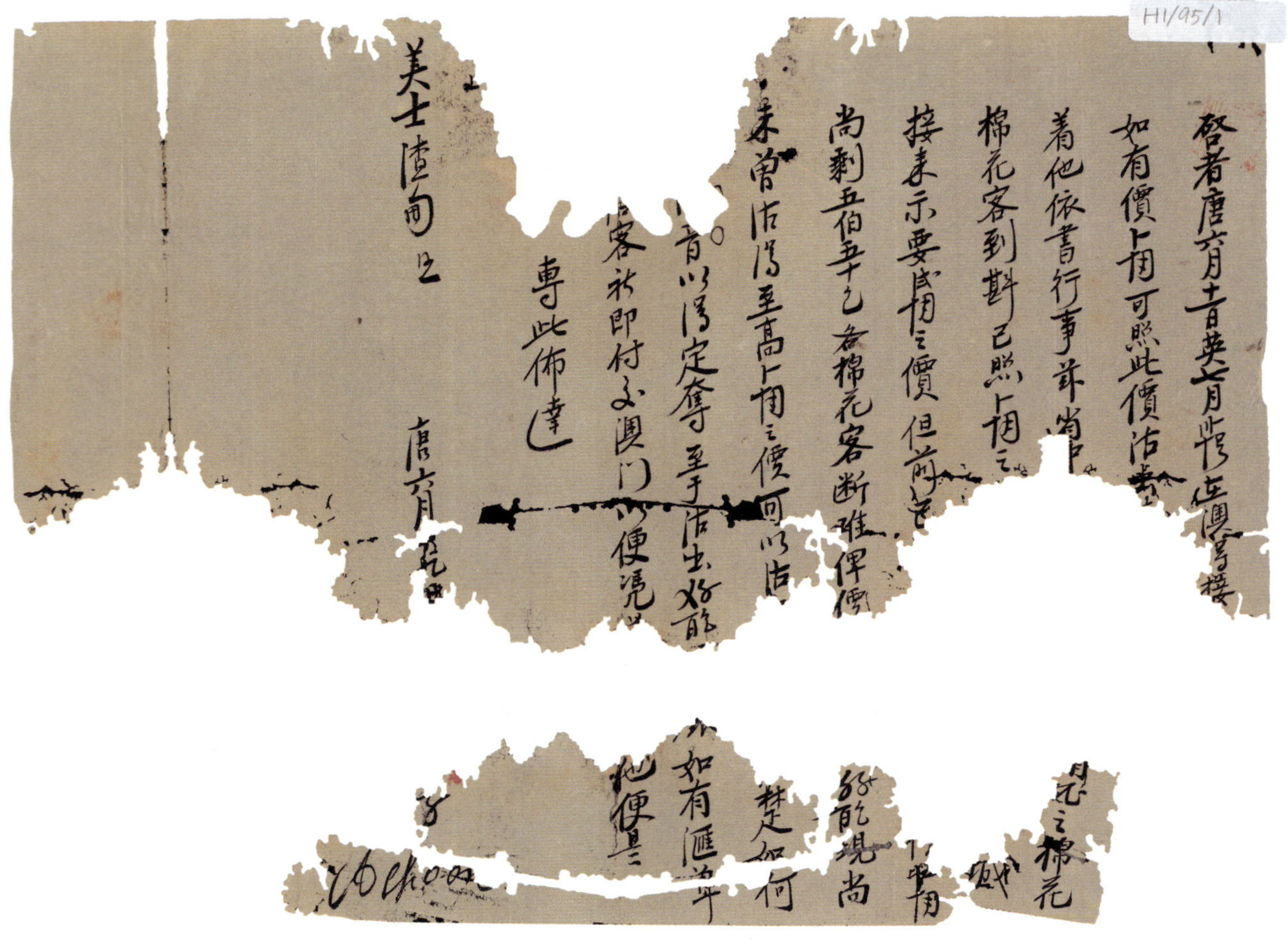

啓者唐六月十二日英七月廿九日在澳奉接

如有價上用可照此價沽出

着他依書行事并尚

棉花客到斟已照上用之

接来示要咸用之價但前

尚剩五伯五十乙包棉花客断难俾價

未曾沽得至高上用之價可以沽

首以得定奪至于沽出好歹

客於即付与澳门以便浼

專此佈達

美士渣甸　台

唐六月

月……之棉花

……也

下用

能現尚

楚如何

如有滙单

他便其

2. 九月二十三日亚中[①]致渣甸[②]的信函（H1/95/2）

九月二十三日，亚中致渣甸的信函，要求其结算货款，盖有方形朱文印章，印文“同德图章”。

Letter re account. A letter (in Chinese) requesting the settlement of Jardine’s account, with a Chinese envelope which includes the English note on the back ‘From Achoone’. The year is not given. 2 items; Fair condition, with damage by insects.

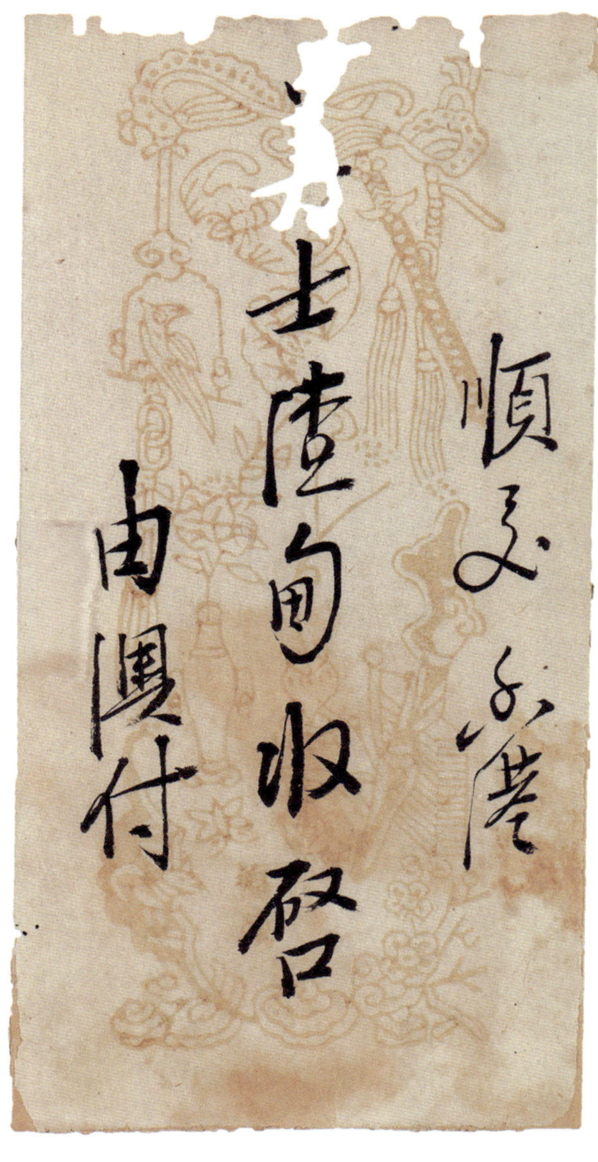

（正）

（反）

---

① 亚中：中国商人，落款英文名写作“Achoon”，信封背面英文作“Achoone”。

② 渣甸：即英国商人威廉·查顿（William Jardine），又译为渣颠、渣顿、赞典，为怡和洋行（Jardine, Matheson & Co.）创始人之一。

啓者，八月十八日奉歸由大班算數除交銀外奉歸
尚欠大班銀叁萬壹仟〇六十肆員，八月廿六日交匯
滙交今麻々捌仟員，廿七日在澳交監嘆嘮艮柒仟
員，九月十七日又交嚧嘆嘮々伍仟員，廿三日又交嚧嘆嘮艮肆
仟員，共計交々貳萬肆仟員，除外尚欠大班艮七〇六四員
待遲日在澳交清，由嚧嘆嘮便是。但上年奉歸立由
大班之存花單，祈為即日付來澳交由監嘆嘮，以便奉歸
截清此數，必要收回此單，以得消繳，至緊至緊。此達

美士渣甸　台上

九月廿三日　亞中字

Achoon

九六、黄埔买办弗即的单据

广州十三行时期，黄埔成为外国水手的居留地，如“丹麦人岛”“法国人岛”等，黄埔村村民都直接或间接地与外国航运有关，充当买办、装卸工、铁匠等等，黄埔村成为外国商船修理中心和后勤补给基地，在十三行海外贸易中扮演了重要角色，在广州乃至中国对外贸易史、中外关系史上均具有重要的地位。黄埔买办弗即的系列单据就是具体的例证。

1. 二月初三日黄埔买办弗即的茶油收据（年份不详）（H1/96/1）

二月初三日，黄埔村买办弗即的茶油收据，盖有印章，印文“黄埔买办弗即”。

Receipt for tea oil. The year is not given. 1 item.

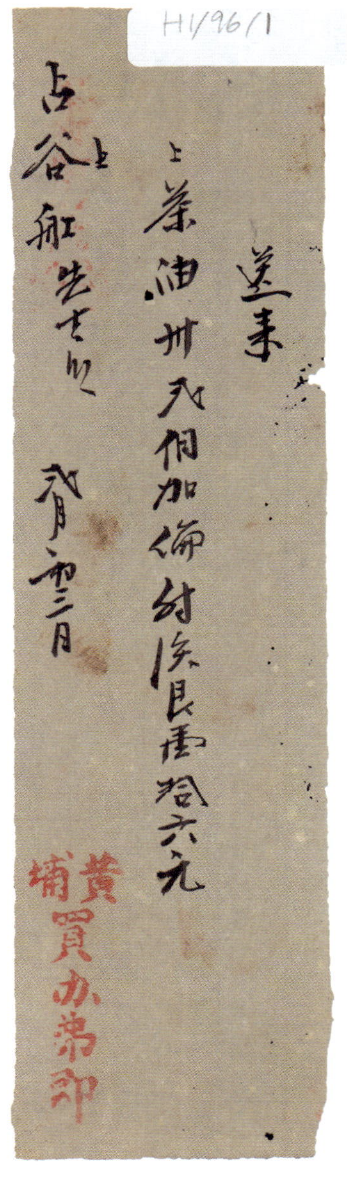

H1/96/1

送来

上茶油卅斤

弍月初三

黄埔買办弗即

2. 三月十一日黄埔买办弗即的啤酒提货单（年份不详）（H1/96/2）

三月十一日，黄埔买办弗即的啤酒提货单，“字来求取啤酒式桶，交来伴带回应用，烦为登记是幸”，盖有印章，印文“黄埔买办弗即”。

Receipt for beer. The year is not given. 1 item.

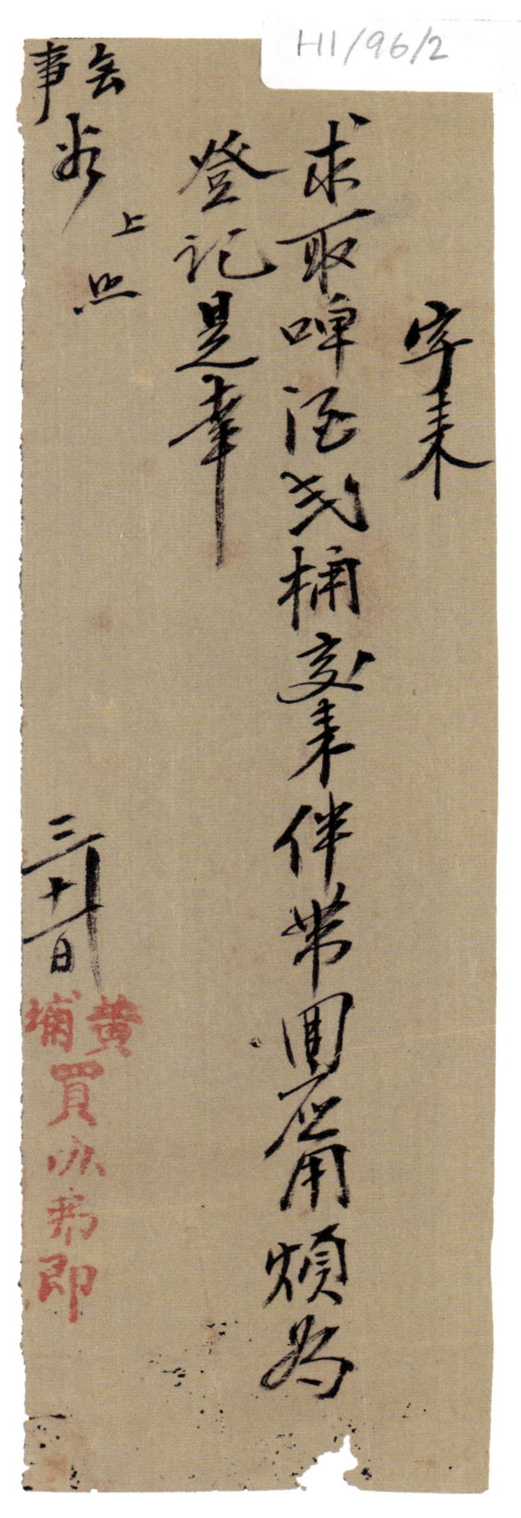
H1/96/2

字来

求取啤酒式桶，交来伴带回应用，烦为

登记是幸

事务

上照

三月十一日

黄埔買办弗即

3. 约道光十七年黄埔买办弗即的苏打粉收据（H1/96/3）

约道光十七年五月二十二日（1837年6月24日），黄埔买办弗即致占谷船（Chan-ku-ch’uan）先生的苏打粉收据，“收到梳打粉壹箱”，盖有印章，印文“黄埔买办弗即”。

Receipt for soda powder. Dated 24 June and from either 1837 or 1856. 1 item.circa 1837

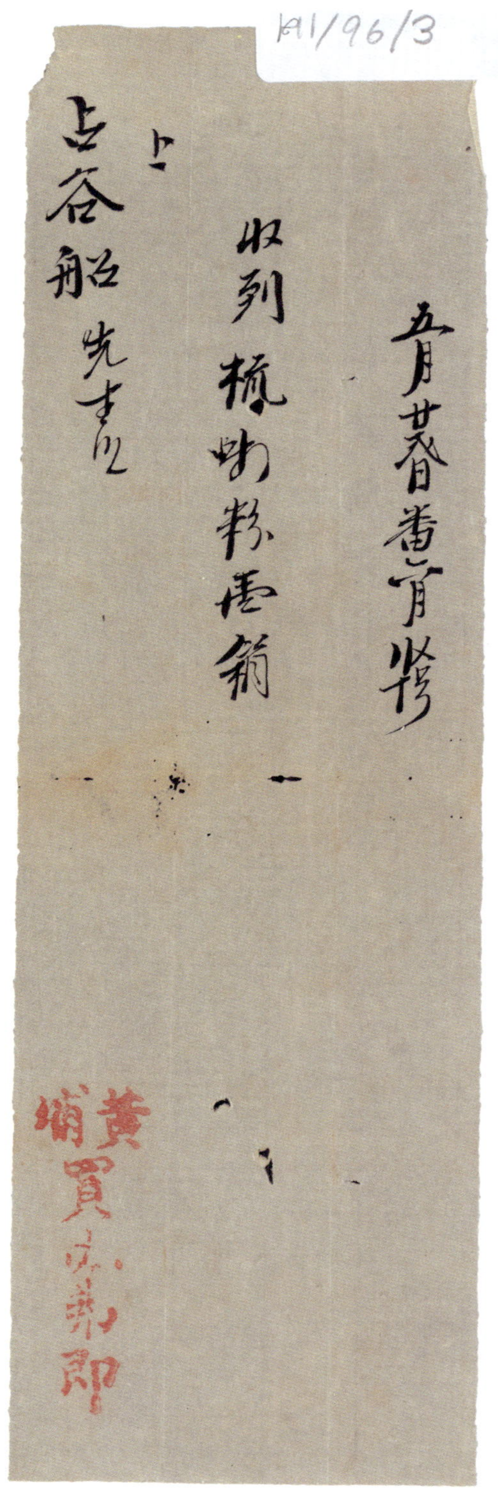

4. 六月二十五日黄埔买办弗即的提货单（年份不详）(H1/96/4)

六月二十五日，黄埔买办弗即给占谷先生的提货单，“字来取橡木圈式打，祈交来伴便是”，盖有印章，印文“黄埔买办弗即”。

Note of collection of goods. The year is not given. 1 item; condition, but damage by insects.

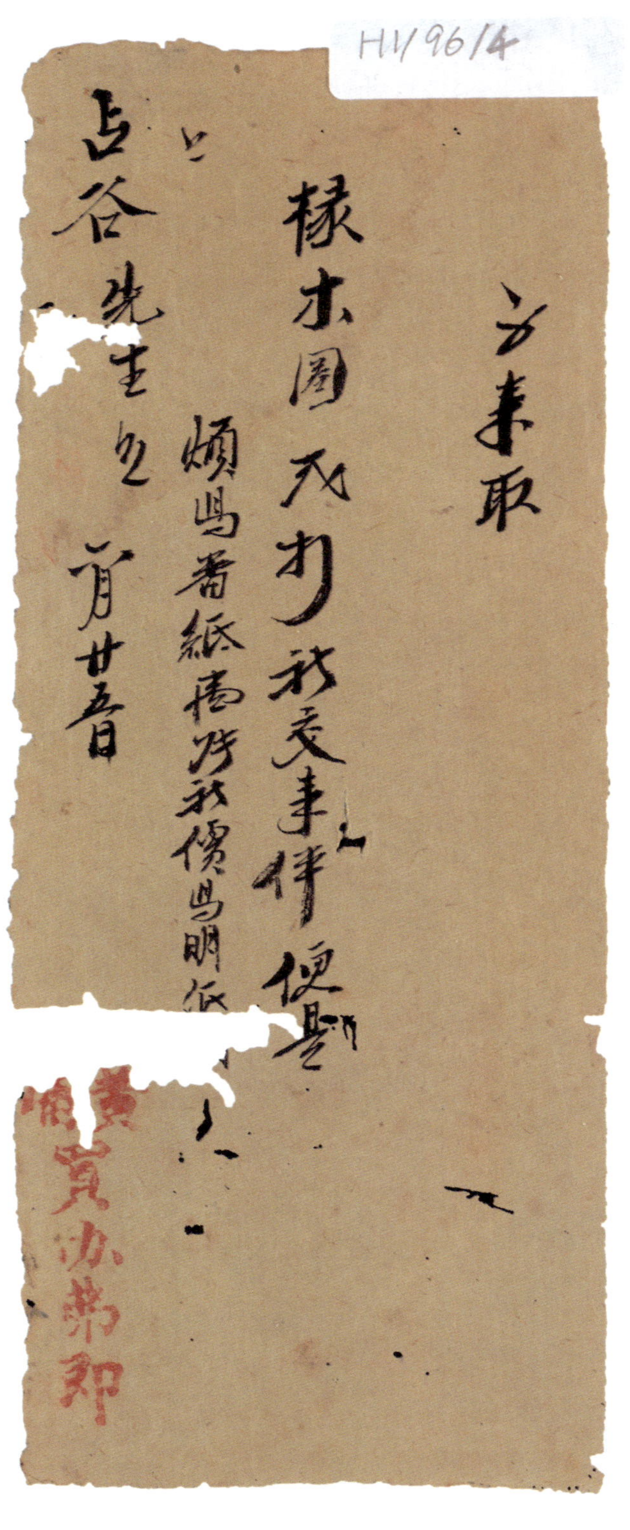

H1/96/4

字來取
橡木圈式打祈交來伴便是
煩為番紙寫明祈價為明[illegible]
占谷先生台
六月廿五日
黃埔買辦弗即

5. 六月二十九日黄埔买办弗即的提货单（年份不详）（H1/96/5）

六月二十九日，黄埔买办弗即给占谷船的提货单，凭此“取鱼油式加伦，白油壹桶，黑油壹桶，番枧壹箱”，盖有印章，印文“黄埔买办弗即”。

Receipt for groceries. The year is not given. 1 item; Moderate condition, with damage by insects and missing sections.

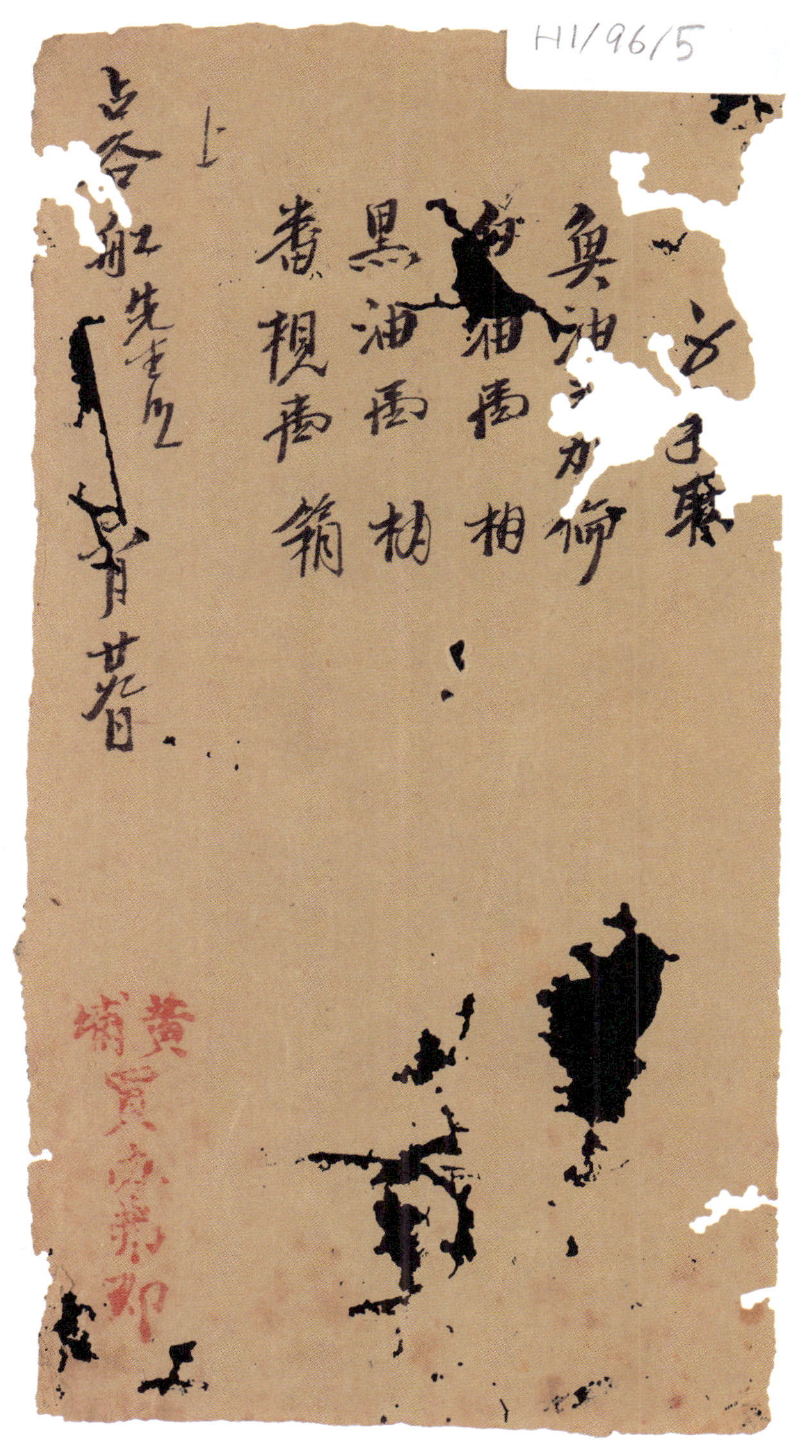

6. 十一月初二日黄埔买办弗即关于咸牛肉的提货单（年份不详）（H1/96/6）

十一月初二日，黄埔买办弗即给占谷船的提货单，“凭单取咸牛肉式桶”，盖有印章，印文“黄埔买办弗即”。

Receipt for pickled beef. The year is not given. 1 item.

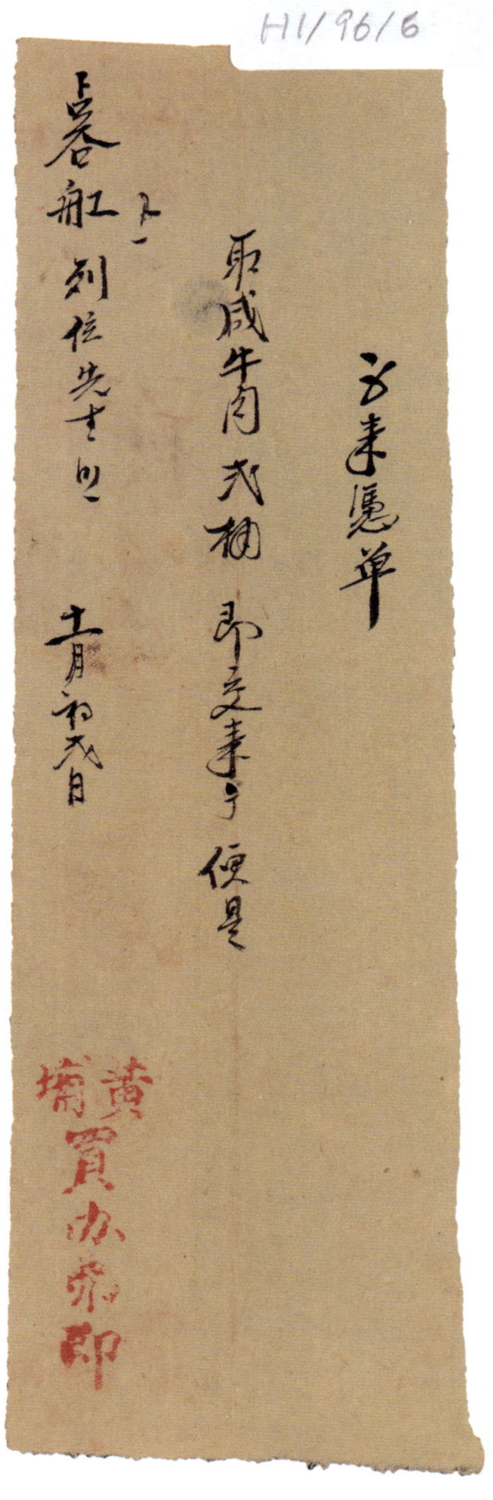
H1/96/6

兹来凭单

取咸牛肉弍桶 即交来手便是

占谷船 列位先生 [illegible]

十一月初弍日

黄埔買办弗即

7. 十一月十九日黄埔买办弗即的提货单（年份不详）（H1/96/7）

十一月十九日，黄埔买办弗即给占谷船的提货单，“字来求取毡酒壹箱，啤酒壹桶”，盖有印章，印文“黄埔买办弗即”。

Receipt for beer, etc.. The year is not given. 1 item.

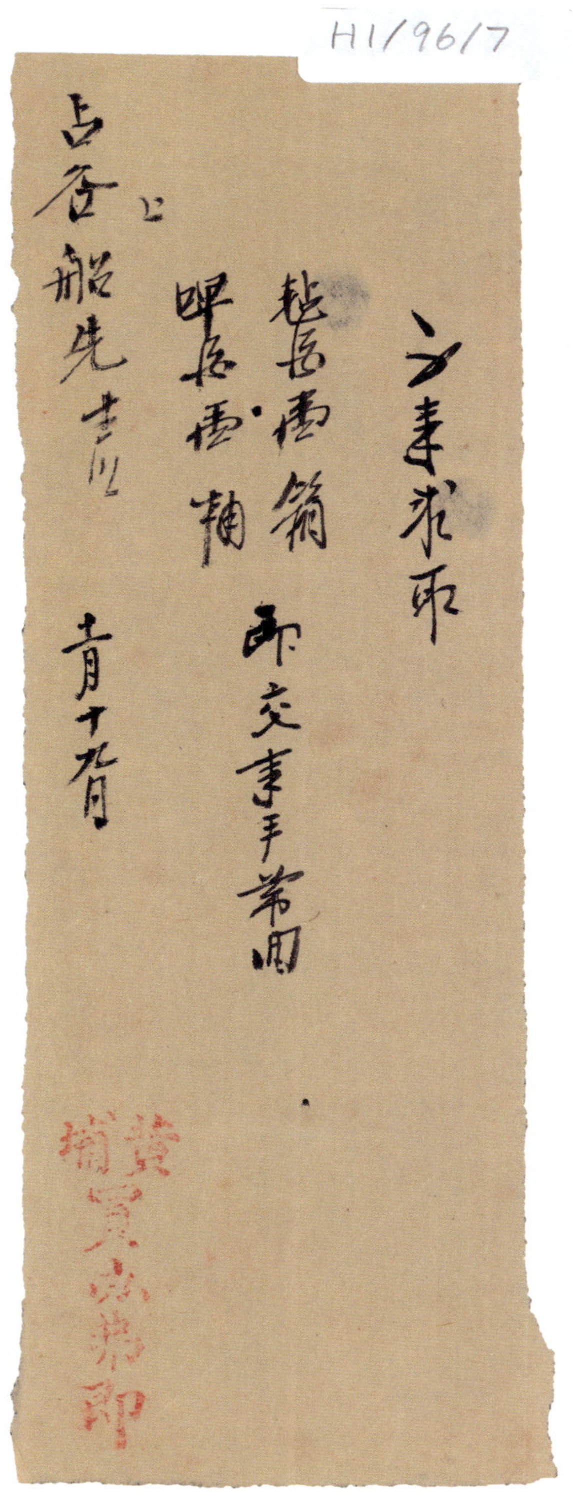

H1/96/7

字来求取
毡酒壹箱
啤酒壹桶
即交来手带回
占谷船先生 [illegible]
十一月十九日

黄埔买办弗即

九七、八月香港福泰号致谦吉宝号的收据（年份不详）（H1/97）

八月，香港福泰号致谦吉宝号的收据，盖有福泰号印章，印文“香港□环福泰号”“香港福泰章，发货图章，余事不用”。

Receipt from Fu-t'ai hao. A receipt (in Chinese) from Fu-t'ai hao, Hong Kong, to Ch'ien-chi (Qianji) hao (Jardine ?), including a brief English note. The year is not given. 1 item.

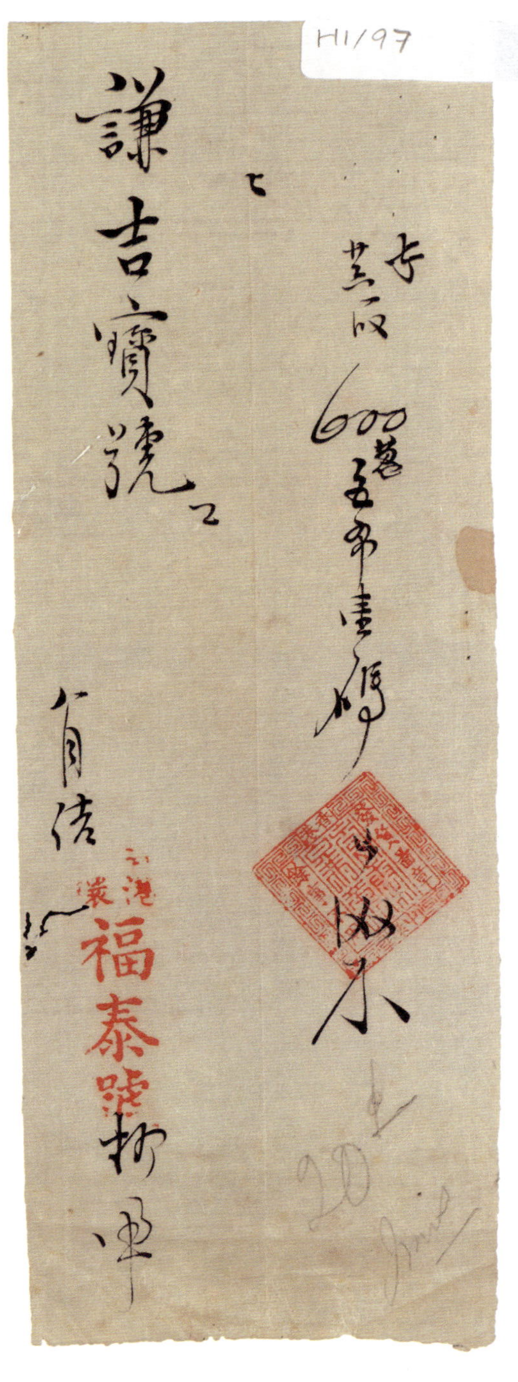

H1/97

謙吉寶號

600

福泰號

九八、省港和合号[①]致渣甸行[②]买办的信函（日期不详）（H1/98）

省港和合号致渣甸行买办的信函，告知他们渡船已准备好，可把渣甸行的铝运至广州，但须提前在港缴纳铝税。盖有和合号印章，印文残损。

Notice from Ho-ho hsiang-tu. A notice from Shen-kong Ho-ho hsiang-tu (Shenggang hehe xiangdu) to the compradore of Jardine, Matheson & Co. reporting that their ferry is ready for Jardine, Matheson & Co.'s cargo of aluminium and that the likin tax should be paid at the port in advance. The year is not given. 1 item; Fair condition, but damage by insects and missing the bottom of the document.

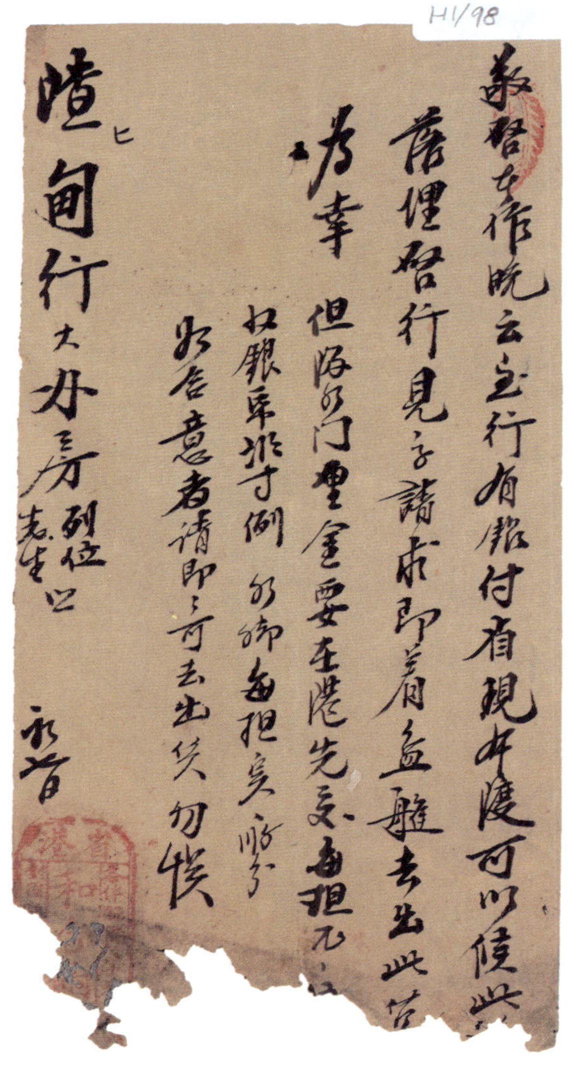

① 和合号：中国商号。

② 渣甸行：即怡和洋行（Jardine, Matheson & Co.），英国商人威廉·查顿（William Jardine）等创办。

九九、二月十四日广长泰[①]付渣甸宝行[②]的收据（年份不详）（H1/99）

二月十四日，广长泰与渣甸宝行关于大蛏干货款结算的收据，盖有广长泰印章，印文“广长泰发货图章，揭借不用”。

Receipt from Kuang-ch’ang-t’ai. A receipt from Kuang-ch’ang-t’ai (Guang chang tai) to the comprador of Jardine, Matheson & Co. for dried razor clam. The year is not given. 1 item; Fair condition, but some damage by insects.

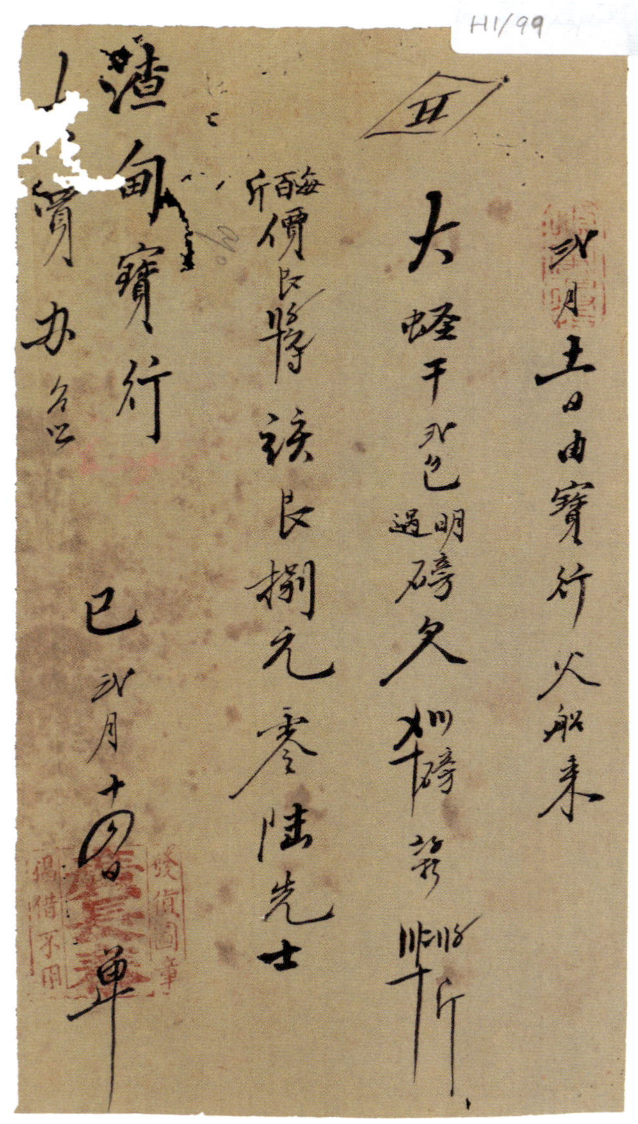

---

① 广长泰：中国商号。

② 渣甸宝行：即怡和洋行（Jardine, Matheson & Co.），英国商人威廉·查顿（William Jardine）等创办。

一〇〇、九月初四日澳门新步头广盛隆收据（年份不详）（H1/100）

九月初四日，澳门新步头广盛隆“铁线缆式条”的收据，盖有广盛隆印章，印文“澳门新步头广盛隆单”。附有英文注释。

Receipt from Kuang-sheng-lung. A receipt (in Chinese) from Kuang-sheng-lung (Guang sheng long), Macao, for iron rope, including a brief English note about the receipt. The year is not given. 1 item.

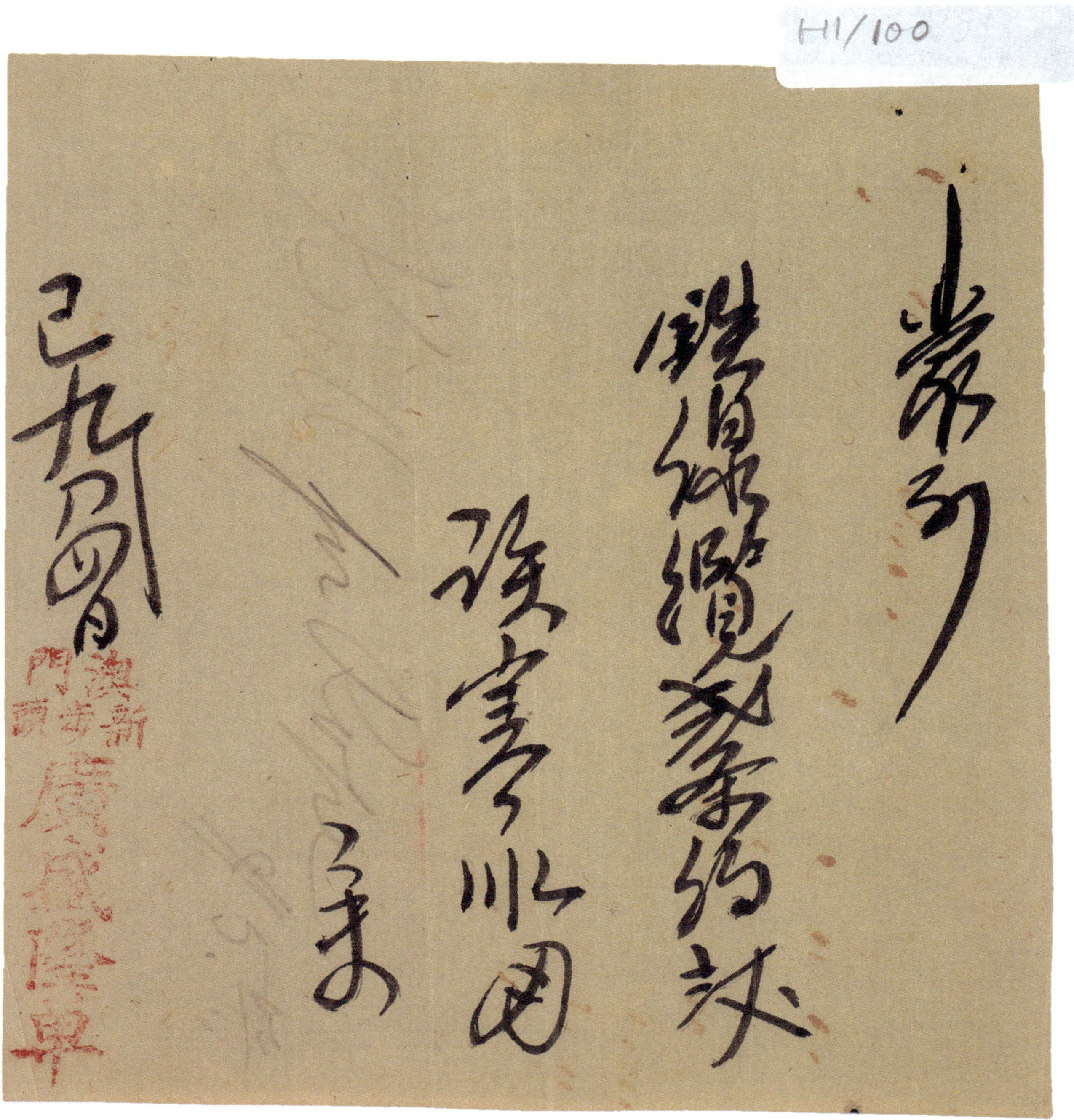

一〇一、四月十三日香港广兴致福茂隆大宝行的信函（年份不详）（H1/101）

四月十三日，香港广兴致信福茂隆，因禅臣屡催起货，要求其立即派人提货。信函盖有广兴印章，印文“香港广兴书柬”。背面附有英文注释。

Order from Kwong Hing. An order (in Chinese) from Kwong Hing (Kuang-hsing, Guangxing), Hong Kong, to Fook Mao Loong (Fu-mao-lung, Fu mao long) to take delivery immediately as result of Ch'an-ch'en firm (Siemens?) pressing for its goods, including a short English note on the back about the order. The year is not given. 1 item.

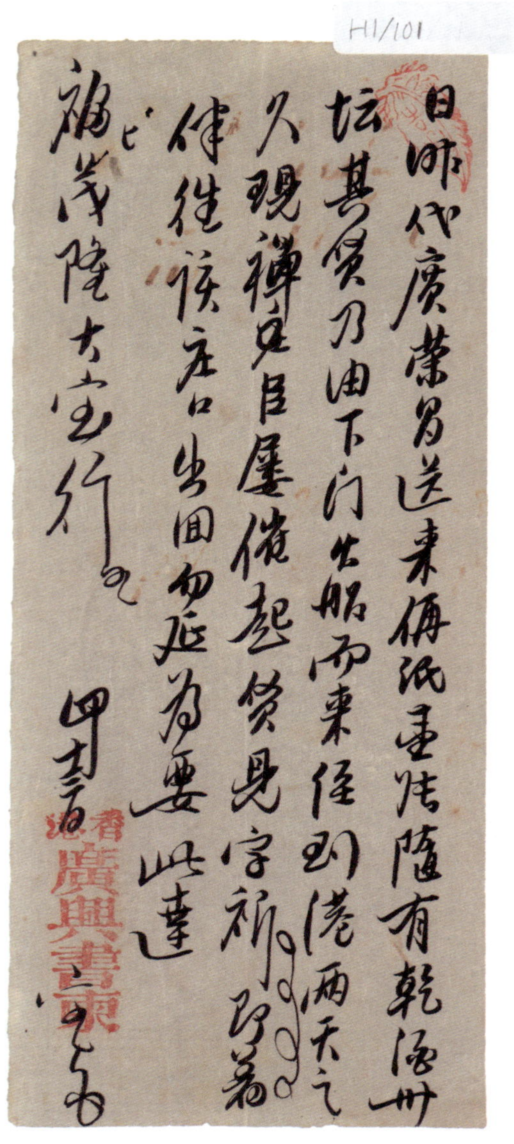

H1/101

日昨代廣榮另送來倆紙壹件隨有乾隆卅壇其貨刀由下門出船而來經到港兩天之久現禪臣屢催起貨見字祈即着伴往該庄口出回勿延為要此達

福茂隆大宝行

四月十三日

香港廣興書柬

（正）

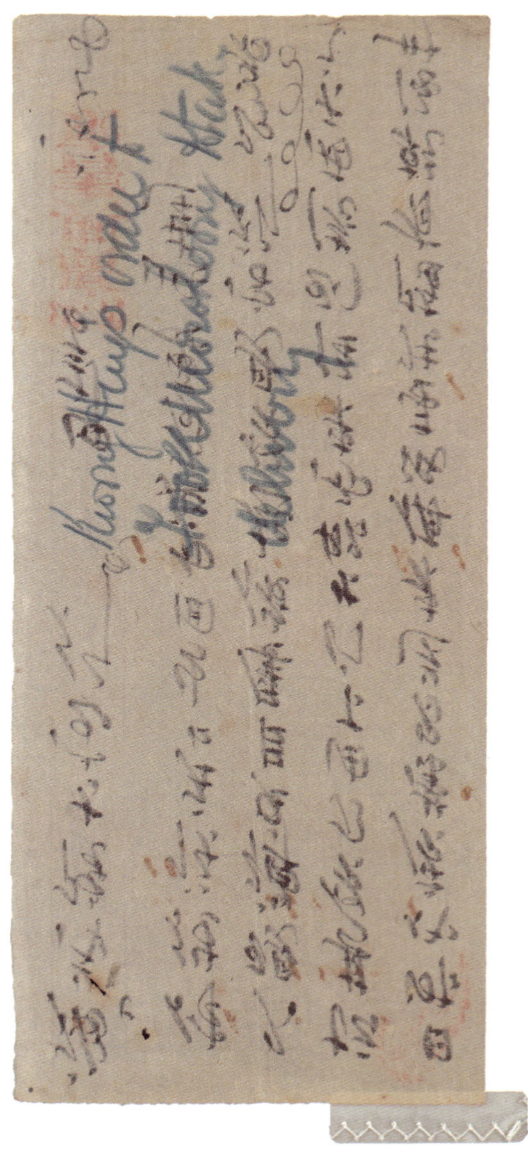

（反）

一〇二、高利治公司[①]收据（年份不详）

1. 二月初二日高利治公司收据（H1/102/1）

二月初二日，高利治公司与英国商人渣顿[②]、孖地臣[③]之间的交易收据，盖有高利治公司印章，印文“高利治公司”。

Receipt from Kao-li-chi Co.. A receipt from Kao-li-chi (Gao li zhi) Co. for ‘gifts and tea’ and money that had been paid by Jardine to Matheson. The year is not given. 1 item.

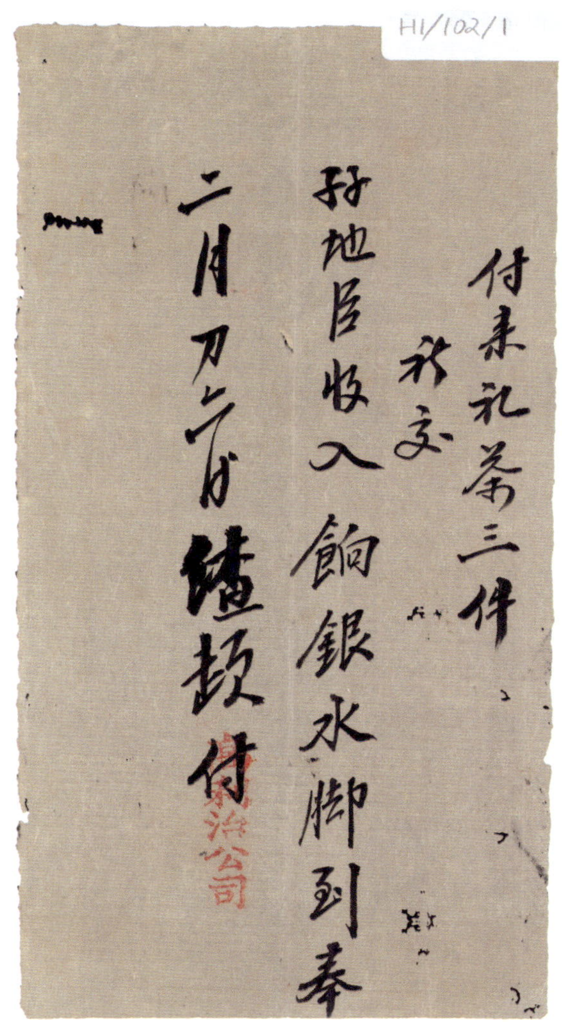
H1/102/1

付来礼茶三件

孖地臣收入餉銀水脚到奉

二月初二日渣顿付

高利治公司

---

① 高利治公司，不一定是中国商号。

② 渣顿：即英国商人威廉·查顿（William Jardine），又译为渣颠、渣甸、赞典，为怡和洋行（Jardine, Matheson & Co.）创始人之一。

③ 孖地臣：英国商人 Matheson，怡和洋行（Jardine, Matheson & Co.）创始人之一。

2. 二月初九日香港药馆收据（H1/102/2）

二月初九日，香港药馆与英国商人孖地臣[①]交易的收据，盖有香港药馆墨色印章，印文“香港药馆”。

Receipt from the Hong Kong Pharmacy. A receipt from the Hong Kong Pharmacy to Matheson in Canton, recording that Hui-chi is bringing three ‘gifts and tea’ and requesting that the delivery man be paid so that the payment can be taken back to Hong Kong. The year is not given. 1 item.

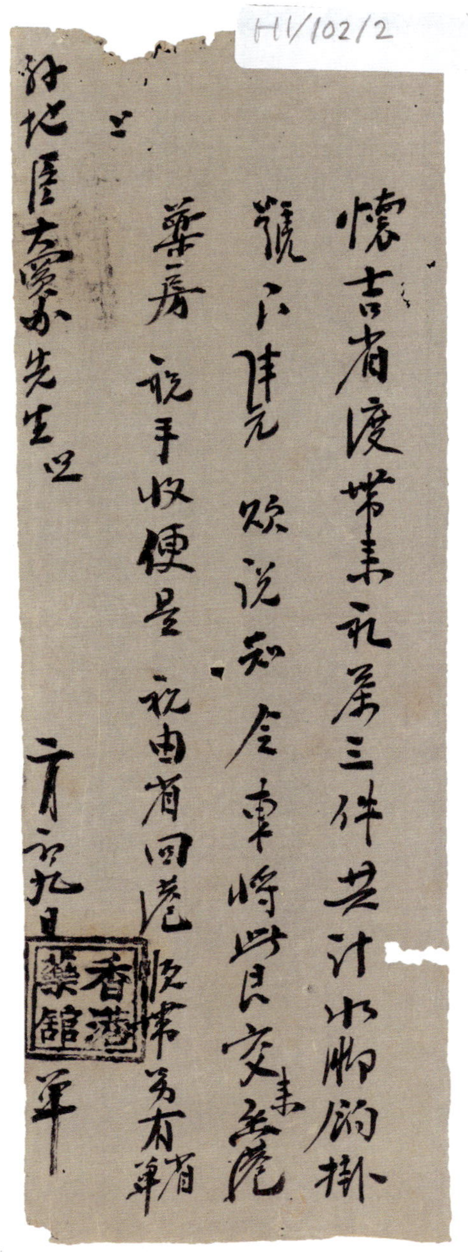

H1/102/2

懷吉省渡帶來礼茶三件共計水脚尚掛

鏡下肆元　欲說知令東將此艮交來港

藥房　親手收便是　礼由省回港　收帶另有單省

孖地臣大爺先生　二

二月初九日　香港藥館　單

① 孖地臣：英国商人 Matheson，怡和洋行（Jardine, Matheson & Co.）创始人之一。

一〇三、沙梨文船长[①]致广成宝号[②]的信函（年份不详）

1. 三月二十二日沙梨文船长致广成宝号的信函（H1/103/1）

三月二十二日，沙梨文（Sullivan）船长致汕头广成宝号的信函，他报告说，香港燕疏公司[③]曾两次写信询问该失事船只是何人租的（是广成宝号所租或是为别号代理），希望该商行尽快回复。

Letter from Captain Sullivan. A letter from Captain Sullivan to Kuang-ch’eng hao (Guangcheng) in Swatow, including the original Chinese envelope. Sullivan reports that the cargo on the wrecked ship has been unloaded and moved to the recipient’s firm. He records that Hong Kong Yen-shu (Yan shu) Co. has written twice to ask who hired the ship and whether it was a joint renting or not, and Sullivan requests that a person be sent to discuss the matter. The year is not given. 2 items.

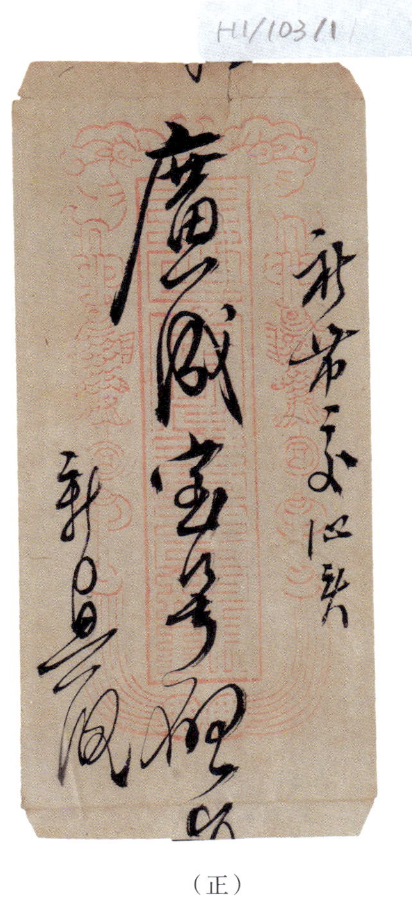

（正）

（反）

---

① 沙梨文船长：Captain Sullivan，英国船长。

② 广成宝号：中国汕头商号。

③ 燕疏公司：保险公司，“燕疏”有时亦写作“燕梳”，是保险的英文“Insure”的音译。

旧岁遇风打破三喼板共货往于
宝号起清，各人均见。今承香港燕梳行
来信嘱问该船是何人租的，是望何字号。
早日信二函内，仅未覆音，不知该船是
宝号租的，抑是合号代理，望示回陈
示知，以便回覆香港燕梳行，何以
宝号将货物起清，还王不即望来遂
即前来设可，争能延迟，恐误专此致
近日佳
广盛宝号 收
三月廿二 汕梨文 顿

2. 三月二十五日广珍源记[1]信函（H1/103/2）

三月二十五日，广珍源记信函，询问沙梨云[2]（Sullivan）船长有关货物下落的事。失事船只“佛时达时利兀打”去年八月二十二日中标，这批货全是豆饼。盖有广珍源记印章，印文“广珍源记”，抬头为“护封”章。

Letter from Kuang-chen-yuan-chi. A letter from Kuang-chen-yuan-chi (Guang zhen yuan ji), Swatow, regarding Captain Sullivan's enquiry about the whereabouts of a cargo. It reports that the wrecked ship 'Fu-shih-ta-shih-li-wu-ta' (Fo shi da shi li wu da) was put to tender last August, and that they won the bid by offering the highest price. The cargo was comprised solely of bean cakes. This information has been confirmed by Sullivan and K'a-le (Ka Le), who had a personal enquiry with the manager of Kuang-ch'eng hao (Guangcheng). The year is not given. 1 item.

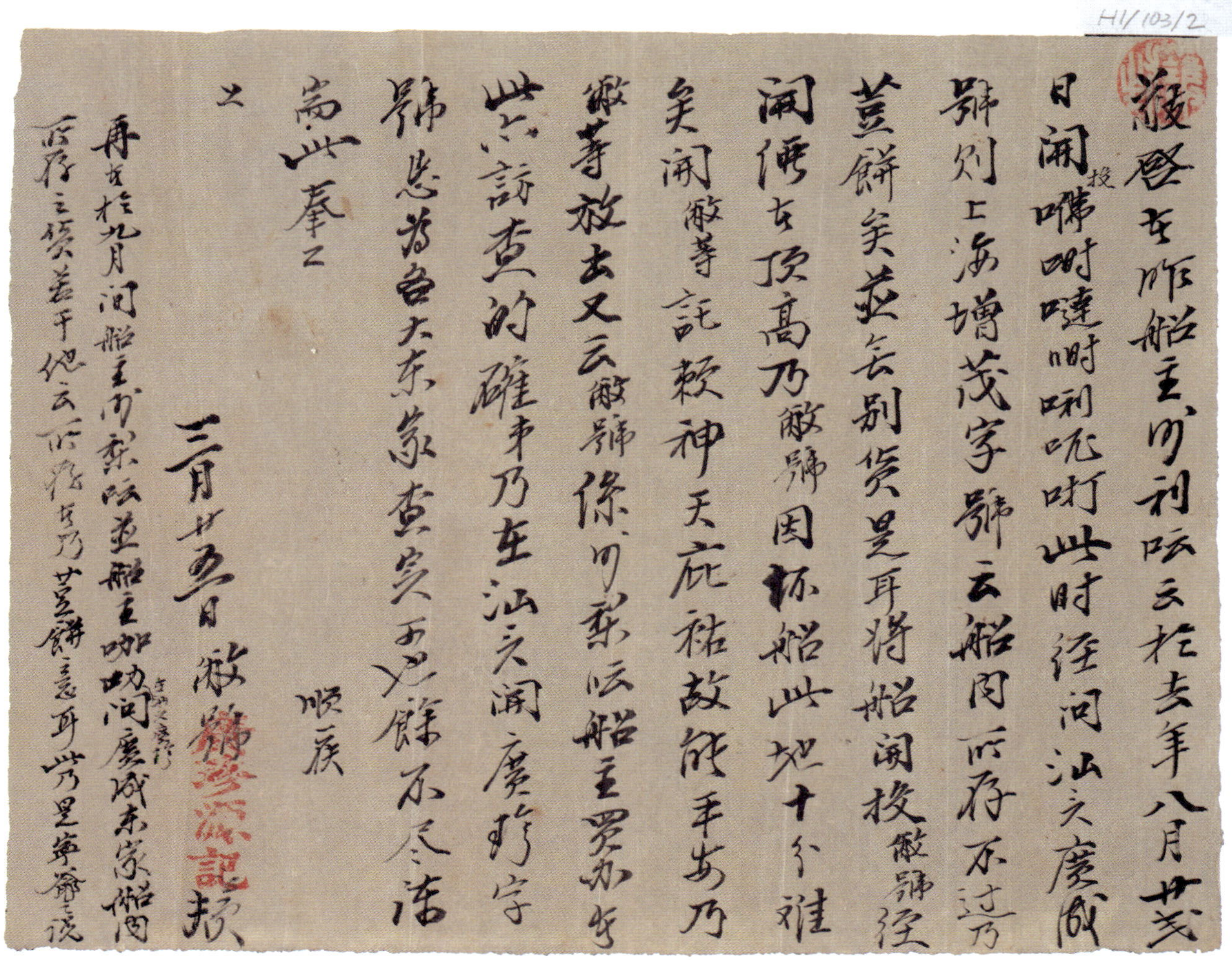

H1/103/2

敬启者，昨船主叫利呅云：于去年八月廿二日闻投佛时达时利兀打，此时经同汕之广成号则上海增茂字号云，船内所存不过乃荳饼矣，并无别货，是耳将船闻投，敝号经闻价出顶高，乃敝号因标船此地十分难矣，闻敝等托赖神天庇祐，故能平安，乃敝等放去，又云敝号系叫利呅船主罗弥步此，访查的確，来乃在汕之闻广，将字号恳着向大东家查实，不见余不尽陈，为此奉之

顺候

三月廿五日　敝号广珍源记拜

再者，于九月间船主叫利呅并船主咖叻问广成东家船所存之货若干，他云所存乃荳饼並耳……

---

① 广珍源记：中国商号。

② 沙梨云：Sullivan，英国船长，上文写作“沙梨文”。

一〇四、九月初五日建昌办馆[①]收据（年份不详）（H1/104）

九月初五日，建昌办馆波臣积致痕行大买办的收据，盖有建昌办馆印章，印文“建昌办馆”。

Receipt from Pan-kuan. A receipt from Po-ch’en Chi (Bo chen ji) (Boston Jack) of Pan-kuan (Banguan) in Chien-chang, Jianchang, to Hen hong. The year is not given. 1 item; Fair condition, but some damage by insects.

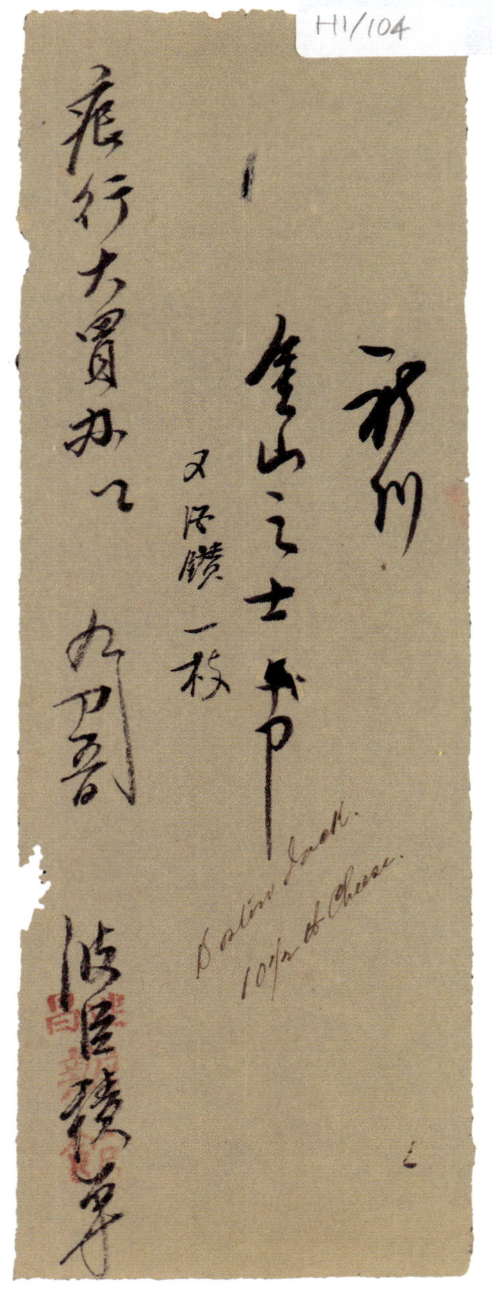

H1/104

① 建昌办馆：为外国商人提供零售批发业务的中国杂货店。

一〇五、元月初八日松盛号[①]杨锦樑收单（年份不详）（H1/105）

元月初八日，松盛号杨锦樑（致吴宗蕃）收单，上面记录着孖地臣[②]公司从孟埠[③]运到香港的货物已经收到并储存在松盛号的船上。盖有松盛号印章，印文不清。

Receipt from Song-sheng hao. A receipt from Yang Chin-liang, Achu (Yahu), of Song-sheng hao to Wu Tsung-fan (Wu Zongfan) recording that the cargo shipped by Matheson's firm from India to Hong Kong has been received and stored in the Song-sheng hao. The year is not given. 1 item.

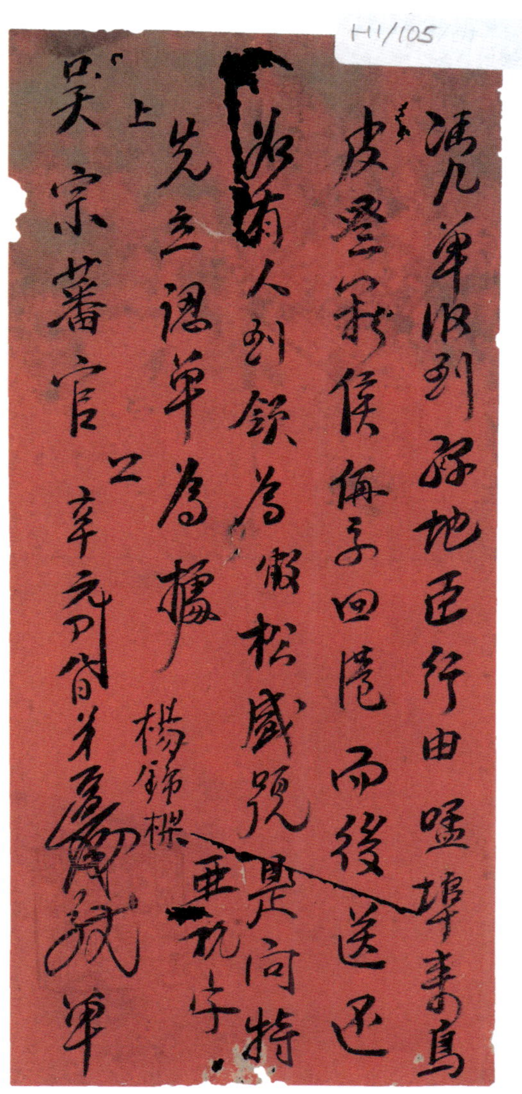
H1/105

① 松盛号：中国商号。

② 孖地臣：即 Matheson，外商。

③ 孟埠：印度孟买。

一〇六、八月十二日香港利贞号单据（年份不详）（H1/106）

八月十二日，香港利贞号郑福容赊购船橹的单据，盖有利贞号印章，印文“香港鸾颈利贞号”。

Receipt from Hong Kong luan-ching li-chen hao. A receipt from Cheng Fu-jung (Zheng Furong) of Hong Kong luan-ching li-chen (Lizhen) hao for the purchase of a scull on credit. The year is not given. 1 item.

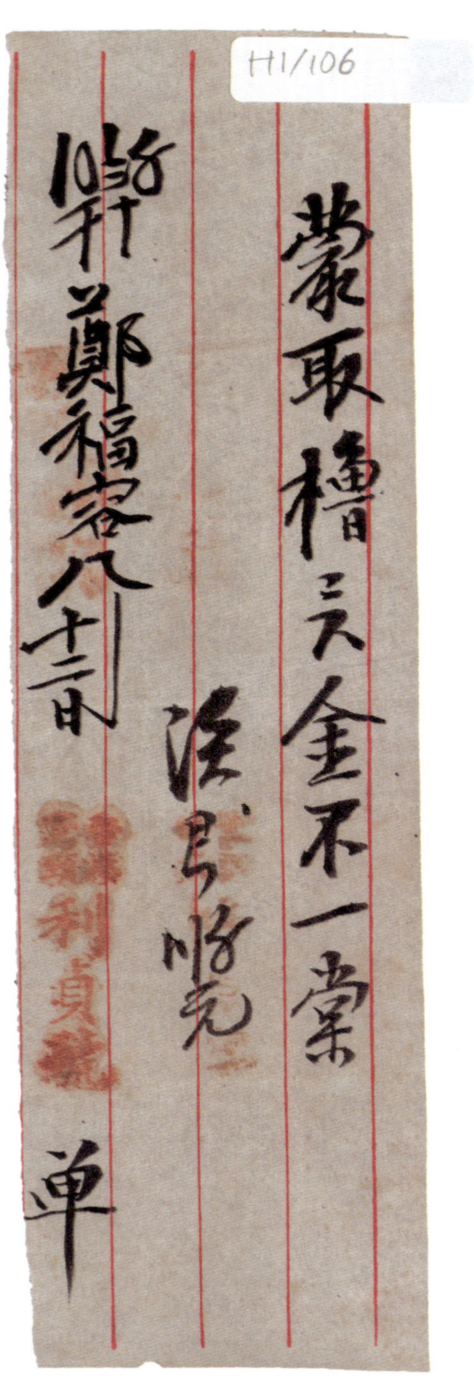

H1/106

蒙取櫓二只金不一彙

准?日收兑?

鸞頸利貞號鄭福容八月十二日

利貞號

單

一〇七、十二月初一日联昌单据（年份不详）（H1/107）

联昌单据，说明“拾弍月初一日付顺邑龙潭圩茂聚纸店[1]收食物壹笠，吉信壹封”。盖有联昌店印章，印文不清。背面为报纸广告局部。

Receipt from Lien-ch’ang. A receipt from Lien-ch’ang (Lianchang) to Mao-chu chih-tien (Maoju zhidian) for stationery and food. The year is not given. 1 item.

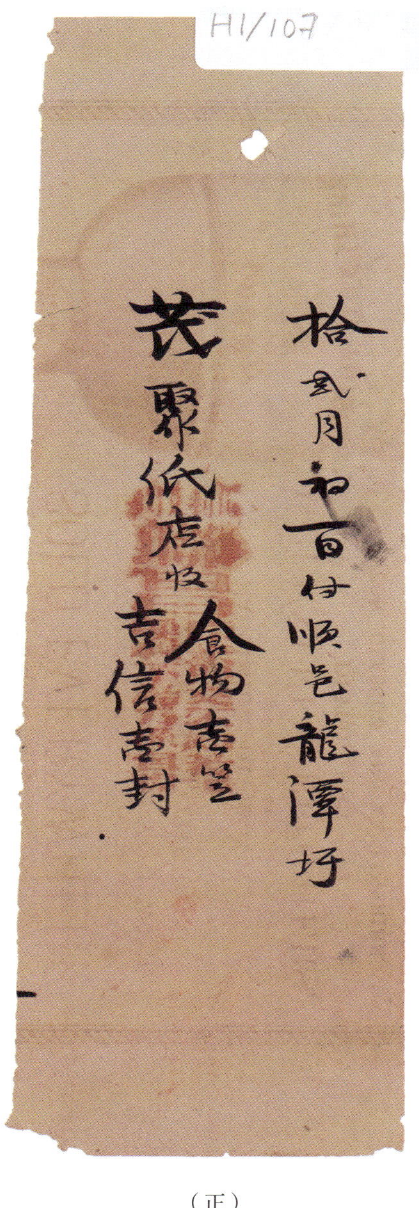

H1/107

拾弍月初一日付順邑龍潭圩

茂聚紙店收食物壹笠

吉信壹封

（正）

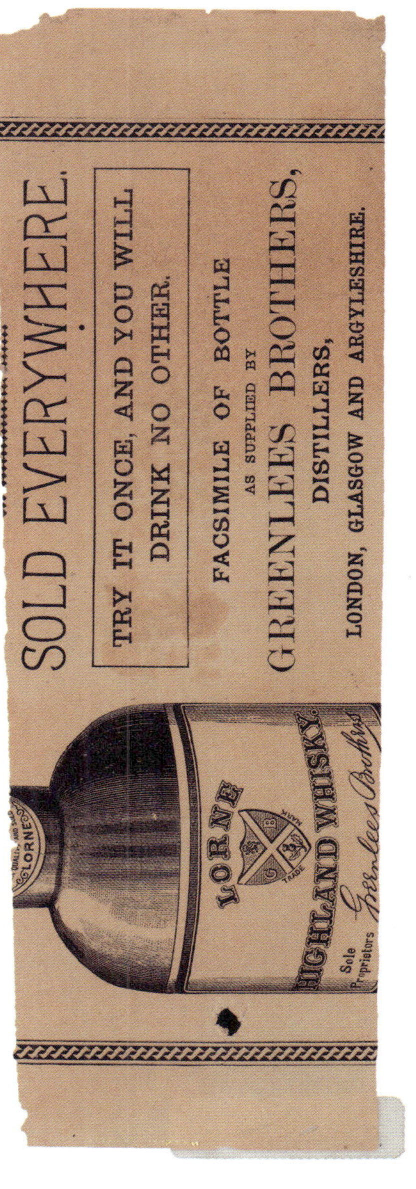

（反）

① 茂聚纸店：中国商号，位于顺邑龙潭圩。

一〇八、九月初六日京戳[①]与万益[②]的茶叶贸易单据（年份不详）（H1/108）

九月初六日，京戳与万益的茶叶贸易单据。

Receipt from Ching-chien. A receipt from Ching-chien (jingjian) to Man-i or Wan-i (Wanyi) (Magniac) for tea. The year is not given. 1 item; Moderate condition, including damage from the ink and some part of the writing missing.

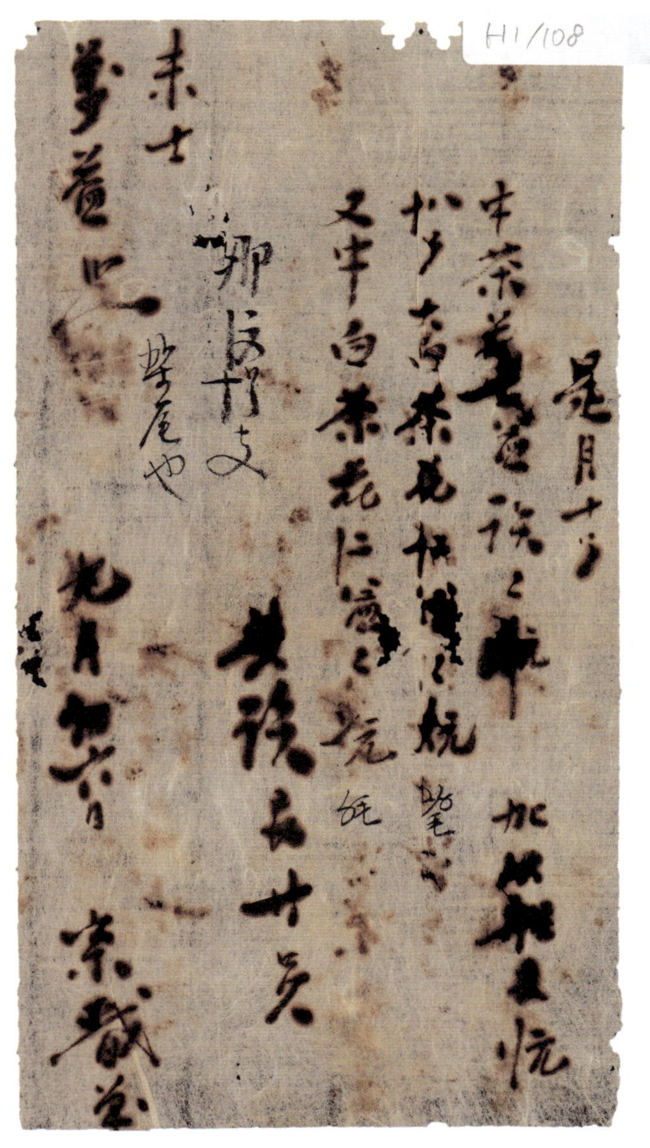

① 京戳：中国商号。

② 万益：英国商行。

一〇九、七月初七日荣昌盛[①]与源生贸易单据（年份不详）（H1/109）

七月初七日，荣昌盛与源生贸易单据，盖有荣昌盛印章，印文不全，有“荣昌盛发货章”字样；另一枚方形印章，印文不清。

Receipt from Jung-ch’ang-sheng.A receipt from Jung-ch’ang-sheng (Rong chang sheng) to Yuan-sheng. The year is not given. 1 item.

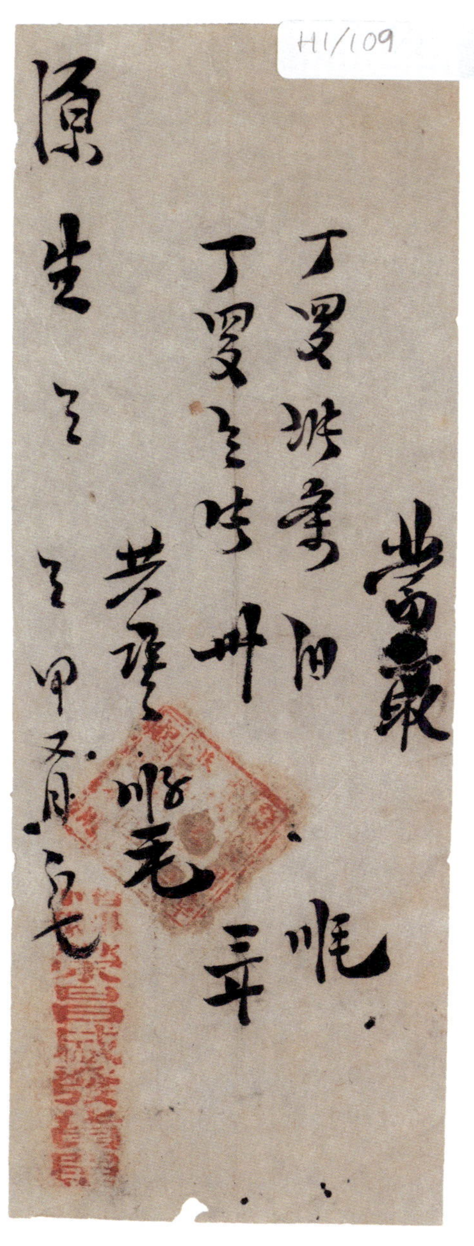

① 荣昌盛：中国商号。

一一〇、四月二十八日香港三和号与成记大宝号的贸易单据（年份不详）（H1/110）

四月二十八日，香港下环三和号与成记大宝号关于杉木的贸易单据，盖有三和号印章，印文“下环三和号”。

Receipt from San-ho hao. A receipt (in Chinese) from San-ho (Sanhe) hao in Hsia-huan (Xiahuan) to Ch’eng-chi (Chengji) for beams, including a brief English note about the receipt. The year is not given. 1 item.

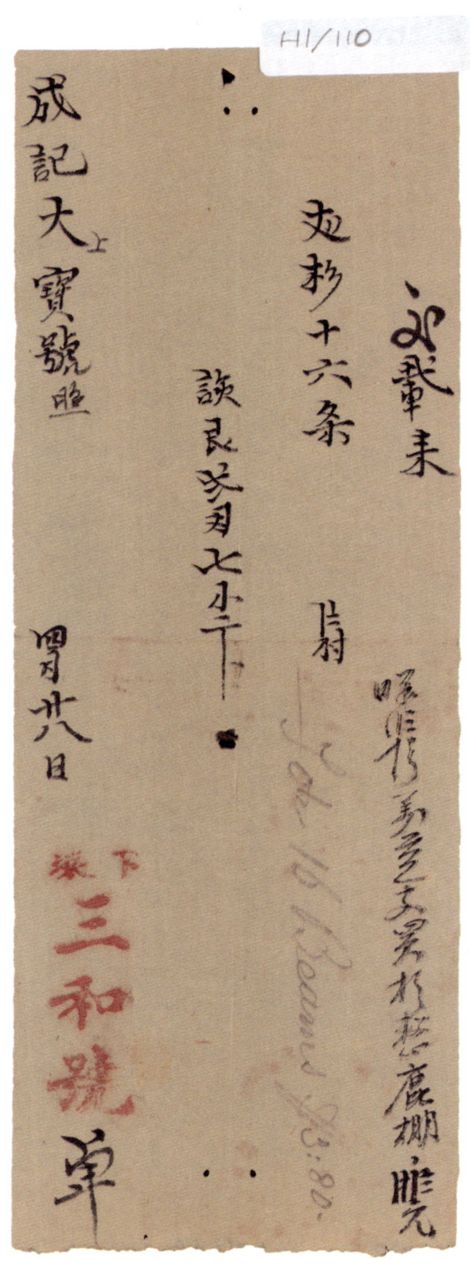
H1/110

成記大寶號照

四月廿八日

下環三和號單

For 16 Beams $3.80

一一一、六月初五日香港泰顺店与德合大宝号的贸易单据（年份不详）（H1/111）

六月初五日，香港泰顺店与德合大宝号关于铁钉等五金器具的贸易单据，盖有泰顺店印章，印文“香港泰顺店”“泰顺图记”。另有一枚朱文印章，内容为“本行出店规矩每两叁分担工搬运贵客自理”。

Receipt from T’ai-shun tien. A receipt from T’ai-shun tien (Taishen dian), Hong Kong, to Te-ho (Dehe) for its order of hardware. The year is not given. 1 item.

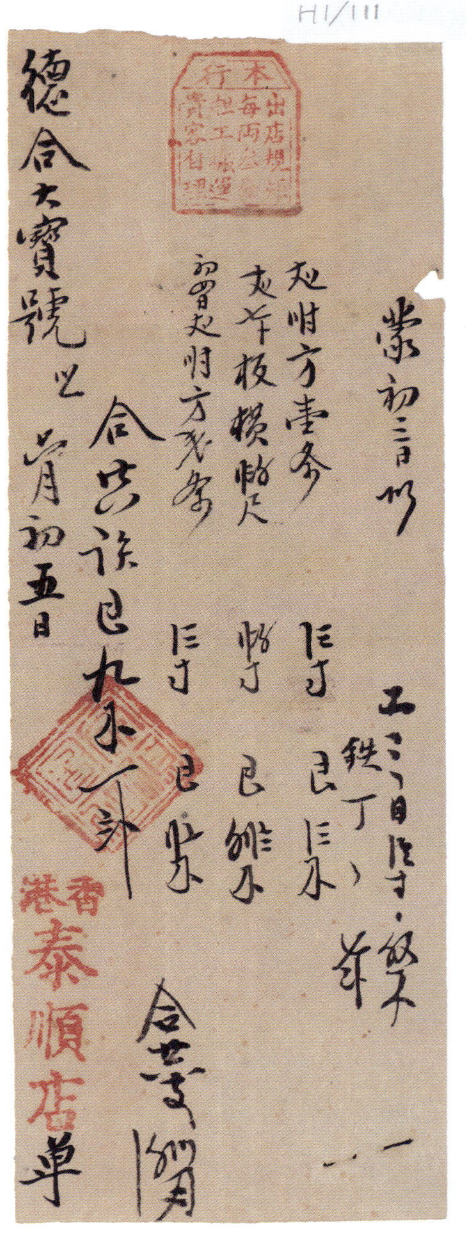

一一二、七月初三日泰隆[①]与占谷船的贸易单据（年份不详）（H1/112）

七月初三日，泰隆与占谷船关于油桶等货物的贸易单据，盖有三枚印章，方形印章印文“泰隆图记”，随形印印文“顺利图记”，另有一枚圆形白文印章，印文“护封”。

Receipt from T’ai-lung. A receipt (in Chinese) from T’ai-lung (Tailong) to Mr. Chan-ku-ch’uan (Zhan gu chuan) for iron rings, including a brief English note about the receipt. The year is not given. 1 item.

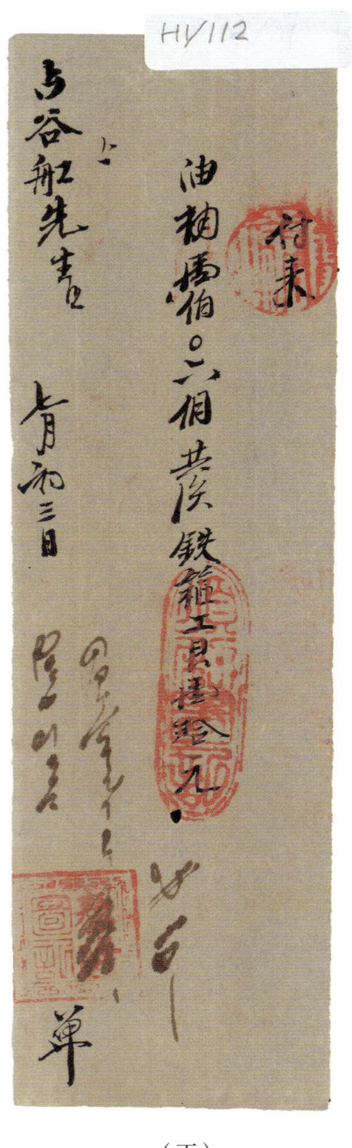

（正）

（反）

① 泰隆：中国商号。

一一三、九月初九日同茂[1]与班市佛[2]师头的贸易单据（年份不详）（H1/113）

九月初九日，同茂与班市佛（Pan-shih-fo）师头关于洗身桶的贸易单据，盖有同茂店印章，印文“同茂图记”。

Receipt from T’ung-mao. A receipt from T’ung-mao (Tongmao) to Mr. Pan-shih-fo (Ban shi fo) for wood buckets. The year is not given. 1 item.

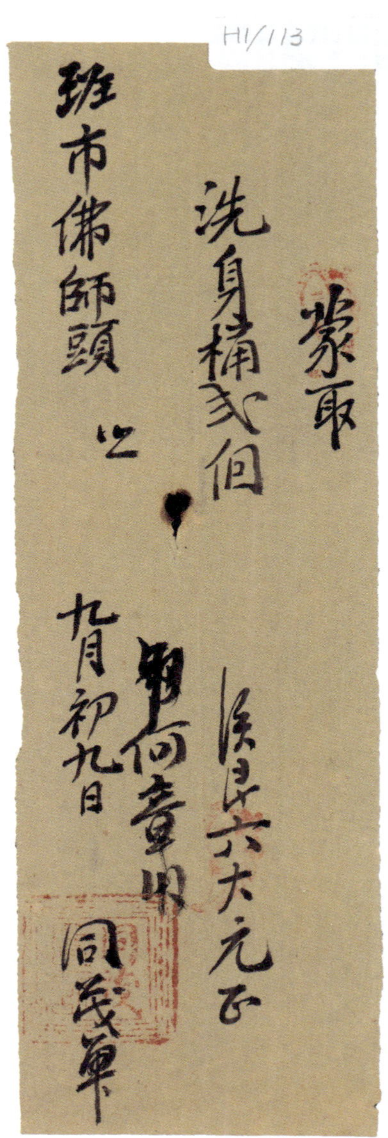
H1/113

蒙取

洗身桶弍佰

班市佛師頭 之

該艮六大元正

九月初九日

同茂單

---

① 同茂：中国商号。

② 班市佛：外国商人。

一一四、八月初九日同盛[1]与渣颠大买办[2]的贸易单据（年份不详）（H1/114）

八月初九日，同盛与渣颠大买办关于油纸的贸易单据，盖有同盛店印章，其中一枚印文“同盛图记”；另一枚印章未完全显示，印迹“图记”。

Receipt from T’ung-sheng. A receipt from T’ung-sheng (Tongsheng) to Jardine for paper. The year is not given. 1 item; Fair condition, but missing the top right corner of the document.

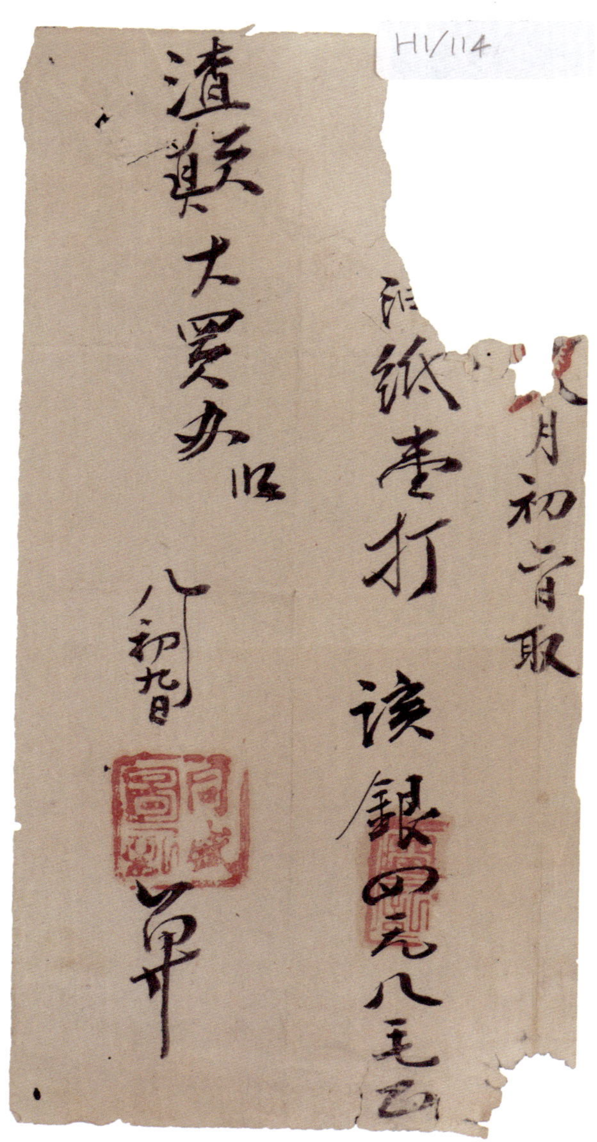

[八]月初[illegible]取

油纸壹打　该银四元八毛[illegible]

渣颠大买办　收

八月初九日

同盛图记

单

① 同盛：中国商号。

② 渣颠大买办：Jardine，英国商人。

一一五、二月二十九日西盛[①]与霸列度[②]的贸易单据（年份不详）（H1/115）

二月二十九日，西盛与霸列度（Pa-lie-tu）关于大米的贸易单据，盖有两枚西盛印章，印文“西盛图记”。另有英文注释。

Receipt from His-sheng. A receipt (in Chinese) from His-sheng (Xisheng) to Mr. Pa-lie-tu (Ba lie du) for rice, including an English note: ‘Chainam’s (?) friend’s Chop for the Coeur de Lion (?)’s Rice.’ The year is not given. 1 item.

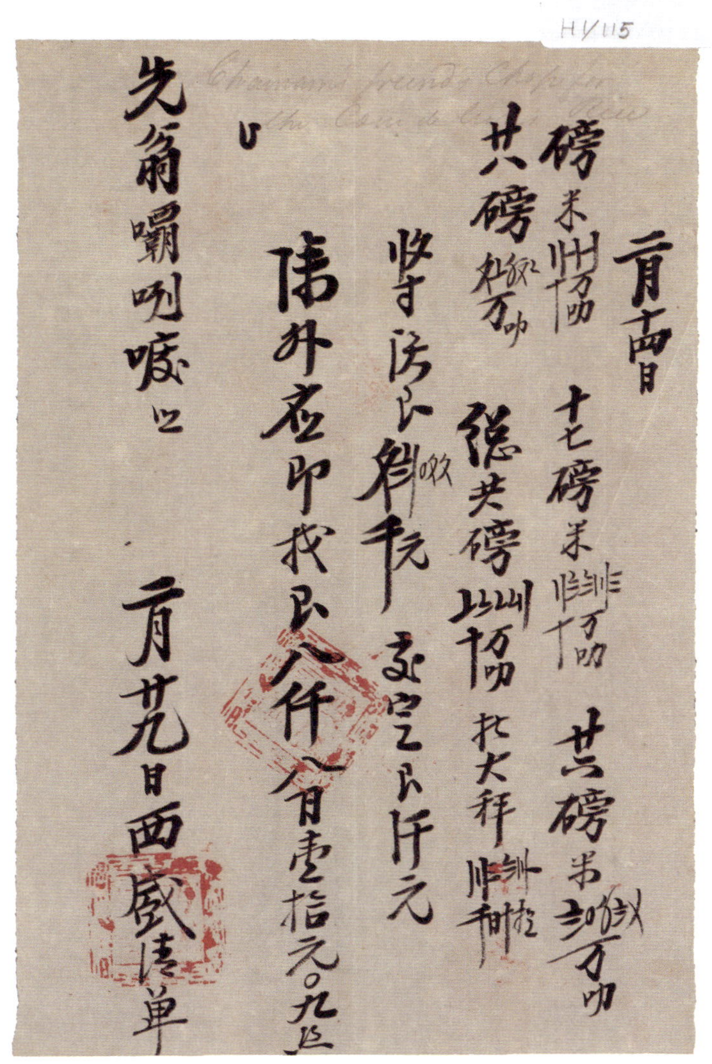

① 西盛：中国商号。

② 霸列度：外国商人。

一一六、十月初五日兴和馆[①]与英国谷姓商人的贸易单据（年份不详）（H1/116）

十月初五日，兴和馆与英国谷姓商人关于布匹的贸易单据。

Receipt from Hsing-ho kuan. A receipt from Hsing-ho kuan (Xing he guan) to Mr. Ku (Gu) for cloth. The year is not given. 1 item.

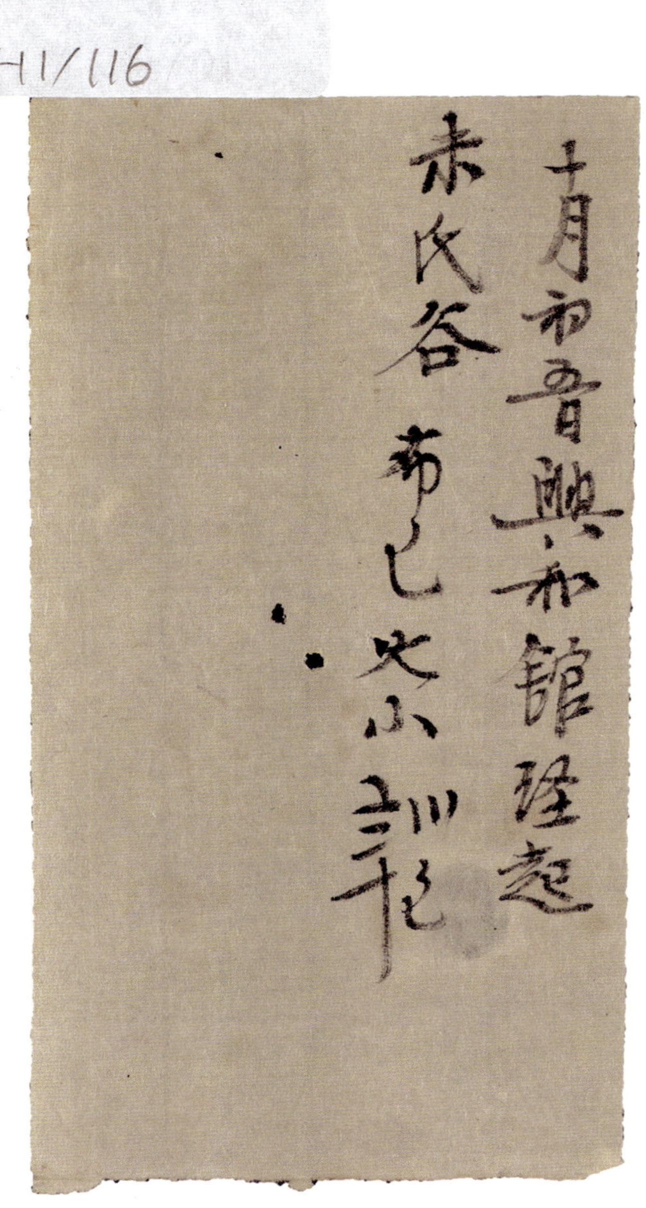

H1/116

十月初五日興和館經起

赤氏谷布乙[illegible]

---

① 兴和馆：中国商号。

一一七、六月初七日益记[1]贸易单据（年份不详）（H1/117）

六月初七日，益记代麦记连[2]（Maclean）大班购买白丝手巾的单据，盖有白文印章，印文“护封”。另有英文注释。

Receipt from I-chi. A receipt (in Chinese) from I-chi (Yi ji) for silk ordered under the name of Mr. Maclean, including an English note about the receipt. The year is not given.1 item.

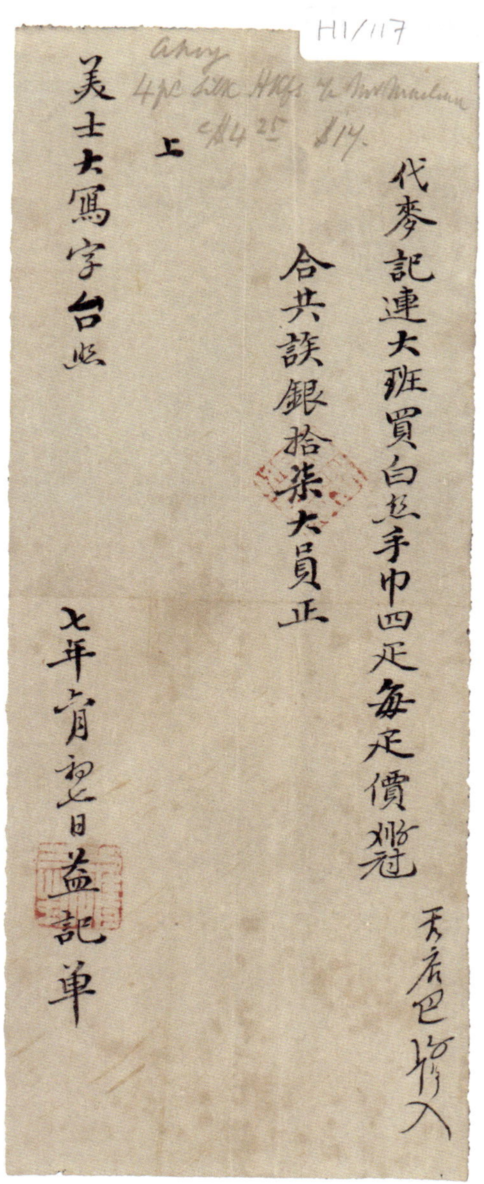

H1/117

代麥記連大班買白絲手巾四疋每疋價[illegible]

天后巴[illegible]入

合共該銀拾柒大員正

上

美士大寫字台照

七年六月初七日益記單

① 益记：中国商号。

② 麦记连：Maclean，外国商人。

一一八、五月二十七日怡兴号[①]与怡和宝行[②]的贸易单据（年份不详）（H1/118）

五月二十七日，怡兴号与怡和宝行关于松柴的贸易单据，盖有朱文印章，印文不全，有“怡兴号”字样以及白文印章“怡和堂印”。

Receipt from I-hsing. A receipt from I-hsing (Yi xing) to Ewo for firewood, including Ewo’s stamp. The year is not given. 1 item.

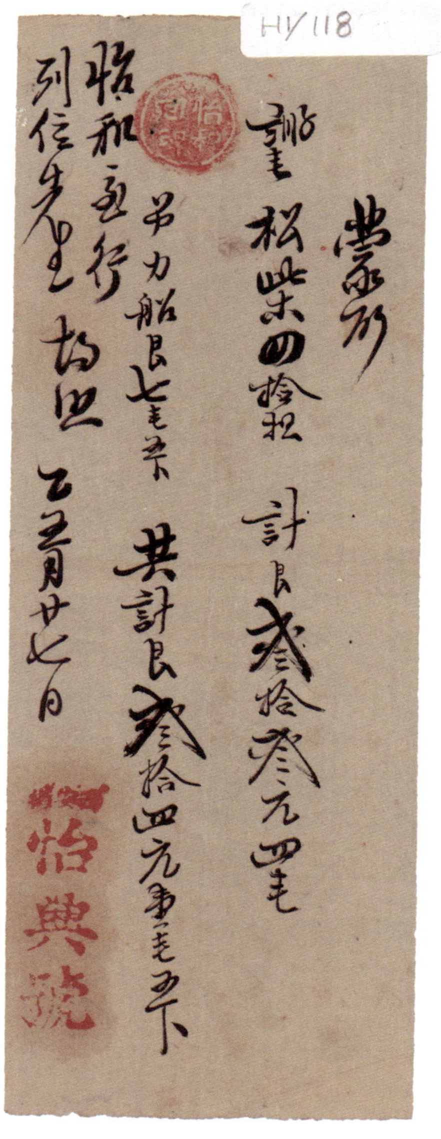
H1/118

松柴四拾担　計銀貳拾叁元四毛

苦力船銀七毛五　共計銀貳拾四元一毛五

怡和寶行

列位先生　收照

五月廿七日

怡興號

---

① 怡兴号：中国商号。

② 怡和宝行：即怡和洋行（Jardine, Matheson & Co.）。

一一九、香港溢隆兴记贸易单据（年份不详）

1. 七月香港溢隆兴记与谦吉大宝号关于布料的贸易单据（H1/119/1）

七月，香港溢隆兴记与谦吉大宝号关于布料的贸易单据，盖有溢隆兴记印章，印文“溢隆兴记”“香港溢隆兴记”，另有一枚随形印。

Receipt for cloth. The year is not given. 1 item.

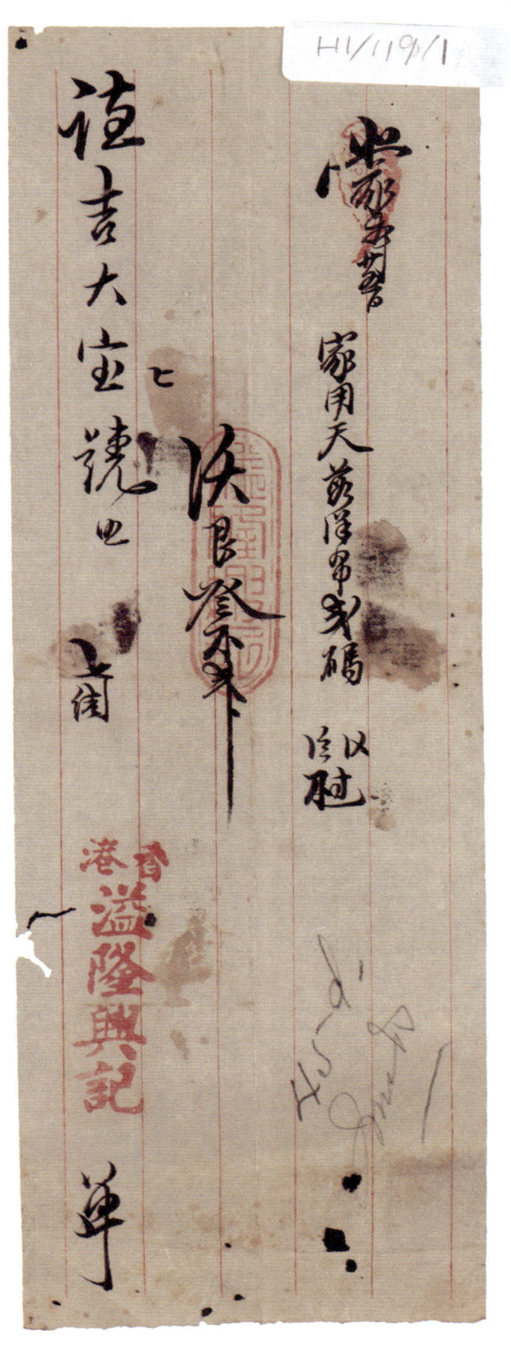
H1/119/1

謙吉大寶號

香港
溢隆興記

2. 八月香港溢隆兴记与谦吉大宝号关于布料的贸易单据（H1/119/2）

八月，香港溢隆兴记与谦吉大宝号关于布料的贸易单据，盖有溢隆兴记印章，印文“溢隆兴记”“香港溢隆兴记”。

Receipt for cloth. The year is not given. 1 item.

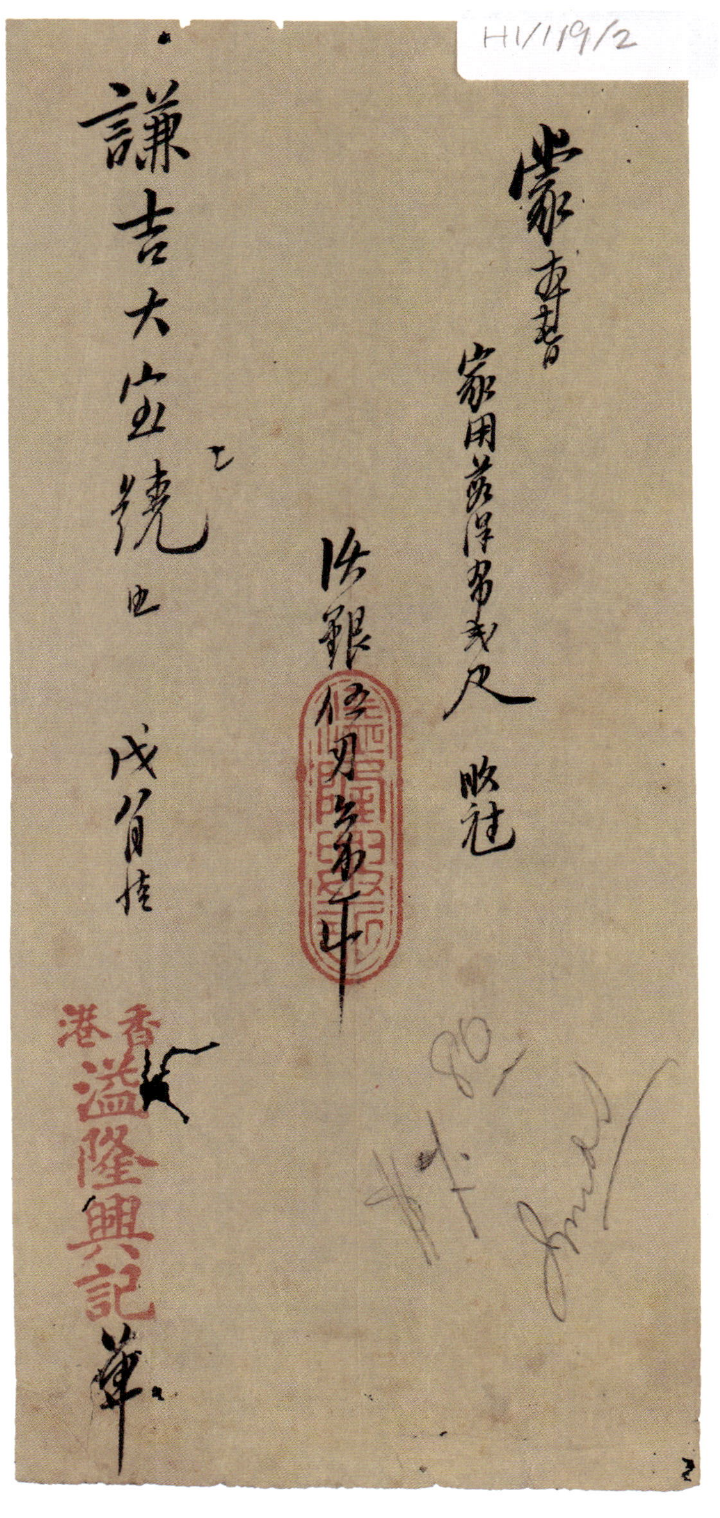
H1/119/2

謙吉大寶號

香港溢隆興記

一二〇、正月十三日香港远芳斋与高路云大状师的贸易单据①（年份不详）（H1/120）

正月十三日，香港中环远芳斋与高路云大状师的贸易单据，盖有远芳斋印章，印文“中环远芳斋”“远芳图章”。贴有一枚印花税票。

Receipt from Yuen-fang-chai. A receipt (in Chinese) from Yuen-fang-chai (Yuan fang zhai), Hong Kong, to Kao Yun-lu (Gao Yunlu) for groceries, including two short English notes about the receipt. The year is not given. 1 item.

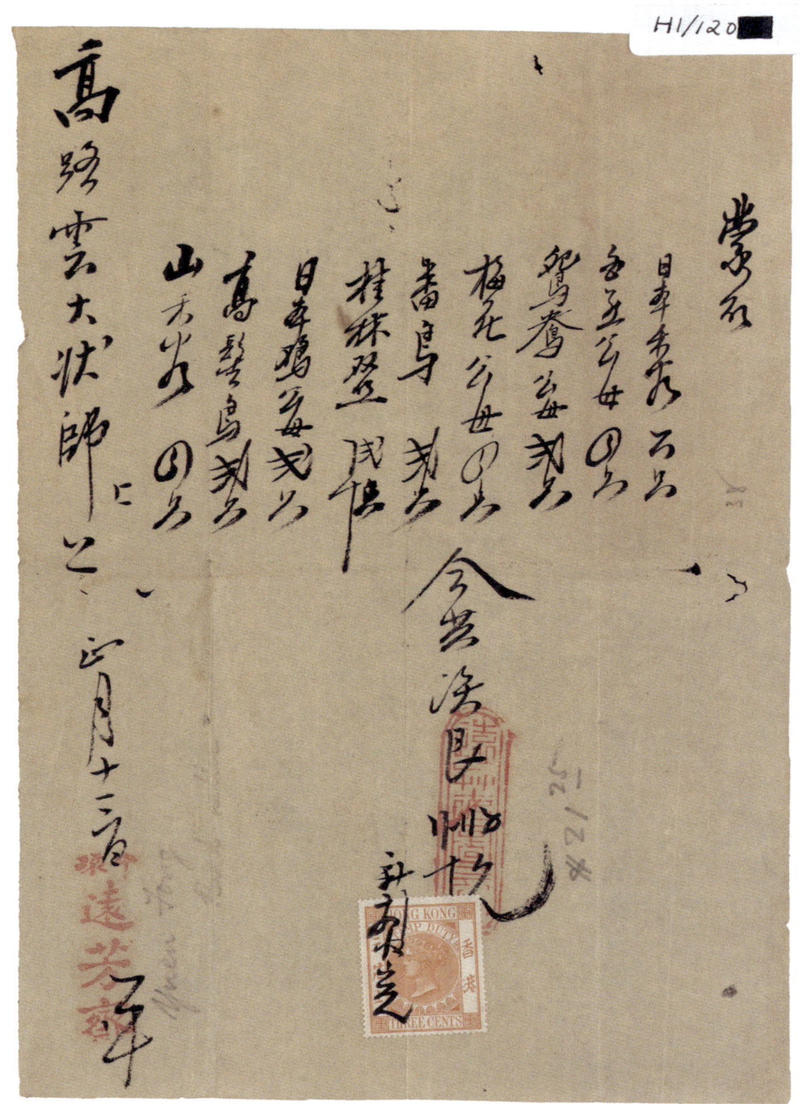

① 单据上贴有一枚印花税票（不是邮票，上面注明是“Stamp Duty”），通常纳税人自贴自销。

一二一、五月十七日香港源广和发货单（年份不详）（H1/121）

五月十七日，香港源广和发货单，盖有源广和印章，印文“香港源广和发货单”。

Receipt from Yuan-kuang-ho. A receipt from Yuan-kuang-ho (Yuan guang he), Hong Kong. The year is not given. 1 item; Fair condition, but some damage by insects.

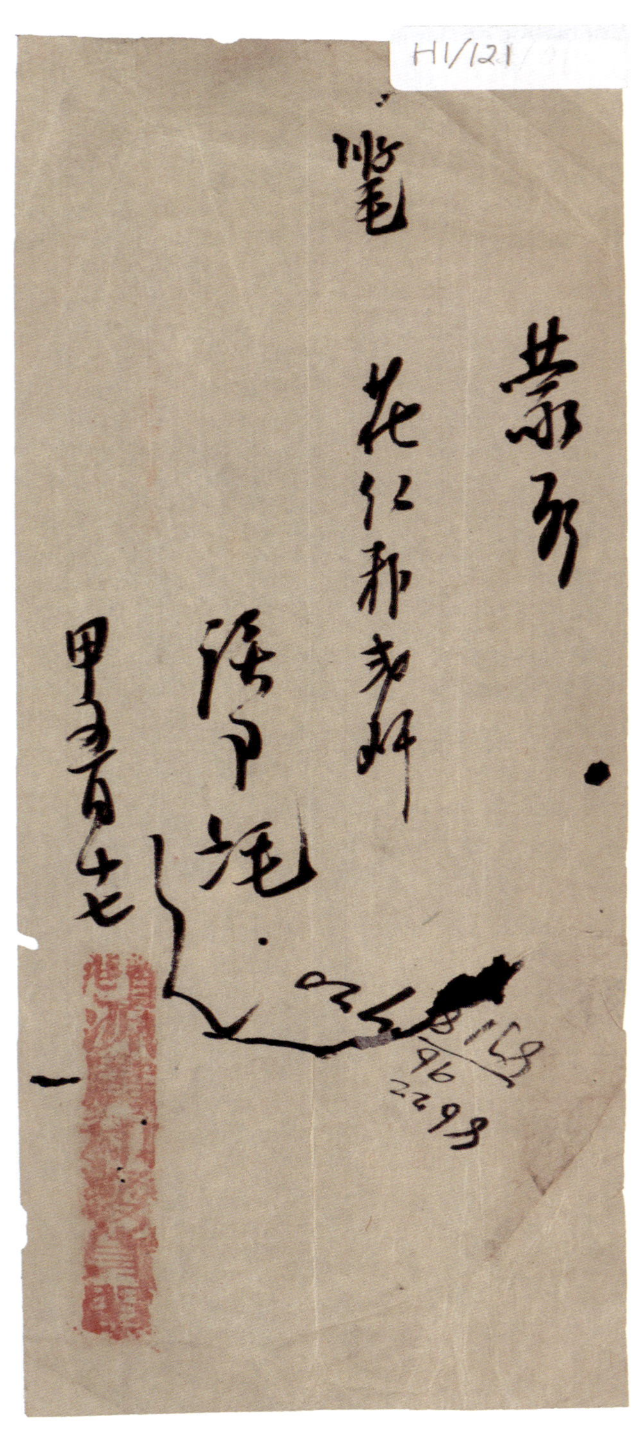
H1/121

一二二、五月十七日香港湾仔远利号发货单（年份不详）（H1/122）

五月十七日，香港湾仔远利号发货单，盖有远利号印章，印文“香港湾仔远利号书柬”。

Receipt from Yuan-li hao. A receipt from Yuan-li (Yuanli) hao, Hong Kong. The year is not given. 1 item; Fair condition, but some damage by insects.

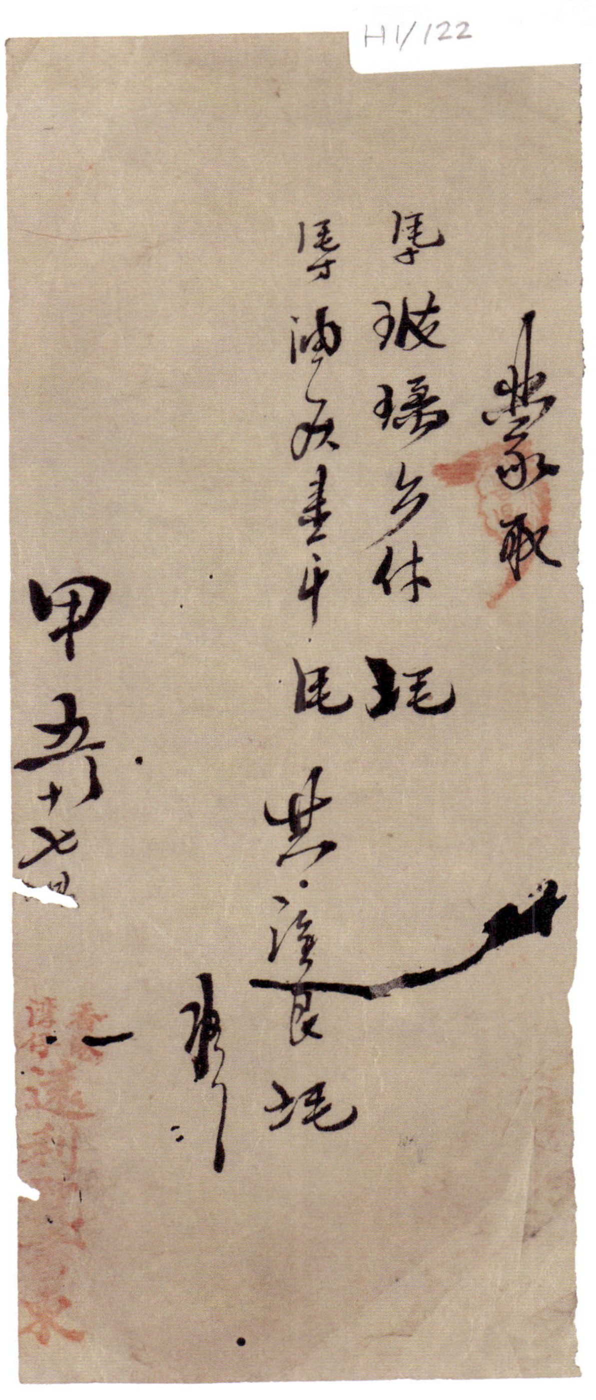

一二三、同治十一年香港报纸关于保险的广告（H1/123）

同治十一年十二月初六日（1873年1月4日），香港报纸广告，刊有两则广告：其一是“壬申年六月初六日”剌士厘公司[①]关于航运保险的广告；其二是“壬申年十二月初六日”禅神公司[②]关于火灾保险的广告。背面有铅笔撰写的英文注释。

Advertisements. A newspaper cutting of 4 January 1873 containing two advertisements (in Chinese) from 1) La-shih-li Co., regarding shipping insurance, dated on the 6th day, 6th month, 11th year of Tongzhi's (T'ung-chih) reign (1 July 1872[③]), and 2) Ch'an-shen (Chanshen) Co., regarding fire insurance, dated on the 6th day, 12th month, 11th year of Tongzhi's reign. On the reverse are English notes in pencil regarding Mr. William Laage (?) and Paul Sittig Esq. of San Francisco. 1 item. 1873

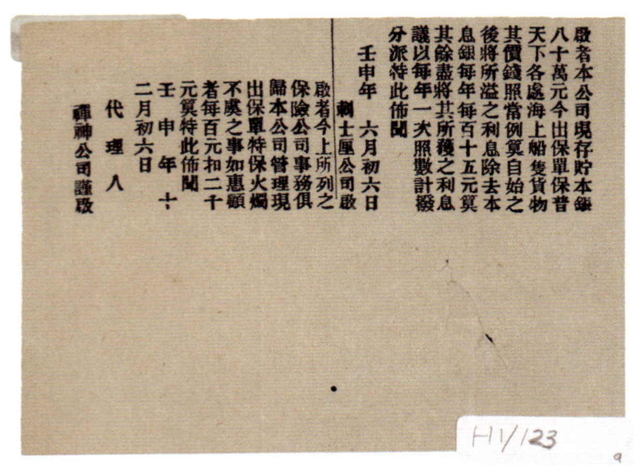
啟者本公司現存貯本銀八十萬元今出保單保昔天下各處海上船隻貨物其價錢照常例算自始之後將所溢之利息除去本息銀每年每百十五元算其餘盡將其所獲之利息議以每年一次照數計撥分派特此佈聞

壬申年　六月初六日

剌士厘公司啟

啟者今上所列之保險公司事務俱歸本公司管理現出保單特保火燭不虞之事如惠顧者每百元扣二十元算特此佈聞

壬申年十二月初六日

代理人

禪神公司謹啟

H1/123　a

（正）

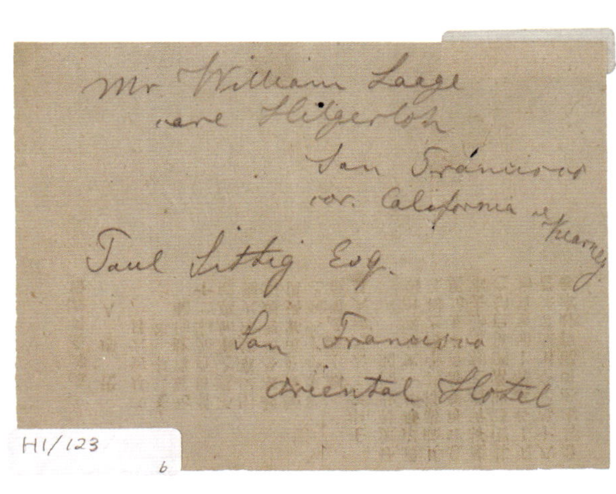
Mr William Laage

care Hilgerloh

San Francisco

cor. California & Kearny

Paul Sittig Esq.

San Francisco

Oriental Hotel

H1/123　b

（反）

① 剌士厘公司：保险公司。

② 禅神公司：保险公司。

③ 勘误：英文提要中谓第一则广告的时间为1872年7月1日（1 July 1872），按原中文文献“壬申年六月初六日”，应为1872年7月11日。

一二四、贞侯系列单据

1. 光绪三十三年凤池[①]付贞侯的单据（H1/124/1）

光绪三十三年八月初九日（1907年9月16日），凤池付贞侯的单据，涉及往法国兵船交炭砖的费用。

Receipt from Mr. Feng-ch'ih. A receipt from Mr. Feng-ch'ih (Fengchi) for charcoal delivered to a French warship, 16 September 1907. 1 item. 1907

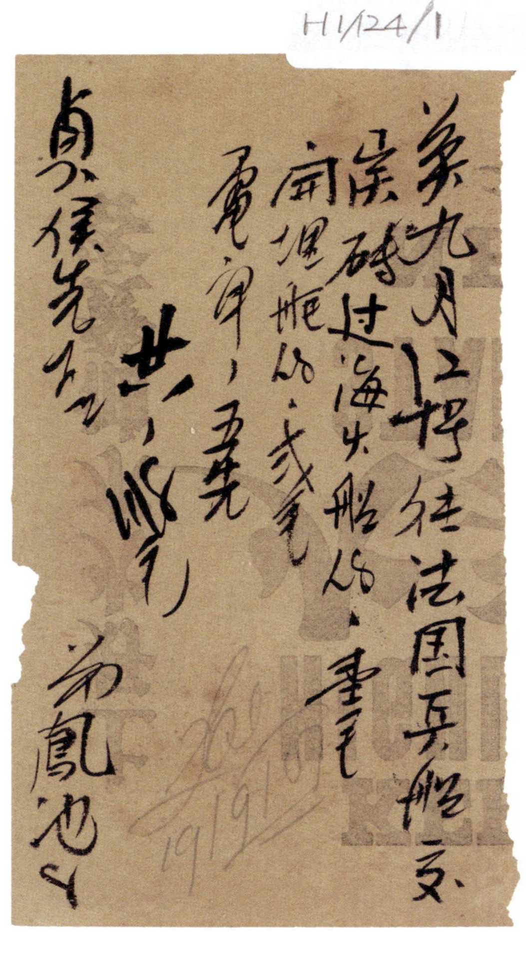

（正）

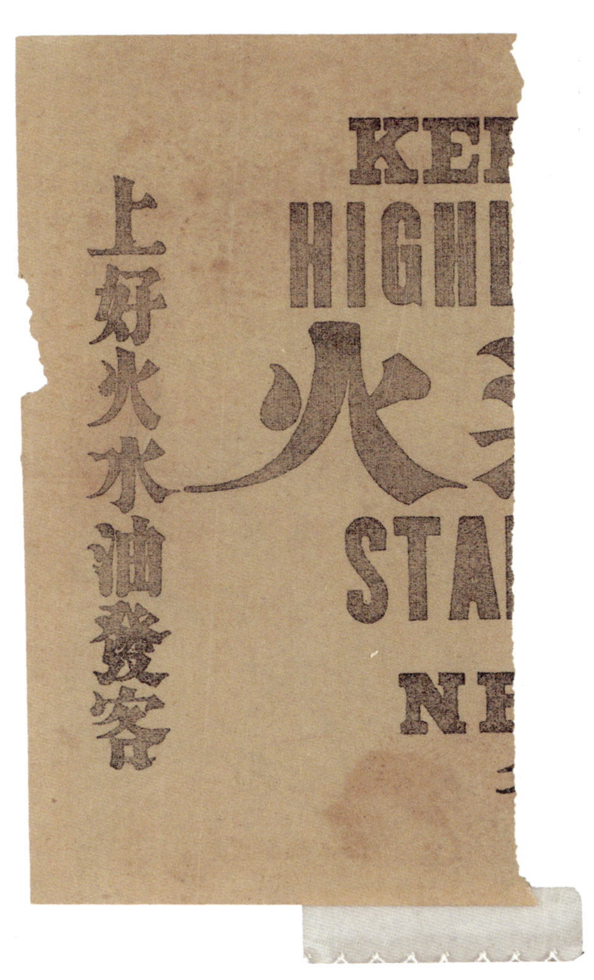

（反）

① 凤池：买办。

2. 光绪三十三年荣佳[①]付祯侯[②]的单据（H1/124/2）

光绪三十三年八月初十日（1907年9月17日），荣佳付祯侯的单据，内容为："英九月十七号往吉生交炭，开埋艇仔[③]弍毛五仙。"

Receipt from Mr. Jung-chia. A receipt from Mr. Jung-chia (Rongjia) for charcoal delivered to the boat K'ai-mei (Kaimai), 17 September 1907. 1 item. 1907

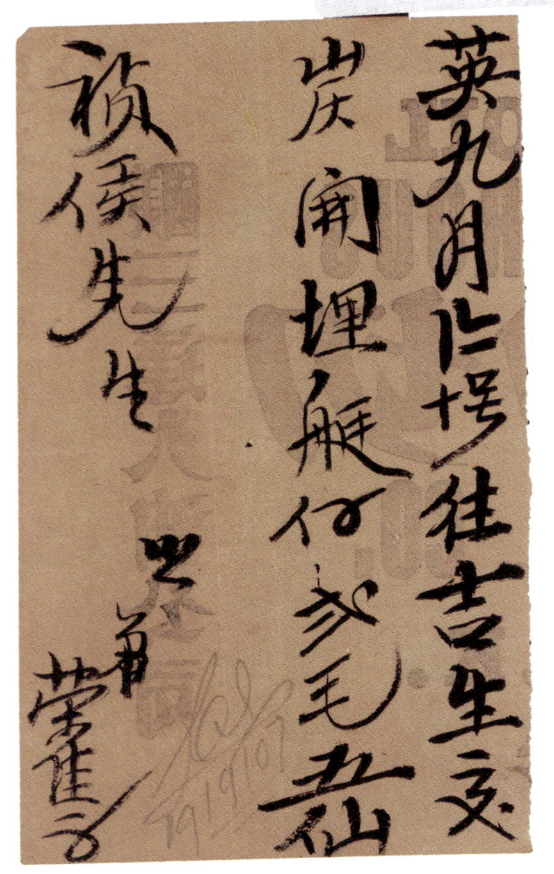
英九月十七号往吉生交
炭开埋艇仔弍毛五仙
祯侯先生
照单
荣佳

（正）

（反）

---

① 荣佳：买办。
② 祯侯：上文写作"贞侯"，商人。
③ 开埋艇仔：小型船舶。可能是粤语，表示开艇仔送炭的费用。

3. 光绪三十三年凤池[①]付贞侯的单据（H1/124/3）

光绪三十三年八月十二日（1907年9月19日），凤池付贞侯的单据，涉及往“昌升”船交炭的费用。

Receipt from Mr. Feng-ch-ih. A receipt from Mr. Feng-ch’ih (Fengchi) for charcoal for Ch’ang-sheng (Changsheng), 19 September 1907. 1 item. 1907

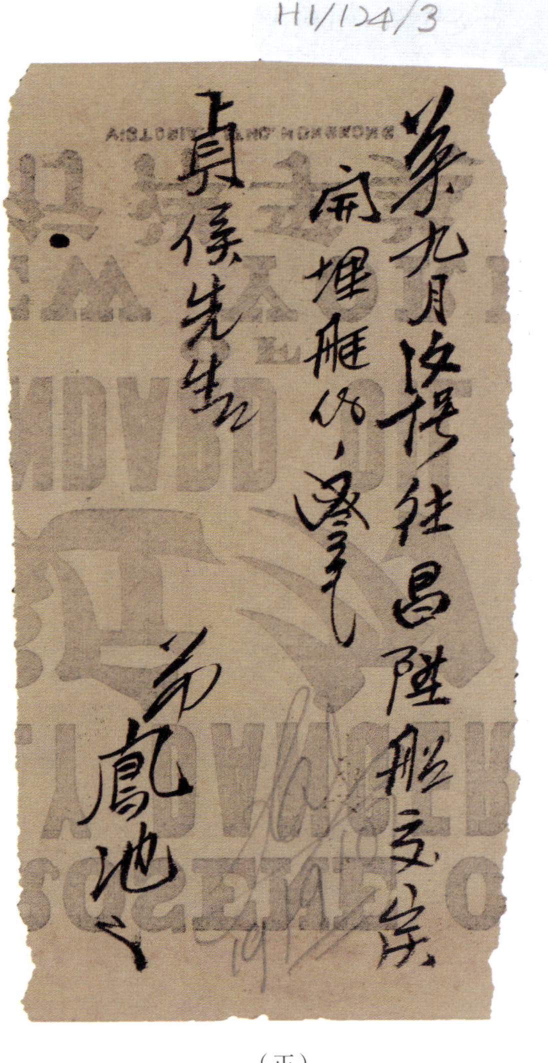
H1/124/3

贞侯先生

弟 凤池

（正）

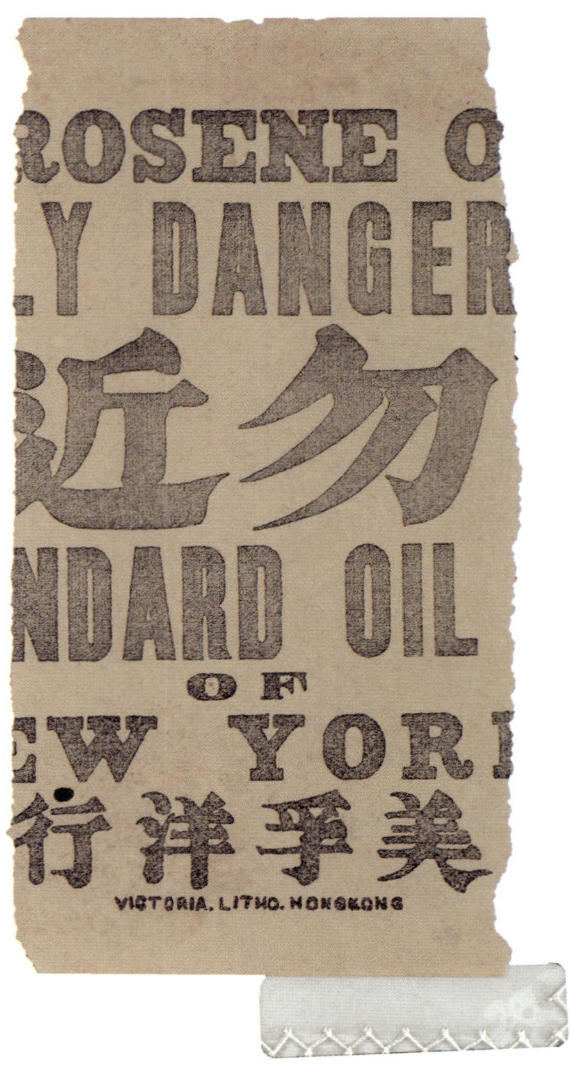

（反）

① 凤池：买办。

4. 七月十九日单据（年份不详）（H1/124/4）

七月十九日，达□给贞侯先生的单据。

Receipt. Receipt from Ta [...](Da [...])[...], 19 July (no year). 1 item.

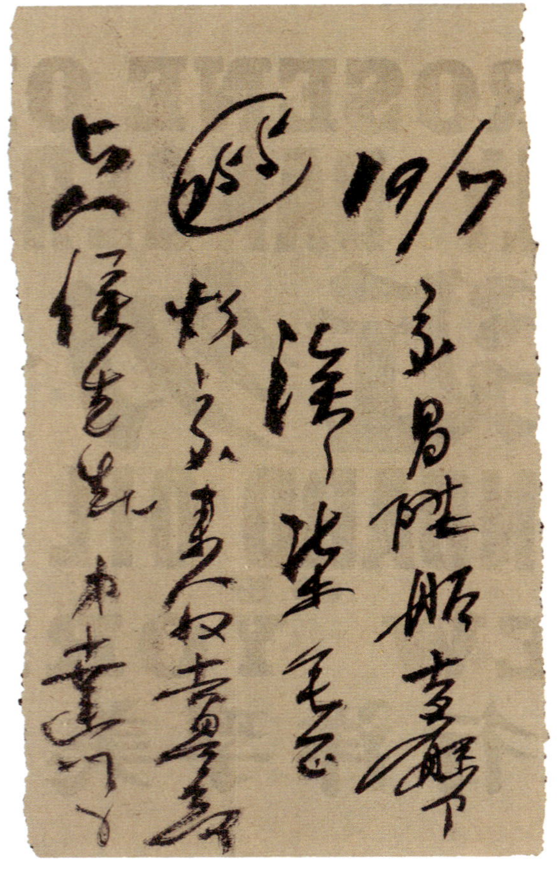

（正）

（反）

5. 顺利[①] 给贞侯的单据（日期不详）(H1/124/5）

顺利给贞侯的单据，内容显示“昌升”船购买的木炭已交货，费用共35.47元。

Receipt from Shun-li. An undated receipt from Shun-li (shunli) for charcoal for Ch’ang-sheng (Changsheng). 1 item.

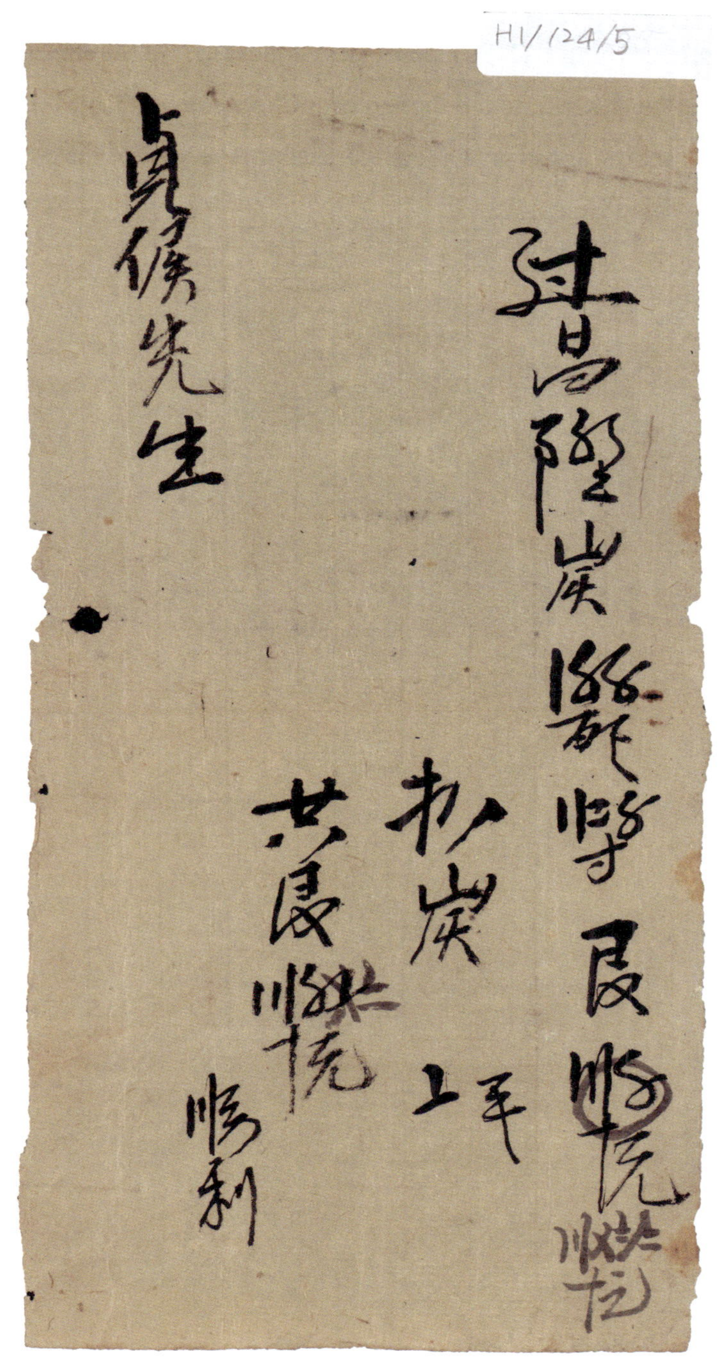

H1/124/5

貞侯先生

付昌隆炭[illegible]

[illegible]炭 [illegible]

共[illegible]

順利

---

① 顺利：买办。

一二五、二月十三日香港中环忠信铜铁号[①]单据（年份不详）（H1/125）

二月十三日，香港中环忠信铜铁号给吉地士大洋行[②]以赊购60张铜片的收据，盖有中环忠信铜铁号印章，印文“香港中环忠信铜铁号□”。另有随形印三枚，印文不清。附有简要英文注释。

Receipt from Chung-hsin t’ung-t’ie. A receipt (in Chinese) from Chung-hsin t’ung-t’ie (Zhongxin tongtie) Hao in Chunghuan, Hong Kong, to the foreign firm Chi-ti-shih (Jidishi) for its purchase of 60 copper sheets on credit, including a short English note about the receipt. The year is not given. 1 item.

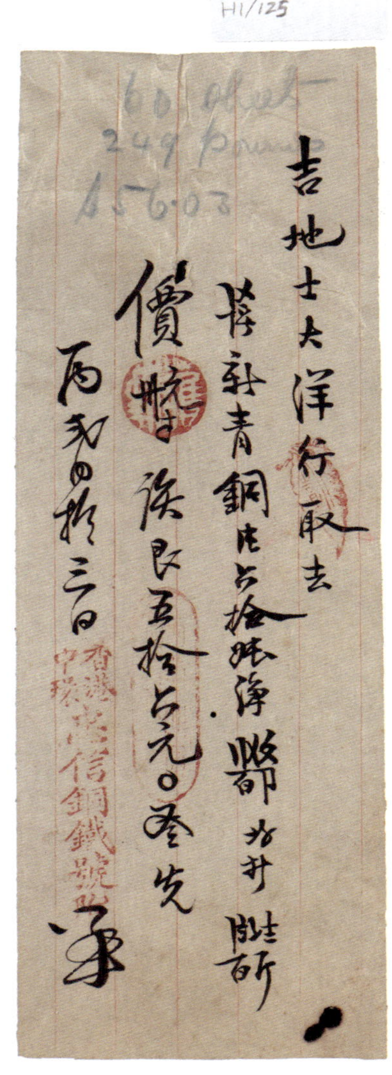
H1/125

吉地士大洋行取去

香港中環忠信銅鐵號

---

① 香港中环忠信铜铁号：金属制品商店。

② 吉地士大洋行：外国商行。

一二六、怡和洋行相关信函（日期不详）

该文献包括三件信函，均谈及怡和洋行的不良贸易行为。

1. 溪镇郭和记[①]致树攀信函（H1/126/1）

二十二日，溪镇郭和记致树攀信函，告知其有关怡和洋行的不良行为，并叮嘱其切勿配货该行。盖有印章，印文“溪镇郭和记书柬”。

Letter from Kuo-ho chi. Part of a letter from Kuo-ho chi in His-chen, Hankow, to Shu-p’an (Shupan) regarding stopping the loading of Ewo’s ship due to the company’s bad behaviour. The year is not given. 1 item.

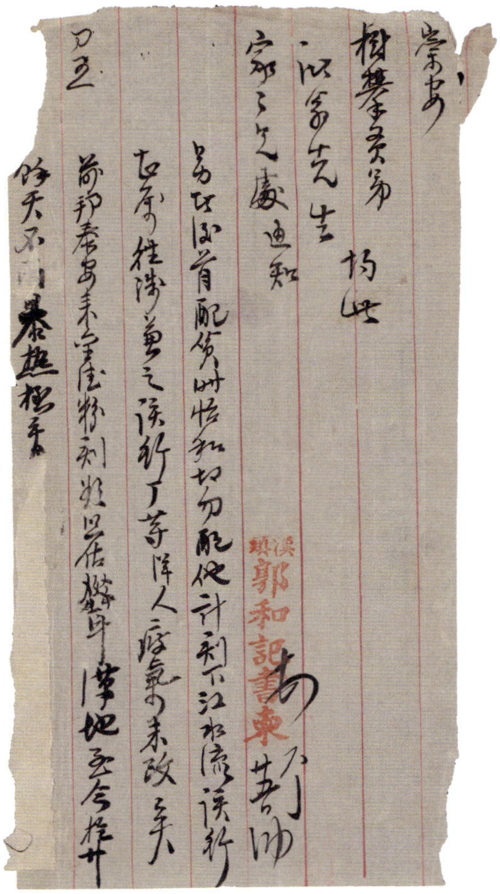

① 郭和记：中国商号。

2. 汉口益丰信函（H1/126/2）

汉口益丰信函，谈及怡和洋行以往贸易中的狡猾，建议其切勿用该行船只载运货物。

Letter from I-feng. An undated part of a letter from I-feng (Yifeng), Hankow, regarding stopping the loading of Ewo's ship. 1 item.

H1/126/2

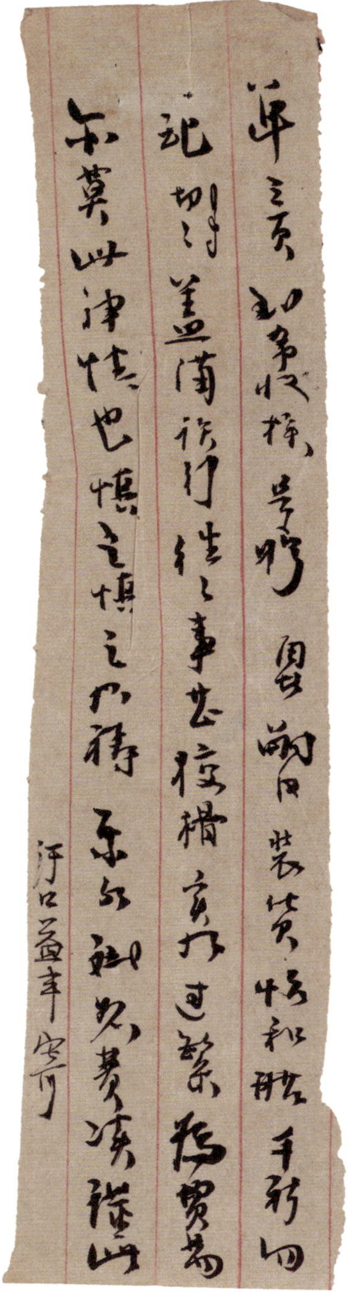

单三页知弟收存，是所恳留装货怡和船，千祈勿
託，切切。盖该行往之事甚狡猾，贵行过繁[illegible]贵为
尔莫此律情也，慎之慎之为特[illegible]谨此
汉口益丰字行

（正）

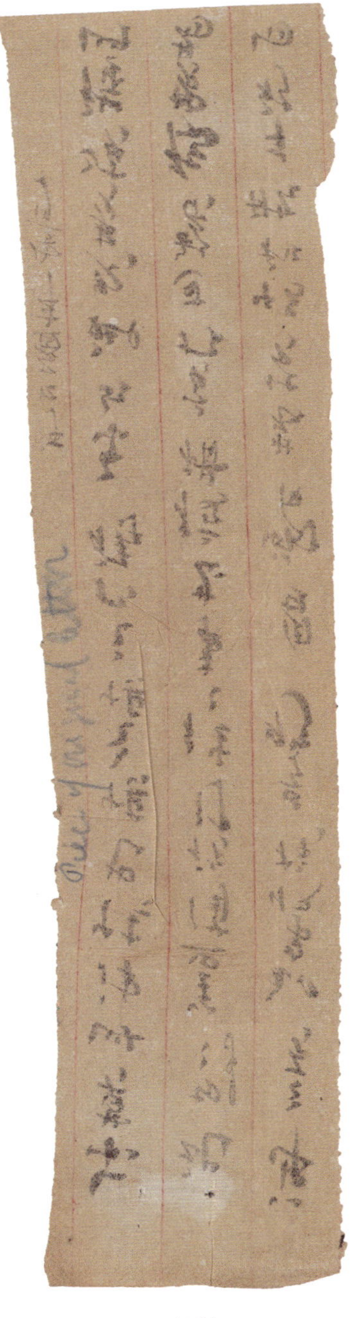

（反）

3. 某人信函（H1/126/3）

信函不完整，写信人与收信人均没注明。信中指出“怡和洋行格外狡猾”“不认赔”，叮嘱切勿用该行船只载运货物。

Letter re Ewo. An undated part of a letter (in Chinese) regarding Ewo’s refusal to pay a cargo claim, including an English note: ‘copy of extract from letter.’ The author and recipient are not known. 1 item.

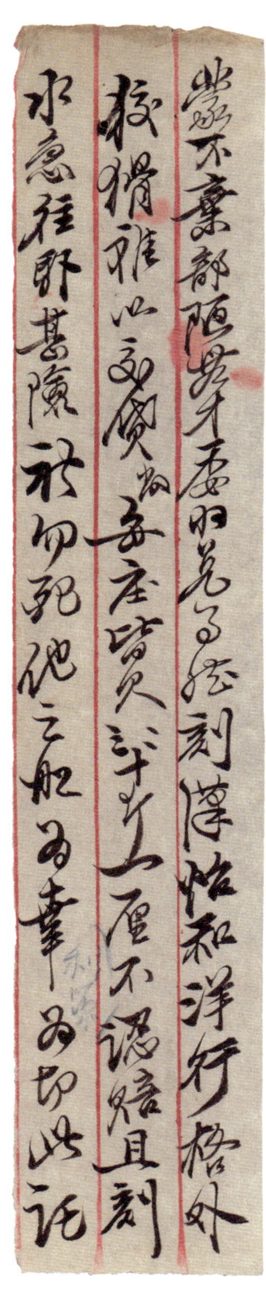

（正）

（反）

一二七、四月十八日周胜[1]收到孖地臣[2]款项的单据（年份不详）（H1/127）

四月十八日，周胜收到孖地臣款项的单据（油漆匠周胜为孖地臣的船只进行油漆作业，费用45元），附有英文注释。

Receipt from Chow Sheng. A receipt from Chow Sheng (Zhou Sheng) to Matheson for painting a boat, including part of an English note at the top of the document. The year is not given. 1 item; Fair condition, but the top of the document, including the English note, has been damaged by the ink and is missing the top part (the Chinese text is unaffected).

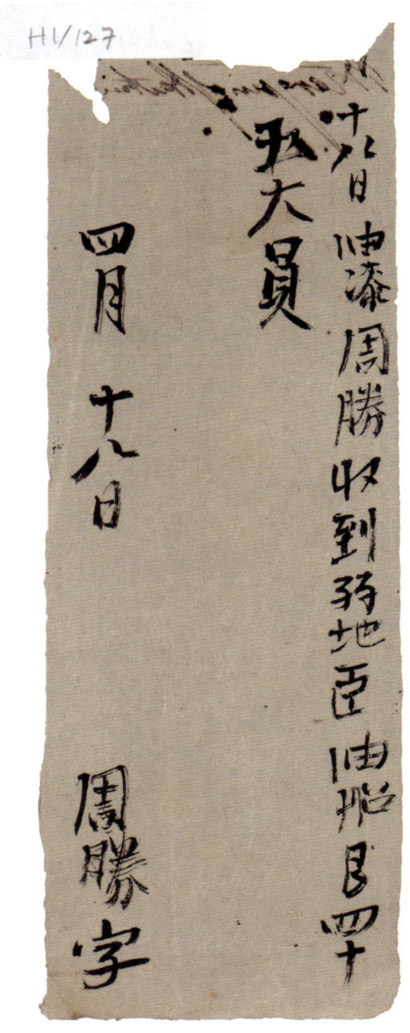
H1/127

十八日油漆周勝收到孖地臣由船艮四十
五大員
四月十八日
周勝字

① 周胜：中国油漆匠。

② 孖地臣：英国商人 Matheson，怡和洋行（Jardine, Matheson & Co.）创始人之一。

一二八、维盛等五家商号的交易清单（日期不详）（H1/128）

交易清单，包括香港维盛、和栈、公源、永祥盛及义生栈的交易款项，共133.46元。

List of bills. An undated list of bills (in Chinese), including those of Wai Sing (Weisheng), Wo chan (He zhan), Kung Yuen (Gongyuan), Wung chian sheng (Yong xiang sheng) and E sheng chan (Yi sheng zhan), totalling $133.46. The document includes English annotations. 1 item; Fair condition, but damage by insects.

H1/128

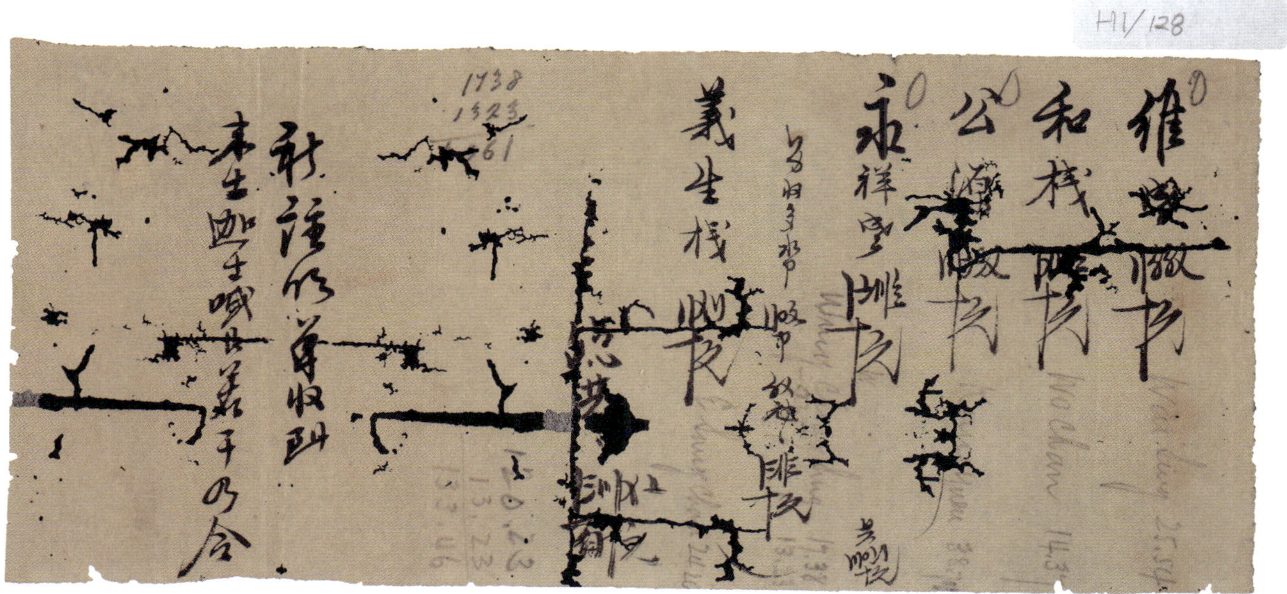

一二九、藤器店收支清单（日期不详）（H1/129）

一家藤器店的收支清单，包括“行内共用伙食工金各项计银2574.37两”“新装造驳茶艇五条计银987.12两”，以及用去籐、唛绵纸等各项开支，最后注明“除收之外仍少2604.98两”。另有铅笔标注的阿拉伯数字汇总计算。

Annual report. An undated annual report (in Chinese) of a firm’s domestic expenditure, including annotations comprised of Western numbers. 1 item.

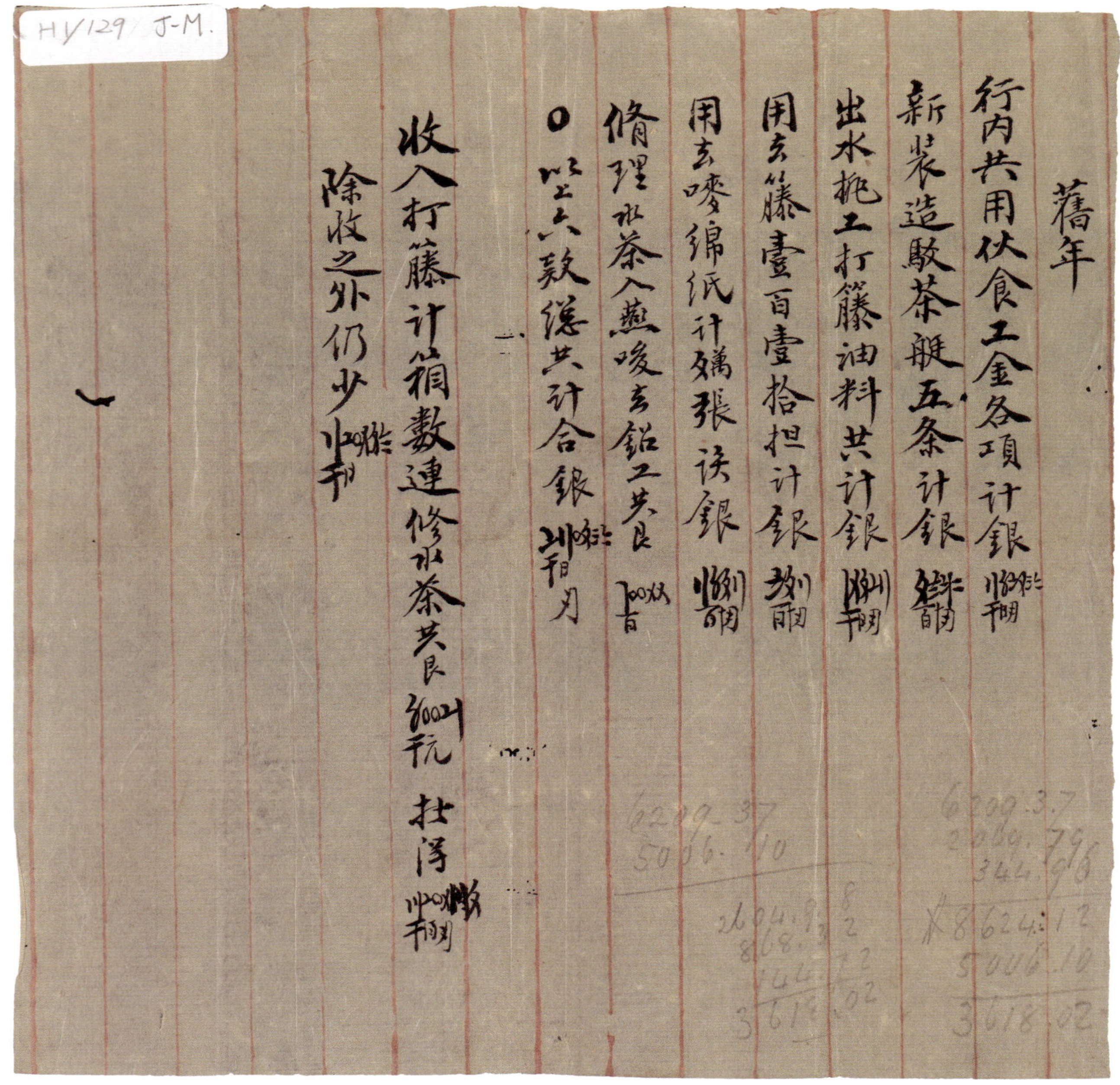

H1/129 J-M.

舊年

行内共用伙食工金各項計銀 [illegible]

新装造駁茶艇五条計銀 [illegible]

出水拖工打籐油料共計銀 [illegible]

用去籐壹百壹拾担計銀 [illegible]

用去嘜綿紙計[illegible]張該銀 [illegible]

脩理水茶入燕嘜去鉛工共艮 [illegible]

〇坐六數總共計合銀 [illegible]

收入打籐計箱數連脩水茶共艮 [illegible] 扯洋 [illegible]

除收之外仍少 [illegible]

6209.37
5006.10

2604.98
868.32
144.72
3618.02

6209.37
2069.79
344.96
8624.12
5006.10
3618.02

一三〇、南昌店[①]大柑提货单（日期不详）（H1/130）

南昌店大柑提货单，由该店亚生写给火船大事头，要求提货15箩大柑。盖有南昌店印章，印文“南昌图记”。背面有英文注释。

Note from Asing. An undated note (in Chinese) from Asing (Yasheng) to the manager of a steamer regarding taking delivery of 15 boxes of oranges ex ‘Hellespont’ (?) from Swatow. An English note on the reverse describes the note as a guarantee for Asing taking delivery.1 item.

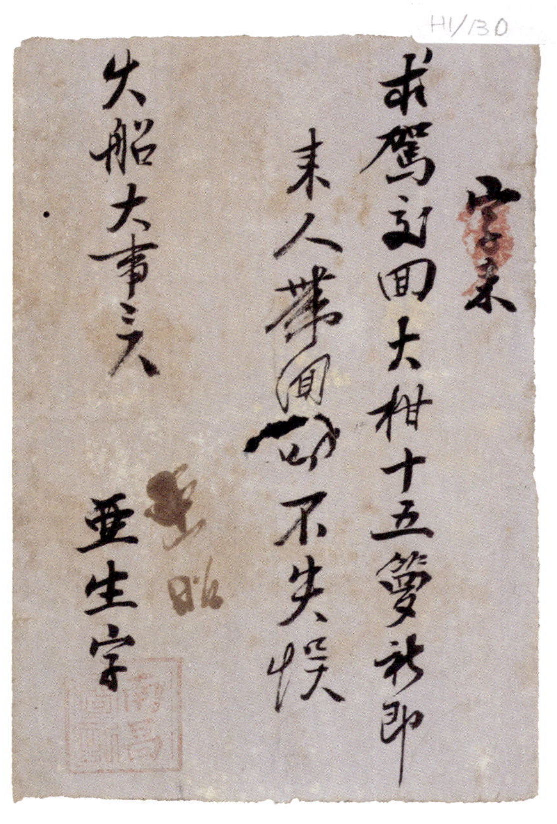

（正）

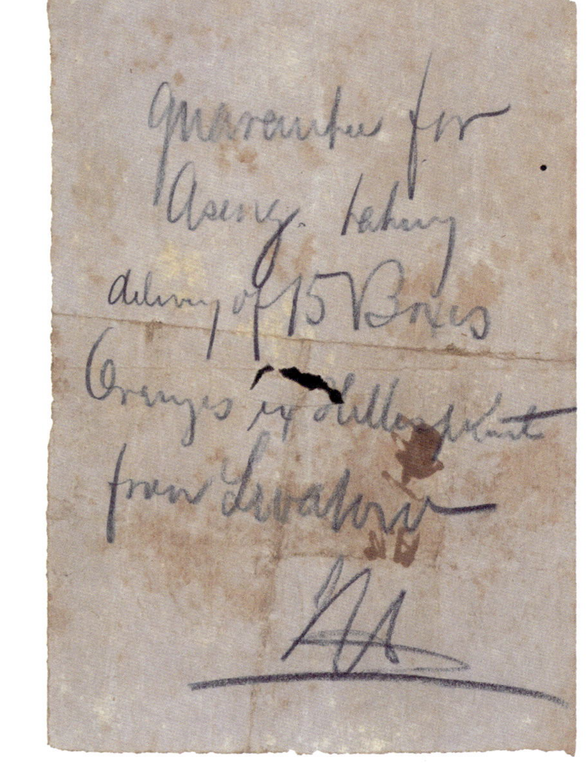

（反）

① 南昌店：中国水果店铺。

一三一、正月初三日打伦行[1]收据（年份不详）（H1/131）

正月初三日，打伦行杨兴给多臣的收据（杨兴于正月初三日收到多臣5元）。

Receipt from Ta-lun. A receipt from Yang Hsing (Yang Xing) of Ta-lun (Dalun) hong to Mr. Tuo-ch'en (Duochen) for his payment, 16 February (no year). 1 item; Fair condition, but damage by insects.

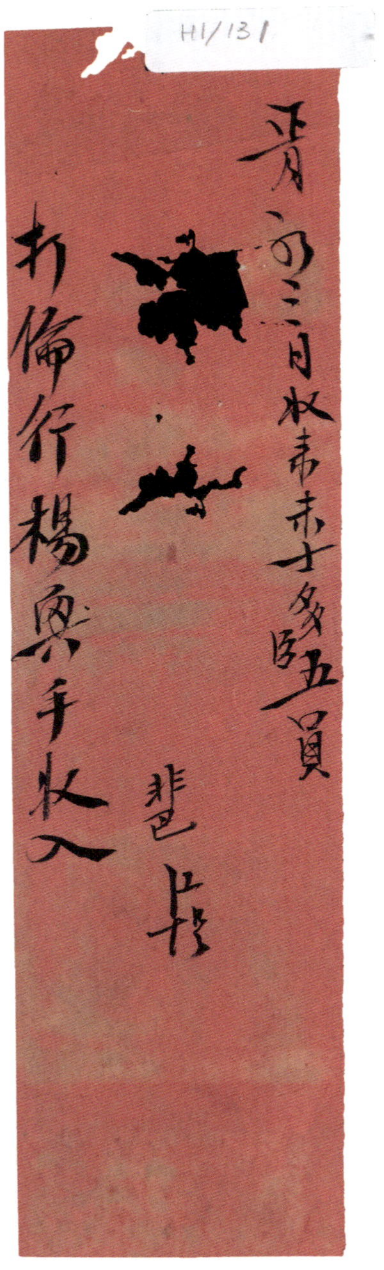

H1/131

正月初三日收来未士多臣五員

打倫行楊興手收入

---

① 打伦行：中国店铺。

一三二、大米报价单（日期不详）（H1/132/1-11）

大米报价单，共有11张报价单，每张单均包含18个大米品种，分别报出当日市价的最高价和最低价。没有注明年份，但有具体日期，分别为“正月初十日、十三日、十四日（2张）、十六日、二十日、二十一日、二十五日、七月初八日、九月十七日、十月十七日”，其中九月十七日备注：“此三四日内连日市淡，不过低三几个先士”。

132 Market quotations. 11 items.

Quotations of prices on the rice market, including ceiling and floor prices, featuring 18 names. The year is not given.

Manuscripts/MS JM/H1/132 contains:

（1）Market quotations. Dated 10 January (no year). 1 item.

（2）Market quotations. The month and year are not given. 1 item.

（3）Market quotations. The month and year are not given. 1 item

（4）Market quotations. The month and year are not given. 1 item.

（5）Market quotations. The month and year are not given. 1 item.

（6）Market quotations. The month and year are not given. 1 item.

（7）Market quotations. The month and year are not given. 1 item.

（8）Market quotations. The month and year are not given. 1 item.

（9）Market quotations. The year is not given. 1 item.

（10）Market quotations. The year is not given. The document includes a note recording that in the last three to four days business was dull and the price dropped. 1 item.

（11）Market quotations. The year is not given. 1 item.

H1/132/1

上三猫玉

上吹录咕

百架四嚨

呂宋花朴

上宣粘玉

䟷谷宣粘

多谷宣粘

上天華玉

上天華朴

上扒厘玉

上扒厘朴

上寧波坩

上夏門朴

上安南朴

庇姑粳朴

石辣粘朴

石辣粳朴

黄洋粘玉

正月初十日市

H1/132/2

黄洋粘玉

石辣粳朴

又粘朴

庇姑粳朴

上安南朴

上夏門朴

上寧波玉

上扒厘朴

又玉

上腰華朴

又玉

多谷宣粘朴

䟷谷宣粘朴

又玉

呂宋花朴

百架四嚨

上噫緑咕

上三猫玉

十三日市

H1/132/3

十四日

H1/132/4

十四日

黄洋梹玉
石辣梗豹
又梹朴
庇姑梗朴
上安南朴
上廈門朴
上寧波玉
上扒厘朴
又玉
上腰華朴
又玉
谷多宣糕朴
谷肆宣糕朴
又玉
呂宋花朴
陌架四哤
上噫嚒咕
上三蒞玉

十六日 市

黄洋梹玉
石辣梗豹
又梹朴
庇姑梗朴
上安南朴
上廈門朴
上寧波玉
上扒厘朴
又玉
上腰華朴
又玉
谷多宣糕朴
谷肆宣糕朴
又玉
呂宋花朴
百架四哤
上噫嚒咕
上三蒞玉

十四日 市

H1/132/7

黄洋粘玉　上次
石辣粳朴
又粘朴
庇姑粳朴　次上
上安南朴
上夏門朴
上寧波玉
上扒厘朴
又玉
上腰華朴
又玉
谿宣粘朴
谿宣粘朴
又玉
呂宋花朴
咟奈四嚨
上噫嗦咕
上三茵玉

廿日帝

收　收之

H1/132/8

黄洋粘玉
石辣粳朴
又粘朴
庇姑粳朴
上安南朴
上夏門朴
上寧波玉
上扒厘朴
又玉
上腰華朴
又玉
谿宣粘朴
谿宣粘朴
又玉
呂宋花朴
百架四嚨
上噫嗦咕
上三茵玉

廿五日

好一毛已足

收　收之

H1/132/9

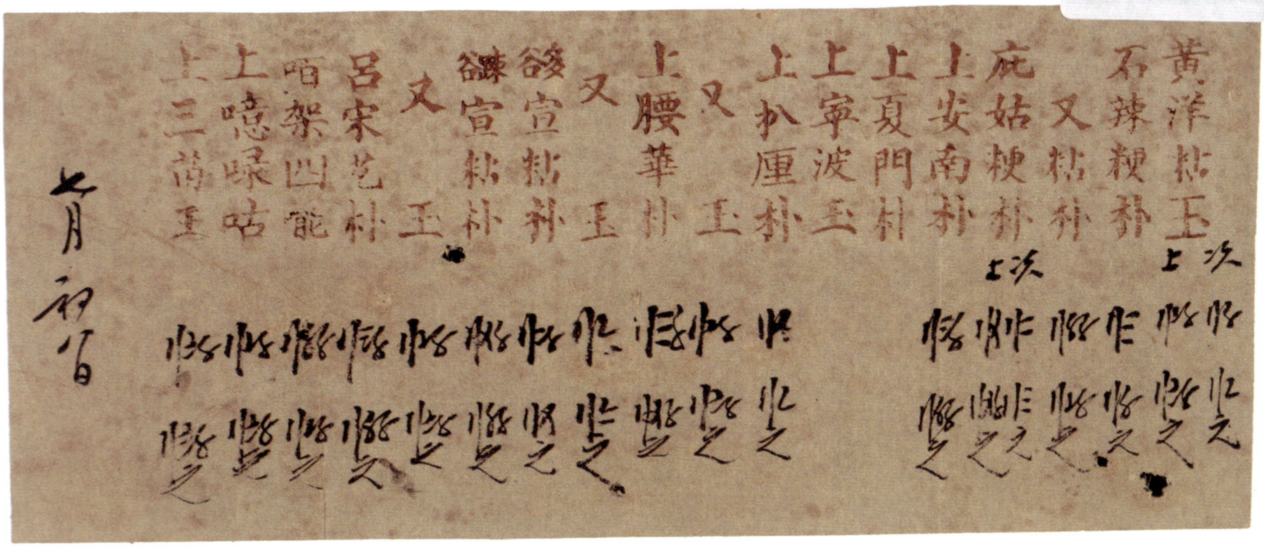

黃洋粘玉 上次
石辣粳朴
又粘朴 上次
庇姑粳朴
上安南朴
上夏門朴
上寧波玉
上扒厘朴
又玉
上腰華朴
又玉
發宣粘朴
陳宣粘朴
又玉
呂宋芑朴
唔架四能
上噫啰咕
上三苘玉

七月初旬

H1/132/10

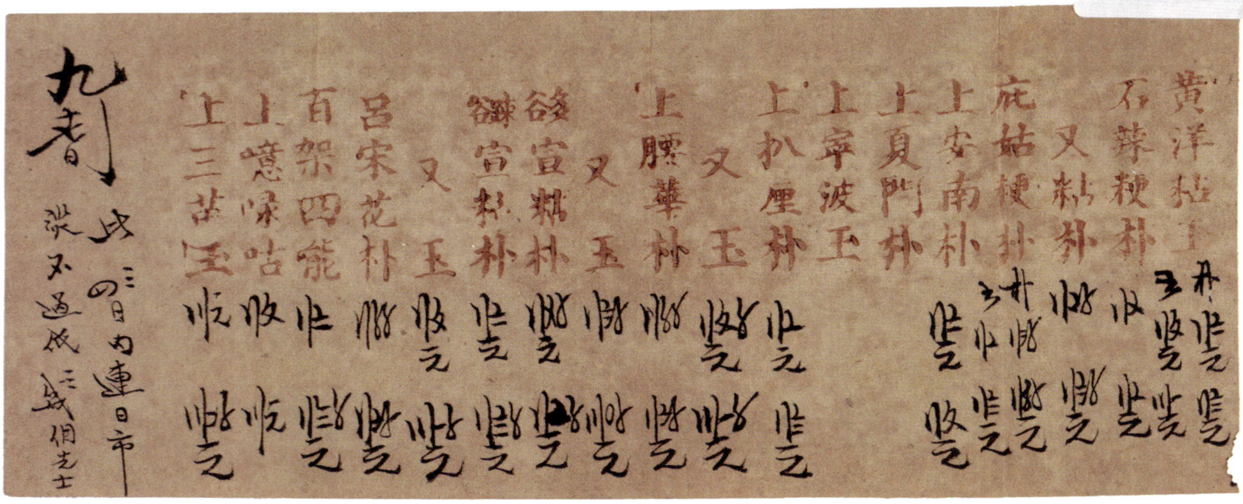

黃洋粘玉
石辣粳朴
又粘朴
庇姑粳朴
上安南朴
上夏門朴
上寧波玉
上扒厘朴
又玉
上腰華朴
又玉
發宣粘朴
陳宣粘朴
又玉
呂宋芑朴
百架四能
上噫啰咕
上三苦玉

九月

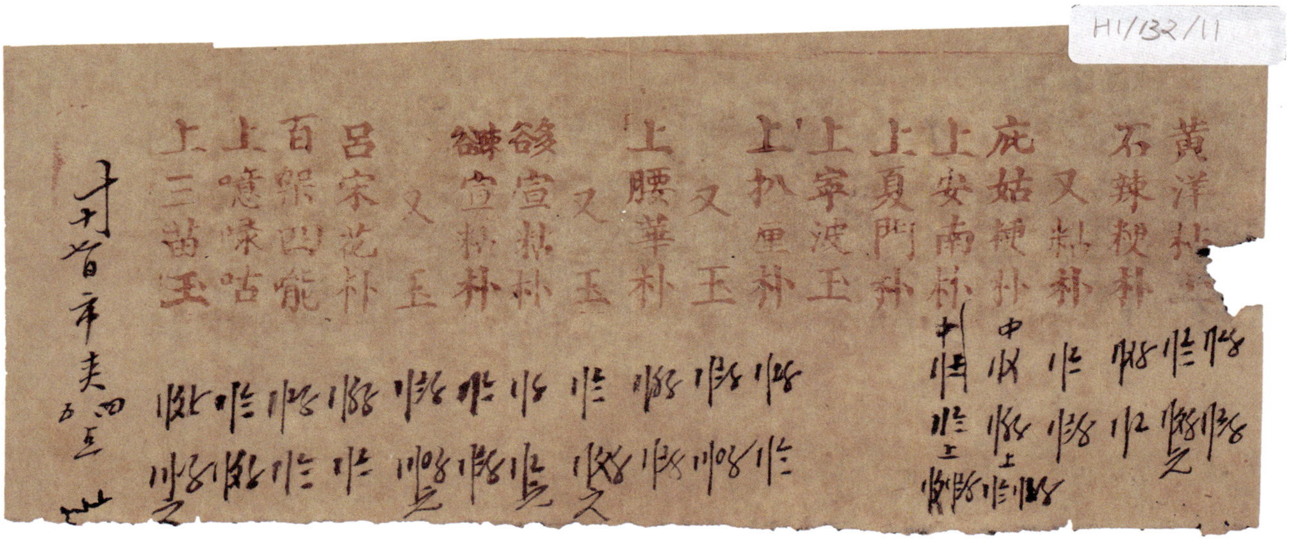

H1/132/11

黃洋朴玉

石辣梗朴

又粘朴

庇姑梗朴

上安南朴

上夏門升

上寧波玉

上扒里朴

又玉

上腰華朴

又玉

篘宣梗朴

篘宣梗朴

又玉

呂宋花朴

百槑四能

上噫喙咕

上三茴玉

一三三、腊月二十日徐发茂[①]致五十家宝栈的《知单》（年份不详）（H1/133）

腊月二十日，徐发茂致50家宝栈的《知单》，其内容包括四个部分：标题、正文、去年四月十六日出具的10包经线保单（徐发茂立，程阿和经手）以及50家宝栈的名称。《知单》正文反映，其供货给怡和洋行410包经线[②]，该洋行尚欠四万四千五百五十四两一钱七分，屡次催收仍拖延不付款，并借口经线售出发现内有次货，要求徐发茂的商号算还1955两银。徐发茂指出，成交之日验货，已把次货剔出，其中10包次货，在怡和洋行知情的情况下，于四月十六日出保单，且由“管栈陈洪浦亲向丝客读明”，按保10包计算，应算还140两，而非1955两银。因此，徐发茂奉请50家宝栈至丝茶公所商议酌办此事。

Notice from Hsu Fa-mao. A notice from Hsu Fa-mao (Xu Famao) to 50 shops inviting them to the Silk and Tea Guild for a hearing of the issue at stake between his shop and Ewo Co. with regard to compensation for substandard cotton yarn. The document is in four parts: title, text, a copy of the guarantee note dated in the 4th month and 16th day, and the 50 shop names. The year is not given. 1 item.

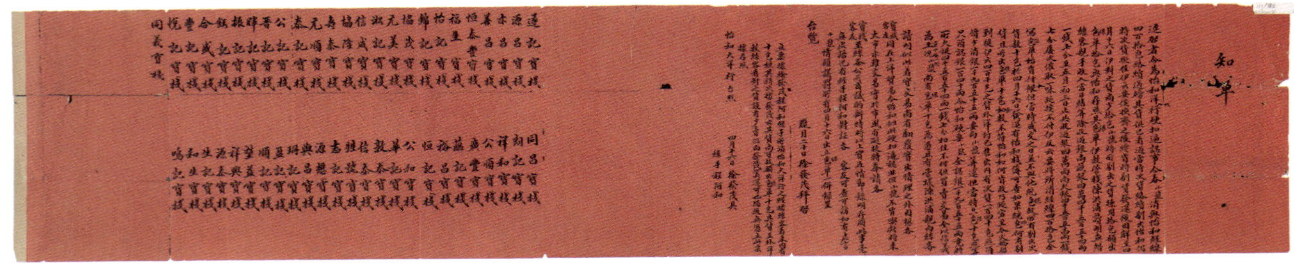

2 | 1

① 徐发茂：中国商人。

② 经线：是纺织丝绸的原丝和主线。丝绸纺织中的原丝分类为经线丝和纬线丝。

（局部图1）

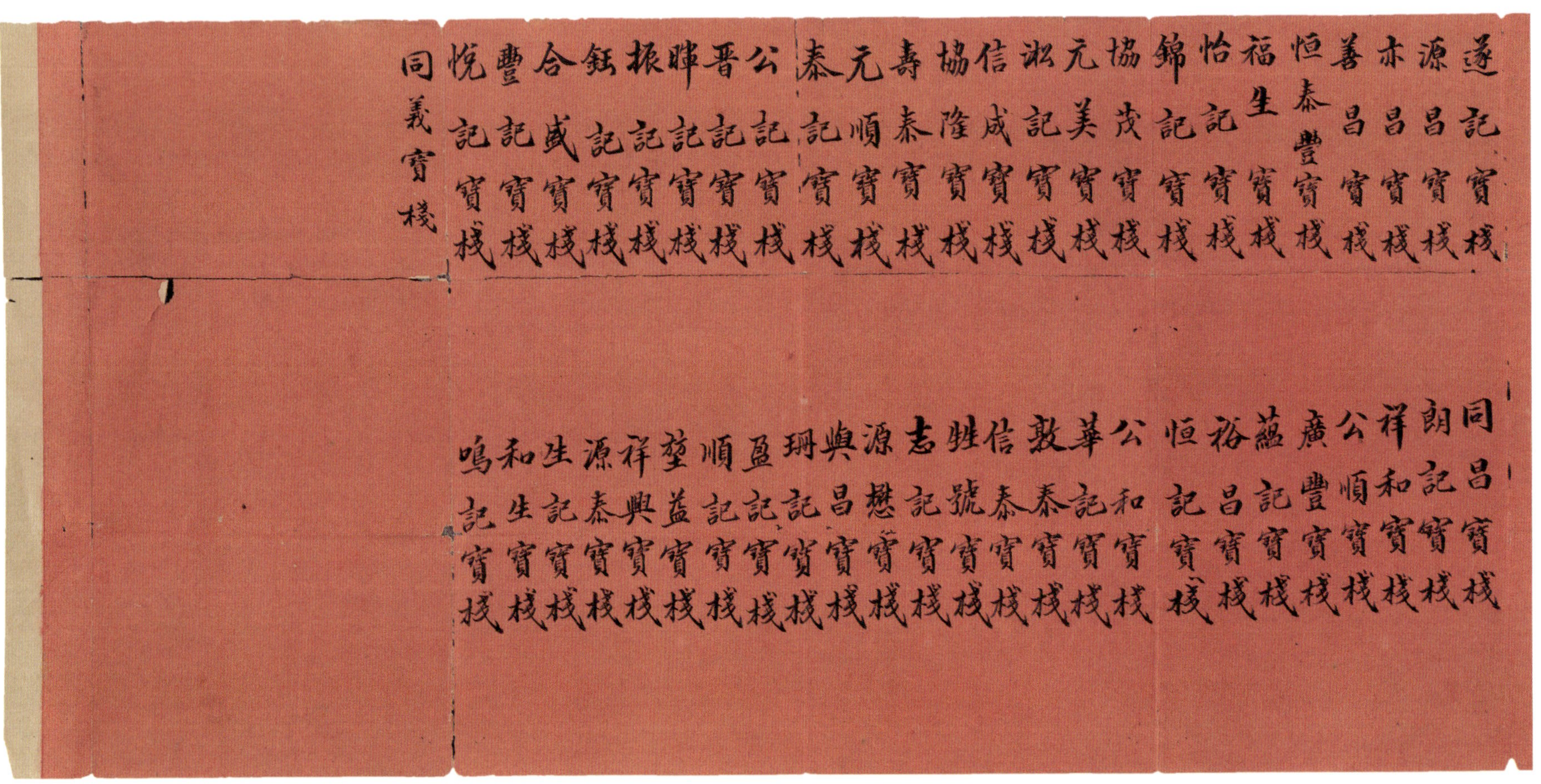

遂記寶棧
源昌寶棧
赤昌寶棧
善昌寶棧
恒泰豐寶棧
福生寶棧
怡記寶棧
錦記寶棧
協茂寶棧
元美寶棧
淞記寶棧
信成寶棧
協隆寶棧
壽泰寶棧
元順寶棧
泰記寶棧
公記寶棧
晋記寶棧
肆記寶棧
振記寶棧
鈺記寶棧
合盛寶棧
豐記寶棧
悅記寶棧
同義寶棧

同昌寶棧
朗記寶棧
祥和寶棧
公順寶棧
廣豐寶棧
蘊記寶棧
裕昌寶棧
恒記寶棧
公和寶棧
華記寶棧
敦泰寶棧
信泰寶棧
甡號寶棧
志記寶棧
源懋寶棧
與昌寶棧
珊記寶棧
盈記寶棧
順記寶棧
堃益寶棧
祥興寶棧
源泰寶棧
生記寶棧
和生寶棧
鳴記寶棧

（局部图2）

一三四、出口茶叶清单（日期不详）（H1/134）

“Childeharold”号船的茶叶清单，记录了“J M F 公司”装运的91个字号的茶叶，由苏州码子、阿拉伯数字标出茶叶数量和重量。

Tea inventory. An undated inventory of 91 brands of tea shipped on the ‘Childeharold’ for ‘J M F Co.’. The inventory gives the name of the tea, the weight in Suchow number, and an Arabic number, probably that of the teacase. 1 item.

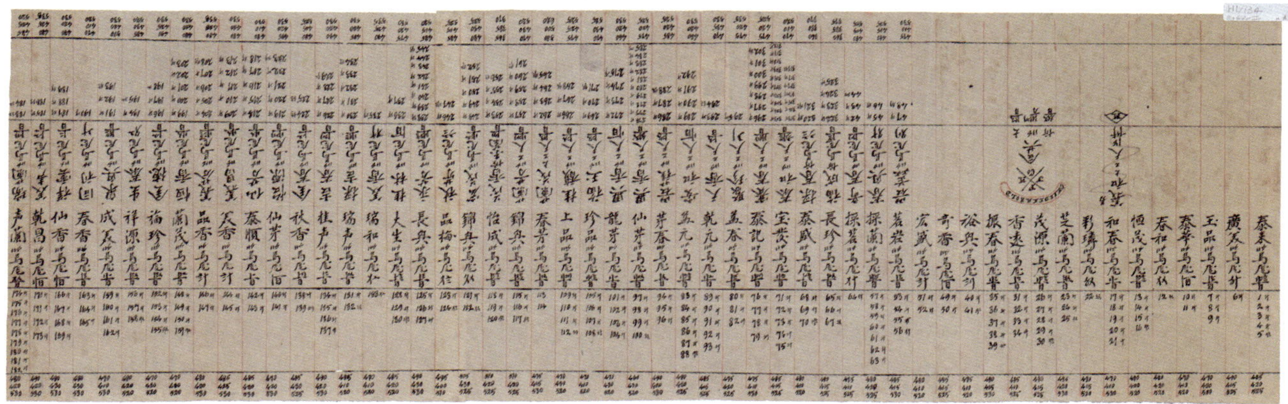

2 | 1

（局部图1）

（局部图2）

一三五、约道光六年巴斯商人[①]信函

1. 约道光六年巴斯商人信函（H1/135/1）

约道光六年（1826）广州巴斯商人的信函。

Letter to Framjee Pestonjee. A letter (in Parsi) to Framjee Pestonjee in China. The date 1826 has been written in pencil at the end of a paragraph in Western characters. 1 item. circa 1826

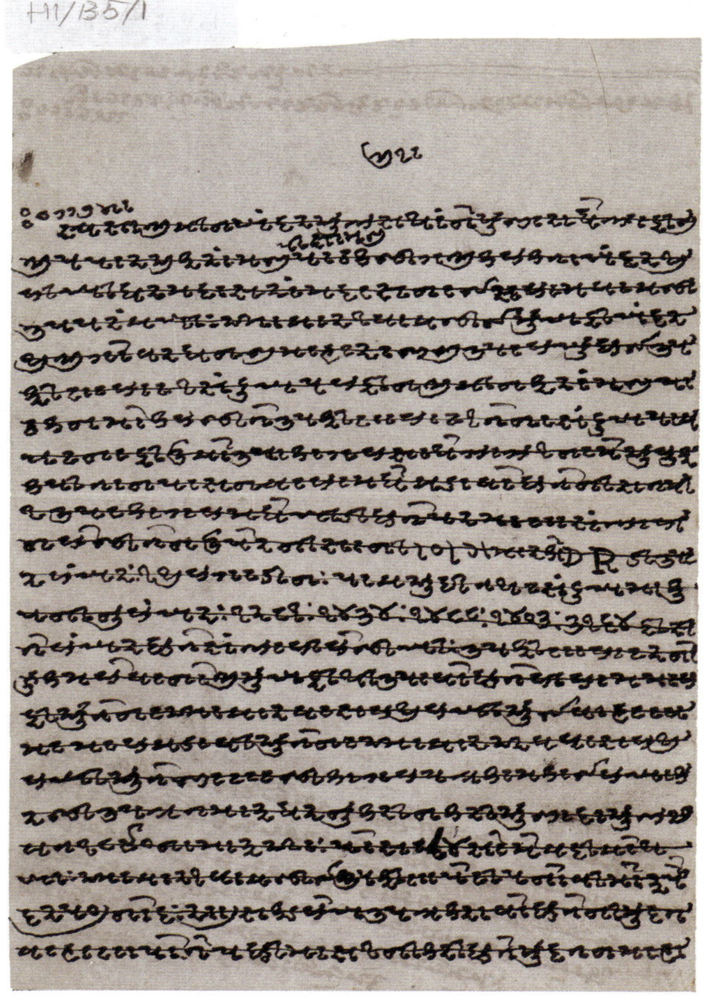

（正）

① 巴斯人（Parsee或Parsi）是波斯人的后代，信奉琐罗亚斯德教，又称“拜火教”。波斯被阿拉伯人征服后，部分拜火教徒移居印度苏拉特、孟买等地，成为巴斯人的起源。鸦片战争前夕，不少巴斯人跟随英国商人来华贸易，因为拜火教徒头缠白布，也被粤港民众称之为“白头摩罗”。他们曾是广州十三行的常客，人数占来穗外商的三分之一，以贸易和金融借贷闻名，广州最早的一位“大耳窿”，便出现在这个商人群体里，并以从事鸦片贸易而闻名。

（反）

2. 约道光六年巴斯商人信封（H1/135/2）

约道光六年（1826）巴斯商人的信封，上有英文注释，可知此信寄往中国。

Envelope to Framjee Pestonjee. An envelope including writing in English and Parsi, addressed (in English) to 'Framjee Pestonjee at China'. The senders' names, H. & O.J.S. Ramdass (?), are written in English on the back. 1 item. circa 1826

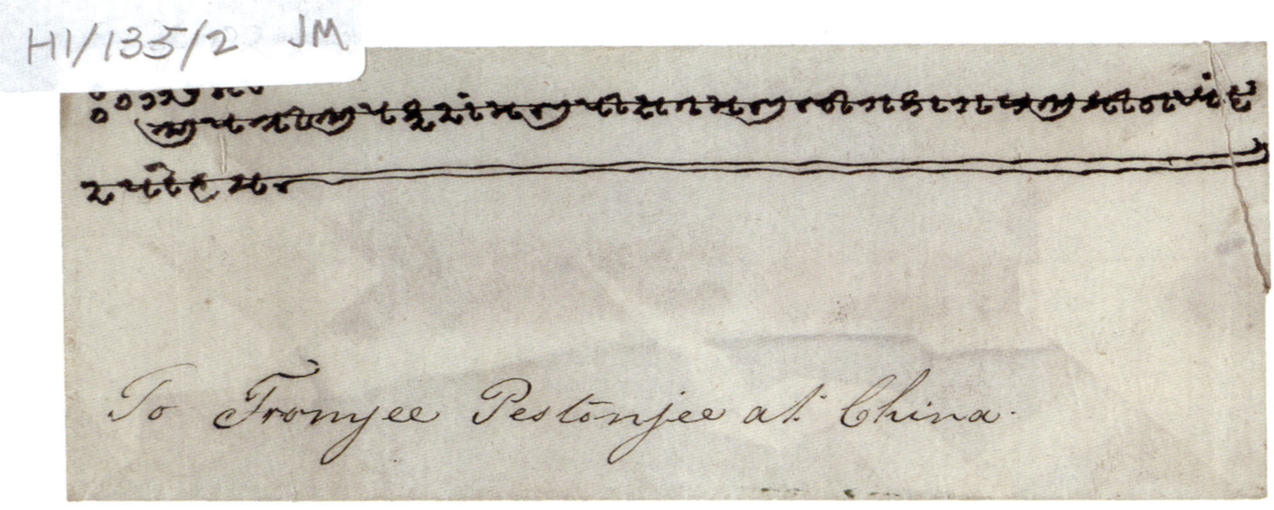

（正）

（反）

一三六、寄给英国商人渣甸[①]的信封（日期不详）（H1/136）

寄给英国商人渣甸的信封。

Envelope for chop to Jardine. An envelope addressed to Mr. Jardine on the front (in Chinese), with an English note on the reverse of a chop from Aymee (?) holding himself responsible for any damage resulting from the bad packing of silk. The document is undated. 1 item.

（正）

（反）

① 渣甸：即英国商人威廉·查顿（William Jardine），又译为渣颠、渣顿、赞典，为怡和洋行（Jardine, Matheson & Co.）创始人之一。

一三七、民国三年香港先施公司[①]广告（H1/137）

民国三年（1914），香港先施公司广告，盖有两枚蓝色印章，其中方形印章印有中文“中西药品电灯钟表恕不退换”。

Advertisement of Sincere Co. Ltd. A printed advertisement (in Chinese and English) of the Sincere Co. Ltd, Universal Providers, Queen’s Road, Hong Kong, supplier of clothes and shoes for men and women, with a receipt below, including two stamps. The document is dated in the third year of the Republic［1914］(no month or day). 1 item.

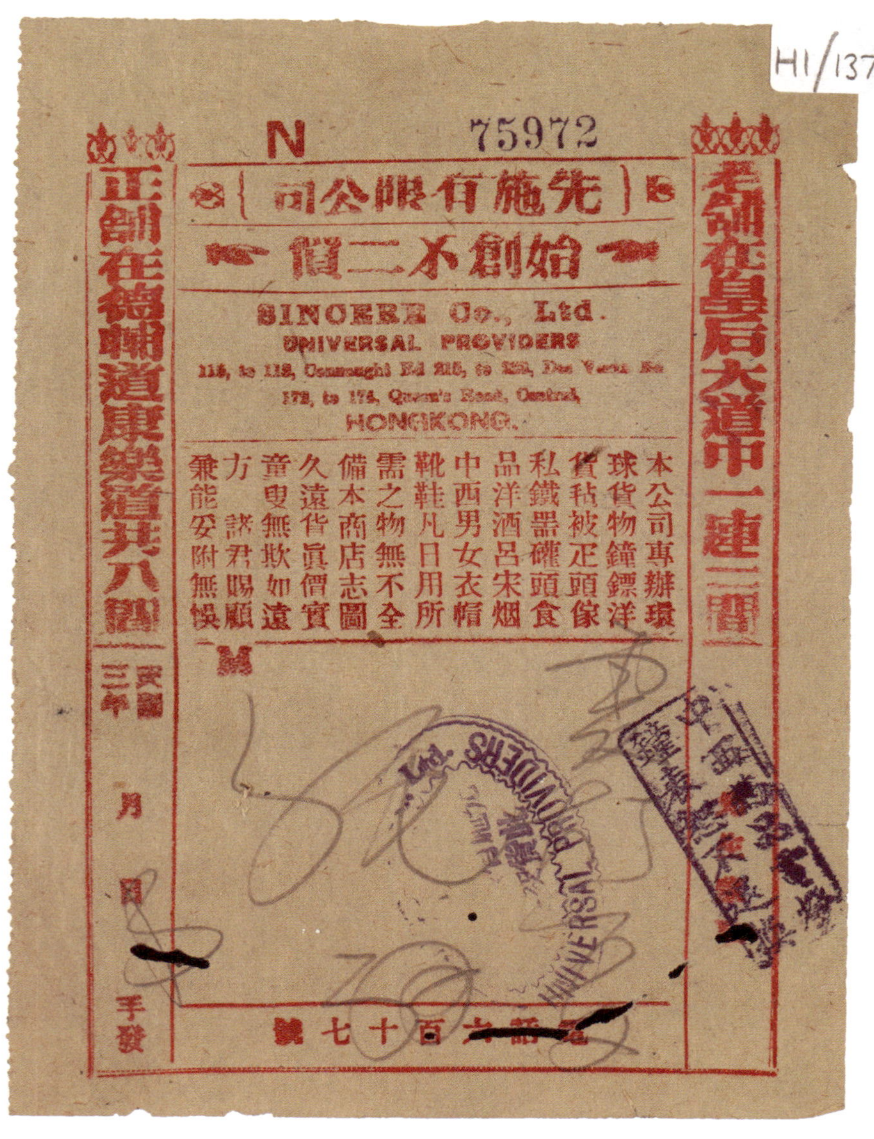

---

① 先施公司：著名百货公司。

Chapter Two

第二章

法律文件

法律文件时间涵盖1766—1868年，共计35件。其中有广州十三行街回澜桥房产物业系列买卖文件17件，时间为1766—1826年；福建闽县观音街土地、物业销售文书9件；有关出售及出租广州十三行之东生行物业的文件4件，1827—1832年；及1853—1865年之间其他地区的房产契约5件。有些文件是白契，即没有在公共记录中登记并得到官方认可的材料，时间为1780—1855年。

一、乾隆、道光年间回澜桥房屋买卖契约

1. 乾隆三十一年温紫光回澜桥房产售予蔡德远立的卖契[①]（H2/1/1）

房屋卖契。乾隆三十一年（1766）三月，由温紫光订立契约，陈平可代笔，将其回澜桥脚的房屋（此房产原为行商聚丰行[②]所有）永卖给蔡家。售房成交价9000两的契税已由广州府南海县县令确认完税。附一枚印花税票。契约署名买家姓名蔡德远，此外有买卖中介人和见证人签字。盖南海县衙官印，共盖印四处，其中两枚分别在“验契价玖千两正”笔迹上和各人签名下方。另外两枚印章为一半，左侧半个印章应是与契尾相连的骑缝章，右侧半个印章则是与税契相连的骑缝章。各人签名下方的一枚黑文方印的印文显示，乾隆三十二年十一月（1767年12月21日—1768年1月19日）已支付360两税银。

Sale papers for Huilan Bridge property Deed poll. A deed-poll by Wen Tzu-kuan (Wen Ziguan), April 1766, drafted by Ch’en P’ing-k’e (Chen Pingke), for the irrevocable sale of his property at the foot of Huilan Bridge to Cai zhai (Cai family). The tax on the deed of sale of Tls 9000 is confirmed by Lu, Magistrate of Nanhai County, Canton. A stamp indicates that the payment of a tax of Tls 360 was made in the 11th month of the 32nd year of Xinglong’s reign (December 1767). 1 item; Fair condition, but damage by insects.

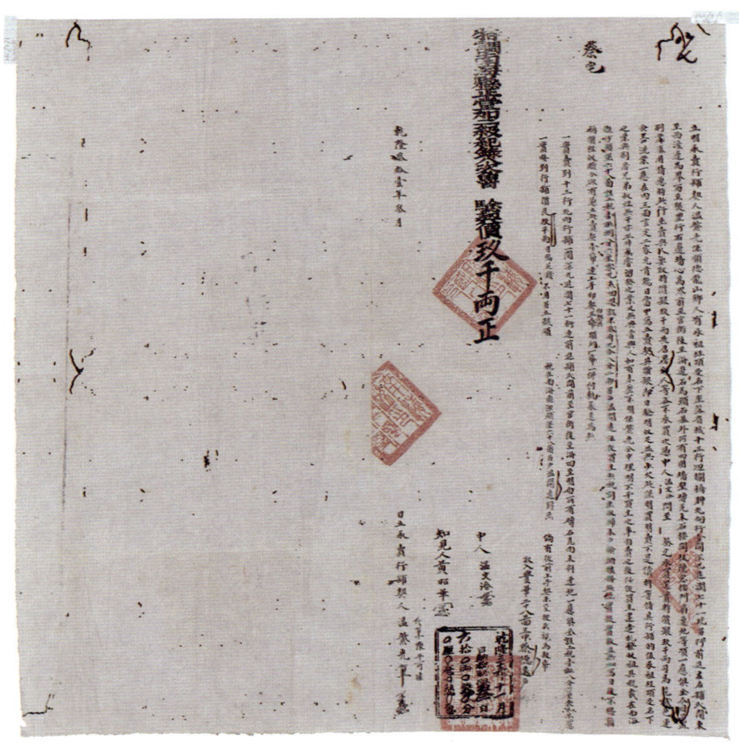

① 中人：温文洽（签字）；知见人：黄昭华（签字）；永卖行铺契人：温紫光笔（签字）；代笔：陈平可（签字）。

② 聚丰行：行商蔡国辉，乾隆二十四年（1759）成立，后欠夷人番银十六万六千两，乾隆四十九年（1784）倒闭。

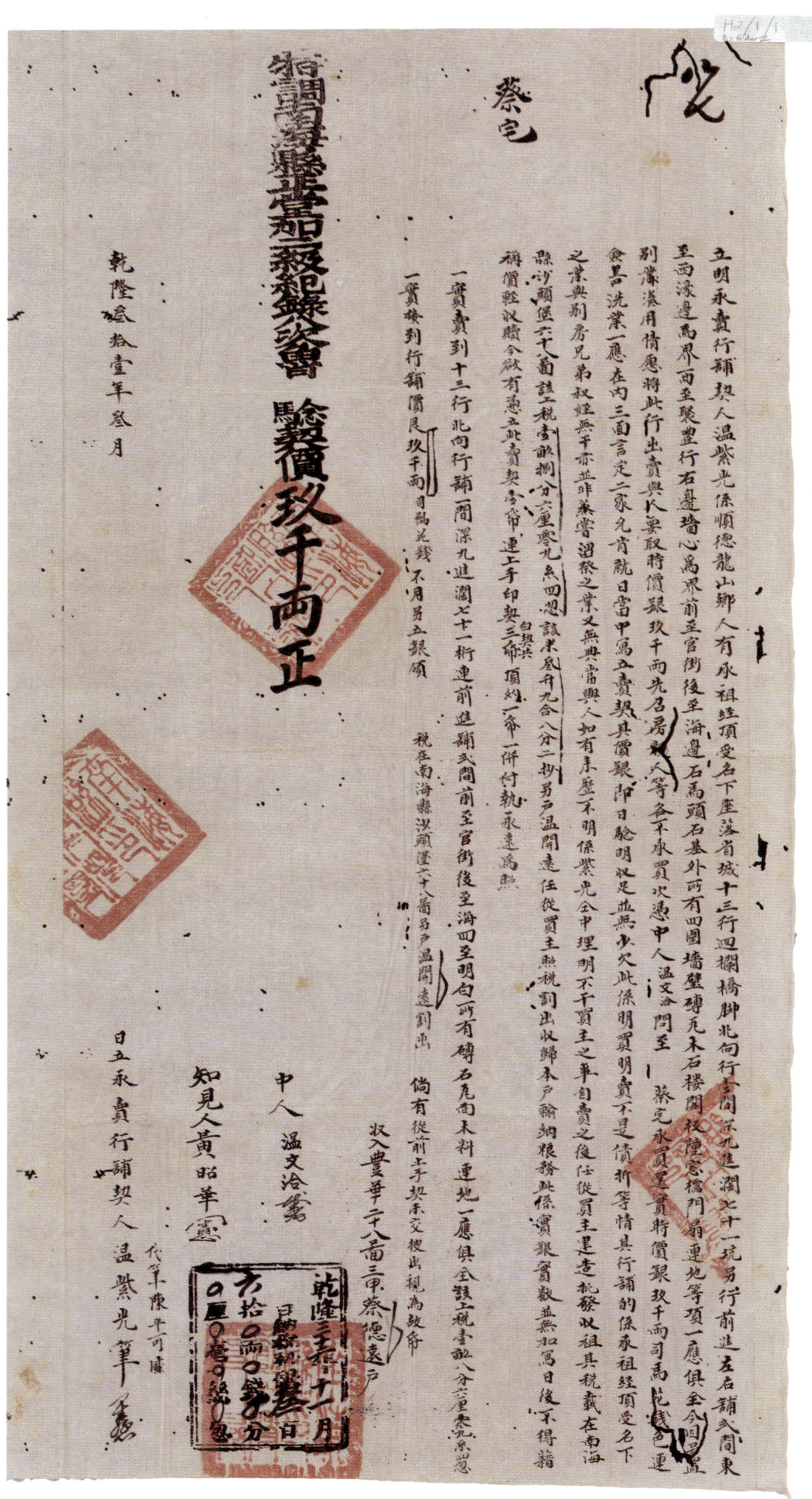

蔡宅

立明承賣行鋪契人温紫光係順德龍山鄉人有承祖經項受名下坐落省城十三行迴欄橋脚北向行鋪壹間深九進濶七十一坑另行前進左右鋪弍間東至西濠邊為界西至聚豐行右邊墻心為界前至官街後至海邊石碼頭石基外所有四圍墻壁磚瓦木石樓閣杉壁窓櫺門扇連地等項一應俱全今因要置別業湊用情願將此行出賣與人要取時價銀玖千両先召房親人等各不承買次憑中人温文洽問至　蔡宅承買足實時價銀玖千両司馬花錢色連食墨□洗業一應在內三面言定二家允肯就日當中寫立賣契具價銀即日驗明收足並無少欠此係明買明賣不是債折等情其行鋪的係承祖經項受名下之業與別房兄弟叔姪無干亦並非蒸嘗瀏祭之業又無典當與人如有來歷不明係紫光全中理明不干買主之事自賣之後任從買主建造批發收租其稅載在南海縣沙頭堡六十八啚該工稅壹畝捌分六厘零九毫四忽該米壹升九合八勺二抄另戶温開遠任從買主照稅割出收歸本戶輸納粮務此係實銀實數並無加寫日後不得藉稱價輕收贖今欲有憑立此賣契壹帋連上手印契三帋白契共頂約一帋一併付執永遠為照

一實賣到十三行北向行鋪一間深九進濶七十一桁連前進鋪弍間前至官街後至海四至明白所有磚石瓦面木料連地一應俱全該工稅壹畝八分六厘零九毫四忽

稅在南海縣沙頭堡六十八啚另戶温開遠割出　倘有從前上手契未交抽出視為故帋

一實接到行鋪價艮玖千両司碼花錢不用另立銀領

特調南海縣正堂加三級紀錄四次曾　驗契價玖千両正

收入豐華二十八啚三甲蔡德遠戶

中人　温文洽（押）

知見人黃昭華（押）

乾隆叁拾壹年叁月

日立承賣行鋪契人温紫光（押）

代筆陳平可據

乾隆三十[illegible]年十一月　日納[illegible]　六拾○両○錢○分○厘○毫○絲○忽

（局部图）

2. 乾隆三十二年蔡德远购买回澜桥房产的契尾[①]（H2/1/2）

乾隆三十二年十一月（1767年12月21日—1768年1月19日），蔡德远购买回澜桥房屋的契尾。契尾由布政使司统一印发，编列号数，其中有如下说明："前半幅照常细书业户等姓名、买卖田房数目、价银税银若干；后半幅于空白处预钤司印，以投税时将契价税银数目大字填写钤印之处。令业户看明，当面骑字截开，前半幅给业户收执，后半幅同季册汇送布政司查核。"

Tail of deed. A tail of a deed (the official endorsement of the transaction) for H2/1/1, issued by Wang, Magistrate of Nanhai County, Canton, December 1767, numbered 87, including the official stamps of Nanhai County and another office. 1 item. 1767

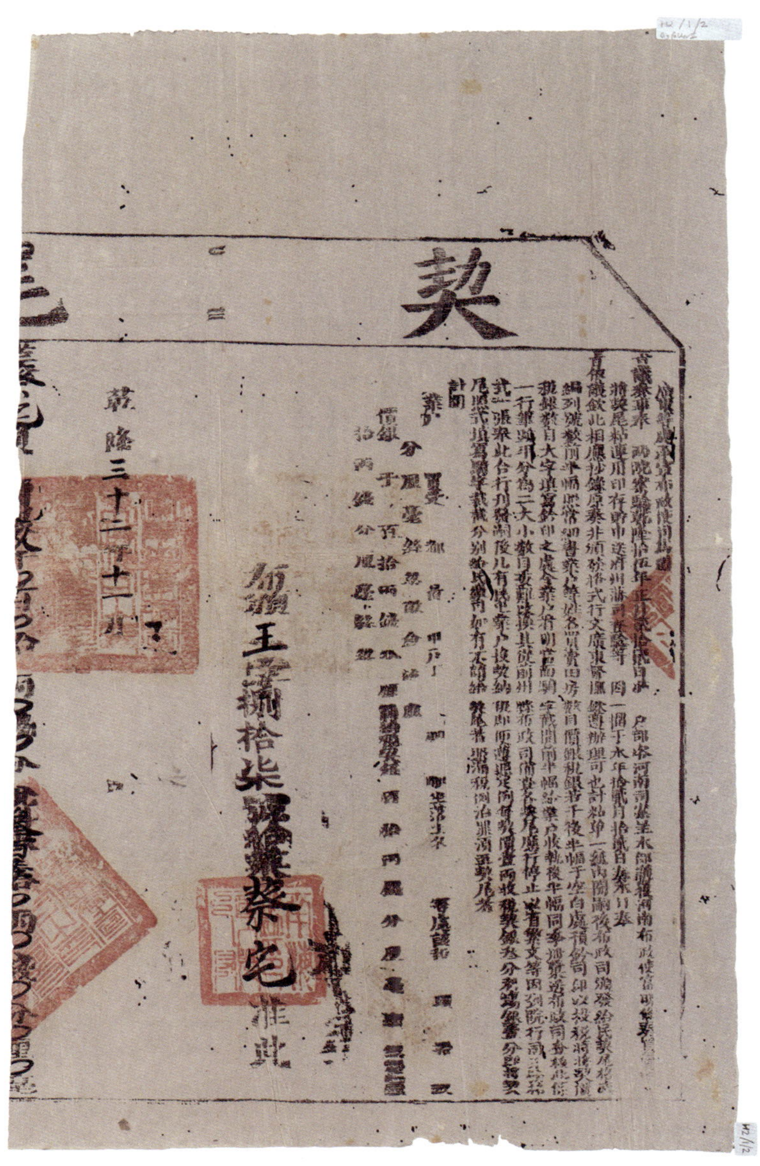

① 卖方：温紫光。买方：蔡德远。

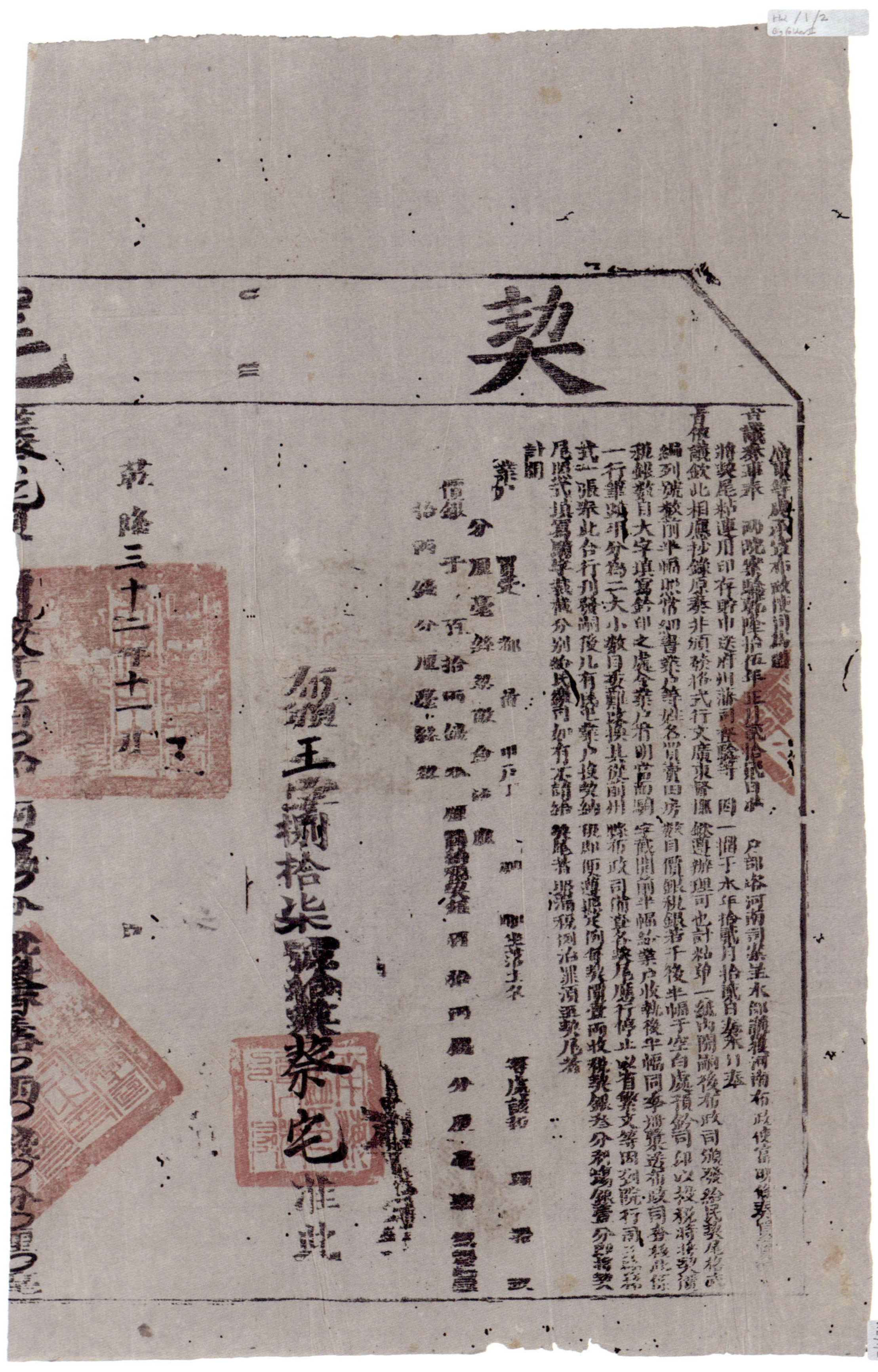

（局部图）

3. 乾隆三十二年蔡德远购买回澜桥房产的卖主推照①（H2/1/3）

乾隆三十二年十一月（1767年12月21日—1768年1月19日），此为蔡德远购买温开远回澜桥脚房产的卖主推照，标明此次买卖房产的位置为“沙头堡六十八图”，纳税面积为“一亩八分六厘〇毫九丝四忽”。

Land tax registration certificate. A registration certificate for the transfer of the land tax due on the Huilan Bridge property which has been sold by Wen K’ai-yan, known as Tzu-kuang, to the Ts’ai (Cai) family, headed by Ts’ai Te-yuan (Cai Deyaun), December 1767. The new proprietor is liable for the payment of the tax, numbered 87.

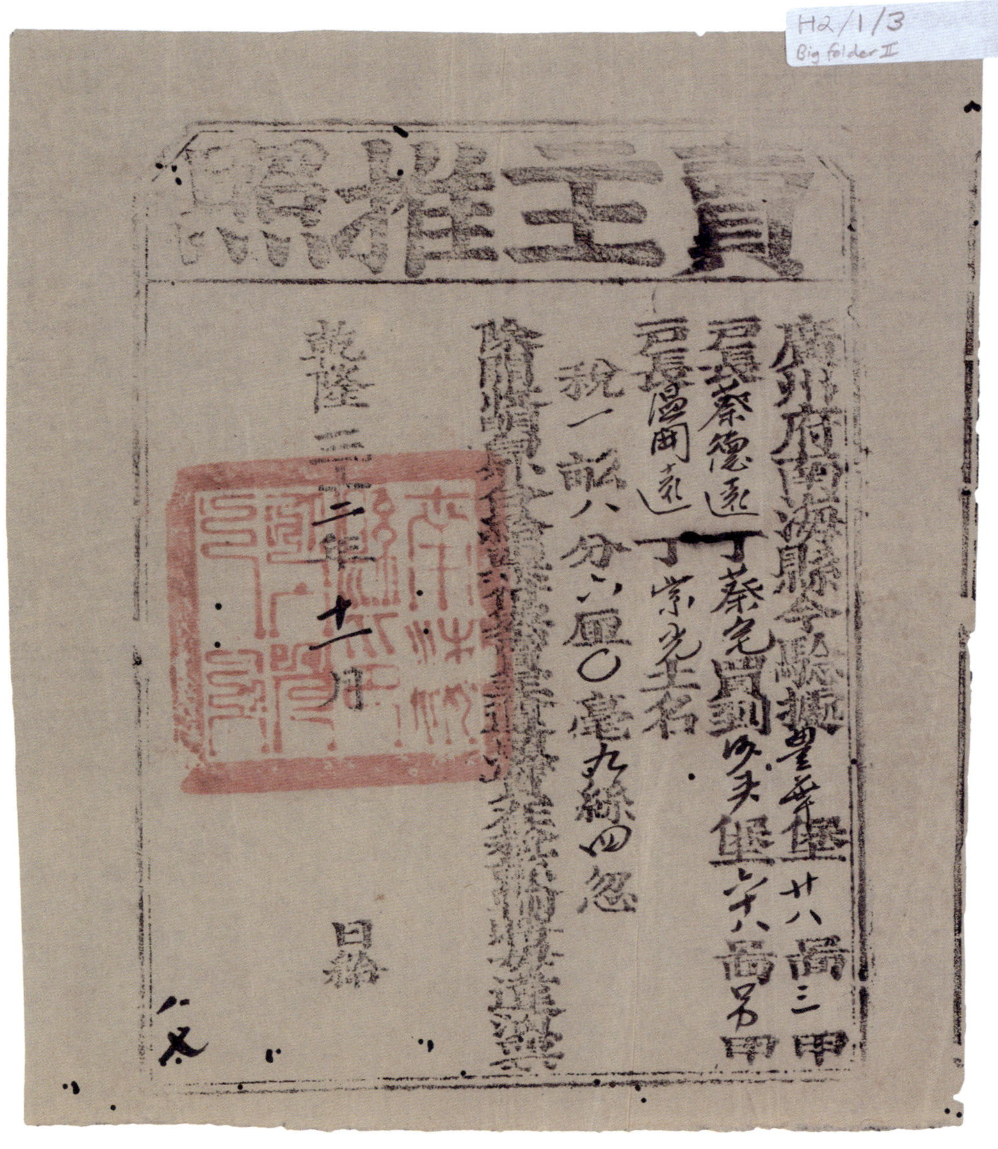

賣主推照

廣州府南海縣[illegible]堡廿八圖三甲

戶長蔡德遠　丁蔡兆買到沙頭堡六十八圖另甲

戶長溫開遠　丁崇光土名

稅一畝八分六厘〇毫九絲四忽

乾隆三十二年十一月　日給

H2/1/3
Big folder II

---

① 卖主推照：清代房产交易的税务登记证明。

4. 乾隆三十一年蔡德远购买回澜桥房产的税契（H2/1/4）

乾隆三十一年（1766）三月，蔡德远购买温开远房产的税契，税契字第87号。

Tax certificate. A certificate (Shui-ch'I) of the payment in the form of manony and grain of a legal tax on the sale of property, issued by the Magistrate of Nanhai County, Kwangchow fu, to the Ts'ai (Cai) family, for the Huilan Bridge property, December 1767[①].1 item.

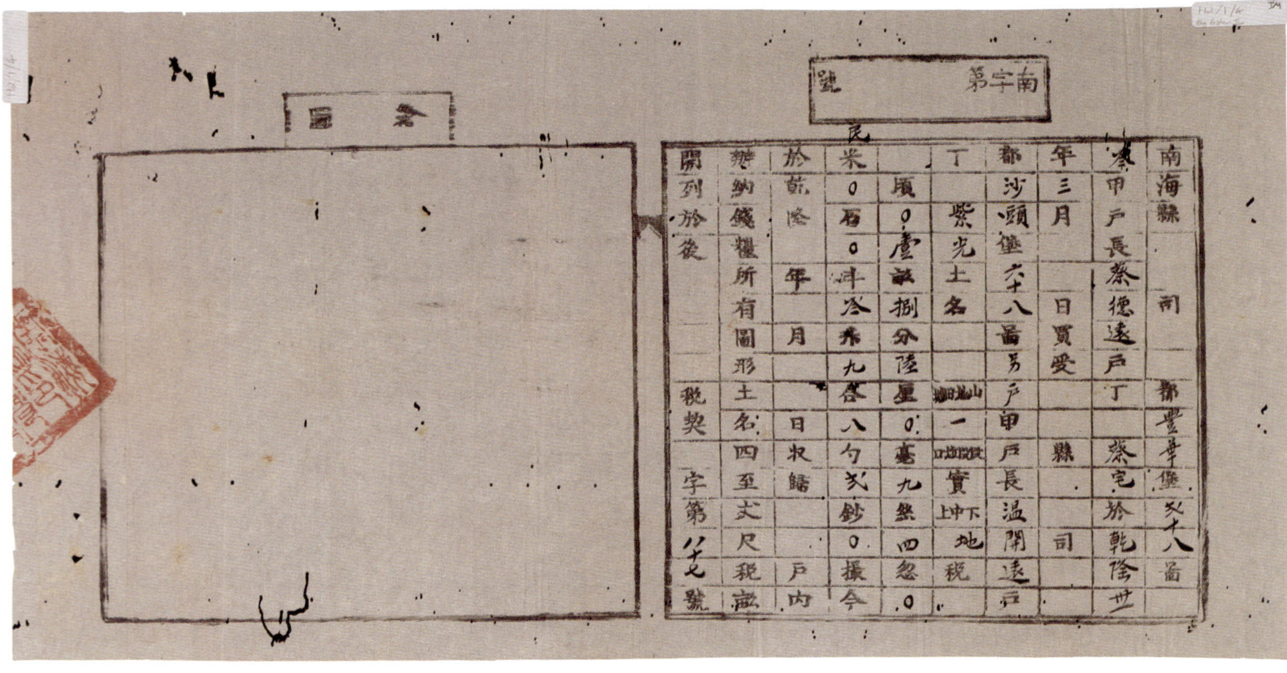
南字第　　號

南海縣　　司　都豐亭堡又十八啚
承甲戶長蔡德遠戶丁　蔡宅於乾隆卅
年三月　日買受　縣　司
都沙頭堡六十八啚另戶甲戶長溫開遠戶
丁　紫光土名　一　實　上中下地稅
項　0壹畝捌分陸釐0毫九絲四忽0
民米0石0斗叁升九合八勺弍鈔0撮令
於乾隆　年　月　日收歸　戶內
辦納錢糧所有圖形土名四至丈尺稅畝
開列於後　稅契　字第八十七號

① 勘误：英文提要日期为1767年12月（December 1767），按原中文文献“乾隆卅一年三月”，此时间有误。

5. 乾隆四十一年蔡家回澜桥房产售予潘宅的卖契[①]（H2/1/5）

乾隆四十一年（1776）六月房屋契据。1775年4月[②]蔡璋把回澜桥脚的房屋以15,000两的价格永卖给潘家的正式签署的契据。房产旧为集和行的商馆，房产的契税已由南海县张县令确认完税。契约上的一枚钤印显示，乾隆四十一年（1776）六月已经支付了契税600两。此外有两条附加说明：房屋的六大庭院原属义和馆，嘉庆十三年六月十二日（1808年8月3日）被卖给西成行；房产剩余部分仍属潘家。

Deed poll. An officially endorsed deed-poll of Ts'ai Chang (Cai Zhang) et la for the irrevocable sale of his property at the foot of Huilan Bridge to the P'an (Pan) family for Tls 15,000, April 1775. The property is currently a merchant house named Chi-ho hong (Jihe). The tax on the deed of sale is confirmed by Ch'ang (Chang), Magistrate of Nanhai County, Canton. A stamp indicates that the payment of a tax of Tls 600 was made in the 6th month of the 41st year of Qinglong's reign (July 1776). There are two additional notes, one of which indicates that the six courtyards used to be I-ho Kuan, which was sold to Exchin on the 12th day, 6th month, 13th year of Jiaqing's reign (3 August 1808), the rest of property belonging to the P'an (Pan) family.1 item.

---

① 此卖契署印为南海县衙官印，共盖印四处：其中两枚完整地分别盖在"验契价壹万伍千两"和表明完税时间及税银的钤印上，左侧有一枚与契尾相连的骑缝章，右侧有一枚与税契相连的骑缝章。

② 此时间由英文提要翻译而来，为公历时间，因无法直接推出阴历月份时间，故此处直录为公历时间。

二十

立明永賣行屋契人蔡璋等今有承父遺下行屋一所坐落太平門外十三行街迴瀾橋現開集和行坐南向北上蓋自下地基共深連水亭十一進前門左右舖面二間每進一排三間前五進每進闊五拾九桁中心二進每進闊六十三桁後四進每進闊七十九桁每進上樓下房後進水亭各進門窗板障天井石砌一切俱全東至河澇西至顏宅行墻心為界前至官街後至官河四至明白兹因闵餉急需母子商議將此行屋出賣先召房親人等各不願受次憑中友引就與　潘宅承買一寔還到行價銀壹萬伍千両良水花不司碼連簽書洗業折席花枝一應在內二家允肯即日當中三面立契其銀的係璋親手接回銷驗明白並無低偽短少其行亦即日當中交與　潘宅掌管另自批租永為己業此係明買明賣并非債折等情實銀實契亦無加寫乃屋係此行的係璋兄弟承父遺下之業與叔兄弟姪人等無干亦不是蒸嘗流祭物業又無重復典當情弊日後不得称言價輕索找索贖如有來歷不明以及別人爭論係璋等同中理明不干買主之事今欲有憑立此永賣行屋文契一紙連上手印契一紙一併交與　潘宅收執永遠為照

此義和夷館共深六大進已於嘉慶拾叁年陸月拾貳日賣與　西成行管業其餘尚存夷館後坐南向北棧屋壹間深肆進左右舖弍間各深壹進仍係潘宅管業批明文契為據隨於

嘉慶拾肆年七月十二日收足價銀書立大契交執

此行屋一門深四進左右舖二間各深一進
經分二房培春堂管業收租批明為照

一稅載在　　堡　　畨戶內聽憑收割

一實收到永賣行屋價銀花不壹萬伍千両不再另立銀領

廣州府南海縣正堂常　驗契價銀壹萬伍千兩

中友蔡煥臣（押）

同賣行屋長姪　（押）

廣東等處承宣布政使司為遵

6. 乾隆四十一年潘宅购买回澜桥房产的契尾[①]（H2/1/6）

乾隆四十一年（1776）六月，潘家购买蔡家回澜桥房屋的契尾，与卖契粘连并盖有官府的骑缝章。契尾由布政使司统一印发，编列号数，其中有如下说明："前半幅照常细书业户等姓名、买卖田房数目、价银税银若干；后半幅于空白处预钤司印，于投税时将契价税银数目大字填写钤印之处。令业户看明，当面骑字截开，前半幅给业户收执，后半幅同季册汇送布政司查核。"

Tail of deed. A tail of a deed (the official endorsement of the transaction) for H2/1/5, issued by the office of the provincial treasurer to the P'an (Pan) family, July 1776, numbered Ben/20, and including the stamp of the Magistrate of Nanhai County, Canton.1 item.

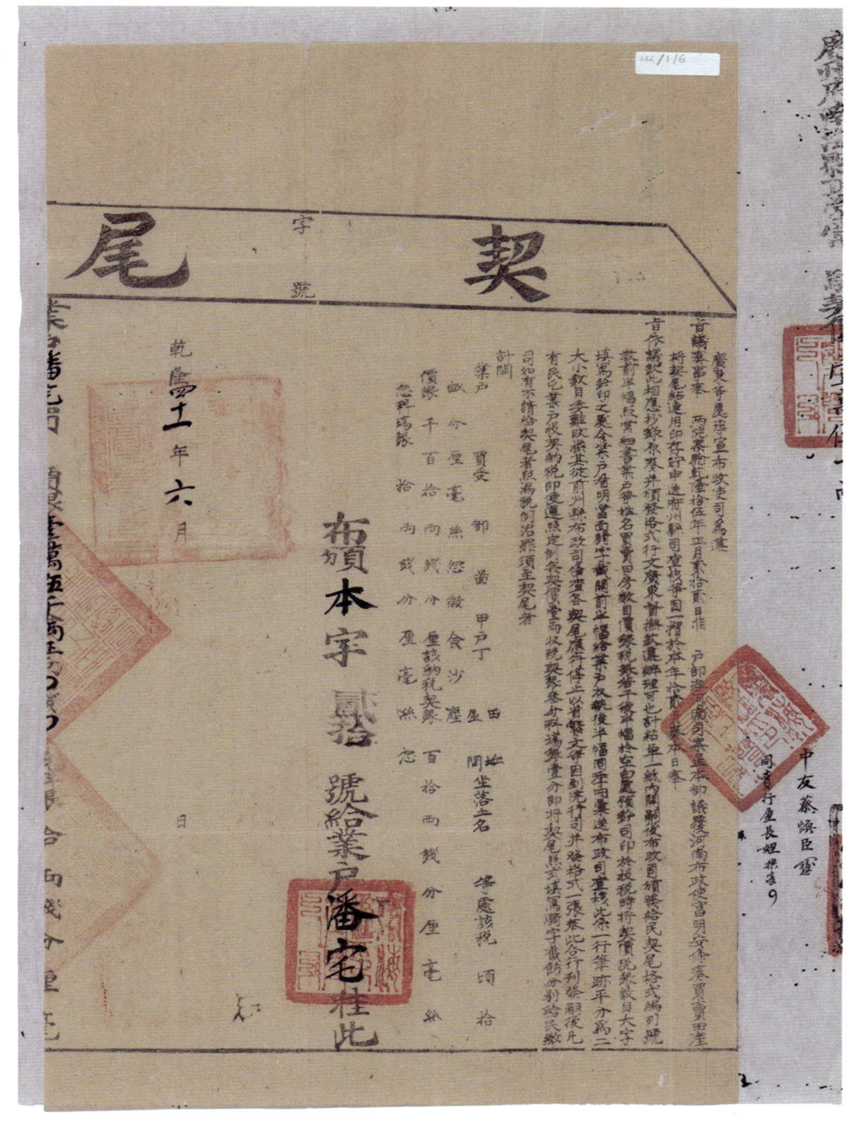

契尾

字 號

布 本字貳拾號給業戶潘宅 准此

乾隆四十一年六月 日

① 本份契尾盖有两枚完整的官府署印，其中一枚盖在新业主名"潘宅"上，另一枚盖在房屋完税日期"乾隆四十一年六月"上面。

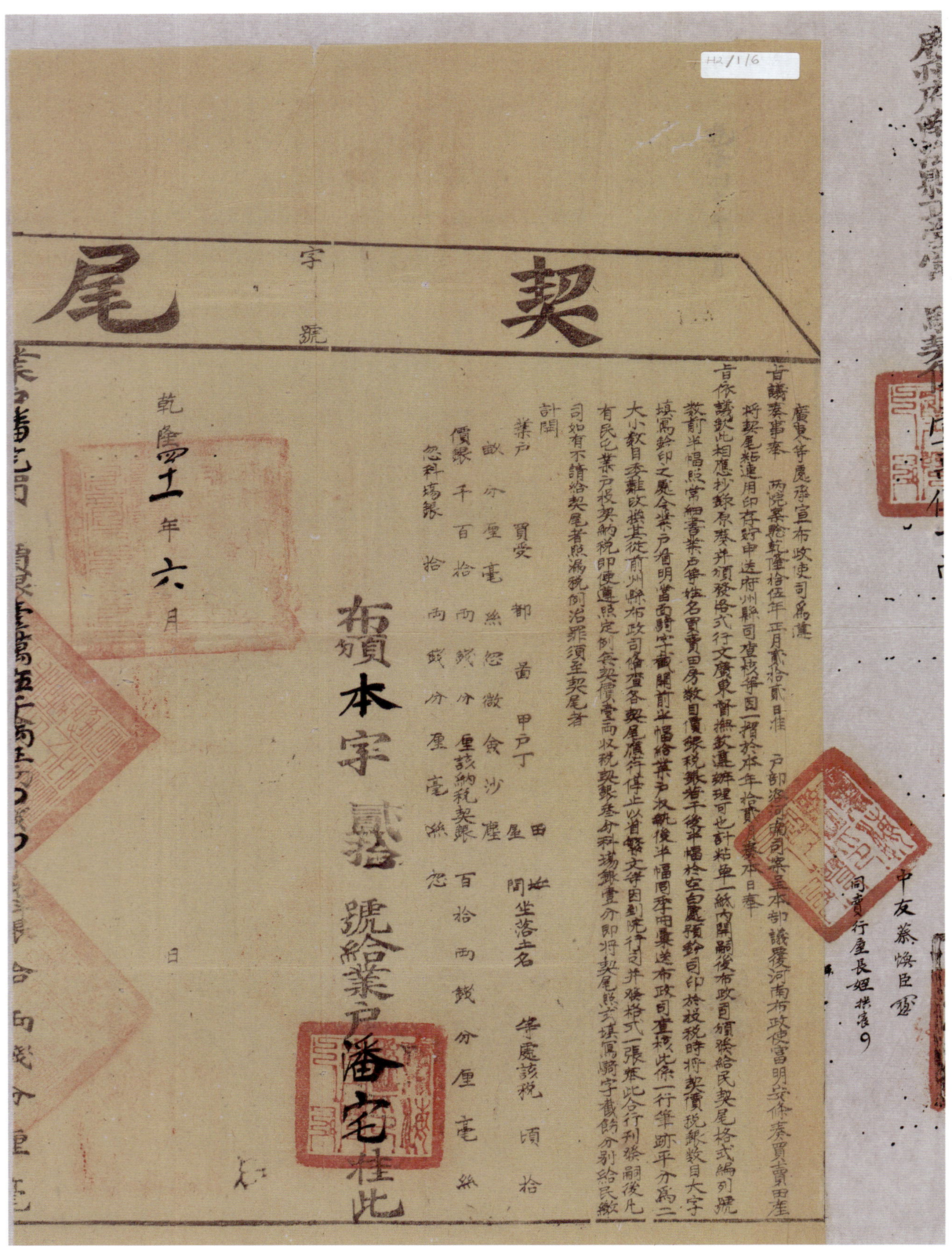

（局部图）

7. 乾隆四十一年潘宅购买回澜桥房产的卖主推照①（H2/1/7）

乾隆四十一年（1776）六月，潘宅购买蔡家回澜桥房屋的卖主推照。蔡璋回澜桥的房屋卖给潘家，并登记房产交易的土地税，新业主有义务付清税银。

Land tax registration certificate. A registration certificate for the transfer of the land tax due on the Huilan Bridge property, July 1776, which has been sold by Ts'ai Chang (Cai Zhang) to the P'an (Pan) family. The new proprietor is liable for the payment of the tax, numbered 20. 1 item.

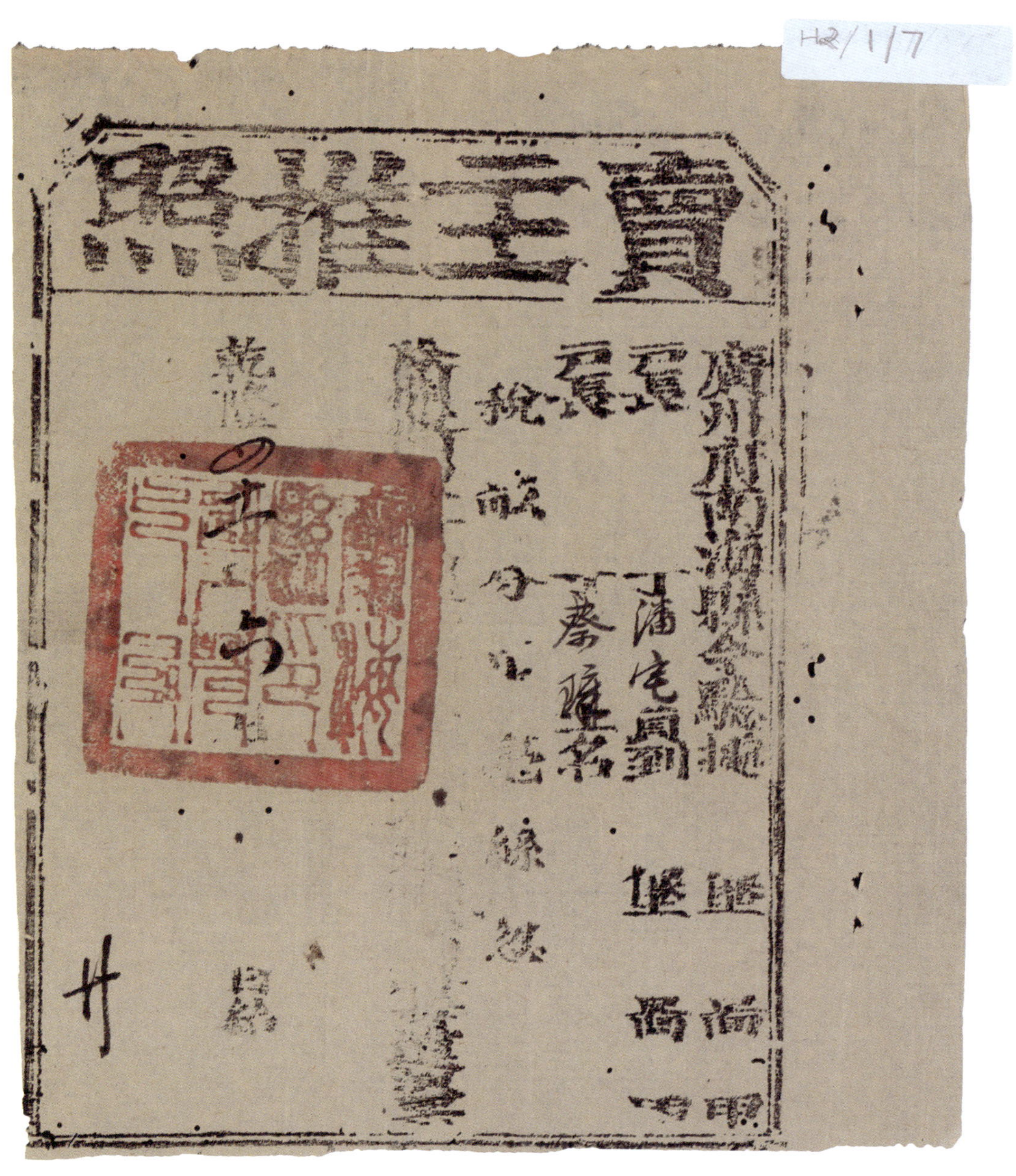
H2/1/7

賣主推照

廣州府南海縣令據　堡　圖　甲

買主潘宅戶　堡　圖　甲

賣主蔡璋名

稅　畝　分　厘　毫　絲　忽

乾隆四十一年六月廿　日給

---

① “堡”与“图”之间没有填写具体地址，是因蔡家当初购买此房产的卖主推照已清楚标明其具体地理位置为“沙头堡六十八图”。

8. 乾隆四十一年潘宅购买回澜桥房产的税契①（H2/1/8）

乾隆四十一年（1776）六月，由南海县县令签发的关于潘家在回澜桥房屋买卖的税契。

Tax certificate. A certificate (Shui-ch'I) of the payment in the form of manony and grain of a legal tax on the sale of property, issued by the Magistrate of Nanhai County, to the P'an (Pan) family for the Huilan Bridge property, July 1776.1 item.

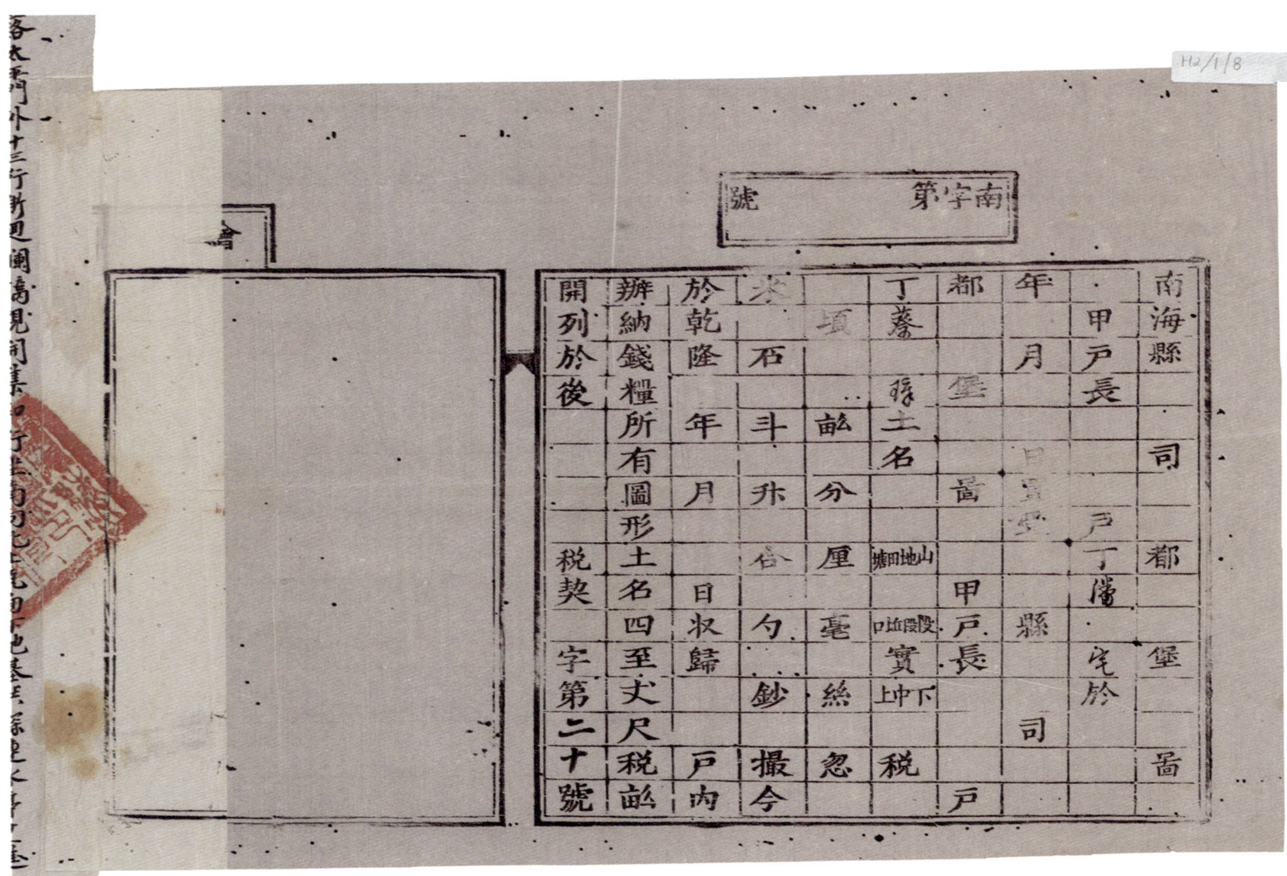

H2/1/8

南字第　號

南海縣　司　都　堡　啚
甲戶長　戶丁潘　宅於
年　月　縣　司
都　堡　啚　甲戶長　戶
丁蔡　土名　山地田塘　段　上中下　稅
頃　畝　分　厘　毫　絲　忽
石　斗　升　合　勺　鈔　撮　今
於乾隆　年　月　日　收歸　戶內
辦納錢糧所有圖形土名四至丈尺稅畝
開列於後　稅契　字第二十號

① 此税契标示为“第二十号”，没有官印，但内容写明是纳税人由蔡璋转至潘宅，与潘宅购买蔡璋回澜桥房产的正契相连并盖有骑缝章，时间应亦为乾隆四十一年（1776）六月。“堡”与“图”之间没有填写具体地址，是因蔡家最初购买此房产的税契已清楚标明其具体地理位置为“沙头堡六十八图”。

9. 乾隆四十一年潘宅购买回澜桥房产的税契副本[①]（H2/1/9）

乾隆四十一年（1776）六月，由南海县县令签发的关于潘家在回澜桥房屋买卖的税契副本。

Tax certificate. A copy of H2/1/8, a certificate (Shui-ch'I) of the payment in the form of manony and grain of a legal tax on the sale of property, issued by the Magistrate of Nanhai County, to the P'an (Pan) family for the Huilan Bridge property, July 1776.1 item.

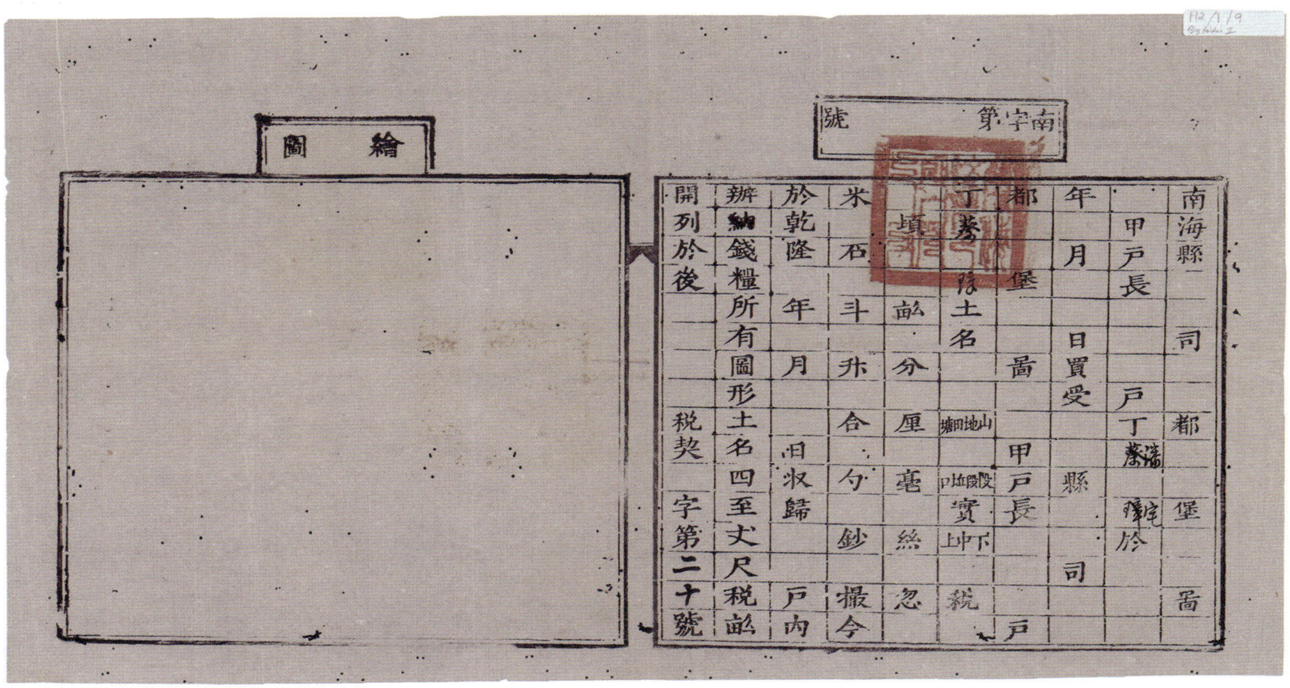
繪圖

南字第　號

南海縣　司　都　堡　啚
甲戶長　戶丁　　於
年　月　日買受　縣　司
都　堡　啚　甲戶長　戶
丁　土名　山地田塘　實　上中下　稅
頃　畝　分　厘　毫　絲　忽
米　石　斗　升　合　勺　鈔　撮　令
於乾隆　年　月　日收歸　戶內
辦納錢糧所有圖形土名四至丈尺稅畝
開列於後　稅契　字第二十號

① 此为文献“乾隆四十一年潘宅购买回澜桥房产的税契”副本，证上盖有官印。

10. 约道光五年回澜桥潘培春堂房产的说明[①]（H2/1/10）

此文书简要记述了潘宅从蔡璋处购买回澜桥房产的交易时间、地理位置、契据清单以及目前的租赁情况。

Copy of deed of sale. A sheet of wrapping paper containing a brief account of the deed of sale for the Huilan Bridge property, including the date of transfer, the property's location, a list of the title deeds enclosed, and the current position of the tenancy, recording that the present occupier is John Henry Cox (foreign clock maker). The document is undated, but originates from after 1782.

---

① 此文书内容有："查此行系旧义和行，后七进现租与整钟夷人及各国居住，前四进系租与旧集和行。此义和夷馆深六进，已卖与西成行管业，其余夷馆后栈屋一间，深四进，左右铺一间，各深一进，仍系潘宅管业。"其中提及的西成行成立于嘉庆九年（1804），可知此文书出现时间必定晚于1804年（英国剑桥大学图书馆撰写的"英文提要"对该文献的时间判断为1782年以后）。此文书应是东升行购买潘培春堂回澜桥房屋之前，找相关部门对此房产出售的合法性进行核验，并对此房产的来龙去脉撰写详细说明（参H2/1/11件），时间疑为1825年。

乾隆肆拾年叁月潘宅買受蔡瑋等行屋乙所
深十乙進前門左右鋪面二間前五進每濶五十九
桁中二進每濶六十三桁後四進每濶七十九桁
坐落太平門外十三行街廻欄橋脚坐南向北
契價銀壹萬伍千兩
内賣契乙紙乾隆四十年叁月印契本字貳拾號
上手印契乙紙
查此行係將義和行後七進現租與澄鐘夷人及各國居住
前四進係租與蕭崗集和行
此義和夷館深六進已賣與西成行管業其餘夷館後棧屋一間深四
進左右[illegible]一間各深一進仍係潘宅管業

（局部图）

11. 道光五年回澜桥潘培春堂房产售予东生行所立的定帖[①]（H2/1/11）

道光五年七月初八日（1825年8月21日），潘培春堂关于永售回澜桥的商馆晋孚行及地皮给东生行所订立的最终契约，包括一张300两的定银收据。

Deed-roll. The final draft version of the deed-roll of P’an P’ei-ch’un (Pan Peichun) for the irrevocable sale of his merchant house Chin-fu (Jinfu) Hong and its ground at Huilan Bridge to Tung-sheng (Dongsheng) Hong, 21 August 1828[②], including a record of the receipt of a deposit of $300.1 item.

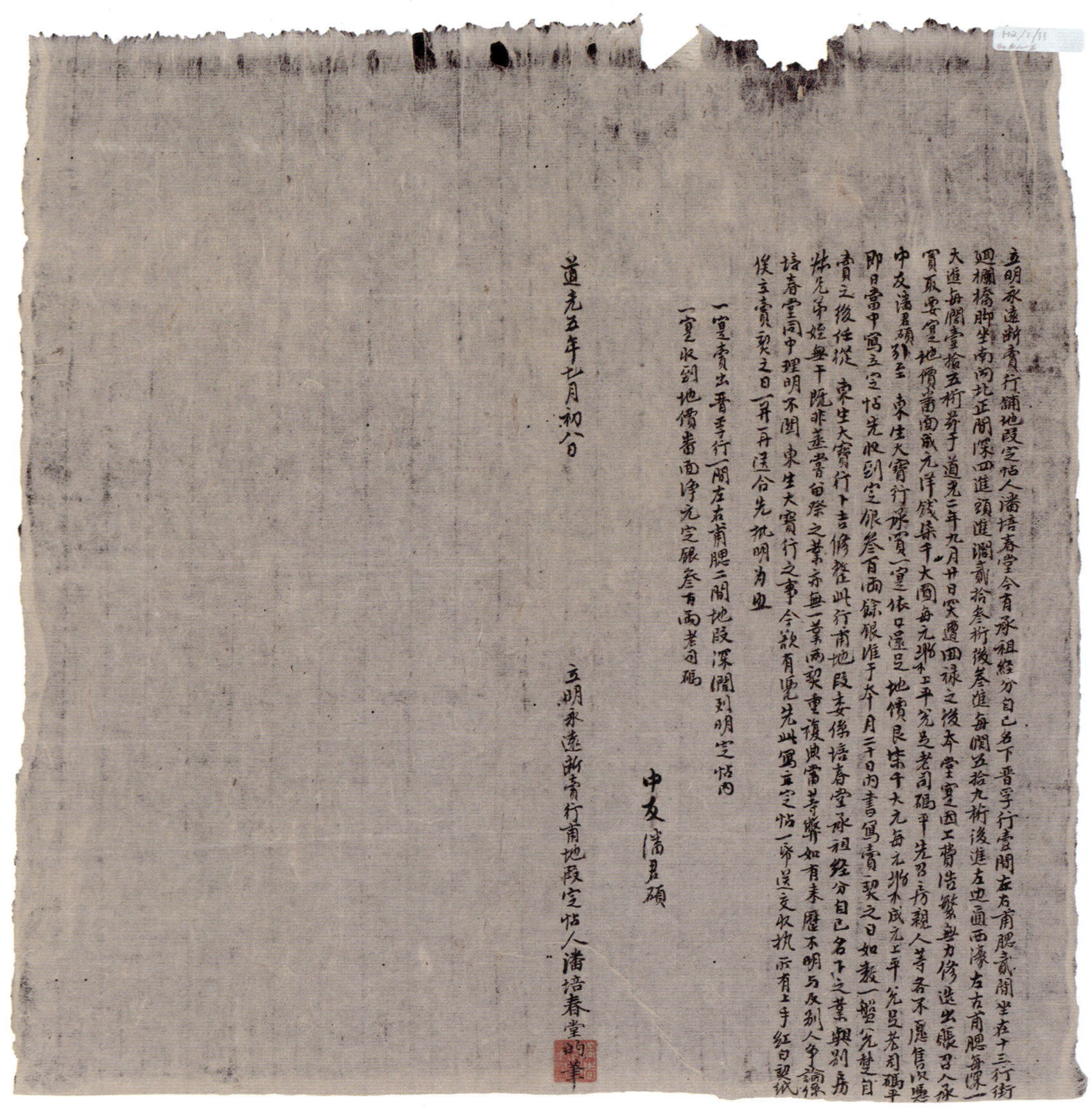

立明永遠斷賣行舖地段定帖人潘培春堂今有承祖經分自己名下晉孚行壹間左右甬腮貳間坐在十三行街廻欄橋脚坐南向北正間深四進頭進闊貳拾叁桁後叁進每闊五拾九桁後進左邊面西滴右古甬腮每深一大進每闊壹拾五桁并于道光三年九月廿日突遭回祿之後本堂定因工費浩繁無力修造出賬召人承買取要定地價番面銀元洋錢柒千大圓每元柒錢上平兑足老司碼平先召房親人等各不愿承受後憑中友潘君碩引至東生大寶行承買一定依口還足地價艮柒千大元每元柒錢上平兑足老司碼平即日當中寫立定帖先收到定銀叁百兩餘銀准于本月二十日內書寫賣契之日如數一盤兑楚自賣之後任從東生大寶行卜吉修整此行甬地段委係培春堂承祖經分自己名下之業與別房叔兄弟姪無干既非蒸嘗自祭之業亦無一業兩契重複典當等弊如有來歷不明與及別人爭論係培春堂同中理明不關東生大寶行之事今欲有憑先此寫立定帖一帋送交收執所有上手紅白契紙俟立賣契之日一并一再送合先批明為照

一定賣出晉孚行一間左右甬腮二間地段深闊列明定帖內

一定收到地價番面淨元定銀叁百兩老司碼

中友潘君碩

道光五年七月初八日

立明永遠斷賣行甬地段定帖人潘培春堂的筆

---

① 本契约没有官府署印，是潘培春堂单方所立的定帖，有中介人签字，并盖有潘培春堂印章。买方：东生行。十三行行商之一，行商刘德章，商名章官（Chunqua），嘉庆十六年（1811）成立，道光年间倒闭。卖方：潘培春堂，为著名行商家族潘家分支二房第三世潘正绵所用印章。潘正绵（1786—1826年），号韶石，嘉庆十八年（1813）举人，拣选知县，即用内部员外郎，例授文林郎。正绵之子潘仕徵（1809—1852年），字聘三，号莘农，候选盐知事，著有《培春堂吟草》。

② 勘误：英国剑桥大学图书馆所撰的“英文提要”将该文献的时间写成1828年，应为1825年之误。

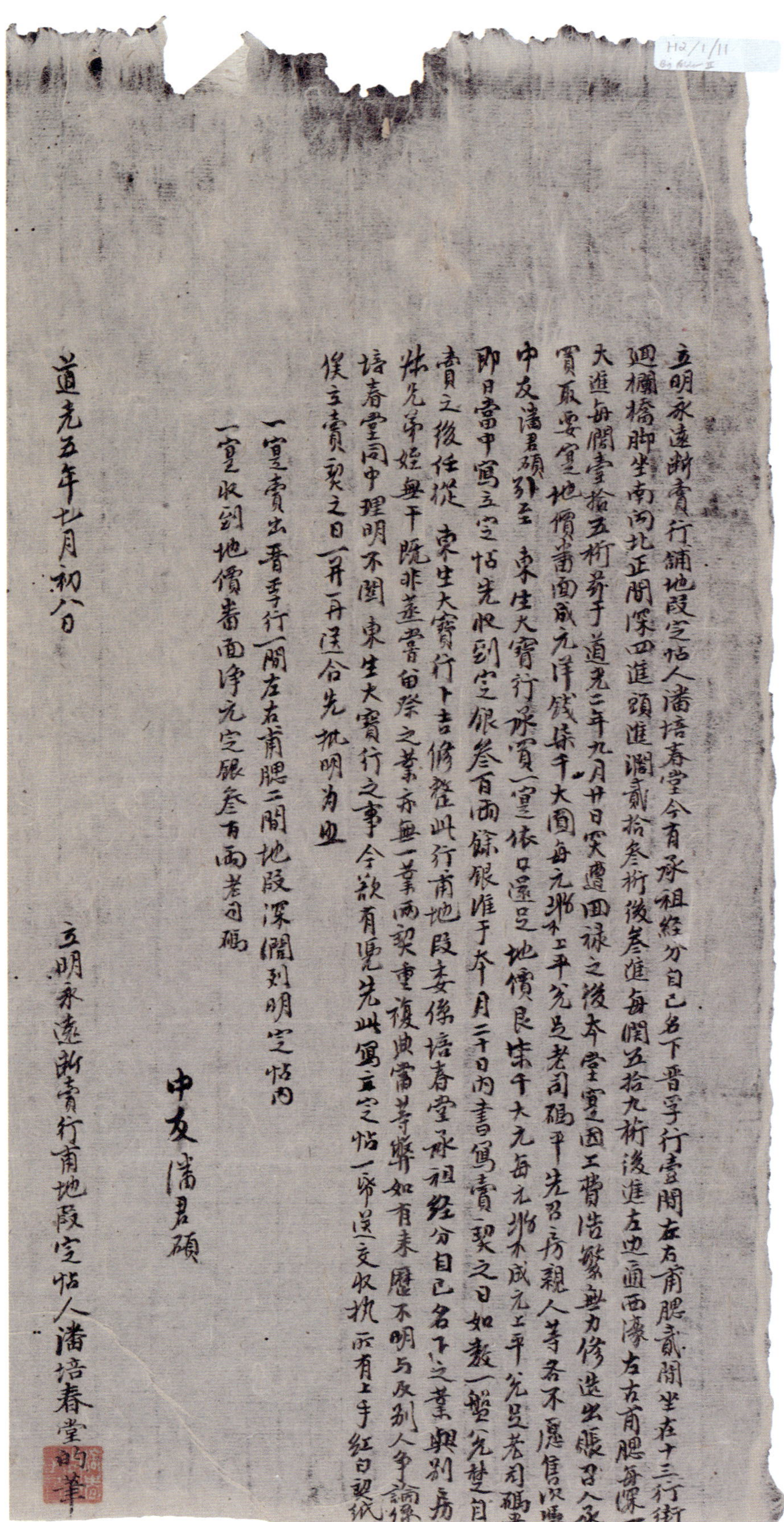

立明永遠斷賣行舖地段字帖人潘培春堂今有承祖經分自己名下晉孚行壹間左右甫腮貳間坐在十三行街廻欄橋脚坐南向北正間深四進頭進濶貳拾叁桁後叁進每濶五拾九桁後進左邊通西濠左右甫腮每深一大進每濶壹拾五桁於于道光二年九月廿日突遭回祿之後本堂實因工費浩繁無力修造出賬召人承買取要實地價番面成元洋錢柒千大圓每元淅木上平兌足老司碼平先召房親人等各不愿售次憑中友潘君碩引至東生大寶行承買（實）依口還足地價良柒千大元每元淅木成元上平兌足老司碼平即日當中寫立字帖先收到定銀叁百兩餘銀准于本月二十日內書寫賣契之日如數一盤（交）兌楚足自賣之後任從東生大寶行卜吉修整此行甫地段妥係培春堂承祖經分自己名下之業與別房叔先弟姪無干既非蒸嘗留祭之業亦無一業兩契重複典當等弊如有來歷不明與及別人爭論係培春堂同中理明不關東生大寶行之事今欲有憑先此寫立字帖一紙交收執所有上手紅白契紙俟立賣契之日一并一再送合先批明為照

一實賣出晉孚行一間左右甫腮二間地段深濶列明字帖內

一實收到地價番面淨元定銀叁百兩老司碼

中友　潘君碩

道光五年七月初八日

立明永遠斷賣行甫地段字帖人潘培春堂的筆

（局部图）

12. 道光五年回澜桥潘培春堂房产售予东生行所立的卖契[1]（H2/1/12）

道光五年七月二十八日（1825年9月10日），潘培春堂将其在回澜桥的商馆晋孚行及其土地以番银7000元（即5005两白银）永卖给东生行的正式契约，盖有南海县令印章。

Deed-roll. An officially endorsed deed-roll of P’an P’ei-ch’un (Pan Peichun) for the irrevocable sale of his merchant house Chin-fu (Jinfu) Hong and its ground at Huilan Bridge to Tung-sheng (Dongsheng) Hong for $7000 (Tls 5005), 21 August 1825[2], endorsed by Hsu (xu), magistrate of Nanhai County. 1 item.

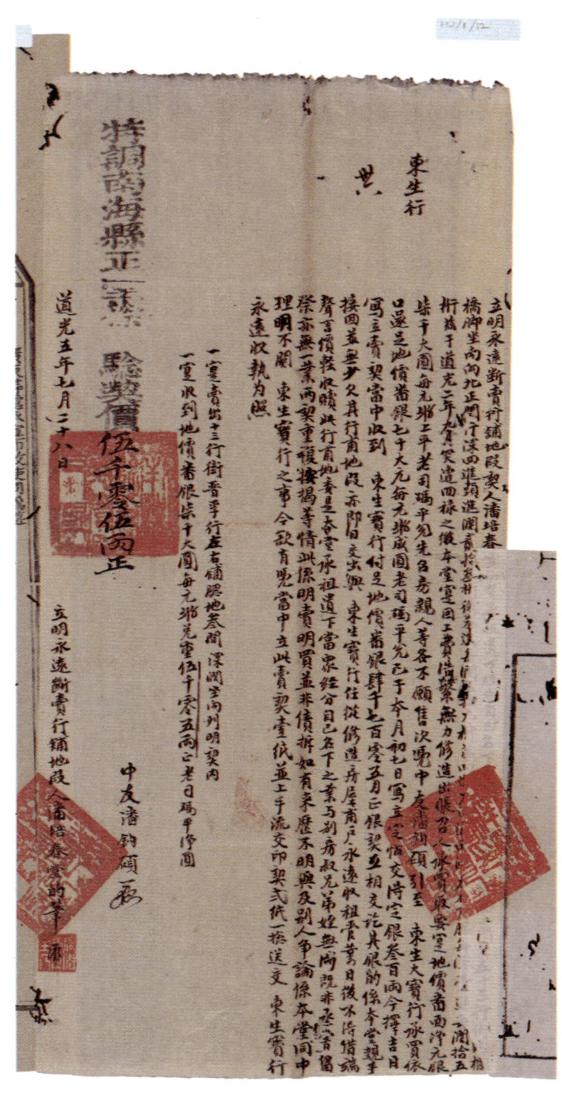
特調南海縣正堂
東生行
道光五年七月二十八日
驗契價伍千零伍兩正

---

① 卖契中注明“一，实收到地价番银柒千大圆，每元〦〡〥，兑重伍千零五两正，老司码平净圆”“验契价伍千零伍两正”（上面还加盖了红色官印）。可知当时七千元外国银元，兑换为中国白银即五千零五两。此卖契中使用的是中国特有的商业数字“花码”。这是南宋时期从算筹中分化出来的一种进位制计数系统，使用特殊符号来代表数字，汉字计数“一、二、三、四、五、六、七、八、九、十”，相对应的符号分别为“〡、〢、〣、〤、〥、〦、〧、〨、〩、十”，因其最早产生于苏州，故又称“苏州码子”。卖契中的“〧〡〥”即“715”，说明一千元外国银元兑换中国白银七百一十五两。

② 勘误：英文提要日期为1825年8月21日（21 August 1825），按原中文文献“道光五年七月二十八日”，应为1825年9月10日。

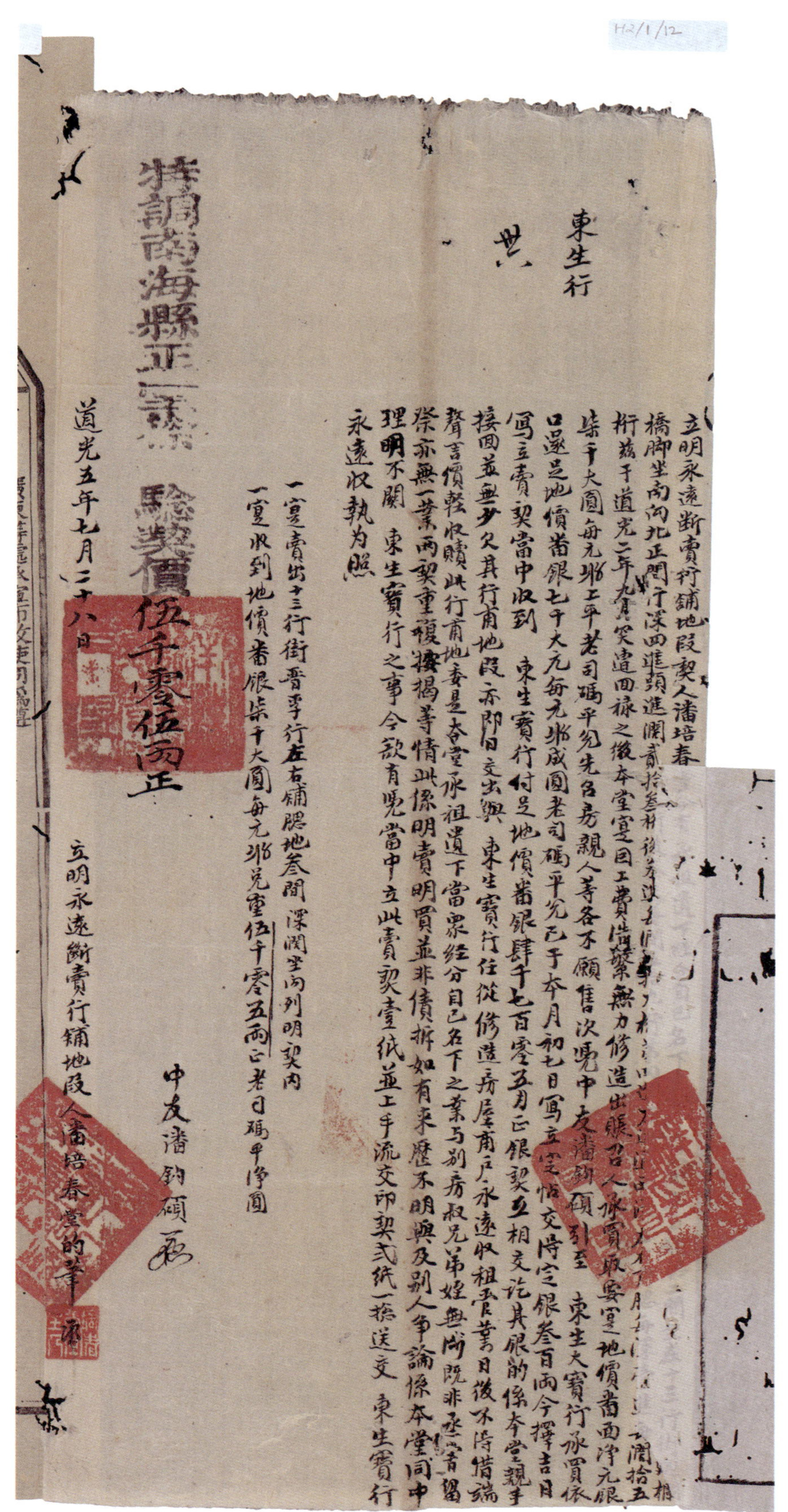

東生行

世

立明永遠斷賣行舖地段契人潘培春……
橋脚坐南向北正門行深四進頭進闊貳拾叁……拾五
桁茲于道光二年九月哭遣回祿之後本堂寔因工費浩繁無力修造出賬召人承買取要寔地價番面淨元銀
柒千大圓每元八錢工平老司碼平兌先召房親人等各不願售次憑中友潘鈞碩引至　東生大寶行承買依
口遂是地價番銀七千大元每元八錢成圓老司碼平兌己于本月初七日寫立定帖交得定銀叁百兩今擇吉日
寫立賣契當中收到　東生寶行付足地價番銀肆千七百零五兩正銀契兩相交訖其銀的係本堂親手
接回並無少欠其行舖地段亦即日交出與　東生寶行任從修造房屋商戶永遠收租管業日後不得借端
聲言價輕收贖此行舖地委是本堂承祖遺下當衆經分自己名下之業與別房叔兄弟侄無涉既非烝嘗留
祭亦無一業兩契重複按揭等情此係明賣明買並非債折如有來歷不明與及別人爭論係本堂同中
理明不關　東生寶行之事今欲有憑當中立此賣契壹紙並工手流交印契弍紙一揔送交　東生寶行
永遠收執為照

特調南海縣正堂　驗契價伍千零伍兩正

一宗賣出十三行街晉亨行左右舖腳地叁間深闊坐向列明契內
一宗收到地價番銀柒千大圓每元八錢兌重伍千零五兩正老司碼平淨圓

中友潘鈞碩　押

道光五年七月二十八日　立明永遠斷賣行舖地段人潘培春堂的筆

（局部图）

13. 道光六年东生行购买回澜桥房产的契尾①（H2/1/13）

道光六年（1826）七月，东生行购买回澜桥的契尾，盖有广州府南海县县令印章。

Tail of deed. A tail of deed (the official endorsement of the transaction) for H2/1/12, issued by the office of the provincial treasurer to Tung-sheng (Dongsheng) Hong, August 1826, numbered Shi/36, and including the stamp of the magistrate of Nanhai County, Canton.1 item.

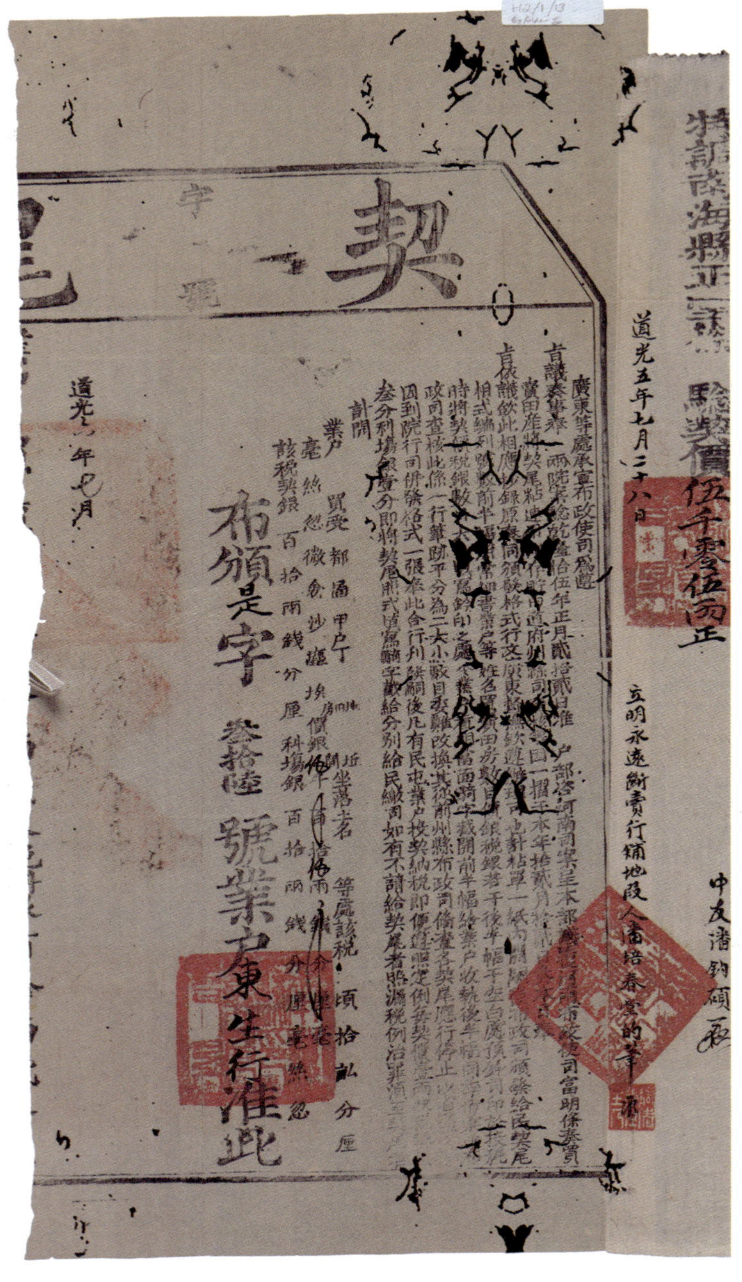

① 东生行购买潘培春堂位于回澜桥房产的契尾，盖有南海县印章。东生行行商刘德章，商名章官（Chunqua），祖籍安徽，于乾隆五十九年（1794）开始充当行商。

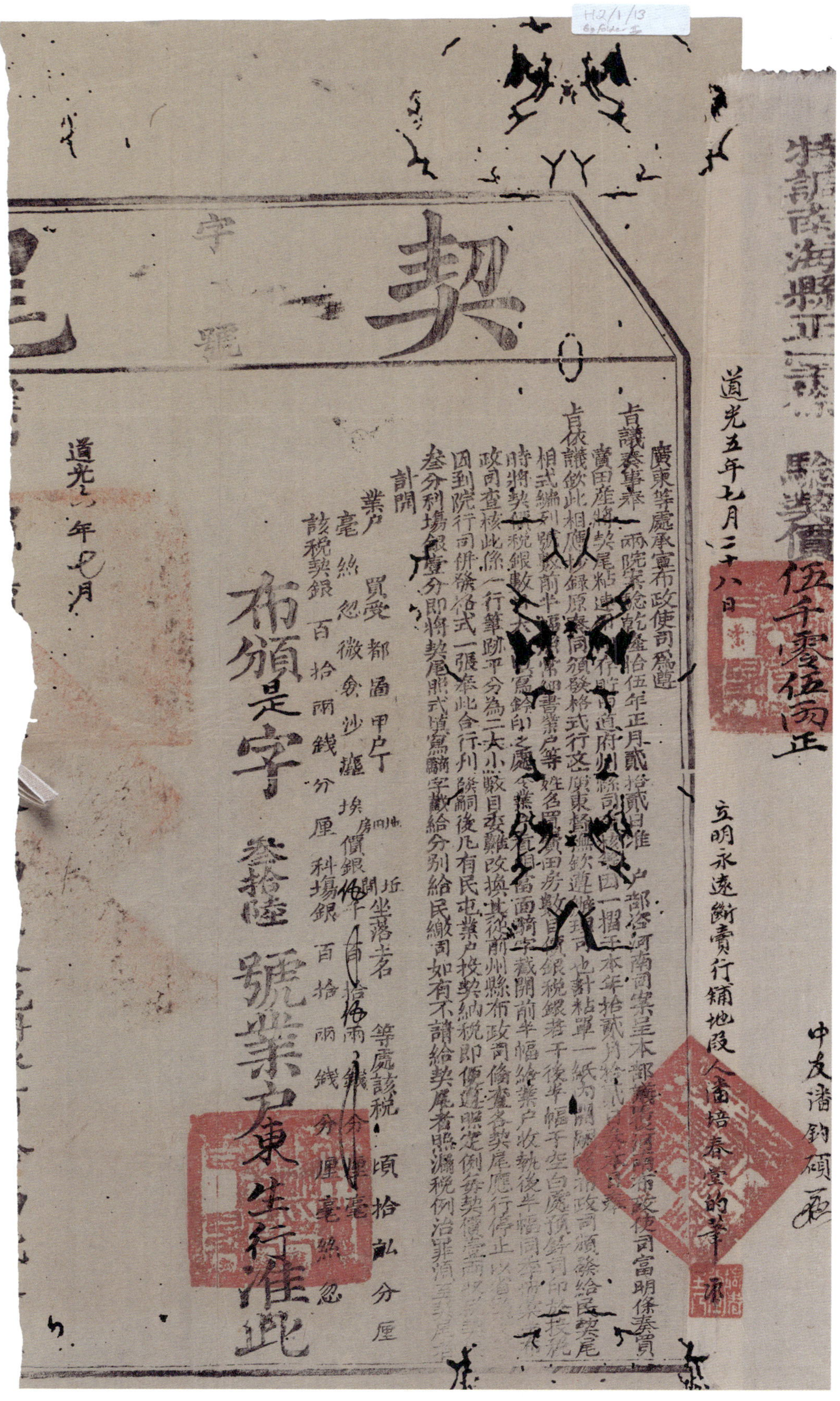

契

字　號

廣東等處承宣布政使司為遵

旨議奏事奉兩院憲案[illegible]乾隆拾伍年正月貳拾貳日准户部咨河南司案呈本部議覆廣東布政使司富明條奏買

賣田產將契尾粘連[illegible]道府州縣司[illegible]一摺于本年拾貳月[illegible]

旨依議欽此相應抄錄原奏同頒發格式行文廣東督撫欽遵[illegible]也其粘單一紙為開[illegible]布政司頒發給民契尾

相式編列號數前半幅[illegible]書業户等姓名買賣田房數目價銀稅銀若干後半幅于空白處預鈐司印於投稅

時將契價稅銀數目大寫鈐印之處令業户看明當面騎字截開前半幅給業户收執後半幅同季冊彙[illegible]

政司查核此係一行筆跡平分為二大小數目委難改換其從前州縣布政司備查各契尾應行停止以省[illegible]

因到院行司併發格式一張奉此合行刊發嗣後凡有民屯業户投契納稅即便遵照定例每契價壹兩[illegible]

叁分科場銀壹分即將契尾照式填寫騎字截給分別給民繳司如有不請給契尾者照漏稅例治罪須至契尾者

計開

業户　買受　都　啚　甲　户丁　坐落土名　等處該稅　頃　拾　畝　分　厘

毫　絲　忽　微　纖　沙　塵　埃　價銀伍千零伍拾兩　錢　分　厘　毫

該稅契銀　百　拾　兩　錢　分　厘　科場銀　百　拾　兩　錢　分　厘　毫　絲　忽

布頒是字叁拾陸號業户廣東生行准此

道光五年七月

道光五年七月二十八日

[illegible]價伍千零伍両正

立明永遠斷賣行鋪地段人潘培春堂的筆　承

中友潘鈞碩

（局部图）

14. 道光六年东生行购买回澜桥房产的卖主推照（H2/1/14）

道光六年（1826）七月，潘培春堂把回澜桥物业卖给东生行，并登记房产交易的土地税，新业主有义务付清税银，税契编号第36号。

Land tax registration certificate. A registration certificate issued by the Magistrate of Nanhai County for the transfer of the land tax due on the sale of the Huilan Bridge property, which has been sold by P'an P'ei-ch'un (Pan Peichun) to Tung-sheng (Dongsheng) Hong, August 1826. The new proprietor is liable for the payment of the tax, numbered 36.1 item.

H2/1/14

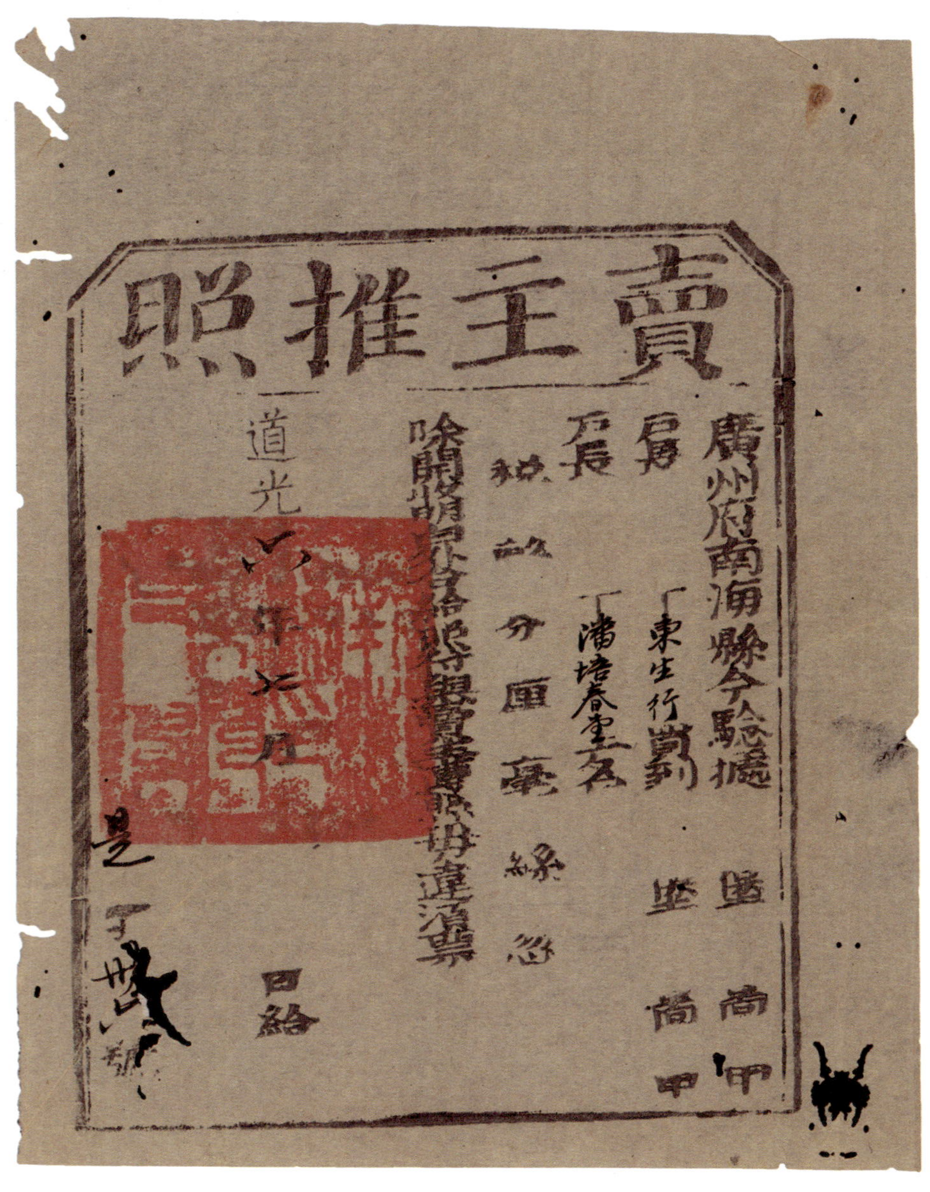
賣主推照

廣州府南海縣令驗據 圖 啚 甲

戶 東生行戶 堡 啚 甲

戶長 潘培春堂

稅 畝 分 厘 毫 絲 忽

道光六年七月 日給

15. 道光六年东生行购买回澜桥房产的税契（H2/1/15）

道光六年（1826），南海县县令发给东生行所购回澜桥脚房屋的税契。

Tax certificate. A certificate (Shui-ch'i) of the payment in the form of manony and grain of a legal tax on the sale of property, issued by Magistrate of Nanhai County to Tung-sheng (Dongsheng) Hong for the Huilan Bridge property, August 1826.1 item.

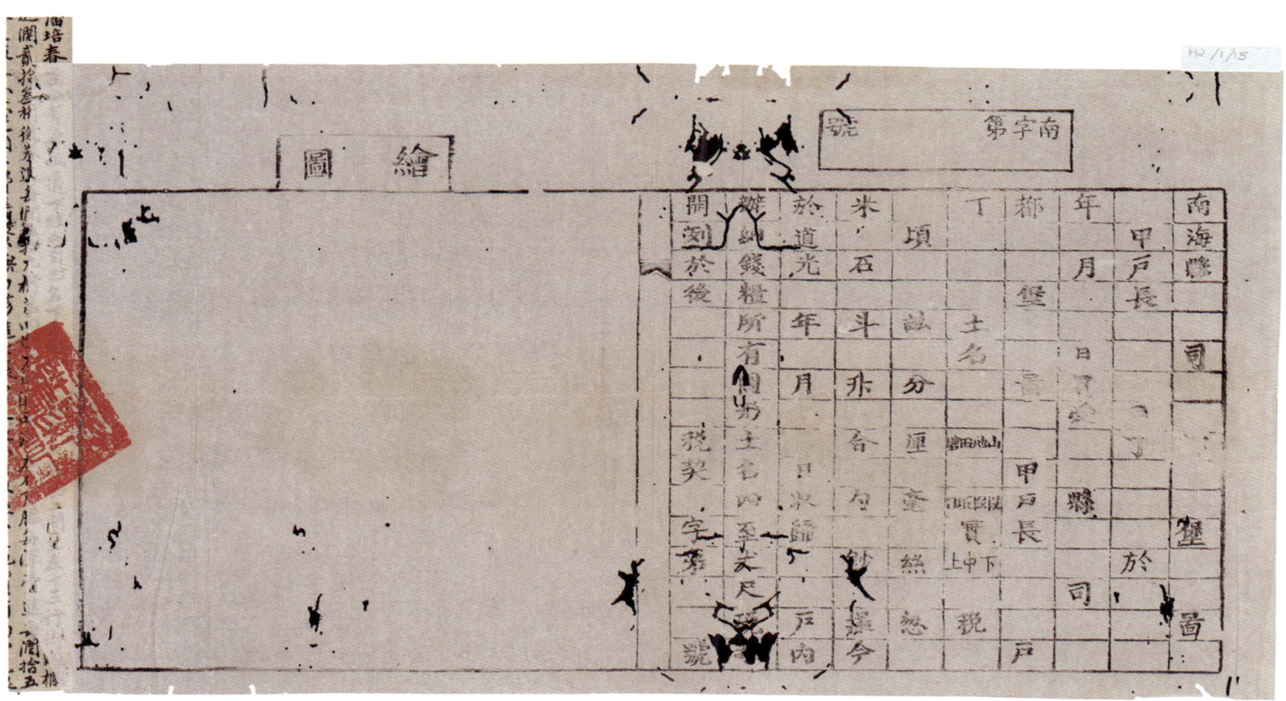

16. 道光五年潘培春堂售卖回澜桥房产的说明[①]（H2/1/16）

道光五年（1825）八月，潘培春堂把房产卖给东升行的交易补充说明。

Note of land sale. A sheet of wrapping paper containing a brief note of August 1826[②] recording the purchase of land from P'an P'ei-ch'un (Pan Peichun) in the 8th month of the 5th year of Daoguang's reign for $7000, and listing enclosures: a new deed-roll, two previous deed-rolls and the final draft version of the deed-roll. 1 item; Fair condition, but damage by insects.

① 此文书内容为："道光五年八月买潘培春堂晋孚行地基壹块，坐落地名回澜桥脚，去价银柒千元。新文契壹纸、老文契式纸、定帖字壹纸在内。"可知潘培春堂售卖房产时除订立新文契，还附上了此房产之前的两次售卖交易的"老文契"。老文契包括两部分，其一是指潘培春堂祖上于乾隆四十一年（1776）向蔡璋购买此房产的相关契约文书，包括蔡璋所立卖契、卖主推照、契尾、税契及其副本，即本章英国剑桥大学怡和洋行档案H2/1/5至H2/1/9，共5份契约文书；其二是指蔡璋家族于乾隆三十一年（1766）向温紫光购买此房产的相关契约文书，包括温紫光所立卖契、契尾、卖主推照、税契，即本章英国剑桥大学怡和洋行档案H2/1/1至H2/1/4，共4份契约文书。

② 应为1825年。

17. 道光六年官方催促东生行交税[①]饷银的文书（H2/1/17）

县令谕告。道光六年（1826），南海县县令要求地保向东生行收取购买潘培春堂在回澜桥脚的店铺的契税。

Magistrate’s order. A copy of an order issued by Hsu (Xu), magistrate of Nanhai County, to the police to collect a tax from Tung-sheng (Dongsheng) Hong for its purchase of property belonging to P’an P’ei-ch’un (Pan Peichun) in 1825.1 item.

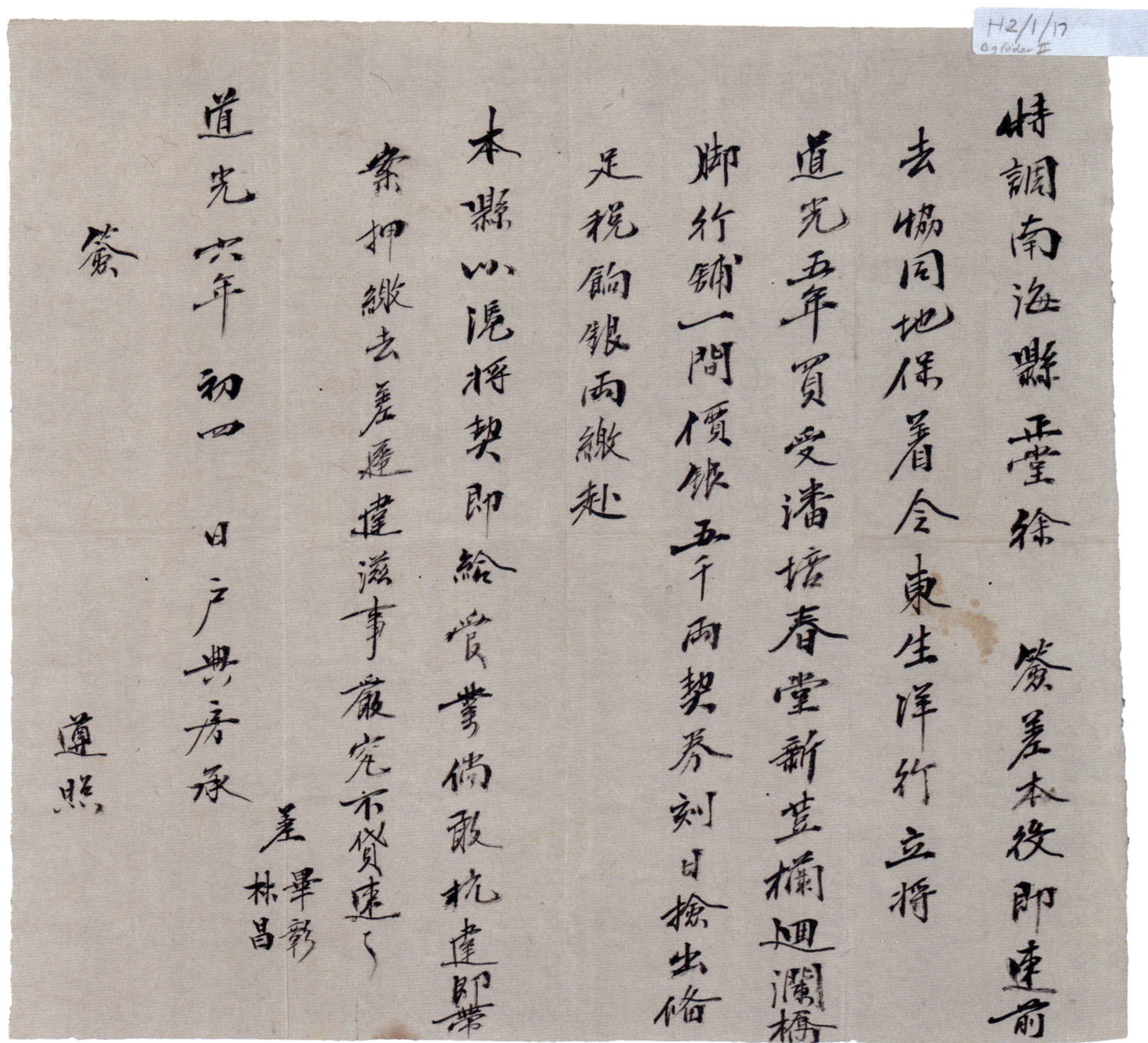

① 当时购买房产所纳税项包括“税契银”和“科场银”。

二、乾隆至咸丰年间福建闽县观音街房屋买卖契约

福建闽县观音街土地、物业销售文书9件。有些文件是白契，即没有在公共记录中登记并得到官方认可的材料。

1. 乾隆四十五年何素云、何素海售地的卖契[①]（H2/2/1）

何素云、何素海的售地契约。乾隆四十五年（1780）九月，何素云和她的弟弟何素海在保长余子静的见证下，由中间人代笔，签署契约把观音井的地卖给郑发祥。

Deed-roll of Ho Ssu-yun and Ho Ssu-hai. A deed-roll of Ho Ssu-yun (He Suyun) and his brother Ho Ssu-hai (He Suhai), subscribed by middlemen, for the irrevocable sale of their spare land in Kuan-yin ching to Cheng Fa-hsiang (Zheng Faxiang), October 1780, confirmed by Yu Tzu-ching (Yu Zijing), village headman in charge of order and peace in Kuan-yin ching region.1 item.

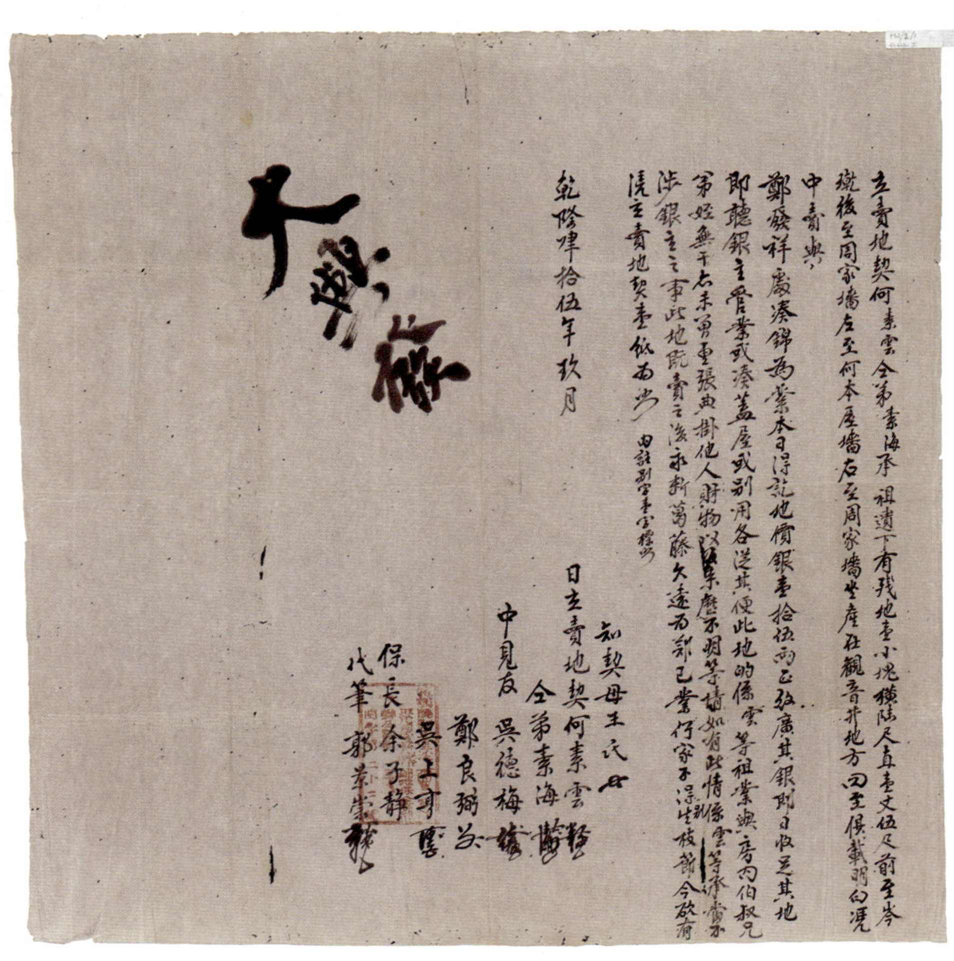
立賣地契何素雲仝弟素海承祖遺下有殘地壹小塊橫闊尺直壹丈伍尺前至岑
璈後至周家墻左至何本厝墻右至周家墻坐產在觀音井地方四至俱載明白憑
中賣與
鄭發祥處湊錦為業本日得訖地價銀壹拾伍兩正紋廣其銀即日收足其地
即聽銀主管業或湊蓋厝或別用各從其便此地的係雲等祖業與房內伯叔兄
弟姪無干亦未曾重張典掛他人財物以及來歷不明等情如有此情係雲等承當不
涉銀主之事此地既賣之後永斷葛藤久遠為鄭己業任從子孫世代管業[illegible]今欲有
憑立賣地契壹紙為照 内註別字壹字[illegible]
乾隆肆拾伍年玖月
日立賣地契何素雲
仝弟素海
知契母王氏
中見友吳德梅
鄭良璠
吳上守
保長余子静
代筆郭[illegible]

---

① 卖方：何素云、何素海。买方：郑发祥。保长：余子静。

立賣地契何素雲仝弟素海承　祖遺下有残地壹小塊横陆尺直壹丈伍尺前至岑
璇後至周家墻左至何本屋墻右至周家墻坐落在觀音井地方四至俱載明白凴
中賣與
鄭發祥處湊錦爲業本日得訖地價銀壹拾伍両正親收足其地
即聽銀主管業或湊蓋屋或别用各從其便此地的係雲等祖業與房内伯叔兄
弟姪無干亦未曾重張典掛他人財物以及來歷不明等情如有此情係雲等承當不
涉銀主之事此地既賣之後永斷葛藤久遠爲鄭己業何家不得生枝節今欲有
凴立賣地契壹紙爲炤

内註别字壹字標明

乾隆肆拾伍年秋月　日立賣地契何素雲

知契母王氏

仝弟素海

中見友　吳德梅

鄭良瑞

保長　吳上可

余子静

代筆　郭景崇

大發祿

（局部图）

2. 乾隆五十九年郑起元兄弟四人售地的卖契[①]（H2/2/2）

郑起元及其兄弟的售地契约。乾隆五十九年（1794）九月，郑起元兄弟四人在保长余子静的见证下，由中间人、见证人及代笔等人签字画押，签署契约把观音井铺的物业卖给林家。

Deed-roll of Cheng Chi-yuan and his brothers. A deed-roll of Cheng Chi-yuan (Zheng Qiyuan) and his three brothers, subscribed by witnesses and middlemen, for the irrevocable sale of their property at Kuan-yin-ching-p'u (Guanyin jing pu) to the Lin family, 24 September 1794, confirmed by Yu Tzu-ching (Yu Zijing), village headman in charge of order and peace in Kuan-yin ching (Guanyin jing) region. 1 item; Fair condition, but damage by insects.

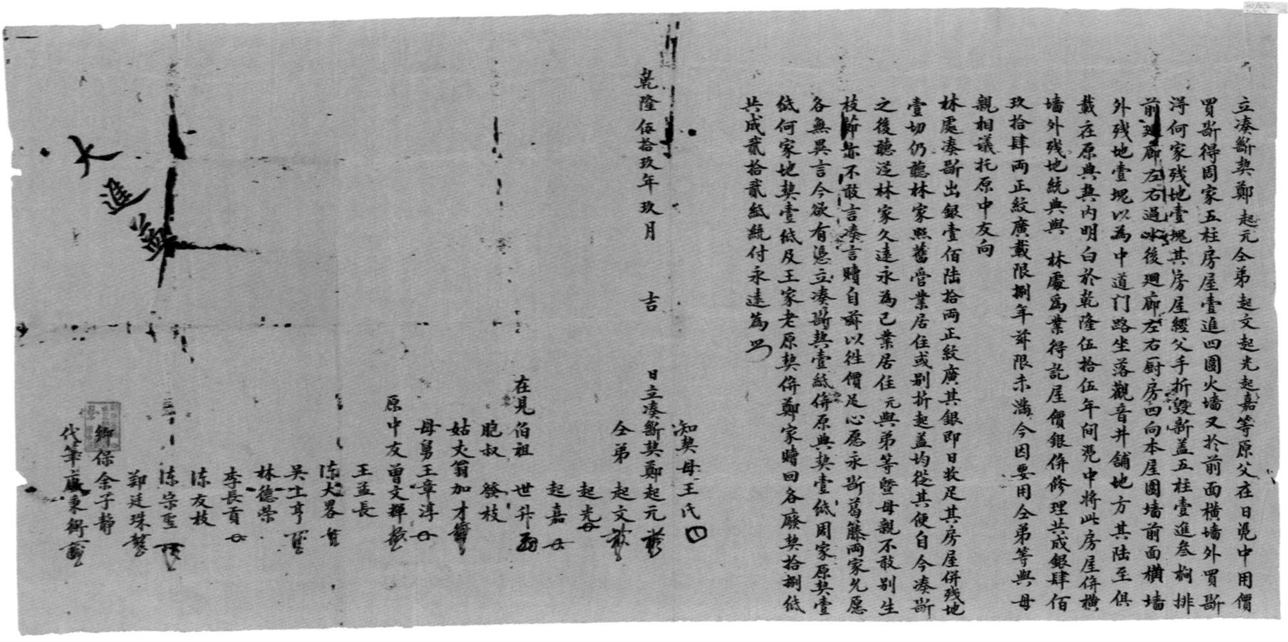

立湊斷契鄭起元仝弟起文起光起嘉等原父在日憑中用價
買斷得周家五柱房屋壹進四圍火墻又於前面横墻外買斷
浔何家残地壹塊其房屋經父手拆毁新蓋五柱壹進叁榀排
前廻廊左右過水後廻廊左右厨房西向本屋圍墻前面横墻
外残地壹塊以為中道门路坐落觀音井舖地方其陸至俱
載在原典契内明白於乾隆伍拾伍年間憑中將此房屋併横
墻外残地統典與　林慶為業得訖屋價銀併修理共成銀肆佰
玖拾肆两正紋廣載限捌年贖限未滿今因要用仝弟等與母
親相議托原中友向
林處湊斷出銀壹佰陸拾两正紋廣其銀即日收足其房屋併残地
壹切仍聽林家照舊管業居住或剔折起蓋均從其便自今湊斷
之後聽從林家久遠永為已業居住元與弟等暨母親不敢别生
枝節紛不敢言湊言贖自爵以往價足心愿永斷葛藤两家允愿
各無異言今欲有憑立湊斷契壹紙併原典契壹紙周家原契壹
紙何家地契壹紙及王家老原契併鄭家贖回各廢契拾捌紙
共成貳拾貳紙統付永遠為照

乾隆伍拾玖年玖月　吉　日立湊斷契鄭起元

知契母王氏

仝弟　起文
起光
起嘉

在見伯祖　世升
胞叔　發枝
姑丈翁加才
母舅王章淳
原中友曾文輝
王孟長
陳大碁
吳士亨
林德崇
李長青
陳友枝
陳宗聖
鄭廷珠
鄉保余子静
代筆嚴東衡

大進

---

① 卖方：郑起元、郑起文、郑起光、郑起嘉。买方：林家。

立凑斷契鄭起元仝弟起文起光起嘉等原父在日凴中用價
買斷得周家五柱房屋壹進四圍火墻又於前面横墻外買斷
浮何家残地壹塊其房屋經父手折毀新盖五柱壹進叁榀排
前廻廊左右過水後廻廊左右厨房四向本屋圍墻前面横墻
外残地壹塊以為中道门路坐落觀音井鋪地方其陸至俱
載在原典契内明白於乾隆伍拾伍年間凴中將此房屋併横
墻外残地統典與　林處爲業得訖屋價銀併修理共成銀肆佰
玖拾肆两正紋廣載限捌年爲限未滿今因要用仝弟等與母
親相議托原中友向
林處凑斷出銀壹佰陸拾两正紋廣其銀即日收足其房屋併残地
壹切仍聽林家照舊管業居住或别拆起盖均從其便自今凑斷
之後聽從林家久遠永為己業居住元與弟等暨母親不敢别生
枝節亦不敢言凑言贖自爺以徃價足心愿永斷葛藤两家允愿
各無異言今欲有憑立凑斷契壹紙併原典契壹紙周家原契壹
紙何家地契壹紙及王家老原契併鄭家贖回各廠契拾捌紙
共成貳拾貳紙統付永遠為照

乾隆伍拾玖年玖月　吉　日立凑斷契鄭起元

知契母王氏

仝弟　起文　起光　起嘉

在見伯祖　世升

胞叔　發枝

姑丈翁　加才

母舅王章淳

原中友曾文輝

王孟長　陈大畧　吴士亨　林德崇　李長貢　陈友枝　陈宗聖　郑廷珠

鄉保余子静

代筆廣秉衡

大進

（局部图）

3. 嘉庆十一年林尔秀、林厚松典当房屋的典契[①]（H2/2/3）

林尔秀和林厚松的典契。嘉庆十一年（1806）七月，林尔秀及其胞侄林厚松由中间人代笔，签署“白契”把观音井铺利通里的房屋典当给叶奕，期限为5年。

Deed of transfer of Lin Er-hsiu and Lin Hou-sung. A ‘white’ deed of Lin Er-hsiu (Lin Erxiu) and his nephew Lin Hou-sung, subscribed by middlemen, for the transfer of their houses at Ta-ling-ting (Dalingding), Kuan-yin ching, to Ye I (Ye Yi) for a term of five years, dated 14 August–3 September 1806. 1 item; Fair condition, but damage by insects.

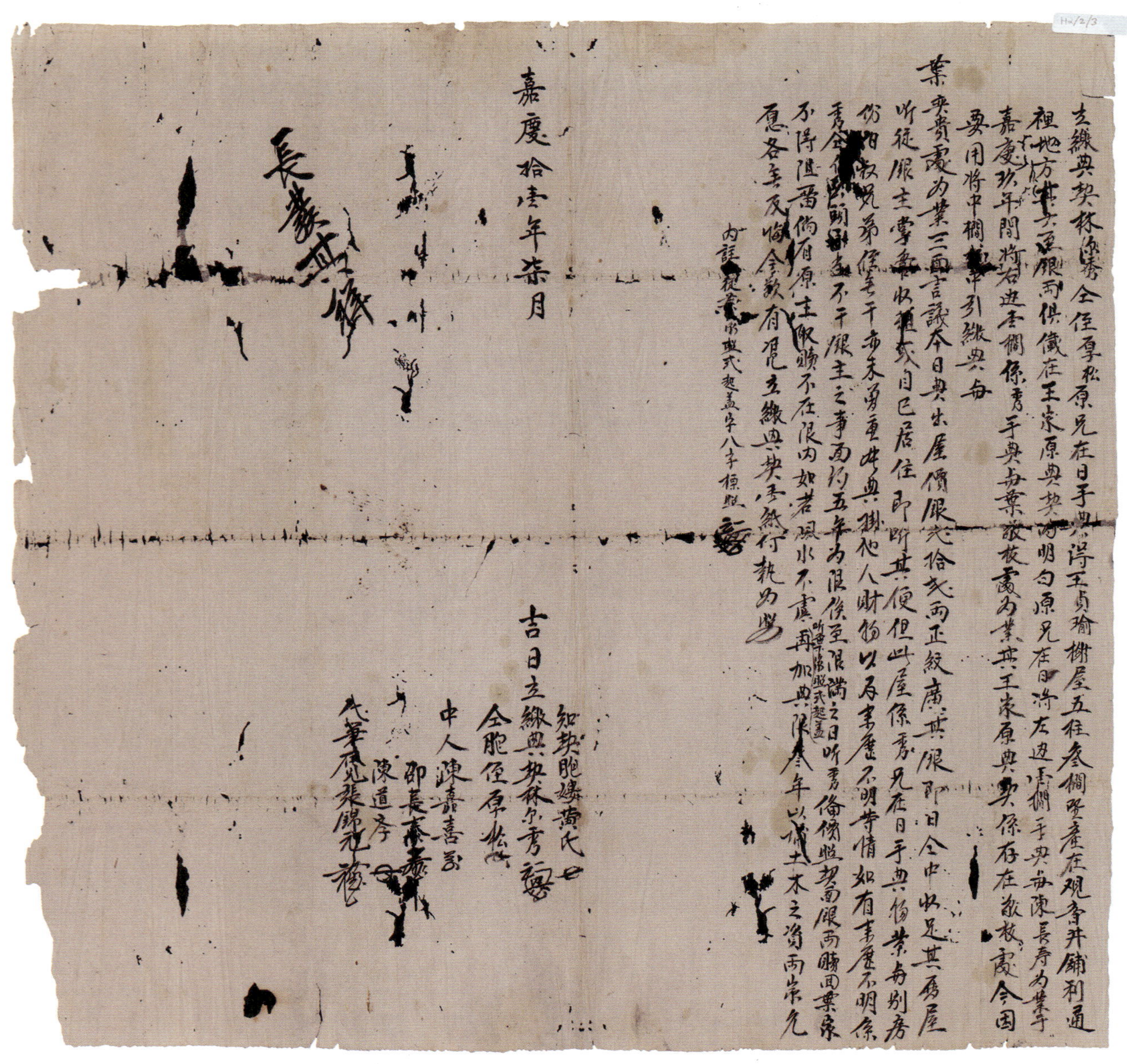

① 出典人：林尔秀、林厚松。承典人：叶奕。

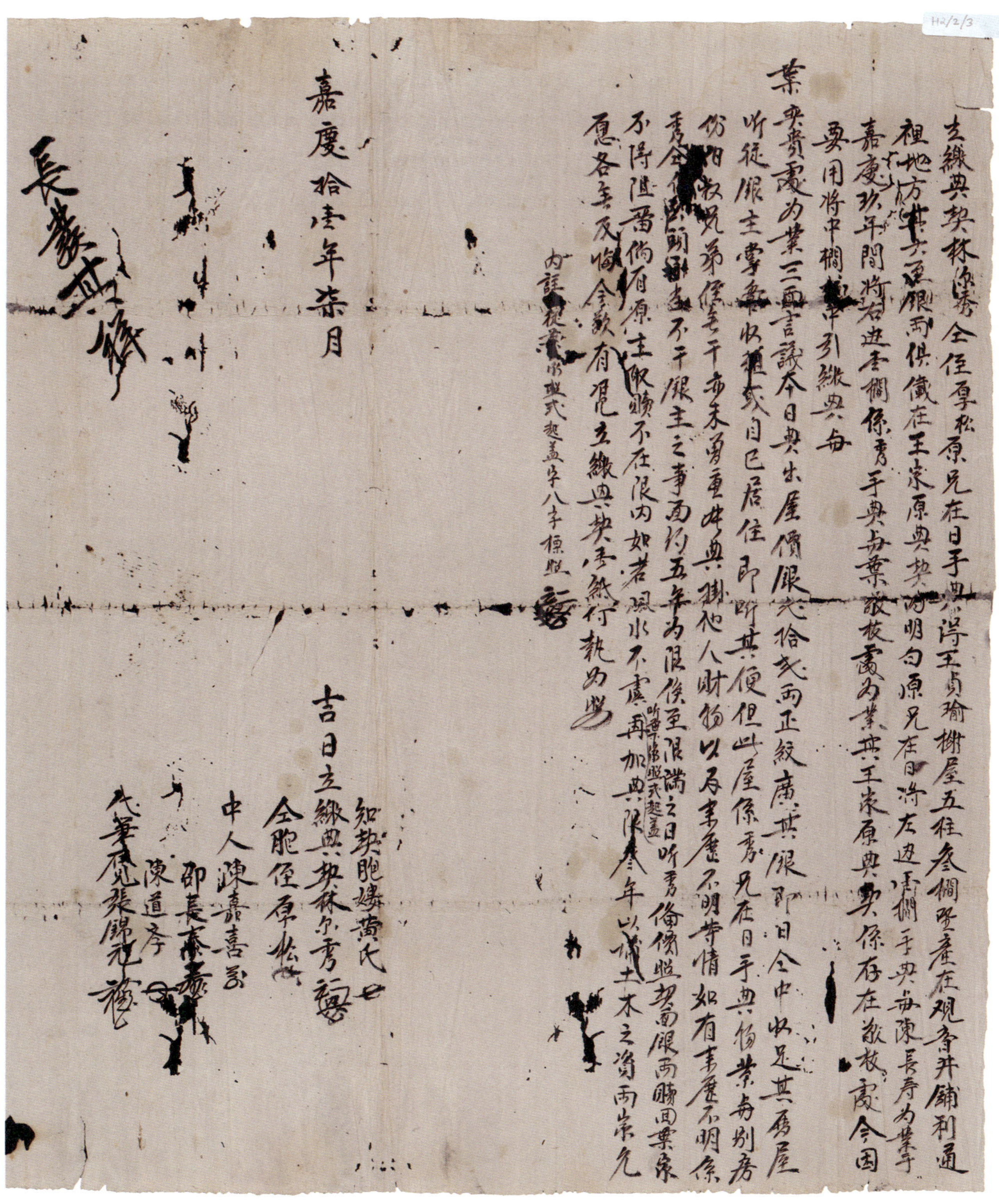

（局部图）

4. 道光二十六年杜文澜、杜文森房产转让契约[①]（H2/2/4）

杜文澜、杜文森房屋转让的契约。道光二十六年（1846）十月，杜文澜和他的弟弟杜文森由中间人代笔，签署契约把观音井铺大岭顶的店屋转让给林家，为期5年，典契盖有乡保的印章。

Deed of transfer of Tu Wen-lan and Tu Wen-sen. A deed of Tu Wen-lan (Du Wenlan) and his brother Tu Wen-sen (Du Wensen), subscribed by middlemen, for the transfer of their house at Ta-ling-ting (Dalingding), Kuan-yin ching, to the Lin family for a term of five years, 19 November 1846, including the stamp of Chang Yu-hua (Zhang Yuhua), village headman of Kuan-yin ching region. 1 item; Fair condition, but damage by insects.

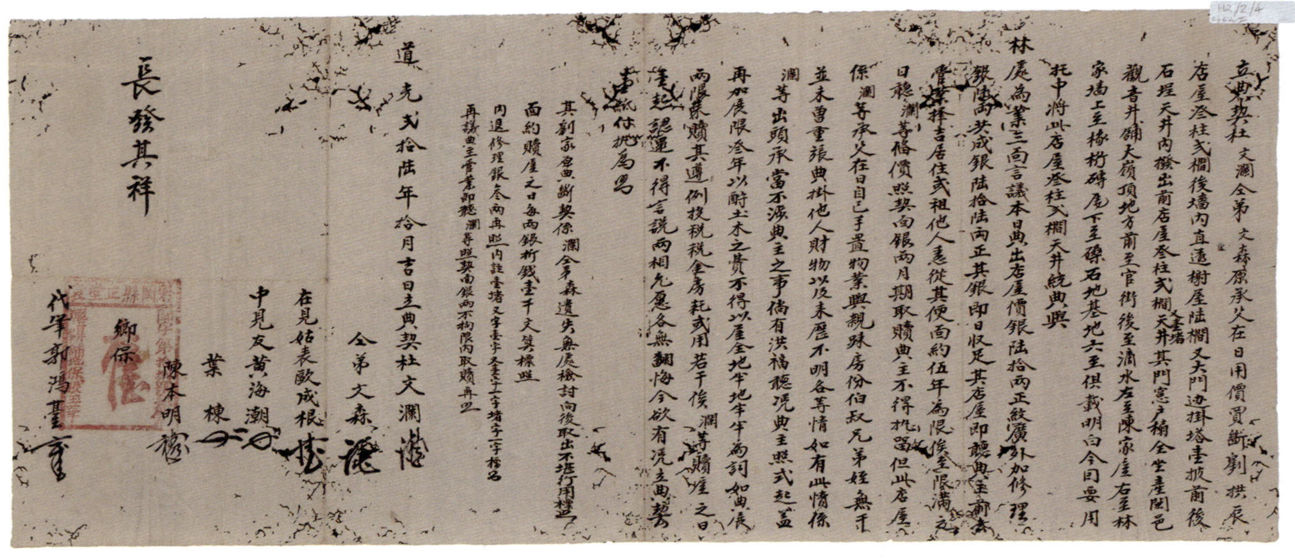
立典契杜文瀾仝弟文森原承父在日用價買断劉拱辰
店屋叁柱弍櫊後墻内直透樹屋陸櫊又大門边掛塔壹披前後
石埕天井内檢出前店屋叁柱弍櫊天井又壹墙其門窓户稱全坐產閩邑
觀音井舖大嶺頂地方前至官街後至濟水左至陳家屋右至林
家墙上至椽桁磚瓦下至磉石地基地六至俱載明白今因要用
托中將此店屋叁柱弍櫊天井統典與
林處為業三面言議本日典出店屋價銀陸拾両正紋廣外加修理
銀陸両共成銀陸拾陸両正其銀即日收足其店屋即聽典主前去
管業擇吉居住或租他人悉從其便面約伍年為限俟至限滿之
日聽瀾等備價照契面銀両月期取贖典主不得執留但此店屋
係瀾等承父在日自己手置物業與親疎房份伯叔兄弟姪無干
並未曾重張典掛他人財物以及來歷不明各等情如有此情係
瀾等出頭承當不涉典主之事倘有洪福聽冼典主照式起蓋
再加展限叁年以酎土木之費不得以屋全地半地半半為詞如典屋
兩限未贖其遵例投税税金房耗或用若干俟瀾等贖屋之日
清还認還不得言說兩相允愿各無翻悔今欲有凭立典契
壹紙付執為照
其劉家原典断契係瀾仝弟森遺失無處檢封向後取出不堪行用批照
面約贖屋之日每両銀折錢壹千文算標照
内退修理銀叁両再照 内註壹堵又字壹字又壹字十一字堵字一字[illegible]
再議典主賣業即聽瀾等照契面銀両不拘限内取贖再照
道光弍拾陸年拾月 吉日立典契杜文瀾
仝弟文森
在見姑表歐成根
中見友黃海潮
葉棟
陳本明
鄉保
代筆郭鴻基
長發其祥

① 业主：杜文澜、杜文森兄弟。

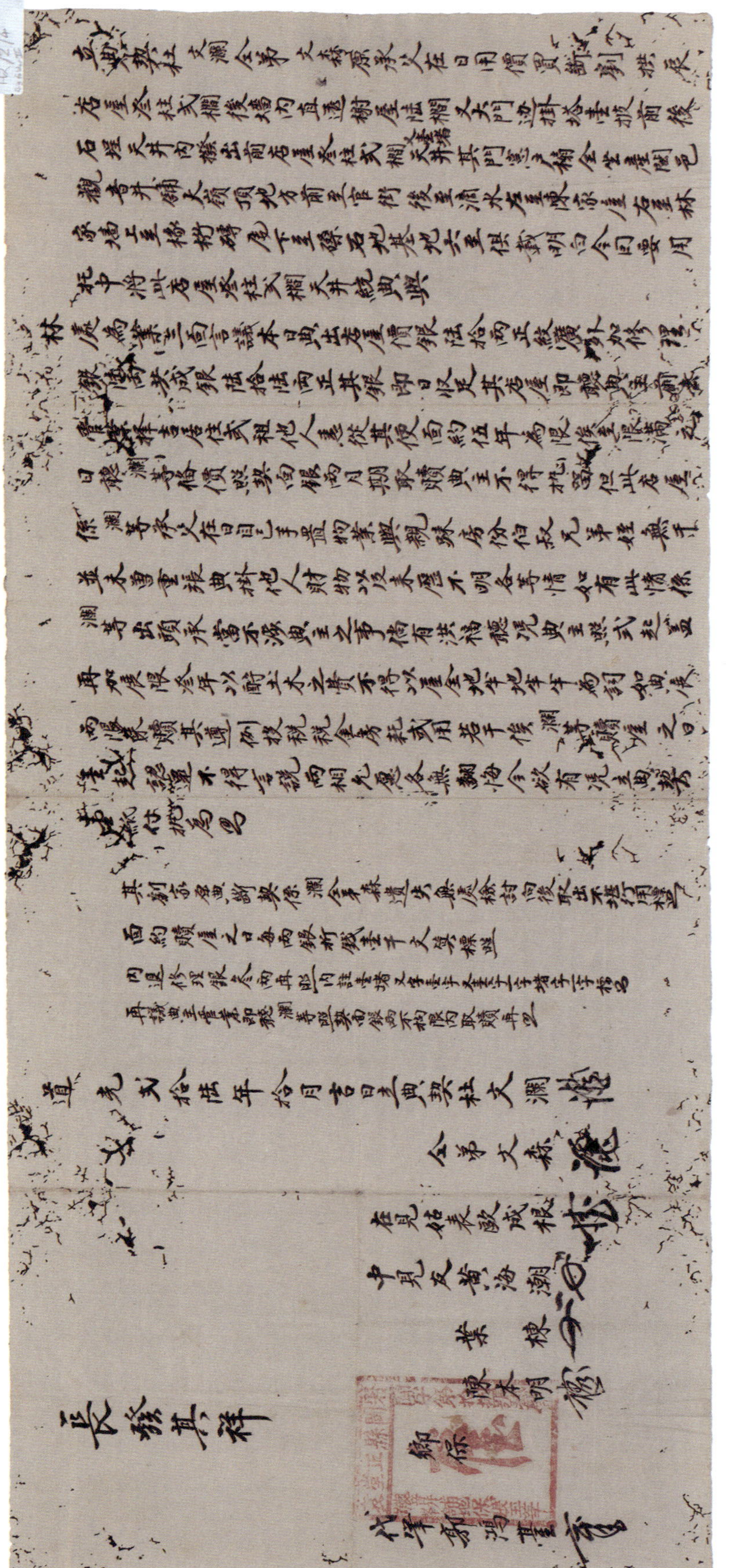

（局部图）

5. 道光三十年杜文澜、杜文森房产转让契约[①]（H2/2/5）

道光三十年（1850）八月，杜文澜、杜文森由王邦章代笔，签订房屋契约，将原先顶典当给林家在观音井铺大岭顶的房产议定期延长5年。

Deed of transfer of Tu Wen-lan and Tu Wen-sen. A 'white' deed of Tu Wen-lan (Du Wenlan) and his brother Tu Wen-sen (Du Wensen), subscribed by middlemen, for the renewal of their earlier deed, transferring their real property at Ta-ling-ting (Dalingding), Kuan-yin ching, to the Lin family for a further term of five years, 6 September 1850. 1 item; Fair condition, but damage by insects.

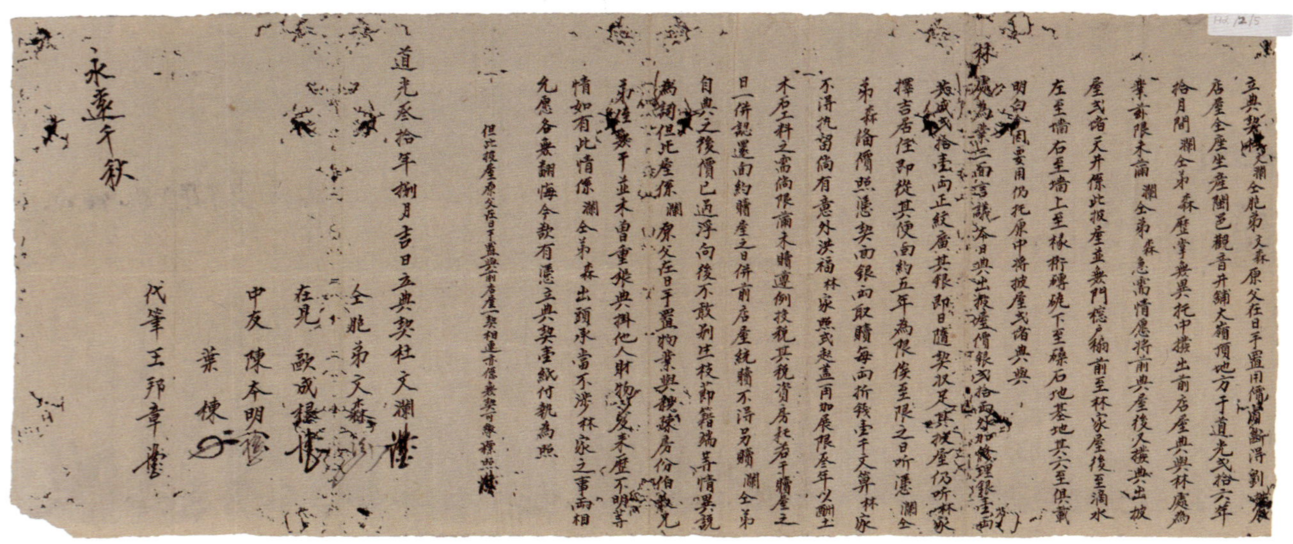

① 业主：杜文澜、杜文森（画押）。在见人：欧成根（画押）。中友：陈本明、叶栋（画押）。代笔：王邦章（画押）。

立典契[illegible]文潮仝胞弟文森原父在日于置用價斷得劉[illegible]
店屋仝座坐落閩邑觀音井鋪大街頂地方于道光貳拾六年
拾月間潮仝弟森[illegible]典與[illegible]出首店屋典與林處為
業言[illegible]限未滿潮仝弟森[illegible]應將前典店屋後又樓典出被
屋貳落天井係此被屋並無門[illegible]前至林家屋後至溝水
左至牆右至牆上至椽桁磚瓦下至磚石地基地址[illegible]至俱載
明白[illegible]要用仍托原中將被屋貳落典與
林[illegible]為業三面言議本日典出被屋價銀貳拾[illegible]
[illegible]主兩正紋番其銀即日隨契收足其被屋仍付林家
擇吉居住即從其便面約五年為限俟五年限之日所憑潮仝
弟森備價照契面銀兩取贖每兩折錢[illegible]千文算林家
不得執留倘有意外[illegible]林家[illegible]年以到
未到五年之期倘限滿未贖[illegible]
日一併認還面約贖屋之日併前店屋統贖不得另贖潮仝弟
自典之後倘已過五年向後不敢刁難[illegible]其情異說
為[illegible]但此屋原係潮原父在日于置[illegible]物業[illegible]
弟[illegible]等干並未[illegible]典與他人財物[illegible]不明等
情如有此情係潮仝弟森出頭承當不涉林家之事兩相
允愿各無翻悔今欲有憑立典契壹紙付執為照

但此被屋原父在日于道光[illegible]前店屋一契相連亦係[illegible]照

道光叁拾年捌月廿日立典契杜文潮
仝胞弟文森
在見[illegible]
中友陳本明
[illegible]
代筆王邦[illegible]
永遠千秋

（局部图）

6. 咸丰三年陈茂茂房产契约①（H2/2/6）

咸丰三年（1853）十月，陈茂茂由中间人和见证人代笔，签署“白契”把观音井铺池里的房产典当给王家，期限为5年。英国剑桥图书馆英文编目年份有误。

Deed of transfer of Ch’en Mao-mao. A ‘white’ deed of Ch’en Mao-mao (Chen Maomao), subscribed by middlemen and witnesses, for the transfer of his property at Ch’I-li (Chili), Kuan-yin ching p’u (Guanyin jing pu), to the Wang family for a term of five years, 1 November 1853.

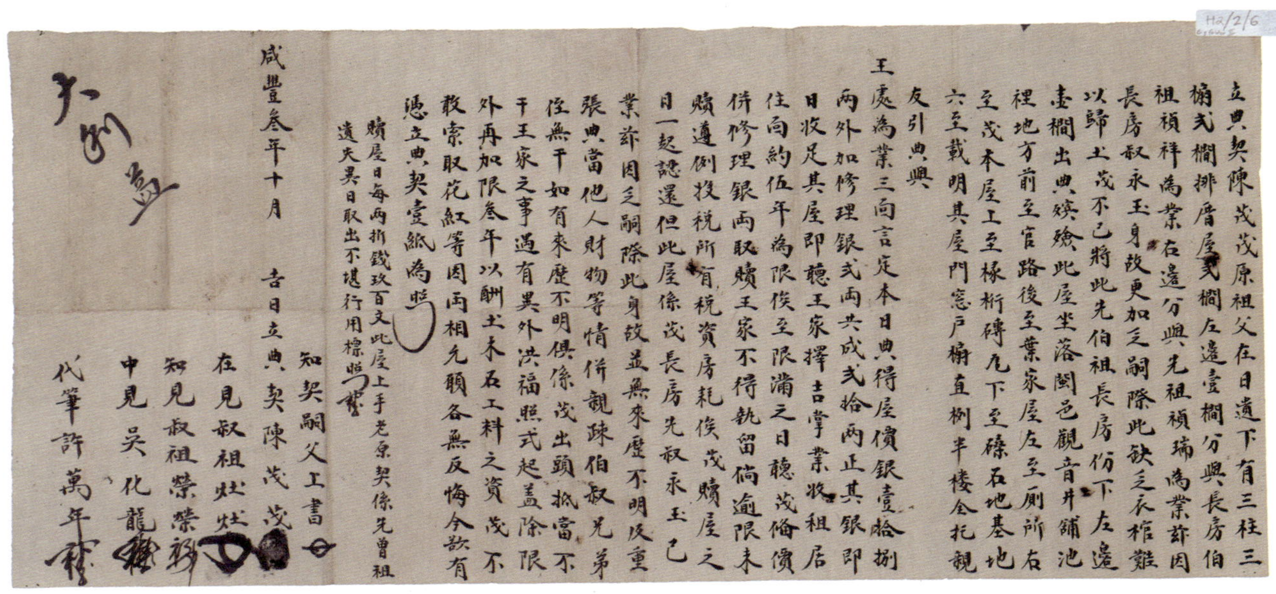

H2/2/6

立典契陳茂茂原祖父在日遺下有三柱三
榆弍櫊排厝屋弍櫊左邊壹櫊分與長房伯
祖禎祥為業右邊分與先祖禎瑞為業茲因
長房叔永玉身故更加乏嗣除此缺乏衣棺難
以歸土茂不已將此先伯祖長房份下左邊
壹櫊出典殯殮此屋坐落閩邑觀音井舖池
裡地方前至官路後至葉家屋左至廁所右
至茂本屋上至椽桁磚瓦下至磉石地基地
六至載明其屋門窓戶榆直桝半樓全托襯
友引典與
王處為業三面言定本日典得屋價銀壹拾捌
兩外加修理銀弍兩共成弍拾兩正其銀即
日收足其屋即聽王家擇吉掌業收租居
住向約伍年為限俟至限滿之日聽茂備價
併修理銀兩取贖王家不得執留倘逾限未
贖遵例投稅所有稅資房耗俟茂贖屋之
日一起認還但此屋係茂長房先叔永玉己
業茲因乏嗣除此身故並無來歷不明及重
張典當他人財物等情併親疎伯叔兄弟
侄無干如有來歷不明俱係茂出頭抵當不
干王家之事遇有異外洪福照式起蓋除限
外再加限叁年以酬土木石工料之資茂不
敢索取花紅等因兩相允願各無反悔今欲有
憑立典契壹紙為照
贖屋日每兩折錢玖百文此屋上手老原契係先曾祖
遺失異日取出不堪行用標照

咸豐叁年十月　吉日立典契陳茂茂
知契嗣父上書
在見叔祖灶灶
知見叔祖榮榮
中見吳化龍
代筆許萬年

① 卖方：陈茂茂（画押）。知契嗣父：上书（画押）。在见叔祖：灶灶（画押）。知见叔祖：荣荣（画押）。中见：吴化龙（画押）。代笔：许万年（画押）。

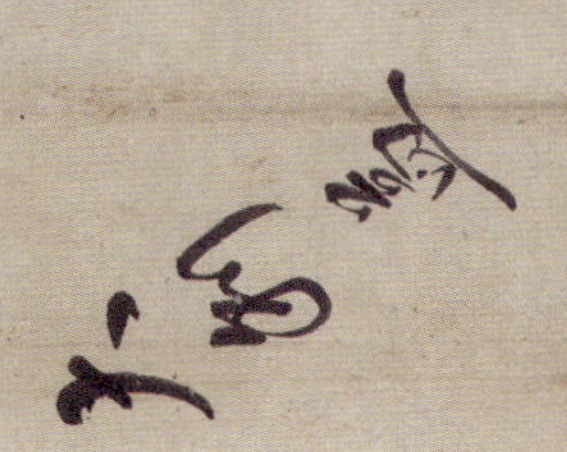

（局部图）

7. 咸丰三年杜文森房产契约[①]（H2/2/7）

咸丰三年十二月（1853年12月30日—1854年1月28日），杜文森由王邦章代笔，签订房屋契约，将原先典当给林家在观音井铺大岭顶的房产改为出售。

Deed-roll of Tu Wen-sen. A deed-roll of Tu Wen-sen (Du Wensen), copied by Wang Pang-chang (Wang Bangzhang), for the conversion of his earlier deed for the transfer of his real property at Ta-ling-ting (Dalingding), Kuan-yin ching, to the Lin family into an irrevocable sale, 30 December 1853. This is a white deed. 1 item; Fair condition, but damage by insects.

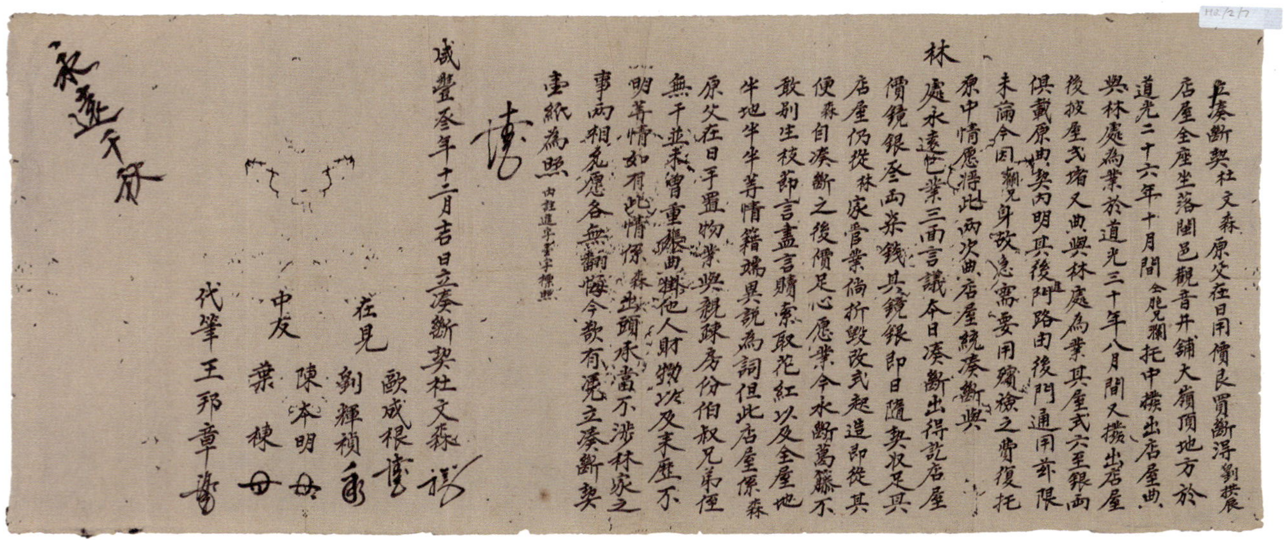

立湊斷契杜文森原父在日用價良買斷得劉拱辰
店屋全座坐落閩邑觀音井鋪大嶺頂地方於
道光二十六年十月間全胞兄瀾托中撥出店屋典
與林處為業於道光三十年八月間又撥出店屋
後披屋弍堵又典與林處為業其屋弍六至銀兩
俱載原典契內明其後門路由後門通用並限
未滿今因瀾兄身故急需要用殯殮之費復托
原中情愿將此兩次典店屋統湊斷與
林
處永遠世業三面言議本日湊斷出得訖店屋
價鏡銀叁兩柒錢其鏡銀即日隨契收足其
店屋仍從林家管業倘折毀改弍起造即從其
便森自湊斷之後價足心愿業今永斷葛藤不
敢別生枝節言盡言贖索取花紅以及全屋地
半地半半等情藉端異說為詞但此店屋係森
原父在日手置物業與親疎房份伯叔兄弟侄
無干並未曾重張典掛他人財物以及來歷不
明等情如有此情係森出頭承當不涉林家之
事兩相允愿各無翻悔今欲有憑立湊斷契
壹紙為照　內註進字壹字標照

懷

咸豐叁年十二月吉日立湊斷契杜文森
在見　歐成根
　　　劉輝禎
中友　陳本明
　　　葉　棟
代筆　王邦章

永遠千秋

① 断契人：杜文森（画押）。在见人：欧成根、刘辉祯（画押）。中友：陈本明、叶栋（画押）。代笔：王邦章（画押）。

立杜斷契杜文森，原父在日同價良買斷得劉棋展
店屋全座，坐落隨邑觀音井鋪大橋頭地方。於
道光二十六年十月間，仝胞兄瀾托中構出店屋典
與林慶為業。於道光三十年八月間又構出店屋
後披屋弍植又典與林慶為業。其屋弍穴至銀兩
俱載原典契內明具。其後披進門路由後披門通同用，言約限
未滿，今因瀾兄身故，急需要用，窮窘之極，復托
原中情愿將此兩次典店屋統歸杜斷與
林
慶承受業，三面言議，本日杜斷出得訖店屋
價錢銀叁百兩，其錢銀即日隨契收足。其
店屋仍從林家管業，倘析毀改弍起造，即從其
便。森自杜斷之後，價足心愿，業今永斷葛藤，不
敢別生枝節，即言盡言贖，索取花紅，以及全屋地
尺地寸半等情，藉端異說為詞。但此店屋係森
原父在日手置物業，與親族房分伯叔兄弟侄
無干，並未曾重張典掛他人財物，以及來歷不
明等情，如有此情，係森出頭承當，不涉林家之
事。兩相甘愿，各無翻悔，今欲有憑，立杜斷契
壹紙為照。內註進字壹字照。

咸豐叁年十二月廿日立杜斷契杜文森

歐成根
在見　劉輝禎
陳本明
中友　葉棟

代筆　王邦章

永遠大吉

（局部图）

8. 咸丰五年杜文森房产契约[①]（H2/2/8）

咸丰五年（1855）六月，杜文森由王邦霖代笔，签订房屋契约，将观音井铺大岭的房产出售给林家。

Deed-roll of Tu Wen-sen. A deed-roll of Tu Wen-sen (Du Wensen), subscribed by middlemen, copied by Wang Pang-lin (Wang Banglin), for the irrevocable sale of his real property at Ta-ling (Daling), Kuan-yin ching p'u, to the foreign firm, Lungshun (Longshun) (Heard & Co. ?), 14 July 1855. This is a white deed. 1 item; Fair condition, but some damage by insects.

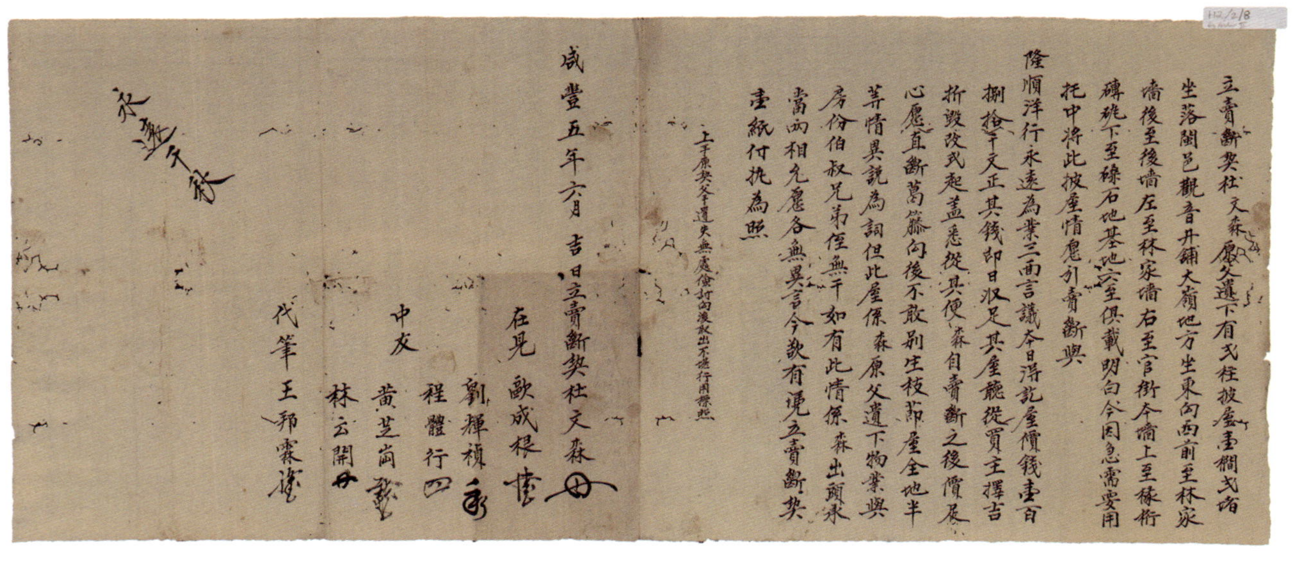

立賣斷契杜文森，原父遺下有弍柱披屋壹間弍堵，坐落閩邑觀音井鋪大嶺地方，坐東向西，前至林家墻，後至後墻，左至林家墻，右至官街，今墻上至椽桁磚瓦，下至磉石地基，地穴全俱載明白。今因急需要用，托中將此披屋情愿引賣斷與
隆順洋行永遠為業。三面言議，本日得訖屋價錢壹百捌拾千文正，其錢即日收足。其屋聽從買主擇吉折毀改弍起蓋，悉從其便。森自賣斷之後，價足心愿，直斷葛籐，向後不敢別生枝節、屋全地半等情異說為詞。但此屋係森原父遺下物業，與房份伯叔兄弟侄無干。如有此情，係森出頭承當。兩相允愿，各無異言。今欲有憑，立賣斷契壹紙付執為照。

上手原契父手遺失無處，僉討向後搜出不堪行用，係照

咸豐五年六月　吉日立賣斷契杜文森（押）

在見　歐成根（押）　劉輝禎（押）

中友　程體行（押）　黃芝崗（押）　林云開（押）

代筆　王邦霖（押）

---

① 立卖断契人：杜文森（画押）。在见人：欧成根、刘辉祯（画押）。中友：程体行、黄芝岗、林云开（画押）。代笔：王邦霖（画押）。

立賣斷契杜文森原承父遺下有弍柱披屋壹間弍堷
坐落閩邑觀音井鋪大嶺地方坐東向西前至林家
墻後至後墻左至林家墻右至官街今墻上至椽桁
磚瓦下至磉石地基地穴至俱載明白今因急需要用
托中將此披屋情愿引賣斷與
隆順洋行永遠為業三面言議今日得訖屋價錢壹百
捌拾千文正其錢即日收足其屋聽從買主擇吉
拆毀改弍起蓋悉從其便森自賣斷之後價足
心愿直斷葛藤向後不敢另生枝節屋全地半
等情異說為詞但此屋係森原父遺下物業與
房份伯叔兄弟侄無干如有此情係森出頭承
當兩相允愿各無異言今欲有憑立賣斷契
壹紙付執為照

上手原契父手遺失無處僉討向後取出不堪行用標照

咸豐五年六月　吉日立賣斷契杜文森（押）

在見　歐成根（押）
　　　劉輝禎（押）
　　　程體行（押）
　　　黃芝崗（押）
中友　林云開（押）
代筆　王邦霖（押）

永遠千秋

（局部图）

9. 咸丰五年陈天然房产契约①（H2/2/9）

咸丰五年（1855）六月，陈天然将其在时升里观音井铺利通里的房产永卖隆顺洋行。这是一份“白契”。买主：隆顺洋行，美资洋行琼记洋行在福州开设的分行。琼记洋行由旗昌洋行前合伙人美籍商人奥古斯丁·赫德（Augustine Heard）创立于1840年，总部设于广州，1856年第二次鸦片战争中商馆被焚，于1857年将总部迁到香港。

Deed-roll of Ch’en Tien-jan. A deed-roll of Ch’en Tien-jan (Chen Tianran) for the irrevocable sale of his real property at Shih-sheng-li, Kuan-yin ching, to the foreign firm Lungshun (Longshun) (Heard & Co. ?), July 1855. This is a ‘white deed’.1 item; Fair condition, but some damage by insects.

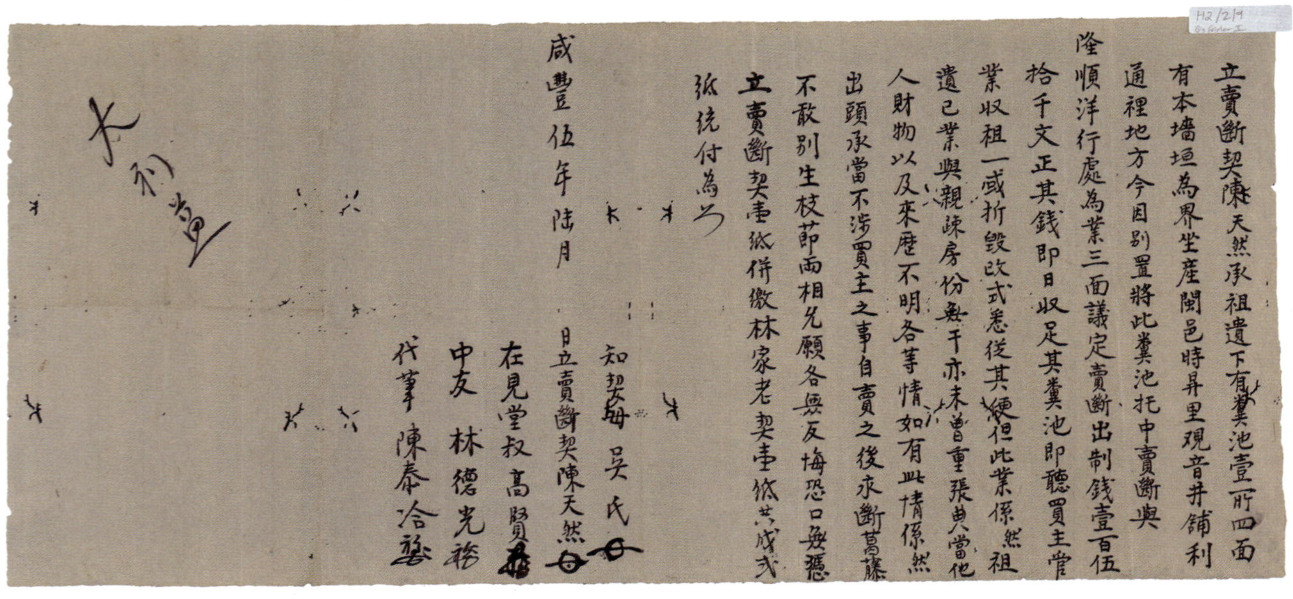

立賣斷契陳天然承祖遺下有糞池壹所四面有本墻垣為界坐産閩邑時昇里觀音井鋪利通裡地方今因别置將此糞池托中賣斷與隆順洋行處為業三面議定賣斷出制錢壹百伍拾千文正其錢即日收足其糞池即聽買主管業收租一概拆毀改式悉從其便但此業係然祖遺己業與親疎房份無干亦未曾重張典當他人財物以及來歷不明各等情如有此情係然出頭承當不涉買主之事自賣之後永斷葛藤不敢别生枝節两相允願各無反悔恐口無憑立賣斷契壹紙併繳林家老契壹紙共成弍張繳付為照

咸豐伍年陸月　日立賣斷契陳天然

知契母　吴氏

在見堂叔　高賢

中友　林德光

代筆　陳泰洽

① 卖主：陈天然（画押）。知契母：吴氏（画押）。在见堂叔：高贤（画押）。中友：林德光（画押）。代笔：陈泰洽（画押）。

三、道光年间东生行[1]房屋买卖契约

1. 道光七年东生行房屋买卖契单（H2/3/1）

道光七年二月十一日（1827年3月8日），东生行房屋买卖契单，购买二和行[2]的卢慎余堂，价银14,400两，税银一千零五十一两九钱二分，房屋大契存放在东生行。

Receipt from Tungsheng hong. A receipt from Tungsheng hong for payment for Lu Shen-yu t'ang (Lu Shenyu tang)'s real property 'Er-ho (Erhe) hong' and for the registration tax at the district magistrate, 8 March 1827. The title deed was to kept by Tungsheng Hong. The document also records that a payment of $1461[3] was made to the Hong on the 2nd moon of the 15th day (12 March 1827).1 item.

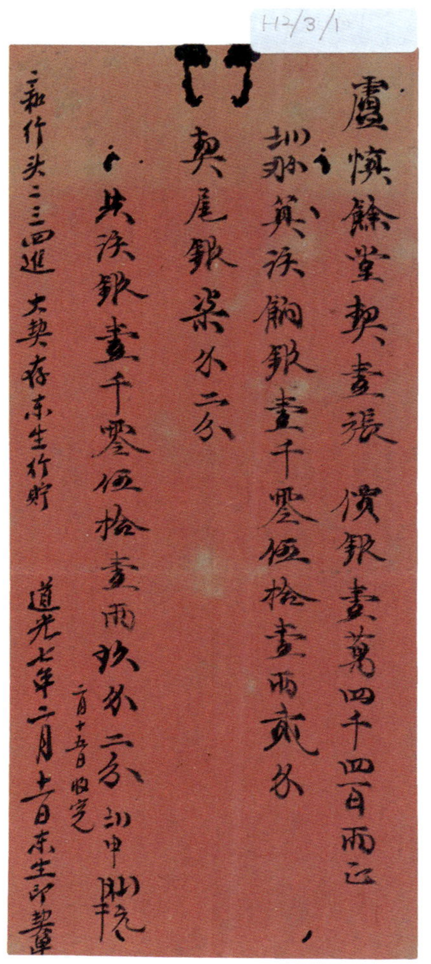

H2/3/1

盧慎餘堂契壹張　價銀壹萬四千四百兩正

計開 契稅餉銀壹千零伍拾壹兩貳錢

契尾銀柒錢二分

共稅銀壹千零伍拾壹兩玖錢二分 [illegible]

二月十五日收完

二和行頭二三四進　大契存東生行貯

道光七年二月十一日東生[illegible]單

---

① 东生行：广州十三行之一，行商刘德章，商名章官（Chunqua），嘉庆十六年（1811）成立，道光年间倒闭。

② 二和行：新发现的广州十三行商行，以前未见记载，详情待考。

③ 勘误：英文提要税银“1461”有误。

2. 道光七年东生行[①] 房屋买卖契单说明（H2/3/2）

道光七年二月十五日（1827年3月12日），在中文信封上的说明便条，说明东生行房屋买卖契单，购买二和行[②] 的卢慎余堂，价银14,400两，税银一千零五十一两二分，房屋大契存放在东生行。

Notes re property payment. A Chinese envelope containing a note in Chinese on the front recording the payment of $1461 to Tungsheng Hong for the registration of a deed of sale at the district magistrate on the 15th day of the 2nd month of the 7th year of the reign of Taokuang (Daoguang). There is a note in English on the reverse: 'No. 17. Cheonqua's H.M: Receipt for Drs 1461[③]: paid Mandarine fees for the Creek Hong Chop - being for Factories Nos. 1, 2, 3 + 4 - dated 11th March 1827–7th Year 2d Moon 14th Day.'[④] 1 item.

H2/3/2

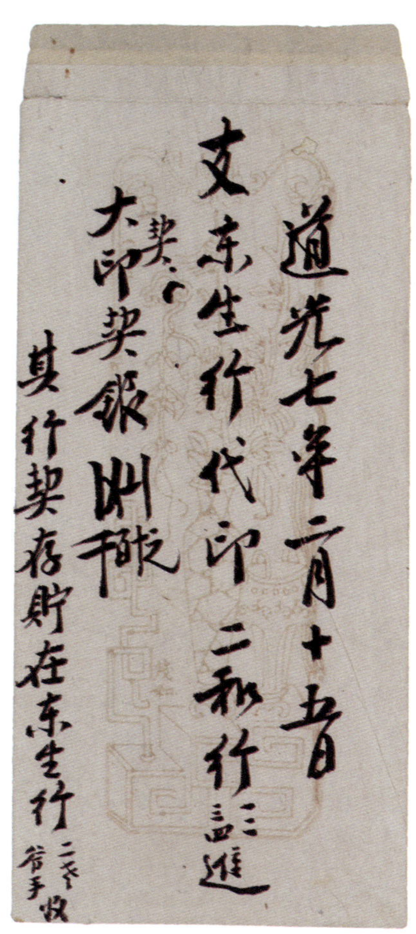

① 东生行：广州十三行之一，行商刘德章，商名章官（Chunqua），嘉庆十六年（1811）成立，道光年间倒闭。

② 二和行：新发现的广州十三行商行，以前未见记载，详情待考。

③ 勘误：英文提要中税银数额有误，应为"1051.2两"。

④ 勘误：英文提要中称信封背面有英文注释，未见。

3. 道光十二年东生行[①]出租义和馆契约（H2/3/3）

道光十二年（1832）三月，东生行将义和馆租给渣典[②]的租约，但因为东生行欠了英国怡和洋行巨额商欠，义和馆的租金不足以补偿债务，因此由外洋会馆出面保证其他债务的赔偿问题，并加盖印章“外洋会馆图记”，以示权威性和可靠性。在“十三行”已显颓势并拖欠巨款的情况下，契约中除了规定债务赔偿和房屋租赁细节外，仍不忘向外商宣示严禁将外国女性带入商馆居住。

Permission to lease. A grant of permission issued by Co-hong, including Tungfoo (Tongfu), Ewo, Kwangli (Guangli), Tungyu (Dongyu), Chongho (Zhonghe), Wanyuan (Wanyuan), Tienpao (Tianbao), Hingtae (Xingtai) and Shunt'ai (Shuntai) to Tungsheng Hong, April 1832, to let its house I-ho to the private businessman Mr. Jardine for a period of three years. Tungsheng's debt to Jardine was to be paid by the Co-hong, and the tenant was to have responsibility for painting and maintenance. Foreign females were strictly forbidden from living in the property. 1 item. 1832

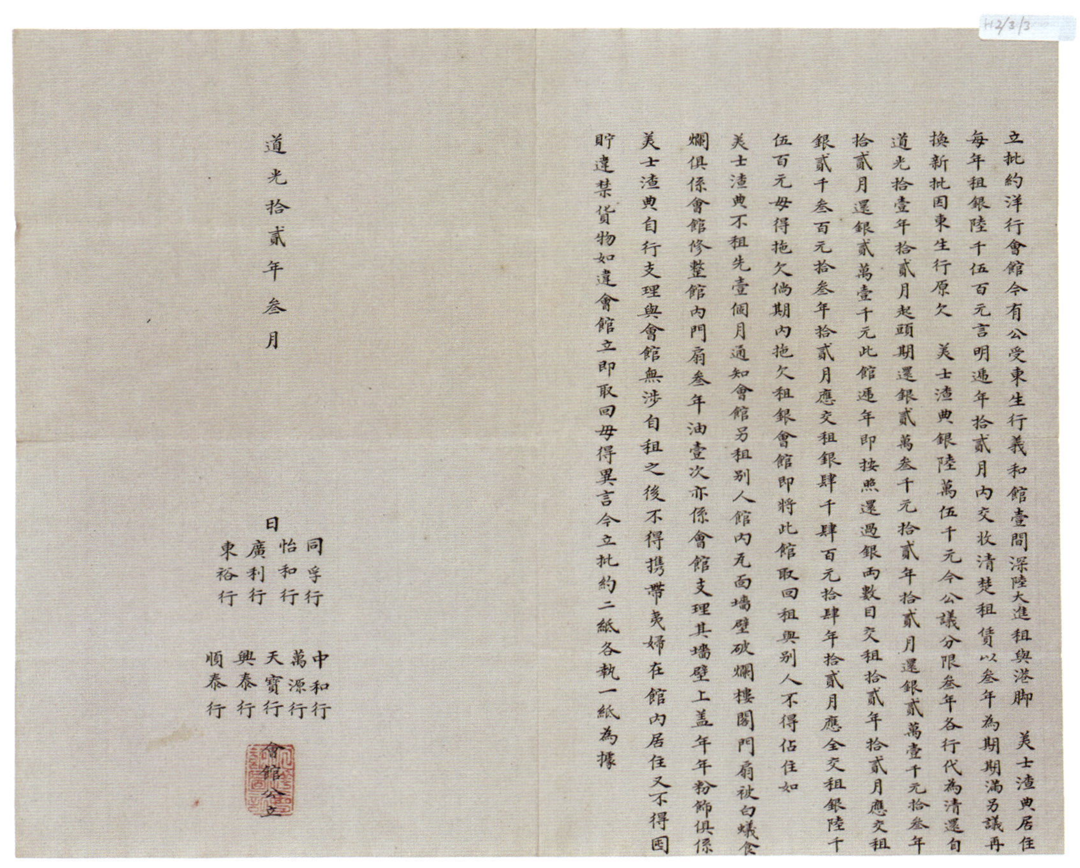
H2/3/3

立批約洋行會館今有公受東生行義和館壹間深陸大進租與港脚　美士渣典居住
每年租銀陸千伍百元言明遞年拾貳月內交收清楚租賃以叁年為期期滿另議再
換新批因東生行原欠　美士渣典銀陸萬伍千元今公議分限叁年各行代為清還自
道光拾壹年拾貳月起頭期還銀貳萬叁千元拾貳年拾貳月還銀貳萬壹千元拾叁年
拾貳月還銀貳萬壹千元此館遞年即按照還過銀両數目交租拾貳年拾貳月應交租
銀貳千叁百元拾叁年拾貳月應交租銀肆千肆百元拾肆年拾貳月應全交租銀陸千
伍百元毋得拖欠倘期內拖欠租銀會館即將此館取回租與別人不得佔住如
美士渣典不租先壹個月通知會館另租別人館內充面墻壁破爛樓閣門扇被白蟻食
爛俱係會館修整館內門扇叁年油壹次亦係會館支理其墻壁上盖年年粉飾俱係
美士渣典自行支理與會館無涉自租之後不得携帶夷婦在館內居住又不得囤
貯違禁貨物如違會館立即取回毋得異言今立批約二紙各執一紙為據

道光拾貳年叁月　日

同孚行
怡和行
廣利行
東裕行
中和行
萬源行
天寶行
興泰行
順泰行

① 东生行：广州十三行之一，行主刘德章，号章官（Chunqua）。义和馆为东生行物业，租赁给查顿洋行作为商馆。为之担保的怡和行（行商伍元华）、广利行（行商卢文锦）、同孚行（行商潘有度）、东裕行（行商谢嘉梧）、天宝行（行商梁经国）、万源行（行商李应桂）、兴泰行（行商严启昌）、中和行（行商潘文涛）、顺泰行（行商马佐良），则是道光十二年（1832）存在的各家商行。

② 渣典：即威廉·查顿（William Jardine），又译渣颠、渣甸、赞典等，为怡和洋行（Jardine, Matheson & Co.）创始人之一。

H2/3/3

立批約洋行會館今有公受東生行義和館壹間深陸大進租與港脚　美士渣典居住
每年租銀陸千伍百元言明遞年拾貳月内交收清楚租賃以叁年為期期滿另議再
換新批因東生行原欠　美士渣典銀陸萬伍千元今公議分限叁年各行代為清還自
道光拾壹年拾貳月起頭期還銀貳萬叁千元拾貳年拾貳月還銀貳萬壹千元拾叁年
拾貳月還銀貳萬壹千元此館遞年即按照還過銀兩數目交租拾貳年拾貳月應交租
銀貳千叁百元拾叁年拾貳月應交租銀肆千肆百元拾肆年拾貳月應全交租銀陸千
伍百元毋得拖欠倘期内拖欠租銀會館即將此館取回租與别人不得佔住如
美士渣典不租先壹個月通知會館另租别人館内冇面墻壁破爛樓閣門扇被白蟻食
爛俱係會館修整館内門扇叁年油壹次亦係會館支理其墻壁上盖年年粉飾俱係
美士渣典自行支理與會館無涉自租之後不得携帶夷婦在館内居住又不得囤
貯違禁貨物如違會館立即取回毋得異言今立批約二紙各執一紙為據

道光拾貳年叁月　　日

同孚行　怡和行　廣利行　東裕行
中和行　萬源行　天寶行　興泰行　順泰行

（局部图）

4. 道光十二年东生行[1]出租义和馆契约副本（H2/3/4）

此为英国剑桥大学怡和洋行档案 H2/3/3“道光十二年东生行出租义和馆契约”的副本，规定将义和馆租给渣典[2]。契约中明文规定“今立批约二纸，各执一纸为据”，按道理是怡和洋行和东生行各保留一份，不知为何两份契约都由怡和洋行保存。

Permission to lease. A grant of permission issued by Co-hong, including Tungfoo (Tongfu), Ewo, Kwangli (Guangli), Tungyu (Dongyu), Chongho (Zhonghe), Wanyuan (Wanyuan), Tienpao (Tianbao), Hingtae (Xingtai) and Shunt'ai (Shuntai) to Tungsheng Hong, April 1832, to let its house I-ho to the private businessman Mr. Jardine for a period of three years. Tungsheng's debt to Jardine was to be paid by the Co-hong, and the tenant was to have responsibility for painting and maintenance. Foreign females were strictly forbidden from living in the property. 1 item. 1832

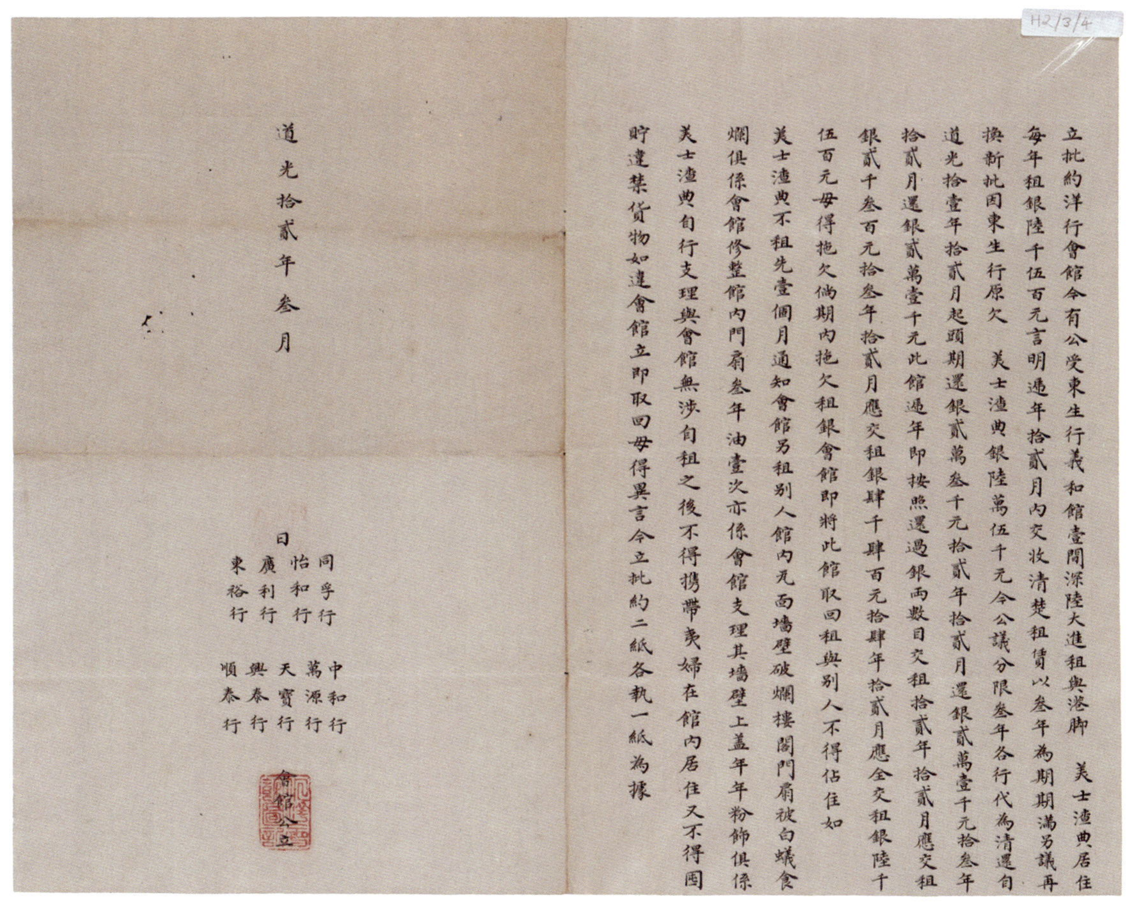
H2/3/4

立批約洋行會館今有公受東生行義和館壹間深陸大進租與港脚　美士渣典居住
每年租銀陸千伍百元言明逓年拾貳月內交收清楚租賃以叁年為期期滿另議再
換新批因東生行原欠　美士渣典銀陸萬伍千元今公議分限叁年各行代為清還自
道光拾壹年拾貳月起頭期還銀貳萬叁千元拾貳年拾貳月還銀貳萬壹千元拾叁年
拾貳月還銀貳萬壹千元此館逓年即按照還過銀両數目交租拾貳年拾貳月應交租
銀貳千叁百元拾叁年拾貳月應交租銀肆千肆百元拾肆年拾貳月應全交租銀陸千
伍百元毋得拖欠倘期內拖欠租銀會館即將此館取回租與別人不得佔住如
美士渣典不租先壹個月通知會館另租別人館內瓦面墻壁破爛樓閣門扇被白蟻食
爛俱係會館修整館內門扇叁年油壹次亦係會館支理其墻壁上蓋年年粉飾俱係
美士渣典自行支理與會館無涉自租之後不得携帶夷婦在館內居住又不得囤
貯違禁貨物如違會館立即取回毋得異言今立批約二紙各執一紙為據

道光拾貳年叁月　日

同孚行　怡和行　廣利行　東裕行
中和行　萬源行　天寶行　興泰行　順泰行

會館公立

---

① 东生行：广州十三行之一，行主刘德章，号章官（Chunqua）。义和馆为东生行物业，租赁给查顿洋行作为商馆。为之担保的怡和行（行商伍元华）、广利行（行商卢文锦）、同孚行（行商潘有度）、东裕行（行商谢嘉梧）、天宝行（行商梁经国）、万源行（行商李应桂）、兴泰行（行商严启昌）、中和行（行商潘文涛）、顺泰行（行商马佐良），则是道光十二年（1832）存在的各家商行。

② 渣典：即威廉·查顿（William Jardine），又译渣颠、渣甸、赞典等，为怡和洋行（Jardine, Matheson & Co.）创始人之一。

立批約洋行會館今有公受東生行義和館壹間深陸大進租與港脚　美士渣典居住每年租銀陸千伍百元言明逓年拾貳月内交收清楚租賃以叁年為期期滿另議再換新批因東生行原欠　美士渣典銀陸萬伍千元今公議分限叁年各行代為清還自道光拾壹年拾貳月起頭期還銀貳萬叁千元拾貳年拾貳月還銀貳萬壹千元拾叁年拾貳月還銀貳萬壹千元此館逓年即按照還過銀両數目交租拾貳年拾貳月應交租銀貳千叁百元拾叁年拾貳月應交租銀肆千肆百元拾肆年拾貳月應全交租銀陸千伍百元毋得拖欠倘期内拖欠租銀會館即將此館取回租與别人不得佔住如美士渣典不租先壹個月通知會館另租别人館内瓦面墻壁破爛樓閣門扇被白蟻食爛俱係會館修整館内門扇叁年油壹次亦係會館支理其墻壁上蓋年年粉飾俱係美士渣典自行支理與會館無涉自租之後不得携帶夷婦在館内居住又不得囤貯違禁貨物如違會館立即取回毋得異言今立批約二紙各執一紙為據

道光拾貳年叁月　日

同孚行　怡和行　廣利行　東裕行　中和行　萬源行　天寶行　興泰行　順泰行

會館公立

（局部图）

四、咸丰年间曾春信房屋买卖契约

1. 咸丰三年曾春信房屋买卖契约①（H2/4/1）

咸丰三年六月二十九日（1853年8月3日），曾春信购买陈国辉房屋契约，注明价银20元。

Assignment to Tsang Chun Sang. An assignment (in Chinese) of the sale of Inland Lot No. 353 from Chun Kok Fie (Ch'en Kuohui/Chen Guohui) chen to Tsang Chun Sang (Tseng Ch'unhsing/Zeng Chunxin), 3 August 1853. The document includes English notes, including the registration number F5, and the signatures of William Chapman and M. C. Morrison, Assistant Chinese Secretary. 1 item.

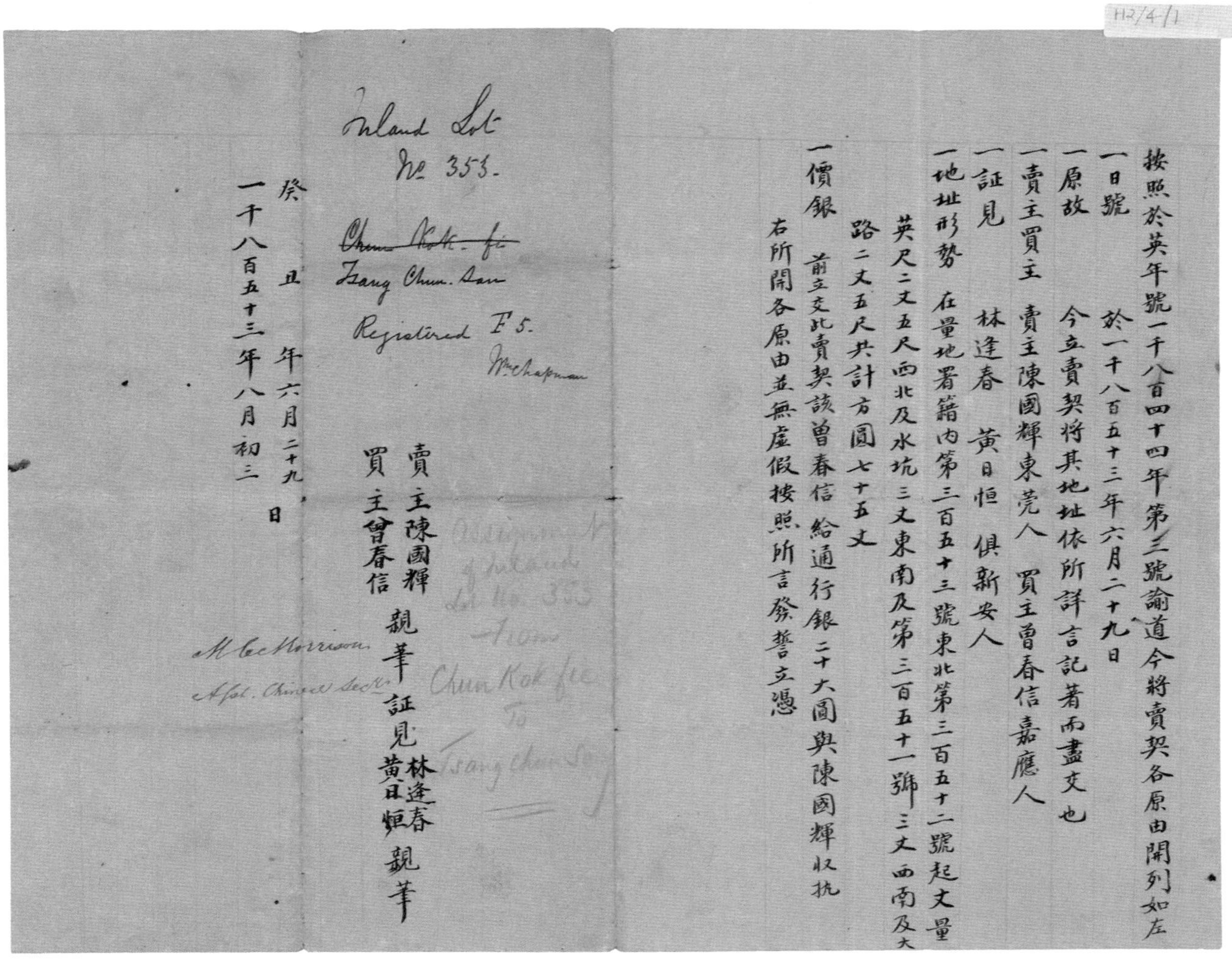

H2/4/1

按照於英年號一千八百四十四年第三號諭道今將賣契各原由開列如左

一日號　於一千八百五十三年六月二十九日

一原故　今立賣契將其地址依所詳言記著而盡文也

一賣主買主　賣主陳國輝東莞人　買主曾春信嘉應人

一証見　林逢春　黄日恒　俱新安人

一地址形勢　在量地署簿內第三百五十三號東北第三百五十二號起丈量英尺二丈五尺西北及水坑三丈東南及第三百五十一號三丈西南及大路二丈五尺共計方圓七十五丈

一價銀　前立此賣契該曾春信給通行銀二十大圓與陳國輝收執

右所開各原由並無虛假按照所言發誓立憑

Inland Lot No. 353.

~~Chun Kok fie~~

Tsang Chun San

Registered F5.

Wm Chapman

賣主陳國輝 親筆

買主曾春信

証見林逢春 黄日恒 親筆

癸丑年六月二十九日

一千八百五十三年八月初三日

M C Morrison

Asst. Chinese Secy.

Assignment of Inland Lot No. 353 from Chun Kok fie to Tsang Chun Sang

① 卖方：陈国辉。买方：曾春信。证见：林逢春、黄日恒。

2. 咸丰七年曾春信房屋买卖契约[①]（H2/4/2）

咸丰七年闰五月初一日[②]（1857年6月22日），曾春信将其在房地署编号353号的房屋卖给曾二，盖有印章，印文不清。

Assignment to Chung Ayei. An assignment (in Chinese) of the sale of Inland Lot No. 353 from Tsang Chun Sang (Tseng Ch'unhsing/Zeng Chunxin) to Chung Ayei (Tseng Erh/Zeng Er), 22 June 1857, including the English signature of the officer and the official stamp of Hong Kong. There is also a short English note describing the assignment.

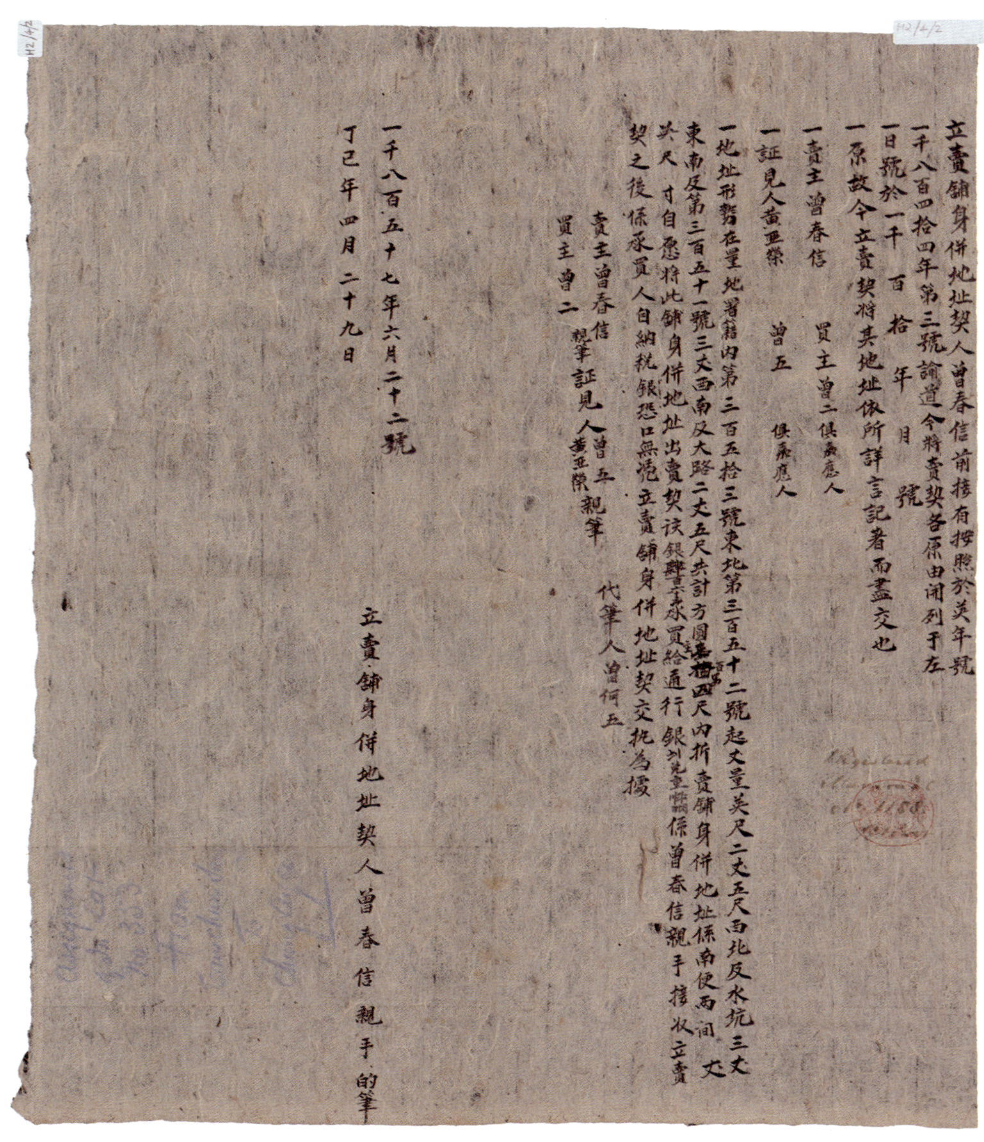

H2/4/2

立賣鋪身併地址契人曾春信前接有按照於英年號

一千八百四拾四年第三號諭道今將賣契各原由開列于左

一日號於一千 百 拾 年 月 號

一原故今立賣契將其地址依所詳言記着而盡交也

一賣主曾春信 買主曾二俱要應人

一証見人黃亞榮 曾五 俱要應人

一地址形勢在量地署籍内第三百五拾三號東北第三百五十二號起丈量英尺二丈五尺西北及水坑三丈

東南及第三百五十一號三丈西南及大路二丈五尺共計方圓[illegible]四尺内折賣鋪身併地址係南便西間丈

尖尺 寸自愿將此鋪身併地址出賣契該銀[illegible]承買給通行銀[illegible]係曾春信親手接收立賣

契之後係承買人自納税銀恐口無憑立賣鋪身併地址契交执為據

賣主曾春信親筆 証見人曾五 黃亞榮親筆 代筆人曾何五

買主曾二

一千八百五十七年六月二十二號

丁巳年四月二十九日

立賣鋪身併地址契人曾春信親手的筆

---

① 卖主：曾春信。买主：曾二。证见人：黄亚荣、曾五。

② 原中文文献中并排所写的两个时间阴历丁巳年四月二十九日（阳历1857年5月22日）、阳历一千八百五十七年六月二十二号（阴历咸丰七年闰五月初一日），二者并非同一天，疑原文献有误。

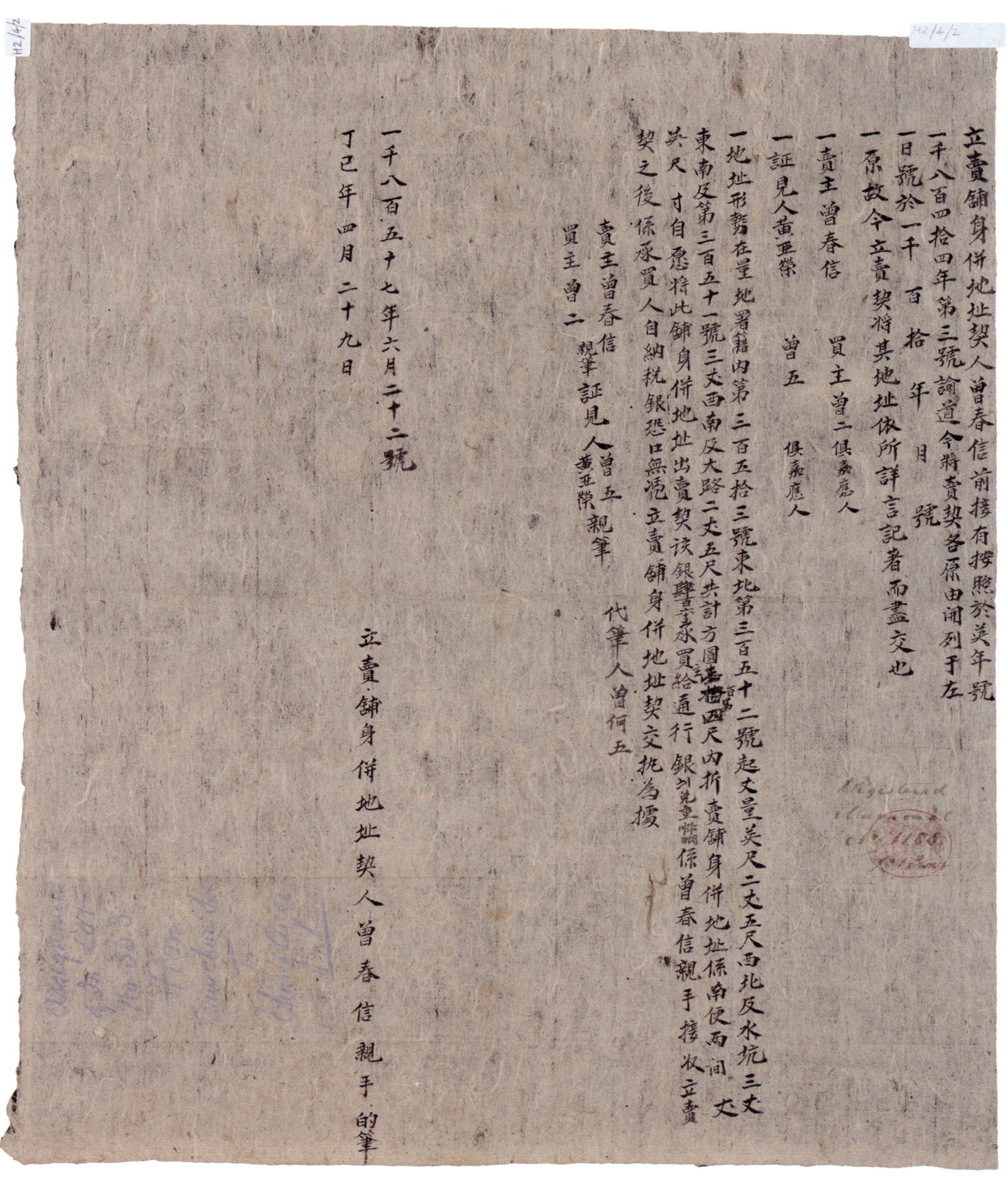

立賣舖身併地址契人曾春信前接有按照於英年號
一千八百四拾四年第三號諭道今將賣契各原由開列于左
一日號於一千　百　拾　年　月　號
一原故今立賣契將其地址依所詳言記者而盡交也
一賣主曾春信　　買主曾二俱嘉應人
一証見人黃亞榮　　曾五　　俱嘉應人
一地址形勢在量地署籍內第三百五拾三號東北第三百五十二號起丈量英尺二丈五尺西北反水坑三丈
東南反第三百五十一號三丈西南反大路二丈五尺共計方圓[illegible]四尺內折賣舖身併地址係南便西間　丈
英尺　寸自愿將此舖身併地址出賣契該銀[illegible]承買給通行銀[illegible]係曾春信親手接收立賣
契之後係承買人自納稅銀恐口無憑立賣舖身併地址契交執為據
賣主曾春信親筆　証見人曾五 黃亞榮親筆　代筆人曾何五
買主曾二
一千八百五十七年六月二十二號
丁巳年四月二十九日
立賣舖身併地址契人曾春信親手的筆

（局部图）

五、咸丰四年英国商人孖地臣①交来晋元馆②租银的收据（H2/5）

咸丰四年二月初九日（1854年3月7日），英国商人孖地臣交来1844年至1854年的晋元馆租银。

A copy of a receipt from Chin-yuen kuan (Jinyuan guan) to Matheson, 7 March 1854, for rents paid during the period from DG 25y 2m 11d (18 March 1835③) to XF 3y 10m 1d (1 November 1853), including a breakdown of the rents.

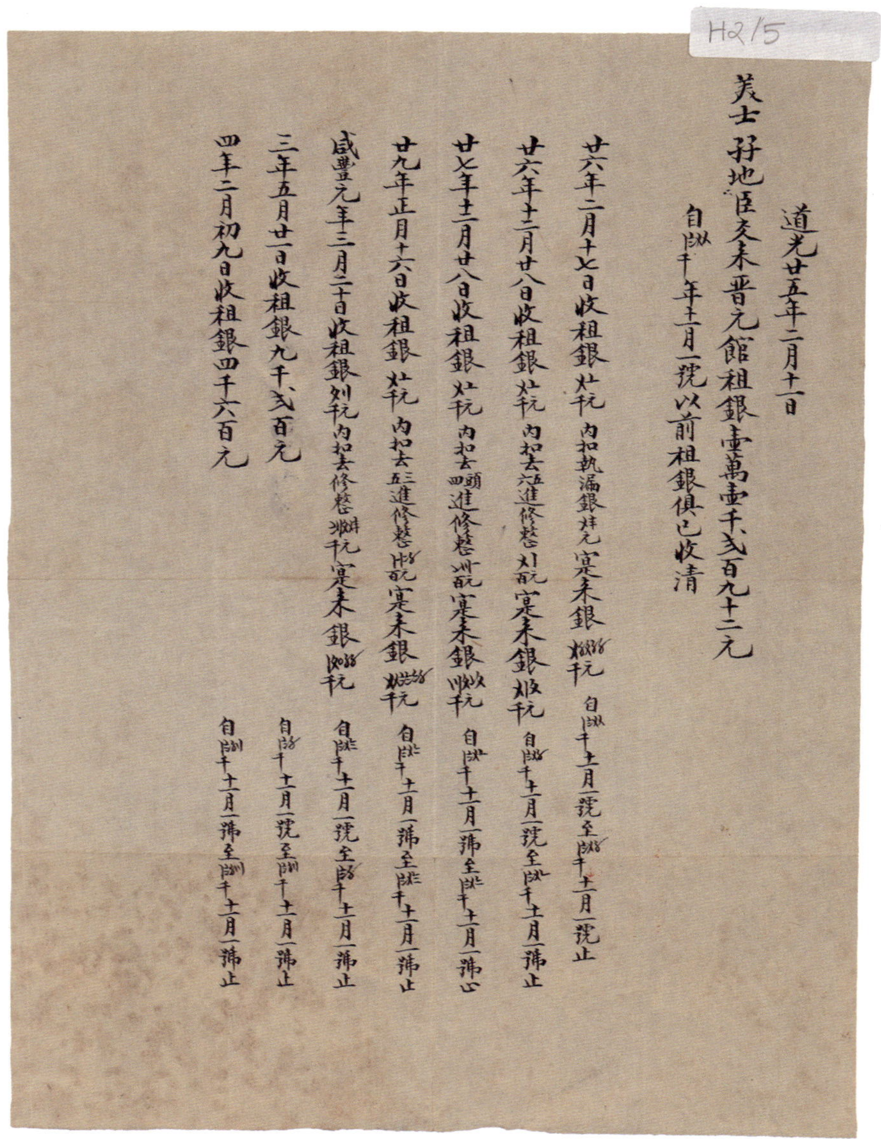

H2/5

道光廿五年二月十一日

美士孖地臣交来晋元館租銀壹萬壹千弍百九十二元

自[illegible]年十月一號以前租銀俱已收清

廿六年二月十七日收租銀[illegible]元　内扣執漏銀[illegible]元　實来銀[illegible]元　自[illegible]年十二月一號至[illegible]年十二月一號止

廿六年十二月廿八日收租銀[illegible]元　内扣去六五進修整[illegible]元　實来銀[illegible]元　自[illegible]年十二月一號至[illegible]年十二月一號止

廿七年十二月廿八日收租銀[illegible]元　内扣去頭四進修整[illegible]元　實来銀[illegible]元　自[illegible]年十二月一號至[illegible]年十二月一號止

廿九年正月十六日收租銀[illegible]元　内扣去五三進修整[illegible]元　實来銀[illegible]元　自[illegible]年十二月一號至[illegible]年十二月一號止

咸豐元年三月二十日收租銀[illegible]元　内扣去修整[illegible]元　實来銀[illegible]元　自[illegible]年十二月一號至[illegible]年十二月一號止

三年五月廿一日收租銀九千弍百元　自[illegible]年十二月一號至[illegible]年十二月一號止

四年二月初九日收租銀四千六百元　自[illegible]年十二月一號至[illegible]年十二月一號止

① 孖地臣：James Matheson，即詹姆斯·马地臣，1796—1878年，与威廉·查顿同为怡和洋行（Jardine, Matheson & Co.）创办人。

② 晋元馆：马地臣租用的商馆。

③ 勘误："道光二十五年二月十一日"换算为公历，应为1845年3月18日，英文提要中误将1845年写作1835年。

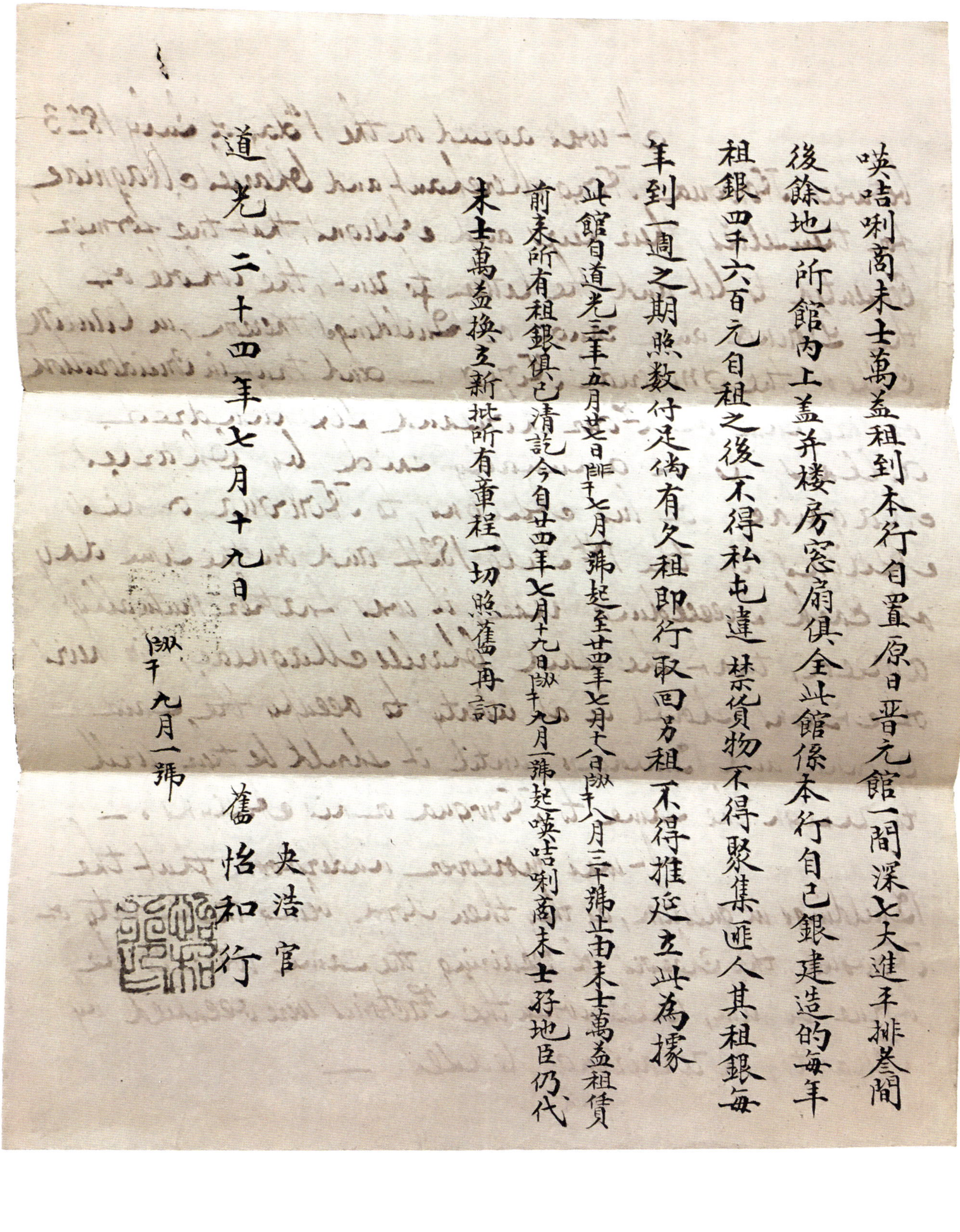

𠸄咭唎商未士萬益租到本行自置原日晋元館一間深七丈進手排叁間

後餘地一所館內上蓋并樓房窗扇俱全此館係本行自己銀建造的每年

租銀四千六百元自租之後不得私屯違禁貨物不得聚集匪人其租銀每

年到一週之期照數付足倘有欠租即行取回另租不得推延立此為據

此館自道光三年五月廿七日陬七月一號起至廿四年七月十八日陬八月三十號止由未士萬益租賃

前來所有租銀俱已清訖今自廿四年七月十九日陬九月一號起𠸄咭唎商未士孖地臣仍代

未士萬益換立新批所有章程一切照舊再訂

道光二十四年七月十九日

陬九月一號

舊怡和行

央浩官

It was agreed on the 1st day of July 1823 between Howqua Hong Merchant and Charles Magniac, for themselves, their heirs and Assigns, that the former Consented to let and the latter to rent, the whole of the Ground and range of Buildings thereon, in Canton called the Imperial Hong — and that in Consideration of the sum of Four thousand Six hundred dollars, to be annually paid by Charles Magniac, or his Assigns, to Howqua or his Assigns, on the 1st July 1824 and on the same day of each succeeding year, it was further mutually agreed, that the said Charles Magniac, his heirs or Assigns, should be at liberty to occupy the said ground and Buildings, until it should be their will to resign the same to Howqua or his Assigns. —

It was moreover understood that the Buildings in question, as they then stood, being the property of Howqua, the charges of repairing the same were to be borne by him, unless when the Factories were occupied by Tenants, on repairing leases. —

The late War having for a time suspended the fulfilment of the foregoing agreement the same has been renewed between Young Howqua, as heir and representative of his late Father and Alexander Matheson as representative of Hollingworth Magniac, heir of the late Charles Magniac, on precisely similar terms – all past accounts having been settled to 1st November 1843 on which date – annually the aforesaid Ground rent is to be paid to Young Howqua by the Agent of Hollingworth Magniac, his heirs or Assigns. –

Signed by both parties in Canton this 18th day of March 1845. in duplicate –

Witness to Signature of Young Howqua

羅照官　　　　央浩官

Witness to Signature of Alexander Matheson
John Millar

Alexr. Matheson

六、同治四年台湾淡水邱氏兄弟出租土地契约

1. 同治四年台湾淡水邱氏兄弟出租土地契约[①]（H2/6/1）

同治四年（1865）七月，台湾淡水邱氏兄弟出租土地给唐隆茂官契约。

Deposit receipt. A copy of a receipt from Ch’iu Ta-man (Qiu Daman) and his two brothers to T’ang Lung-mao (Tang Longmao) for the deposit for a deed of sale for land in Tamsui containing sulphur springs, dated 2 August–19 September 1865, including the names of three witnesses and the stamp of the Tamsui magistrate.1 item.

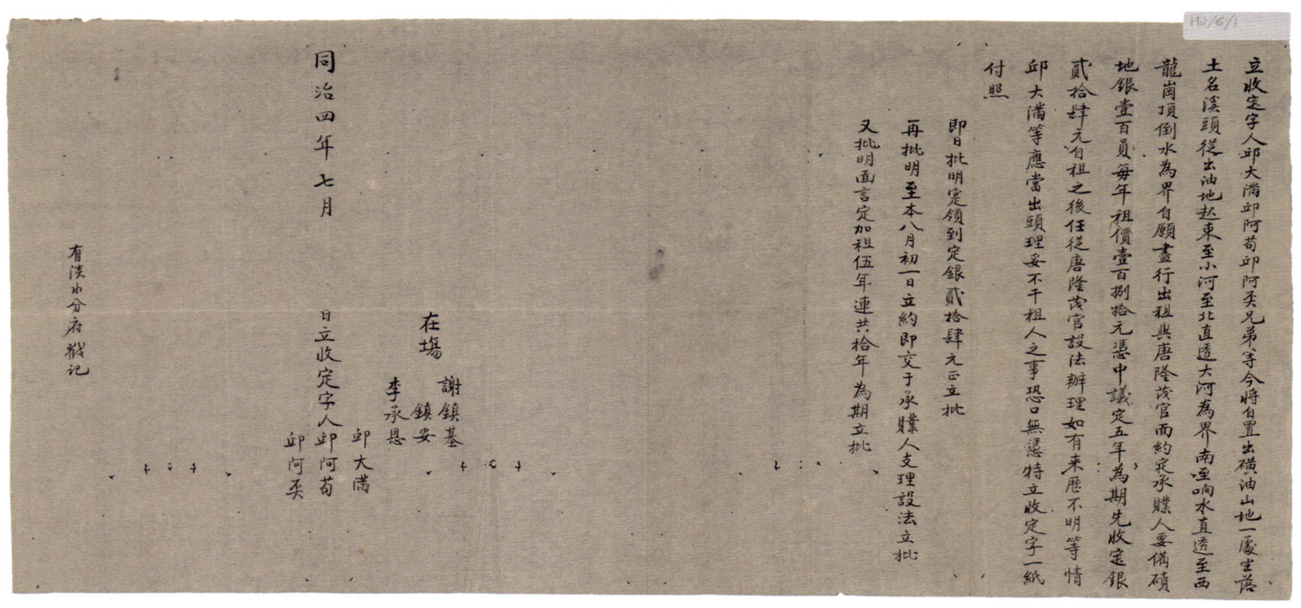
H2/6/1

立收定字人邱大滿邱阿苟邱阿奕兄弟等今將自置出磺油山地一處坐落
土名溪頭從出油地起東至小河至北直透大河為界南至响水直透至西
龍崗頂倒水為界自願盡行出租與唐隆茂官面約定承贌人要備磧
地銀壹百員每年租價壹百捌拾元憑中議定五年為期先收定銀
貳拾肆元自租之後任從唐隆茂官設法辦理如有來歷不明等情
邱大滿等應當出頭理妥不干租人之事恐口無憑特立收定字一紙
付照

即日批明定領到定銀貳拾肆元正立批

再批明至本八月初一日立約即交于承贌人支理設法立批

又批明面言定加租伍年連共拾年為期立批

在場　謝鎮基　謝鎮安　李承恩

同治四年七月　日立收定字人　邱大滿　邱阿苟　邱阿奕

有淡水分府戳記

① 出租方：邱大满、邱阿苟、邱阿弈。承租方：唐隆茂官。在场：谢镇基、谢镇安、李承恩。

立收定字人邱大滿邱阿苟邱阿奀兄弟等今將自置出横油山地一處坐落
土名溪頭從出油地起東至小河至北直透大河為界南至响水直透至西
龍崗頂倒水為界自願盡行出租與唐隆茂官面約定承贌人要備磧
地銀壹百員每年租價壹百捌拾元憑中議定五年為期先收定銀
貳拾肆元自租之後任從唐隆茂官設法辦理如有來歷不明等情
邱大滿等應當出頭理妥不干租人之事恐口無憑特立收定字一紙
付照

即日批明寔領到定銀貳拾肆元正立批

再批明至本八月初一日立約即交于承贌人支理設法立批

又批明面言定加租伍年連共拾年為期立批

在場　謝鎮基　鎮安　李承恩

同治四年七月　日立收定字人邱阿苟　邱大滿　邱阿奀

有淡水分府戳记

（局部图）

2. 同治四年台湾淡水邱氏兄弟出租土地契约[①]（H2/6/2）

同治四年八月初一日（1865年9月20日），台湾淡水邱氏兄弟出租土地给唐隆茂官契约。

Deed of pledge. A copy of a deed of pledge from Ch’iu Akuo (Qiu Agou) and his six brothers, including Ch’iu Ta-man (Qiu Daman), to T’ang Lung-mao (Tang Longmao), for the sale of their land in Tamsui, Taiwan, where sulphur springs have been discovered, 20 September 1865. The document includes the names of the Ch’ius’ mother, four witnesses, a middleman and a copier, and the official stamp of the prefecture magistrate, Tamsui.1 item.

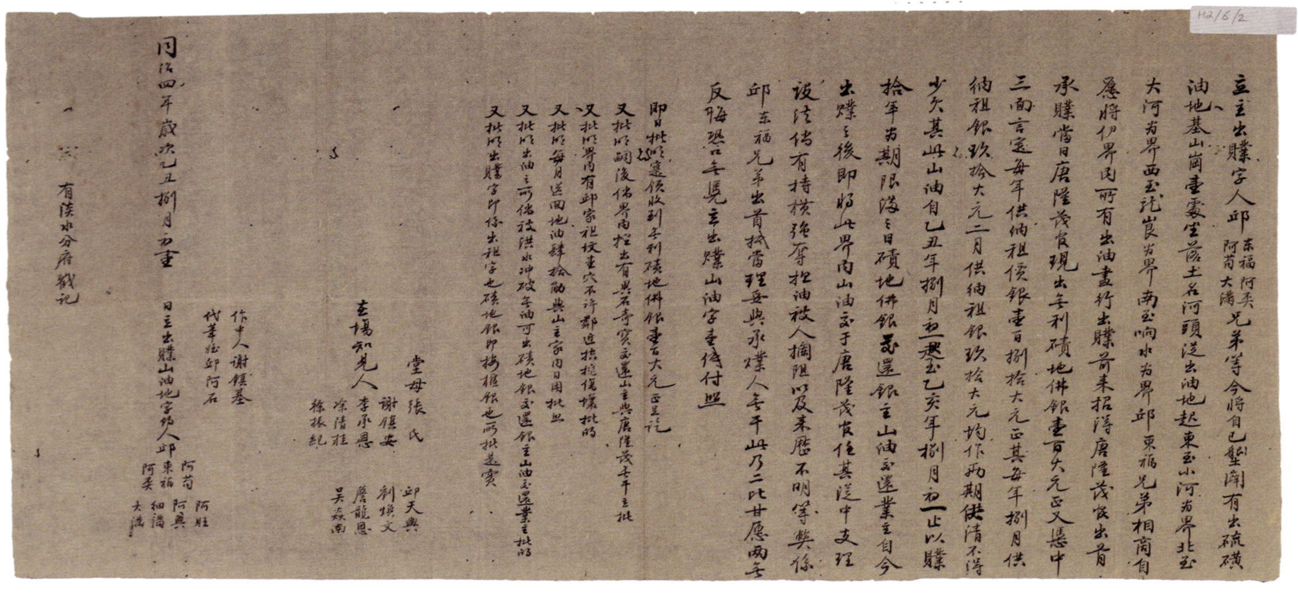

① 卖方：邱东福、邱阿苟、邱阿弈、邱大满、邱阿旺、邱阿兴、邱细满。买方：唐隆茂官。在场：谢镇安、李承恩等人。代笔：邱阿石。中人：谢镇基。

（局部图）

Chapter Three

第三章

海关文件

海关文件时间涵盖1852—1866年，共计17件。其中有粤海关签发的十余件各船户装载白糖等货物前往江浙地区出口关票。此外还有中国其他地方海关的资料，如黄冈海关签发各船户装载白糖等货物前往江浙地区出口关票；江南海关签发给怡和洋行属下轮船装载货物的完纳税钞红单。

一、咸丰二年虎门[1]验单[2]

1. 咸丰二年粤海关发给美国晏庇地[3]船长虎门验单（H3/1/1）

咸丰二年十一月十八日（1852年12月28日），虎门海关商船出入口的袁专员发放给晏庇地（Yen-pi-ti）船长的谕令，告知他要遵守各国领事官议定的章程，必须在出入口办事处登记并出具红牌谕令才能进出虎门。盖有粤海关下属印章，印文“巡查虎门洋面委员钤记”。

Customs notice. A notice issued by Yuan, the inspector in charge of the entry and exit of merchant ships at the Bogue to Captain Yen-pi-ti, 28 December 1852, informing him that according to the regulation agreed by foreign consuls all merchant ships entering and exiting the Bogue must show the Red Note which is issued by his office after registration. 1 item; Fair condition, but damage by insects.

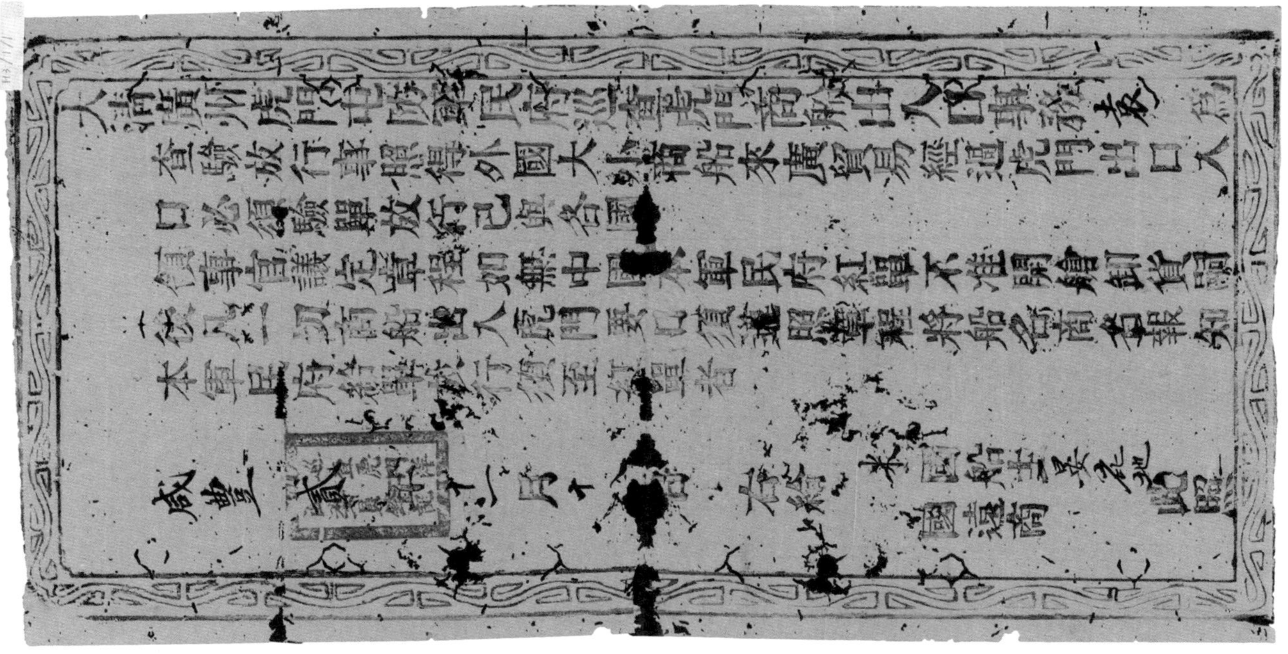

大清署廣州府虎門海防軍民府兼巡查虎門商船出入口事務袁　為
查驗放行事照得外國大小商船來廣貿易經過虎門出口入
口必須驗單放行已與各國
領事官議定章程如無中國本軍民府紅單不准開艙卸貨嗣
後凡一切商船出入虎門要口須遵照新章將船名商名報知
本軍民府給單放行須至驗單者
右給　米國船主晏庇地　照
咸豐二年十一月十[illegible]日

---

① 虎门：《粤海关志》有虎门口图。书云：“此系挂号口，在广州府东莞县，距大关一百六十里。”虎门税馆位于虎门水道中的江中的横档岛，横档岛水道两侧为海防炮台重地。横档岛又称“北横档岛”“上横档岛”。1931年粤海五十里内外常关全部改为海关机构，虎门口划归粤海关管理。清代虎门水道，上横档岛（左）粤海关虎门口（有中式旗幡建筑），面向东航道，对岸为威远炮台（右）。虎门是广州门户，也是西江、北江、东江三江汇集之地，其地受时局的重视而渐有设防。明清时期虎门海防地位逐步提高，特别是清中期以后，虎门水道的珠江防御已成为广东中路乃至全国海防重点，被喻为“海上函谷关”。

② 验单：粤海关颁发的外国商船出入口凭证，因其纸张为红色，称为“红单”。

③ 晏庇地：Yen-pi-ti，美国商船“巴辰士号”船长。

2. 咸丰二年粤海关发给美国晏庇地[①]船长虎门[②]报单[③]（H3/1/2）

咸丰二年十一月十八日（1852年12月28日），虎门海关税口外国商船出入口的申报单，注明美国商船“巴辰士号”，船长“晏庇地”，前往广州贸易，船上载有洋米等货。盖有粤海关英文印章，印文“HOICHONG”。

Import declaration form. An import declaration form from the Bogue customs to Captain Yen-pi-ti, 28 December 1852.

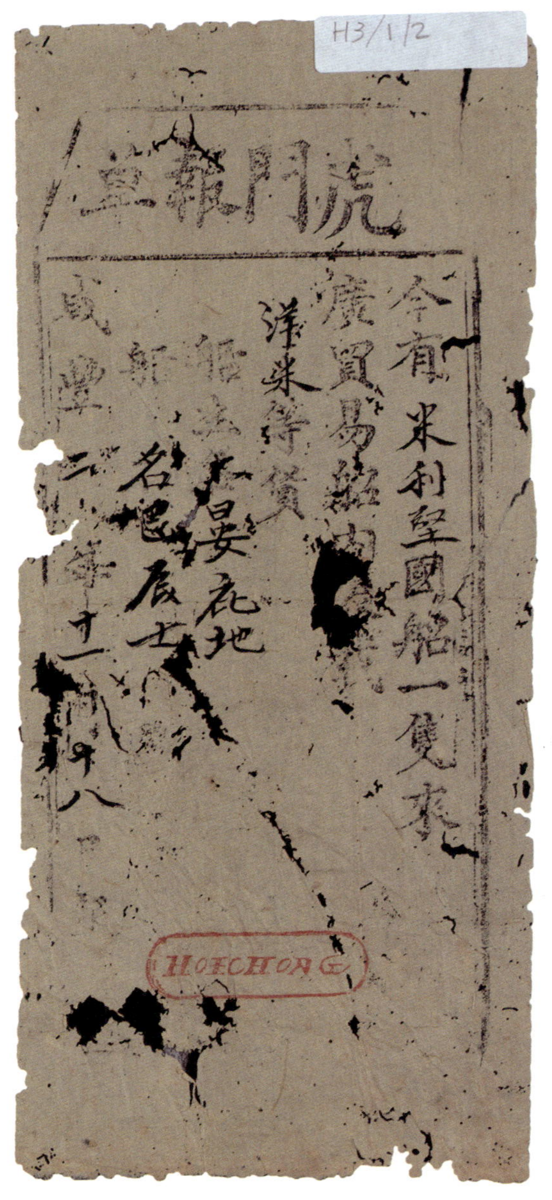

H3/1/2

虎門報單

今有米利堅國船一隻來

廣貿易船內

洋米等貨

船主晏庇地

船名巴辰士

咸豐二年十一月十八日

HOICHONG

---

① 晏庇地：Yen-pi-ti，美国商船“巴辰士号”船长。

② 虎门：粤海关税口，在广州府东莞县，距大关一百六十里。

③ 报单：外国商船出入虎门税口的申报登记证明，注明国籍、船名、船长、所载货物等。

二、咸丰八年黄冈口[①]出口关票

1. 咸丰八年粤海关黄冈口出口关票（H3/2/1）

咸丰八年二月十六日（1858年3月30日），粤海关监督恒祺[②]发给外国货船“德隆号”通过黄冈口赴江浙口出口关票，载有500包白糖，赴江浙口售卖，饷银完讫。盖有粤海关两枚印章，一枚粤海关关防[③]，印文不清，据同时期其他出口关票中的印文判断应为“督理广东省沿海等处贸易税务户部分司关防”；另一枚黄冈口税务印章，印文“黄冈口图记”。

Customs permit to the ‘Te-lung’. A customs clearance permit issued to the ‘Te-lung’, loaded with 500 bags of white sugar, 30 March 1858. The document was originally numbered 35. 1 item.

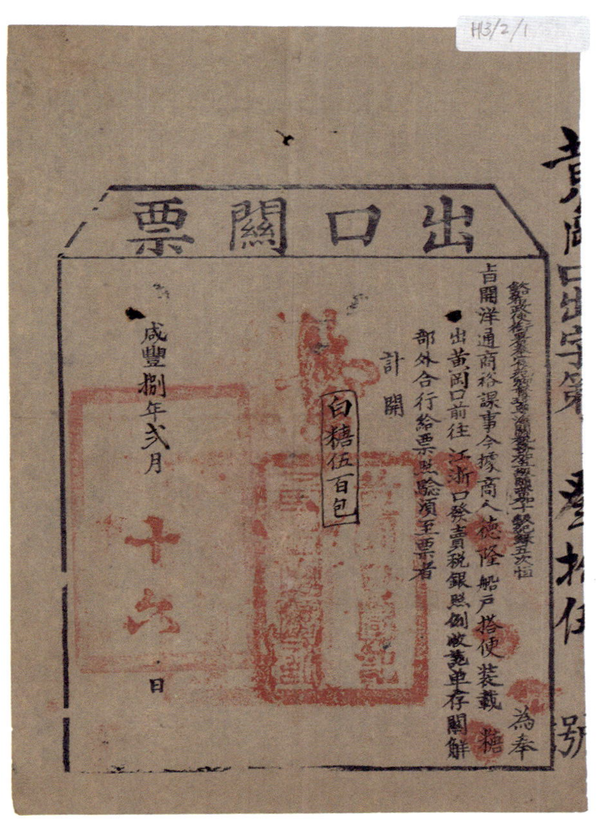

H3/2/1

出口關票

為奉

旨開洋通商務課事今據商人德隆船戶搭使裝載糖

出黃岡口前往江浙口發賣稅銀照例收訖单存關解

部外合行給票照驗須至票者

計開

白糖伍百包

咸豐捌年弍月十六日

---

① 黄冈口：据梁廷枏《粤海关志》记载，为正税口，位于潮州府饶平县，距离庵埠总口一百四十里，距离省城大关一千七百里。黄冈口下辖乌塘口，也在饶平县，为挂号小口。

② 恒祺1856—1859年任粤海关监督。

③ 粤海关关防：为满、汉篆文合璧，长九又二分之一厘米，宽六厘米。粤海关，设于康熙二十四年（1685），位于广东省城五仙门内，其主官为粤海关监督。粤海关监督在英文资料中被称为“Hoppo”。因为粤海关监督是“户部分司”，是中央户部派出驻在广东省负责收税的司员，而粤海关衙门便是户部的派出衙门。而在广州的官场上，较常使用“关部”这样的用语。其实，“关部”就是“海关—户部”的合称，更能显示粤海关监督的特点。

2. 咸丰八年粤海关黄冈口[①]出口关票（H3/2/2）

咸丰八年三月初九日（1858年4月22日），粤海关监督恒祺[②]发给外国货船德隆号通过黄冈税口赴江浙口出口关票，载有700包白糖，赴江浙口售卖，饷银完讫。盖有粤海关两枚印章，一枚粤海关关防[③]，印文不清，据同时期其他出口关票中的印文判断应为“督理广东省沿海等处贸易税务户部分司关防”；另一枚黄冈口税务印章，印文“黄冈口图记”。

Customs permit to the ‘Te-lung’. A customs clearance permit issued to the ‘Te-lung’, loaded with 700 bags of white sugar, 22 April 1858. The document was originally numbered 57. 1 item.

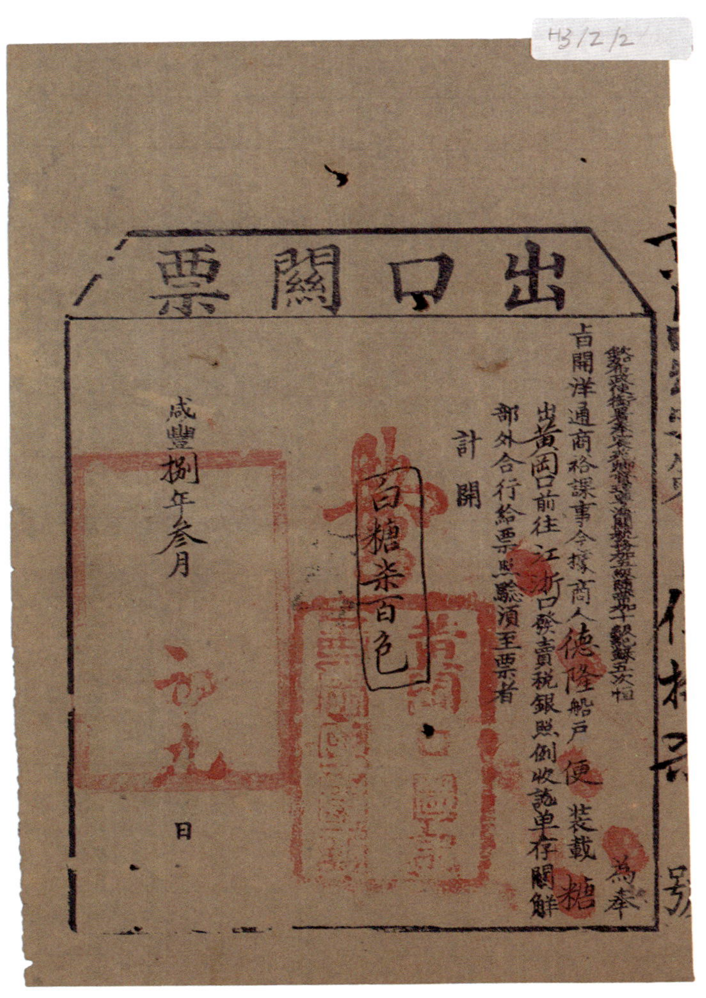
H3/2/2

出口關票

為奉

旨開洋通商裕課事今據商人德隆船戶便裝載糖

出黃岡口前往江浙口發賣稅銀照例收訖單存關

部外合行給票照驗須至票者

計開

白糖柒百包

咸豐捌年叁月初九日

---

① 黄冈口：据梁廷枏《粤海关志》记载，为正税口，位于潮州府饶平县，距离庵埠总口一百四十里，距离省城大关一千七百里。黄冈口下辖乌塘口，也在饶平县，为挂号小口。

② 恒祺1856—1859年任粤海关监督。

③ 粤海关关防：为满、汉篆文合璧，长九又二分之一厘米，宽六厘米。粤海关，设于康熙二十四年（1685），位于广东省城五仙门内，其主官为粤海关监督。粤海关监督在英文资料中被称为“Hoppo”。因为粤海关监督是“户部分司”，是中央户部派出驻在广东省负责收税的司员，而粤海关衙门便是户部的派出衙门。而在广州的官场上，较常使用“关部”这样的用语。其实，“关部”就是“海关—户部”的合称，更能显示粤海关监督的特点。

三、咸丰八年至九年北炮台口[①]出口关票

1. 咸丰八年粤海关北炮台口出口关票（H3/3/1）

咸丰八年二月十七日（1858年3月31日），粤海关监督恒祺[②]发给中国货船“福元号”通过北炮台税口赴江浙口出口关票，载有219包白糖，赴江浙口售卖，饷银完讫。盖有粤海关两枚印章，一枚粤海关关防[③]，印文不清，据同时期其他出口关票中的印文判断应为“督理广东省沿海等处贸易税务户部分司关防”；另一枚北炮台税务印章，印文“北炮台口图记”。

Customs permit to Fu-yuan. A customs clearance permit issued to Fu-yuan (Fuyuan) for 200[④] bags of white sugar, 31 March 1858. The document has the serial number 82. 1 item.

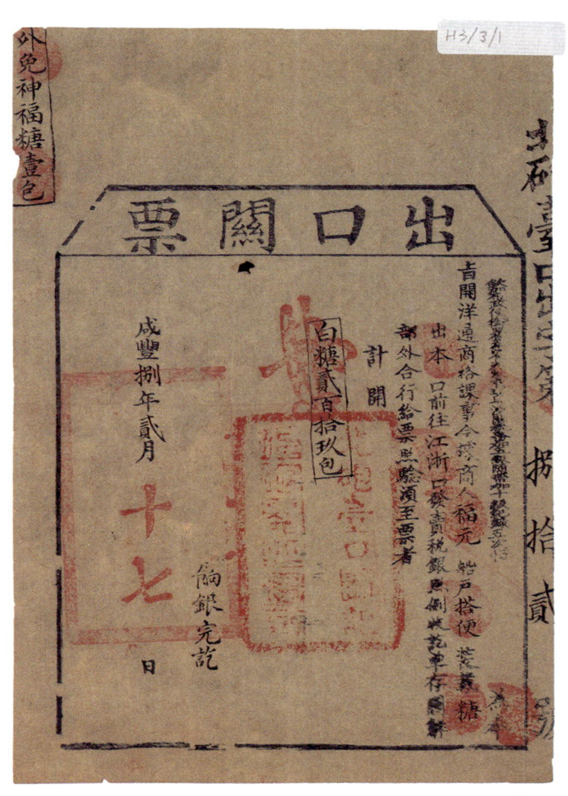
H3/3/1
外免神福糖壹包
出口關票
吉開洋通商給課事今據商人福元 船戶搭便 裝載糖
出本口前往江浙口發賣稅銀照例收訖
部外合行給票照驗須至票者
計開
白糖貳百拾玖包
咸豐捌年貳月十七日
餉銀完訖

---

① 北炮台口：据梁廷枏《粤海关志》记载，为正税口，位于潮州府揭阳县，距离庵埠总口一百二十里，距离省城大关一千六百里。

② 恒祺1856—1859年任粤海关监督。

③ 粤海关关防：为满、汉篆文合璧，长九又二分之一厘米，宽六厘米。粤海关，设于康熙二十四年（1685），位于广东省城五仙门内，其主官为粤海关监督。粤海关监督在英文资料中被称为“Hoppo”。因为粤海关监督是“户部分司”，是中央户部派出驻在广东省负责收税的司员，而粤海关衙门便是户部的派出衙门。而在广州的官场上，较常使用“关部”这样的用语。其实，“关部”就是“海关—户部”的合称，更能显示粤海关监督的特点。

④ 勘误：按原中文文献应为219包，英文提要中此数字疑误。

2. 咸丰八年粤海关北炮台口[①]出口关票（H3/3/2）

咸丰八年二月二十三日（1858年4月6日），粤海关监督恒祺[②]发给中国货船“福源号”通过北炮台税口赴江浙口出口关票，载有293包白糖，赴江浙口售卖，饷银完讫。盖有粤海关两枚印章，一枚粤海关关防[③]，印文不清，据同时期其他出口关票中的印文判断应为“督理广东省沿海等处贸易税务户部分司关防”；另一枚北炮台税务印章，印文“北炮台口图记”。

Customs permit to Fu-yuan. A customs clearance permit issued to Fu-yuan (Fuyuan) for 200[④] bags of white sugar, 6 April 1858. 1 item.

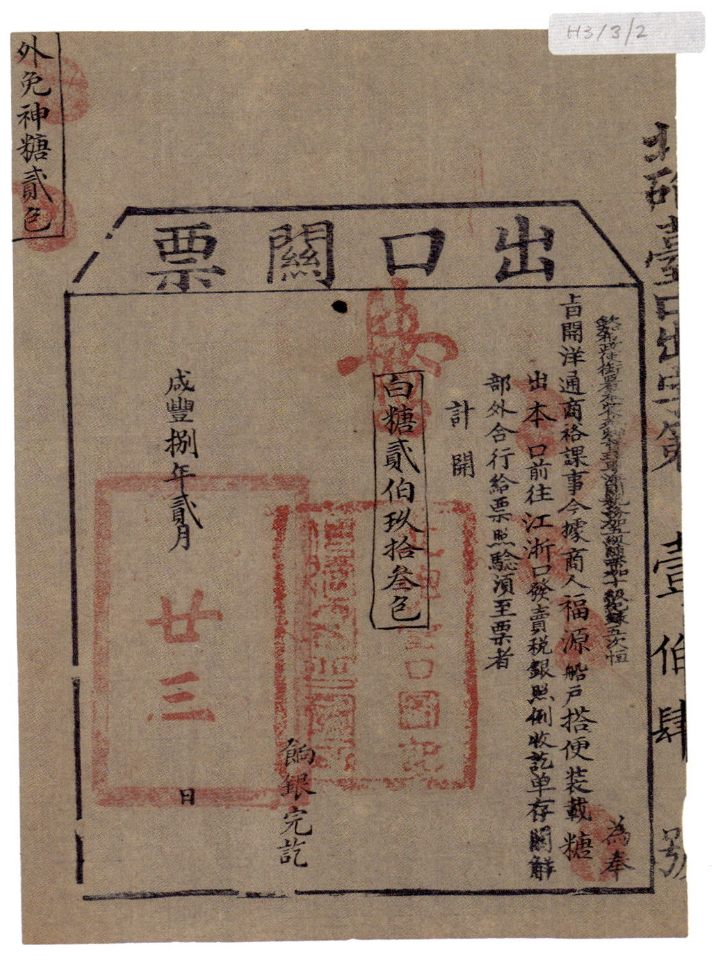

H3/3/2

外免神糖貳包

出口關票

為奉
吉開洋通商裕課事今據商人福源船戶搭便裝載糖
出本口前往江浙口發賣稅銀照例收訖單存關觧
部外合行給票照驗須至票者
計開
白糖貳伯玖拾叁包
餉銀完訖
咸豐捌年貳月廿三日

---

① 北炮台口：据梁廷枏《粤海关志》记载，为正税口，位于潮州府揭阳县，距离庵埠总口一百二十里，距离省城大关一千六百里。

② 恒祺1856—1859年任粤海关监督。

③ 粤海关关防：为满、汉篆文合璧，长九又二分之一厘米，宽六厘米。粤海关，设于康熙二十四年(1685)，位于广东省城五仙门内，其主官为粤海关监督。粤海关监督在英文资料中被称为“Hoppo”。因为粤海关监督是“户部分司”，是中央户部派出驻在广东省负责收税的司员，而粤海关衙门便是户部的派出衙门。而在广州的官场上，较常使用“关部”这样的用语。其实，“关部”就是“海关—户部”的合称，更能显示粤海关监督的特点。

④ 勘误：按原中文文献应为293包，英文提要中此数字疑误。

3. 咸丰八年粤海关北炮台口[①]出口关票（H3/3/3）

咸丰八年二月二十七日（1858年4月10日），粤海关监督恒祺[②]发给中国货船“隆顺号”通过北炮台税口赴江浙口出口关票，载有220包白糖，赴江浙口售卖，饷银完讫。盖有粤海关两枚印章，一枚粤海关关防[③]，印文不清，据同时期其他出口关票中的印文判断应为“督理广东省沿海等处贸易税务户部分司关防”；另一枚北炮台税务印章，印文“北炮台口图记”。

Customs permit to Lung-shun. A customs clearance permit issued to Lung-shun (Longshun) for 200[④] bags of white sugar, 10 April 1858.1 item.

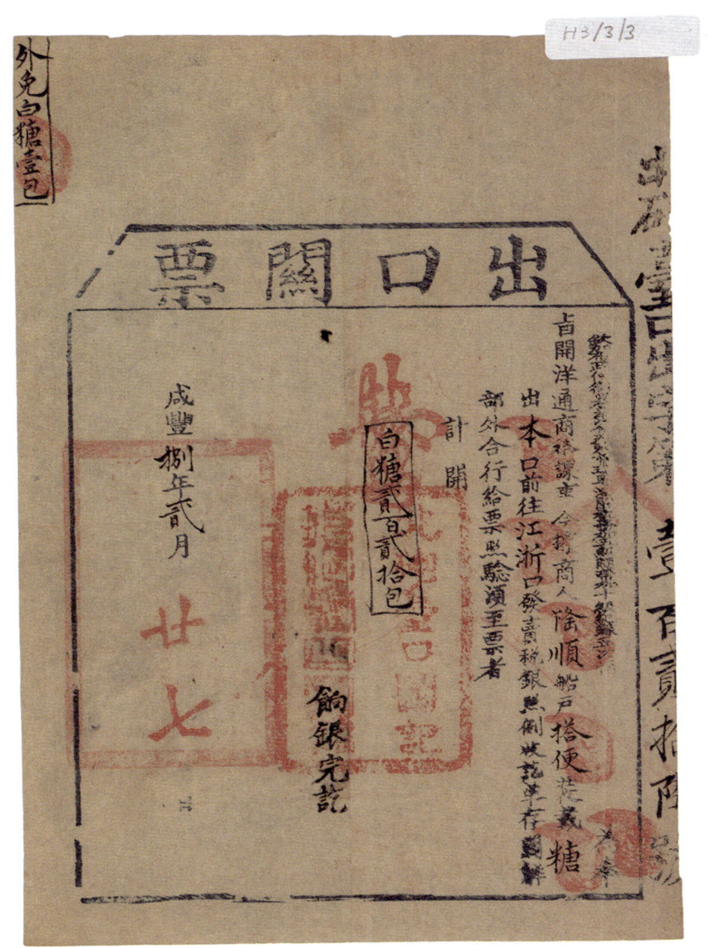
H3/3/3

出口關票

計開

白糖貳百貳拾包

餉銀完訖

咸豐捌年貳月 廿七

---

① 北炮台口：据梁廷枏《粤海关志》记载，为正税口，位于潮州府揭阳县，距离庵埠总口一百二十里，距离省城大关一千六百里。

② 恒祺1856—1859年任粤海关监督。

③ 粤海关关防：为满、汉篆文合璧，长九又二分之一厘米，宽六厘米。粤海关，设于康熙二十四年（1685），位于广东省城五仙门内，其主官为粤海关监督。粤海关监督在英文资料中被称为“Hoppo”。因为粤海关监督是“户部分司”，是中央户部派出驻在广东省负责收税的司员，而粤海关衙门便是户部的派出衙门。而在广州的官场上，较常使用“关部”这样的用语。其实，“关部”就是“海关—户部”的合称，更能显示粤海关监督的特点。

④ 勘误：按原中文文献应为220包，英文提要中此数字疑误。

4. 咸丰八年粤海关北炮台口[①]出口关票（H3/3/4）

咸丰八年三月十四日（1858年4月27日），粤海关监督恒祺[②]发给中国货船“隆顺号”通过北炮台税口赴江浙口出口关票，载有90包白糖，赴江浙口售卖，饷银完讫。盖有粤海关两枚印章，一枚粤海关关防[③]，印文不清，据同时期其他出口关票中的印文判断应为“督理广东省沿海等处贸易税务户部分司关防”；另一枚北炮台税务印章，印文“北炮台口图记”。

Customs permit to Lung-shun. A customs clearance permit issued to Lung-shun (Longshun) for 90 bags of white sugar, 27 April 1858. 1 item.

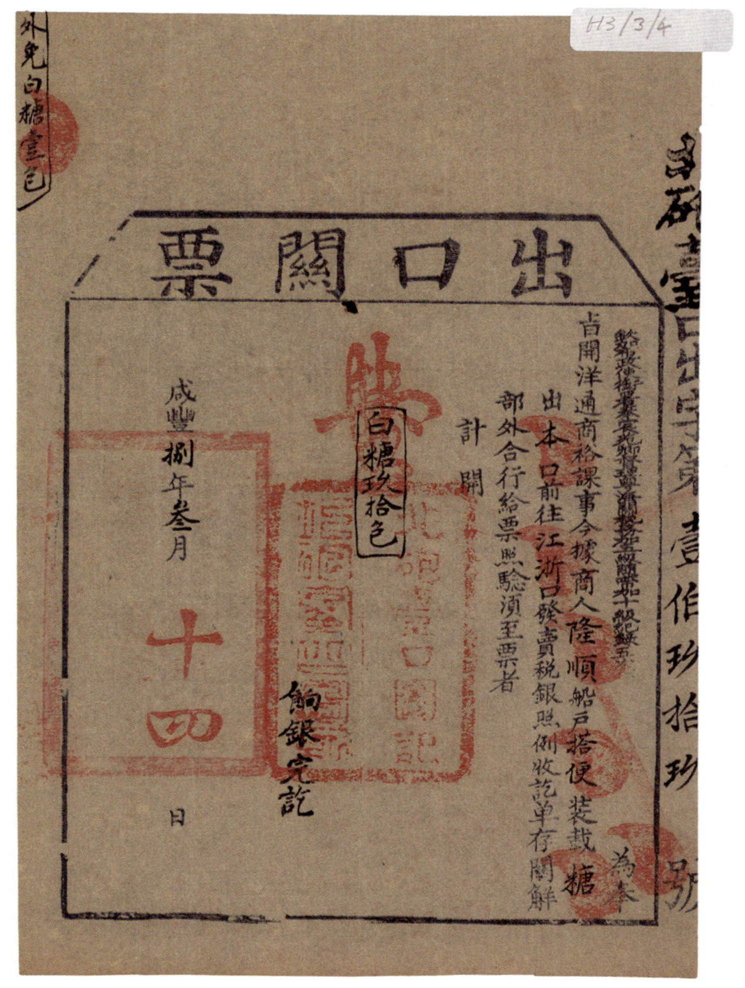

H3/3/4

外免白糖壹包

出口關票

旨開洋通商裕課事今據商人隆順船戶搭便裝載糖

出本口前往江浙口發賣稅銀照例收訖單存關鮮

部外合行給票照驗須至票者

計開

白糖玖拾包

餉銀完訖

咸豐捌年叁月十四日

---

① 北炮台口：据梁廷枏《粤海关志》记载，为正税口，位于潮州府揭阳县，距离庵埠总口一百二十里，距离省城大关一千六百里。

② 恒祺1856—1859年任粤海关监督。

③ 粤海关关防：为满、汉篆文合璧，长九又二分之一厘米，宽六厘米。粤海关，设于康熙二十四年（1685），位于广东省城五仙门内，其主官为粤海关监督。粤海关监督在英文资料中被称为“Hoppo”。因为粤海关监督是“户部分司”，是中央户部派出驻在广东省负责收税的司员，而粤海关衙门便是户部的派出衙门。而在广州的官场上，较常使用“关部”这样的用语。其实，“关部”就是“海关—户部”的合称，更能显示粤海关监督的特点。

5. 咸丰八年粤海关北炮台口[①] 出口关票（H3/3/5）

咸丰八年三月二十八日（1858年5月11日），粤海关监督恒祺[②] 发给中国货船“和合号”通过北炮台税口赴江浙口出口关票，载有203包白糖，赴江浙口售卖，饷银完讫。盖有粤海关两枚印章，一枚粤海关关防[③]，印文不清，据同时期其他出口关票中的印文判断应为“督理广东省沿海等处贸易税务户部分司关防”；另一枚北炮台税务印章，印文“北炮台口图记”。

Customs permit to Ho-ho. A customs clearance permit issued to Ho-ho (Hehe) for 203 bags of white sugar, 11 May 1858. 1 item.

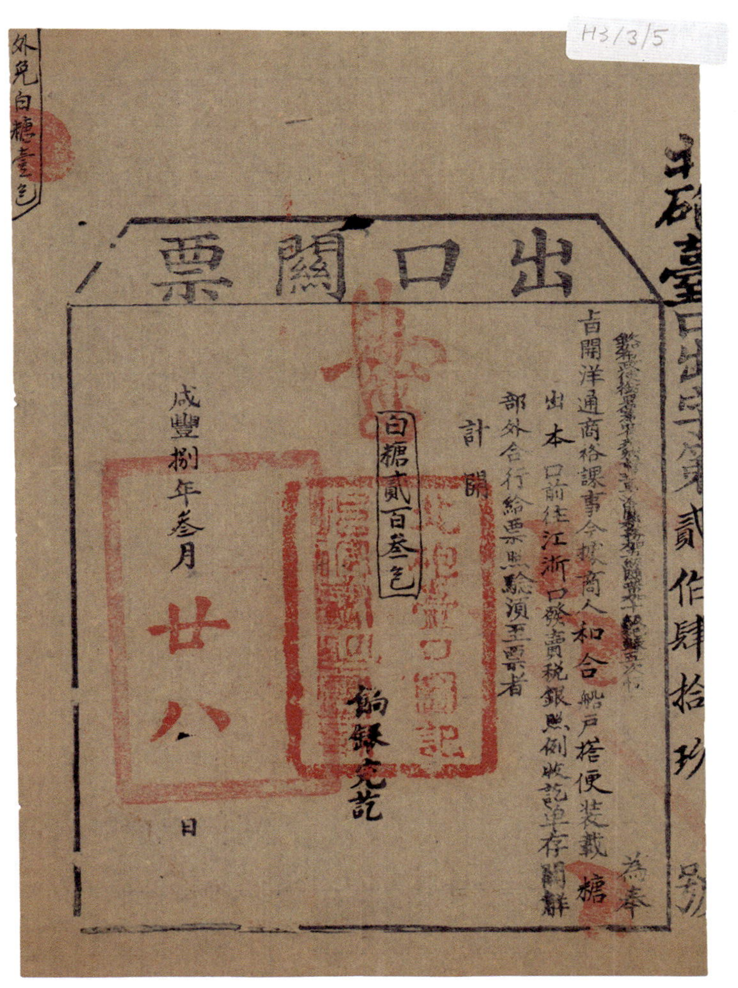
H3/3/5

出口關票

為奉
旨開洋通商裕課事今據商人和合船戶搭便裝載糖
出本口前往江浙口發賣稅銀照例收訖單存關辦
部外合行給票照驗須至票者
計開
白糖貳百叁包
餉銀完訖
咸豐捌年叁月廿八日

---

① 北炮台口：据梁廷枏《粤海关志》记载，为正税口，位于潮州府揭阳县，距离庵埠总口一百二十里，距离省城大关一千六百里。

② 恒祺1856—1859年任粤海关监督。

③ 粤海关关防：为满、汉篆文合璧，长九又二分之一厘米，宽六厘米。粤海关，设于康熙二十四年（1685），位于广东省城五仙门内，其主官为粤海关监督。粤海关监督在英文资料中被称为“Hoppo”。因为粤海关监督是“户部分司”，是中央户部派出驻在广东省负责收税的司员，而粤海关衙门便是户部的派出衙门。而在广州的官场上，较常使用“关部”这样的用语。其实，“关部”就是“海关—户部”的合称，更能显示粤海关监督的特点。

6. 咸丰九年粤海关北炮台口[①]出口关票（H3/3/6）

咸丰九年五月二十六日（1859年6月26日），粤海关监督恒祺[②]发给中国货船“潮兴号”“志合号”通过北炮台税口赴江浙口出口关票，载有64包白糖、321包黄糖，赴江浙口售卖，饷银完讫。盖有两枚印章，一枚粤海关关防[③]，印文不清，据同时期其他出口关票中的印文判断应为“督理广东省沿海等处贸易税务户部分司关防”；另一枚北炮台税务印章，印文“北炮台口图记”。

Customs permit to Ch’ao-hsing and Chih-ho. A customs clearance permit issued to Ch’ao-hsing (Chaoxing) and Chih-ho (Zhihe) for 64 bags of white sugar and 321 bags of brown sugar, 26 June 1859. 1 item.

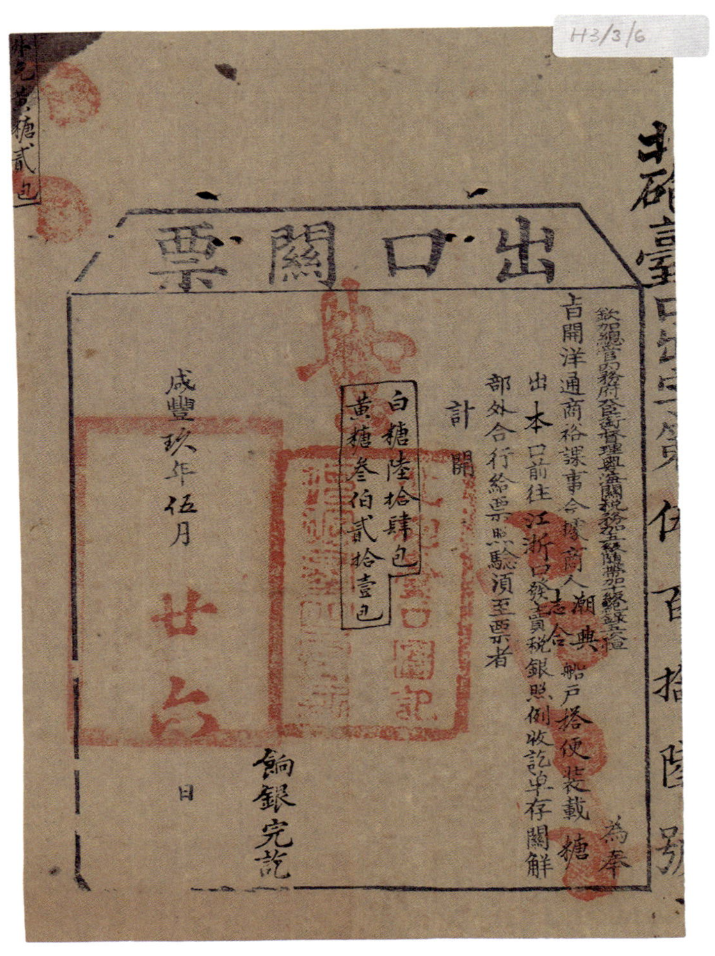

H3/3/6

出口關票

欽加總管內務府銜督理粵海關稅務加五級隨帶加十級紀錄十次恒　為奉

旨開洋通商裕課事今據商人潮興志合船戶搭便裝載糖

出本口前往江浙口發賣稅銀照例收訖單存關解

部外合行給票照驗須至票者

計開

白糖陸拾肆包

黃糖叁伯貳拾壹包

咸豐玖年伍月廿六日

餉銀完訖

北砲臺口圖記

---

① 北炮台口：据梁廷枏《粤海关志》记载，为正税口，位于潮州府揭阳县，距离庵埠总口一百二十里，距离省城大关一千六百里。

② 恒祺1856—1859年任粤海关监督。

③ 粤海关关防：为满、汉篆文合璧，长九又二分之一厘米，宽六厘米。粤海关，设于康熙二十四年（1685），位于广东省城五仙门内，其主官为粤海关监督。粤海关监督在英文资料中被称为“Hoppo”。因为粤海关监督是“户部分司”，是中央户部派出驻在广东省负责收税的司员，而粤海关衙门便是户部的派出衙门。而在广州的官场上，较常使用“关部”这样的用语。其实，“关部”就是“海关—户部”的合称，更能显示粤海关监督的特点。

7. 咸丰九年粤海关北炮台口[①]出口关票（H3/3/7）

咸丰九年十一月十八日（1859年12月11日），粤海关监督恒祺[②]发给中国货船“振瑞号”通过北炮台税口赴江浙口出口关票，载有162包白糖、118包黄糖，赴江浙口售卖，饷银完讫。盖有两枚印章，一枚粤海关关防[③]，印文不清，据同时期其他出口关票中的印文判断应为“督理广东省沿海等处贸易税务户部分司关防”；另一枚北炮台税务印章，印文“北炮台口图记”。

Customs permit to Chen-jui. A customs clearance permit issued to Chen-jui (Zhenrui) for 162 bags of white sugar and 118 bags of brown sugar, 11 December 1859. 1 item.

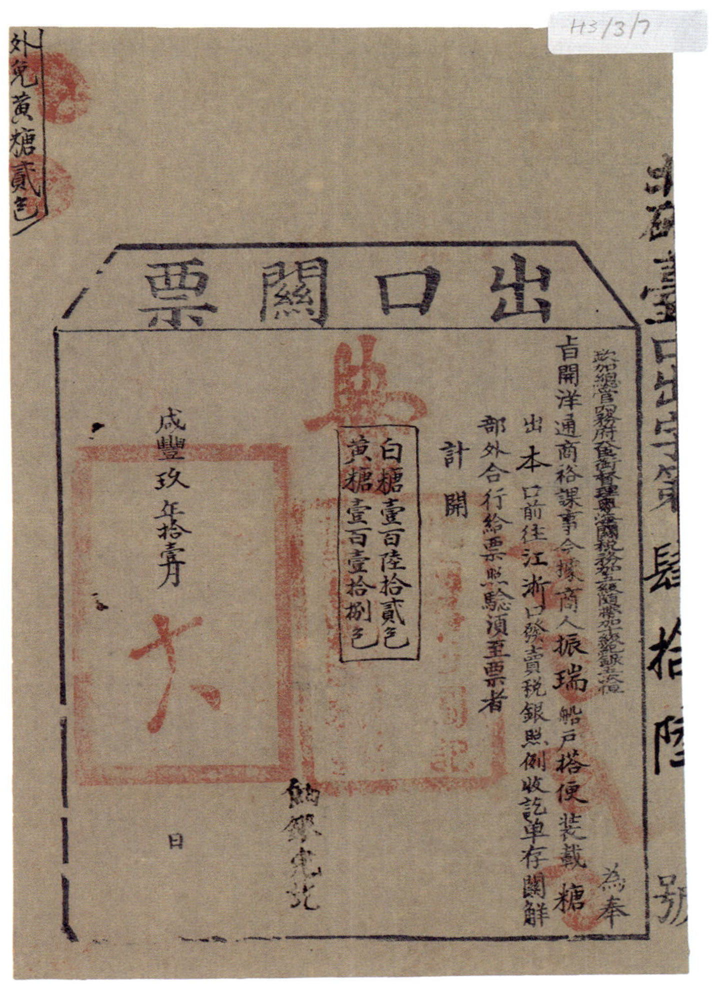

出口關票

為奉
旨開洋通商裕課事今據商人振瑞船戶搭便裝載糖
出本口前往江浙口發賣稅銀照例收訖單存關解
部外合行給票照驗須至票者
計開
白糖壹百陸拾貳包
黃糖壹百壹拾捌包
咸豐玖年拾壹月十八日
納餉完訖

H3/3/7

---

① 北炮台口：据梁廷枏《粤海关志》记载，为正税口，位于潮州府揭阳县，距离庵埠总口一百二十里，距离省城大关一千六百里。

② 恒祺1856—1859年任粤海关监督。

③ 粤海关关防：为满、汉篆文合璧，长九又二分之一厘米，宽六厘米。粤海关，设于康熙二十四年（1685），位于广东省城五仙门内，其主官为粤海关监督。粤海关监督在英文资料中被称为“Hoppo”。因为粤海关监督是“户部分司”，是中央户部派出驻在广东省负责收税的司员，而粤海关衙门便是户部的派出衙门。而在广州的官场上，较常使用“关部”这样的用语。其实，“关部”就是“海关—户部”的合称，更能显示粤海关监督的特点。

8. 咸丰九年粤海关北炮台口[①]出口关票（H3/3/8）

咸丰九年十一月二十二日（1859年12月15日），粤海关监督恒祺[②]发给中国货船“潮兴号”“章记号”通过北炮台税口赴江浙口出口关票，载有35包白糖、64包黄糖，赴江浙口售卖，饷银完讫。盖有两枚印章，一枚粤海关关防[③]，印文不清，据同时期其他出口关票中的印文判断应为“督理广东省沿海等处贸易税务户部分司关防”；另一枚北炮台税务印章，印文“北炮台口图记”。

Customs permit to Ch’ao-hsing and Chang-chi. A customs clearance permit issued to Ch’ao-hsing (Chaoxing) and Chang-chi (Zhangji) for 35 bags of white sugar and 64 bags of brown sugar, 16 December 1859[④]. 1 item.

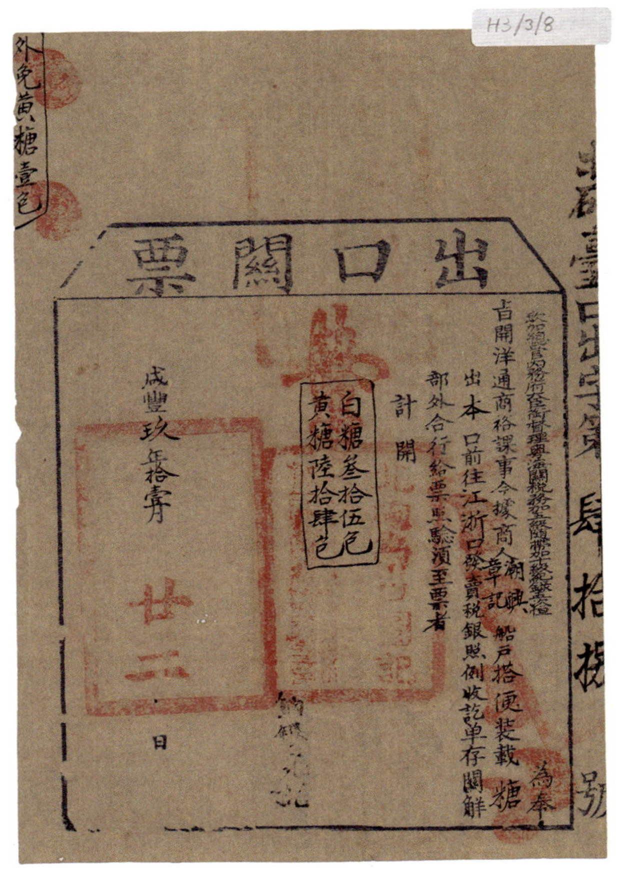
H3/3/8

外免黃糖壹包

出口關票

為奉

旨開洋通商裕課事今據商人潮興、章記船戶搭便裝載糖出本口前往江浙口發賣稅銀照例收訖單存關解部外合行給票照驗須至票者

計開

白糖叁拾伍包

黃糖陸拾肆包

咸豐玖年拾壹月廿二日

---

① 北炮台口：据梁廷枏《粤海关志》记载，为正税口，位于潮州府揭阳县，距离庵埠总口一百二十里，距离省城大关一千六百里。

② 恒祺1856—1859年任粤海关监督。

③ 粤海关关防：为满、汉篆文合璧，长九又二分之一厘米，宽六厘米。粤海关，设于康熙二十四年（1685），位于广东省城五仙门内，其主官为粤海关监督。粤海关监督在英文资料中被称为“Hoppo”。因为粤海关监督是“户部分司”，是中央户部派出驻在广东省负责收税的司员，而粤海关衙门便是户部的派出衙门。而在广州的官场上，较常使用“关部”这样的用语。其实，“关部”就是“海关—户部”的合称，更能显示粤海关监督的特点。

④ 勘误：英文提要日期为1859年12月16日（16 December 1859），按原中文文献“咸丰玖年拾壹月廿二日”，应为1859年12月15日。

四、咸丰八年东陇口[①]出口关票

1. 咸丰八年粤海关东陇口出口关票（H3/4/1）

咸丰八年三月十二日（1858年4月25日），粤海关监督恒祺[②]发给中国货船“顺利号”通过东陇口税口赴江南口的出口关票，载有70包白糖，饷银完讫。盖有两枚印章，一枚粤海关关防[③]，印文不清，据同时期其他出口关票中的印文判断应为“督理广东省沿海等处贸易税务户部分司关防”；另一枚东陇口税务印章，印文“东陇口图记”。

Customs permit to Shun-li. A customs clearance permit for 70 bags of white sugar, 25 April 1858. 1 item.

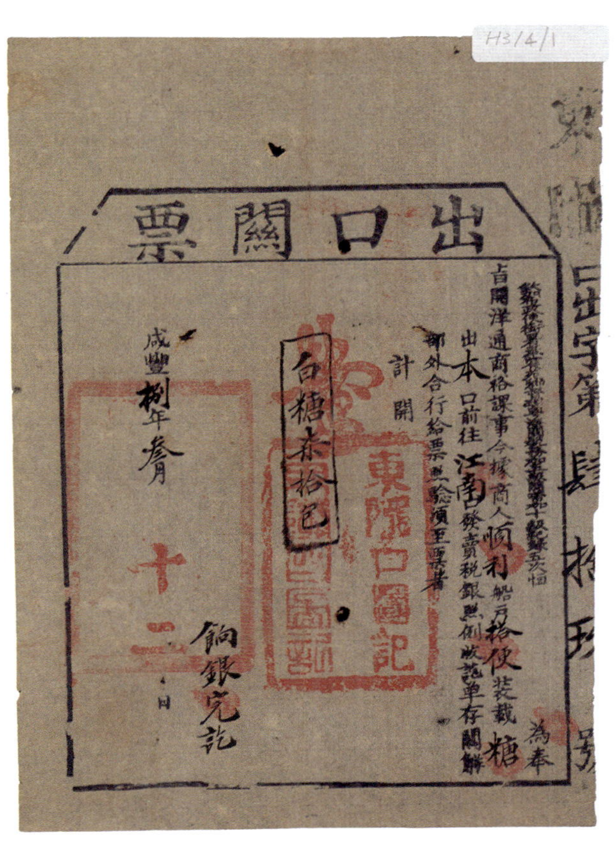

H3/4/1

出口關票

為奉

旨開洋通商裕課事今據商人順利船戶裕使裝載糖

出本口前往江南口發賣稅銀照例繳訖單存關辦

部外合行給票照驗須至票者

計開

白糖柒拾包

東隴口圖記

咸豐捌年叁月十二日

餉銀完訖

---

① 东陇口：据梁廷枏《粤海关志》记载，为正税口，位于潮州府澄海县，距离庵埠总口八十里，距离省城大关一千六百里。东陇口下辖樟林口，也在澄海县，为挂号小口。

② 恒祺1856—1859年任粤海关监督。

③ 粤海关关防：为满、汉篆文合璧，长九又二分之一厘米，宽六厘米。粤海关，设于康熙二十四年（1685），位于广东省城五仙门内，其主官为粤海关监督。粤海关监督在英文资料中被称为“Hoppo”。因为粤海关监督是“户部分司”，是中央户部派出驻在广东省负责收税的司员，而粤海关衙门便是户部的派出衙门。而在广州的官场上，较常使用“关部”这样的用语。其实，“关部”就是“海关—户部”的合称，更能显示粤海关监督的特点。

2. 咸丰八年粤海关东陇口[①]出口关票（H3/4/2）

咸丰八年三月十七日（1858年4月30日），粤海关监督恒祺[②]发给中国货船“顺利号”通过东陇税口赴江南口的出口关票，载有50包白糖，赴江南口售卖，饷银完讫。盖有两枚印章，一枚粤海关关防[③]，印文不清，据同时期其他出口关票中的印文判断应为“督理广东省沿海等处贸易税务户部分司关防”；另一枚东陇口税务印章，印文“东陇口图记”。

Customs permit to Shun-li. A customs clearance permit for 50 bags of white sugar, 30 April 1858. 1 item.

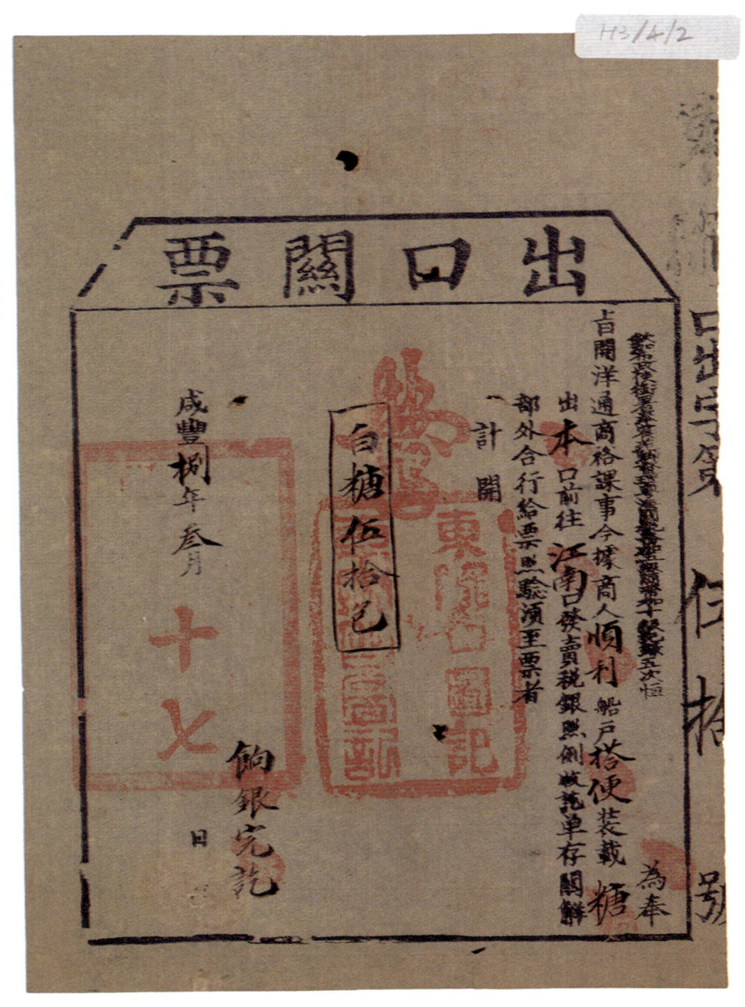
H3/4/2

出口關票

為奉
旨開洋通商裕課事今據商人順利船戶搭便裝載糖
出本口前往江南口發賣稅銀照例徵訖單存關
部外合行給票照驗須至票者
計開
白糖伍拾包
咸豐捌年叁月十七日
餉銀完訖

① 东陇口：据梁廷枏《粤海关志》记载，为正税口，位于潮州府澄海县，距离庵埠总口八十里，距离省城大关一千六百里。东陇口下辖樟林口，也在澄海县，为挂号小口。

② 恒祺1856—1859年任粤海关监督。

③ 粤海关关防：为满、汉篆文合璧，长九又二分之一厘米，宽六厘米。粤海关，设于康熙二十四年（1685），位于广东省城五仙门内，其主官为粤海关监督。粤海关监督在英文资料中被称为“Hoppo”。因为粤海关监督是“户部分司”，是中央户部派出驻在广东省负责收税的司员，而粤海关衙门便是户部的派出衙门。而在广州的官场上，较常使用“关部”这样的用语。其实，“关部”就是“海关—户部”的合称，更能显示粤海关监督的特点。

五、咸丰八年江南海关照验税单

1. 咸丰八年江南海关[①]照验税单（H3/5/1）

咸丰八年十二月二十八日（1859年1月31日），江南海关监督发给英国怡和洋行的第2100号照验税单，注明缴纳出口税银四百四十九两二钱三分二厘，准许搭载零星货物出口。盖有江南海关满汉文长方形关防，印文“监督江南海关兼理铜务关防”。

Conveyance duty and commodity tax certificate. A certificate issued in confirmation of Ewo’s payment of the conveyance duty and commodity tax for the British commercial vessel numbered 2100, 31 January 1859. 1 item.

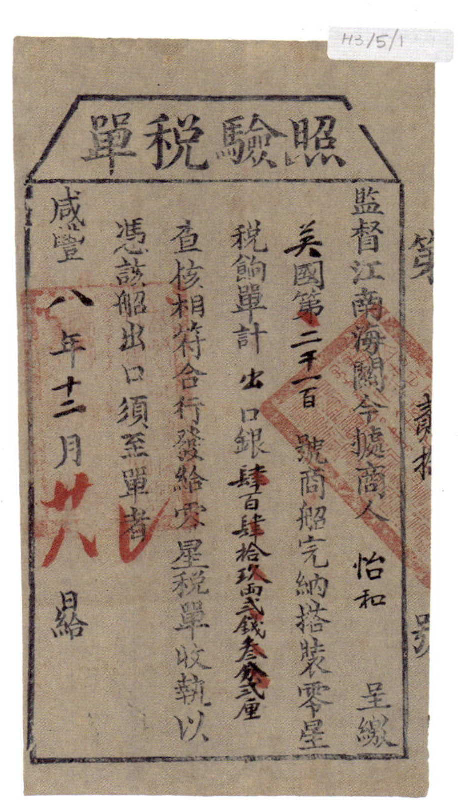

H3/5/1

照驗稅單

監督江南海關給據商人怡和呈繳
英國第二千一百號商船完納搭裝零星
稅餉單計出口銀肆百肆拾玖兩貳錢叁分貳厘
查核相符合行發給零星稅單收執以
憑該船出口須至單者
咸豐八年十二月廿八日給

---

① 江南海关：即江海关。康熙二十四年（1685），始设于江南云台山（今江苏连云港）。后移上海，设在上海县城大东门外黄浦江边（今白渡路），旧地名称为关桥。道光二十五年（1845），根据《南京条约》和英国领事巴富尔的要求，上海海关监督在洋泾浜（今延安东路）设置了“西洋商船盘验所”。1845年12月31日，宫慕久撤销这个盘验所，在上海县城租界内设置了“江海北关”，并为之增设了两个稽查关卡。因和原来江海关差异较大，通常称“新关”“洋关”，办理新式轮船征收关税等事。由江苏省苏松太兵备道（这是一个地方军事长官职务而不是民事长官）兼管，江海关海关监督的正式官职称呼为“护理江南海关道”。咸丰三年（1853），英人乘上海小刀会起义之机，强占江海关。次年，上海道吴健彰与英、法、美驻沪领事签订协定，允由三国各派税务司一人，掌管江海关。同年七月，少关税务管理委员会成立，遂开外国侵略者直接管理中国海关的恶例。

2. 咸丰八年江南海关[①]完纳税钞红单[②]（H3/5/2）

咸丰八年十二月二十八日（1859年1月31日），江南海关监督发给英国怡和洋行完纳税钞红单，注明根据新的规定计吨科钞，按货科税，缴纳船钞[③]银三百三十一两五钱。盖有江南海关满汉文长方形关防，印文“监督江南海关兼管铜务关防”。

Tonnage certificate. A tonnage certificate issued in confirmation of Ewo's payment of the tonnage tax on its vessel, 31 January 1859. 1 item.

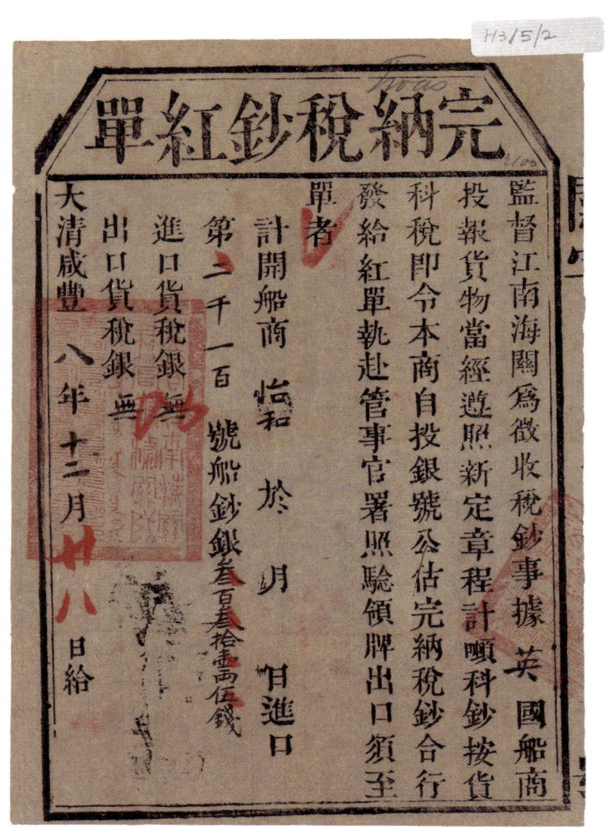

H3/5/2

完納稅鈔紅單

監督江南海關爲徵收稅鈔事據英國船商投報貨物當經遵照新定章程計噸科鈔按貨科稅即令本商自投銀號公估完納稅鈔合行發給紅單執赴管事官署照驗領牌出口須至單者

計開船商怡和於　月　日進口

第二千一百號船鈔銀叁百叁拾壹兩伍錢

進口貨稅銀無

出口貨稅銀無

大清咸豐八年十二月廿八日給

① 江南海关：即江海关。

② 完纳税钞红单：是对船只应缴纳的关税的凭证，红单的内容包括该船名号，计吨科钞、按货科税的数目，分列船钞若干、进口税若干、出口税若干、通共完税若干，因此又有“税票、印票、税单、印单等”名称。

③ 1843年中英《五口通商附粘善后条款》中规定七十五吨以下至一百五十吨的船只，每吨纳钞一钱，一百五十吨以上的船只每吨纳船钞五钱。1844年中美《望厦条约》中明确规定：“凡合众国船只赴五港口贸易者，均由领事等官查验船牌，报明海关，按所载吨数输纳船钞，计所载货物在一百五十吨以上者，每吨纳钞银五钱，不及一百五十吨者，每吨纳钞银一钱，所有以前丈量及各项规费全行裁革。或有船只进口，已在本港海关纳完钞银，因货未全销，复载往别口转售者，领事等官报明海关，于该船出口时，将钞已纳完之处在红牌内注明，并行文别口海关查照，候该船进别口时，止纳货税，不输船钞，以免重征。”也就是说，原来清朝沿袭明代以丈量船只的方式来收取船钞被“一百五十吨以上每吨纳钞银五钱，不满一百五十吨者每吨纳钞银一钱”所代替。船钞的具体含义在此时已经发生了变化，以吨税而不是丈量船只来收取船钞，但仍沿用“船钞”之名。1858年中英《天津条约》中规定：“英国商船应纳钞课，一百五十吨以上，每吨纳钞银四钱，一百五十吨正及一百五十吨以下，每吨纳钞银一钱。凡船只出口，欲往通商他口并香港地方，该船主禀明海关监督，发给专照，自是日起以四个月为期，如系前赴通商各口，俱无庸另纳船钞，以免重输。”

六、同治四年粤海关免钞专照（H3/6）

同治四年八月十四日（1865年10月3日），粤海关监督师曾[①]发给英国商人痕地（Hen-ti）免钞专照，作用就是作为船只已经缴纳吨税即“船钞”的凭证。牌照一页分为两折，正面上方为“免钞专照”标题，在其上方盖有长方形英文印章“TONNAGE DUES CERTIFICATE VALUABLE”，为“免钞专照”英文。执照正面盖有长方形粤海关印章，但是印文不清。背面为船钞执照内容的英文翻译，格式事先印刷成文，标题为：TONNAGE DUES SPECIAL CERTIFICATE，在下文空白处填写名字、船只、吨位、有效时间。并盖有随形印中英文粤海关印章，中间为中文“粤海关税务使司印”，外围下边为“CANTON”，周围为“COMMISSIONER OF CUSTOMS”字样。

Customs documents: Tonnage dues certificate of Canton Customs. A tonnage dues special certificate (in Chinese and English) issued by Mr. Shi, Commissioner of Customs, Canton, to Mr. Hen-ti (Hendi) for the American vessel ‘Jack’ of 42 tons burthen, 3 October 1865, recording that following the payment of the tonnage dues at this port the vessel is cleared for running on the Canton River for a term expiring on 2 February 1866.1 item. 1866

① 师曾：同治朝粤海关监督。清代粤海关监督多从内务府钦点，师曾出身奉宸苑卿，内务府所属三院之一，掌皇室苑囿园林，初名尚膳监，属工部，康熙十年（1671）改属内务府，康熙十六年（1677）并归都虞司，康熙二十三年（1684）设奉宸苑。主官有兼管事务大臣，无定员，卿二人，正三品。所管有景山、瀛台、阐福寺、乐善园、钓鱼台等处行宫，及南苑、圆明园、畅春园、玉泉山等处稻田。师曾即为奉宸苑卿，深受皇帝信任，前后“加五级记录十七次”，同治四年（1865）上任，后因补报同治三年（1864）大关并潮州新关洋税收支总数的奏折，赏给二品顶带，同治九年（1870）离任。

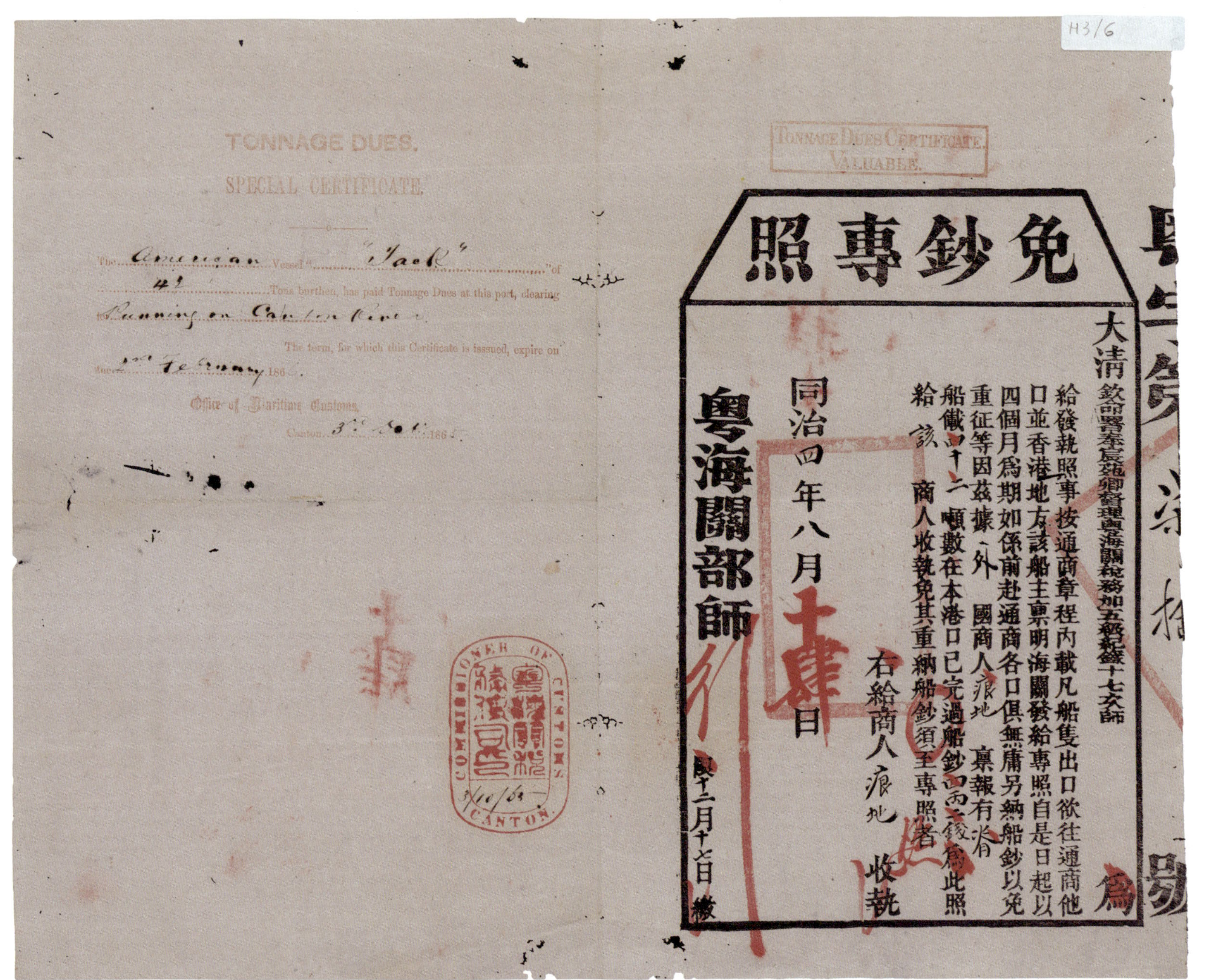

H3/6

免鈔專照

大清
欽命署奉宸苑卿督理粵海關稅務加五級紀錄十七次師　為
給發執照事按通商章程內載凡船隻出口欲往通商他
口並香港地方該船主稟明海關發給專照自是日起以
四個月為期如係前赴通商各口俱無庸另納船鈔以免
重征等因茲據外　國商人痕地　稟報有
船　隻載四十二噸數在本港口已完過船鈔　兩　錢為此照
給該　商人收執免其重納船鈔須至專照者

右給商人痕地　收執

同治四年八月　日

粵海關部師

十二月十七日　繳

TONNAGE DUES CERTIFICATE.
VALUABLE.

TONNAGE DUES.

SPECIAL CERTIFICATE.

The American Vessel "Jack" of 42 Tons burthen, has paid Tonnage Dues at this port, clearing to Running on Canton River.

The term, for which this Certificate is issued, expire on the 1st February 1866.

Office of Maritime Customs.
Canton, 3rd Oct. 1865.

COMMISSIONER OF CUSTOMS CANTON
3/10/65

Chapter Four

第四章

钱庄票据

本章收入编号为Manuscripts/MS JM/H4的档案，时间约1877年，共计15件。在档案目录上标注的标题为“Title Native Bank Documents”，从实际收入的档案文献来看，应称之为“钱庄票据”。该批档案全部以中文和传统苏州码记录，共分为两部分，其一为往来款项账单；其二为钱庄汇票，以系列编号的形式装订成册，保存了大量金融业务的底账。这是19世纪晚期中国传统金融业与国际金融机构结合的珍贵档案，但是非常遗憾，本章第二部分“光绪三年怡和汇票簿”合计72份文件，由于污损比较严重，英国剑桥大学图书馆管理部门不允许影印出版，编者只好忍痛割爱，暂时不能将之公示于世了。但是文献基本内容、中英文提要仍然附录于此，以供管中窥豹。如有兴趣研究的机构和人士，可与编者联系，在可能的范围内进行学术研究。

一、约光绪三年众商曹平公估账单

1. 白银二千五百八十四两七分账单（H4/1/1）

白银二千五百八十四两七分账单，盖有印文为“众商曹平公估图记”的印章。

Shroffing bill. An undated shroffing bill to EPCS for 2580 Tls①. 1 item.

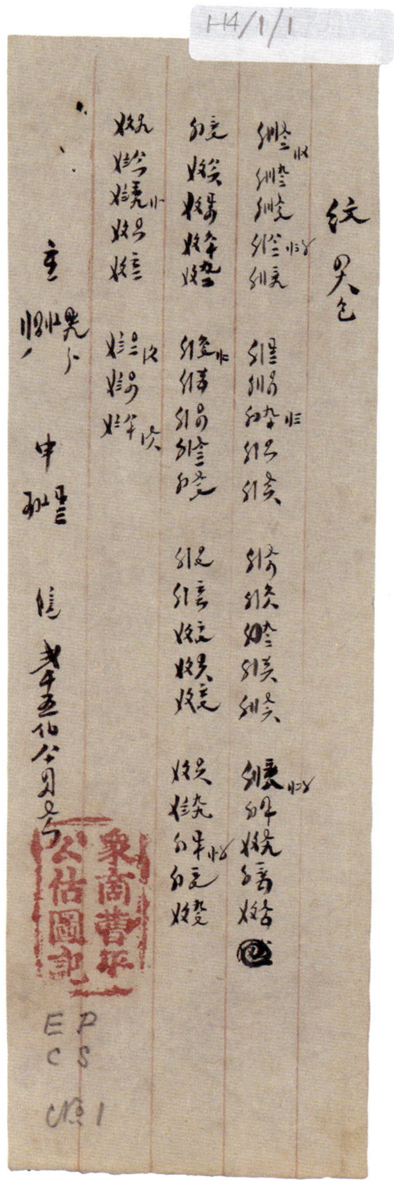

① 勘误：应为二千五百八十四两七分。

2. 白银二千五百九十五两二十九分账单（H4/1/2）

白银二千五百九十五两二十九分账单，盖有印文为“众商曹平公估图记”的印章。

Shroffing bill. An undated shroffing bill to EPCS for 2597 Tls[①]. 1 item.

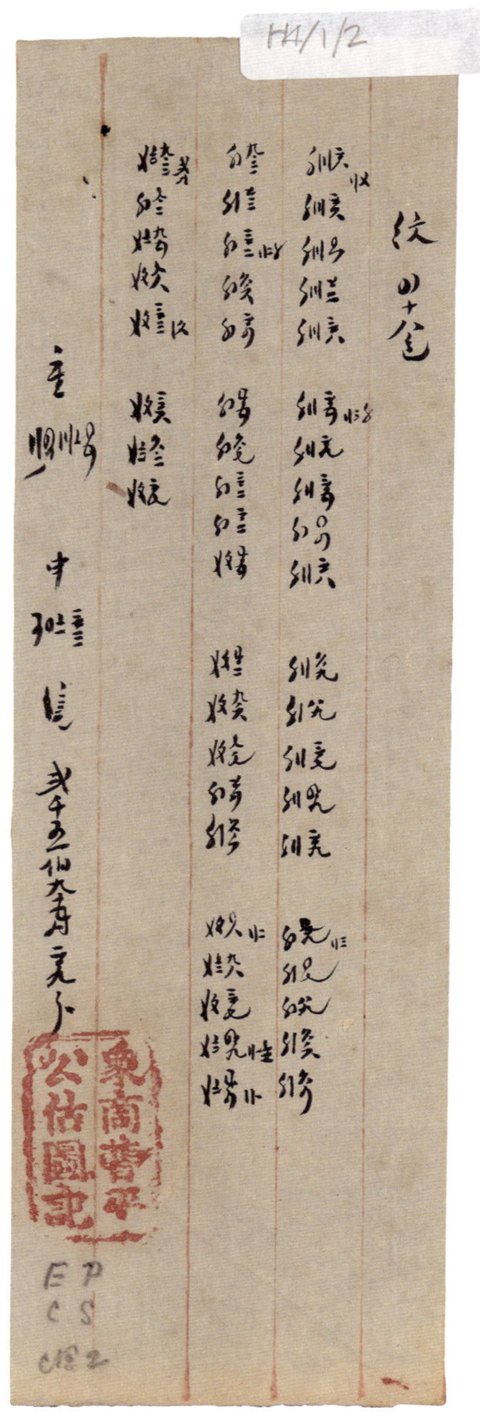

① 勘误：应为二千五百九十五两二十九分。

3. 白银三千四百四十九两账单（H4/1/3）

白银三千四百四十九两账单，盖有印文为“众商曹平公估图记”的印章。

Shroffing bill. An undated shroffing bill to EPCS for 3448 Tls[①]. 1 item.

① 勘误：应为三千四百四十九两。

4. 白银二千五百六十三两四钱四分账单（H4/1/4）

白银二千五百六十三两四钱四分账单，盖有印文为“众商曹平公估图记”的印章。

Shroffing bill. An undated shroffing bill to EPCS for 2563 Tls[①]. 1 item.

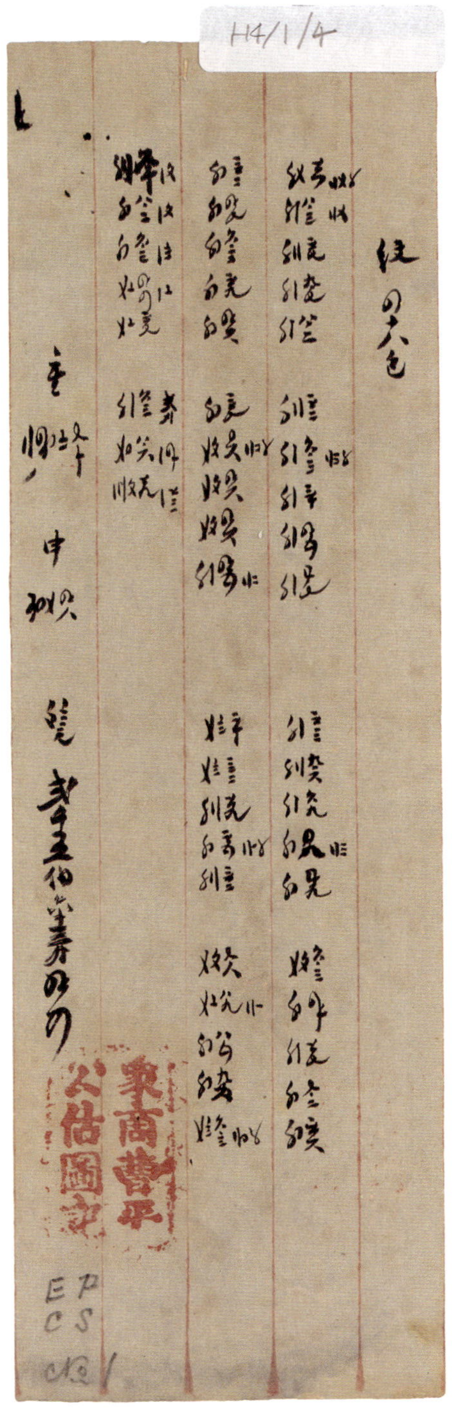

① 勘误：应为二千五百六十三两四钱四分。

5. 白银二千九百一十六两四钱二分账单（H4/1/5）

白银二千九百一十六两四钱二分账单，盖有印文为“众商曹平公估图记”的印章。

Shroffing bill. An undated shroffing bill to EPCS for 2916 Tls[①]. 1 item.

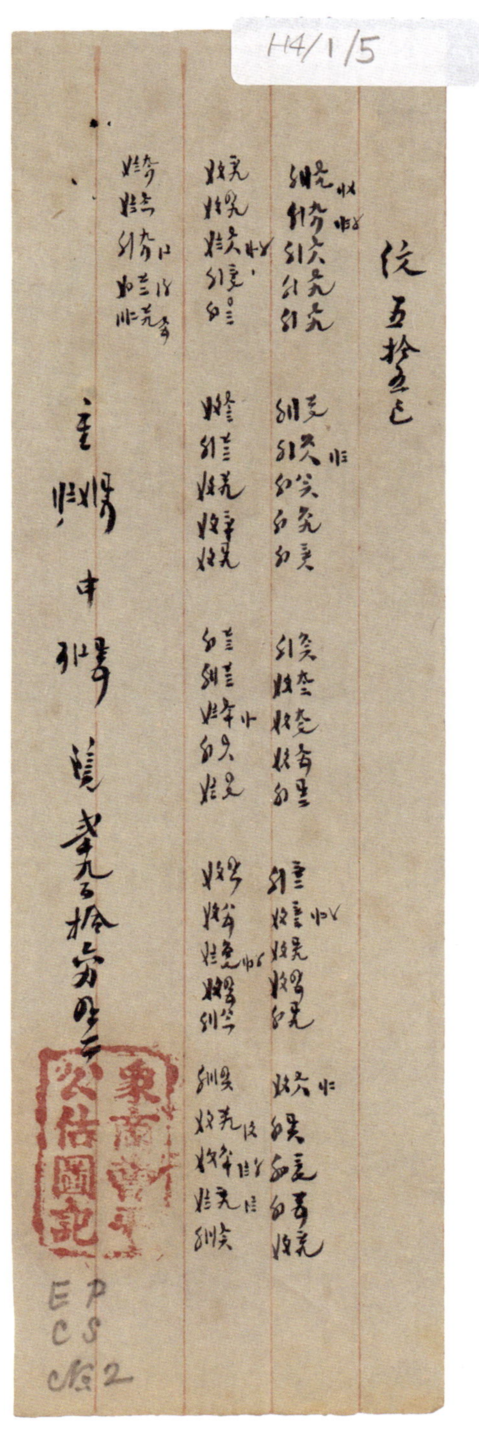

① 勘误：应为二千九百一十六两四钱二分。

6. 白银三千四百五十八两六钱二分账单（H4/1/6）

白银三千四百五十八两六钱二分账单，盖有印文为“众商曹平公估图记”的印章。

Shroffing bill. An undated shroffing bill to EPCS for 3458.62 Tls. 1 item.

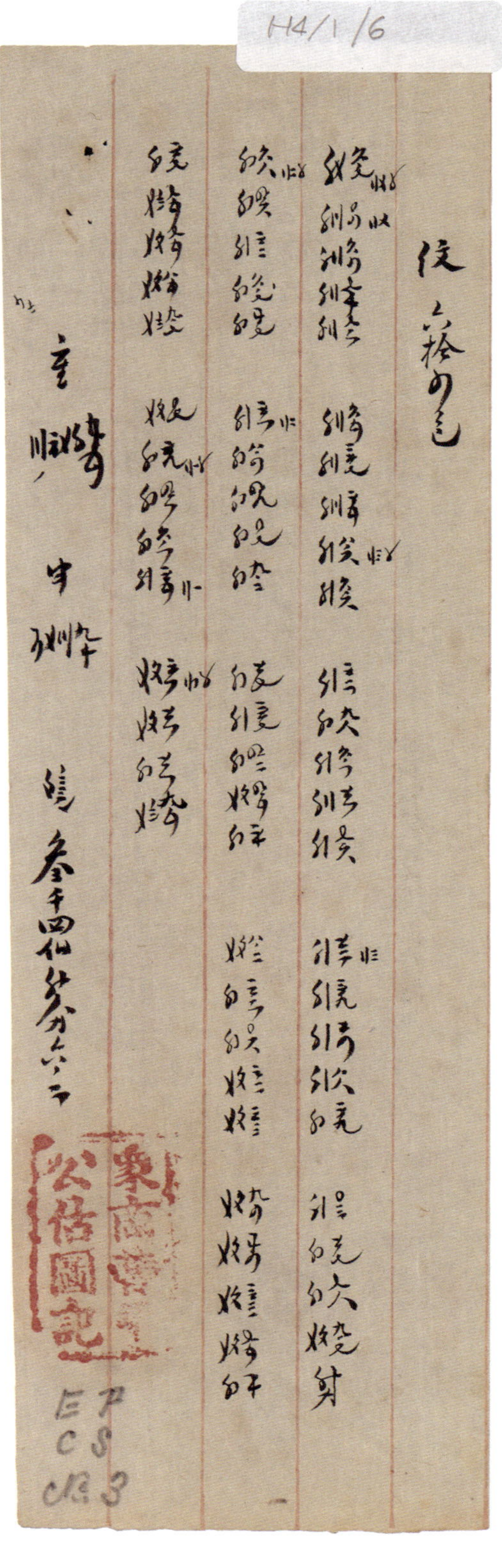

7. 白银三千二百七十五两三钱账单（H4/1/7）

白银三千二百七十五两三钱账单，盖有印文为“众商曹平公估图记”的印章。

Shroffing bill. An undated shroffing bill to EPCS for 3277.3 Tls[1].

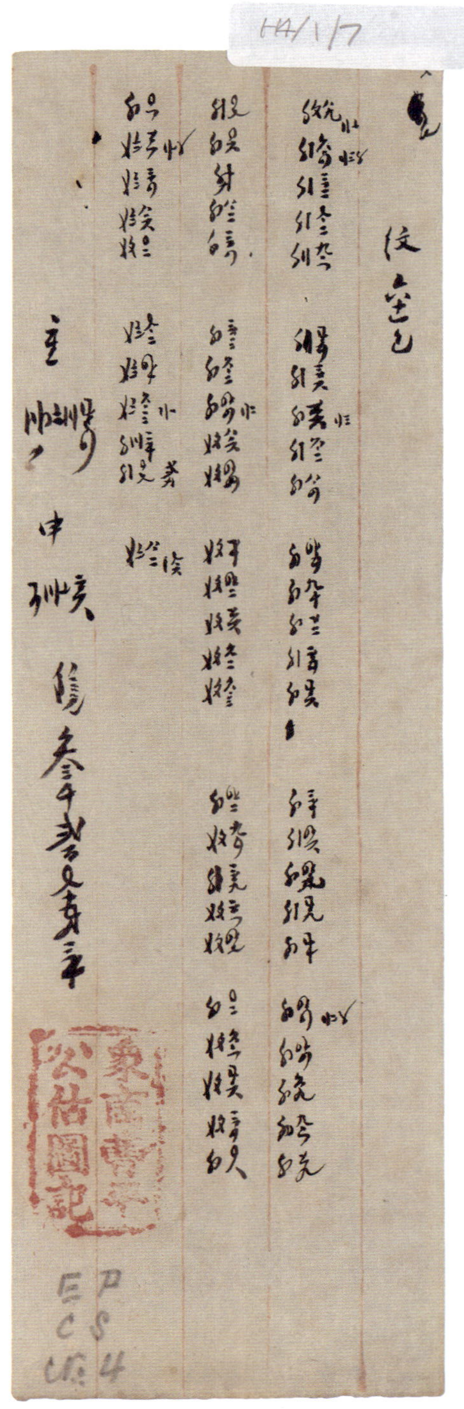

① 勘误：应为三千二百七十五两三钱。

8. 白银三千二百八十三两二钱八分账单（H4/1/8）

白银三千二百八十三两二钱八分账单，盖有印文为“众商曹平公估图记”的印章。

Shroffing bill. An undated shroffing bill to JM for 3283.85 Tls[①]. 1 item.

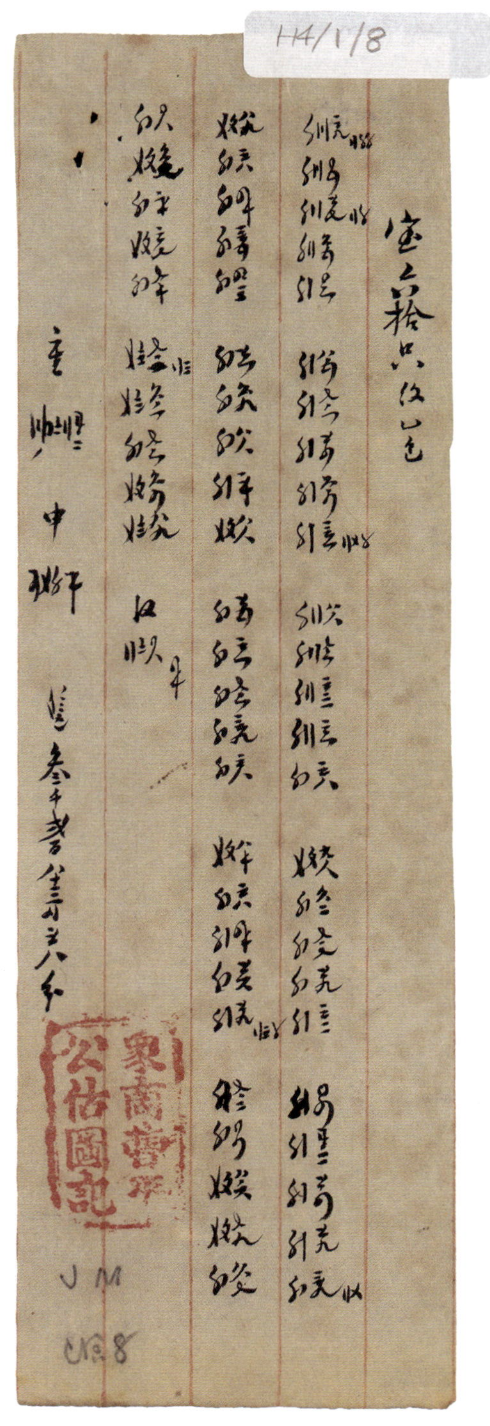

① 勘误：应为三千二百八十三两二钱八分。

9. 白银三千二百八十三两五钱七分账单（H4/1/9）

白银三千二百八十三两五钱七分账单，盖有印文为“众商曹平公估图记”的印章。

Shroffing bill. An undated shroffing bill to JM for 3283.07 Tls[①]. 1 item.

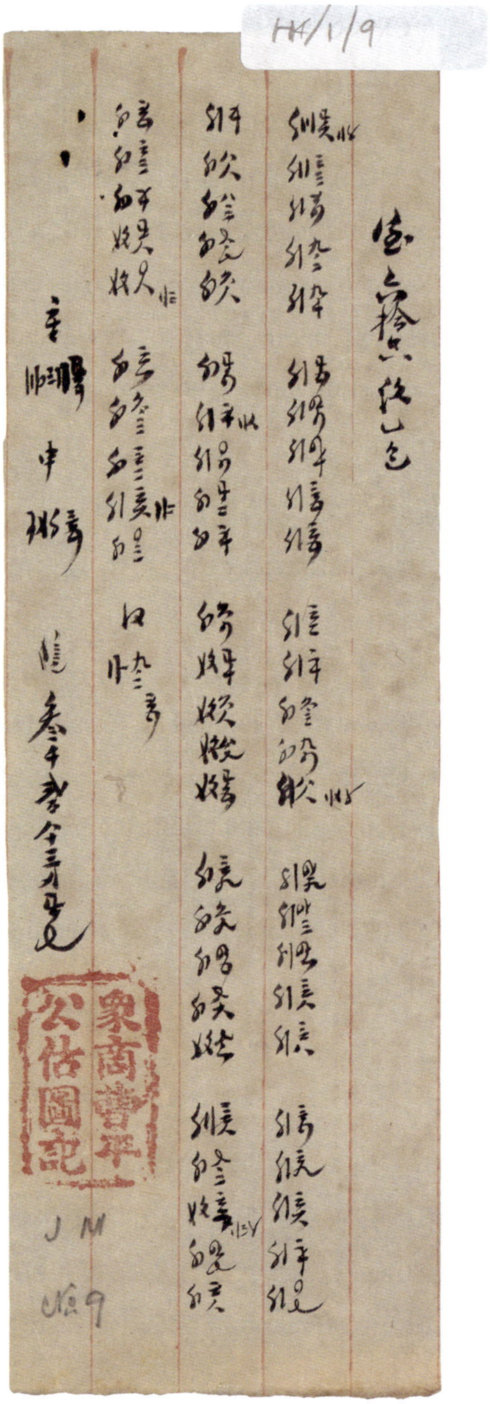

① 勘误：应为三千二百八十三两五钱七分。

二、光绪三年怡和汇票簿

1. 公和邵大全揭票（H4/2/1）

公和邵大全的一本银行汇票簿，内有七张存根和三张空白汇票。序列号是一至十号，时间周期为“周”，存根上盖有“公和”和“万商云集”印章。日期包括1877年5月11日至27日，总金额为白银9500两（根据上海的白银比例）。正面有两个英文注释：“sinyu”和“tls 9500”。

Draft book of Shao Daquan. An Ewo Bank draft book (in Chinese) of Shao Daquan (Shao Ta-ch'uan) of Gonghe containing seven counterfoils and three blank drafts. The book is marked with the serial code 'Zhou'. The counterfoils include the stamp of Kungho (Gonghe). Their entries cover 11–27 May 1877, and amount to Tls 9500 (based on the Shanghai scale for silver). There are two English notes on the front of the book: 'Sinyu' and 'Tls 9500'. 1 item; Moderate condition, including damage by damp and insects. 1877

2. 嵩县陈维贞揭票（H4/2/2）

陈维贞银行汇票，其中有四张存根和六张空白汇票。这本书上有“宙”的序列号。存根上有“公兴”的印章。时间涵盖了1877年5月12日至21日，总金额为白银12,000两（根据上海的白银比例）。书的正面有两个英文注释：“hopo”和“tls 12,000”。盖有“公兴”和“万商云集”印章。

Draft book of Ch'en Wei-chen. An Ewo Bank draft book (in Chinese) of Ch'en Wei-chen of Hao-pa (Haoba Chen Weizhen) containing four counterfoils and six blank drafts. The book is marked with the serial code 'Yu'. The counterfoils include the stamp of 'Kunghsing' (Gongxing). Their entries cover 12–21 May 1877, and amount to Tls 12,000 (based on the Shanghai scale for silver). There are two English notes on the front of the book: 'Hopo' and 'Tls 12,000'. 1 item; Moderate condition, including damage by damp and insects. 1877

3. 阜阳洪字联票（H4/2/3）

唐茂芝银行汇票簿，内有五张存根和五张汇票。书上的序列号是“洪”。存根上盖有“公和”和“万商云集”印章。其中三张存根的日期是5月19日，两张是1877年5月28日。入账总额为白银4500两（根据上海的白银比例）。书的正面有两个英文注释：“fooyang”和“tls 4500”。

Draft book of Tong Mow-chee. An Ewo Bank draft book (in Chinese) of Mr. Tong Mow-chee (Tang Maozhi) containing five counterfoils and five drafts. The book is marked with the serial code 'hung' (hong). The counterfoils include the stamp 'Kung［...］stamp'(Gong［...］tuzhang). Three of the counterfoils are dated 19 May, and two 28 May［1877］. Their entries amount to Tls 4500 (based on the Shanghai scale for silver). There are two English notes on the front of the book: 'Fooyang' and 'Tls 4500'. 1 item; Moderate condition, including damage by damp and insects. 1877

4. 后港桥元字联票（H4/2/4）

后港桥元字银行汇票簿，其中有三张存根和七张空白汇票。序列号是“元”。存根上盖有“公和”和“万商云集”印章。日期分别为4月14日、15日和18日（未注明年份），总金额为白银11,000两（以上海的白银比例计算）。书的正面有两个英文注释：“who(?) hong”和“tls 11,000”。

Draft book of Ch'ien-feng-chuan. An Ewo Bank draft book (in Chinese) of Ch'ien-feng-chuan containing three counterfoils and seven blank drafts. The book is marked with the serial code 'Yuan'. The counterfoils include the stamp of 'Kung-t'ai' (Gong tai tu zhang). Their entries are dated on the 14th day, 15th day and 18th day of the 4th month (the year is not given), and amount to Tls 11,000 (based on the Shanghai scale for silver). There are two English notes on the front of the book: 'Who (?) hong' and 'Tls 11,000'. 1 item; Moderate condition, including damage by damp and insects.

5. 无锡地字联票（H4/2/5）

无锡地字汇票簿。含有四张存根和六张空白汇票的银行汇票簿。这本上有序列号“地”。 存根上盖有“公和”和“万商云集”印章。日期为4月7日至11日（未注明年份），总金额为白银11,000两（按上海银价标准计算）。书的正面有两个英文注释：“woosu”和“tls 9000”，“bank order”后面跟着计算9000—6000=3000。

Draft book. An Ewo Bank draft book (in Chinese) containing four counterfoils and six blank drafts. The book is marked with the serial code 'Ti'. The counterfoils include the stamp of 'Kung-ta' (Gong da tu zhang). Their entries are dated from the 7th to the 11th days of the 4th month (the year is not given), and amount to Tls 11,000 (based on the Shanghai scale for silver). There are two English notes on the front of the book, 'Woosu' and 'Tls 9000', and the words 'Bank Order' followed by the calculation 9000—6000=3000. 1 item; Moderate condition, including damage by damp and insects, and missing part of the back cover.

6. 溧阳黄字联票（H4/2/6）

益丰和唐茂芝先生的银行汇票，内有六张存根和四张空白汇票。这本上有“黄”的序列号。存根上盖有“公和”和“万商云集”印章。日期为4月5日至6日（未注明年份），总金额为白银8000两（按上海市白银比例计算）。一号和二号分别由少生堂的海生和连青制备。书的正面有英文注释：“lyhong”“tls 8000”“drawn 8000”和“draft 4904.867/3095.133”。

Draft book of I-feng and Tong Mow-chee. An Ewo Bank draft book (in Chinese) of I-feng (Yifeng) and

Mr. Tong Mow-chee (Tang Maozhi) containing six counterfoils and four blank drafts. The book is marked with the serial code 'huang'. The counterfoils include the stamp of 'Kung-t'ai' (Gong tai tu zhang). Their entries are dated from the 5th to the 6th days of the 4th month (the year is not given), and amount to Tls 8000 (based on the Shanghai scale for silver). Nos 1 and 2 were prepared by Haisheng and Liench'ing of Shao-sheng-t'ang respectively. There are English notes on the front of the book: 'Lyhong', 'Tls 8000', 'Drawn 8000' and 'Draft 4904.867/3095.133'. The cover also includes the Chinese name of the hall Shao-sheng-t'ang. 1 item; Moderate condition, including damage by damp and insects.

Chapter Five

第五章

官方文件

官方文件时间涵盖1830—1935年，共计41件，是中国和英国政府、领事馆和其他官员之间的官方往来文件。如1830年查顿致函粤海关要求立刻准许商船回国的照会；1843年“香港首席裁判官”发出的禁止在香港过度砍伐森林的中文公告；1853年福建茶帮的公告；1853年潮州向英国领事递交的处罚不法外国商人的请愿书；1855年上海道台发布的新货币取代旧外币的公告；1858年两广总督禁止鸦片的谕令；1859年4月10日福建当局发布的筹集军事资金而征收税的谕令；1859年福建漳州府允许怡和洋行继续经营鸦片生意的通知；1860年粤海关官员向怡和洋行通报鸦片贸易事宜；各地海关颁发的出口关票、外交照会等。

一、道光十年查典①因茂生行②迟未代办出洋红牌③事呈粤海关监督禀帖（H5/1）

道光十年九月十九日（1830年11月4日），查典向粤海关监督禀告茂生行行商林应奎拖延办理出港红牌事宜。

Letter from Jardine re Red Note. A letter (in Chinese) from Jardine, responsible for British private business in Canton, to the Inspector of Canton Customs, 4 November 1830, reporting that 27 days after an English vessel, captained by I (Yi), paid the required tonnage dues and all duties and tax through the guarantee merchant Lim Ying-k'ui (Lin Yingkui) of Maosheng Hong the ship is still waiting for its Red Note (certificate of clearance). He requests that the note be issued immediately, because the ship cannot afford further delay. There is a part of a brief English note about the letter on the reverse. 1 item; Poor condition, including damage by damp and insects, with missing sections.

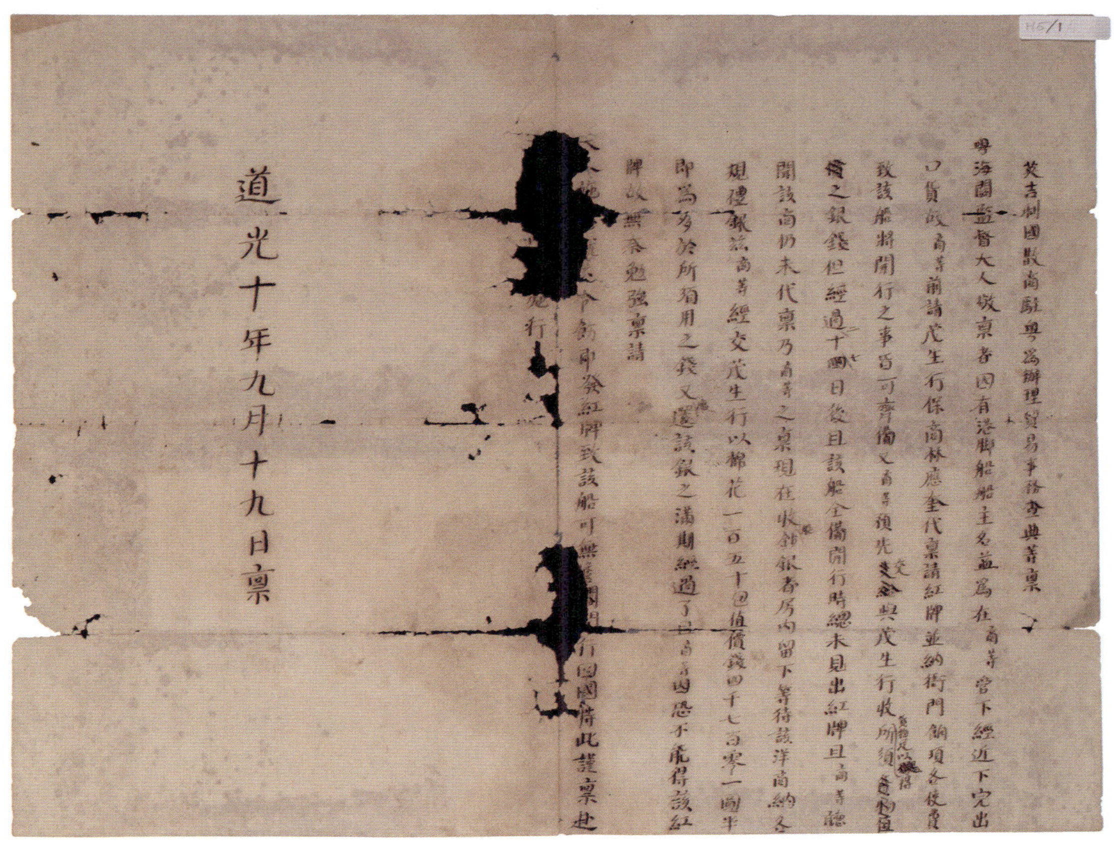

H5/1

英吉利國散商駐粵爲辦理貿易事務查典菁稟

粵海關監督大人敬稟者因有港腳船船主名益爲在商等當下經近下完出

口貨致商等前請茂生行保商林應奎代稟請紅牌並納衙門餉項各使費

致該船將開行之事皆可齊備又商等預先交銀與茂生行收所須[illegible]

費之銀錢但經過十四日後且該船全備開行時總未見出紅牌且商等聽

聞該商仍未代稟乃商等之稟現在收銀銀者房內留下等待該洋商納各

規禮緣該商等經交茂生行以棉花一百五十包值價錢四千七百零一圓半

即爲有於所須用之銭又還該銀之滿期經過了日商等因恐不能得該紅

牌以無奈勉強稟請

大人施[illegible]令飭即發紅牌致該船可無[illegible]開[illegible]行回國備此謹稟赴

[illegible]行

道光十年九月十九日稟

---

① 查典：即威廉·查顿（William Jardine），又译渣颠、渣甸、赞典等，为怡和洋行（Jardine, Matheson & Co.）创始人之一。

② 茂生行：行商林应奎（Linqua），道光八年（1828）成立，道光十八年（1838）倒闭。

③ 红牌：外国船只回国前向粤海关申请的准许离港证明，因为纸张颜色为红色被称为“红牌”。

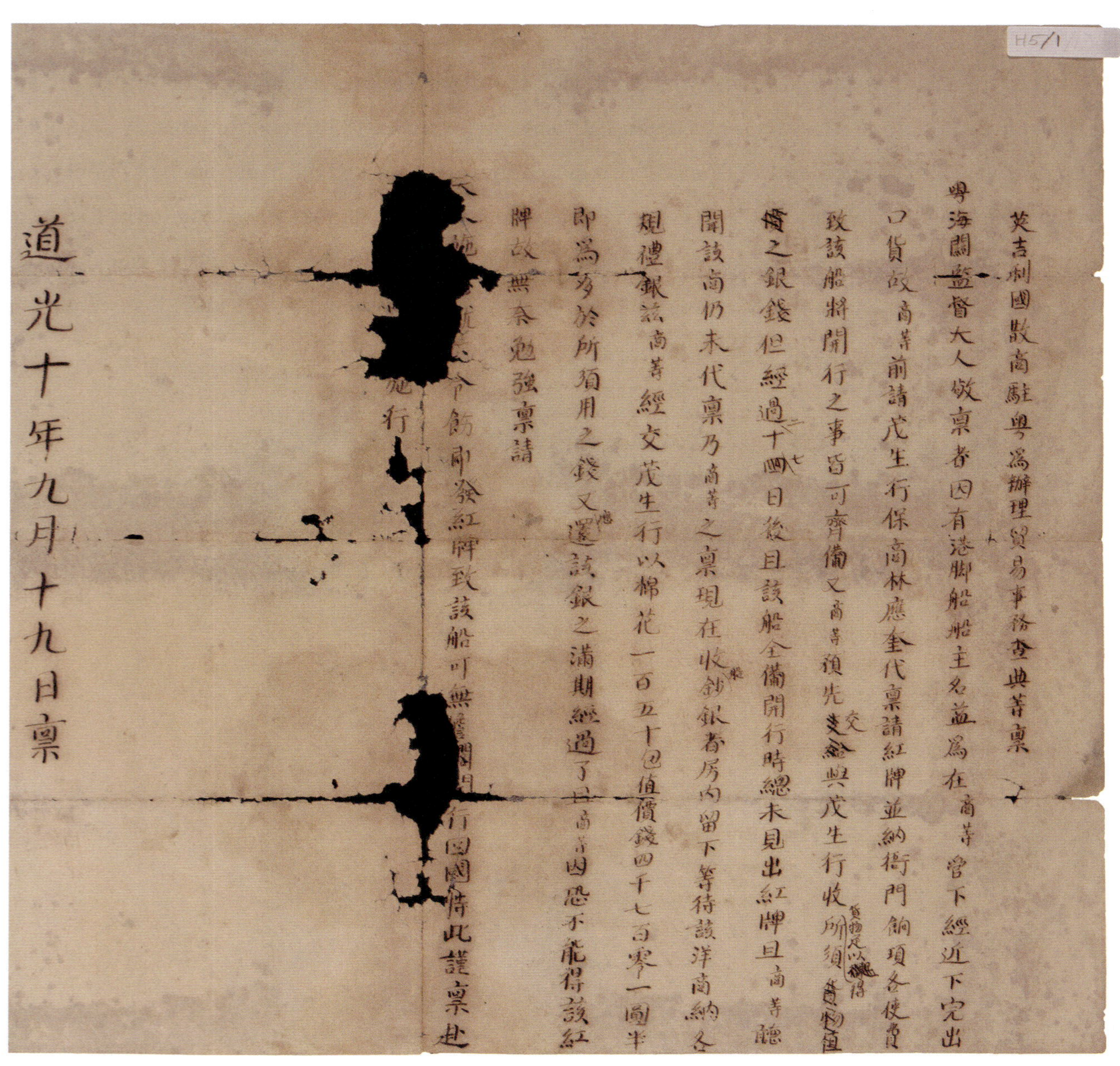

英吉利國散商駐粵爲辦理貿易事務查典等稟
粵海關監督大人敬稟者因有港脚船船主名益爲在商等管下經近下完出
口貨故商等前請茂生行保商林應奎代稟請紅牌並納衙門餉項各使費
致該船將開行之事皆可齊備又商等預先交銀與茂生行收所須貨物值
價之銀錢但經過十四日後且該船全備開行時總未見出紅牌且商等聽
聞該商仍未代稟乃商等之稟現在收鈔銀者房內留下等待該洋商納各
規禮銀該商等經交茂生行以棉花一百五十包值價錢四千七百零一圓半
即爲多於所須用之錢又還該銀之滿期經過了已商等因恐不能得該紅
牌故無奈勉強稟請
大[illegible]施[illegible]令飭即發紅牌致該船可無[illegible]行回國特此謹稟赴
[illegible]施行

道光十年九月十九日稟

（局部图）

二、道光二十三年“香港首席裁判官”告示（H5/2）

道光二十三年三月二十八日（1843年4月27日），“香港首席裁判官”George W. Caine颁布的告示，禁止随意砍伐树木，盖有中英文印章，印文“巡理香港等处地方印”。

Public note re deforestation. A public notice (in Chinese) issued by George W. Caine, Chief Magistrate, Hong Kong, for prohibiting excessive deforestation in Hong Kong, 27 April 1843, including the magistrate's stamp and a short English note about the notice.1 item; Moderate condition, including significant damage by insects.

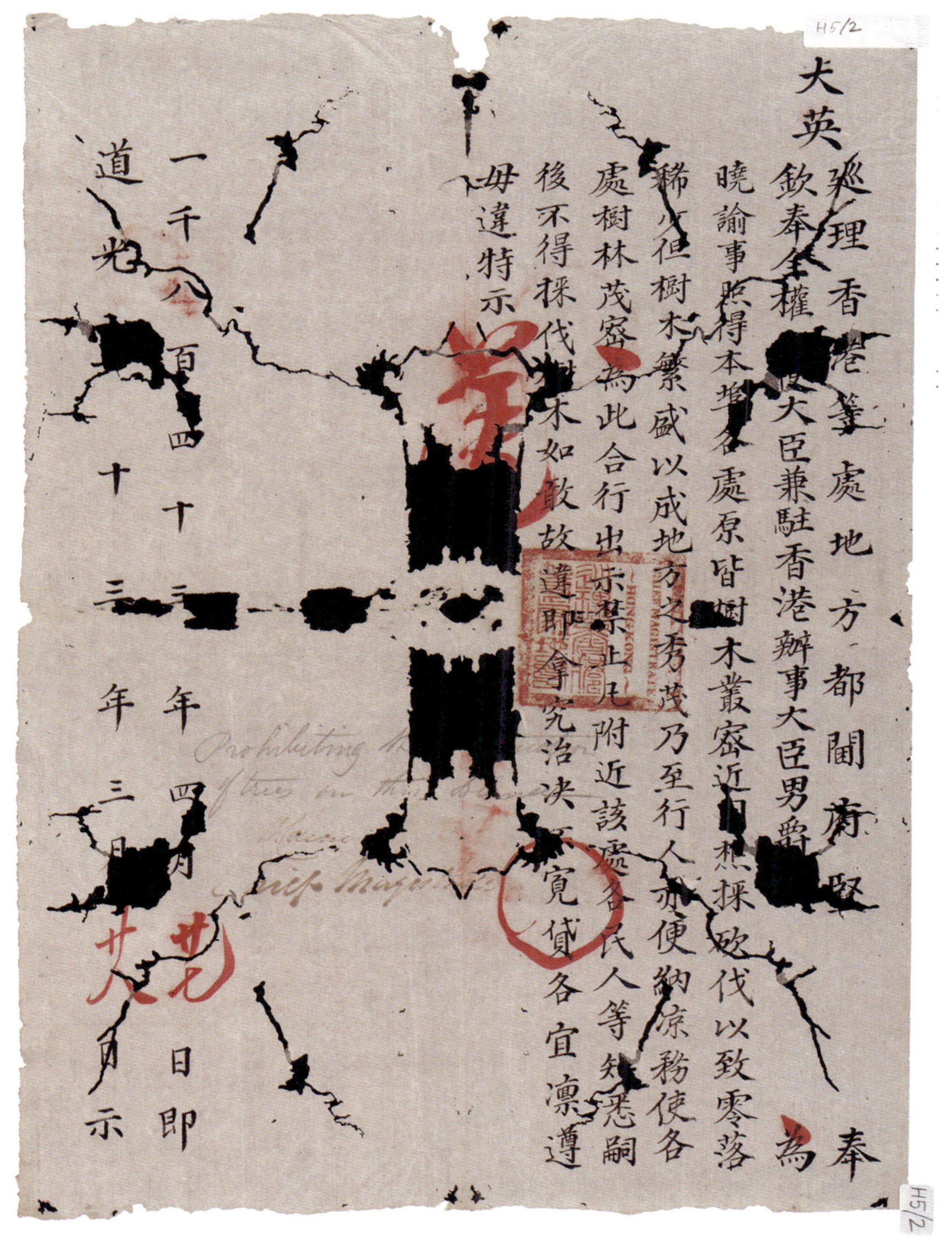

H5/2

大英
巡理香港等處地方都閫府堅　奉
欽奉全權大臣兼駐香港辦事大臣男爵璞　為
曉諭事照得本港各處原皆樹木叢密近日[illegible]採砍伐以致零落
稀少但樹木繁盛以成地方之秀茂乃至行人亦便納凉務使各
處樹林茂密為此合行出示禁止凡附近該處各民人等知悉嗣
後不得採伐樹木如敢故違即拿究治決不寬貸各宜凜遵
毋違特示
一千八百四十三年四月廿七日即
道光二十三年三月廿八日示

三、道光二十八年丹麦[①]驻广州领事通行证明一式两份（H5/3/1-2）

道光二十八年五月十二日（1848年6月12日），丹麦驻广州领事发给渣甸[②]的通行证明两份，注明前往香港办理货物等事宜。盖有印章，印文不详。

Letters from Danish Consulate. 2 items.

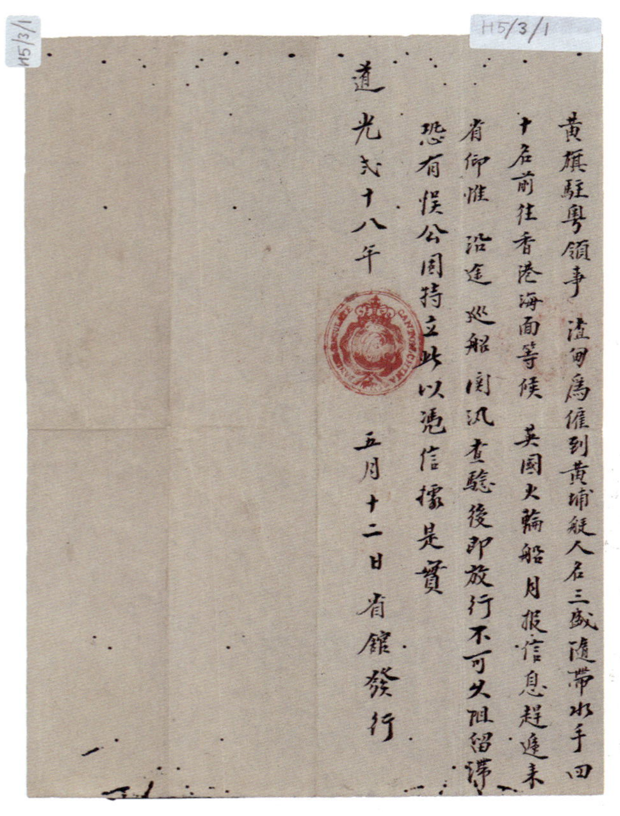

H5/3/1

黄旗駐粤領事 渣甸爲催到黄埔艇人名三盛隨帶水手四
十名前往香港海面等候 英國火輪船月報信息赶速來
省仰惟 沿途巡船関汛查驗後即放行不可久阻留滯
恐有悞公因特立此以憑信據是實
道光弍十八年 五月十二日 省館發行

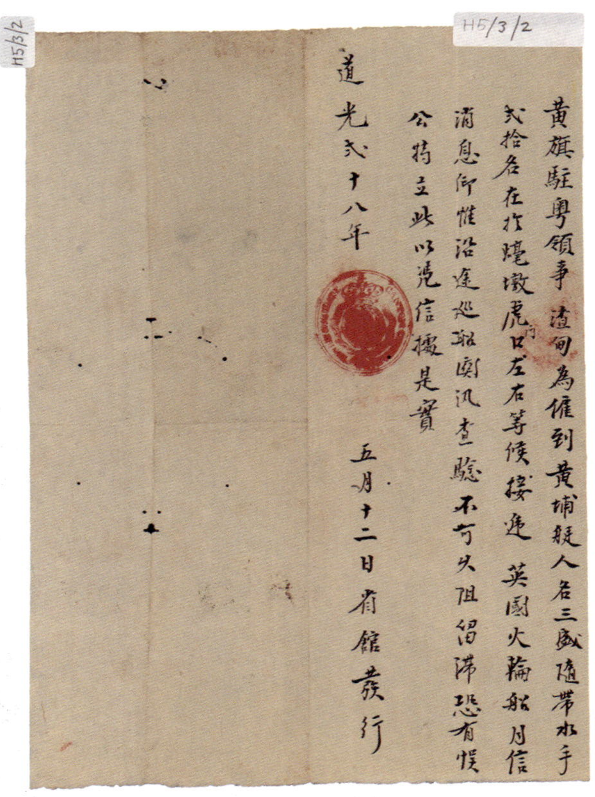

H5/3/2

黄旗駐粤領事 渣甸爲催到黄埔艇人名三盛隨帶水手
弍拾名在於礮墩虎門口左右等候接連 英國火輪船月信
消息仰惟沿途巡船関汛查驗不可久阻留滯恐有悞
公特立此以憑信據是實
道光弍十八年 五月十二日 省館發行

① 丹麦：原中文文献中作“黄旗”，黄旗国即指丹麦。

② 渣甸：即威廉·查顿（William Jardine），又译渣颠、赞典等，为怡和洋行（Jardine, Matheson & Co.）创始人之一。

四、咸丰三年福建茶叶贸易谕令

1. 咸丰三年福州闽县茶叶贸易谕令（H5/4/1）

咸丰三年（1853），福建福州闽县茶叶贸易谕令，申明在福建茶区中外商人进行贸易应该遵守的规定。

Papers re Fukien tea business. 1853

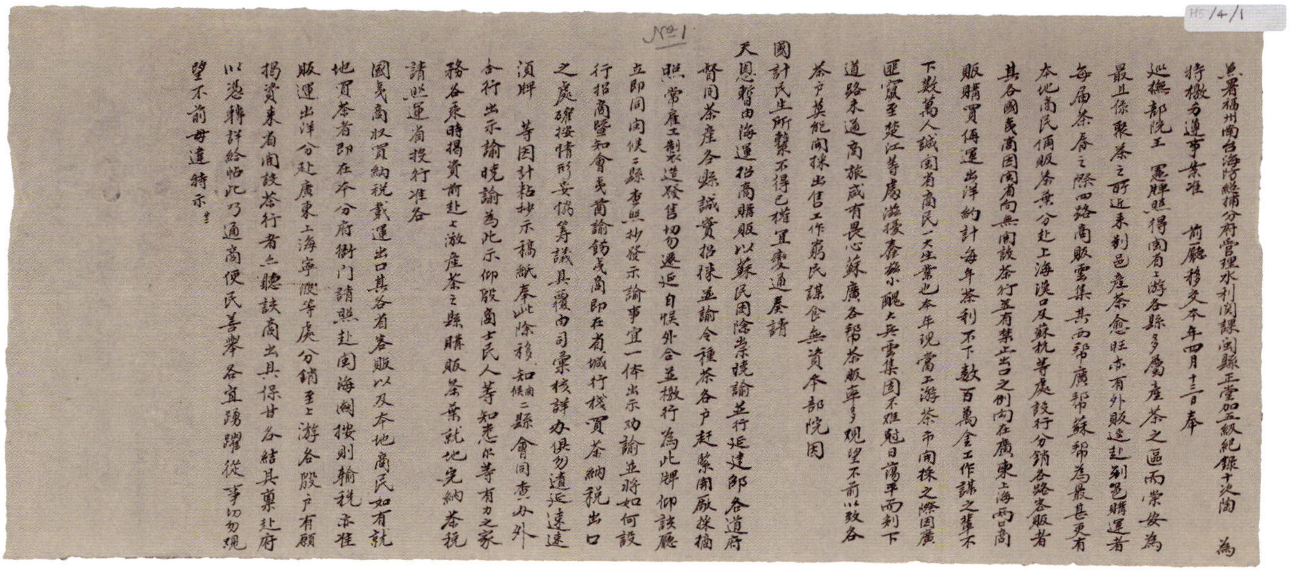

兼署福州南台海防總捕分府管理水利關課關稅正堂加五級紀錄十次胡 為
特授福道事案准 前廳移文本年四月十三日奉
巡撫部院王 憲牌照得閩省上游各縣多屬產茶之區而崇安為
最且係聚茶之所近來新邑產茶愈旺亦有外販運赴新邑購運者
每屆採茶之際四路商販雲集其西路即廣幫北路即蘇幫均為最是更有
本地商民偶販茶葉分赴上海漢口及蘇杭等處設行分銷各路茶販若
其各國來商因閩省向無開設茶行並有禁止出口之例向在廣東上海兩口商
販購買偏運出洋約計每年茶利不下數百萬金工作謀生者不
下數萬人誠閩省商民一大生業也本年現當上游茶市開採之際因廣
匪竄至楚江等處滋擾雖係小醜么魔雲集因不准赴日滿平而利下
道路未通商旅咸有畏心蘇廣各幫茶販寥寥觀望不前以致各
茶戶甚難開採出售工作窮民謀食無資本部院因
國計民生所繫不得已權宜變通奏請
天恩暫由海道招商購販以蘇民困除出示曉諭並行延建邵各道府
督同茶產各縣誠實招徠並諭令種茶各戶趕緊開採以濟
照常產茶售切勿遲延自誤外合亟檄行為此牌仰該廳
立即同閩侯二縣查照抄發示諭事宜一併出示明諭並將如何設
行招商照章會來商諭飭來閩即在省城行棧買茶納稅出口
之處酌議情形妥協籌議具覆由司案核詳辦毋得遲延速速
須牌 等因計粘抄示稿 准此除移知閩侯二縣會同查照外
合行出示曉諭為此示仰該商民人等知悉凡爾等有力之家
務各乘時揭資前赴上游產茶之縣購販茶葉就地完納茶稅
請照運省投行准各
國來商收買納稅載運出口其各省茶販以及本地商民如有就
地買茶者即在本分府衙門請照赴閩海關報明輸稅承准
販運出洋分赴廣東上海寧波等處分銷至上游各戶有願
揭資來省開設茶行者亦聽該商出具保甘各結具稟赴府
以憑核詳給照仍令該商候示遵辦各宜踊躍從事切勿觀
望不前毋違特示

（局部图）

2. 咸丰三年福州闽县茶叶贸易谕令抄录（H5/4/2）

咸丰三年（1853），福州闽县茶叶贸易谕令抄录。

Papers re Fukien tea business.

H5/4/2

№3—

照抄曉示　撫憲全銜

為曉諭事照得閩省上游各縣多屬產茶之區而崇安為最且係聚茶之所云云照海防示稿內叙至以蘇民困合行出示曉諭為此示仰合屬士民人等知悉尔等有力之家務各乘時揭資前赴上游產茶各縣購販茶葉就地完納茶稅請照運省投行准聽各國夷商收買納稅載運出口其各省客販以及本地商民如有就省買茶者即在福防廳衙门請照赴閩縣海關按則輸稅亦准販運出洋分赴廣東上海寧波等處分銷至上游各殷戶有願揭資來省開設茶行者亦听其便此乃通商便民善舉務宜踴躍從事切勿自悞生業其各恪遵特示

3. 咸丰三年福州闽县茶叶贸易谕令抄录（H5/4/3）

咸丰三年（1853），福州闽县茶叶贸易谕令抄录。

Papers re Fukien tea business.

No 2

前事云云等因奉此出示曉諭外合就移知為此移諮貴
縣查照確按抄發示諭事宜一体出示勸諭並將如何
招商設行暨知會夷商諭令夷商即在省城行棧買
茶納稅出口之處查看情形會同妥協際議具覆由
司核轉須至移者

五、咸丰二年潮州商户因重开哈板湾至汕头贸易事致英国领事公函[①]（H5/5）

咸丰二年（1853）十二月，潮州19家商号致信英国领事，希望重开哈板湾至汕头的贸易。

Petition of Ch'ao chow fu merchants. A petition from the Ch'ao chow (Chaozhou) Fu merchants to the British Consul, January 1853, requesting the recall of Hapan (Haban) to Swatow for the good of business and public peace. The signatories are Fuhsing (Fuxing), Chuefa (Jufa), Hochih (Heji), T'ienpao (Tianbao), Shunfa, Fangchih (Fangji), Hoshing (Hexing), Pingchih (Bingji), Chiali (Jiali), Wensheng, I-ho (Yihe), Ch'enssu (Chensi), Tashun (Dashun), Wangho (Wanghe), Lienhsing (Lianxing), Ch'engshun (Shengshun), Ch'engfa (Chengfa), Teho (Dehe) and Luch'eng (Lucheng).

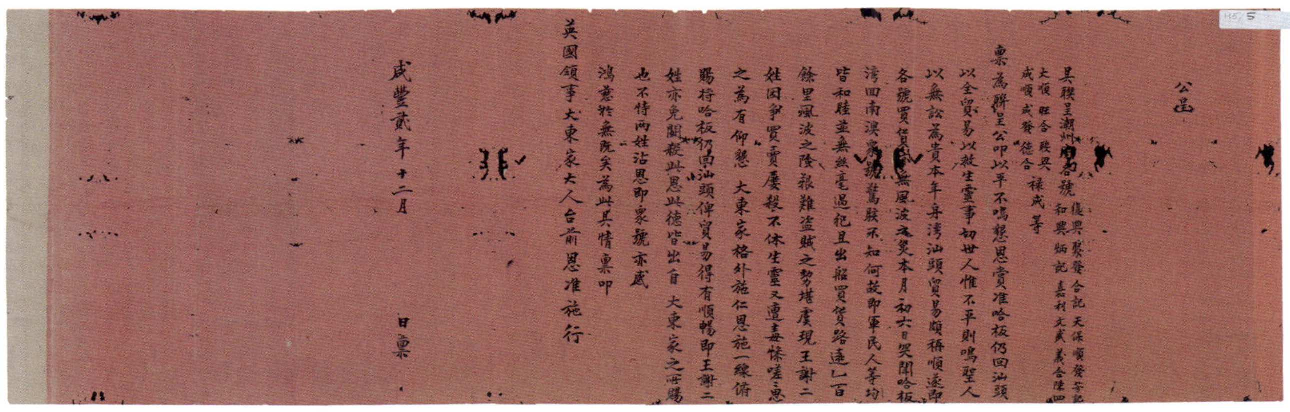

公呈

具稟呈潮州府各號 復興 聚發 合記 天保 順發 芳記 和興 炳記 嘉利 文盛 義合 陳四 大順 旺合 聯興 成順 成發 德合 祿成 等

稟為聯呈公叩以平不鳴懇恩賞准哈板仍回汕頭以全貿易以救生靈事切世人惟不平則鳴聖人以無訟為貴本年舟湾汕頭貿易頗稱順遂即各號買貨並無風波之災本月初六日哭聞哈板湾回南澳衆號驚駭不知何故即軍民人等均皆和睦並無絲毫過犯且出船買貨路遠七百餘里風波之險艱難盜賊之勢堪虞現王謝二姓因爭買賣屢殺不休生靈又遭毒條嗟嗟悲之為有仰懇 大東家格外施仁恩施一線俯賜特哈板仍回汕頭俾貿易得有順暢即王謝二姓亦免鬬殺此恩此德皆出自 大東家之所賜也不特兩姓沾恩即衆號亦感鴻慈於無既矣為此具情稟叩

英國領事大東家大人台前恩准施行

咸豐貳年十二月　日稟

---

① 发信人：复兴、聚发、合记、天保、顺发、芳记、和兴、炳记、嘉利、文盛、义合、陈四、大顺、旺合、联兴、成顺、成发、德合、禄成等。

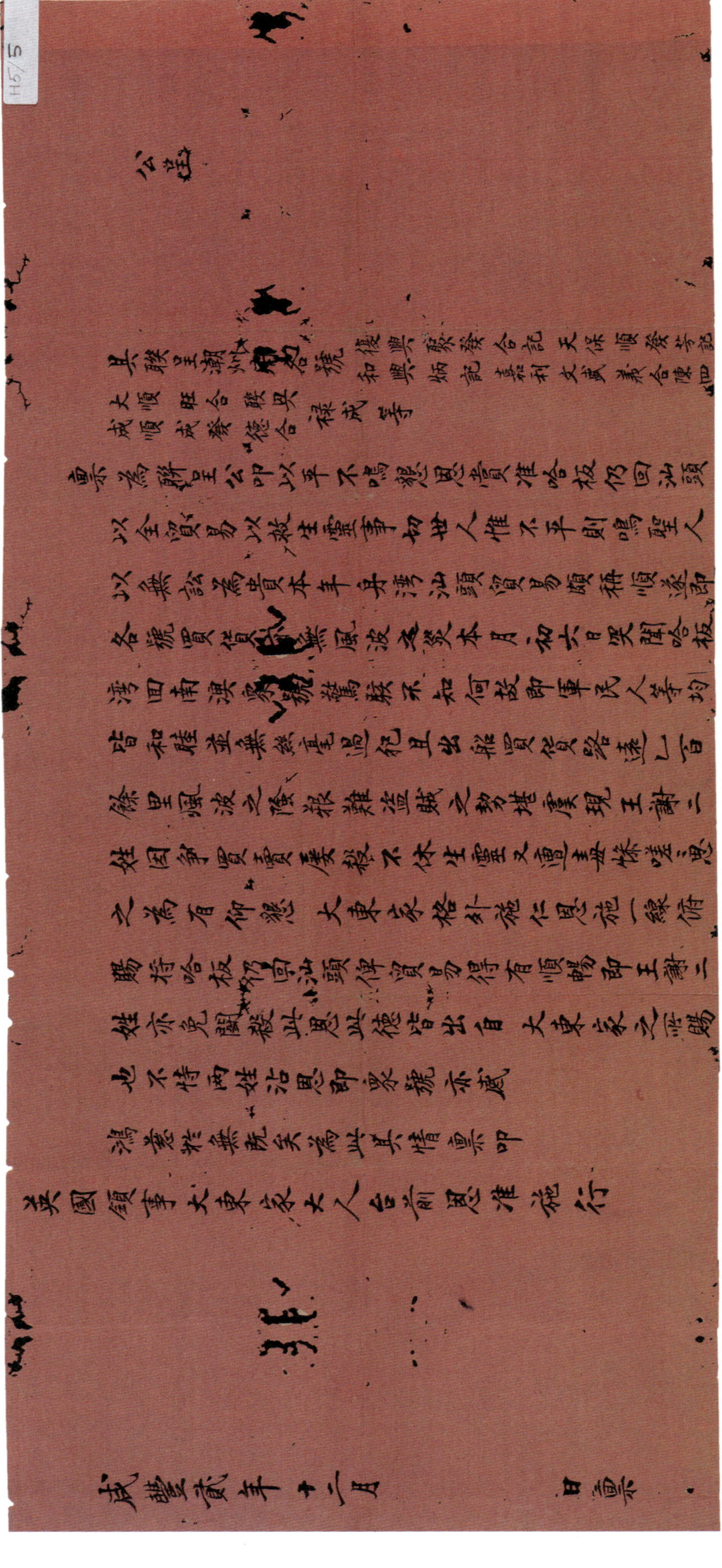

（局部图）

六、咸丰五年上海道台新旧银元兑换①告示（H5/6）

咸丰五年（1855）七月，上海道台公布新旧银元兑换告示事宜。

Public notice of the Taot’ai of Shanghai. A copy of a public notice issued by Chao (Zhao), Taot’ai of Shanghai, regarding replacing the old foreign currency with a new one, dated 13 August–10 September 1855. 1 item.

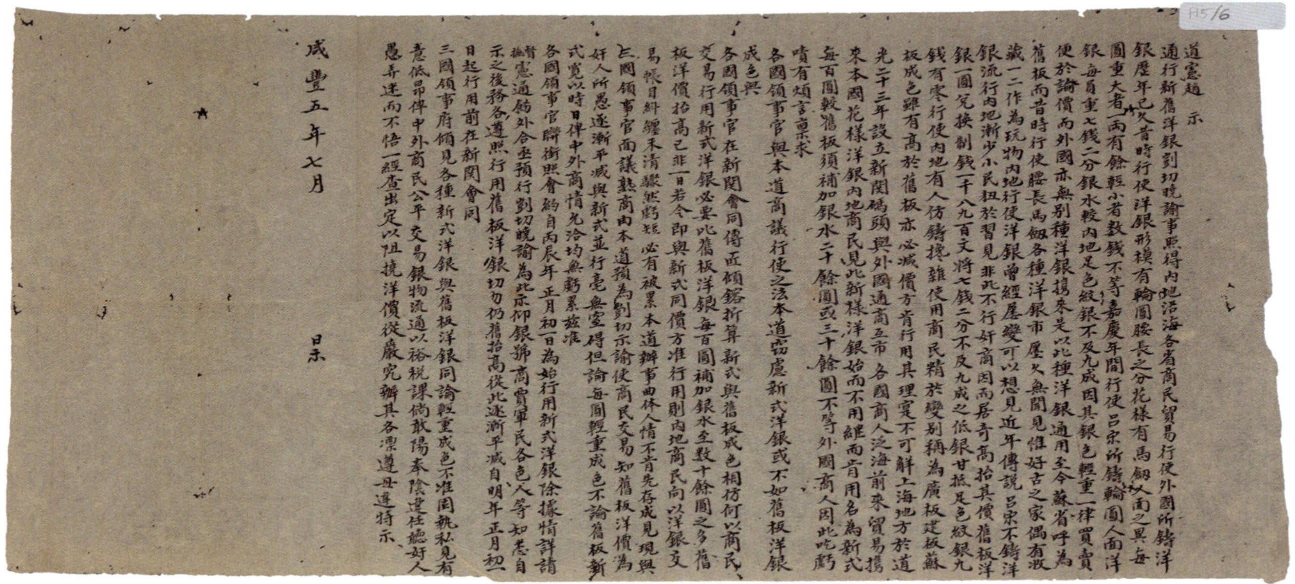

H5/6

道憲趙　示
通行新舊洋銀剴切曉諭事照得内地沿海各省商民貿易行使外國所鑄洋
銀歷年已久昔時行使洋銀形模有輪圍腰長之分花様有馬劍人面之異每
圓重大者一兩有餘輕小者數錢不等嘉慶年間行使呂宋所鑄輪圓人面洋
銀每員重七錢二分銀水較内地足色紋銀不及九成因其銀色輕重一律買賣
便於論價而外國亦無別種洋銀携來是以此種洋銀通用至今蘇省呼為
舊板而昔時行使腰長馬劍各種洋銀市廛久無聞見惟好古之家偶有收
藏一二作為玩物内地行使洋銀曾經屢變可以想見近年傳說呂宋不鑄洋
銀流行内地漸少小民狃於習見非此不行奸商因而居奇高抬其價舊板洋
銀一圓兌換制錢一千八九百文將七錢二分不及九成之低銀甘抵足色紋銀九
錢有零行使内地有人彷鑄攙雜使用商民精於變別稱為廣板建板蘇
板成色雖有高於舊板亦必減價方肯行用其理實不可解上海地方於道
光二十三年設立新閞碼頭與外國通商互市各國商人泛海前來貿易携
來本國花様洋銀内地商民見此新様洋銀始而不用繼而肯用名為新式
每百圓較舊板須補加銀水二十餘圓或三十餘圓不等外國商人因此吃虧
嘖有煩言禀求
各國領事官與本道商議行使之法本道酌處新式洋銀或不如舊板洋銀
成色與
各國領事官在新閞會同傳匠傾鎔折算新式與舊板成色相彷何以商民
交易行用新式洋銀必要比舊板洋銀每百圓補加銀水至數十餘圓之多舊
板洋價抬高已非一日若令即與新式同價方准行用則内地商民向以洋銀交
易帳目糾纏未清驟然虧短必有被累本道辦事曲体人情不肯先存成見現與
三國領事官面議熟商由本道預為剴切示諭使商民交易知舊板洋價為
奸人所愚遂漸平減與新式並行毫無窒碍但論每圓輕重成色不論舊板新
式寬以時日俾中外商情允洽均無虧累茲准
各國領事官聯銜照會約自丙辰年正月初一日為始行用新式洋銀除據情詳請
督撫憲道飭外合亟預行剴切曉諭為此示仰銀號商賈軍民各色人等知悉自
示之後務各遵照行用舊板洋銀切勿仍舊抬高從此逐漸平減自明年正月初一
日起行用前在新閞會同
三國領事府備見各種新式洋銀與舊板洋銀同論輕重成色不准固執私見有
意低昂俾中外商民公平交易銀物流通以裕稅課倘敢陽奉陰違任聽奸人
愚弄迷而不悟一經查出定以阻撓洋價從嚴究辦其各凜遵毋違特示
咸豐五年七月　　日示

① 行商与外商的兑换比率在每枚银元价值纹银0.69两—0.72两之间，这应当是银元的基本汇价。在银元实际流通中会因为各种不同的因素而上下浮动。首先是地域因素，由于广州一口通商的特殊地位，自然银元的保有流通量在全国范围来讲是最大的，因此银元在广东流通的价格低于0.72之比，相反江浙地区银元流通价格则高于0.72之比。

道憲趙　示

通行新舊洋銀剴切曉諭事照得內地沿海各省商民貿易行使外國所鑄洋銀歷年已久昔時行使洋銀形模有輪圓腰長之分花樣有馬劍雙面之異每圓重大者一兩有餘輕小者數錢不等嘉慶年間行使呂宋所鑄輪圓人面洋銀每員重七錢二分銀水較內地足色紋銀不及九成因其銀色輕重一律買賣便於論價而外國亦無別種洋銀攜來是以此種洋銀通用至今蘇省呼為舊板而昔時行使腰長馬劍各種洋銀市歷久無聞見惟好古之家偶有收藏一二作為玩物內地行使洋銀曾經屢變可以想見近年傳說呂宋不鑄洋銀流行內地漸少小民狃於習見非此不行奸商因而居奇高抬其價舊板洋銀一圓兌換制錢一千八九百文將七錢二分不及九成之低銀甘抵足色紋銀九錢有零行使內地有人仿鑄攙雜使用商民精於變別稱為廣板建板蘇板成色雖有高於舊板亦必減價方肯行用其理實不可解上海地方於道光二十三年設立新關碼頭與外國通商互市各國商人泛海前來貿易攜來本國花樣洋銀內地商民見此新樣洋銀始而不用繼而肯用名為新式每百圓較舊板須補加銀水二十餘圓或三十餘圓不等外國商人因此吃虧嘖有煩言稟求

各國領事官與本道商議行使之法本道竊慮新式洋銀或不如舊板洋銀成色與

各國領事官在新關會同傳匠傾鎔折算新式與舊板成色相彷何以商民交易行用新式洋銀必要比舊板洋銀每百圓補加銀水至數十餘圓之多舊板洋價抬高已非一日若令即與新式同價方准行用則內地商民向以洋銀交易帳目糾纏未清驟然虧短必有被累本道辦事曲体人情不肯先存成見現與

各國領事官面議熟商由本道預為剴切示諭使商民交易知舊板洋價為奸人所愚逐漸平減與新式並行毫無窒碍但論每圓輕重成色不論舊板新式寬以時日俾中外商情允洽均無虧累茲准

各國領事官聯銜照會約自丙辰年正月初一日為始行用新式洋銀除據情詳請

督撫憲通飭外合亟預行剴切曉諭為此示仰銀錢商賈軍民各色人等知悉自示之後務各遵照行用舊板洋銀切勿仍舊抬高從此逐漸平減自明年正月初日起行用前在新關會同

三國領事府傾見各種新式洋銀與舊板洋銀同論輕重成色不准固執私見有意低昂俾中外商民公平交易銀物流通以裕稅課倘敢陽奉陰違任聽奸人愚弄迷而不悟一經查出定以阻撓洋價從嚴究辦其各凛遵毋違特示

咸豐五年七月　　日示

（局部图）

七、咸丰八年至九年两广总督谕令

1. 咸丰八年两广总督致伍崇曜[①]谕令（H5/7/1）

咸丰八年五月二十七日（1858年7月7日），两广总督致伍崇曜谕令，《天津条约》签订后北方战事渐渐平息，令其在广东斡旋与外国交涉等事宜。

Papers of Governor-general of Kwangtung and Kwangshi.

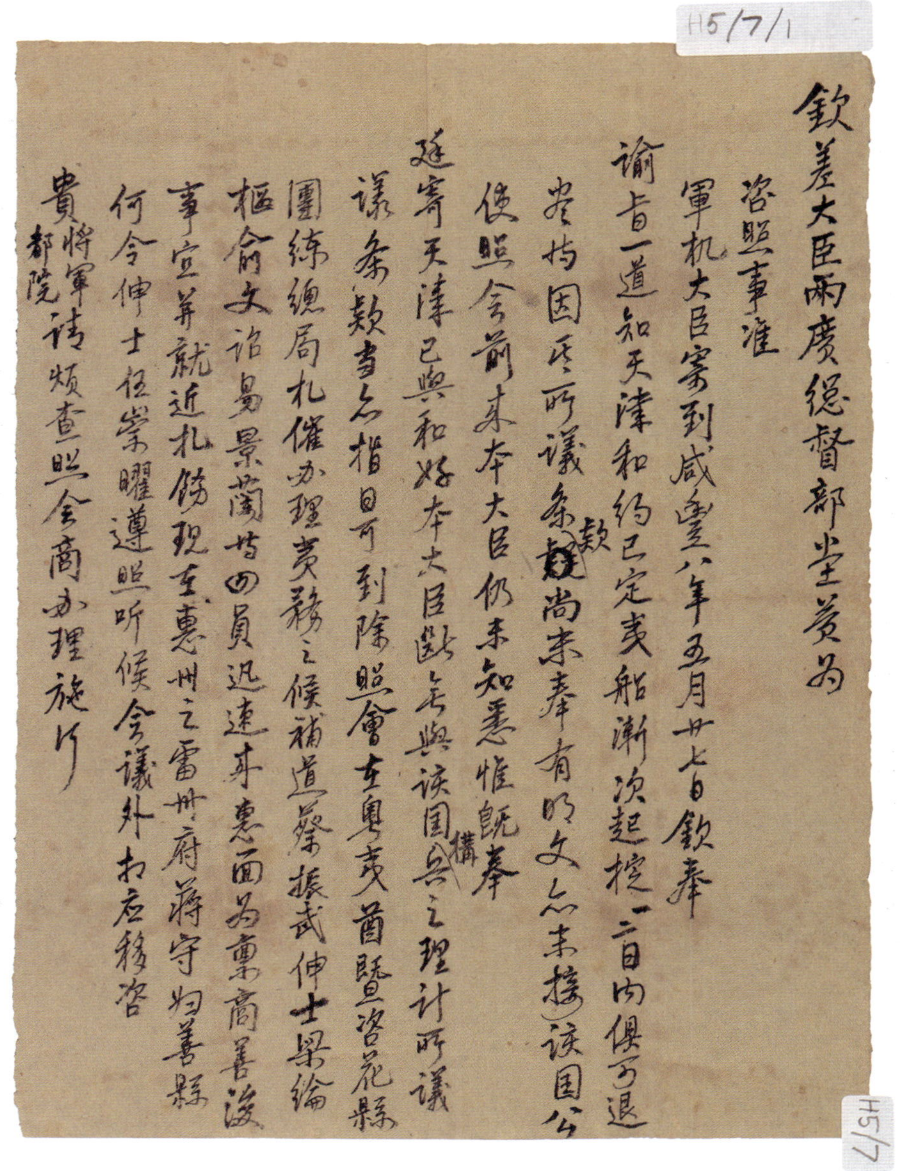

H5/7/1

欽差大臣兩廣總督部堂黃為
咨照事准
軍機大臣寄到咸豐八年五月廿七日欽奉
諭旨一道知天津和約已定夷船漸次起椗一二日內俱可退
出均因臣所議條款尚未奉有明文亦未接該國公
使照會前來本大臣仍未知悉惟既奉
廷寄天津已與和好本大臣斷無與該國兵〔構〕之理計所議
議條款當不指日可到除照會在粵夷酋暨咨花縣
團練總局札催辦理夷務之候補道蔡振武伸士梁綸
樞會同諭易景蘭等四員迅速赴惠面為稟商善後
事宜并就近札飭現在惠州之雷州府蔣守歸善縣
何令伸士伍崇曜遵照听候會議外相應移咨
貴將軍請煩查照會商辦理施行
都院

H5/7

① 伍崇曜：怡和行行商，时任十三行总商。

2. 咸丰九年两广总督讨剿土匪告示[①]（H5/7/2）

咸丰九年（1859），自《天津条约》签订后北方战事渐渐平息，两广总督谕令，加紧剿灭广东境内土匪事宜。

Papers of Governor-general of Kwangtung and Kwangshi.

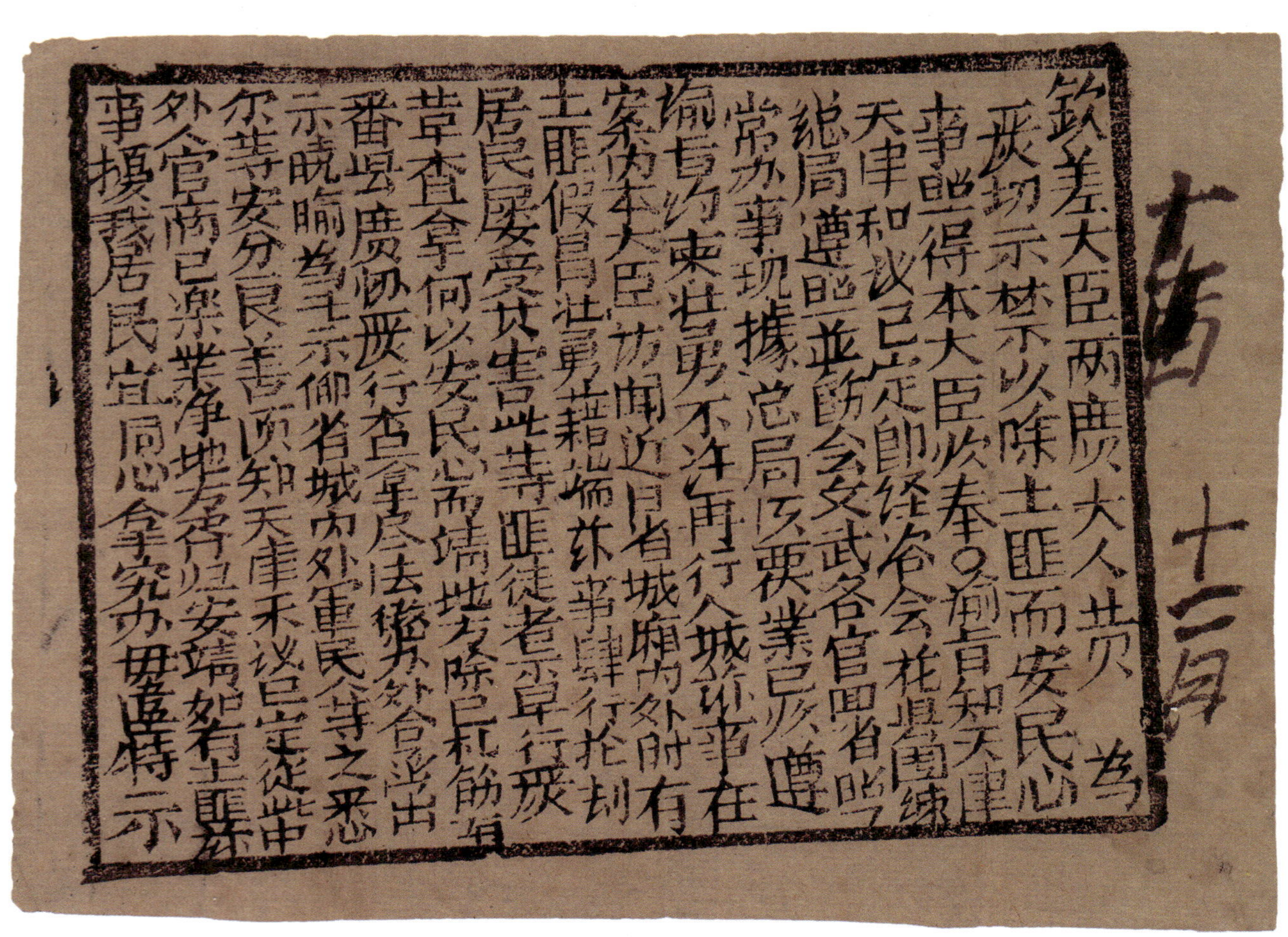
欽差大臣兩廣大人黄　為
嚴切示禁以除土匪而安民心
事照得本大臣欽奉　諭旨知天津
天津和議已定即經洽會花縣團練
總局遵照並飭令文武各官畄省照
常辦事現據總局以業已欽遵
諭旨約束壯勇不准再行入城滋事在
案惟本大臣訪聞近日省城廂內外附有
土匪假冒壯勇藉端訛詐尋衅肆行搶劫
居民屢受其害此等匪徒若不早行嚴
革查拏何以安民心而靖地方除已札飭南
番縣廣協嚴行查拏盡法懲辦外合亟出
示曉諭為此示仰省城內外軍民人等知悉
爾等安分良善須知天津和議已定從中
外官商已樂業淨地方得歸安靖如若土匪
事擾我居民宜同心拏究辦毋違特示

① 1854年广东三合会起义，大举围攻广州城。行商伍崇曜协助两广总督叶名琛筹措军饷，在广州大佛寺、长寿寺等地设劝捐局，筹措500余万军饷及大批粮草军械。凭借一口通商时期与外国的密切联系，筹措得来的粮饷部分是由外国商人提供的。这为叶名琛最终镇压三合会起义提供了重要的物资保障。

八、咸丰九年军需局告示（H5/8）

这是一份于咸丰九年三月初八日（1859年4月10日）由福建军需局发布的公告复件，内容是关于执行清政府征收税饷以筹集军费的命令。附有英文注释，内容为“张贴公告的厦门商铺因此在6月5日关闭”。

Public notice of Bureau of Military Provision. A copy of a public notice issued by the Bureau of Military Provision, Fukien, 10 April 1859, regarding the execution of the imperial mandate for the levying of a likin tax to raise military funds, including an English note: ‘Proclamation Posted in Amoy Shops shut 5th June in Consequence.’ 1 item.

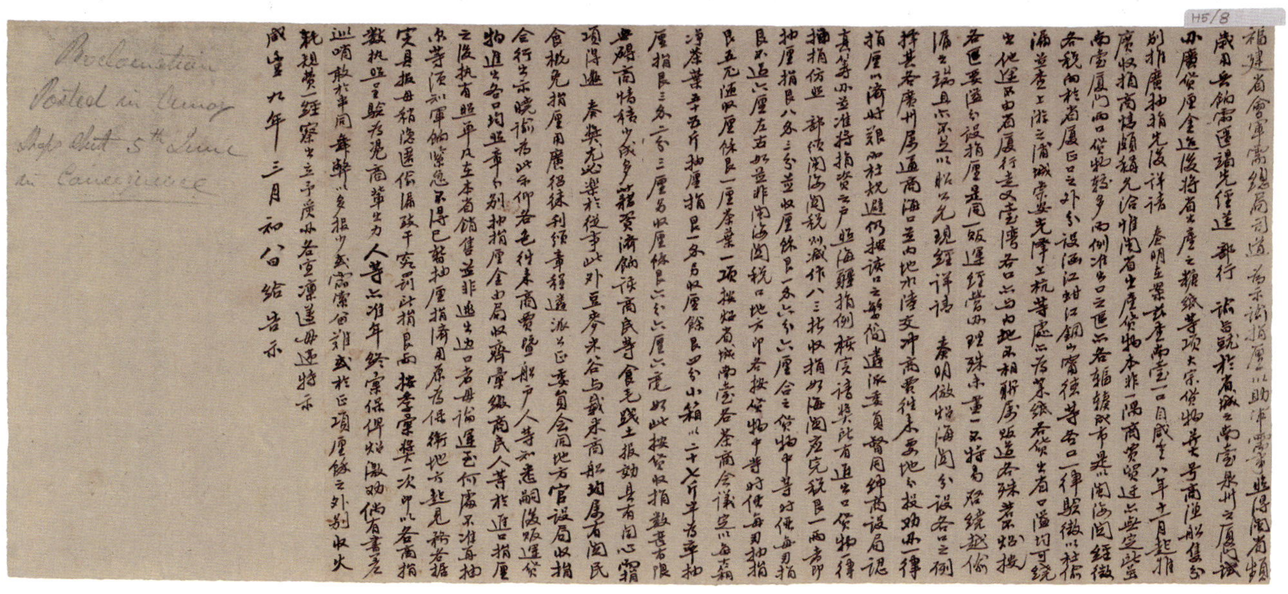
H5/8

Proclamation Posted in Amoy Shops shut 5th June in Consequence

咸豐九年三月初八日給告示

2 | 1

（局部图 1）

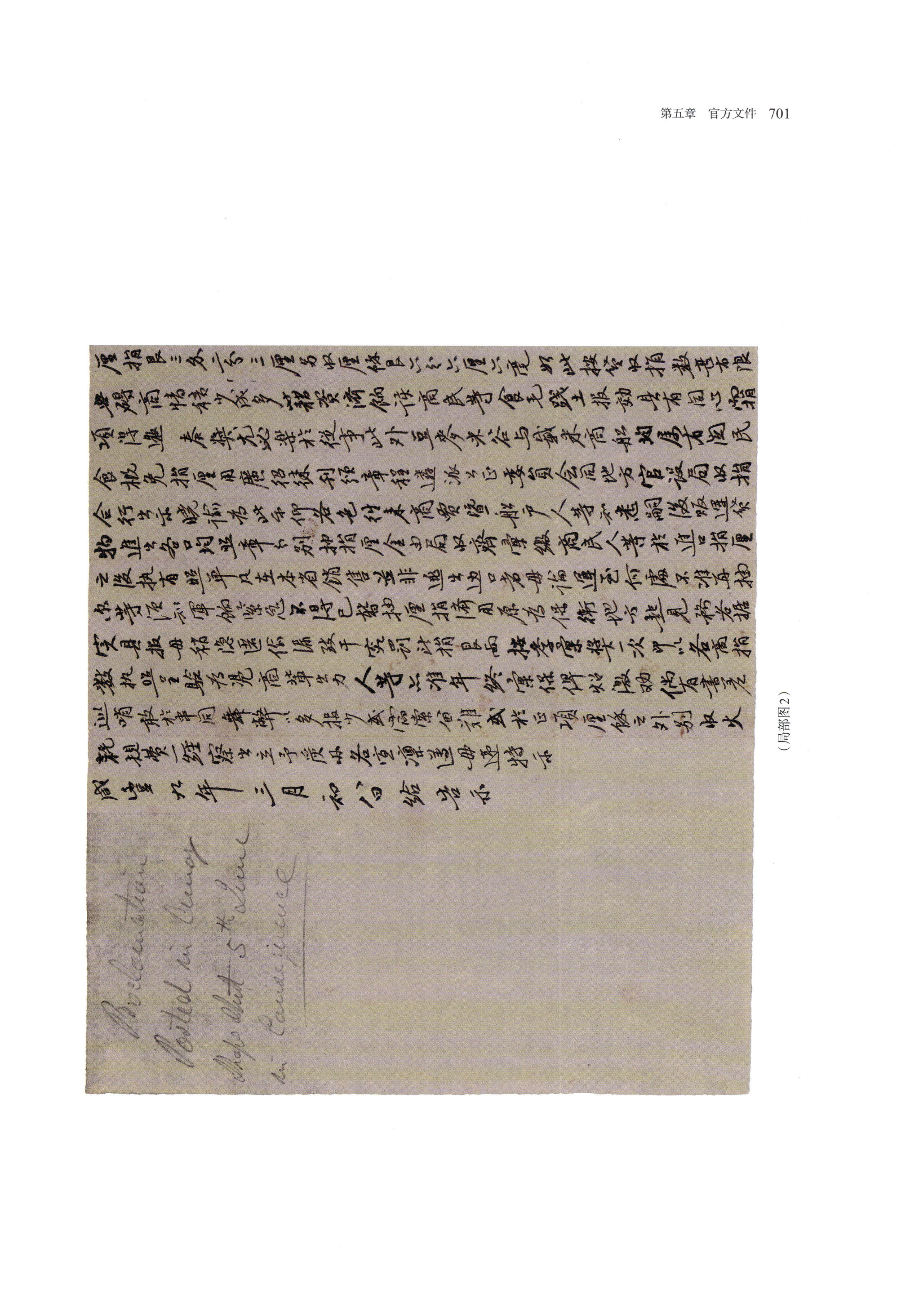

（局部图2）

九、咸丰九年福建泉永海防兵备道禁令（H5/9）

咸丰九年四月二十八日（1859年5月30日），福建泉永海防兵备道陈出示禁令，严禁福建中外商人偷漏税饷。

Public notice of Circuit of Coastal Defence. A copy of a public notice issued by Ch'en (Chen), intendant of the circuit of coastal defence with the title of Provincial Judge, to foreign and Chinese merchants, 30 May 1859, regarding the strict prohibition of the evasion of likin taxes and of the smuggling of opium.1 item.

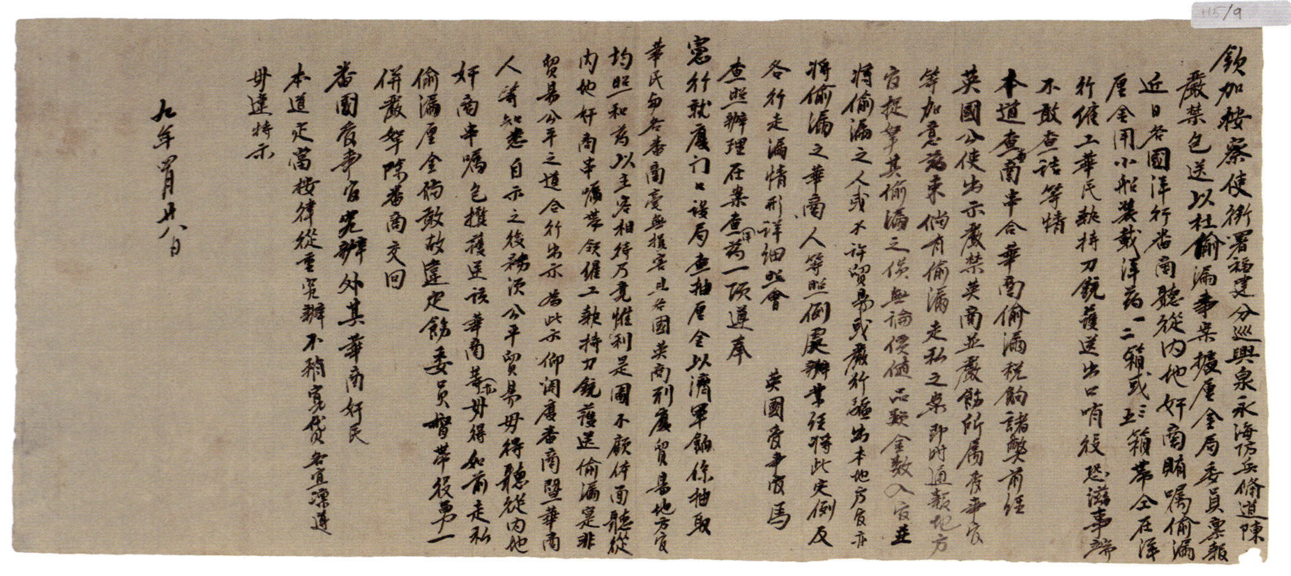

H5/9

欽加按察使銜署福建分巡興泉永海防兵備道陳
嚴禁包送以杜偷漏事案據厘金局委員稟報
近日各國洋行番商聽從内地奸商賄囑偷漏
厘金用小船裝載洋藥一二箱或三五箱帶仝在洋
行僱工華民執持刀銃護送出口哨役懾於事端
不敢查詰等情
本道查番商串合華商偷漏稅餉諸弊前經
英國公使出示嚴禁英商並嚴飭所屬領事官
等加意稽查倘有偷漏走私之案即時通報地方
官捉拿其偷漏之貨無論價值全數入官並
將偷漏之人或不許貿易或嚴行驅出本地方官亦
將偷漏之華商人等照例處辦業經將此定例及
各行走漏情形詳細照會　英國領事官馬
查照辦理在案查茲一項遵奉
憲行就廈門口設局查抽厘金以濟軍餉係抽取
華民向各番商處無損害之各國英商利處貿易地方官
均照和約以主客相待乃竟惟利是圖不顧体面聽從
内地奸商串囑帶領僱工執持刀銃護送偷漏是非
貿易公平之道合行出示　為此示仰闔廈番商暨華商
人等知悉自示之後務須公平貿易毋得聽從内地
奸商串囑包攬護送該華商等亦毋得如前走私
偷漏厘金倘敢故違定飭委員暨帶役勇一
併嚴拏除番商交回
番國領事官究辦外其華商奸民
本道定當按律從重究辦不稍寬貸各宜凜遵
毋違特示

九年四月廿八日

（局部图）

一〇、咸丰九年福建泉州府准许渣颠[①]售卖鸦片谕令（H5/10）

咸丰九年六月二十七日（1859年7月26日），福建泉州府致函渣颠，因其守法，准许其在域内长期从事鸦片贸易，抽税以资国用。

Dispatch from Ch'uan-chow fu magistrate. A dispatch from Jan (Ran), prefecture magistrate of Ch'uan-chow fu, Fukien, to Jardine, 27 June 1859[②], praising him for his positive response to the government's decision to levy a likin tax and granting him permission to stay and conduct his opium business.

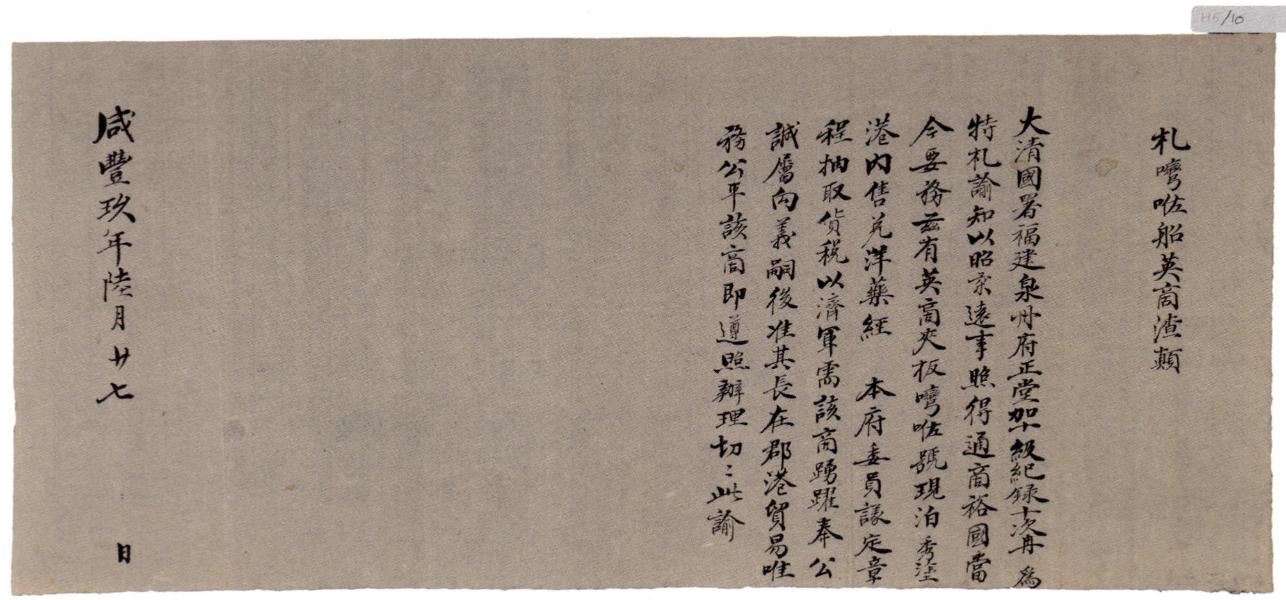
H5/10

札哼咗船英商渣顛

大清國署福建泉州府正堂加十級紀錄十次冉　為
特札諭知以昭柔遠事照得通商裕國當
今要務茲有英商夾板哼咗號現泊秀塗
港內售兌洋藥經　本府委員議定章
程抽取貨稅以濟軍需該商踴躍奉公
誠屬向義嗣後准其長在郡港貿易唯
務公平該商即遵照辦理切切此諭

咸豐玖年陸月廿七　日

① 渣颠：即英国商人威廉·查顿（William Jardine），又译为渣顿、渣甸、赞典，为怡和洋行（Jardine, Matheson & Co.）创始人之一。

② 勘误：英文提要日期为1859年6月27日（27 June 1859），按原中文文献"咸丰玖年陆月廿七日"，应为1859年7月26日。

一一、咸丰九年督理厦门海关官员给英国领事的照会[①]（H5/11）

咸丰九年十月二十九日（1859年11月23日），督理厦门海关官员给英国领事的照会，表明鸦片进口需在福州和厦门进行征税，而非在地方征税。

Dispatch from Amoy Customs. A dispatch (in Chinese) from Jung (Rong), regimental commander, in charge of taxation at Amoy, to the British consul, Amoy (A. R. Johnston?), 23 November 1859, containing the transcript of edicts for the levying of tax on the opium trade, and rejecting the proposal that payment be made at local ports instead of at the Maritime Customs at Fuchow and Amoy. There is also an English note describing the document as a copy of a circular to the foreign consuls from the Collector of Customs at Amoy.

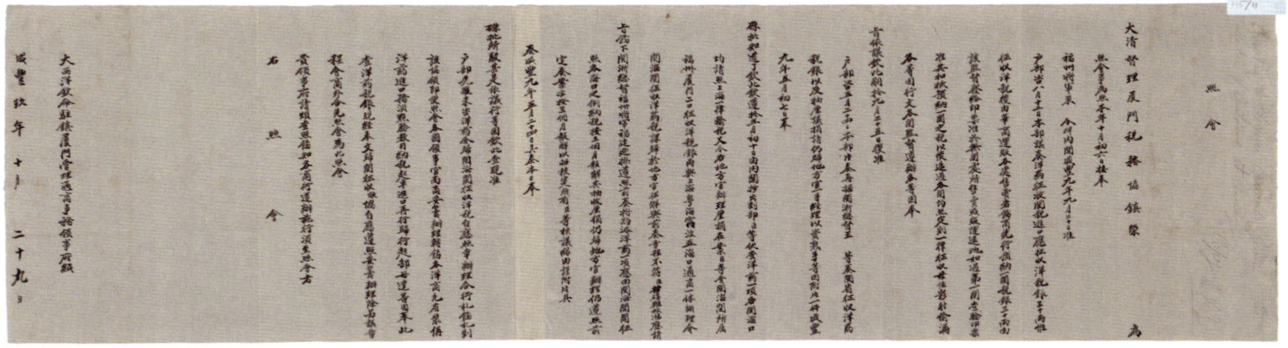

2 | 1

① 照会：近代以后国家之间各级机构文书往来的形式。

Circular to Foreign Consuls from the Collector of Customs at Amoy
Copy

照會

大清督理厦門稅務協鎮榮　為

照會事。為照本年十月初六日接奉

福州將軍東　今牌內開咸豐九年九月二十日准

戶部咨八月十二日本部議奏洋药征收関稅進口應征收洋稅銀三十兩惟

征收洋稅後由華商運販各處售賣者飭商先行預納一関稅銀三十兩由

該監督發給印票准於無関處所售賣或販運遠地如過第一関查驗印票

准其扣抵預納一関之稅以後運過各関均照定則一律征收毋任影射偷漏

各等因行文各関監督遵辦各等因奉

旨依議欽此嗣於九月二十五日復准

戶部咨五月二十四日本部片奏再据閩浙總督王　等奏閩省征收洋药

稅銀以及抽厘議捐請仍歸地方官一手經理以資熟手等因附片一件咸豐

九年五月初七日奉

硃批知道了欽此欽遵於五月初十日由內閣抄出到部臣等伏查洋药一項各関海口

均請照上海一律輸稅又令各地方官辦理厘捐在案臣等查閩海関所屬

福州厦門二口征收洋稅銀兩與上海粵海寧波五海口通商一体辦理今

閩海関征收洋药稅課歸於地方官征解與前奏章程不符臣韓礙難核准應請

（局部图1）

福州廈門二口征收洋稅銀兩與上海粵海寧波五海口通商一体辦理今
閩海關征收洋藥稅課歸於地方官征解與前奏章程不符臣部礙難核准應請
旨飭下閩浙總督福州將軍福建巡撫遵照前奏將酌添洋藥一項應由閩海關征
照各海口之例納稅按三個月報解其抽收厘捐仍歸地方官辦理仍遵照前
定奏案亦按三個月報解以昭核實所有臣等核議緣由謹附片具
奏咸豐九年五月二十四日具奏本日奉
硃批所駁甚是依議行等因欽此查現准
户部先後來咨洋藥今歸閩海關征收洋稅自應照章辦理合行札飭札到
該協領即便照會各國領事官而商妥籌辦理轉飭各洋商凡有裝備
洋藥進口務須照驗數目納稅起單進口再行歸行起卸毋違等因奉此
查洋藥稅銀現經奉文歸閩征收敝協自應遵照妥籌辦理除另議章
程會商外合先照會為此照會
貴領事府請煩查照飭知各商行遵辦施行須至照會者
右　照　會
大西洋欽命駐鎮廈門管理通商事務領事府綫
咸豐玖年十月二十九日

（局部图2）

一二、咸丰十年福建陵水海关官员严禁偷漏税饷、鸦片走私的告示（H5/12）

咸丰十年四月十七日（1860年6月6日），福建陵水海关官员严禁偷漏税饷、鸦片走私的告示，盖有新兴栈的印章，印文“妈屿新兴栈来往图书支取不准”。

Public notice of Ling-shui county Customs. A public notice issued by Yu, magistrate of Ling-shui county, with associated duties as Superintendent of Customs at Ch’aochow, and Hua, officer of foreign trade, 6 June 1860, proclaiming again the levying of an opium tax and strictly forbidding opium smuggling and evasion of the transit tax. The document was copied by Hsinhsing chan, Mayu bu, Swatow.1 item.

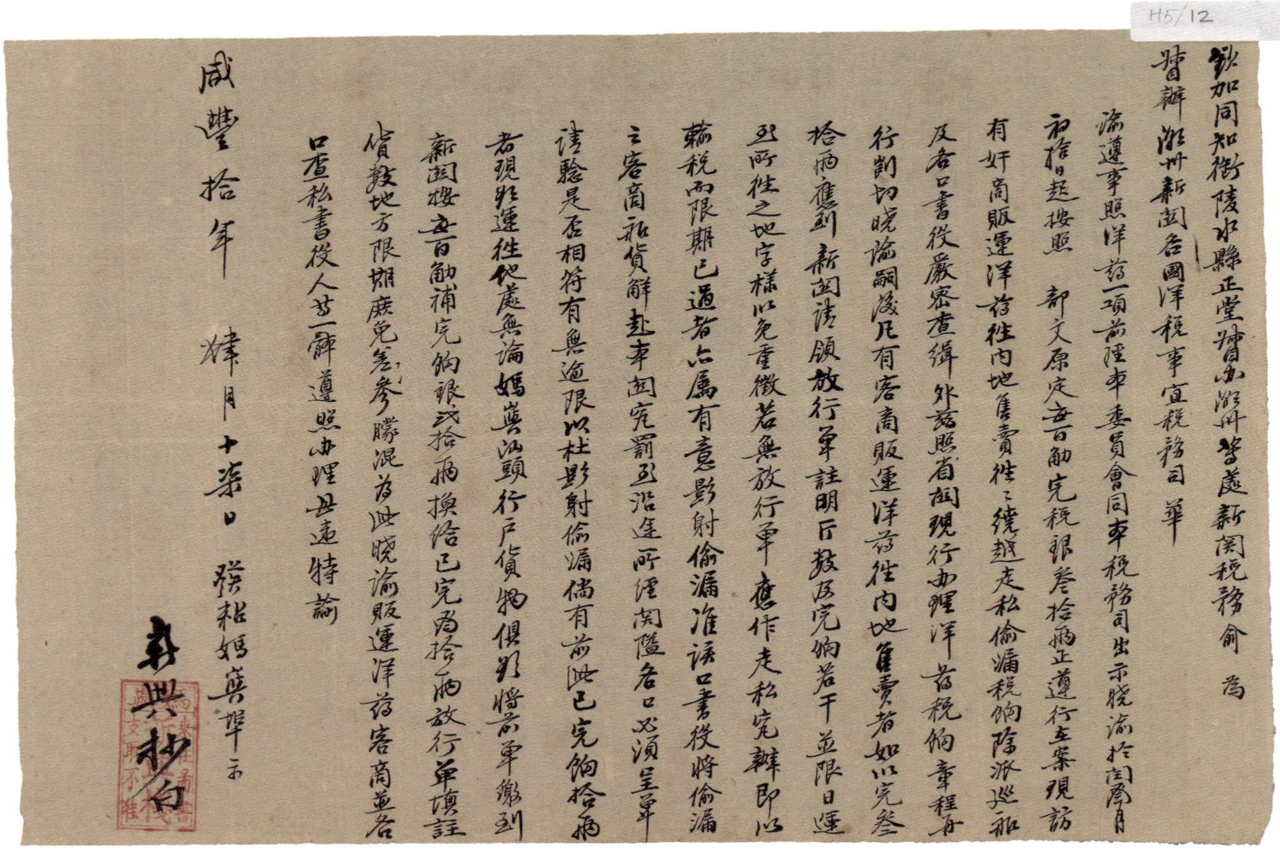
H5/12

欽加同知銜陵水縣正堂署理潮州等處新關稅務俞　為
署辦潮州新關各國洋稅事宜稅務司華
諭遵事照洋藥一項前經本委員會同本稅務司出示曉諭於閏叁月
初拾日起按照　部文原定每百觔完稅銀叁拾兩正遵行在案現訪
有奸商販運洋藥往內地售賣往往繞越走私偷漏稅餉除派巡船
及各口書役嚴密查緝外茲照省關現行辦理洋藥稅餉章程再
行剴切曉諭嗣後凡有客商販運洋藥往內地售賣者如已完叁
拾兩應到　新關請領放行單註明斤數及完餉若干並限日運
到所往之地字樣以免重徵若無放行單應作走私究辦即以
漏稅而限期已過者亦屬有意影射偷漏准該口書役將偷漏
之客商私貨解赴本關究罰至沿途所經關隘各口必須呈單
請驗是否相符有無逾限以杜影射偷漏倘有前此已完餉拾兩
者現販運往他處無論媽嶼汕頭行戶貨物俱照將前單繳到
新關按每百觔補完餉銀贰拾兩換給已完叁拾兩放行單填註
貨數地方限期庶免蒙混為此曉諭販運洋藥客商並各
口查私書役人等一體遵照辦理毋違特諭

咸豐拾年肆月十柒日　發粘媽嶼曉示

新興抄白

媽嶼新興棧來往圖書支取不准

一三、咸丰十年某海关官员发给运输鸦片船只信函（H5/13）

咸丰十年（1860），某海关官员发给运输鸦片船只信函，说明鸦片征税有关规定。

Customs letter. A letter from an unknown customs regarding the regulation and taxation of the opium trade. 3 items.

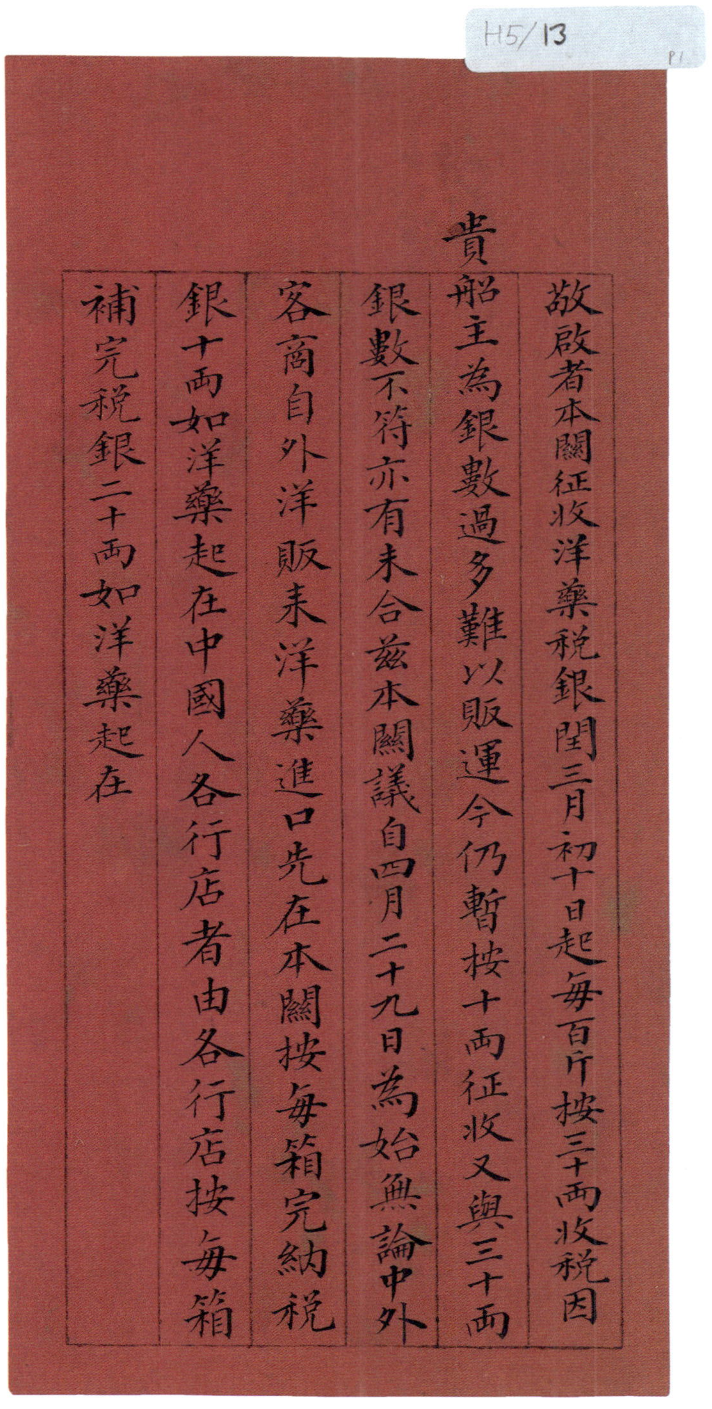

H5/13

敬啟者本關征收洋藥稅銀閏三月初十日起每百斤按三十兩收稅因

貴船主為銀數過多難以販運今仍暫按十兩征收又與三十兩

銀數不符亦有未合茲本關議自四月二十九日為始無論中外

客商自外洋販來洋藥進口先在本關按每箱完納稅

銀十兩如洋藥起在中國人各行店者由各行店按每箱

補完稅銀二十兩如洋藥起在

貴躉船者中國客人到

貴躉船買洋藥販運內地各處銷賣該客人先到本關亦按

每箱補完稅銀二十兩請領出水照單填明洋藥件數運

往某處銷賣註明地方限期以杜中國客人走漏稅餉

之弊尚祈

貴船主查照信內情節凡有中國客人在

貴臺船買運洋藥有本關出水照单者即照单上填明件
數賣給倘無出水照单及數目不符者即是漏稅請
貴船主飭令該客来本關補領照单發給可也如此通融辦
理則中外兩便彼此和氣遇事相商豈不美哉特此順候
時祺亨嘉惟希
朗照不一　名另具

一四、咸丰十一年宁波金顺兴[①]等涉外讼案

1. 咸丰十一年宁波金顺兴等涉外讼案甘结[②]（H5/14/1）

咸丰十一年（1861）七月，宁波金顺兴船户禀告英国商人霍仕（C. J. Fox）强抢截留货物一案经浙江官府与英国领事裁决后判定，由英国商人霍仕赔偿一切损失。盖有各方印章，印文“宁帮金顺兴泉公许图章”“金瑞庆”“伍成丰记”。

Papers re legal claim against C. J. Fox.

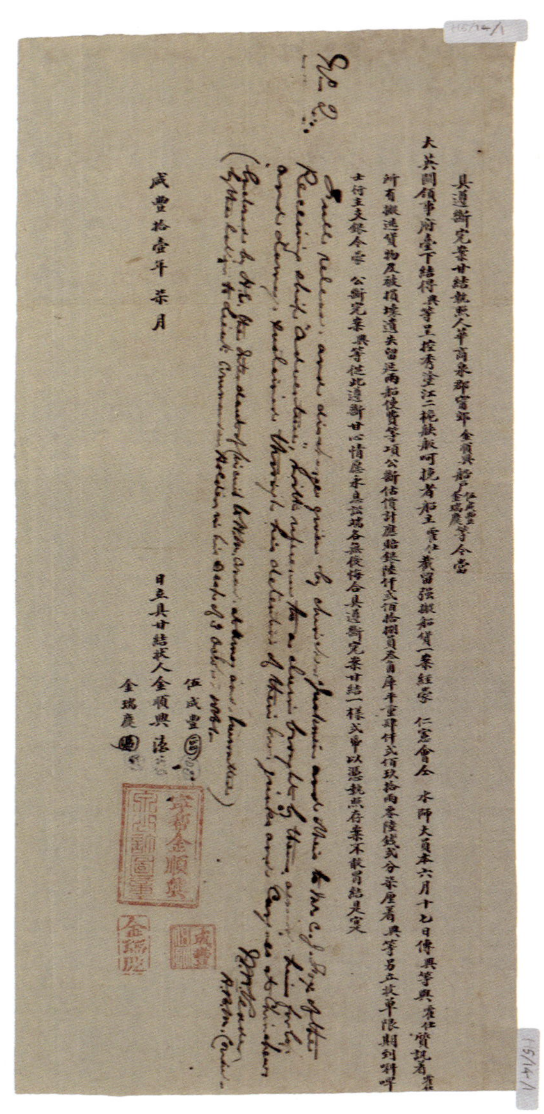

具遵断完案甘结船户金顺兴伍成丰金瑞庆等今当

大英国领事府台下结得兴等呈控霍仕截留强搬船货一案经蒙 仁宪会同 本师大员本六月十九日传兴等与霍仕质讯着霍仕

所有搬过货物及被损坏遗失留延两船使费等项公断估价……着兴等另立收单限期到时呼

士行主交银全领 公断完案兴等从此遵断甘心情愿并无反悔各无後悔合具遵断完案甘结一样贰纸以凭执照存案不敢冒结是实

咸丰拾壹年柒月　日立具甘结状人金顺兴　伍成丰　金瑞庆

---

① 金顺兴：宁波船户。

② 甘结：清代司法案件中的保证书。

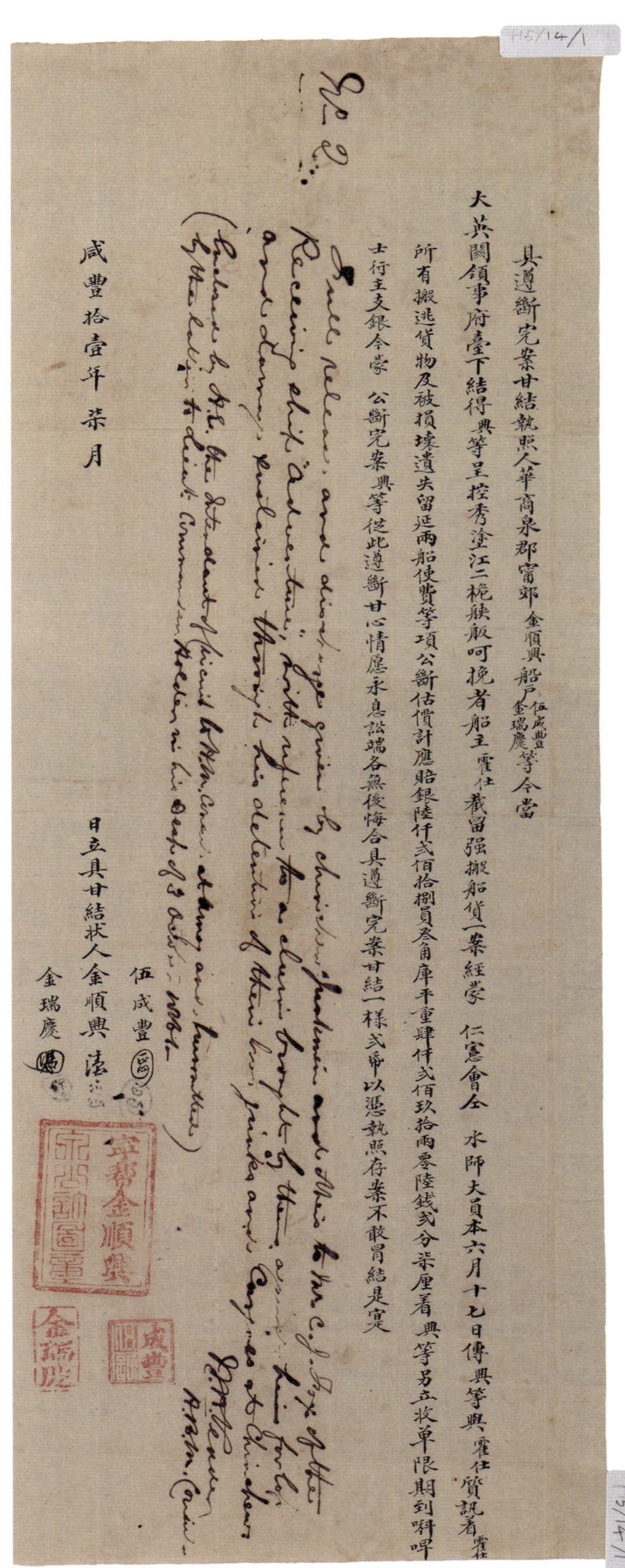
具遵斷完案甘結執照人華商泉郡甯郊金順興船戶伍成豐金瑞慶等今當
大英國領事府臺下結得興等呈控秀塗江二桅兵艇叼挽者船主霍仕截留强搬船貨一案經蒙　仁憲會仝　水師大員本六月十七日傳興等與霍仕質訊着霍仕
所有搬逃貨物及被損壞遺失留延兩船使費等項公斷估價計應賠銀陸仟貳佰拾捌員叁角庫平重肆仟貳佰玖拾兩零陸錢貳分柒厘着興等另立收單限期到𠺝呼
士行主支銀令蒙　公斷完案興等從此遵斷甘心情愿永息訟端各無後悔合具遵斷完案甘結一樣弍帋以憑執照存案不敢冒結是寔

咸豐拾壹年柒月　日立具甘結狀人金順興　伍成豐　金瑞慶

（局部图）

2. 咸丰十一年宁波金顺兴[①]等的甘结（H5/14/2）

咸丰十一年（1861）八月，宁波金顺兴等船户禀告英国商人霍仕强抢截留货物的甘结，盖有各方印章，印文“宁帮金顺兴泉公许图章”“金瑞庆”“伍成丰记”。有英文注释。

Papers re legal claim against C. J. Fox.

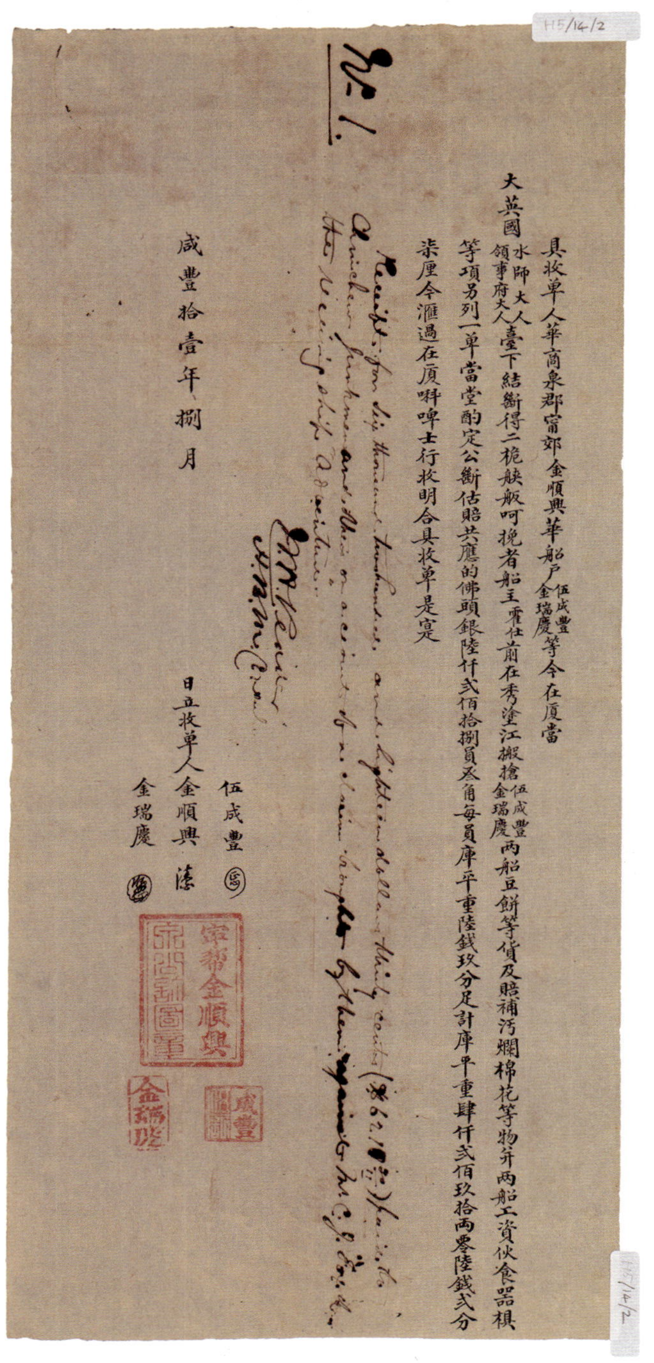

No. 1.

具收單人華商象郡甯郊金順興華船户（伍成豐、金瑞慶）等今在廈當

大英國水師大人、領事府大人臺下結斷得二桅艇舨呵挽者船主霍仕前在秀塗江搬搶（伍成豐、金瑞慶）兩船豆餅等貨及賠補污爛棉花等物并兩船工資伙食器椇

等項另列一單當堂酌定公斷估賠共應的佛頭銀陸仟弍佰拾捌員叁角每員庫平重陸錢玖分足計庫平重肆仟弍佰玖拾兩零陸錢弍分

柒厘今滙過在廈㗎嗶士行收明合具收單是寔

Receipt for six thousand two hundred and eighteen dollars thirty cents ($6218.30)

咸豐拾壹年捌月　日立收單人 伍成豐 金順興 漆 金瑞慶

寧幫金順興泉公許圖章

成豐

金瑞慶

① 金顺兴：宁波船户。

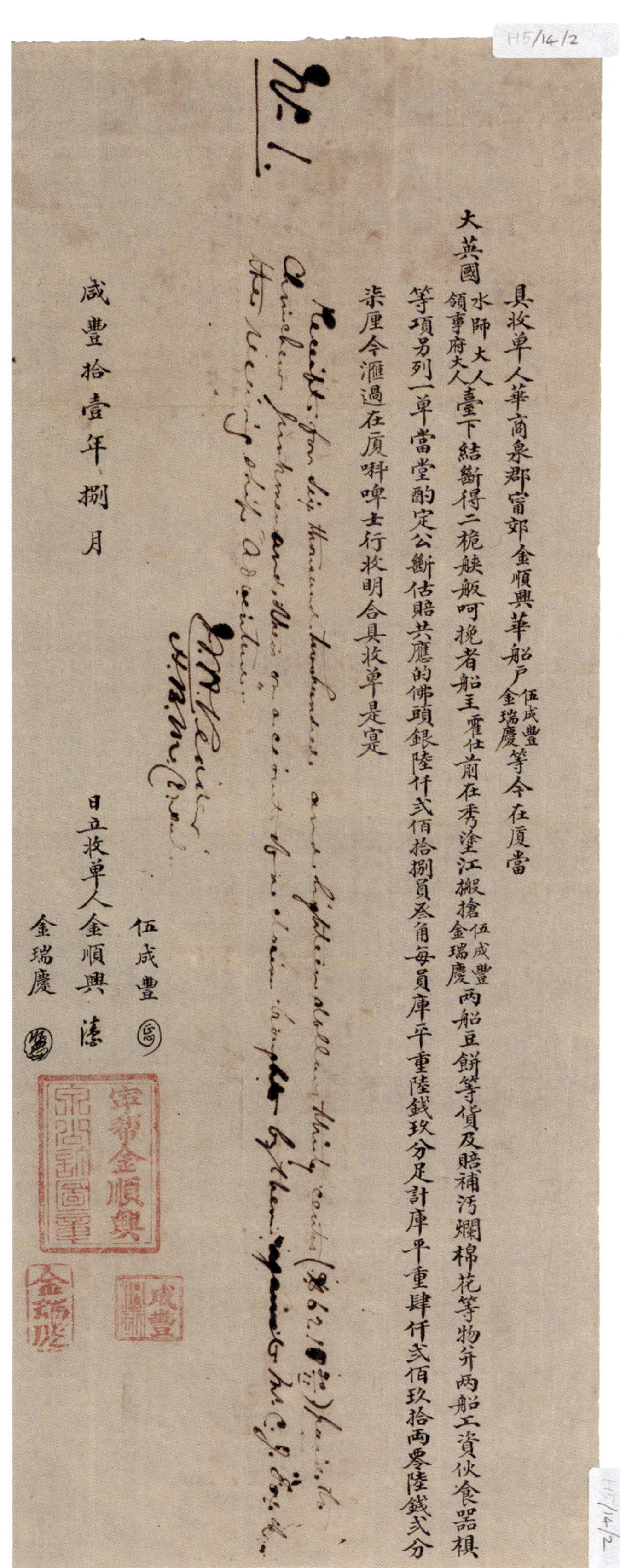

No. 1

具收單人華商泉郡甯郊金順興華船戶伍成豐金瑞慶等今在廈當

大英國水師大人
領事府大人臺下結斷得二桅艇舨呵挽者船主雇任前在秀塗江搬搶伍成豐金瑞慶兩船豆餅等貨及賠補汚爛棉花等物并兩船工資伙食器棋

等項另列一單當堂酌定公斷估賠共應的佛頭銀陸仟弍佰捌拾捌員叁角每員庫平重陸錢玖分足計庫平重肆仟弍佰玖拾兩零陸錢弍分

柒厘今滙過在廈㖞嗶士行收明合具收單是寔

咸豐拾壹年捌月　日立收單人金順興　伍成豐　金瑞慶

（局部图）

一五、咸丰十一年淡水海关禁止鸦片走私谕令（H5/15）

咸丰十一年九月初五日（1861年10月8日），台湾厘捐署淡水海关，颁布谕令，严禁一艘停泊在沪尾港的夷船走私鸦片和非法销售。谕令盖有海关印章，印文不清；另有一枚“内号”印章印迹。

Dispatch from the Taiwan Customs. A dispatch from Ch’iu (Qiu), Tamsui branch of Likin station, Taiwan, with the honorary title of Prefect, to a foreign opium clipper mooring at Hu-wei port (Hu wei gang), 8 October 1861, regarding opium smuggling and illegal sales.

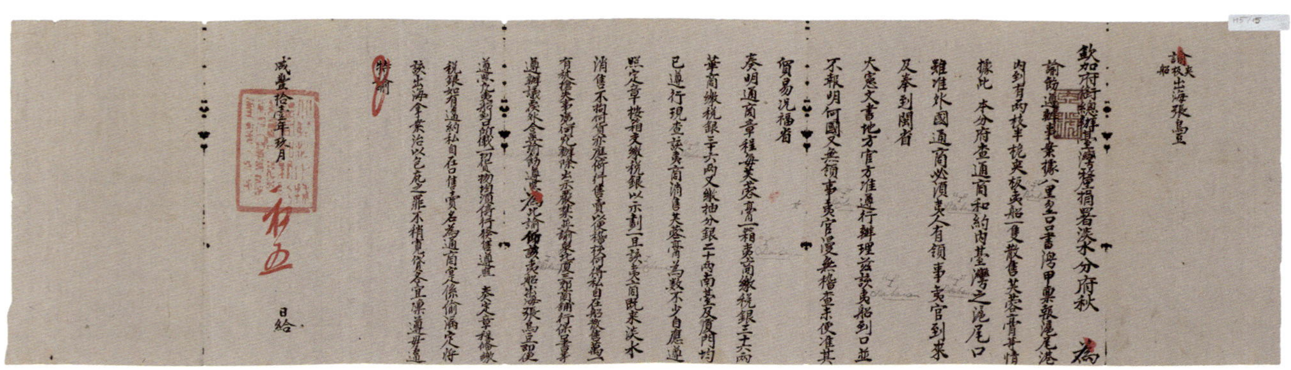

諭夾板船出海張島豆

欽加府銜總辦臺灣釐捐署淡水分府秋　為

諭飭遵辦事案據八里坌口書灣甲稟報滬尾港內到有兩枝半桅夾板夷船一隻散售英荅膏等情

據此　本分府查通商和約內臺灣之滬尾口雖准外國通商必須夷人有領事夷官到來

及奉到閩省

大憲文書地方官方准遵行辦理茲該夷船到口並不報明何國又無領事夷官漫無稽查未便准其

貿易況福省

奏明通商章程每英荅膏一箱夷商繳稅銀三十六兩

華商繳稅銀三十六兩又繳抽分銀二十兩南臺及廈門均已遵行現查該夷商消售英荅膏為數不少自應遵

照定章按箱交繳稅銀以示劃一且該夷商既來淡水消售不拘何貨亦應向行售賣從無稽核任私自在船散售為一

[illegible]

遵辦據[illegible]合再諭飭遵照　為此諭飭該夷船出海張島豆即便

遵照[illegible]所繳一切貨物均須[illegible]遵照　奏定章程備繳

稅銀如有違約私自在船售賣名為通商實係偷漏定將該出海拿案治以包庇之罪不稍寬貸各宜凜遵毋違

特諭

咸豐拾壹年玖月　初五　日給

（局部图）

一六、同治元年严禁私自制造军器谕令（H5/16/1-2）

同治元年闰八月十五日（1862年10月8日），按察使司分巡台澎兵备道兼提督学政洪毓琛发布的谕令，严禁私自炼制樟脑油，不许私制私售与武器相关的物品。盖有印章，印文不清。

Proclamation of the Taotai.2 items.

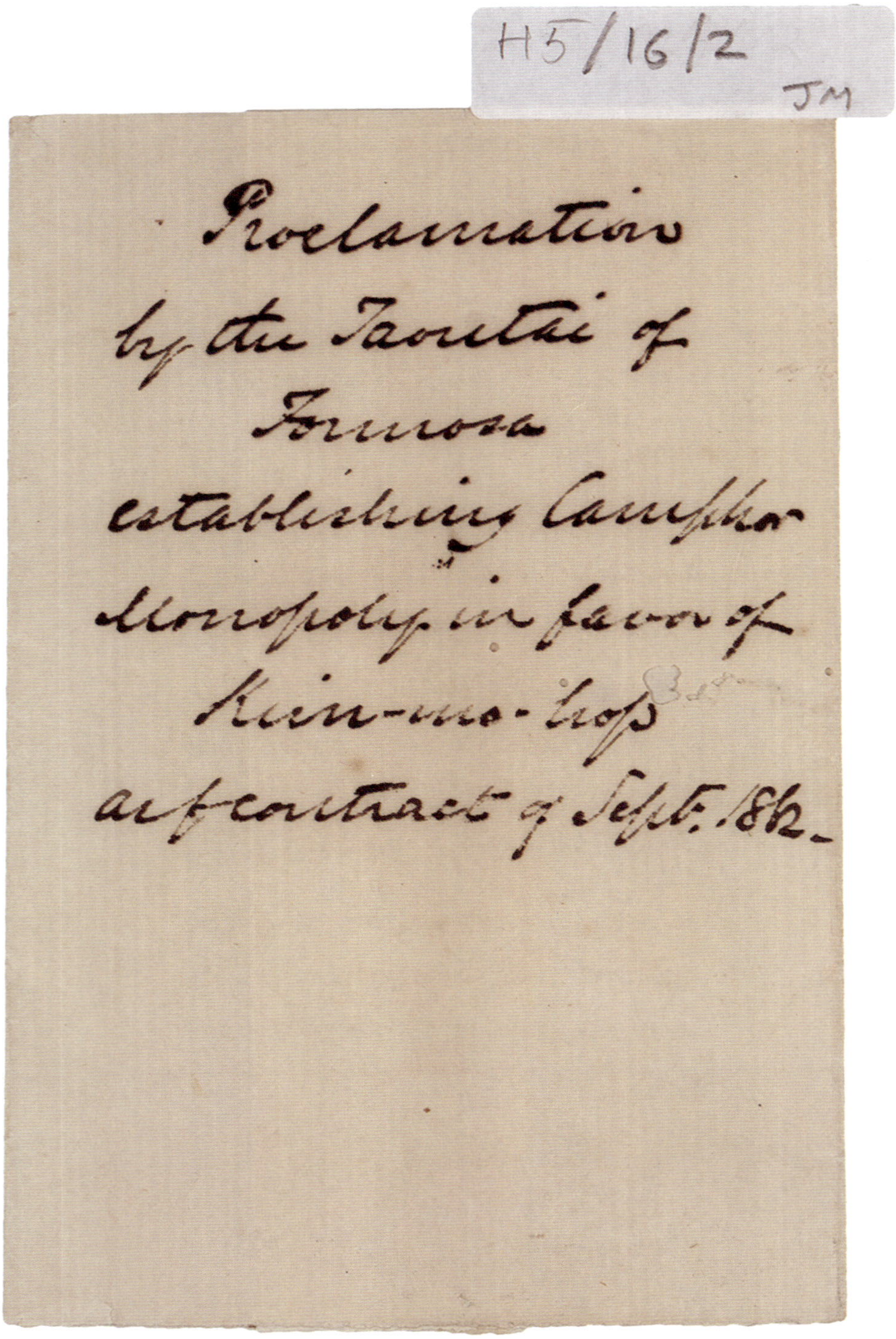

Proclamation
by the Taoutai of
Formosa
establishing Camphor
Monopoly in favor of
Kein-mo-hop
as p contract of Sept. 1862

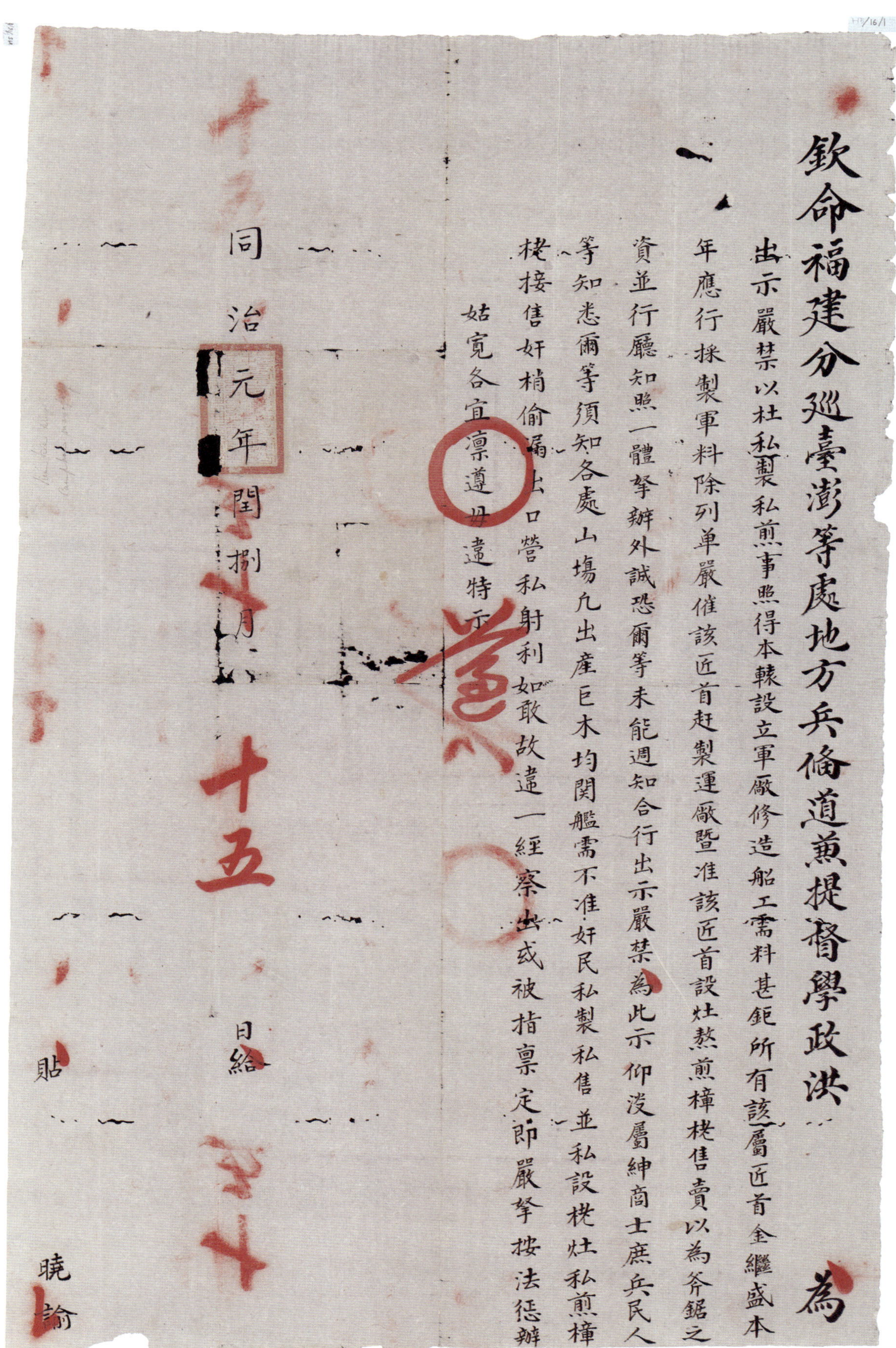

欽命福建分巡臺澎等處地方兵備道兼提督學政洪　為

出示嚴禁以杜私製私煎事照得本轅設立軍廠修造船工需料甚鉅所有該廠匠首金繼盛本年應行採製軍料除列单嚴催該匠首赶製運廠暨准該匠首設灶熬煎樟栳售賣以為斧鋸之資並行廳知照一體拏辦外誠恐爾等未能週知合行出示嚴禁為此示仰淡屬紳商士庶兵民人等知悉爾等須知各處山場凡出產巨木均関艦需不准奸民私製私售並私設栳灶私煎樟栳接售奸梢偷漏出口營私射利如敢故違一經察出或被指禀定即嚴拏按法懲辦姑寛各宜凛遵毋違特示

同治元年閏捌月十五日給

貼曉諭

一七、同治三年台湾海关照会副本（H5/17）

同治三年三月二十九日（1864年5月4日），外国麦姓税务司照会台湾海关副本，申述海关政策影响外国进出口贸易，要求调整事宜。

Dispatch from the Taiwan Customs. A copy of a dispatch from Mr. Mei (Mai), Revenue Department, Maritime Customs, Taiwan, to Mr. Ch'en (Chen), magistrate of Taiwan, 4 May 1864, reporting that the export and import business has increased rapidly at the port of Ta-kou-k'ou (Da gou kou), the prohibition against foreign trade there cannot be carried out properly, and the absence of a customs office will no longer be used as excuse for not opening the port to foreign trade.

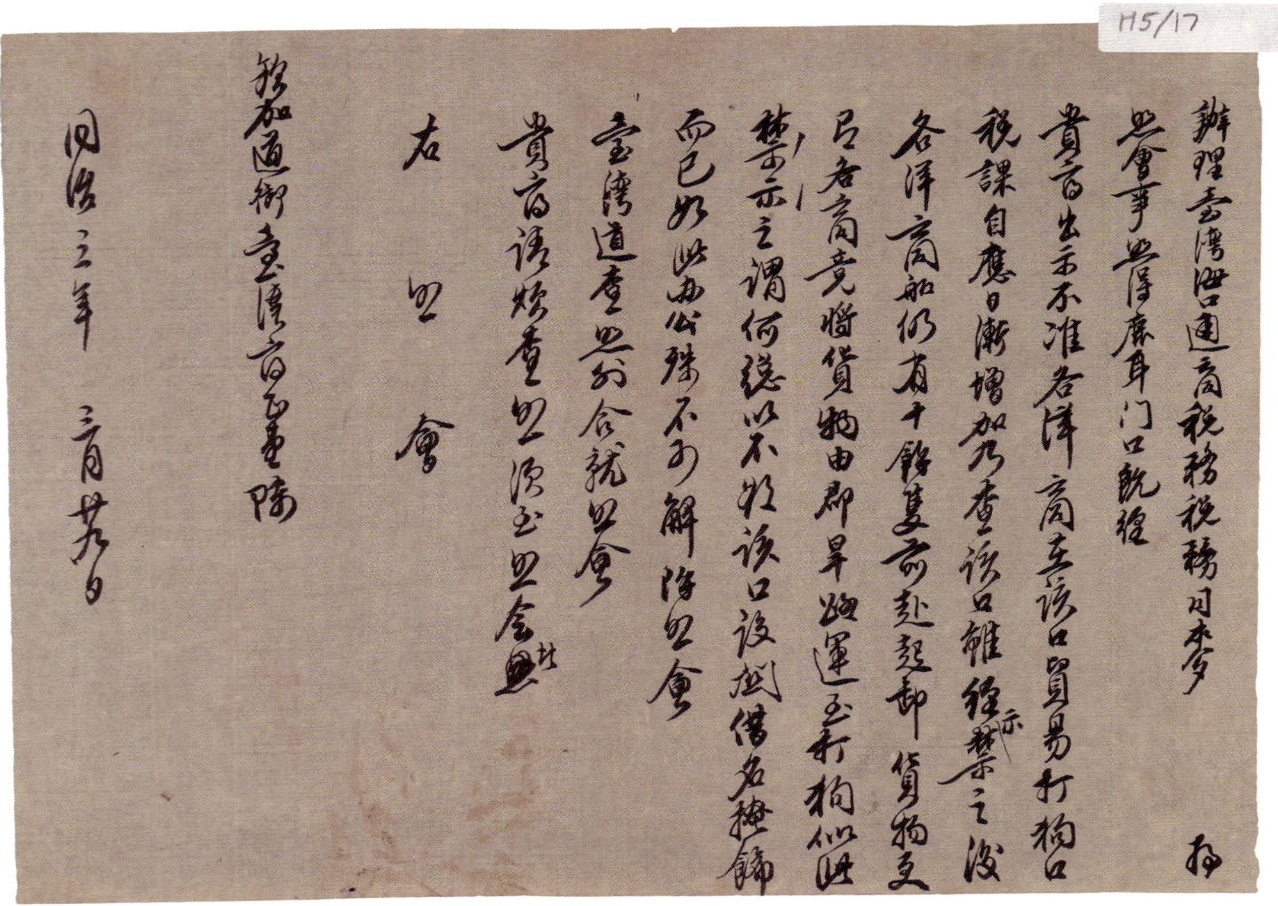

H5/17

辦理臺灣滬口通商稅務稅務司麥　為
照會事：照得康耳門口既經
貴府出示不准各洋商在該口貿易，打狗口
稅課自應日漸增加。旋查該口雖經出示禁止之後，
各洋商船仍有十餘隻前赴起卸貨物，更
且各商竟將貨物由郡旱路運至打狗，似此
禁示之謂何？總以不收該口設關借名推諉
而已。如此無益公務，不可解除照會
臺灣道查照外，合就照會
貴府請煩查照，須至照會者。
右照會
欽加道銜臺灣府正堂陳
同治三年三月廿九日

一八、同治六年隆顺行[①]护照（H5/18）

同治六年二月二十五日（1867年3月30日），福州将军颁发给隆顺行前往香港购买洋硝的护照。

Pass from the Tartar General of Foochow. A special pass issued by Ying, Tartar General of Foochow, with associate duties as Intendant of Custom Affairs, to Messrs Heard & Co. (Lungshun/Longshun), authorising them to go to Hong Kong to purchase fifteen hundred piculs of saltpetre for the Chinese Government and transport it back to Fukien, 30 March 1867. The document includes a short English note about the pass by the Commissioner of Customs, Foochow, accompanied by his stamp. 1 item; Fair condition, but some damage by insects.

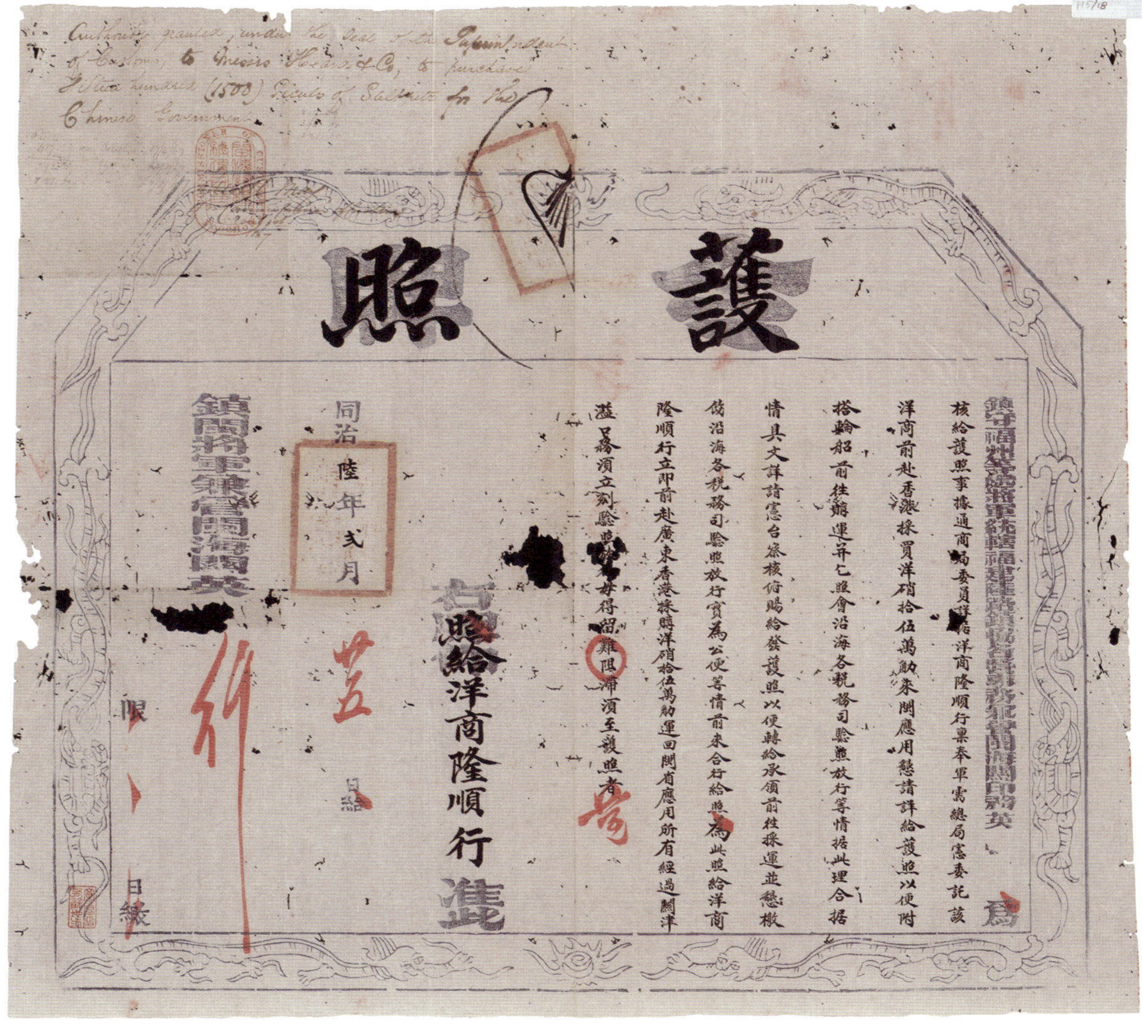

Authority granted, under the Seal of the Superintendent of Customs, to Messrs Heard & Co, to purchase fifteen hundred (1500) Piculs of Saltpetre for the Chinese Government.

護照

鎮守福州[illegible]英

為核給護照事據通商局委員[illegible]據洋商隆順行稟奉軍需總局憲委託該洋商前赴香港採買洋硝拾伍萬觔來閩應用懇請詳給護照以便附搭輪船前往購運并乞照會沿海各稅務司驗照放行等情據此理合据情具文詳請憲台察核俯賜給發護照以便轉給承領前往採運並懇檄飭沿海各稅務司驗照放行實為公便等情前來合行給照為此照給洋商隆順行立即前赴廣東香港採購洋硝拾伍萬觔運回閩省應用所有經過關津隘口務須立刻驗照[illegible]毋得留難限[illegible]須至護照者

右照給洋商隆順行準此

同治陸年貳月　日

鎮閩將軍兼管閩海關英

限　日繳

---

① 隆顺行：美资洋行琼记洋行（Heard & Co.）在福州开设的分行。琼记洋行由旗昌洋行前合伙人美籍商人奥古斯丁·赫德（Augustine Heard）创立于1840年，总部设于广州，1856年第二次鸦片战争中商馆被焚，于1857年将总部迁到香港。

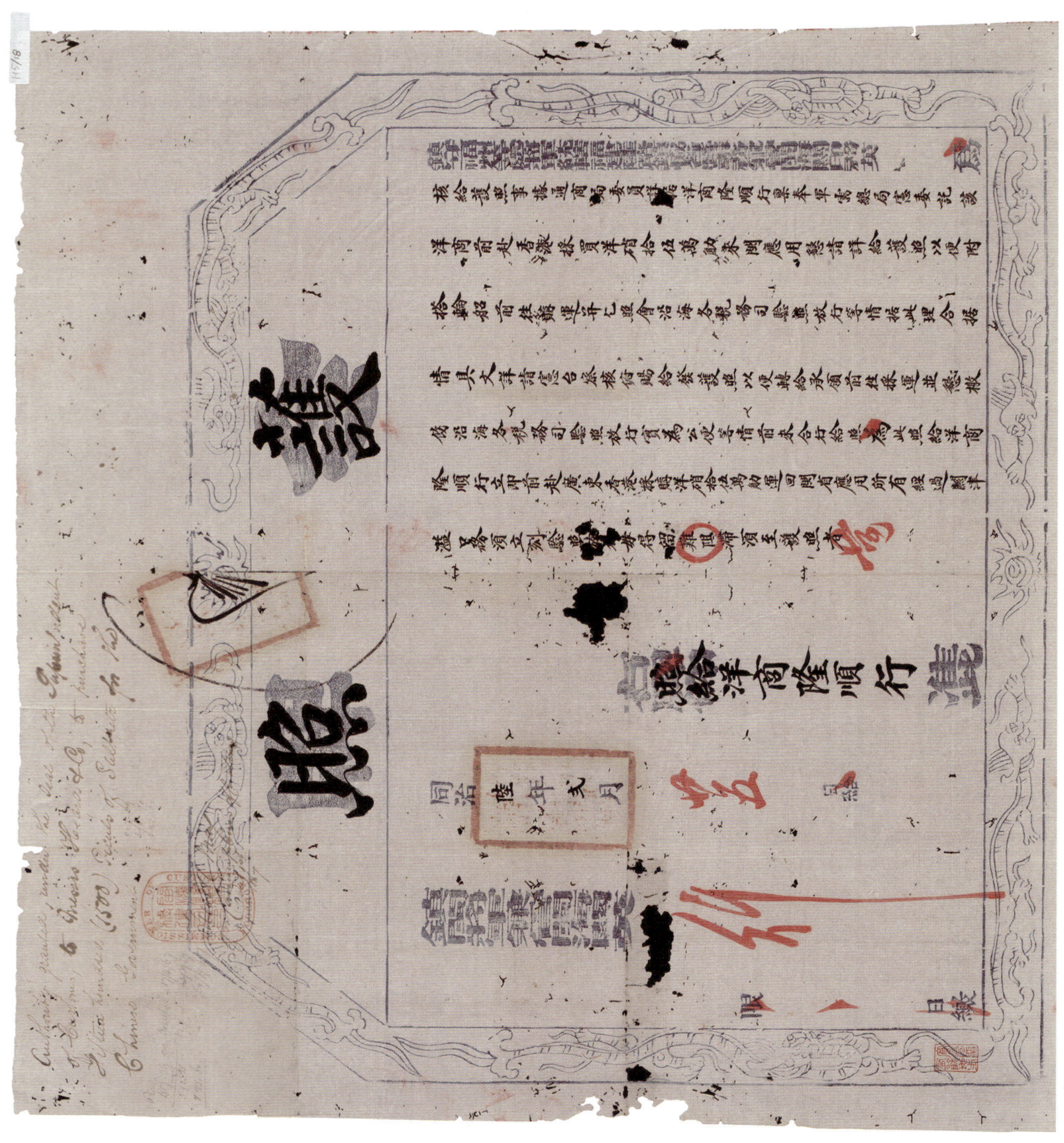

（局部图）

一九、同治七年装封两广总督印约信封（H5/19）

同治七年四月初二日（1868年4月24日），装封两广总督印约信封，加盖两广总督关防，致法国驻广州领事。

Envelope from Governor-general of Kwangtung and Kwangshi. An envelope from Jui (Rui), Minister of War and Governor-general of Kwangtung and Kwangshi, to Li [Tienchia/Tianjia] (G. de Trenqualye), French Consul at Canton, 24 April 1868, including a note recording that it enclosed 'One [letter] with an enclosure of an agreement'.1 item.

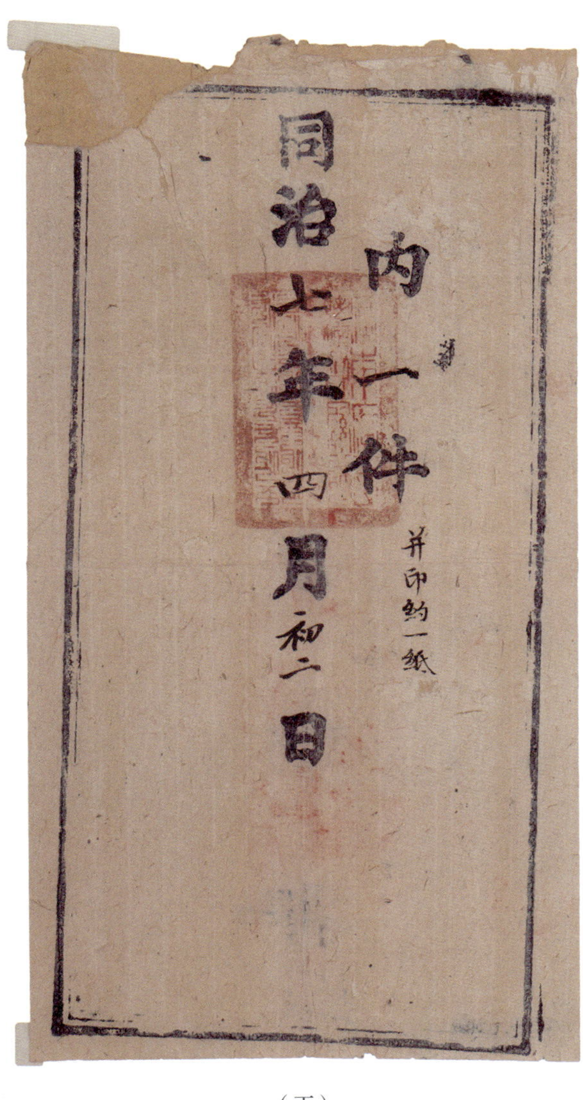

（正）

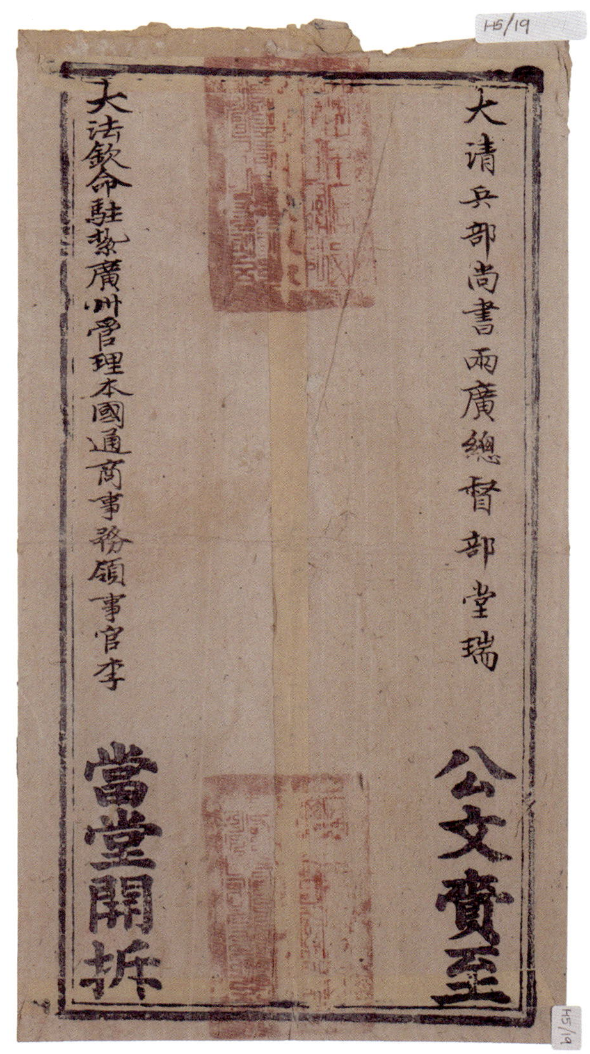

（反）

二〇、同治七年严禁栽种罂粟谕旨副本（H5/20/1-2）

同治七年十二月二十日（1869年2月1日），同治皇帝严禁栽种罂粟谕旨副本，登载京报[①]之上。

Imperial edict against opium.2 items.

H5/20/1

上諭御史游百川奏請飭嚴禁栽種罌粟以濟民生一摺栽種罌粟之害至妨民食始於甘肅延及陝西山西近復江蘇河南山東等省亦有漸行栽種者小民貪利忘害僅顧目前勢必至膏腴之產盡種無用之物於百姓生計大有關碍前曾嚴行申禁著該督撫迅飭各地方官再行剴切曉諭一體禁止倘有不法匪徒故意抗違即治以應得之罪各州縣官如不認真辦理任令吏胥餙詞朦敝並著該管上司從嚴叅辦毋稍徇隱特此通諭知之

欽此

同治七年拾二月二十日 京報

① 京报：清朝晚期在北京发行的早期报纸。

Edict prohibiting the growth of the poppy in China —

上諭御史游百川奏請飭嚴禁栽種罌粟以濟民生一摺栽種罌粟
之害至妨民食始於甘肅延及陝西山西近復江蘇河南山東等省
毋有漸行栽種者小民貪利忘害僅顧目前現勢必至膏腴之產
盡種無用之物於百姓生計大有關碍前曾嚴行申禁著該省督
撫迅飭各地方官再行剴切曉諭一體禁止倘有不法匪徒故意
抗違即治以應得之罪各州縣官如不認真辦理任令吏胥飾
詞朦蔽並著該管上司從嚴參辦毋稍徇隱將此通諭知之欽此

同治七年拾貳月貳十日京報

二一、光绪十年台湾军情汇报（H5/21/1-3）

盛宣怀[①]致福建总督刘铭传[②]的信函，落款日期为1884年10月28日。盛宣怀在八月二十日（即10月8日）的电信中说没有宣战的消息。他后来读了法将孤拔（Courbet）发来的关于台湾海峡被封锁的消息（10月21日），委托机昔[③]（William Keswick）运送军费到台湾。他说目前还没有派增援到台湾，并说他提出要和平谈判的奏折已上交到朝廷讨论。据税务司德璀琳（Detring）汇报，讨论已有进展，可能接下来几天就会有消息。他要求台湾再扼守半个月，并要求奖励李在电报局出色的工作表现。

A letter from Sheng Hsuan-huai (Sheng Xuanhuai) to Liu Ming-ch'uan (Liu Mingchuan), Governor-General of Fukien, 28 October 1884. He writes that in the telegram of the 20th day of the 8th month (8 October) there was no news of a war declaration. He then read Courbet's dispatch concerning the closing of the sea surrounding Taiwan (21 October) and entrusted William Keswick with transmitting military funds to Taiwan. He states that no reinforcements have been sent to Taiwan yet, and that his memorial urging peace talks has been submitted to the court for discussion. According to Detring, there is a hint, and news will come out in a couple of days. He asks that Taiwan be held for a half of a month. He also requests that Li be rewarded for his outstanding work at the telegram office.

---

① 盛宣怀：1844年11月4日—1916年4月27日，字杏荪（杏生、荇生）、幼勖，号补楼、愚斋、次沂、止叟等，出生于江苏常州府武进县龙溪，清末政治家，洋务运动的代表人物。北洋西学学堂（今天津大学）和南洋公学（今西安交通大学、上海交通大学、台湾交通大学）创始人，同时也是一位实业家和福利事业家。

② 刘铭传：1836年9月7日—1896年1月12日，字省三，室号盘亭、大潜山房，谥号壮肃，是一位出身安徽合肥的淮军将领和台湾巡抚，在中法战争中于台湾地区率军击退法军，后被任命为台湾建省后首任巡抚，积极于当地推行各种现代化建设并为其奠定相关基础。

③ 机昔：英国怡和洋行（Jardine, Matheson & Co.）大班。

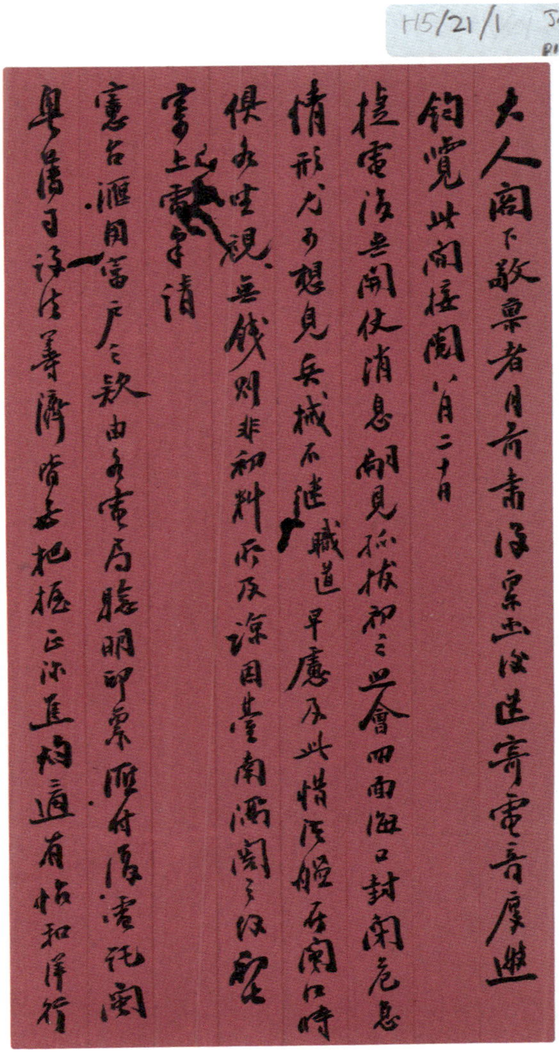

H5/21/1 JM B1

大人閣下敬稟者月前肅陳寸悃並寄電音度邀
鈞覽此間接閣八月二十日
提電後無閩仗消息詢見孫拔初之四會西南海口封閉危急
情形尤爲想見兵械不繼 職道早慮及此惜海船不開以時
俱在坐視無錢則非和料所及諒因臺南滬閩之款
憲上電尊請
憲台滙閩富戶之款由本電局聽明即票滙付後電託閩
粵紳日諒法籌濟皆無把握正不匠內適有怡和洋行

H5/21/1 JM B2

東家機昔來津職道與其崇南北相有洋行與之密商
議法匯兑查其法甚爲妥如該閩官紳借行力匯以機昔
爲美國銀行有行在臺之人託爲買糖價可運銀入口如
該官紳允將和行定單到台以其洋行出票向富戶借銀匯臺
鈞處備用當經今日函致 中堂在於吾廬據請迅速稟
覆并擬每銀十萬兩交與怡和副已就向照來先須作票
與機昔面議 中堂即發復照之後一面由怡和行書明
惟其所作一面怡和行速銀兩後照賣棧再作濟渡付等語

H5/21/1 JM P4

H5/21/1 JM P3

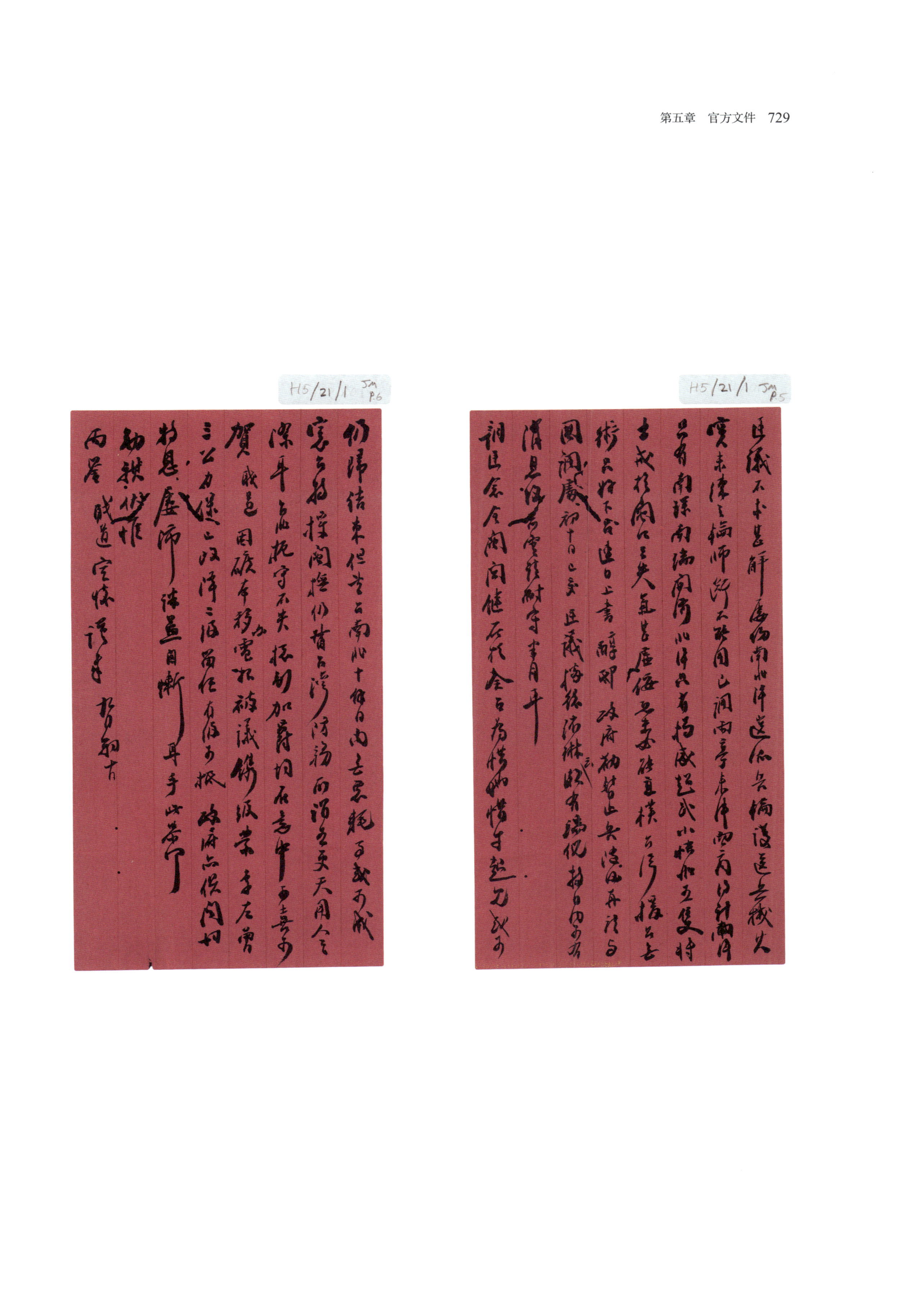

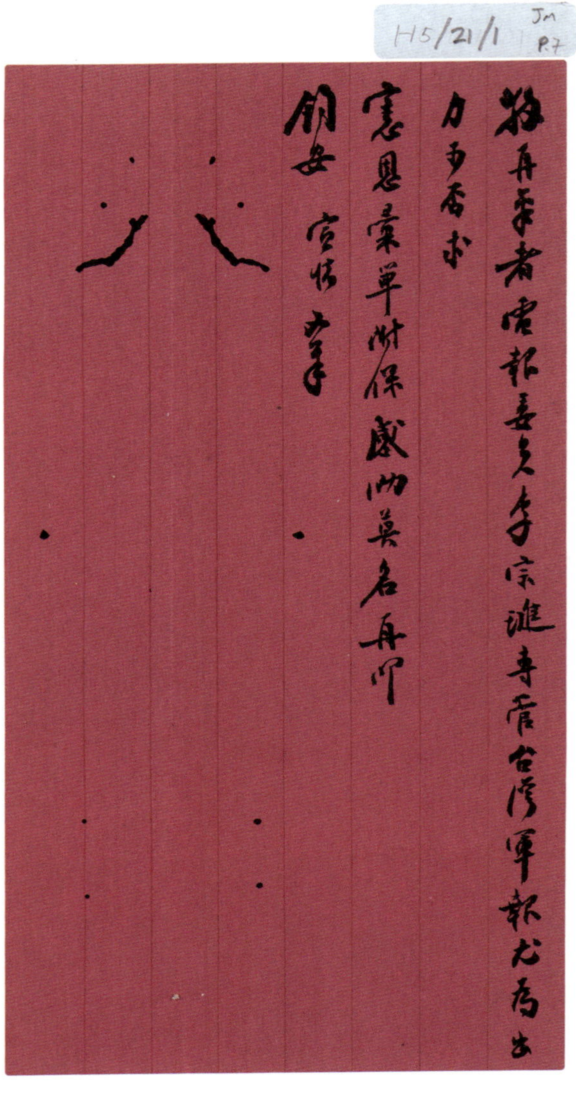

敬再禀者，電報委員李宗濂專管台灣軍報，尤為出力，可否求

憲恩彙單附保，感激莫名。再叩

鈞安 宣怡 等

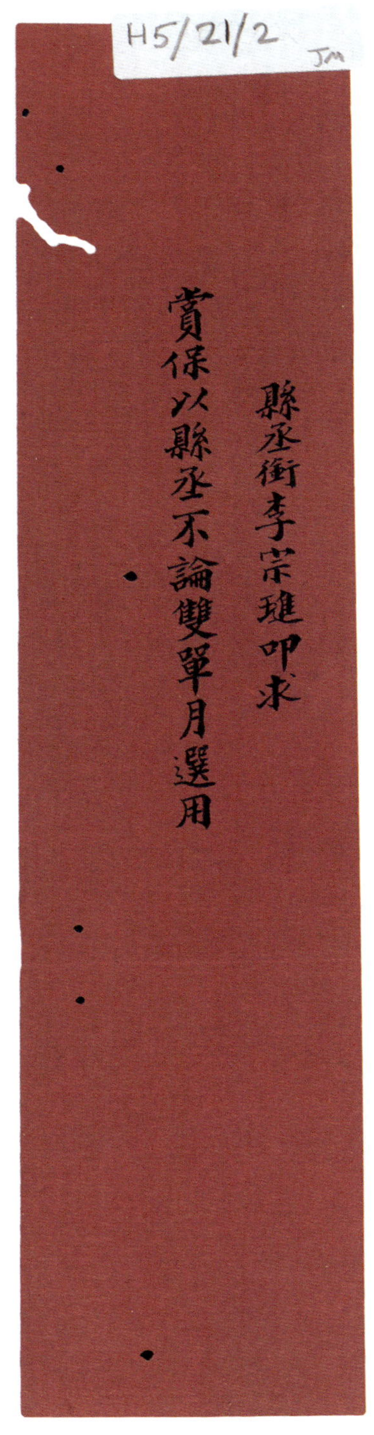

H5/21/2 JM

縣丞銜李宗璡叩求

賞保以縣丞不論雙單月選用

H5/21/3 JM

大人

宗

李

二二、光绪十年台湾战事护票（H5/021/04-05）

机昔的护票。光绪十年九月十二日（1884年10月30日），直隶总督李鸿章[①]给机昔发放的护票，让其运送军费到台北府刘铭传[②]大将军的行营。右上角的红色标签指明有两份护票，一份给机昔，一份给刘铭传。护票上还有英语译文。

Passport for William Keswick. A special passport (in Chinese) issued by Li Hungchang (Li Hongzhang), Imperial High Commissioner, to William Keswick, 30 October 1884, for the conveyance of military funds to the Camp of Governor-general Liu Ming-ch'uan at Taipei Fu or Tamsui. A red strip glued to the top right records that two copies were issued, one to Keswick, and one to Governor-General Liu. The document also includes an English translation. 1 item.

---

① 李鸿章：1823年2月15日—1901年11月7日，字子黻、渐甫，号少荃、仪叟、省心，谥文忠，人称李中堂、李傅相。安徽合肥人，晚清重臣，建立中国第一支西式海军北洋水师，因其尽忠辅清，才干了得而闻名。官东宫三师、文华殿大学士、北洋通商大臣、直隶总督，爵位一等肃毅伯，追赠太傅，追晋侯爵。中国近代地方武装淮军的创建者和领导者。历经太平天国运动、捻军起义、洋务运动、中法战争、甲午战争、义和团运动。著作收于《李文忠公全集》。在经济上与大财阀罗斯柴尔德家族有私人来往，李鸿章曾被英国维多利亚女王授予皇家维多利亚勋章。李鸿章与曾国藩、左宗棠、张之洞并称"晚清四大名臣"。

② 刘铭传：1836年9月7日—1896年1月12日，字省三，室号盘亭、大潜山房，谥号壮肃，是一位出身安徽合肥的淮军将领和台湾巡抚，在中法战争中于台湾地区率军击退法军，后被任命为台湾建省后首任巡抚，积极于当地推行各种现代化建设并为其奠定相关基础。

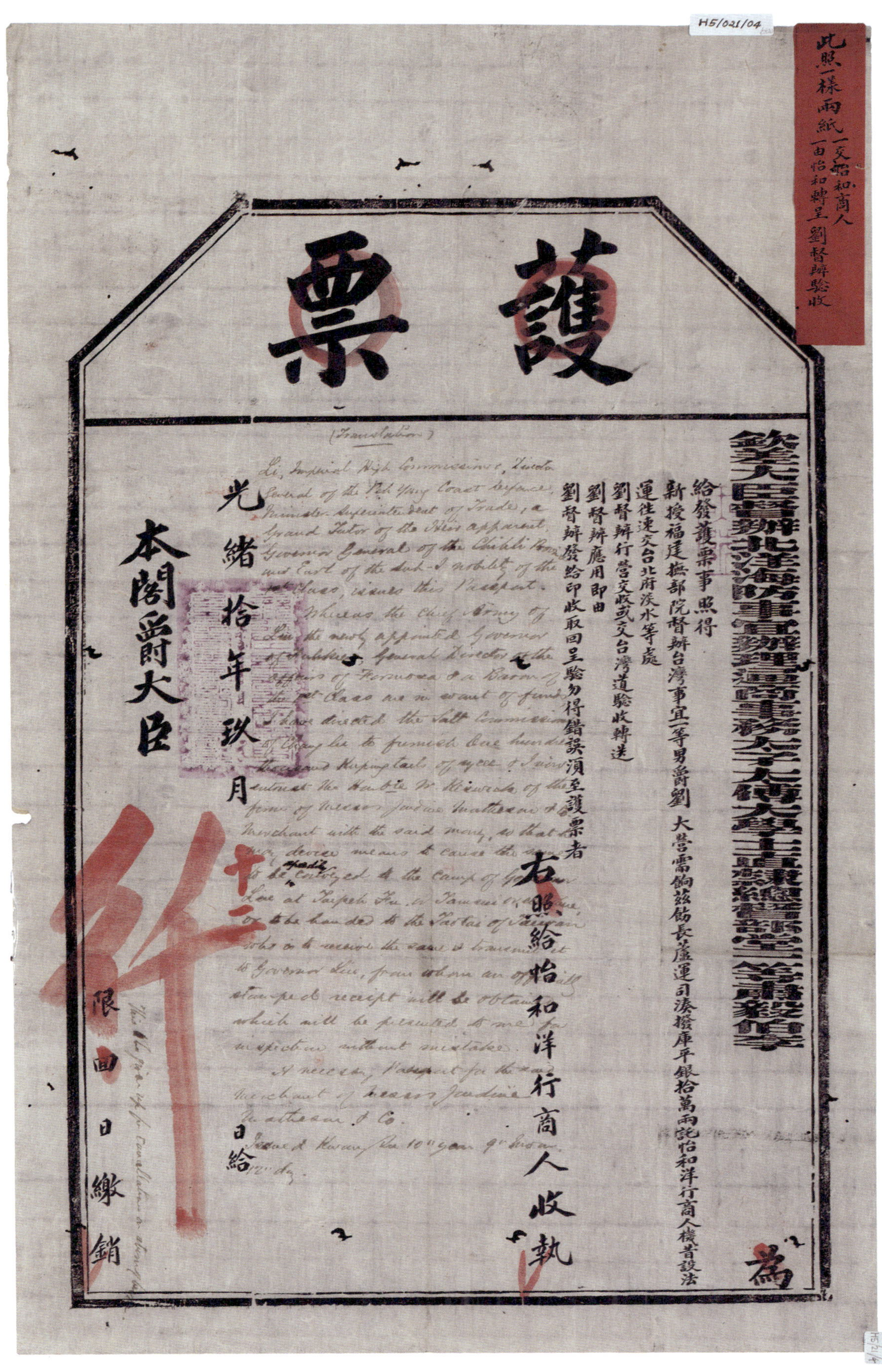

此照一樣兩紙，一交怡和商人，一由怡和轉呈劉督辦驗收

護票

欽差大臣督辦北洋海防事宜兼辦通商事務太子太傅大學士直隸總督部堂一等肅毅伯李

為

給發護票事照得

新授福建撫部院督辦台灣事宜一等男爵劉　大營需餉，茲飭長蘆運司湊撥庫平銀拾萬兩，諗怡和洋行商人機昔設法

運往速交台北府淡水等處

劉督辦行營交收，或交台灣道驗收轉送

劉督辦應用，即由

劉督辦發給印收取回呈驗，勿得錯誤。須至護票者

右照給怡和洋行商人收執

光緒拾年玖月十二日給

本閣爵大臣

限回日繳銷

(Translation)

Li, Imperial High Commissioner, Director General of the Peh Yang Coast Defence, Minister Superintendent of Trade, a Grand Tutor of the Heir apparent, Governor General of the Chihli Province and Earl of the 1st nobility of the 1st class, issues this Passport.

Whereas the Chief Army of Liu the newly appointed Governor of Fukien, General Director of the affairs of Formosa & a Baron of the 1st class are in want of funds I have directed the Salt Commissioner of Changlu to furnish One hundred thousand Kuping taels of sycee & I now entrust the Hon<u>ble</u> W. Keswick of the firm of Messrs Jardine Matheson & Co. Merchant with the said money, so that he may devise means to cause the same to be speedily conveyed to the Camp of Governor Liu at Taipeh Fu, or Tamsui or elsewhere, or to be handed to the Taotai of Taiwan who is to receive the same & transmit it to Governor Liu, from whom an officially stamped receipt will be obtained which will be presented to me for inspection without mistake.

A necessary Passport for the said Merchant of Messrs Jardine Matheson & Co.

Issued at Kwang Hsu 10th year 9th moon 12th day.

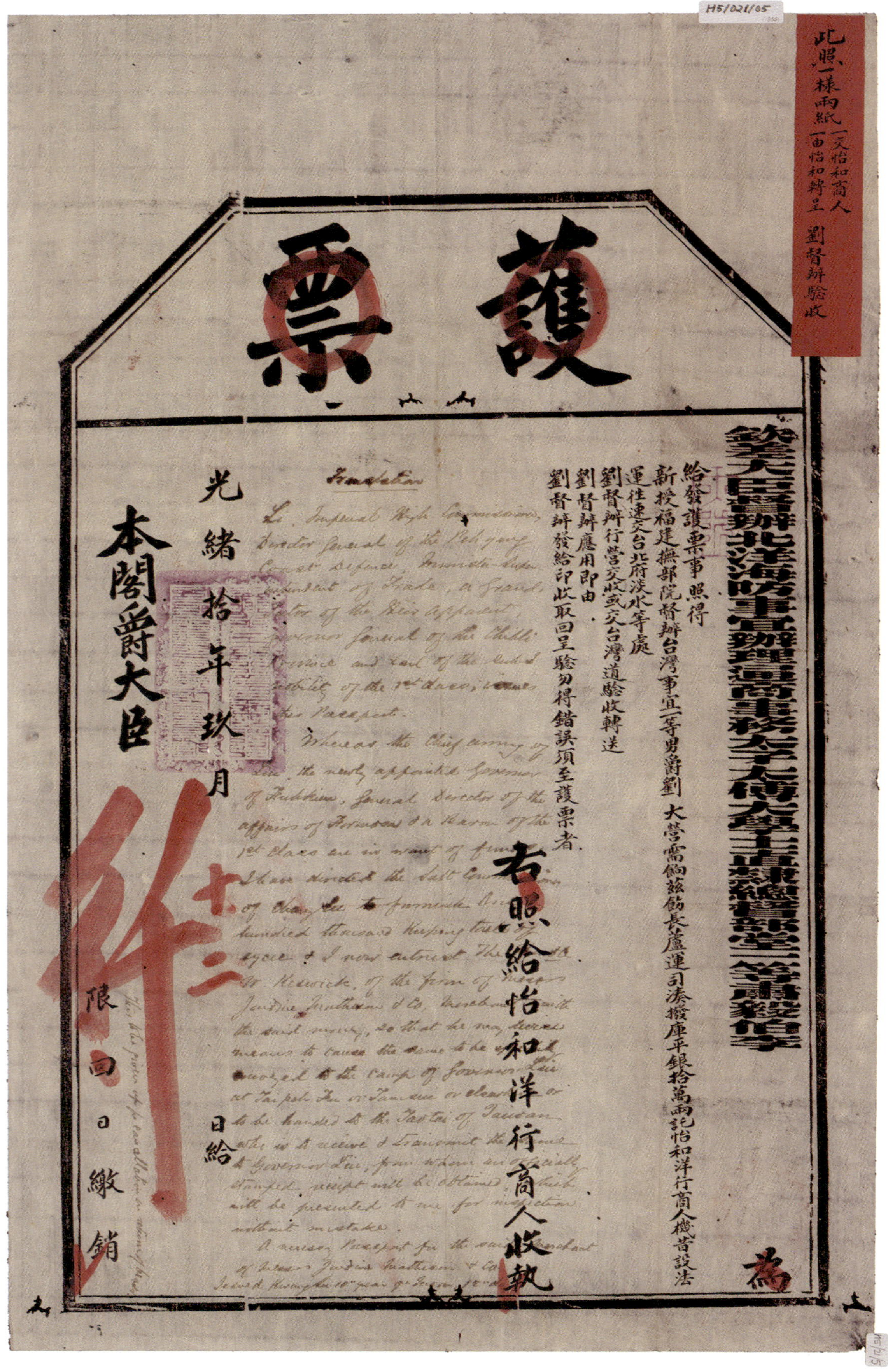

此照一樣兩紙，一交怡和商人，一由怡和轉呈劉督辦驗收

護票

欽差大臣督辦北洋海防事宜辦理通商事務太子太傅文華殿大學士直隸總督部堂一等肅毅伯李
給發護票事照得
新授福建撫部院督辦台灣事宜一等男爵劉 大營需餉兹飭長蘆運司湊撥庫平銀拾萬兩記怡和洋行商人機昔設法
運往速交台北府淡水等處
劉督辦行營交收或交台灣道驗收轉送
劉督辦應用即由
劉督辦發給印收取回呈驗勿得錯誤須至護票者

右照給怡和洋行商人收執

光緒拾年玖月十二日給

本閣爵大臣

限 回日繳銷

Translation

Li, Imperial High Commissioner, Director General of the Peh-yang Coast Defence, Imperial Superintendent of Trade, a Grand Tutor of the Heir Apparent, Governor General of the Chihli Province and Earl of the [illegible] Nobility of the 1st class, issues this Passport.

Whereas the Chief army of Liu, the newly appointed Governor of Fukhien, General Director of the affairs of Formosa & a Baron of the 1st class are in want of funds, I have directed the Salt Commissioner of Chang Lu to furnish One hundred thousand Kuping taels of sycee & I now entrust the same to Mr Keswick, of the firm of Messrs Jardine Matheson & Co, merchants, with the said money, so that he may devise means to cause the same to be speedily conveyed to the camp of Governor Liu at Taipeh Fu or Tamsui or elsewhere, or to be handed to the Taotai of Taiwan who is to receive & transmit the same to Governor Liu, from whom an officially stamped receipt will be obtained, which will be presented to me for inspection without mistake.

A necessary Passport for the said merchant of Messrs Jardine Matheson & Co. Issued Kwanghsu 10th year 9th moon 12th day.

二三、麦士尼名片（日期不详）（H5/22）

麦士尼为能[①]的中文名称名片，上有中文“权授中国副将颖勇巴图鲁[②]麦士尼为能”，并有英文笔迹注明其英文名及头衔。另有英文笔迹“c/o Commissioner of Customs. Hankow”。

Card of William Mesny. The official title card of William Mesny, Major-General of the Chinese Army, with an English note giving his name and title and the words ‘c/o Commissioner of Customs. Hankow’. 1 item.

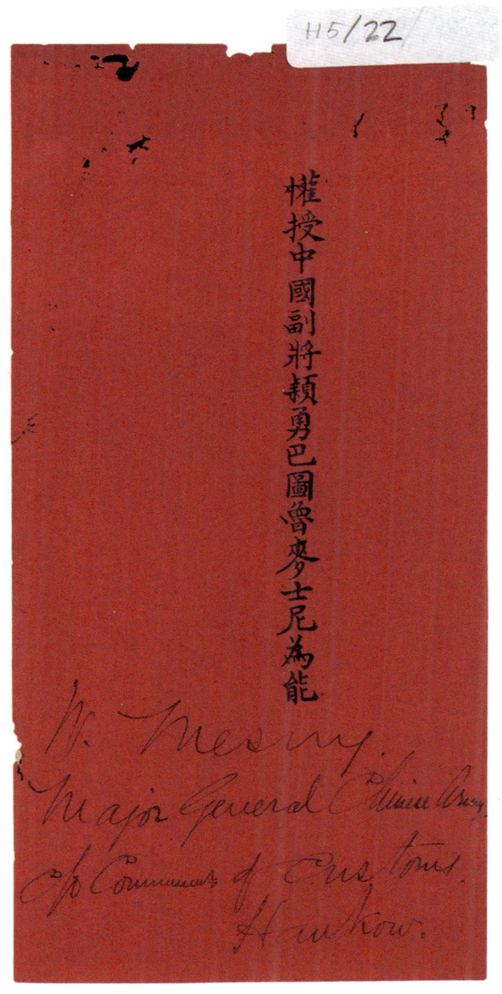
H5/22

權授中國副將頴勇巴圖魯麥士尼為能

W. Mesny.
Major General Chinese Army
c/o Commissioner of Customs.
Hankow.

① 麦士尼为能：即威廉·麦士尼（William Mesny，1842—1919年），“为能”即“William”的音译。麦士尼出生于英国，1863年进入中国海关工作，后参加英国人戈登组织的“常胜军”镇压太平天国运动，随后一直在清军中任职，官至总兵，获赏“颖勇巴图鲁”勇号。1895年在上海创办华英日报馆，主编的英文刊物《华英会通》，内容庞杂，涉及中国的政治、经济、产业、风俗、植物、城市、礼仪、秘密会社等各方面信息，是当时西方了解中国的重要刊物。此外，麦士尼还是英国皇家地理学会、园艺学会研究员，皇家学院研究员。1919年于汉口去世。

② 巴图鲁：满语中“勇士”的音译，是清朝时期赏赐有战功之人的封号。

二四、咸丰三年番禺南海新旧银元通用告示（H5/23）

咸丰三年（1853）八月，番禺南海新旧银元通用告示，宣布新旧银元一律在中外贸易中通行，并附有该告示1935年的英文翻译。

Public notice of Kwongtung magistrates. A public notice (in Chinese) from the Magistrates of the Nam Hoi [Foshan] and Pun Yu [Panyu] Districts, by order of the Viceroy, commanding that silver dollars should be used in all business transactions and treated as legal currency. The notice bemoans the recent depression in the business and commerce of Kwongtung province [Canton] and states that steps should be taken to remedy this. It proceeds to discuss the problems arising from the different valuations of the various types of foreign dollars, and commands that in the future all dollars should be deemed to have the same value. The notice is dated in the 3rd year of the reign of Emperor Ham Fung (Xiangfeng). There is also a two-page English translation, dated Hong Kong, 27 February 1935, giving the Chinese date of the document, which it also dates as 'about 83 years ago'.2 items.

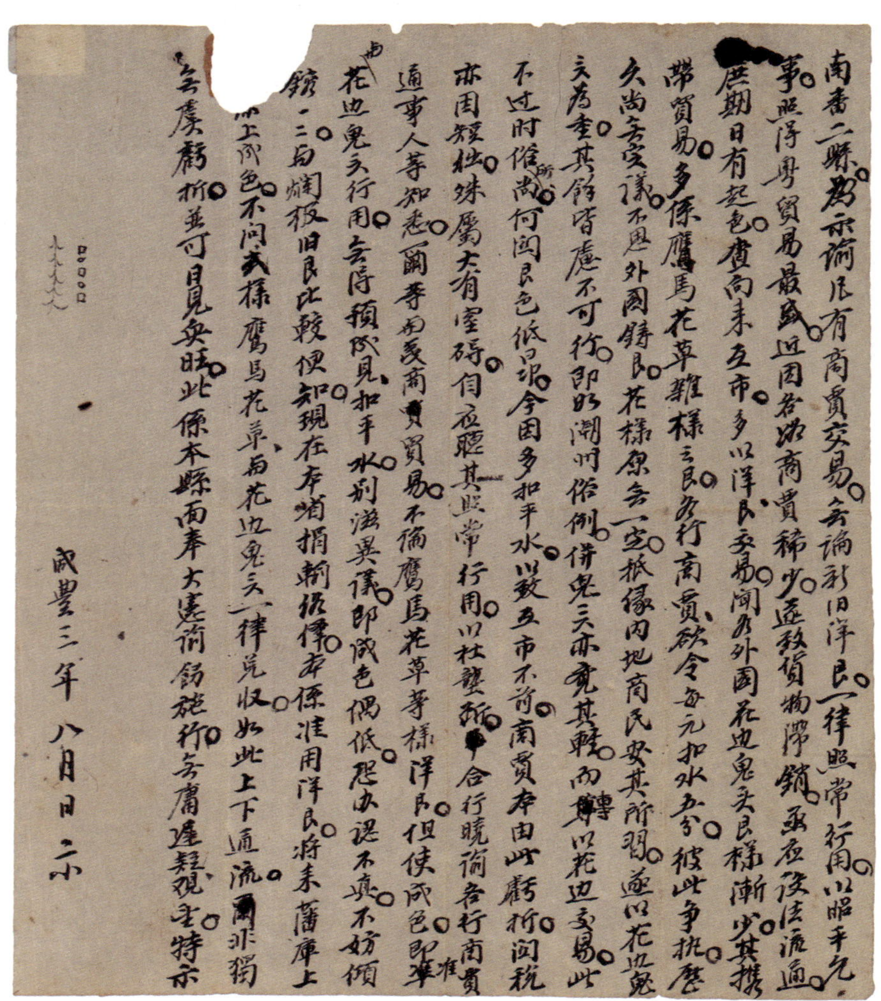

南番二縣為示諭民有商賈交易無論新旧洋銀一律照常行用以昭平允
事照得粵省貿易最盛近因各路商賈稀少遂致貨物滯銷亟應設法流通
歷期日有起色查向來互市多以洋銀交易聞各外國花边鬼头銀樣漸少其攜
帶貿易多係鷹馬花草雜樣之銀各行商賈欲令每元扣水五分彼此爭執歷
久尚無定議不思外國鑄銀花樣原無一定祗緣內地商民安其所習遂以花边鬼
头為重其餘皆慮不可行即如潮州俗例併鬼三头亦竟其輕而轉以花边交易此
不过時俗所尚何關銀色低昂今因多扣平水以致互市不前南賈本由此虧折關稅
亦因短絀殊屬大有窒礙自应聽其照常行用以杜壟斷合行曉諭各行商賈
通事人等知悉爾等與夷商貿易不論鷹馬花草等樣洋銀但使成色準
花边鬼头行用無得預先扣平水致滋異議即成色偶低恐亦退不真不妨價
錢一二分閑扳旧銀比較便知現在本省捐輸概係准用洋銀將來藩庫上
兑上成色不問式樣鷹馬花草與花边鬼头一律兑收如此上下通流商非獨
無虞虧折並可日見興旺此係本縣面奉大憲諭飭施行毋庸遲疑觀望特示

咸豐三年八月日示

H5/23

HONGKONG. 27th February, 1935.

TRANSLATION.

Notice is hereby jointly given to the public by the Magistrates of the Nam Hoi and Pun Yu Districts that in all business transactions silver dollars of all descriptions shall hereafter be used and treated as legal currency.

In the province of Kwongtung business and commerce has been prospering and flourishing until recently. The cause for this recent depression may be found in the decrease in the number of merchants which has caused a comparative stagnation in the movement of goods. Efforts should now be made to remedy this.

It has been the custom for foreign dollars to be used and the older-types, ~~are~~ one with the floral designs round the edge and the other with a "Devil's -head", have been popular. Later other types with the designs of eagles, horses and flowers were introduced. These have not been regarded with the same favour as the older types, owing to merchants having become used to the older types and looking upon them as being of greater value. The new types have therefore only been used at a discount of five per cent. As a result of this discount there have been continuous disputes between dealers and no recognized rule has been followed. There is no reason for this regard of the older types of dollars as being of greater value.

115/23

(2)

In Chiu Chow (Swatow), for example, merchants contend that dollars bearing the "Devil's head" are lighter than those with the floral design round the edge, and that the latter type is the kind acceptable to them. Differentiation between the different types of coins is wrong and has played some part in depressing trade and has decreased customs revenue. It is hereby notified that all merchants and interpreters who have business dealings with foreigners shall not differentiate between different types of coins but that all dollars shall be deemed to have the same value. Should there be any doubt as to the silver content of any particular type of coin, it may be tested by melting down a certain number and comparing its silver content with those of others. Furthermore, with regard to payments by the provincial government to the Imperial Treasury all dollars irrespective of design shall be deemed to be of full value as long as they are genuine.

The above notice is by order of His Excellency, the Viceroy.

This notification was issued in the 3rd year of Emperor Ham Fung about 83 years ago.

Chapter Six

第六章

其他文件

其他文件时间约为1852—1885年，共计51件。包括如怡和洋行商人查顿和马地臣与各方人士通信后保留的各式中文信封，以及各式收据（含茶叶、药房、杂货店、衣服盥洗、房屋修缮等收据）、中英文对照中国鸦片名称、新发行货币信息、棉纱仓库发票、账户附注、电报底稿、工资条、各式名片、运费账单、铁匠的设计图和付款单、杂货清单、老式日历等。

一、信封12件（日期不详）（H6/001/01-12）

信封12件，部分为空白信封，部分有中文及英文邮政信息。

（1）Envelope to ‘Consul’. An undated Chinese envelope. 1 item; Poor condition, including significant damage by insects.

（2）Envelope to Jardine Matheson, Hong Kong. An undated Chinese envelope including Chinese and English writing. 1 item.

（3）Envelope with chop note. An undated Chinese envelope including an English note: ‘Teungsings (?) Chop for advance in Tea shroff on his acct to England.’ 1 item.

（4）Blank envelope. 1 item.

（5）Envelope to L. d’Almeida, Macao. An undated envelope including Chinese and English writing. 1 item.

（6）Envelope to L. d’Almeida, Macao. An undated envelope including Chinese and English writing. 1 item.

（7）Blank envelope. An undated and unaddressed Chinese envelope with a short faded English note on the reverse. 1 item.

（8）Blank envelope. An undated Chinese envelope with Chinese writing on the front. 1 envelope.

（9）Blank envelope. An undated Chinese envelope with two Chinese symbols on the front. 1 item.

（10）Blank envelope. A blank Chinese envelope. 1 item; Fair condition, but some damage by insects.

（11）Envelope to Shih-tie-pu. Undated. 1 item; Fair condition, but some damage by insects.

（12）Envelope with chop note. An undated envelope including an English note: ‘Duty Chops for 3207 Bags Sugar.’ 1 item.

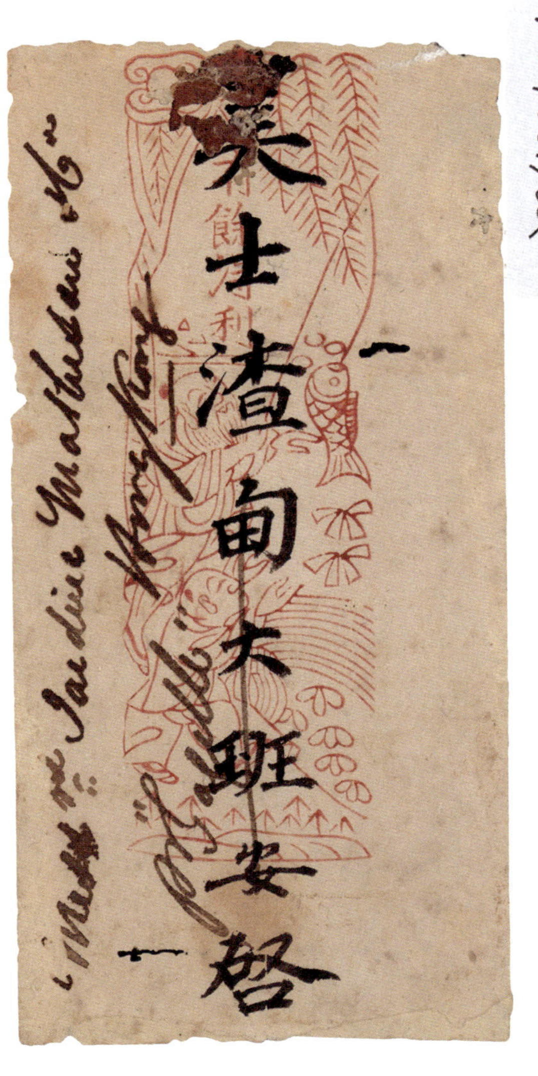

（正）

（反）

H6/001/03

H6/001/04

（正）

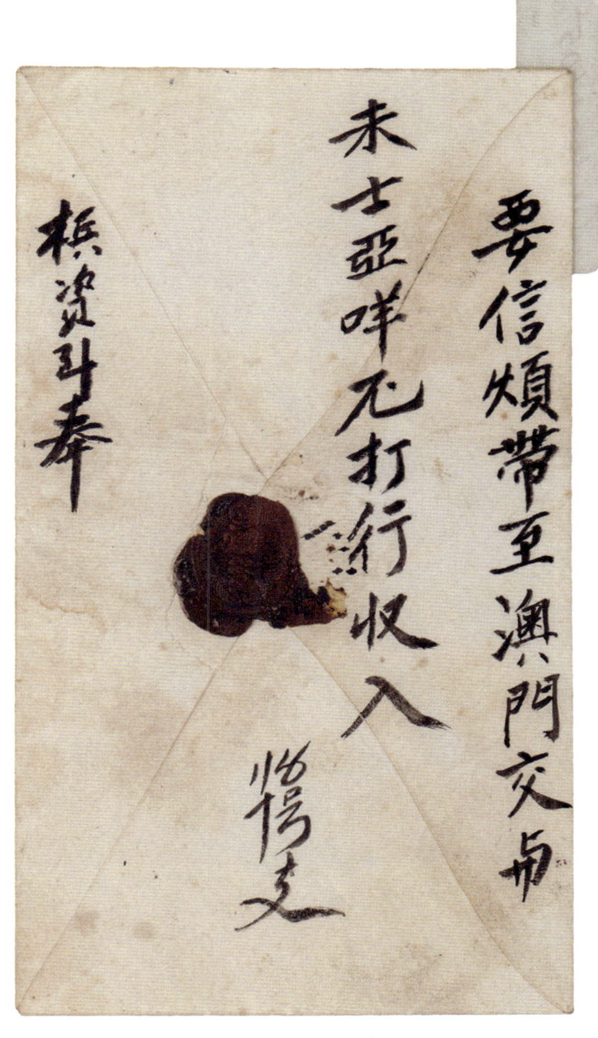

（反）

（正）

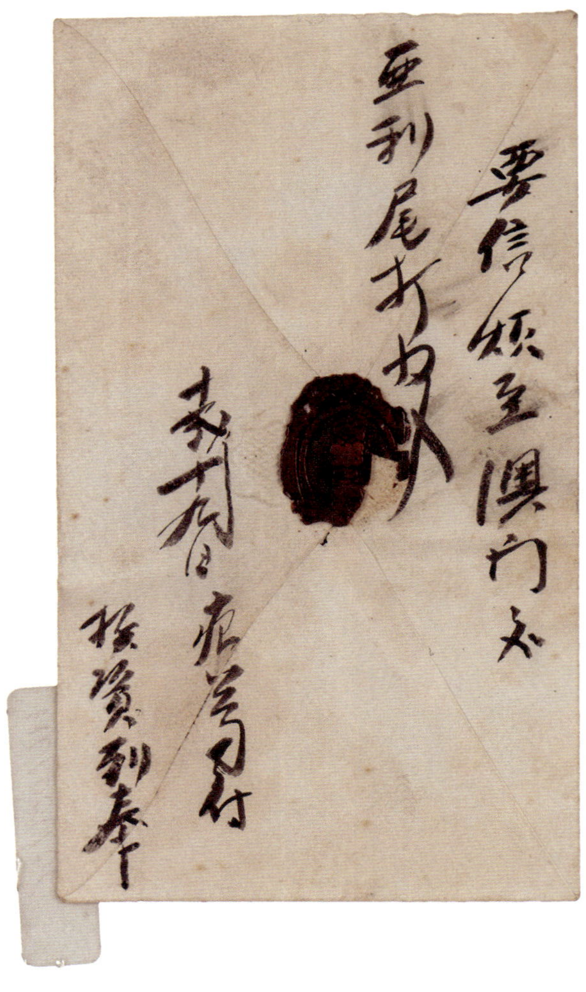

（反）

H6/001/07

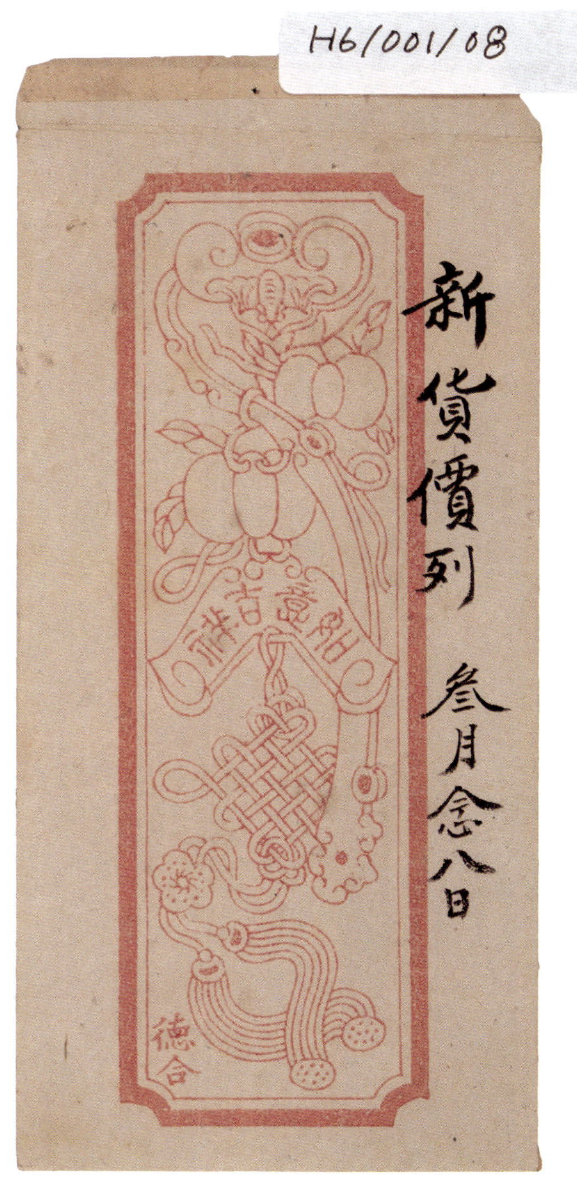
H6/001/08
新貨價列
叁月念八日
如意吉祥
德合

H6/001/09
吉星

H6/001/10
逢春館

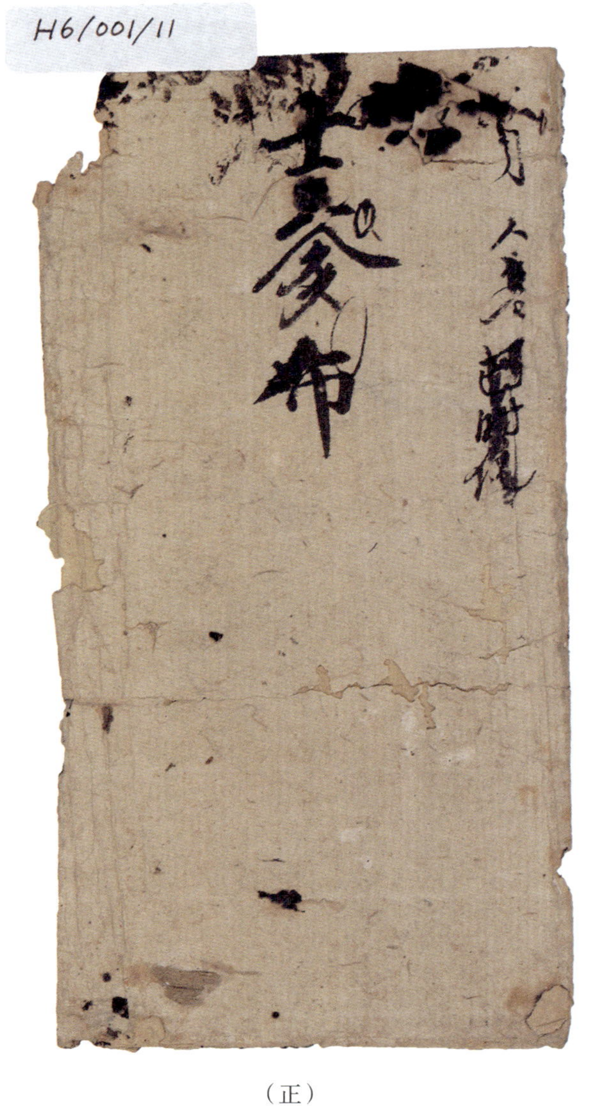

（正）

（反）

H6/001/12
Duty Chits for

二、信封残片两件（日期不详）（H6/2/1-2）

信封残片两件。

（1）Fragment of envelope. Date unknown. 1 item.

（2）Fragment of envelope. Date unknown. 1 item.

三、咸丰二年收据便条（H6/3）

中文收据便条，上有英文注释，写有1852年11月11日的日期。

Note of receipt. A note of receipt (in Chinese) for goods from the ‘Hornet’, including an English note dated 11 November 1852. 1 item; Fair condition, but slight damage by insects.

H6/3

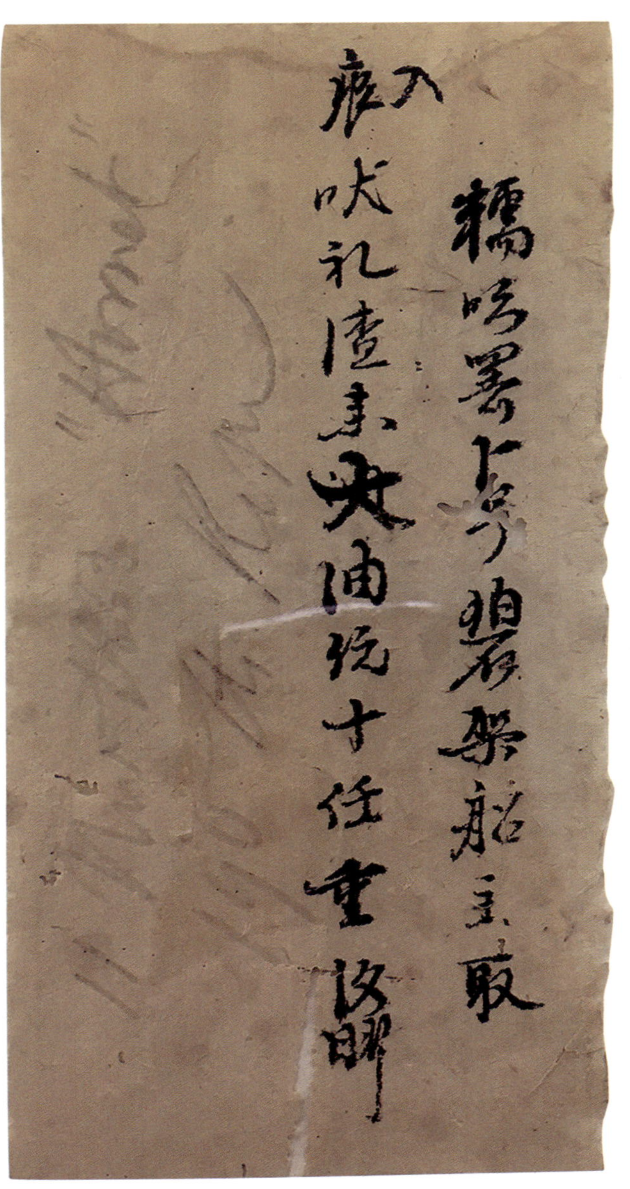

四、糖饷单（日期不详）（H6/4）

糖饷单，单上有“八年九年的”中文笔迹。

Sugar tax roll. Undated. 1 item.

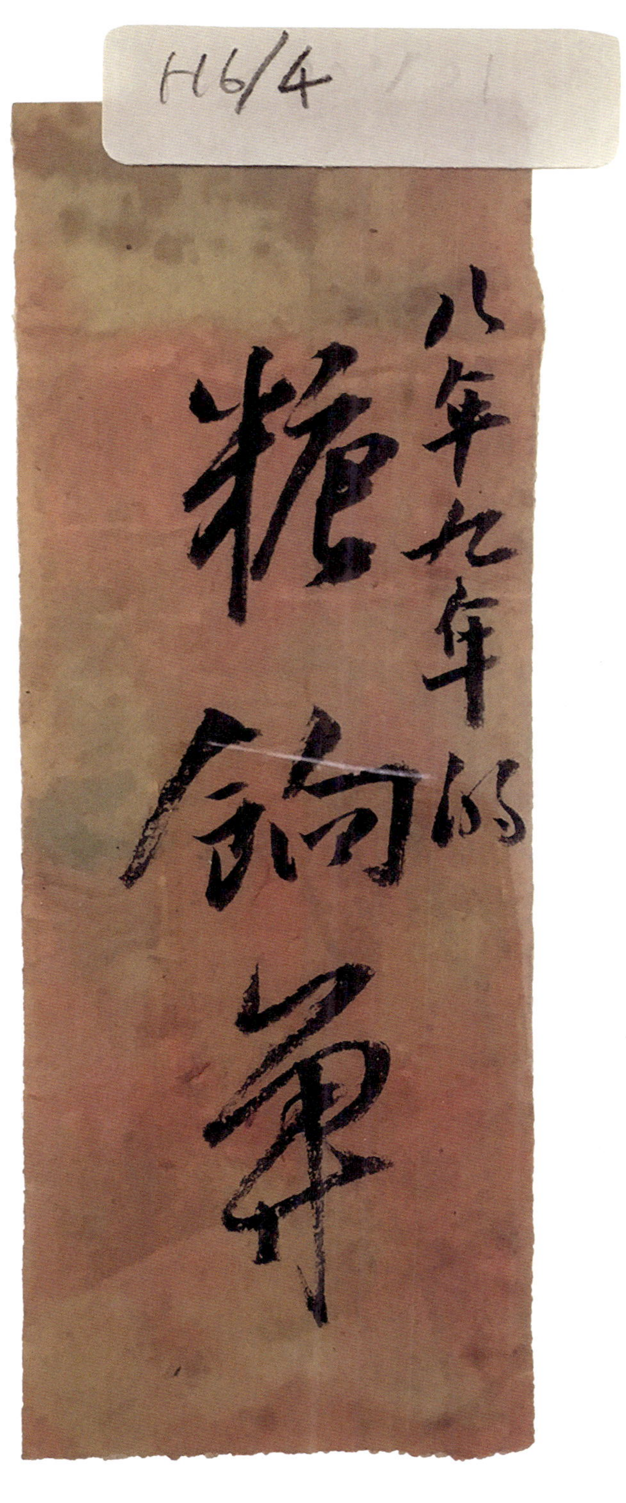

五、鸦片名称便条[1]（日期不详）（H6/5）

鸦片中文名称便条，有英文注释。

Note of Chinese opium name. A note of a Chinese name of opium, undated, including an English note below.

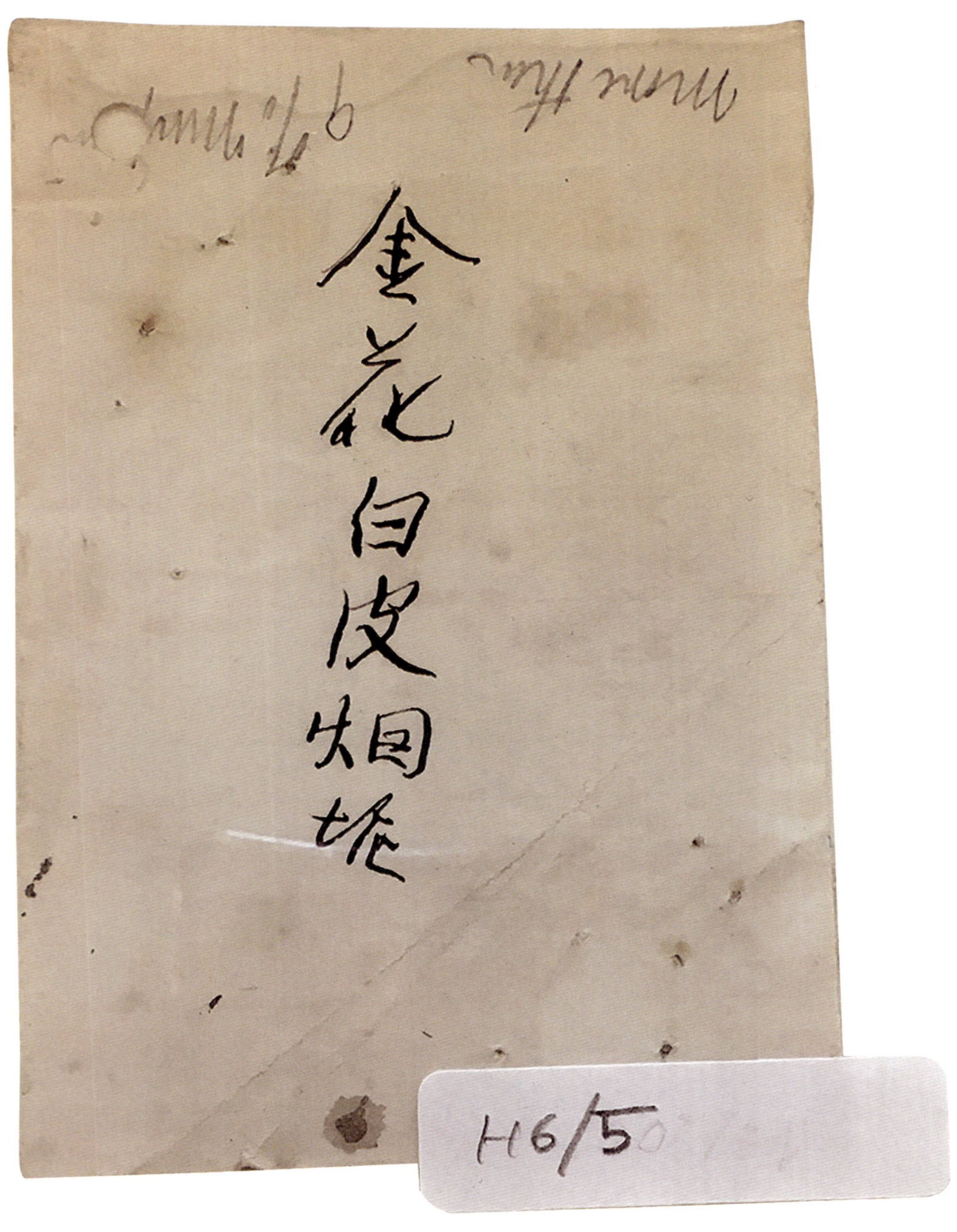

① 便条上的金花、白皮皆为鸦片烟土种类。

六、写有新元新叶对应银两的纸条三张（日期不详）（H6/6/1-3）

第一张纸条写有新元现银345两，新叶36两。

第二张纸条写有新元36,625两，新叶36,625两。

第三张纸条写有新元355两，新叶365两。

Manuscripts/MS JM/H6/6 contains:

（1）Note re new yuan and new leaves. Undated. 1 item.

（2）Note re new yuan and new leaves. Undated. 1 item.

（3）Note re new yuan and new leaves. Undated. 1 item.

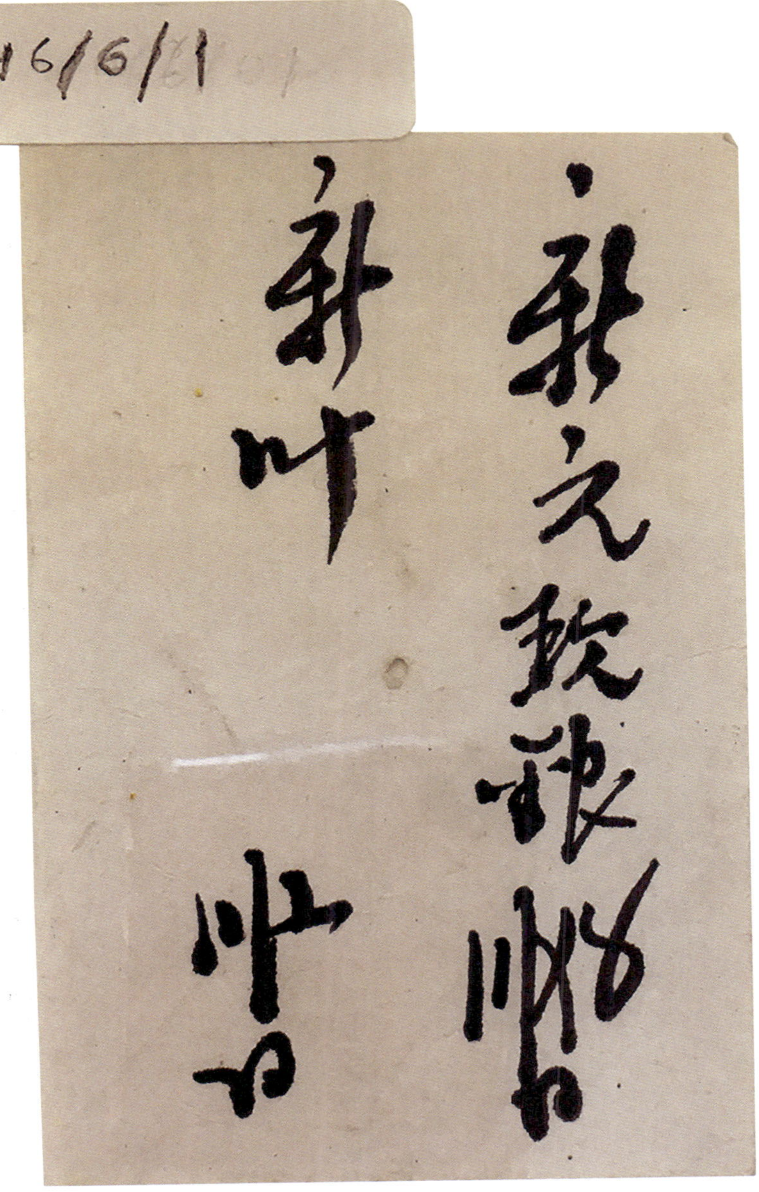

H6/6/1

新元現銀

新叶

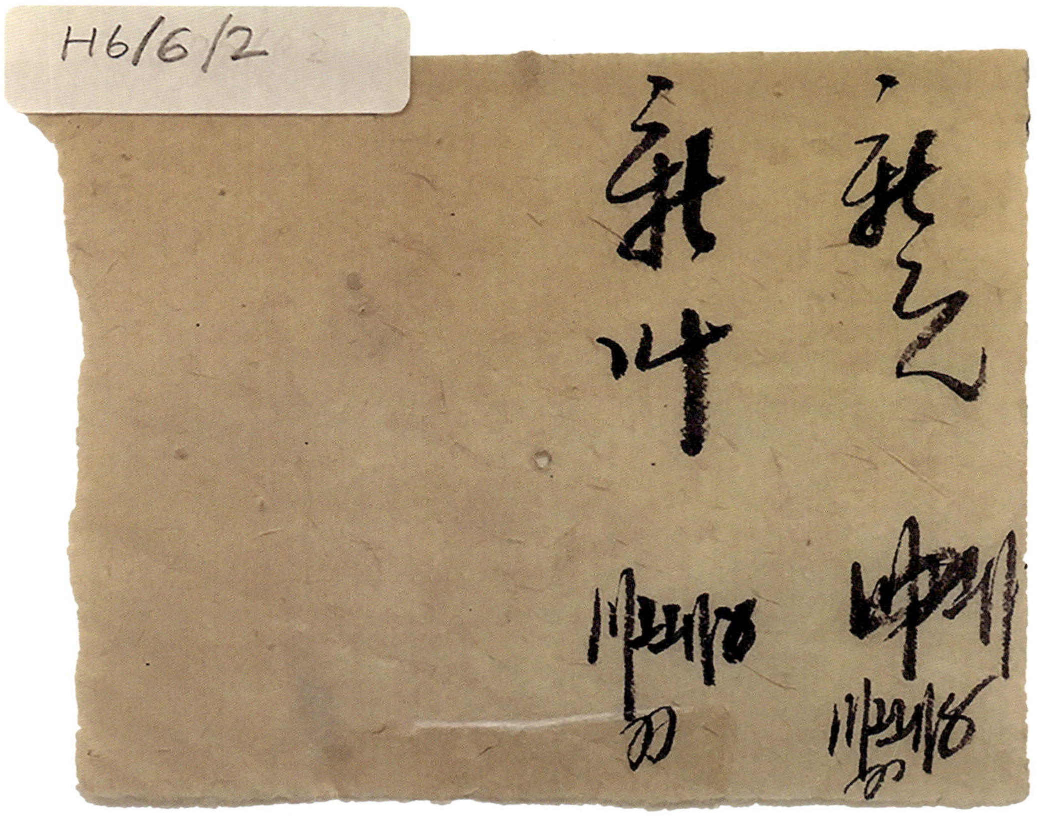

H6/6/2

新元

新叶

H6/6/3

新元

新叶

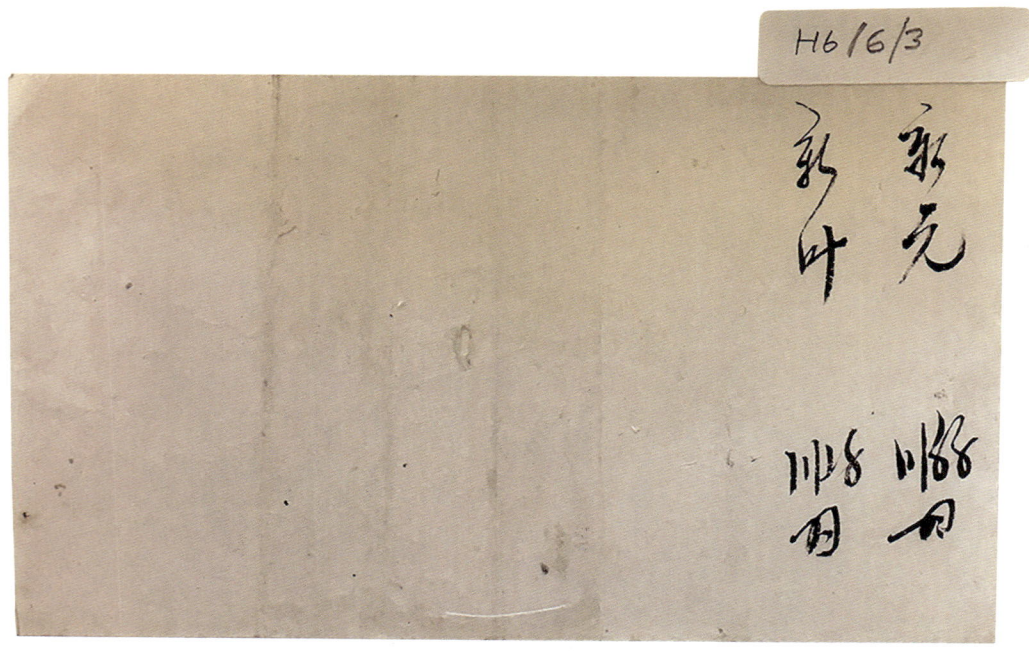

七、纱线仓库单据（日期不详）（H6/7）

纱线仓库单据。

Note of invoice of yarn warehouse. Undated. 1 item.

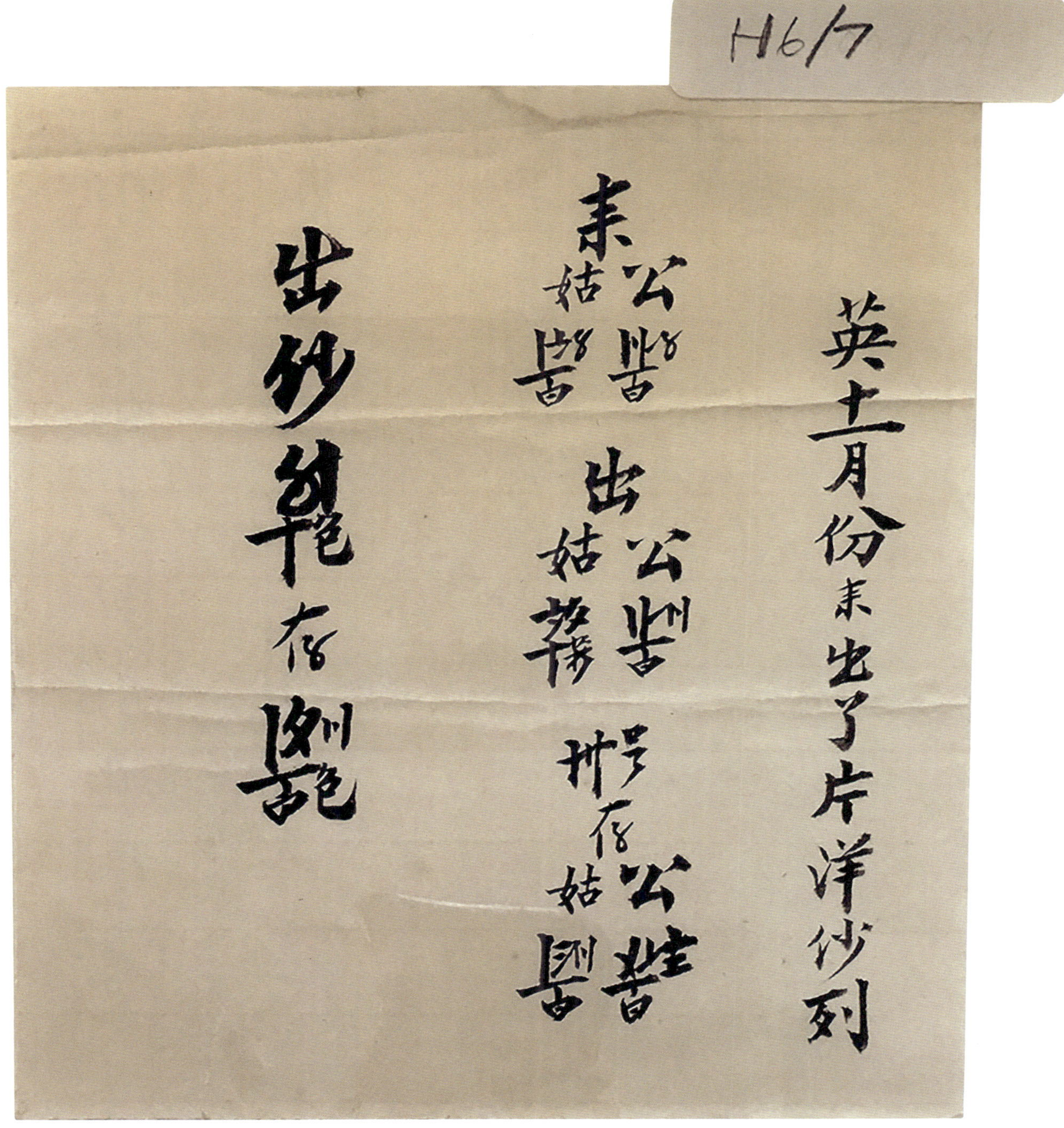

H6/7

英十二月份来出了片洋纱列

八、洗衣收据（日期不详）（H6/8）

洗衣收据，有英文注释。

Laundry receipt. An undated receipt for laundry (in Chinese), including English annotations.

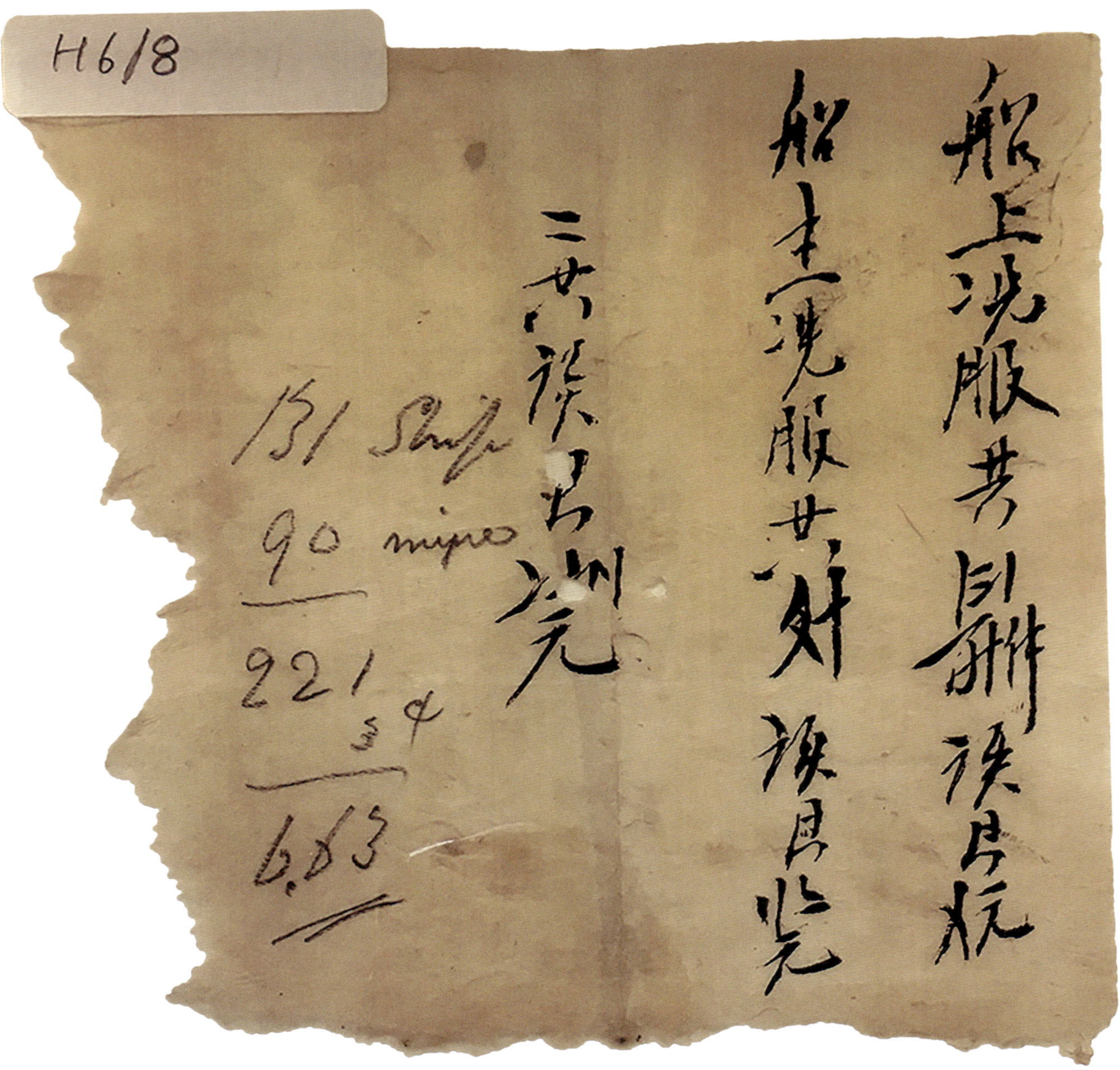

H6/8

船上洗服共[illegible]件該艮[illegible]

船主洗服廿[illegible]該艮[illegible]

二共該艮[illegible]

131 Shirts
90 wipes
221
3¢
6.63

九、茶叶收据（日期不详）（H6/9）

茶叶收据。

Tea receipt. Undated.

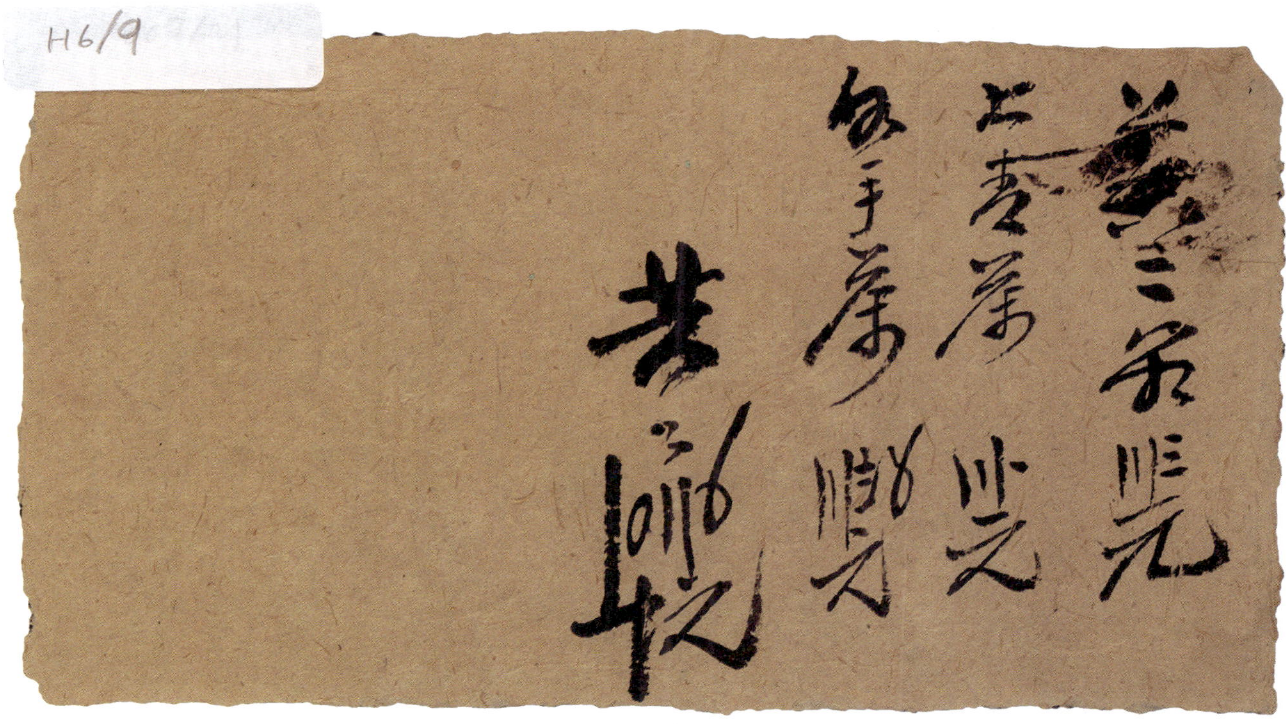

一〇、中文信件残片（日期不详）（H6/10）

中文信件残片，有英文注释。

Fragment of letter. A fragment of a Chinese letter, including English notes. The date is not unknown.

一一、五月十六日香港药房收据（年份不详）（H6/11）

五月十六日，香港药房收据。

Pharmacy receipt. An undated receipt from a Hong Kong pharmacy for a collected debt.

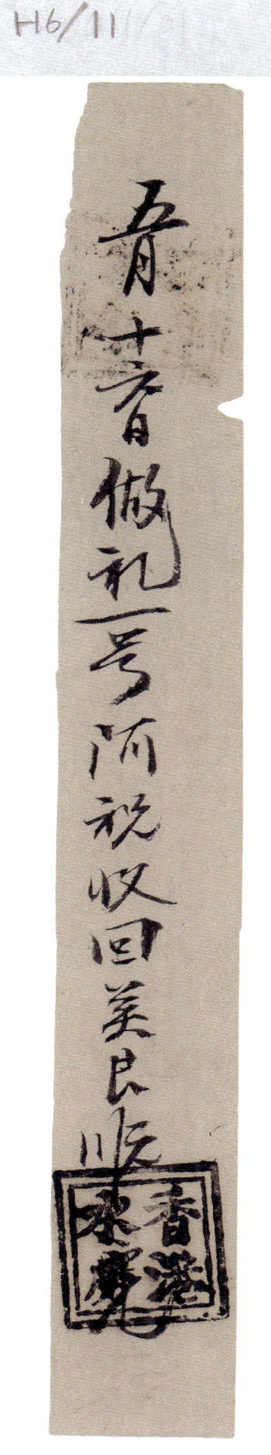

一二、中文信件残片（日期不详）（H6/12）

中文信件残片，上有“内信呈交阿绵官收展”笔迹。末尾盖有朱文印章“尘茂利记”。

Letter to Amain. An undated fragment of a letter. 1 item; Moderate condition.

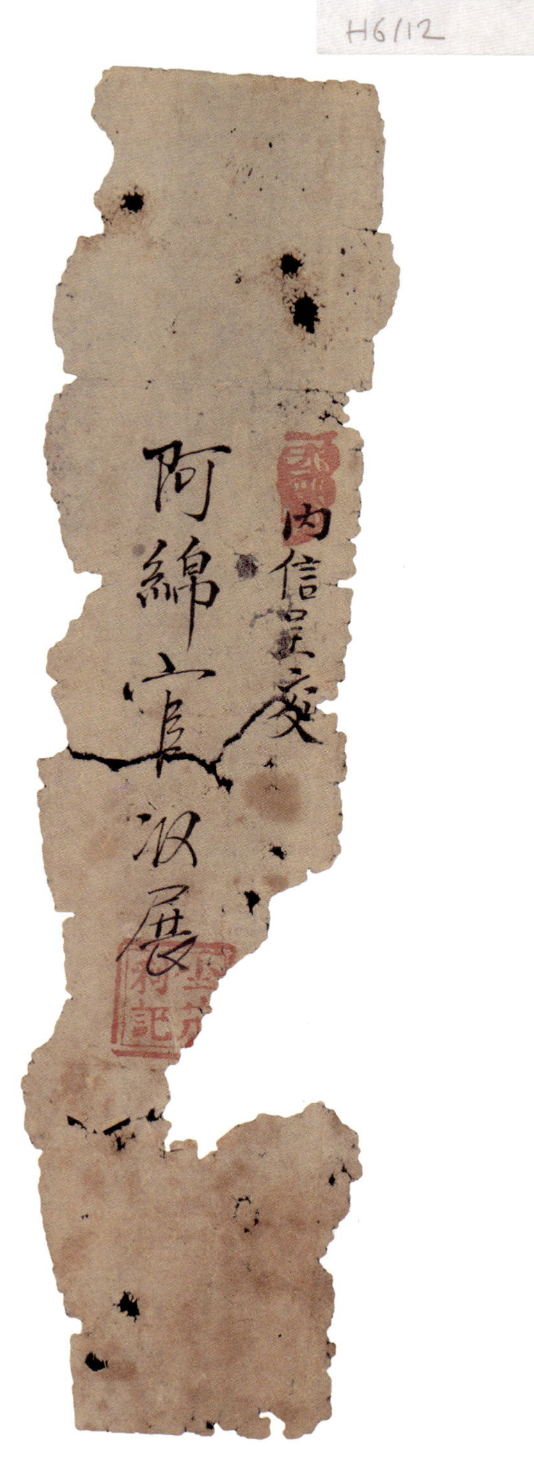
H6/12

内信呈交

阿綿官收展

一三、中文信件残片（日期不详）（H6/13）

中文信件残片，有“李船主收拆”中文字样。

Letter to Captain Li. An undated fragment of a letter. 1 item.

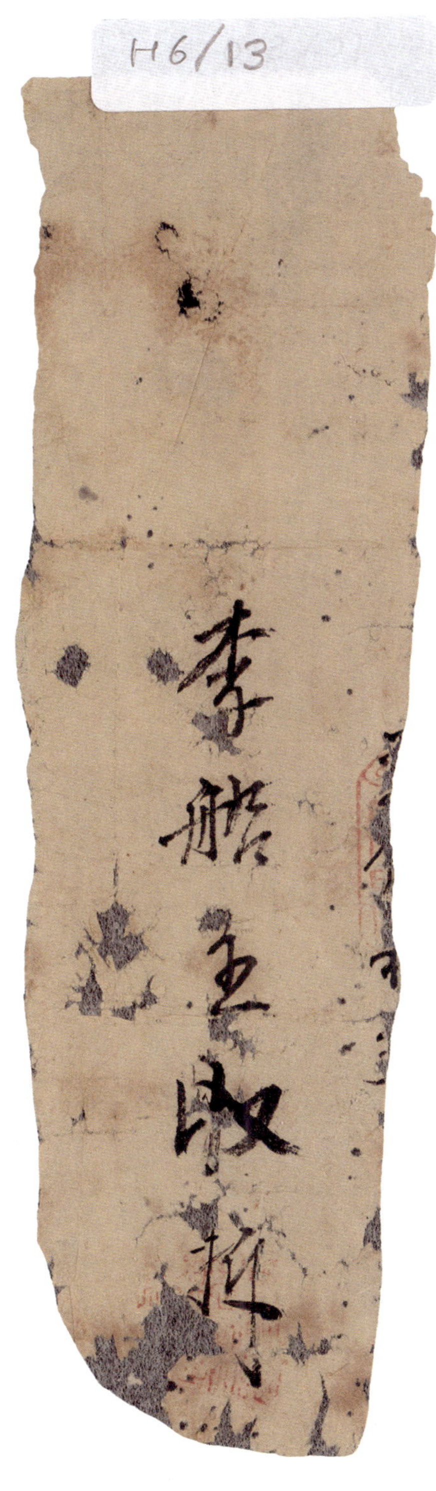

H6/13

李船主收拆

一四、中文谚语（日期不详）（H6/14）

中文信件残片，有中文谚语“岂容故智复萌”，另有英文注释。

Note of a Chinese idiom. An undated note (in Chinese and English) regarding a Chinese idiom. 1 item; Moderate condition and missing two large sections.

一五、送信要求便条（日期不详）（H6/15）

送信要求便条。

Note of request. An undated note of a request for the sending of a letter. 1 item.

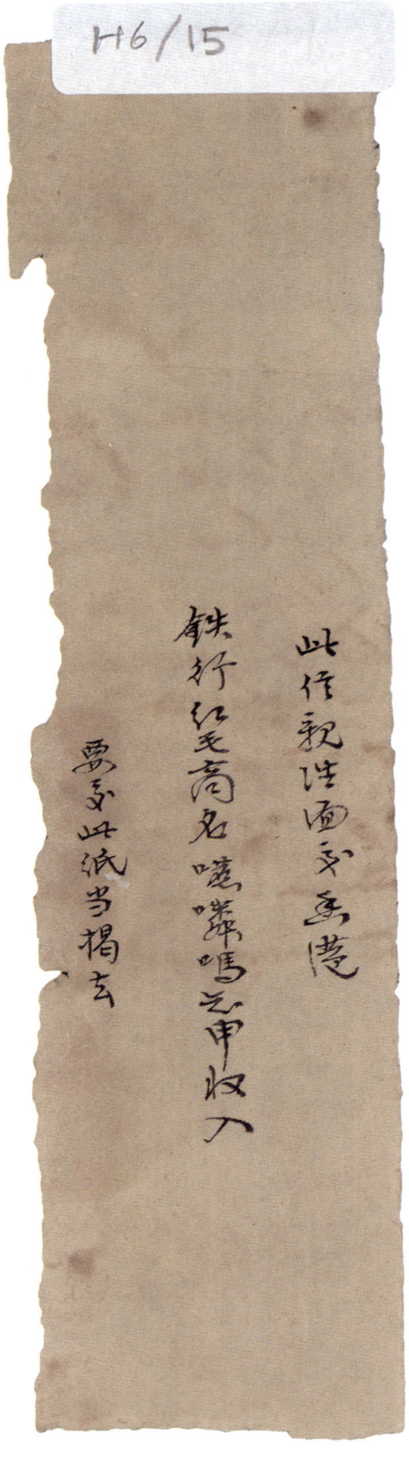
H6/15

此信親往面交香港
鉄行紅毛商名嘰喋嗎之申收入
要交此紙當揭去

一六、收支便条（日期不详）（H6/16）

收支便条。

Note of an account. Undated. 1 item.

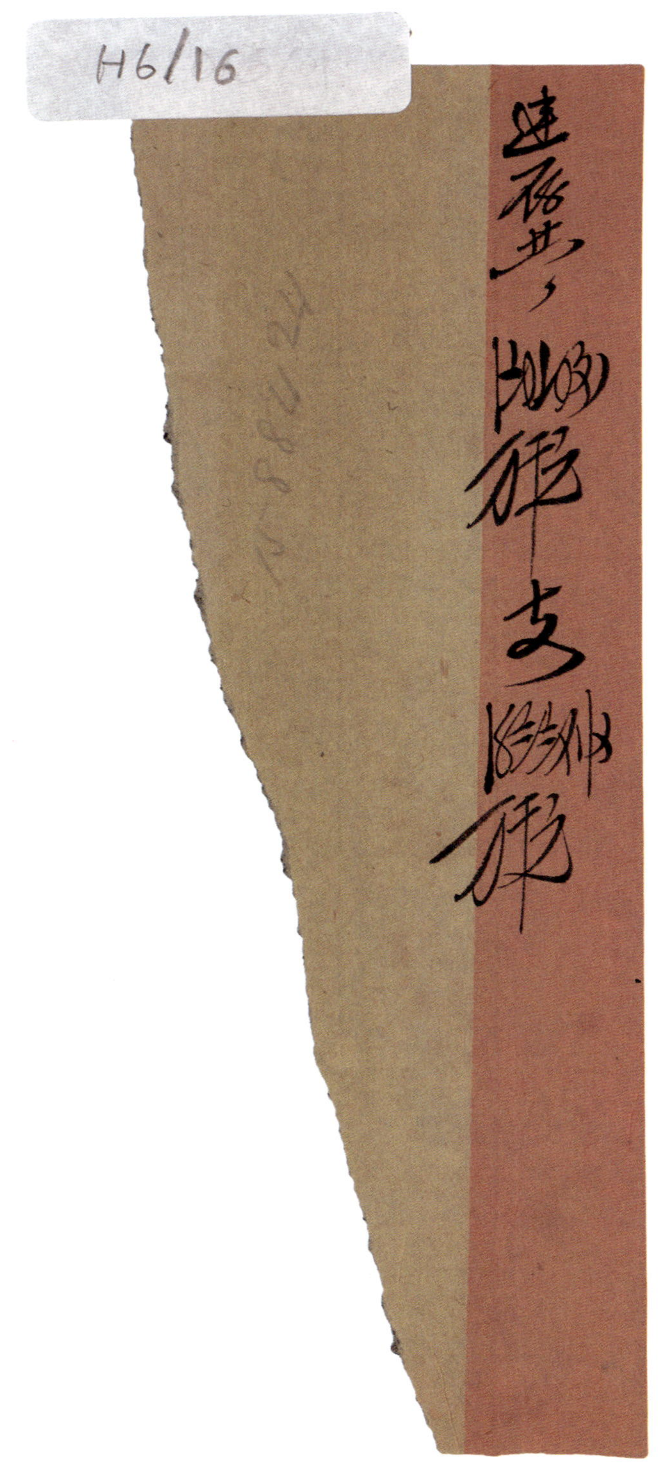

一七、收支便条（日期不详）（H6/17）

收支便条。

Note of an account. Undated. 1 item.

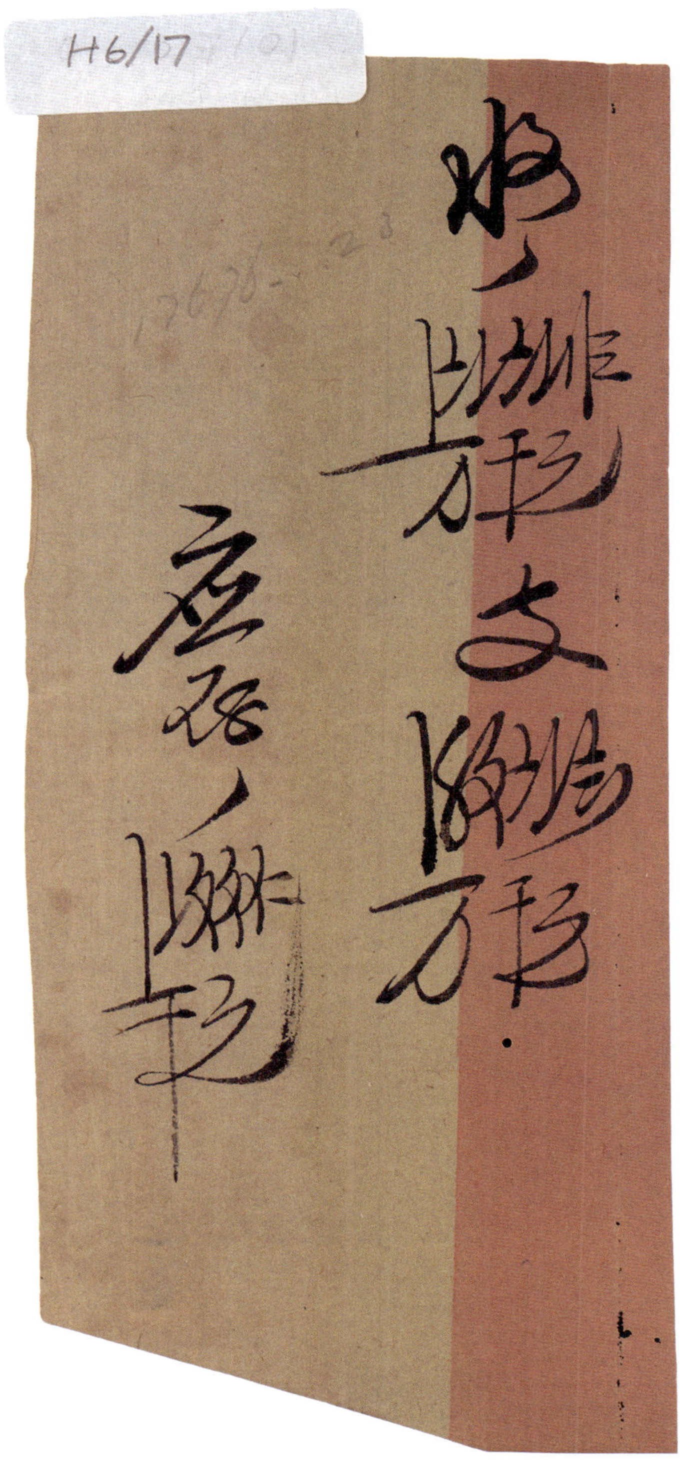

一八、催促搬迁通知（日期不详）（H6/18）

催促搬迁通知。

Note of removal deadline. An undated note of the deadline for removal from a house.

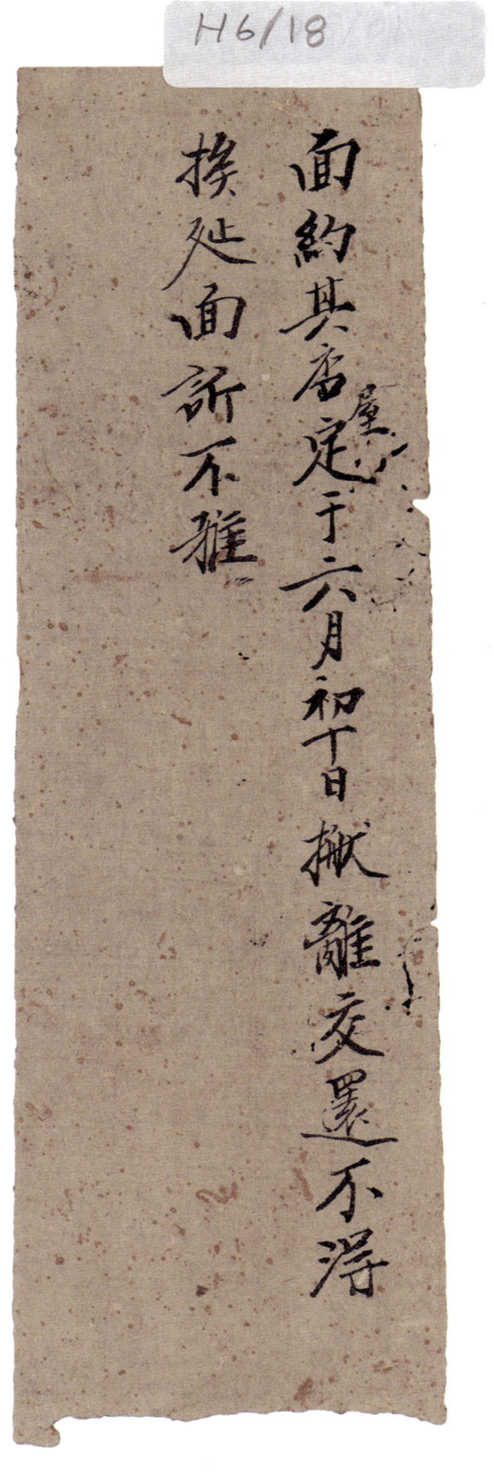

面約其居屋定于六月初十日撤離交還不得

挨延　面訴不准

一九、购房通知（日期不详）（H6/19）

购房通知。

Note re house purchase. An undated note informing that it is the time to buy a house. 1 item.

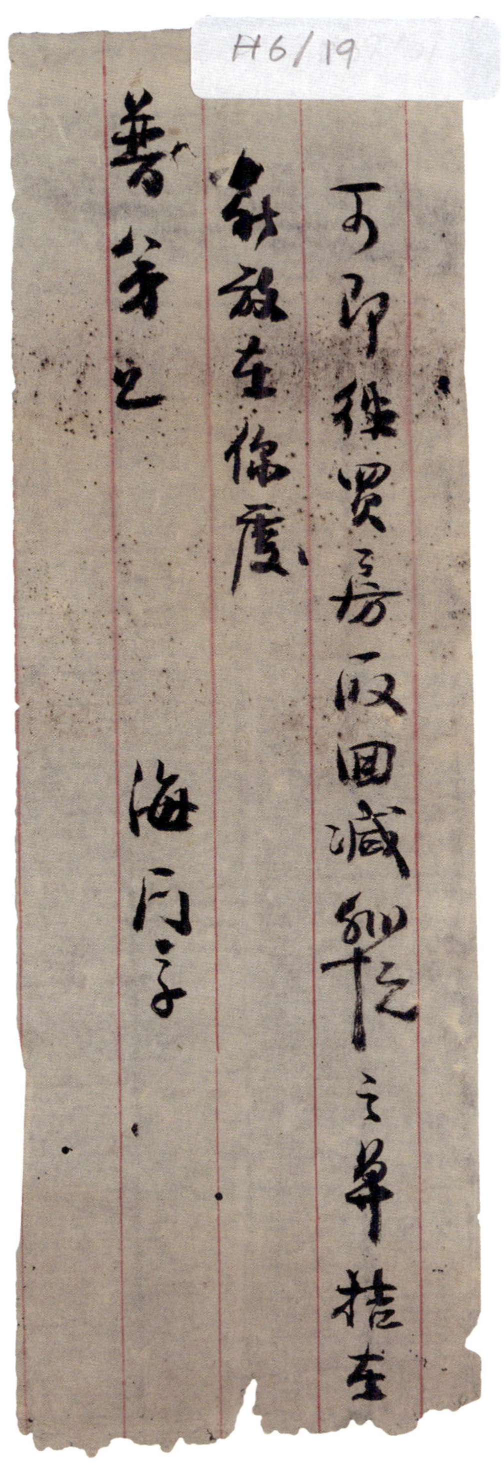

H6/19

可即往買房取回減契之單據存

[illegible]放在你處

善芳兄

海同字

二〇、拍卖货品记录（日期不详）（H6/20）

疑为拍卖鸦片的记录。

Note of auction. Undated.1 item.

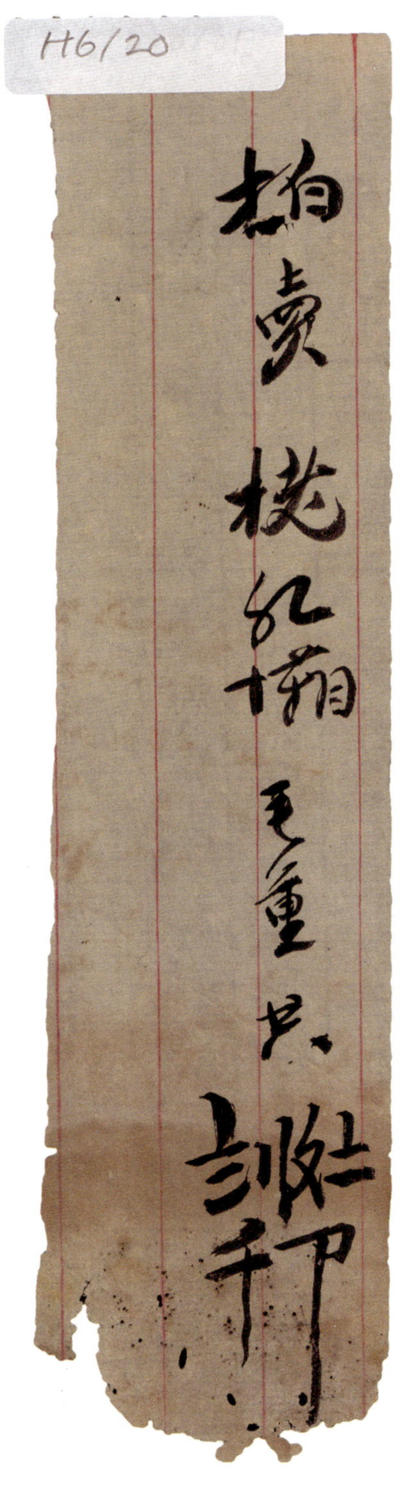

二一、修整门窗收据（日期不详）（H6/21）

修整门窗收据。

Receipt for doors and windows repairs. Undated.1 item.

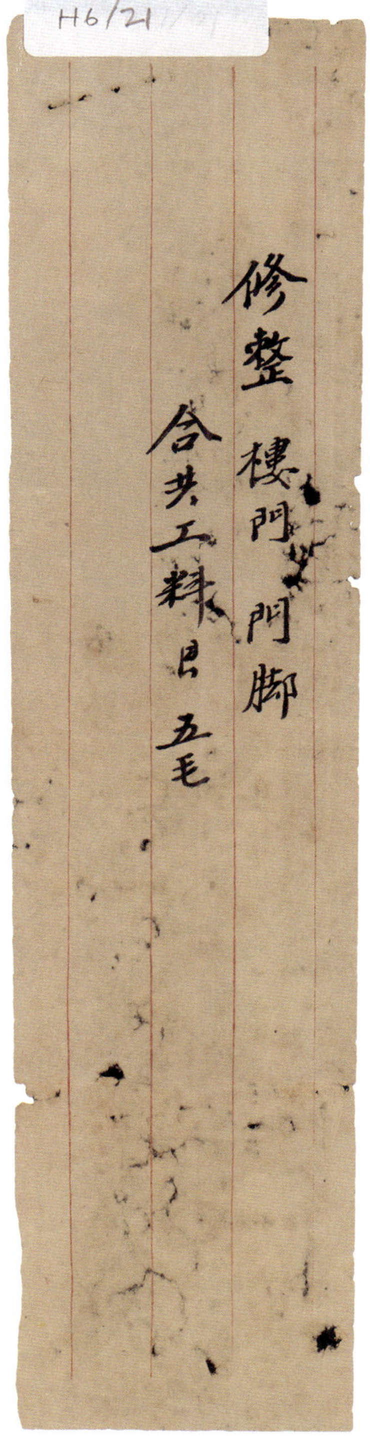

H6/21

修整樓門門脚

合共工料艮五毛

二二、光绪十年电报文稿（H6/22）

光绪十年十二月十二日（1885年1月27日），上海电报局电报文稿。

Telegram from Yuan. A telegram (in Chinese and English) from Yuan, Port Arthur, to Mandl, Shanghai, 27 January 1885, informing him that his two telegrams have been received and requesting that he go directly to Tientsin where they can consult in person. The telegram's message is in Chinese. There is an accompanying English translation. 2 items. 1885

Mandl

— Your two Telegrams received. no need to come to Port Arthur, please go directly to Tientsin, ~~J & K~~ I and Saimber – will ~~probably~~ leave for Tientsin on the 2nd ult. (Chinese) you can consult with ~~them~~ us in person.

~~you~~ Yuan
from Port Arthur

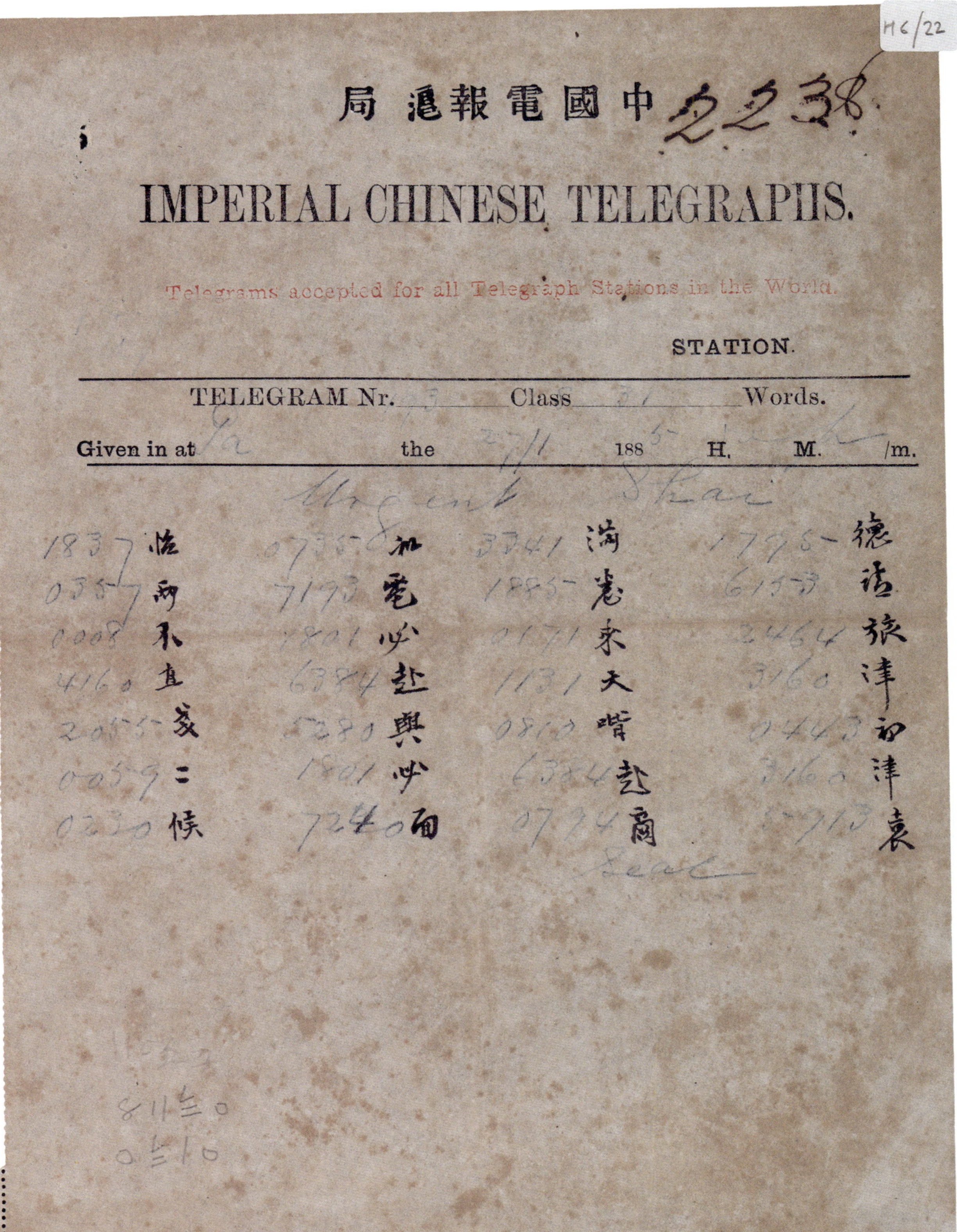

中國電報滬局　2238

IMPERIAL CHINESE TELEGRAPHS.

Telegrams accepted for all Telegraph Stations in the World.

STATION.

TELEGRAM Nr. 　　Class 　　Words.

Given in at 　　the 　　188 　H. 　M. 　/m.

Urgent

二三、工资单（日期不详）（H6/23）

工资单。

Wage slip. An undated wage slip (in Chinese) for a temporary worker, with an English note on the reverse[①]. 1 item; Moderate condition, with damage by insects and missing large sections.

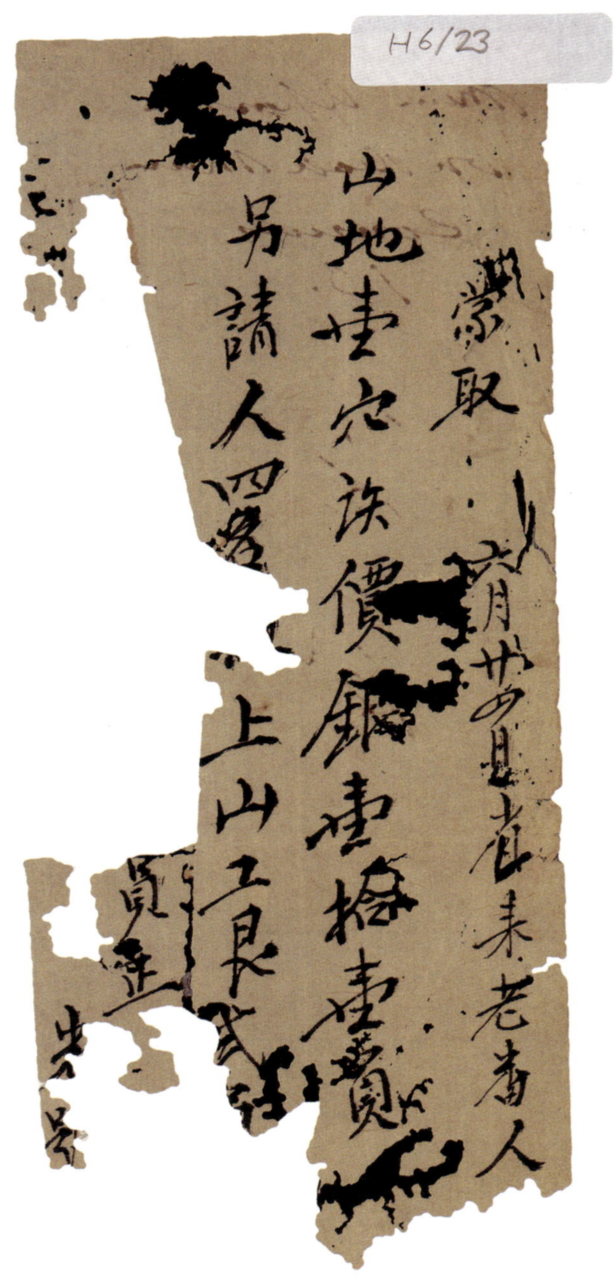
H6/23

崇取　六月廿四日在未老者人

山地壹穴該價銀壹拾壹員

另請人四

上山工良弍拾

① 档案背面图片缺失，英文提要所提有英文注释内容不详。

二四、收据（日期不详）（H6/24）

收据。

Receipt to Lien-t’an-shih-tan. Undated. 1 item.

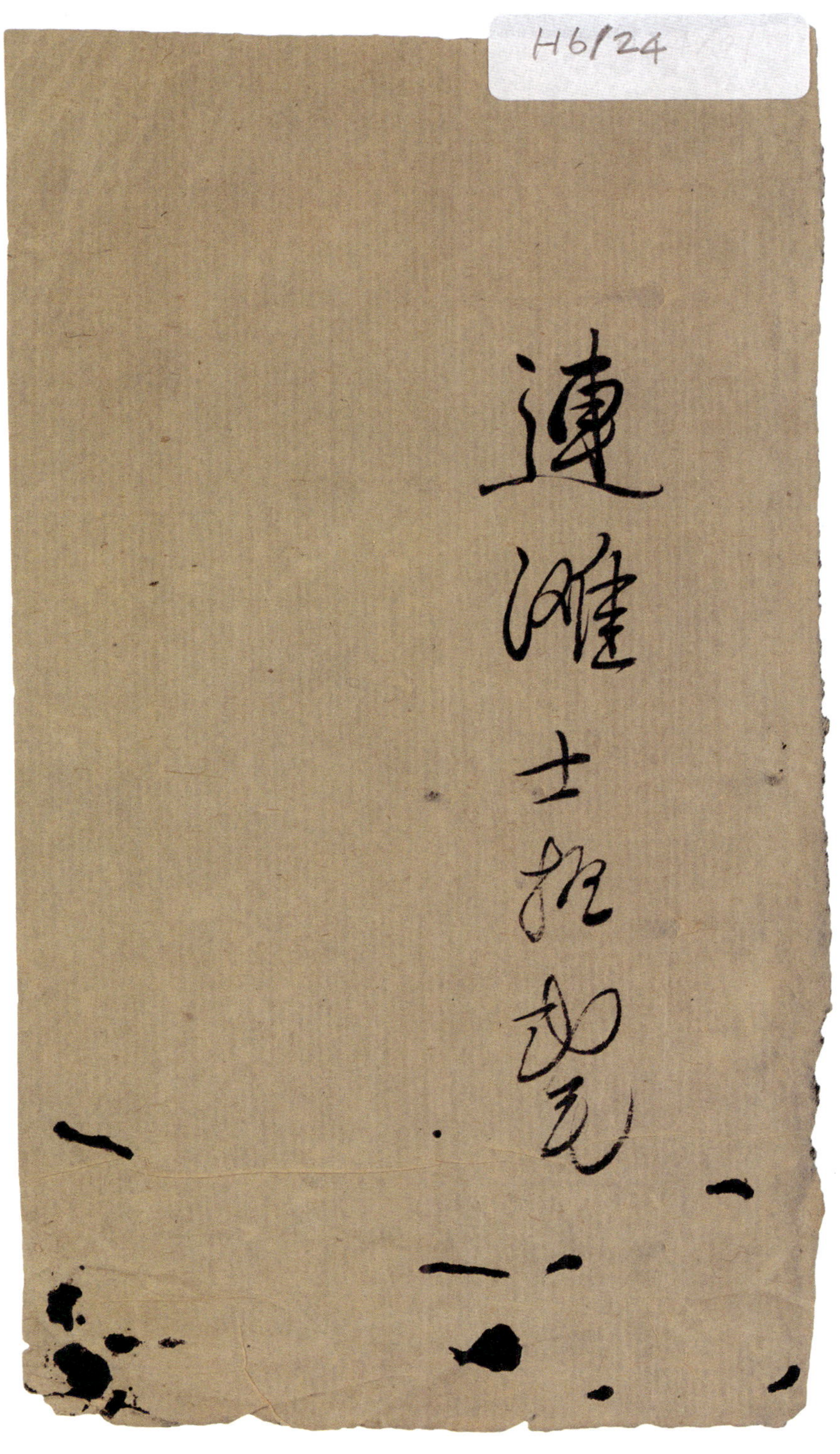

二五、俞思益名片（日期不详）（H6/25）

俞思益名片。

Business card of Yu Ssu-I (Yu Siyi). Undated. 1 item.

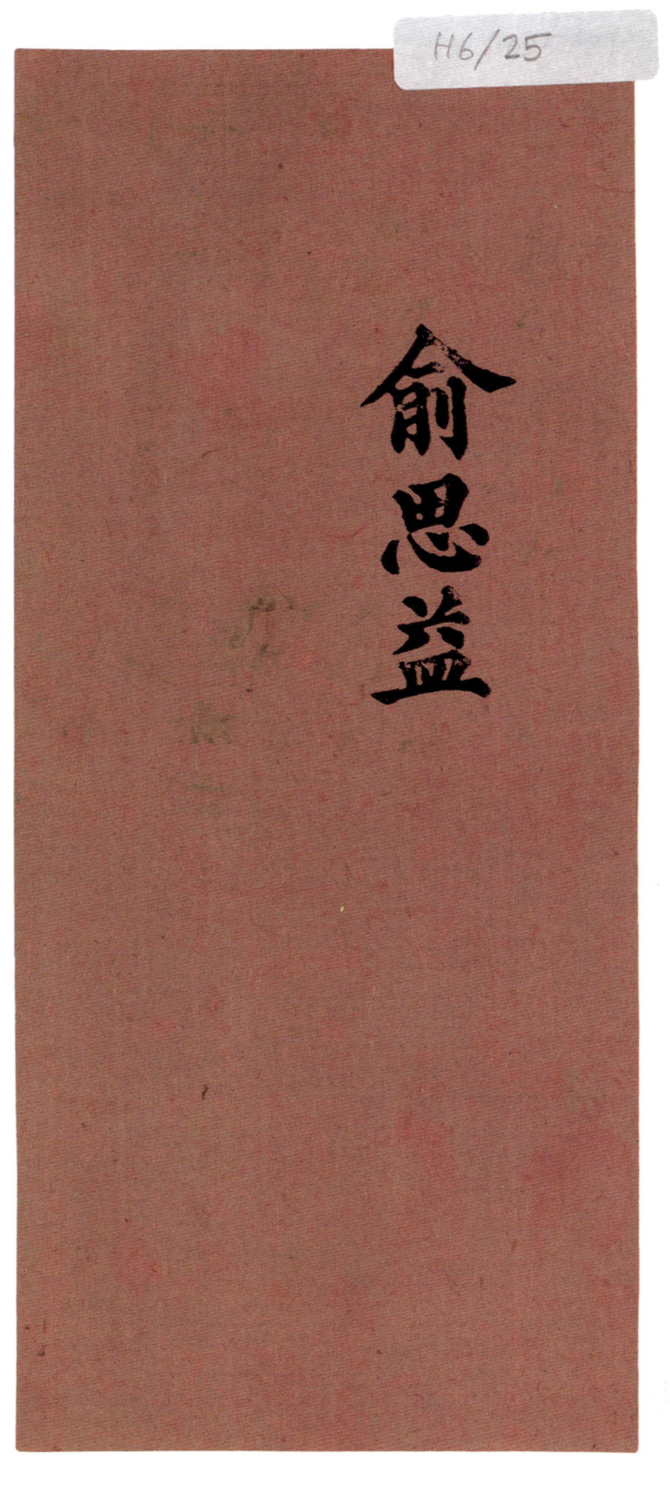

二六、广利源名片（日期不详）（H6/26）

广利源名片。

Card of Kwang-li-yuan. Undated. 1 item.

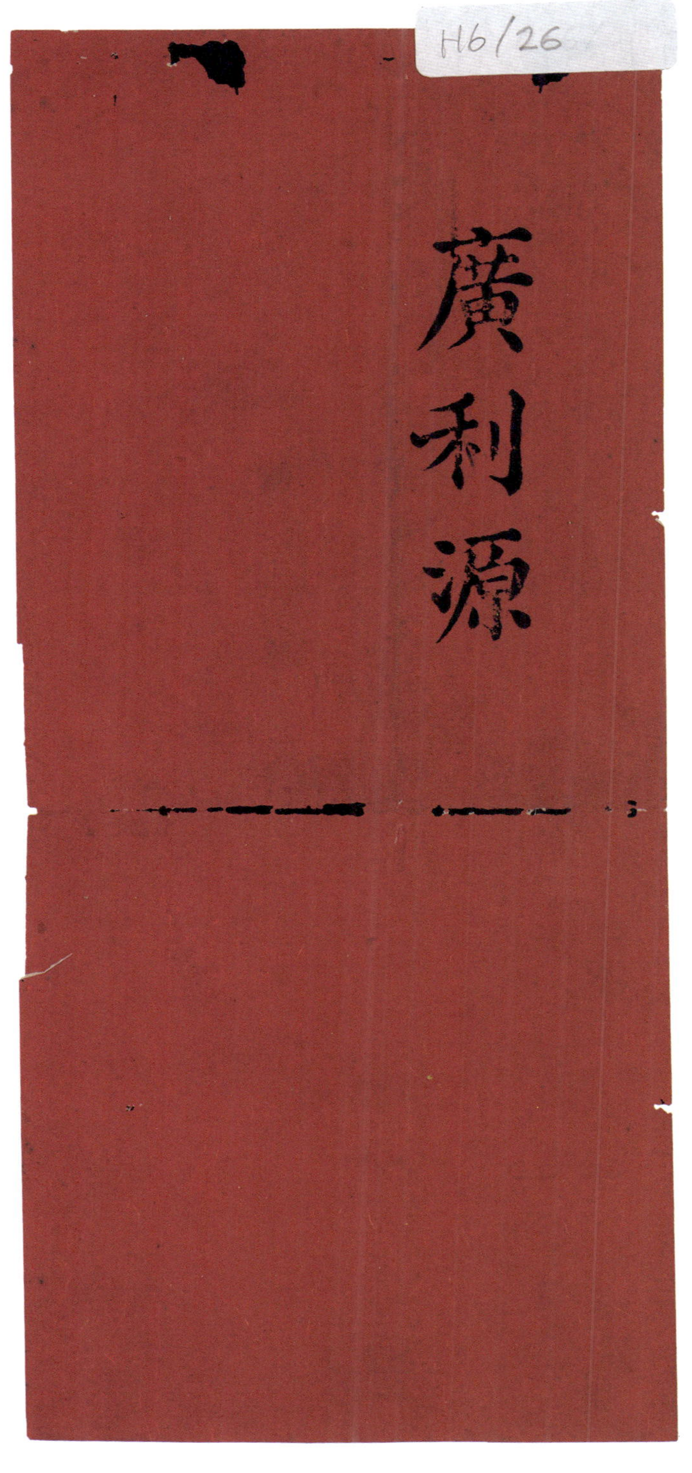

二七、茶叶收据（日期不详）（H6/27）

茶叶收据。上有“茶款　乌龙[①]　工夫　色种　小种”中文字样，左下有“式桅船恒兴”印文。

Tea receipt. An undated title page of a receipt for two Woolong teas. 1 item.

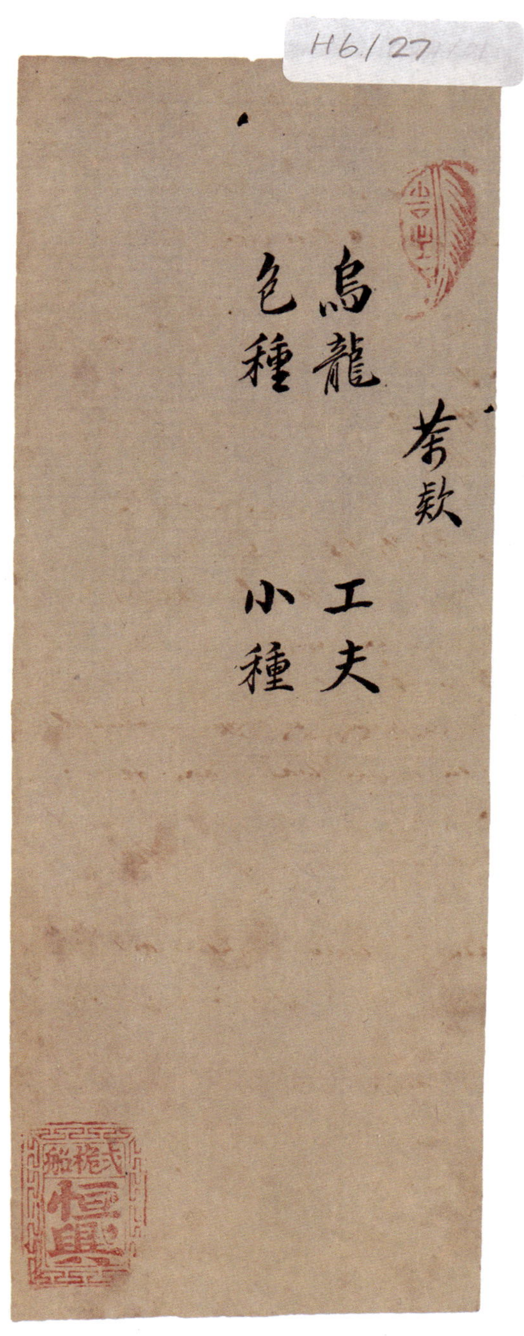
H6/27

茶款

烏龍　工夫

色種　小種

---

① 乌龙：茶叶种类名目。其后的工夫、色种、小种亦为茶叶种类名目。

二八、八月初三日船运货物清单（年份不详）（H6/28）

八月初三日，船运货物清单，有外文辨识。

Shipping bill. An undated shipping bill containing Chinese and Western characters. 1 item.

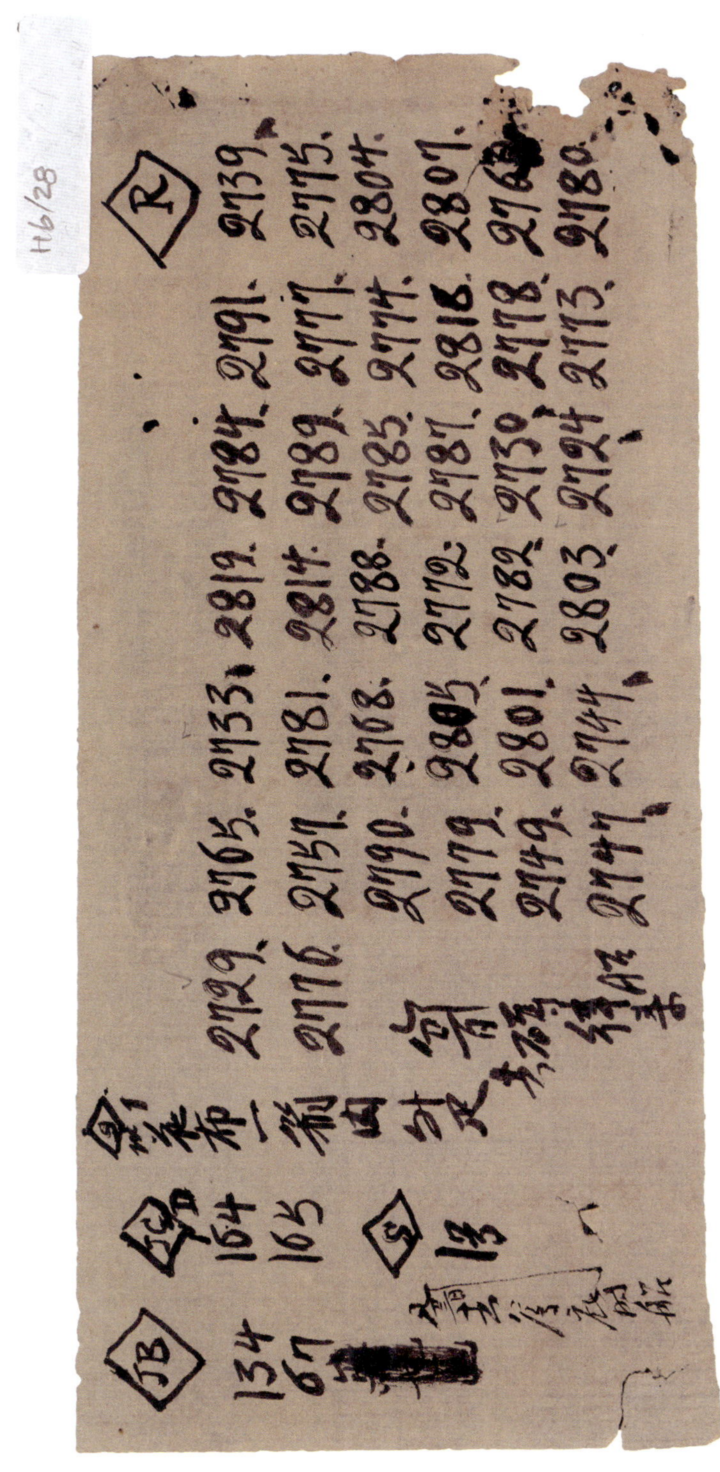

二九、林钦的个人信息（日期不详）（H6/29）

有关林钦的个人信息。上有中文笔迹“林钦，字畅钟，系香山人，在澳门上麻湾涌外堡村居住”，另有简短英文笔迹。

Information re Lin Ch’in. An undated note (in Chinese) containing personal information about Lin Ch’in, including a brief English note. 1 item; Fair condition, but some damage by insects.

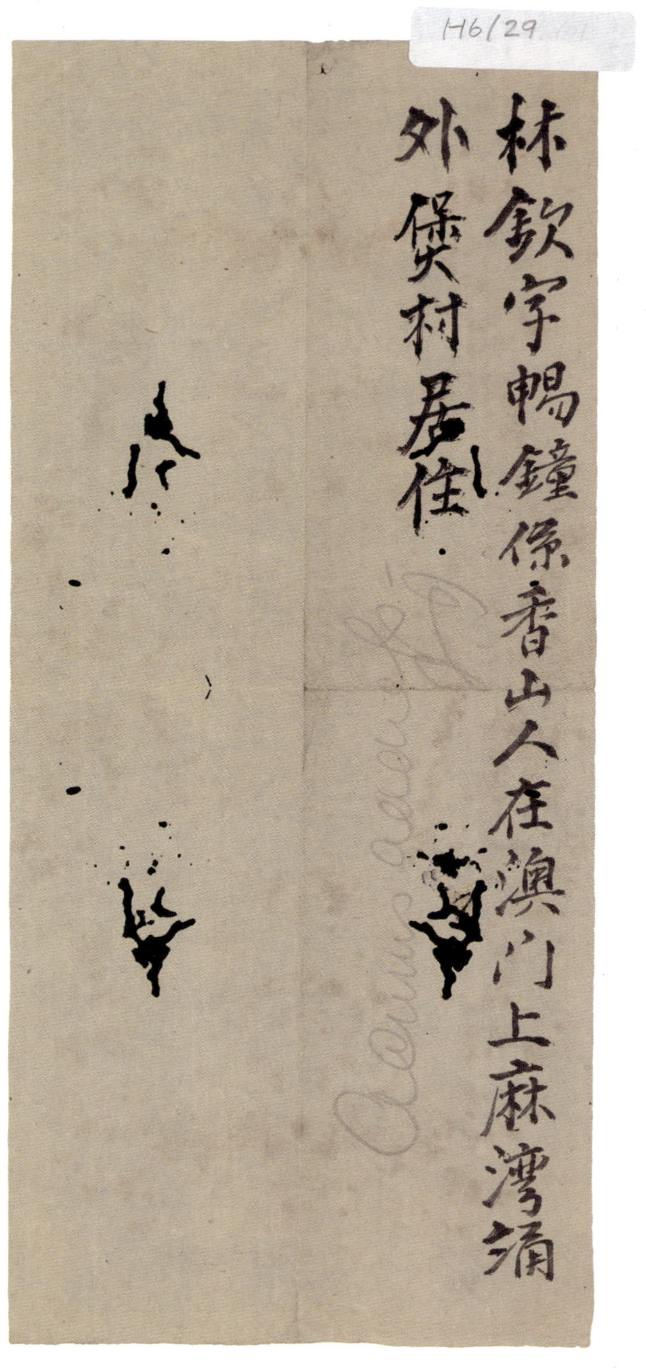

H6/29

林欽字暢鐘係香山人在澳门上麻灣涌
外堡村居住

三〇、铁匠支出（日期不详）（H6/30）

铁匠支出。

Note of payment for blacksmith. Undated. 1 item.

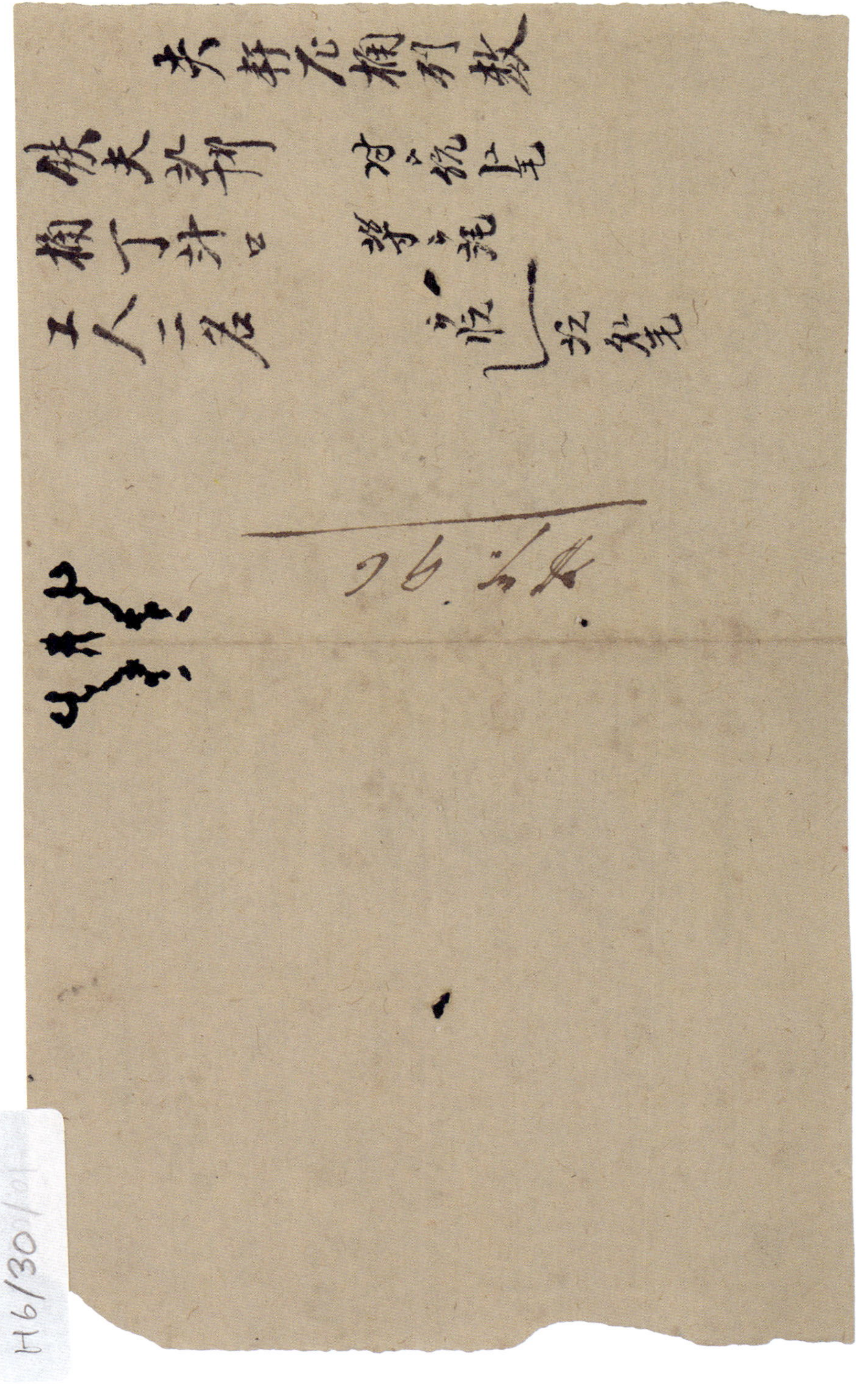

三一、灯饰支出（日期不详）（H6/31）

灯饰支出。

Receipt. Undated. 1 item.

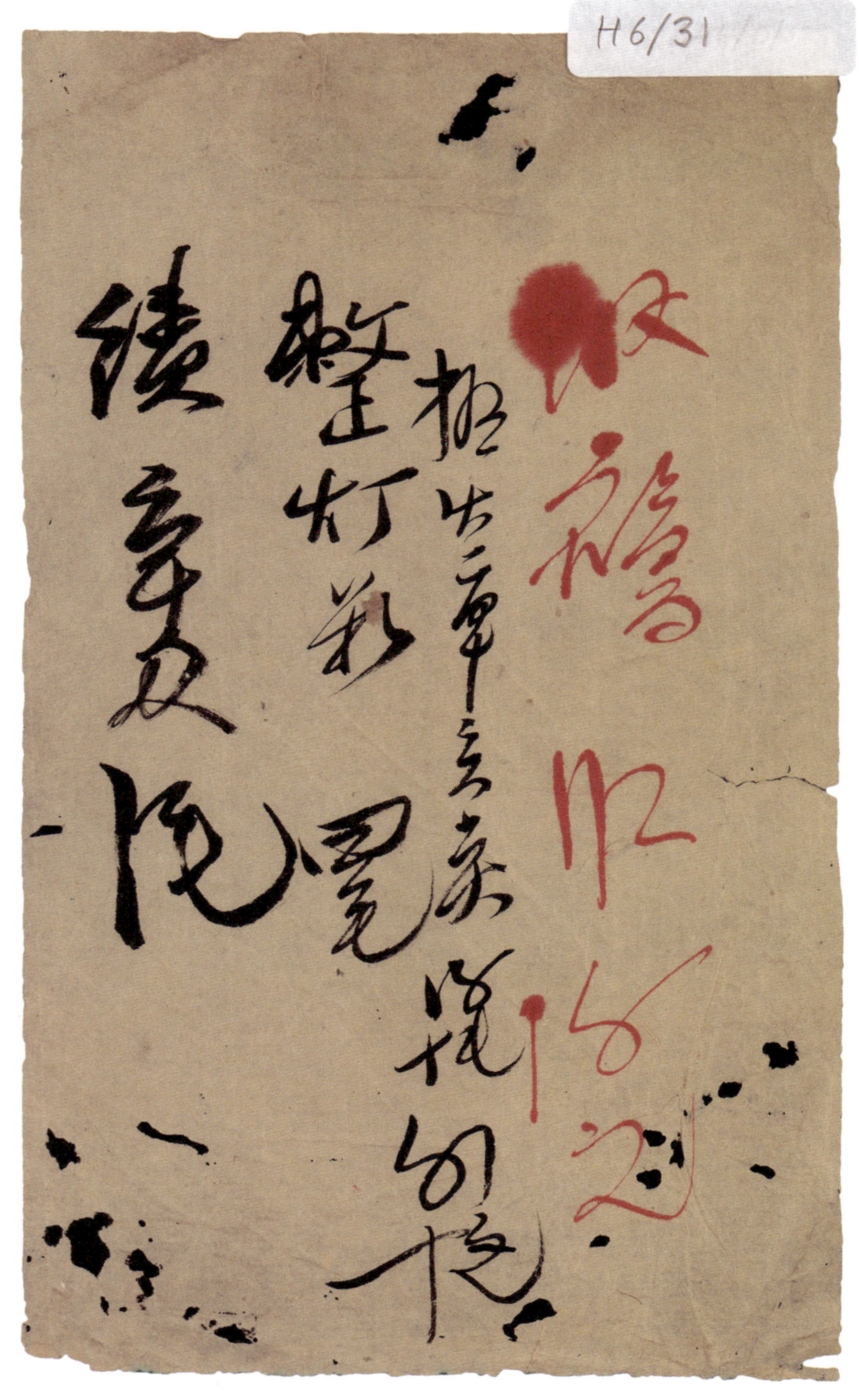
H6/31

三二、货运收据（日期不详）（H6/32）

货运收据。

Receipt to Na-shih. A undated receipt (in Chinese) for 12 cases sent to Hong Kong, including an English note about the receipt on the reverse. 1 item; Moderate condition, in two parts, with damage by insects, and missing large sections.

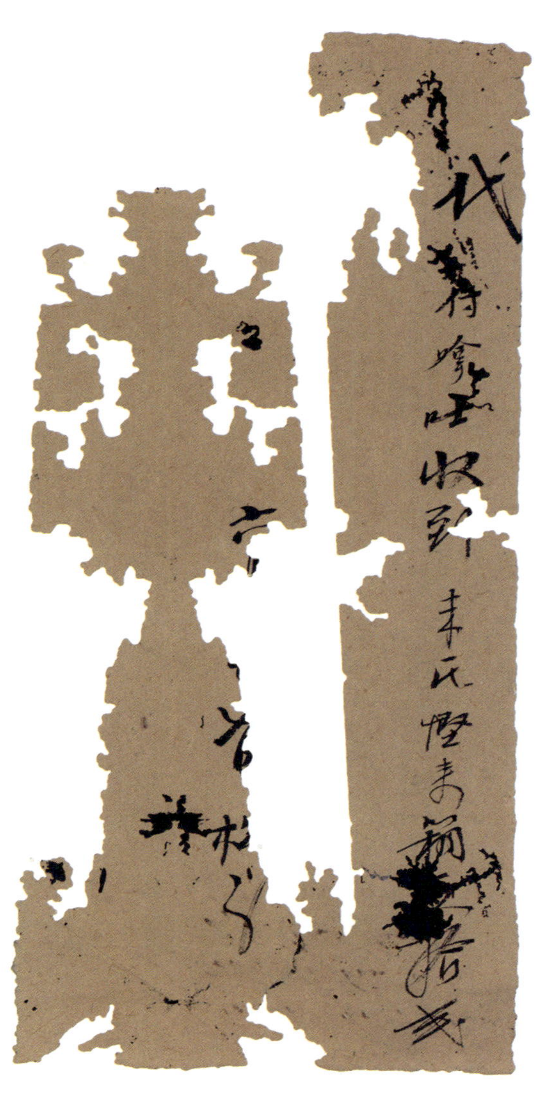

（正）

（反）

三三、不明收据（日期不详）（H6/33）

不明收据。

Su-chow code. Undated. 1 item; Fair condition, but damage by insects and missing significant sections.

三四、杂货店收据（日期不详）（H6/34）

杂货店收据。

Grocery list. Undated. 1 item; Fair condition, but some damage by insects.

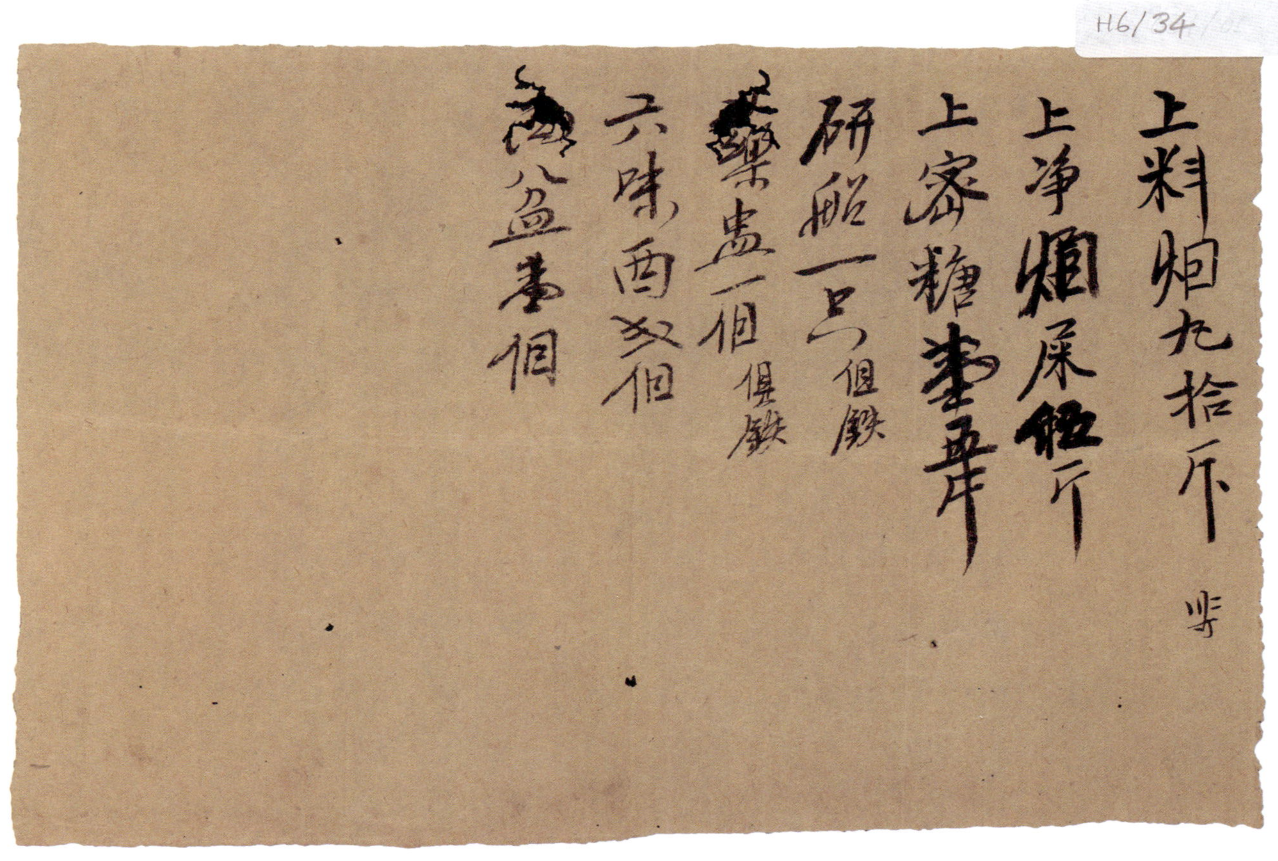

三五、餐具清单（日期不详）（H6/35）

餐具清单。

Cutlery list. Undated. 1 item.

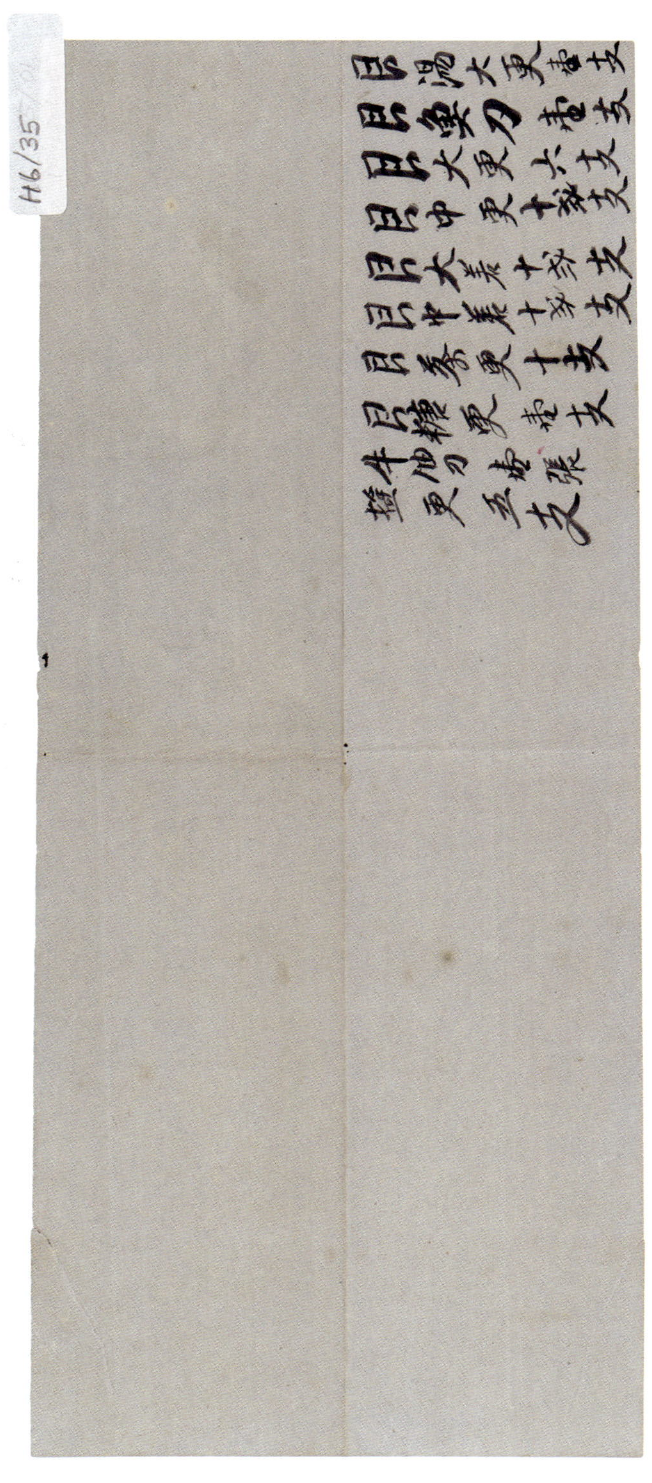

三六、否认担保外国商人船只事宜的声明（日期不详）（H6/36）

华人买办“五馆”的声明，否认担保外国商人船只事宜。

Letter fragment re five hongs. An undated fragment of a letter regarding five hongs, denying that they have given a guarantee to a ship. 1 item.

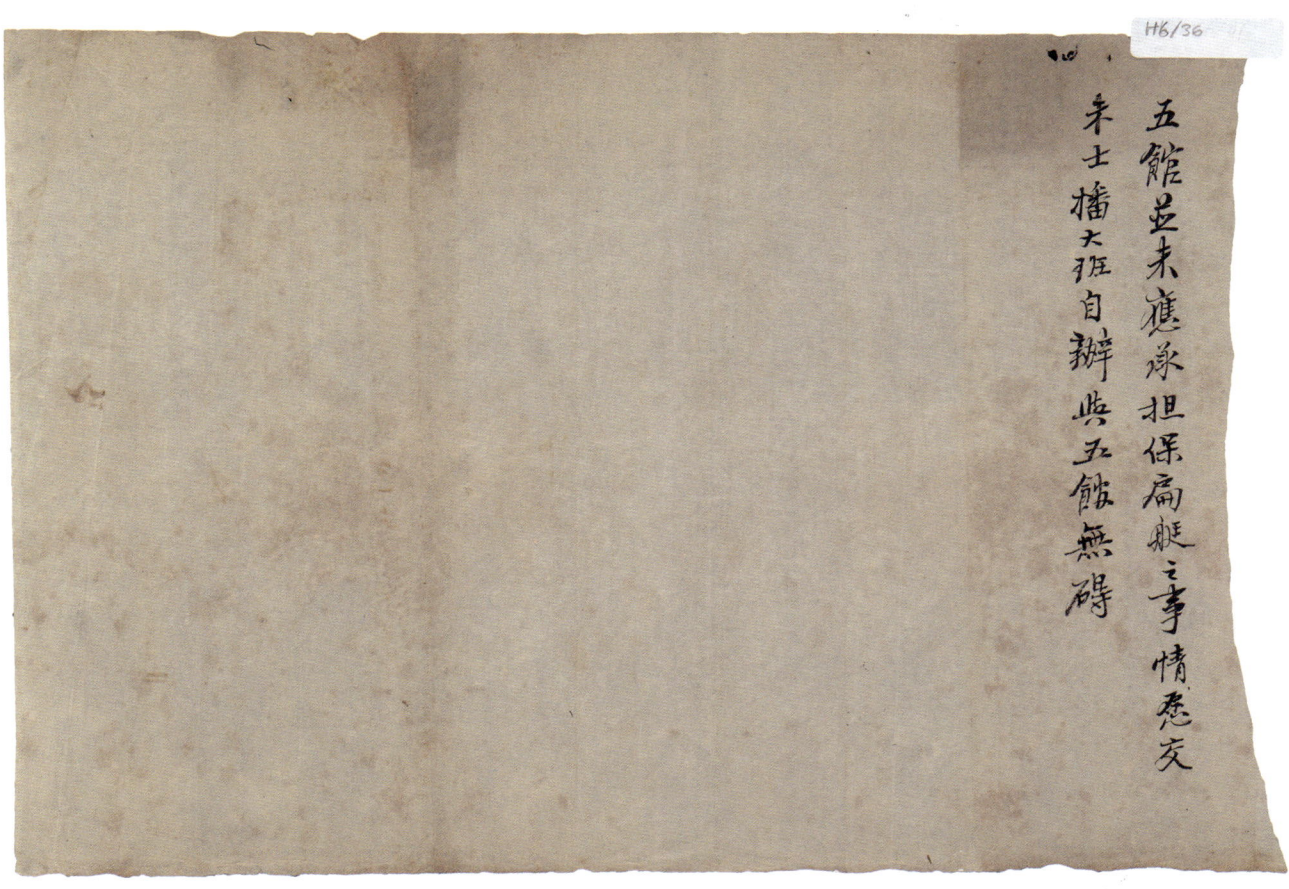

H6/36

五館並未應承担保扁艇之事情懇交

來士播大班自辦與五館無碍

三七、闰五月初九日日历单页（年份不详）（H6/37）

闰五月初九日，日历单页，有中文提要。

Calendar leaf. A leaf removed from a calendar giving the date of Wednesday, 1 July (no year), and ‘5th Moon, 9(th Month)’ in English, followed by additional information in Chinese. Further writing in Chinese has been added down the left-hand side.1 item.

（正）

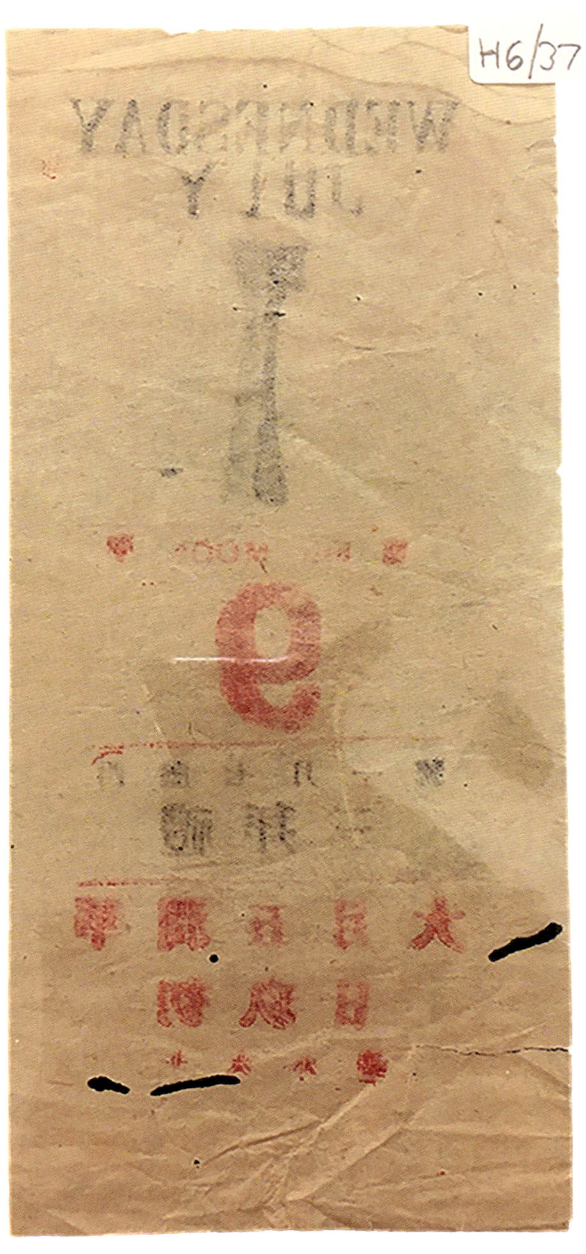

（反）

后 记

2019年1月3日，中国社会科学院中国历史研究院在北京成立，中共中央总书记、国家主席、中央军委主席习近平在贺信中指出："历史是一面镜子，鉴古知今，学史明智。重视历史、研究历史、借鉴历史是中华民族5000多年文明史的一个优良传统。当代中国是历史中国的延续和发展。新时代坚持和发展中国特色社会主义，更加需要系统研究中国历史和文化，更加需要深刻把握人类发展历史规律，在对历史的深入思考中汲取智慧、走向未来。……希望中国历史研究院团结凝聚全国广大历史研究工作者，坚持历史唯物主义立场、观点、方法，立足中国、放眼世界，立时代之潮头，通古今之变化，发思想之先声，推出一批有思想穿透力的精品力作，培养一批学贯中西的历史学家，充分发挥知古鉴今、资政育人作用，为推动中国历史研究发展、加强中国史学研究国际交流合作作出贡献。"

档案文献的整理研究，是加强中国史学研究暨国际交流合作的重要领域。17—19世纪，广州十三行在经营活动中逐步形成信函、公牍、凭信、票据等数量庞大的档案。由于时代更迭和战争的破坏，这些档案多已被焚毁或散佚，仅少数留存于国内外众多档案馆、博物馆、图书馆中，弥足珍贵。因此，英国剑桥大学图书馆所藏怡和洋行中文档案，既是了解、研究怡和洋行最重要的史料依据，也是中西商贸文化交流及广州十三行的历史见证。这批珍贵商业档案得以以影印出版的方式回归祖国，具有重要的文献价值和社会意义。

本书出版之际，我们要向在编写过程中给予我们帮助与支持的单位及个人表示感谢。感谢任职于广州大学的美国学者安乐博教授（Robert Antony），在收集资料的前期，与怡和洋行管理机构和剑桥大学图书馆联系并落实了相关手续；在我们去英访学交流以及在英期间的资料收集与翻译识读等方面，他和夫人张兰馨女士也给予了大量帮助。现在安乐博教授任职于哈佛大学费正清中国研究中心，这部书见证了我们多年同事的深厚友谊。

感谢英国剑桥大学图书馆（Cambridge University Library）及其工作人员。优美的环境、优良的设施、优秀的服务给我们留下了深刻的印象。他们不仅保存了几百年前珍贵的中文文献，而且积极配合和支持后期的出版事宜，方使本书得以顺利出版。同时，感谢英国剑桥大学图书馆工作人员Domniki Papadimitriou为我们购买档案高清图及版权所付出的努力！在此衷心祝愿中英人民友谊长存，文化交流缔结出丰硕果实。

感谢致力于中国商业文化遗产整理与保护的用友基金会，使本课题获得2019年第三届"商的长城”重点立项保障。感谢冯丽婕女士热情细致的管理工作，鼓励课题组克服新型冠状病毒肺炎肆虐造成的种种困难，使课题组取得了较为丰富的前期成果，提交合乎要求的书稿，顺利结项。

感谢梅州市地方志办公室廖晓鹏编审（中国书法家协会会员、中华诗词学会会员、梅州印社社长、嘉应诗社秘书长）、广东嘉应学院政法学院曾旭博士、邝以明博士（西泠印社社员、中央文史研究馆书画院研究员、中国美术家协会会员、中国书法家协会会员），在印玺学领域提供了专业指导，使几百年前文献上模糊的印章印迹得以被识读，从而提升了书稿的学术质量。

感谢广西师范大学出版社集团有限公司。四年前，笔者在复旦大学研讨会上的发言提到了这部书稿。肖爱景女士对此极为关注，并积极地与笔者进行联系与沟通，最终使书稿得以彩印问世，造福学界。感谢文献分社的编辑，耐心细致地处理了书稿中的诸多难题，为书稿顺利出版提供了保障。

这是一部用热情、心血和团结协作孕育出来的书稿。课题组成员无私奉献，精诚合作，为书稿出版奠定了基础。本书主编之一为冷东教授，香港大学博士，现为澳门科技大学社会和文化研究所访问教授、博士生导师；本书主编之二为潘剑芬，暨南大学历史学博士，广州市海珠区文物博物管理中心副研究馆员，邓世昌纪念馆（海珠博物馆）馆长；本书主编之三为沈晓鸣，澳门科技大学社会和文化研究所历史学博士研究生。我们将继续努力，为广州历史文化名城建设和海上丝绸之路研究做出新的贡献。

《英国剑桥大学图书馆藏怡和洋行中文商业档案辑考》的出版，仅是海外中文珍稀档案收集整理过程中一个新的成果，在档案的识读和研究中难免存在不当之处，恳望方家批评指正。

2022年1月